MARINE POLICY
IN SOUTHEAST ASIA

MARINE POLICY IN SOUTHEAST ASIA

edited by
George Kent
and Mark J. Valencia
East-West Environment and Policy Institute

University of California Press
Berkeley   Los Angeles   London

UNIVERSITY OF CALIFORNIA PRESS

Berkeley and Los Angeles, California

UNIVERSITY OF CALIFORNIA PRESS, LTD.

London, England

Library of Congress Cataloging in Publication Data
Main entry under title:

Marine policy in Southeast Asia.

   Includes bibliographical references.
   1. Marine resources — Government policy — Asia,
Southeastern. 2. Maritime law — Asia, Southeastern.
I. Kent, George, 1939–   . II. Valencia, Mark J.
HC92.M36   1985   333.95'2'095   84-16182
ISBN 0-520-05366-4

PRINTED IN THE UNITED STATES OF AMERICA

1 2 3 4 5 6 7 8 9

CONTENTS

PART II. OCEAN USE SECTORS

PART III.   MANAGEMENT OF OCEAN SPACE

TABLES

FIGURES

ACRONYMS AND ABBREVIATIONS

AAW	antiair warfare
ADB	Asian Development Bank
ASCOPE	ASEAN Council on Petroleum
ASEAN	Association of Southeast Asian Nations
ASW	antisubmarine warfare
bbl	barrel
BE	Buddhist Era
BOD	biochemical oxygen demand
BOPD	barrels of oil per day
CCI-WGFAF	Chamber of Commerce and Industry/Working Group on Forestry and Fisheries
CIDA	Canadian International Development Agency
CITES	Convention on International Trade in Endangered Species of Wild Fauna and Flora
CLS	Convention on the Law of the Sea
CMSN	China Merchants Steam Navigation
COFAF	Committee on Food, Agriculture, and Forestry
COIME	Committee on Industry, Minerals, and Energy
COLREG 1960	Convention on International Regulations for Preventing Collisions at Sea of 1960
COST	Committee on Science and Technology
COTAC	Committee on Trade and Communication
CPUE	catch per unit effort
DDT	dichloro-diphenyl-trichloro-ethane
DSLB	Domestic Shipping Licensing Board
DWT	deadweight ton

EEC	European Economic Community
EEZ	exclusive economic zone
EQA	Environmental Quality Act
ESCAP	Economic and Social Commission for Asia and the Pacific

FAO	Food and Agriculture Organization of the United Nations
FASA	Federation of ASEAN Shipowner's Associations
FASC	Federation of ASEAN Shippers' Councils
FEFC	Far Eastern Freight Conference
FESCO	Far Eastern Shipping Company of Vladivostok
FMO	Fish Marketing Organization
FMS	Federated Malay States
FPA	Fertilizer and Pesticide Authority

g	grams
GNP	gross national product
GRT	gross register ton
GT	gross tons

ha	hectare

IBRD	International Bank for Reconstruction and Development
ICLARM	International Center for Living Aquatic Resources Management
IGA	Inter-Group Agreement
IGGI	International Government Group on Indonesia
IHI	Ishikawajima-Harima Heavy Industries
IMCO	Intergovernmental Maritime Consultative
IMO	Intergovernmental Maritime Organization
INSA	Indonesian Shipowners' Association
IOC	Intergovernmental Oceanographic Commission
IPFC	Indo-Pacific Fisheries Commission
IUCN	International Union for the Conservation of Nature and Natural Resources

kg	kilogram
km	kilometers
km²	square kilometers
km/hr	kilometers per hour

LNG	liquefied natural gas
LPG	liquefied petroleum gas

m	meters
m^2	square meters
m^3	cubic meters
MARINA	Maritime Industry Authority
MCF	million cubic feet
MCFD	million cubic feet per day
MCS	monitoring, control, and surveillance
mg/1	milligrams per liter
mi	miles
MISC	Malaysian International Shipping Corporation
MNLF	Moro National Liberation Front
mph	miles per hour
MSY	maximum sustainable yield
MT	metric ton
NEPC	National Environmental Protection Council
NIEO	New International Economic Order
nmi	nautical miles
nmi^2	square nautical miles
NOL	Neptune Orient Line
NPA	New People's Army
NPCC	National Pollution Control Commission
OBO	Ore-Bulk-Oil
OECD	Organization for Economic Cooperation and Development
OECF	Overseas Economic Cooperation Fund
PCB	polychlorinated biphenyl
PIL	Pacific International Lines
PISC	Philippines International Shipping Corporation
PLA	People's Liberation Army
PNSL	Perbadanar Nasional Shipping Line
ppb	parts per billion
ppm	parts per million
PRC	People's Republic of China
PSA	Port of Singapore Authority
PTPANN	PT Pengembangan Armada Niaga National
RA	Republic Act
SCSP	South China Sea Fisheries Development Programme
SEAFDEC	Southeast Asian Fisheries Development Center
SLBM	submerged launch ballistic missile
SRV	Soviet Republic of Vietnam

SSA   Singapore Shipowners' Association
STOL   short-take-off-and-landing

TCF   trillion cubic feet
teus   20-foot equivalent units

ULCC   ultra large crude carriers
UN   United Nations
UNCLOS   United Nations Conference on the Law of the Sea
UNCLOS III   Third United Nations Conference on the Law of the Sea
UNCTAD   United Nations Conference on Trade and Development
UNDP   United Nations Development Programme
UNEP   United Nations Environment Programme
UNITHAL   United Thai Lines

VLCC   very large crude carriers

WESTPAC   IOC Working Group for the Western Pacific
WHO   World Health Organization

ZOPFAN   Zone of Peace, Freedom, and Neutrality

FOREWORD

The Environment and Policy Institute (EAPI) was established by the East-West Center in 1977 to respond to one of the most urgent challenges of the coming decades: How do countries, individually and collectively, manage and use the natural environment to assure its sustained productivity?

Governmental and private organizations are continuously adopting, adapting, and implementing policies designed to meet a broad range of human and societal needs. To be implemented, these policies often depend to a large degree on the use of some part of the natural environment — the biophysical systems and the natural resources that constitute our planet. This environment is finite and responds to demands on it within the limits of the natural laws that govern it. The pressures of growing populations, rising expectations, and sophisticated technologies combine to make it difficult to meet the numerous policy objectives that rely on a common environment.

EAPI conducts research and education programs on issues related to the management of natural systems and natural resources that are of central concern to the United States and the nations of Asia and the Pacific. These programs are conducted with a multidisciplinary approach through multinational cooperation consistent with the mandate and style of the East-West Center, which is a public, non-profit, educational institution with an international board of governors.

The programs of EAPI deal with many parts of the natural environment, from tropical forests to ocean resources, and with many policies, from those designed to meet energy and food needs to those aimed at expanding the limits of national jurisdiction and control. The program area on Marine Environment and Extended Maritime Jurisdictions has been an integral part of EAPI's work for the past six years.

This volume is a major product of the Marine Environment Program Area. It combines the results of other EAPI products with new material and presents the synthesis in a policy context. It is hoped that this combination of scientific information and policy considerations for a variety of ocean-related activities will assist both the technical and the policymaking communities in better understanding and responding to the challenges and opportunities that lie ahead as new approaches are formulated to effectively utilize the vast resource base of the oceans.

William H. Matthews
Director
Environment and Policy Institute
East-West Center

PREFACE AND
ACKNOWLEDGMENTS

The extension of maritime jurisdiction out to 200 nmi or more from shore and the new Convention on the Law of the Sea create both possibilities for conflict and opportunities for cooperation in the management of the semi-enclosed seas of Southeast Asia. Since 1978, the Environment and Policy Institute of the East-West Center has sponsored an interdisciplinary, multinational program of research and workshops under the coordination of Mark J. Valencia to address these problems and opportunities. The overall goal of this program has been to contribute to a maritime perspective among policymakers based on the understanding that the ocean is a link among nations and a resource to be managed. The goals of the program were (1) to delineate and evaluate both the interests of nations in the Southeast Asian marine region and opportunities for facilitating achievement of these interests through regional approaches, and (2) to disseminate the research results to policymakers by providing an independent forum for the discussion of these interests and opportunities.

Central research questions were (1) What is to be managed?; (2) How are these resources and resource-related activities to be managed?; and (3) Who will manage these resources and resource-related activities in these jurisdictional areas, and who will be affected? Research has been conducted in four substantive areas: transnational efforts on transboundary tuna stocks, regional marine environmental management issues, energy material transportation and environmental policies, and transnational oil and gas resource management issues. Each of these areas has been examined with respect to three fundamental components of transnational ocean management issues: the natural environment, juridical regimes, and political and socioeconomic factors (national marine interests). For the Southeast Asian seas, the program area has defined the general national marine interests and present and potential transnational ocean management conflicts. Published program area results are included in the reference section of this volume.

In addition to specific results of research that were published as they developed, a major objective of this program for the past three years has been the preparation of this volume, together with its companion, the *Atlas for Marine Policy in Southeast Asian Seas*, edited by Joseph R. Morgan and Mark J. Valencia (Berkeley: University of California Press, 1983). They are closely linked and maps essential to the policy discussions in this volume have been adapted from the atlas; others providing important background information may be found in the atlas.

The analyses in this volume are based upon and are an outgrowth of the work of many people in many disciplines from many countries. Several of the chapter authors have contributed considerable first-hand knowledge based on long experience in the region dealing with their chapters' subject matter (e.g., Donald Fryer, Southeast Asia marine geography; Elizabeth Samson, fisheries; George Lauriat, shipping; Abu Bakar Jaafar, marine pollution; Alan White, conservation in the marine environment; and Mark J. Valencia, hydrocarbons and pollution.

These works should help to equalize knowledge among nations and increase mutual understanding of various perspectives on transnational marine issues, thereby raising the quality of discussions concerning them. By pointing out possibilities for conflict, it is hoped that conflict can be avoided or better managed. By examining possibilities for cooperation in marine policy, it is hoped that when cooperation is undertaken it will be in a manner likely to yield positive results and with full awareness of the pitfalls.

Marine managers in the region are becoming more aware of each other and of the role of the sea in development. It is hoped that this volume and the atlas will encourage international discussions and cooperative approaches where appropriate and reinforce the growth of this incipient intellectual community. It is to this community and to the peaceful and sustained use of the oceans that these works are dedicated.

The editors and authors acknowledge the support of the East-West Environment and Policy Institute and its Director, William H. Matthews. Special thanks are due to Senior Editor Sheryl R. Bryson of the East-West Center Publications Office who arranged for the work to be published, edited the text in her usual highly professional manner and even helped rewrite some of more the difficult sections. Helen Takeuchi and Mariet Mendoza assisted with the editing, and Sheryl Bryson also prepared the index. The following people gave us their valuable comments on parts of the manuscript during its preparation: M. A. Warga-Dalem, Donald C. Daniel, Donald K. Emmerson, Jesse M. Floyd, Robert L. Friedheim, Norton Ginsburg, Edgardo D. Gomez, B. A. Hamzah, Ron D. Hill, Lim Joo-Jock, Benedict Kerkvliet, Joel Larus, Micheal Leifer, Mario C. Manansala, Michael MccGwire, James A. Nathan, Twesukdi Piyakarnchana, Veronica R. Villavicencio, Ronald Weidenbach, and Helen T. Yap. We would also like to thank the reviewers for the University of California Press who provided excellent advice that helped to strengthen this volume. We are grateful to the many persons at the East-West Center and in Asia and the Pacific who contributed encouragement, constructive suggestions, and data. Cartography was ably accomplished by Barbara Trapido. Numerous drafts and revisions were efficiently typed by Laura Miho, Avery DuBay, Carol Wong, and Elizabeth Figel. The authors and editors are responsible for the substantive accuracy of the text.

George Kent
and Mark J. Valencia

May, 1984

INTRODUCTION

The ocean has become a natural geopolitical link among nations, providing the basis for their interactions and interdependent policies in shipping, fishing, hydrocarbon exploitation, naval maneuvers, and environmental pollution and protection. The peoples of Southeast Asia and of states outside the region have used the Southeast Asian seas for trade, naval warfare, and fishing since ancient times.

The seasonal winds made it possible for the Chinese, the Indians, and the Arabs to sail to Southeast Asia for trade. But the Chinese junks and Arab *dhows* were essentially coasting vessels; regular voyages across open oceans had to await the Europeans, whose deeper-draft ships possessed both the necessary navigational equipment and the ability to sail closer to the wind. Thus, when Europeans using the same wind systems later arrived in the region, they found some flourishing and highly organized trade emporia, of which Malacca was foremost. European traders and voyagers soon found that existing ports and trade locations were ill suited to their needs, and by the end of the sixteenth century they began establishing the trading ports and "factories" that have become the great metropolitan centers and national capitals of the present-day independent states.

The region now produces valuable exports to world markets. More than 85 percent of the world's production of natural rubber comes from Southeast Asia, and virtually all of the supply is exported. Southeast Asian countries produce 55 to 60 percent of the world's tin, much of it dredged from shallow offshore waters. The spices that initially attracted Europeans to the region are still one of Southeast Asia's most important exports. Pepper, cinnamon, nutmeg, and mace, comprising more than 80 percent of the world's supply, are shipped from Southeast Asian ports. Rice, coffee, tea, and sugar are important agricultural exports. Southeast Asian palm oil accounts for approximately 80 percent of world production, and since 1960 the region has been the only producer of abaca, an important cordage fiber.[1] Southeast Asia in 1980 was expected to produce 7 percent of the world's hydrocarbons, the most important commodity by value produced in the region.[2]

In spite of this rich export market, sea trade and transport has had its price. Local

1

rulers have often levied a toll on traffic moving through waters over which they could establish jurisdiction, to establish a "staple" by compelling shippers to use particular ports and markets under their control. Pirates have long been active in the Strait of Malacca, the Sulu Sea, and parts of the South China Sea, though the advent of steam-powered vessels greatly reduced their depredations. The fate of some Vietnamese "boat people" and recent attacks even on large tankers clearing the Strait of Malacca are evidence they still exist.[3] In addition, intricate coastlines with a profusion of off-shore islands allow smuggling and illegal barter trade to flourish.

As with shipping, fishing is a part of the traditions and cultures of the nations of Southeast Asia and provides the livelihood for many of its people. The fisheries of Southeast Asia are extremely rich, with more than 2,500 fish and invertebrate species providing a total marine catch in recent years of approximately 7 million metric tons (MT).[4] Because fish migrate among national zones, Southeast Asian nations and others who have fishery interests in the region are finding it increasingly important to manage fisheries with the goals of maintaining both fish stocks and good international relations.

Within the past decade, increased marine awareness among the world's nations has resulted in the widespread unilateral extensions of national jurisdictions up to 200 nautical miles (nmi) from shore. This "world sea enclosure movement" has transferred one-third of former high seas and most known ocean resources and related activities to the control of individual nations. In the semi-enclosed Southeast Asian seas, all coastal nations except China have extended their maritime jurisdictions, leaving almost no marine area unclaimed and many areas where claims overlap. The historic Convention on the Law of the Sea (CLS) signed by 119 nations in December 1982* recognizes those extensions of jurisdiction in international law and serves as a framework within which nations may carry out their ocean management rights and responsibilities.

The venue for addressing issues of ocean law and policy is now moving from the global to the regional and bilateral level. With few exceptions, Southeast Asia is involved in all of the major issues raised in the debate on the CLS. The juxtaposition of land and sea, the varied geography of a region that includes archipelagic and continental states, states with minuscule territories, and states with large land areas and lengthy coastlines, and living and nonliving marine resources of potentially great value have made the Southeast Asian seas an arena for innovative marine policy. Jurisdictional controversies over marine territories are numerous and, although many are being or have been resolved amicably in bilateral negotiations, there are some that could result in conflict. Southeast Asian nations have taken a leading position in developing the law with respect to the regimes of archipelagos and passage through straits, and they have implemented a safe navigation scheme for traffic in the straits of Malacca and Singapore.

In this century, Southeast Asia has become a major hub of maritime activities,

---

*The CLS is the draft document of the Law of the Sea Treaty, which must be signed by 60 nations.

with oil and gas drawn from the continental shelves, significant fisheries production and trade, and oil tankers and foreign navies using the straits as major transit routes. The region has also become an arena of great power rivalries where the superpowers frequently show their flags. Most of the nations of the region are now engaged in a systematic effort to identify and pursue their national interests in the ocean. The new resources, activities, and concomitant responsibilities create new opportunities and challenges for national development. Yet national management policies for these zones of extended jurisdiction may be developed and implemented with insufficient understanding and consideration of the transnational and interdependent character of the ocean environment and the resources and activities that the ocean harbors and supports. Superimposing a mosaic of national policies on these transnational resources and activities creates possibilities for conflict as well as opportunities for cooperation.

As a center of great political interest and as an area in which most important ocean issues arise and interact, the Southeast Asian region already has received considerable attention from those concerned with marine policy questions. Important studies of international scope include Peter Polomka's *Ocean Politics in Southeast Asia*, Lim Joo-Jock's *Geo-Strategy and the South China Sea Basin*, Lee Yong Leng's *Southeast Asia and the Law of the Sea*, Chia Lin Sien and Colin MacAndrews' edited collection, *Southeast Asian Seas: Frontiers for Development*, and Phiphat Tangsubkul's *ASEAN and the Law of the Sea* (see References for Further Reading). These works selectively describe and explain specific national policies and perspectives.

This volume provides comprehensive descriptions and analyses of transnational marine policy issues in Southeast Asia that are created or exacerbated by the new CLS and, in particular, by the extension of maritime jurisdictions. Moreover, it suggests what might be done about these issues at the national and international level. Rather than provide concrete action plans, the purpose here is to suggest lines of approach to interested policymakers. The chapters in this volume explore a wide variety of approaches to ocean issues, but they try to emphasize the regional perspective and to suggest what policies might be advisable for the nations of Southeast Asia acting together.

The outer limits of the Southeast Asian region are not precisely set, but core nations under study in this volume include Brunei, Burma, Indonesia, Kampuchea, Laos, Malaysia, the Philippines, Singapore, Thailand, and Vietnam. Other nations and territories are included to the extent that they are involved in or affected by ocean-related activities and interests in the core area due to proximity, trade relations, global concerns, or navigation routes. This list varies for different purposes but may include Australia, China, the Chinese province of Taiwan, Hong Kong, Japan, Papua New Guinea, the Soviet Union, and the United States.

This volume is divided into three major parts. Part I sketches the marine geographic setting as a foundation for marine policy studies. Chapter 1, The Marine Geography of Southeast Asia, describes the physical, political, and economic marine geography of Southeast Asia as well as the major subregions that form the geographic context in which specific issues arise.

Although development may well be the driving force behind national interest in the oceans, guiding influences include historical, social, and cultural perspectives, national security, and international relations. Chapter 2 defines the prime interests of the region's nations in the marine sphere and of those foreign nations using the region. It looks at ways that these marine interests can be explained, measured, and compared, and it outlines their similarities, differences, and complementarities.

Resolution or muting of boundary disputes may be a prerequisite for the orderly national and international development of marine resources in Southeast Asia. Chapter 3, Maritime Jurisdictional Issues, delineates the boundaries that have been agreed upon and those that remain to be resolved. It also analyzes the factors that contribute to the complexity of boundary resolution and the possible or likely responses.

Part II examines the policy issues that arise in connection with each of the major uses of the ocean: fisheries, oil and gas exploration, shipping, and defense. The chapters for these ocean use sectors provide background information, systematically delineate the major issues, and explore the different forms of response to these issues.

Fisheries issues are high on policymakers' agendas because fishing plays an important role in employment, nutrition, and foreign exchange. Chapter 4, Fisheries, describes the fisheries interests of the nations both in the region and outside the region and determines which fisheries interests are common to which nations. The chapter also describes jurisdictional and resource access issues, and it analyzes national perspectives and possible responses.

Oil and gas are perhaps the most hoped for resources in many of the newly claimed jurisdictional areas. Chapter 5, Oil and Gas Potential, Overlapping Claims, and Political Relations, describes the present status and trends in hydrocarbon exploration in the region. It then delineates areas of overlapping claims that have hydrocarbon potential, and it examines the effect of international relations on the positions of the claimants. The possible responses to these situations are reviewed, as are the factors that influence the degree of cooperation in the possible response.

Development of national shipping lines to carry more national cargo is a common aspiration in the region. The present practices and problems in shipping of the nations of the region are described in Chapter 6, Shipping, and possible models for shipping development are analyzed. The implications of the United Nations Conference on Trade and Development (UNCTAD) codes and the Far Eastern Freight Conference for the development of national shipping lines are discussed, as are the available responses and the prognosis for regional cooperation in shipping.

Naval defense of national marine and land areas is paramount to the nations of Southeast Asia, many of which have been involved in or near military action in recent years. Chapter 7, Defense, delineates the major maritime defense issues common to Southeast Asian countries and summarizes the concerns, resources, and possible responses to conflict for each of the nations in the region.

Part III examines the challenges to management of ocean space. Extension of jurisdiction brings new meaning and emphasis for transnational marine pollution. Chapter 8, Marine Pollution, describes the major marine pollutants, their sources, and their distribution as well as the present national responses. Actual and possible transnational responses to transnational pollution issues are discussed, as are the issues that may in turn be created by these responses.

Conservation of marine ecosystems and species is an increasing concern in the region, and Chapter 9, Conservation of the Marine Environment, looks at the region's special marine ecosystem types and associated valuable and vulnerable species. It delineates the major threats to their conservation and the possible modes of protection.

Enforcement is the key to management of the newly acquired space and resources. Chapter 10, Enforcement of Maritime Jurisdictions, describes the major activities requiring enforcement and the national priorities and resources for enforcement. It also analyzes the advantages and disadvantages of the possible unilateral or multilateral responses to common enforcement problems.

The policy issues reviewed in this volume are likely to remain on the public agenda for years to come. Moreover, they raise interest in the possibility that these problematic issues might be turned into fruitful arenas of cooperation. Accordingly, Chapter 11, Opportunities, Problems, and Prospects for Cooperation, integrates the conclusions of the prior chapters and explores the potential for international marine policymaking. It delineates those issues for which cooperation may be the appropriate response, and the advantages, disadvantages, and the constraints to such a response.

PART I.
THE SETTING

CHAPTER 1

THE MARINE GEOGRAPHY OF SOUTHEAST ASIA

Joseph R. Morgan
Donald W. Fryer

The geography of a region — the distribution of land and sea, climate, topography, natural resources, and a host of political and economic factors — is the foundation for analytical policy studies. Marine geography, the application of geographic principles to the study of a marine region rather than a terrestrial one, includes physical, political, and economic geography. The concerns in political geography here are primarily with maritime boundaries, marine jurisdictions according to the Convention on the Law of the Sea (CLS), sea power, and the general classification of states according to the degree they benefit politically and economically from the new principles and rules. The economic geography of an ocean area includes patterns of interactions of marine resources and uses for fisheries, offshore oil and gas exploration and development, shipping, maritime defense, and waste disposal, each of which is discussed in a chapter in this volume. Political and economic geography both are concerned not only with a specific region, such as maritime Southeast Asia, but with the relationship of the region to the rest of the world, because the oceans are used with varying degrees of freedom by outside powers. Emphasis here is on those geographic factors most relevant to the formulation of marine policy by Southeast Asian states.

PHYSICAL GEOGRAPHY

The lands and seas defined here as the Southeast Asian marine region (Figure 1.1) occupy some 18 million square kilometers (km^2) (approximately 7 million square miles [mi^2]) of the earth's surface, an area broadly comparable to that of South America. A region so large inevitably has a substantial variety of physical characteristics. However, the degree of basic uniformity in the region, particularly in climate[1] and physical oceanographic features, both latitudinally and longitudinally, is remarkable. This broad physical unity is paralleled by an equally remarkable

9

Figure 1.1   Southeast Asian seas (modified from Joseph R. Morgan and Mark J. Valencia, eds., *Atlas for Marine Policy in Southeast Asian Seas*, Berkeley: University of California Press, 1983, p. 5).

degree of human and cultural unity. Indeed, "unity and diversity" has long been recognized as the regional *leitmotiv*.[2]

Aspects of physical geography important for marine policy analysis include the size of the region and the distribution of land and sea; characteristics of coasts, including natural harbors and port development; bathymetry; marine climate, particularly wind systems; ocean currents and vertical circulation patterns; sea surface temperatures; organic productivity; tides and tidal currents; waves; and natural hazards.

Land and Sea in Marine Southeast Asia

Extending from approximately 15°S to 25°N latitude and from 92°E to 145°E longitude, Southeast Asia is a rectangle approximately 5,800 kilometers (km) (3,596 miles [mi]) east to west and 4,500 km (2,790 mi) north to south. Seas occupy approximately two-thirds of the area. Peninsulas surrounded by gulfs and bays extend south and southeast from southwest China and collectively constitute mainland or continental Southeast Asia. The Malay Peninsula separates the Andaman Sea and the Strait of Malacca from the Gulf of Thailand, and the Indochinese Peninsula separates the Gulf of Thailand from the South China Sea and the Gulf of Tonkin. Archipelagic Southeast Asia, consisting of the Indonesian and Philippine archipelagos, contains thousands of islands that divide the ocean area into several individual seas.[3] The largest and most well-known seas are in the Indonesian island chain: the Java, Bali, Flores, Savu, Timor, Banda, Arafura, Celebes, Molucca, and Ceram seas. The Sulu Sea is the largest body of water within the Philippine Archipelago.

Important straits provide shipping routes into and through marine Southeast Asia; among the most important, all in Indonesian waters, are Sunda, Lombok, Ombai, Wetar, and Makassar. The Makassar Strait, connecting the Bali and Java seas with the Celebes Sea, is large enough to be designated as a sea in its own right. The San Bernardino Strait and Verde Island Passage and the Surigao Strait via the Sulu Sea connect the Pacific Ocean with the South China Sea. Thus the Philippines both separates and provides connections between the Pacific Ocean and Southeast Asian seas. The other important body of water joining the Pacific and the South China Sea is the Luzon Strait, between Luzon and the Chinese province of Taiwan. The control of these straits figures prominently in naval defense issues as do safety regulations for control of pollution within them (see Chapters 7 and 8).

The region's extraordinary geography reflects its geologic complexity. The area may be likened to a "mediterranean" region between the Asian and Australian continents. The term has also been applied to the Gulf of Mexico–Caribbean area, which has been described as the "American Mediterranean."[4] While the appropriateness of such designations may be questioned, the three "mediterranean" regions do indeed present many common characteristics. A brief comparison serves to highlight the essential features of the Southeast Asian marine region.

All three are enclosed or partially enclosed systems of interconnecting seas physically cut off from but with access to major oceanic basins. All are regions of extreme geologic instability with volcanism and seismic activity and in which substantial changes in coastlines have occurred in historic times.[5] The Southeast Asian maritime region, however, is much more vast. It is more than twice as large as the Central America–Caribbean region and almost four times as large as the Mediterranean Basin and its encircling lands. The Southeast Asian region is also more complex geologically and physiographically and in its more intricate patterns of distribution of land and sea.[6]

The distribution of land and sea in the region is of very recent geologic origin, largely a product of the retreat of the continental glaciers of the northern hemisphere and their final disappearance perhaps as recently as 10,000 years ago.[7] Before then the islands of Sumatera, Java, and Borneo were joined to the mainland, and much of the southern portion of the South China Sea was dry land. Volcanism, coastal instability, and the high rate of erosion and deposition associated with a humid tropical climate historically have produced substantial changes in land distribution, and such changes still are occurring, such as in the vital Strait of Malacca.

The distribution of land and sea, particularly in the extensive archipelagic regions, makes for extraordinary coastal lengths in Southeast Asia. Extensive coastal plains are found on the Chinese mainland opposite the island of Hainan, on the west coast of the island of Taiwan, in central and extreme southern Vietnam, on the south coast of the Malay Peninsula, on the northeast coast of Sumatera, in north Java, in southern Sulawesi, and on almost all of Borneo. Where the large rivers enter the sea, deltas are formed, and shallow offshore waters are turbid but rich in nutrients providing the basis for the rich fisheries of the region (see Chapter 4). The Red and Mekong rivers of Vietnam, Thailand's Mae Nam Chao Phraya, the Irrawaddy of Burma, and the Kupuas on the island of Borneo have produced the largest deltas.

Coral reefs and mangroves are predominant coastal features in Southeast Asia. Reefs occur along the more exposed coasts and around small islands where river runoff is minimal. Mangroves, on the other hand, are found in association with rivers, estuaries, and sheltered bays where the influx of silt and nutrients is beneficial to mangrove species but detrimental to the coral polyps. Both ecosystems support many valuable but vulnerable species and their conservation is becoming an increasing concern in the region (see Chapter 9).

Bathymetry

In addition to the complex geography associated with the distribution of land and seas in the region, deep trenches and basins, innumerable coral islands, and broad continental shelves form a complex pattern not found over such an extended area in any other part of the world.[8] In the Indian Ocean south of Java and Sumatera is the Java Trench, with an extreme depth of 7,450 meters (m) and part of a system of trenches that includes the shallower (5,160 m) Bali Trench parallel to it. East of the Philippine Archipelago lies the Mindanao Trench, which with an extreme depth of 11,299 m is one of the deepest on earth. These two trench systems form natural bathymetric boundaries for the Southeast Asian marine region, separating the area from the Indian and Pacific oceans.

The Southeast Asian seafloor is characterized by a relatively flat continental shelf that extends from the coasts to about 200 m deep and has numerous islands. The Southeast Asian continental shelf includes as separately named components the Mainland, Sunda, Arafura, and Sahul shelves, which are some of the most extensive in the world.[9] No country can extend its jurisdiction over these shelves to 200 nautical miles (nmi) without overlapping the claim of a neighboring or opposite state; thus jurisdictional disputes abound. The numerous islands and multiple claims to them compound the jurisdictional picture (see Chapter 3).

The Mainland Shelf reaches a maximum depth of 278 m between the islands of Hainan and Taiwan and is relatively featureless. It continues along the mainland Chinese coast and narrows to about 50 nmi south of Hainan. Depths are 60–80 m in the Taiwan Strait and 20–40 m in the Hainan Strait. The Mainland Shelf includes all of the Gulf of Tonkin, which has a central valley 70 m deep. The shelf narrows off the coast of Vietnam and broadens into the Sunda Shelf south of Cam Ranh Bay. The Sunda Shelf is as wide as 216 nmi and connects Sumatera, Borneo, and Java with the Southeast Asian mainland; it also includes the floor of the Gulf of Thailand. Under the South China Sea, continental shelf depths are between 40 and 100 m, and depths in the Gulf of Thailand are no greater than 80 m. Although the shelf is relatively flat, a number of island groups rise from the floor; these include the Natuna and Anambas groups on the Indonesian portion of the shelf; various shoals and islets off Sarawak, Brunei,* and Sabah; and a number of banks and small islands on the Vietnamese portion. The Arafura Shelf, which connects Australia and the island of New Guinea, ranges in depth from 30 to 90 m but has a slightly deeper channel leading eastward toward the Torres Strait, which itself is shallow due to the coral reefs. The Sahul Shelf, with average depths of 80–100 m, extends about 300 km (186 mi) from the northwest coast of Australia. Near the shelf edge are many reefs, banks, and islands.[10]

The bottom topography is complex in the South China Sea northeast of the Sunda Shelf, with a number of unusual, broad, intermediate-depth benches from which rise many islands. The more well known of these are the Paracels, which are on a broad bench with depths between 200 and 1,500 m, and the Spratly Islands, shown on many nautical charts as the "Dangerous Ground," north of Brunei and east of the Philippine island of Palawan.

Climate

The principal determinants of climate in Southeast Asia are its tropical location straddling the equator, the distribution of land and sea with marine influences dominating, and the seasonal wind and precipitation patterns associated with monsoonal circulation. Southeast Asian waters are located between the large land masses of Asia and Australia and are the "ideal monsoon region."[11] The equatorial

---

*The official name of Brunei as of 1 January 1984, when the country achieved full independence, became Brunei Darussalam (Brunei, the abode of peace).

low-pressure trough moves north and south seasonally; in the northern hemisphere summer it is over the Asian mainland, and atmospheric pressure over the
seas is greater than over the land. Winds are predominantly from sea to land in the
northern part of the marine region; this is the south monsoon.[12] During the northern hemisphere winter, conditions are the reverse; the high pressure system is over
the Asian mainland, and the oceans have relatively low pressure. Consequently,
winds are predominantly from the northerly quadrant and are referred to as the
north monsoon. Actual wind directions deviate from the norm depending on the
distribution of land and sea. In the north monsoon (referred to as the northwest
monsoon by many climatologists and Southeast Asian regional specialists), northwest winds prevail only over the Indonesian Archipelago; in much of the region,
including the Philippines and the South China Sea, the winds are northeasterly
and are influenced and increased by the northeast trade winds.[13]

The north monsoon is most fully developed in January and February as the atmospheric high over Asia is formed and the equatorial trough is just north of Australia. Over the South China and Andaman seas strong northeasterly winds sometimes exceed wind-force 5 (24 miles per hour [mph] or 39 kilometers per hour
[km/hr]) in the South China Sea. Just south of the equator the prevailing winds are
northwesterly rather than northeasterly, and southwesterly winds prevail farther
south, over the region between Java and Australia.

The south monsoon is most fully developed during July and August. In the
summer season of the northern hemisphere there is a low pressure system over
Asia and a high pressure system over Australia, which is experiencing winter.
Southeast Asian waters lie between the two, and wind forces over the open sea may
reach wind-force 4 (13–18 mph or 20–29 km/hr) but are generally less over the
Indonesian and Philippine archipelagos.

In April and May and September through November, conditions shift from the
north to the south monsoon and the south to the north monsoon, respectively.
Winds are generally weaker and less constant in direction, but during June they
may reach wind-force 4 over the Arafura Sea, and northeasterly winds over the
South China Sea in November occasionally exceed wind-force 4.[14]

Ocean Currents

The prevailing monsoon winds in Southeast Asian waters drive the ocean currents,
and strong circulation patterns are favored by the orientation of the principal seas
of the region. The South China Sea, with its general northeast-southwest orientation, has a circulation pattern "with its axis exactly in the main wind direction of
both monsoons."[15] Likewise, the circulation patterns of waters between Sumatera
and Borneo are in a north-south direction, the same direction as the north and
south monsoon winds.

The Banda, Flores, and Java seas are oriented predominantly east-west, as are
the monsoonal winds. In other parts of Southeast Asia the influence of the steady
monsoon winds is less apparent due to different shapes of the ocean basins, and
circulation of the waters is more irregular. In some cases the Southeast Asian seas

are freely connected with Pacific Ocean waters, and circulation patterns are affected accordingly.[16]

Figure 1.2 (a and b) shows ocean circulation patterns in the region for the north and south monsoons, respectively. Despite the relatively strong currents, their flushing action on pollutants tends to be weak due to their reversing directions. Pollutants in some surface waters may remain in the same seas indefinitely or may be transported to other countries' waters (see Chapter 8). There are small subregions (e.g., through narrow straits) where current velocities are extremely high, but in many semi-isolated ocean basins such as in the Gulf of Thailand and the Gulf of Tonkin circulation is weak.

Vertical circulation patterns are of interest because zones of upwelling influence the biological productivity of the waters and may lead to the establishment of important fisheries. Upwelling is caused either by offshore coastal winds, which transport the surface water seaward to be replaced by water that rises from moderate depths, or by diverging surface currents. Upwelling may be stationary and occurring throughout the year, or it may be periodic or alternating as conditions of wind and current direction shift seasonally.[17] Upwelled water is usually rich in nutrients, resulting in large concentrations of phytoplankton, zooplankton, and fish. In the region northwest of Australia, upwelling occurs seasonally, while in the Banda and Arafura seas, upwelling and sinking of surface waters occur alternately. In the South China Sea there is considerable vertical circulation, with upwelling along the edge of the shelf southeast of Vietnam during the north monsoon and with descending water movements during the south monsoon.[18]

Sea Surface Temperatures

In general, sea surface temperatures vary little in Southeast Asian seas, primarily due to the region's equatorial and tropical location and the high heat capacity of sea water, resulting in relatively constant temperatures despite variations in heat input and transfer to the atmosphere. The temperature of the sea surface is important in controlling the distribution of surface or near-surface fish such as the skipjack tuna.[19]

Productivity

Organic productivity of the seas can be measured directly or estimated by the concentration of nutrients such as phosphates, silicates, and nitrates. High productivity is correlated with high fisheries potential (see Chapter 4). Few nutrient data are available for Southeast Asian waters, but some generalizations are possible. As in most tropical seas, productivity is relatively low in the deeper basins, with only isolated upwelling areas showing evidence of significant concentrations of nutrients and organic productivity. Over the extensive continental shelves, however, vertical mixing processes are more effective in bringing nutrients into the euphotic zone where photosynthesis can take place.[20]

Productivity is generally low in the South China Sea, Philippine waters, and the Celebes Sea. It is relatively high over the Sunda Shelf and in the Gulf of Thailand,

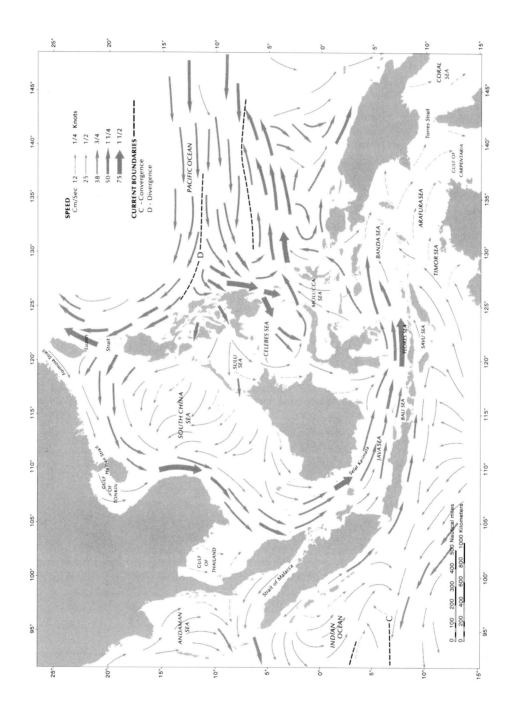

SPEED
Cm/Sec   Knots
12 ———→   1/4
25 ———→   1/2
38 ———→   3/4
50 ———→   1 1/4
75 ———→   1 1/2

CURRENT BOUNDARIES - - - - - -
C - Convergence
D - Divergence

PACIFIC OCEAN

Luzon Strait

Formosa Strait

GULF OF TONKIN

Hainan Strait

SOUTH CHINA SEA

GULF OF THAILAND

Strait of Malacca

ANDAMAN SEA

INDIAN OCEAN

Selat Karimata

JAVA SEA

BALI SEA

FLORES SEA

SAVU SEA

SULU SEA

CELEBES SEA

MOLUCCA SEA

BANDA SEA

TIMOR SEA

ARAFURA SEA

GULF OF CARPENTARIA

Torres Strait

CORAL SEA

0   100 200 300 400 500 Nautical miles
0   200 400 600 800 1000 Kilometers

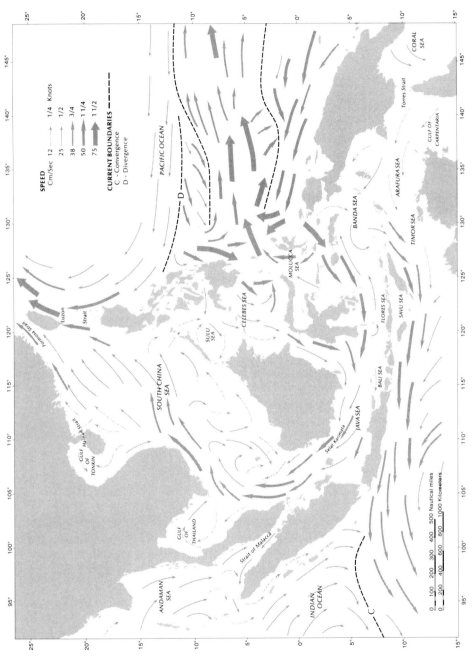

Figure 1.2   Surface currents: (a) February, (b) August (modified from Joseph R. Morgan and Mark J. Valencia, eds., *Atlas for Marine Policy in Southeast Asian Seas*, Berkeley: University of California Press, 1983, pp. 10–11).

the Strait of Malacca, the Java Sea, and waters between Sumatera and Borneo. Productivity is high in the Banda Sea, presumably due to upwelling. Southeast Asian productivity patterns are complicated by the distribution of land and sea, with large rivers sometimes providing concentrations of nutrients to the surface waters, and by the exchanges of both surface and deeper waters between Southeast Asian seas and the Pacific and Indian oceans. Seasonal wind and current patterns that lead to mixing of surface and deep waters are further complicating factors.

Tides

Tides and tidal currents are important to navigation, and they also influence mixing processes that disperse pollutants. Southeast Asian tides are characterized by low-to-moderate tidal ranges and a variety of tidal types — semidiurnal, diurnal, and mixed. They are influenced by conditions in the Indian and Pacific oceans, with the characteristic semidiurnal tide of the Indian Ocean prevailing in the Andaman Sea and the Strait of Malacca, and the mixed tides of the Pacific occurring in eastern Indonesian and Philippine waters. In the South China and Java seas, mixed tides prevail.

Nowhere in the region do tidal ranges exceed 4.6 m (15 feet [ft]), and most are less than 3 m (10 ft). The greatest ranges are found in the northern Andaman Sea where the Burmese port of Rangoon is affected, west of the Leizhou Peninsula in the Gulf of Tonkin, and on the west coast of Taiwan in the Taiwan Strait.[21]

Tidal currents reach considerable strength in some of the narrower passages between islands, despite the generally low tidal range. At spring tides, currents reach 5 to 6 knots in some of the passages in the Sunda area, in the Philippines, and in the Torres Strait. In other passages tidal currents usually do not exceed 3 knots, but even these speeds can be troublesome to shipping. In the most difficult of the navigational passages, the Malacca–Singapore straits, the tidal range is generally 1.5–3 m (5–10 ft), but this moderate range is quite significant in view of the generally shallow depths there and the deep draft vessels that use the main shipping channel.

Waves

In general, wave heights are not troublesome in the more sheltered waters of the Southeast Asian region. In the South China Sea, however, the strong monsoon winds cause high waves, and typhoons that cross the northern part of the sea can cause mountainous seas. Eastward-facing coasts are subject to high surf during periods of northerly and easterly winds that prevail during the north monsoon season affecting the patterns of local fishing activity. Coastal wave heights are likewise high during southerly to westerly winds on the Indian Ocean coasts of Sumatera, Java, Bali, Lombok, and Sumbawa. In the Andaman Sea the coasts of Burma and Thailand experience high surf during southerly to westerly winds, and the Burmese coast north of 16°N is also occasionally subject to Indian Ocean cyclones.

Natural Hazards

Natural hazards are characteristic of maritime Southeast Asia (Figure 1.3). The area is probably the most volcanic of any region of comparable size in the world. The Indonesian island arc extending from Sumatera through Seram, the western Pacific Ocean from the island of New Guinea through the Philippines and the island of Taiwan, and a region of submarine volcanism in the South China Sea are foci of volcanic activity. The 1815 eruption of Gunung Tambora, which killed 92,000 people, and the explosive eruption of Krakatoa in the Sunda Strait in 1883 indicate the potentially violent nature of eruptive activity in the region. Tsunamis, spawned by undersea earthquakes and volcanic eruptions, have struck coasts in the Philippines and Indonesia.

Seismicity, generally high in Southeast Asia, is concentrated in a broad belt along the Indonesian island arc and in a portion of the Circum-Pacific zone of earthquake activity extending from New Guinea through Taiwan. The Philippine islands are probably the most seismic in the world; with about 5 percent of the earthquakes of 6 or greater on the Richter scale and only about 0.1 percent of the earth's land area, the rate of seismicity is approximately fifty times greater than average.

In the northern part of the region typhoons are the most serious of the natural hazards. Eight or more of these intense storms can be expected in an average year, with seven occurring during July through November. The Philippines, Vietnam, and the south China coast are most vulnerable. Rains, violent winds, and waves destroy crops, roads, and port facilities, and loss of life is sometimes great.[22]

MARINE POLITICAL GEOGRAPHY

The nations of Southeast Asia may be divided into three categories by marine political geography. *Richly endowed states* are those with archipelagic status under the CLS, i.e., Indonesia and the Philippines. *Moderately endowed states,* those with long coastlines relative to the national territorial area or in an alignment that maximizes jurisdictional claims, include Vietnam, Malaysia, Burma, and Thailand. *Underendowed states* include landlocked Laos plus Kampuchea and Singapore whose coastlines are small and whose jurisdictional suites are restricted by those of other states. The degree of endowments helps to determine their national interests in the marine regime (see Chapter 2).

Through their positions as archipelagic states under the criteria of the CLS, Indonesia and the Philippines are entitled to claim the full suite of maritime jurisdictions. The area enclosed by the line demarcating Indonesia's exclusive economic zone (EEZ) amounts to almost 8 million km^2, roughly equivalent to the area of Australia. The area of the Philippines, if drawn according to the principles adopted by the CLS, would amount to a little less than half this amount. The Philippines has also added Kalayaan to its claim. The CLS recognizes Indonesia's claims to enormous marine resources in fisheries and in hydrocarbons. Conspicuously

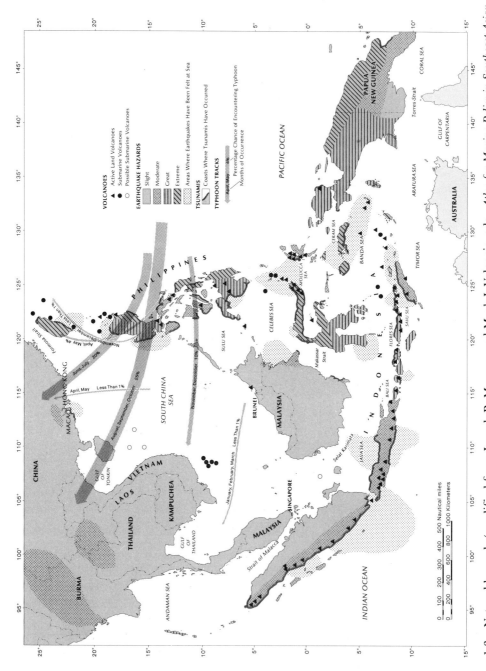

Figure 1.3 Natural hazards (modified from Joseph R. Morgan and Mark J. Valencia, eds., *Atlas for Marine Policy in Southeast Asian Seas*, Berkeley: University of California Press, 1983, p. 15).

lacking so far in Philippine marine resources is any major source of hydrocarbons. There is little doubt that this lack has been a factor in the Philippines' claim to Kalayaan.

The jurisdictions in claimed areas under the CLS greatly enlarge the strategic importance of the two archipelagos due to their positions commanding the vital trade routes between the Indian and Pacific oceans. The naval forces at present available to each country for maintaining security and surveillance over such enormous marine areas face responsibilities greatly exceeding their capacities (see Chapters 7 and 10).

Moderately endowed states are favored by geography in that their coastlines form the basis for a suite of large jurisdictional claims. Foremost is Vietnam, whose generally convex eastern and southern coasts maximize the extent of its claims on the South China Sea. Thailand's concave coast around the Gulf of Thailand, on the other hand, restricts the size of its claims, although this shortcoming is in part offset by a lengthy west coast on the Andaman Sea. Burma's coasts also enable it to make jurisdictional claims to a large area from a baseline that some authorities judge extravagant (see Chapter 3). Malaysia's marine claims by virtue of its eastern wing of Sarawak and Sabah are also substantial despite the intrusion of Indonesian jurisdiction northward into the South China Sea through the Anambas and Natuna islands.

The underendowed or so-called landlocked and geographically disadvantaged states include Laos, Kampuchea, and Singapore. Kampuchea, a large state, is the truncated remnant of a once-great empire. Encroachments by Thais from the west and Vietnamese from the east have reduced its coastline to but a few hundred kilometers along the Gulf of Thailand.

Singapore's allocation to the underendowed category is arguable. Singapore lacks an EEZ, it has little continental shelf, and its minuscule maritime territory is surrounded by that of other states. Nevertheless, describing Singapore as geographically disadvantaged may seem unreasonable. Its geographic position makes it the linch-pin of the Indian Ocean–Strait of Malacca–South China Sea–Pacific Ocean trade route. Singapore's economy, larger than that of Burma or Vietnam, depends more on the sea and on seafaring than does that of any other state in the region, and although its national marine resources are restricted, its influence on maritime affairs in the region is second to none. One of the world's foremost ports by any criteria and the principal center for the supply and maintenance of the offshore oil industry in Southeast Asia, Singapore is an outstanding example of the enormous advantages conferred by a favorable geographic location.

MARINE ECONOMIC GEOGRAPHY

Southeast Asia and its seas do not exist in isolation from the rest of the world, and relations with other nations are an important aspect of the region's economic geography. Major uses of the Southeast Asian marine region are the basis for studying its marine economic geography. Discussed here briefly and covered fully in subsequent chapters are fisheries, hydrocarbons, shipping and trade, maritime defense, and waste disposal. All are of interest not only to the nations of Southeast Asia but to many outside nations as well.

Fisheries

All states in the region (except Laos) have an interest in the fishery resources of Southeast Asian waters. A number of demersal and pelagic species, including the skipjack tuna, are economically valuable and are sought not only by Southeast Asian states but by other nations as well. Expanded maritime jurisdictions, particularly EEZs, have complicated the task of fisheries management. The CLS requires that states allow other nations to fish in their EEZs for any stocks that are surplus to the coastal nation's harvesting capacity. To establish the extent of this surplus requires research in fisheries biology, catch and effort statistics, and oceanographic factors controlling productivity. Based on this research, fishery policy can be established.

Several Southeast Asian states have been particularly active in managing their fishery resources. Indonesia, for example, has established a number of zones in which various types of fishing activities are prohibited. Thus far, Vietnam and Kampuchea have taken the view that they alone should fish in their respective EEZs and have sometimes taken military action to protect their waters from outsiders. The Philippines and Malaysia are establishing procedures designed to protect their own fishermen from competition and to conserve stocks. Thailand, an important distant-water fishing nation, appears to be the chief victim of regulations established by other Southeast Asian countries. The Thais have been unable to gain official permission to fish in other states' EEZs, and on numerous occasions their boats have been confiscated and crews arrested.

Fisheries policy involves social and cultural factors as well as the obvious economic and biological conditions. Many fishermen in the region are owners of small boats and are capable of fishing only shallow, nearshore waters using relatively primitive technology. For them fishing is a way of life, and governments need to consider their social as well as economic needs. Some fisheries policy is designed to protect artisanal fishermen from more highly capitalized and technologically advanced competitors.

Hydrocarbons

The offshore geology of the Southeast Asian region indicates a number of areas where hydrocarbon resources are likely to be abundant. Three countries — Indonesia, Malaysia, and Brunei — are oil exporters. Other states in the region, particularly the Philippines, Vietnam, and China, are actively searching for offshore oil and gas. Burma, an important oil producer until the nation changed its policy regarding foreign trade, is once again looking to the seas under its jurisdiction for hydrocarbons.

In a number of areas where hydrocarbon potential is high, there are overlapping jurisdictional claims. The likely presence of valuable hydrocarbon deposits tends to harden the negotiating positions and makes resolution of any problem more difficult. Much of the exploration and geophysical prospecting, as well as some of the actual development of producing wells, is done by oil companies of developed nations under contract to Southeast Asian countries. Serious jurisdictional controversies in regions with promising petroliferous geological formations are therefore likely to involve not only the competing Southeast Asian states but outside powers as well. Thus, while hydrocarbons are by far the most valuable resource of the Southeast Asian seas, they are also the most potentially dangerous.

Shipping

Lying between the Indian and Pacific oceans, the Southeast Asian seas are a throughway for ship traffic between the Persian Gulf oil ports and Japan. The most important of the sea routes traverses the southern Andaman Sea, the straits of Malacca and Singapore, the South China Sea, and the Luzon Strait. An alternative route for tankers too large to navigate the Malacca–Singapore straits safely goes south of Sumatera and Java before entering Indonesian archipelagic waters via the Lombok Strait. Thereafter, the route follows a navigational channel through the Makassar Strait and the Celebes Sea before passing south of the Philippine island of Mindanao into the Pacific Ocean. While maritime Southeast Asia has other trade links with the rest of the world and intraregional trade by sea is important in its own right, it is the oil routes, particularly the one through the heart of the South China Sea, that form the basis for many of the marine policies of nations within the region as well as marine policies of outside powers.[23]

In addition to the oil routes through the region, there are trade routes within the region, though of lesser importance. Singapore, at the end of the Malacca–Singapore straits and the entrance to the South China Sea, is the principal shipping hub and one of the busiest ports in the world. The principal routes for trade within the Southeast Asian region fan out from Singapore.

There are numerous harbors in the region, but the great majority are little more than open or unprotected roadsteads, accessible only to small coasting vessels and native craft. Very few ports, apart from the major ports of entry, many of which were developed during European occupation and are now national capitals, have modern facilities capable of serving the average size of vessels operating on the high seas. Often too, the facilities at the major national ports are inadequate, making congestion and delay inevitable.

On the low-lying margins of the Sunda Shelf, economically the most important portion of the region, good natural harbors with deep water close inshore are rare, so most modern ports are largely artificial. Investment in improving and extending port facilities has often been laggard, although Singapore is a striking exception. Specialized terminals for the oil industry are another exception to the pattern of generally inadequate investment.

Maritime Defense

Maritime defense and security considerations are yet another factor in both the political and economic geography of Southeast Asian waters. The regional states, grouped generally into an Association of Southeast Asian Nations (ASEAN) faction and the Indochinese nations, are concerned with national security and economic development. Outside powers — Japan, the United States, and the USSR — have military interests in Southeast Asian seas; China, which could be thought of as either a Southeast Asian state or an outside power, has a long coastline on the South China Sea and a dominating influence on the region.

In addition to the classical function of navies — defense of a nation's territory against aggressors — Southeast Asian states have a number of other defense- and security-related problems. Piracy and smuggling are activities that most nations feel must be controlled. Indonesia and the Philippines not only have vast areas to patrol but have dissident elements in their populations, many residing on islands hundreds of kilometers from the national core.

A major issue in maritime defense policy is the optimum size and composition of a state's navy. In Southeast Asian waters there are several narrow, strategically important straits that can be controlled by relatively small, well-armed craft. On the other hand, extensive archipelagic waters and EEZs require much larger ships if adequate surveillance is to be maintained.

Waste Disposal

As Southeast Asian states industrialize in the pursuit of economic development, the disposal of wastes becomes an ever-increasing problem. It is exacerbated by increasing population densities and the resultant sewage. Traditional activities such as agriculture and forestry also are big waste producers. The capability of Southeast Asian waters to act as a reservoir or sink for wastes has been exploited by all states in the region to some extent. Offshore mining, principally for tin, and oil exploration activities are other sources of pollution that must be regulated and controlled if the marine environment is to be protected. Other economic activities, chiefly fisheries and tourism, depend on pollution-free waters.

Knowledge of the physical characteristics of Southeast Asian seas is a necessary prerequisite to establishing reasonable waste disposal policies. Pollutants can be dispersed by prevailing winds and ocean currents, but the capacity of ocean waters to accept toxic and noxious wastes of both biological and industrial origin can be determined only after careful study.

Because of the numerous overlapping jurisdictional claims and the number of Southeast Asian states using the waters, waste disposal activities by one nation may affect many others. Pollution problems can readily become international. A serious oil spill, either from a drilling rig or a large tanker, could cross marine boundaries and foul the beaches of several nations with a disastrous effect on nearshore fisheries, aquaculture, and tourism.

MARINE SUBREGIONS

The successful solution of marine policy problems in a region as complex as Southeast Asia can be facilitated by selecting suitable subregions for analysis. Conditions

Table 1.1   Distances and Travel Times from Singapore to Other Southeast Asian Ports

Route	Distance (nmi)	Travel Time (at 15 knots)
Singapore to Manila	1,330	3 days, 17 hours
Singapore to Bangkok	842	2 days, 8 hours
Singapore to Ho Chi Minh	649	1 day, 19 hours
Singapore to Jakarta	525	1 day, 11 hours
Singapore to Surabaya	763	2 days, 3 hours
Singapore to Torres Strait	2,468	6 days, 21 hours
Singapore to Rangoon	1,109	3 days, 2 hours
Singapore to Hong Kong	1,454	4 days, 1 hour

Source: U.S. Defense Mapping Agency, *Sailing Directions (Planning Guide) for Southeast Asia,* Washington, D.C.: DMA Hydrogeographic/Topographic Center, 1979, p. 345.

of physical, political, and economic geography differ widely in each subregion of the larger Southeast Asian marine area. For example, in some areas ocean currents provide ideal conditions for the flushing of pollutants, while in others the seasonal reversals of winds and currents result in the retention of the polluted water within the subregion indefinitely. Likewise, some subregions are beset with problems of conflicting and overlapping jurisdictional claims that inhibit efforts by bordering nations to arrive at agreements that would be effective for the entire subregion. In other subregions such political controversies do not exist, and regional cooperation is more possible. Where there are important resources claimed by more than one country, marine policy tends to be established by each nation separately, without cooperation or consultation with its neighbors. Subregional cooperation and the development of policies for the protection of the marine environment is easier when there is less at stake economically.

In the discussion that follows, important marine subregions are considered in the order that a vessel proceeds from the Indian Ocean through Southeast Asian seas to Japan (see Table 1.1). For each Southeast Asian subregion, factors of physical, political, and economic geography relevant to marine policy analysis are synthesized.

The Andaman Sea

The vessel first enters Southeast Asian waters by way of the Andaman Sea. The sea is bounded by the Andaman and Nicobar islands to the west, by Burma to the north and northeast, and by Thailand to the east. As usually delineated, the southern boundary of the Andaman Sea is a line drawn from the northwestern tip of Sumatera to the border between the long proruption of Thailand and peninsular Malaysia.

The continental shelf in the northern part of the sea is formed mainly from sediments brought into the region by the outflow of the many distributaries of the Irrawaddy River. Depths shallower than 200 m are found in the Gulf of Martaban and in a broad zone seaward of the Mergui Archipelago. South and west of the continental shelf is the Andaman Basin, with depths to about 3,000 m. The main route through the sea is between the small islands north of Sumatera and Great Nicobar Island, which is under Indian jurisdiction.

Prevailing winds in the Andaman Sea are northerly and northeasterly during the winter monsoon and southwesterly in the summer months. Surface currents, however, are affected less by the winds than by general oceanographic conditions in the Indian Ocean and are southeasterly in the northern part of the sea, circling clockwise and becoming westerly in the southern part. In general, the typhoons of the Indian Ocean are not a serious hazard in the Andaman Sea, but the Burmese coast south to the Thai border has high waves during strong southerly to westerly winds.

The outflows of the Burmese rivers bring great quantities of nutrients into the northern waters, creating conditions beneficial for fishery development. Tidal ranges between 3 and 4.6 m (10 and 15 ft) are a problem for ships entering ports in the Gulf of Martaban, including Burma's principal port of Rangoon. Rangoon, a river port, is also beset with navigational problems because of shallow water, a narrow channel, and silting.

The Andaman Sea is a physical region based on a general uniformity of oceanographic features. It can be thought of as a "backwater" because most of the sea is off the main strategic shipping route for oil, and the littoral states are not politically powerful.

The Straits of Malacca and Singapore

The straits connect the Andaman Sea with the South China Sea and other subregions of maritime Southeast Asia; together they are one of the most important navigational passages in Southeast Asia, and they rank among the most strategic in the world. With an overall length of about 500 nmi they are more than 200 nmi wide at their northwest end, between Phuket, Thailand, and Sabang on the northeast coast of Sumatera. The Strait of Malacca narrows to 8 nmi where it joins the Singapore Strait, which becomes less than 2 nmi wide. Navigable channels within the straits are, of course, much narrower, but it is not just the narrowness of the channels that adds to the difficulties of navigation; they are shallow as well. The *Pilots* or *Sailing Directions* of the principal maritime nations advise vessels drawing more than 19.8 m (65 ft) to use alternate passages, and the Intergovernmental Maritime Organization (IMO) has approved the recommendation of Indonesia, Malaysia, and Singapore that all vessels maintain an underkeel clearance of at least 3.5 m. This effectively limits passage to fully loaded tankers not larger than 220,000 deadweight tons (DWT). Danger of collisions due to the large number of ships using the navigable channels is lessened when ships follow traffic lanes that separate eastbound and westbound vessels. Three of these traffic separation schemes have been established: at One-Fathom Bank, in the Singapore Strait near the intersection of the Main and Philipps channels, and at Horsburgh Light.

There is much cross-traffic in the region because small vessels cross the straits bound for the many ports on the north coast of Sumatera and the west coast of peninsular Malaysia. In addition to Singapore, preeminent in the region, Port Kelang, Port Dickson, and Malacca in Malaysia, and Dumai and Palembang on the

Sumatera coast are important ports. Dumai can accommodate tankers of 304,000 DWT, although vessels that large can only navigate the straits in ballast due to draft limitations.

Charted depths in the straits are not always reliable due to sand waves that move up and down the channel. Tidal ranges vary from 3.8 m (12 ft) at the north entrance to the Strait of Malacca to 1.4 m (4.5 ft) in the Singapore Strait. Since some of the relatively shallow areas cannot be avoided by seagoing ships, accurate predictions of tide height are required. Compounding navigation problems are the occasional local storms, or sumatras, which cause heavy rains and reduced visibility. Strong tidal currents in some inshore areas also may be a hazard to navigation.

Where the Malacca–Singapore straits are narrower than 24 nmi, their waters are part of the territorial seas of the coastal states, but since the straits connect one part of the high seas or an EEZ with another part of the high seas or EEZ, they are "straits used for international navigation," as defined in the CLS. They also are subject to navigation rules approved by the IMO.

The straits can be classed as a physical marine region, owing to unique physical features of bathymetry, or as a management region, since the three coastal states now "manage" shipping through the region by having established traffic separation zones and underkeel clearance requirements for large ships.

The South China Sea

After leaving the Singapore Strait most large vessels take a northeasterly course into the South China Sea. Almost all of Southeast Asia's important ports are on the peripheries of the South China Sea or the gulfs of Thailand and Tonkin. Transit through the sea and to the main ports is generally free of navigational hazards, provided the master of the vessel avoids the shallow water of the "Dangerous Ground" as well as locations of political controversy.

During December through April the northeast trades, which extend from the Pacific Ocean into the South China Sea, are strong, and sea conditions are frequently difficult for small ships that still follow the old trade routes. Ocean currents in the winter months are strong along the western shores of the sea, particularly off the central Vietnam coast where currents exceed 1.5 knots. Elsewhere in the South China Sea surface currents are much weaker and generally circle the region counterclockwise. During the summer, conditions are reversed, with winds predominantly from the southwest and surface currents circling the sea clockwise.

Typhoons periodically sweep the region north of 10°N causing damage and loss of life in the Philippines, the Chinese province of Taiwan, on the Chinese coast near Hong Kong, and on the coast of Vietnam. During the time of strong northeasterly monsoon winds, waves are high along the east coast of peninsular Malaysia and Mindanao, and the coasts may be visited by typhoons. Tidal ranges throughout the South China Sea are generally less than 3 m (10 ft) and cause little navigational difficulty. Upwelling of cold, nutrient-rich waters occurs off the central Vietnam coast in midsummer, resulting in highly productive fisheries.

The littoral states, each claiming its 200-nmi-wide EEZ, and the relatively narrow east-west extent of the sea make for a multiplicity of jurisdictional controversies as nations claim overlapping areas of EEZ and continental shelf. When the overlap areas are rich in fish resources or have good hydrocarbon potential, the prospects for conflict are greater. The CLS encourages states bordering enclosed or semi-enclosed seas such as the South China Sea to resolve problems associated with their marine regions through appropriate multilateral arrangements and agreements.

The South China Sea is a geostrategic region *par excellence*, for in it the military and economic interests of a great number of states are paramount. There are the coastal nations bordering the sea, powers vying for influence in the region, and states using the important sea passages linking the Indian Ocean with the Pacific. Moreover, there are valuable hydrocarbon and fishery resources sought by virtually all of the bordering states.

The Luzon Strait

The principal exit from the South China Sea for ships bound for Japan or across the Pacific to North America is one of three navigable channels — the Bashi, the Balintang, or the Babuyan. The three channels comprise the Luzon Strait between Taiwan and Luzon. Each channel is wide and deep enough to permit transit by large ships, and the northernmost of the three, the Bashi, is most often used by ships bound for Japan and ports on the Asian coast north of the South China Sea. The Balintang Channel, at about 19°45′N, is the recommended route for ships enroute to Seattle, San Francisco, and other ports on the west coast of the United States. Ships enroute to Honolulu from Manila or other Southeast Asian ports usually use the southernmost Babuyan Channel. The strong northeasterly trade winds encountered during the northeast monsoon make for rough seas in the Luzon Strait, and the frequent typhoons make the channels hazardous during the July–December season.

The strait is a geostrategic region in that it is an important route for ships entering or leaving the South China Sea, but it is one of only minor importance since there are alternative passages.

The Gulf of Thailand

Not all vessels pass through the South China Sea from Singapore to the Luzon Strait; some are bound for ports within Southeast Asia. One such port is Bangkok at the northern end of the Gulf of Thailand. The gulf is considered by some to be part of the South China Sea, and it is logical in many ways to consider it a tributary or appendage of the larger marine region. But oceanographic conditions clearly separate the gulf from the larger sea. The Gulf of Thailand is under the influence of the same monsoon wind systems as the other Southeast Asian seas; winds are generally easterly during the winter monsoon and southwesterly in the summer months. Surface currents are sluggish during both seasons, averaging 0.25 knot during February and between 0.25 knot and 0.5 knot in August. Consequently, there is little to flush pollutants out of the gulf, and the large outflow of polluting matter from Bangkok and the surrounding industrial area is slowly degrading the marine environment. Fishing for a number of demersal and pelagic species is an important economic activity, but overfishing and pollution are reducing catches. The Gulf of Thailand can best be classified as a physical marine region, and it is so described in standard descriptive oceanographic literature.[24]

The Gulf of Tonkin

Called Beibu Wan by the Chinese and Bac Bo by the Vietnamese, the Gulf of Tonkin is another appendage of the South China Sea that nevertheless has a distinct identity. As in the case of the Gulf of Thailand, the physical geography of the Gulf of Tonkin separates it from its larger neighbor, and ocean current patterns again are primary among the important distinguishing factors. While surface currents off the central Vietnamese coast are strong, particularly in the winter months, currents in the gulf are not, averaging but 0.5 knot during February and 0.5 knot or less in August. In the northern part of the Gulf of Tonkin winter sea surface temperatures fall to 18 degrees centigrade from their summertime maximum of 29 degrees centigrade. On the Chinese coast west of the Leizhou Peninsula the tidal range is 3.46 m (10–15 ft); elsewhere in the gulf it is 1.5–3 m (5–10 ft). Although somewhat sheltered by Hainan Island, the Chinese mainland and Vietnamese coasts are subject to high wave energies during northerly to easterly winds and when typhoons strike the region. The Gulf of Tonkin is a physical region if uniformity of oceanographic conditions is considered, an economic region if the prime concerns are with the oil and gas resource potential, and a geostrategic region since the economic, strategic, and geopolitical interests of Vietnam and China come together and conflict there.

The Java Sea

Southeast of the South China Sea is the Java Sea, bounded by Sumatera on the west, Indonesian Kalimantan on the north, and Java to the south. With an area of 162, 662 square nautical miles (nmi²) it is the second largest and most important of the marine regions in the Indonesian Archipelago. Java is Indonesia's most populous island; the nation's capital, Jakarta, with its port of Tanjungpriok, is on its southern shore, and there are important oil fields and fishing grounds off its shores.

Ships can enter the Java Sea via Selat Karimata after leaving the Singapore Strait. Selat Bangka, between Bangka and Sumatera, and Selat Gaspar, between Bangka and Belitung islands, are other passages from the northwest. The principal route from the Indian Ocean is via Selat Sunda, until recently one of the most widely used straits in the region. However, the much greater drafts of modern vessels, particularly tankers, have made the passage more difficult, and a longer but safer route is Selat Lombok, which is wide and deep enough for the largest tankers. Most vessels using this route, however, are not bound for ports in the Java Sea but for the Makassar Strait, which leads to the Celebes Sea and ultimately south of Mindanao to the Pacific Ocean and Japan.

As in other Southeast Asian seas, the surface currents reverse seasonally with the prevailing winds. In both monsoons currents are strongest in Selat Karimata, reaching 1.5 knots in February but averaging somewhat less than 1 knot in August. Sea surface temperatures remain near 28 degrees centigrade year around. Tidal ranges are 1.5–3 m (5–10 ft) on the south coast of Borneo, the northeast coast of Java, and the south coast of Madura. Elsewhere they are less than 1.5 m (5 ft). In general, high waves are not a problem in the Java Sea, and the typhoons that make other areas in Southeast Asia hazardous do not extend south of about 5°N latitude.

There are important oil fields in the western Java Sea. Offshore moorings, handling tankers in the 150,000–175,000-DWT range are located at the Cinta, Arjuna, and Balungan terminals on the northwest coast of Java. With Tanjungpriok and Surabaya, these are the largest ports in the Java Sea. The other important economic activity in the region is fishing for both pelagic and demersal species. Seafood canneries and cold-storage facilities are located at Tanjungpriok, Cerebon, Kali Pekalongan, Semarang, Surabaya, and Banyuwangi on the north coast of Java, and at Banjarmasin on the south coast of Borneo.

The Java Sea can be classed as a political region since it is completely within Indonesian archipelagic waters. It is also an economic region due to its resource potential, and as with many of the Southeast Asian seas it also is a physical region.

The Banda Sea

The largest body of water completely within Indonesian archipelagic baselines is the Banda Sea, with an area of 202,157 nmi². In this part of eastern Indonesia, the northern hemisphere winter monsoon brings north-northwesterly winds, driving east-flowing currents. These currents are generally weak over the central part of the sea but reach velocities of about 1 knot in the northwestern region. In the northern hemisphere, summer winds are from the southwest, and currents are generally sluggish and variable in direction over the greater part of the sea. Only in the extreme northwest, where the Banda Sea joins the Flores Sea, do speeds reach as much as 1 knot. Generally uniform sea surface temperatures of 28–29 degrees centigrade, low tidal ranges, and coasts sheltered from strong winds and waves characterize the region.

The chief economic resource is fisheries, but catches of oceanic species are only moderate, and there are few productive demersal fishing grounds. Nevertheless, Japanese tuna fishermen were active in the region under an agreement with the Indonesian government. The Banda Sea is notable from the standpoint of political geography because as early as 1968 Japan recognized Indonesia's jurisdiction over the sea as part of its claimed archipelagic waters. An example of a management region, the Banda Sea Fishing Region established in 1968 was in effect through 1979[25] to manage joint-venture fishery operations of Japan and Indonesia. Management included delineations of prohibited fishing areas and access routes into and out of the region. In 1980 both sides decided that the arrangement should not be continued. The Banda Sea also may be considered a political region since it is entirely under Indonesian jurisdiction, an economic region with fish as the prime marine resource, and a physical region since oceanographic parameters indicate a considerable degree of uniformity.

Selat Lombok, the Makassar Strait, and the Celebes Sea

Selat Lombok is wide and deep enough for the world's largest tankers, and the Makassar Strait presents no serious navigational obstacles to the ultra large crude carriers (ULCCs) that traverse the Celebes Sea before leaving Southeast Asian waters south of Mindanao. During the southeast monsoon, winds over the region are southeasterly, while the northern hemisphere winter brings winds with a more northerly component to the region. Northerly winds predominate in the Makassar Strait and north-northeasterlies occur in the Celebes Sea. The ocean currents are much more complicated, however, with a southerly flow in the Makassar Strait and a generally counterclockwise circulation in the Celebes Sea during the southeast monsoon season. In February, strong southwesterly currents prevail in the eastern Celebes Sea, with velocities sometimes exceeding 1.5 knots. Vessels bound for Japan meet these strong currents and brisk northeasterly trade winds as they pass south of Mindanao and enter the Pacific.

There are several oil terminals on the east coast of Kalimantan, and the port of Ujung Pandang is on Sulawesi. The largest of the oil ports, Balikpapan, can handle tankers of up to 250,000 DWT at an offshore mooring. Fishing for several species of tuna occurs in the Celebes Sea, with Philippine and Indonesian boats sharing the generally high catch. In the past, Japanese fishermen were active in the region, but their take was only a small percentage of the total, and now that the waters are under the jurisdictions of Indonesia and the Philippines, the Japanese no longer find the region profitable. The Makassar Strait is almost as productive as the Celebes Sea, although the catch has been smaller due to the size of the region. Only Indonesian fishermen have been active there, since the waters are part of the Indonesian archipelagic claim.

The Sulu Sea

With an area of 93,460 nmi² the Sulu Sea is the largest of the semi-enclosed seas largely under Philippine jurisdiction. It serves as a pathway for ships bound for the South China Sea from the Pacific Ocean via the Surigao Strait north of Mindoro or the Balabac Strait. Ships enroute to Manila from Selat Lombok also transit the sea. Fishing for skipjack and yellowfin tuna, as well as piracy and smuggling, are economic activities with a long history in the region. Zamboanga on Mindanao and Sandakan in Sabah are the principal ports, but neither is particularly large or important.

Other Straits

Other straits worthy of mention in the region include the Taiwan Strait, between the island of Taiwan and the Chinese mainland, and the Torres Strait, between Australia and Papua New Guinea. The Torres Strait is too shallow for the larger tankers but serves as a route for smaller vessels. The San Bernardino Strait–Verde Island Passage is an important route from the Pacific Ocean through the Philippine Archipelago to the South China Sea, and the Ombai and Wetar straits provide additional routes from the Indian Ocean into Indonesian archipelagic waters. The Sunda Strait was once a far more important passageway into the Southeast Asian region than it is now, due largely to the larger modern vessels and navigational problems.

CONCLUSION

Uses of the Southeast Asian seas and problems associated with these uses derive from their geographic context. National interests and specific economic and political issues that arise are shaped by the physical configurations of the land and the sea. Southeast Asia, like other regions in the world, is geographically unique, but also similar in many ways to other regions. With careful adaptation, the study of marine policy issues in Southeast Asia, grounded in an understanding of its geography, can be of value elsewhere. Marine policymakers who are aware of the geographical framework within which they must make decisions should be able to formulate better policies. This chapter has provided a description of Southeast Asia's marine geography for policymakers and scholars who are concerned with the formulation or the study of marine policy. The following chapters review the full range of current issues of marine policy in the Southeast Asian region.

CHAPTER 2

NATIONAL MARINE INTERESTS IN SOUTHEAST ASIA

Mark J. Valencia

INDICATORS OF MARINE INTERESTS

There have been several attempts to derive qualitative and quantitative indices that could serve as measures of national marine interests.[1] While these studies have provided considerable data useful for preparing national profiles and for comparing sectors among nations, the correlations of such indices with actual ocean policy formulation are inconsistent. Their predictive utility is thus uncertain. These difficulties arise because policy formulation for the marine arena is seldom considered separate from and dominant to other national and international concerns. Indeed, ocean management policies are strongly influenced by the intersection of ocean concerns with such factors as historical and cultural perspectives and inertia, development priorities, internal and external security considerations, and international relations. This chapter provides some quantitative indicators of national interest in the oceans, tabulates and summarizes these indicators for the countries of the region, characterizes both the region as a whole and the countries within it according to their outstanding indicators, and then assesses — within the larger milieu of national and international concerns — the prime interests of each nation in the marine arena.

The major indicators of national marine interests used here include marine accessibility, dependence, investment, and control. Table 2.1 summarizes indicators of marine interests for ten Southeast Asian states, and Table 2.2 shows marine interests for those states plus several outside states with significant interests in the region. Although many more specific indicators might have been used, those chosen were considered most significant among those for which synchronous comparable data were available for all nations treated.

Accessibility

Accessibility to the sea and its resources can be considered from both technology-capital and legal-political perspectives; the former is influenced by economic mea-

Table 2.1 Indicators of National Marine Interests

Political Entity	General			Accessibility		Dependence		
	Land[a] Area (thousand km²)	Population[a]	GNP per Capita, 1981[a] (U.S. $)	Length of Coastline[b] (km)	Extended Jurisdiction Area[c] (km²)	Marine Fisheries Production[b] (% of GNP)	Consumption of Fish per Capita[b] (kg/yr)	Fisheries Workers as Percentage of Labor Force[b] (%)
Brunei	5.77	155,000[d]	6,100[d]	161	7,100	0.8	24.1	1.1
Burma	679.00	34,100,000	190	3,060	148,600	1.9	16.8	2.8
Indonesia	1,906.00	149,500,000	530	54,716	1,577,000	1.8	12.0	2.5
Kampuchea	181.00	n.a.	n.a.	443	16,200	6.7	25.4	3.0
Laos	237.00	3,500,000	80	0	0	0	–	0
Malaysia	332.00	14,200,000	1,840	4,675	138,700	2.2	25.7	2.4
Philippines	300.00	49,600,000	790	22,540	551,400	4.8	30.0	6.3
Singapore	0.58	2,400,000	5,240	193	100	0.2	30.0	0.5
Thailand	513.00	48,000,000	770	3,219	94,700	1.0	15.0	0.8
Vietnam	330.00	55,700,000	150[e]	3,444	210,600	4.1[f]	15.1[f]	5.4
TOTAL	4,254.35	357,155,000		92,451	2,744,400			

sures such as gross national product (GNP), the latter by geographic circumstances. The political entities of the South China Sea marine region are, in general, developing countries with a low per capita GNP and high population growth rates. The greater the GNP, the more resources available that could be allocated to marine activities. China's GNP of US$315 billion is an order of magnitude greater than that of Indonesia, the state with the next highest GNP; Brunei, landlocked Laos, and Kampuchea apparently have the fewest resources available for marine investment.

In general, marine activities represent only a small portion of total national activity. The higher the ratio of total shoreline length to total land area, the greater the opportunity for the inhabitants to interact with the sea and thus the greater the

Dependence (continued)							Investments		
Oil Resources[g] (billion MT)	Seaborne Trade[h] (million MT)	Petroleum Trade by Sea[i] (million MT)	Merchant Fleet[h] (no.)	(GT)	Oil Tankers[k] (no.)	(GT)	Total Naval Fleet[l] (number of vessels)	Marine Scientific Research Vessels[m] (no.)	(GT)
10–100(?)	13	0.2 (export)	1	616	0		35	0	0
?	?	?	109	87,972	4	2,986	89	0	0
10–100	88	57.6 (export)	1,319	1,846,824	130	317,924	123	5	3,965
1–10	0.6	0.3 (import)	3	3,558	0	0	40	0	0
0	–	–	0	0	0	0	0	0	0
10–100	16	5.6 (export) and import)	329	1,195,411	37	37,661	45	0	0
10–100	31	9.3 (import)	882	2,773,855	66	577,304	193	3	1,036
0.1–1	62	44.9[j] (export) and import)	849	7,183,326	141	2,582,871	14	4	1,968
1–100	20	9.8 (import)	197	441,949	59	140,470	155	2	461
1–10[f]	7[f]	4.8[h] (import)	106	261,847	11	35,384	603	0	0
452	237.6	132.5	3,795	13,795,358	448	3,694,600	1,297	14	7,430

national marine interest or awareness. On this basis, the two city-states of Hong Kong and Singapore would have the greatest marine interest. The Philippines, Indonesia, and Brunei would have high interest, and Kampuchea and Laos would have the least national marine interest.

Kampuchea, Hong Kong, and Singapore are shelf-locked, and Brunei is disadvantaged nearly equally. Thailand is shelf-locked in the South China Sea. Its jurisdiction over ocean space and resources extends beyond the continental margin only in the Andaman Sea. Indonesia gained more than 1.5 million square nautical miles (nmi^2) of offshore area under extended maritime jurisdiction, whereas the Philippines, Vietnam, Malaysia, and Thailand have acquired between 114,000 and 551,000 nmi^2. Singapore and Hong Kong, and to a lesser extent Kampuchea, Bru-

Table 2.1   Indicators of National Marine Interests (Continued)

Political Entity	Extended Jurisdiction		Territorial Sea[a,o]	
	Area/Total Fleet (km² per vessel)	Area/Total Military Aircraft[n] (km² per aircraft)	Width (nmi)	Date
Brunei	203	2,367	3[p] (12)	1982[p]
Burma	1,670	9,288	12	15 Nov 68
Indonesia	12,821	35,044	12 Archipelago principle[q]	1957
Kampuchea	405		12	27 Sep 69
Laos	0	0		
Malaysia	3,082	3,749	12	2 Aug 69
Philippines	2,857	4,209	Treaty limits, archipelago principle[q]	1961
Singapore	7	1	3 12 (fishing) limits)	1978
Thailand	611	538	12	6 Oct 68
Vietnam	349	488	12	12 May 77

Sources:

[a] *World Development Report 1983,* New York: World Bank/Oxford University Press, 1983, pp. 148–149.

[b] *Yearbook of Fishery Statistics, 1980,* Rome: Food and Agriculture Organization of the United Nations, 1981; J. C. Marr, *Fishery Resource Management in Southeast Asia,* Washington, D.C.: Resources for the Future, 1976, p. 11, Table 2; *Asia Yearbook 1982,* Hong Kong: *Far Eastern Economic Review,* 182, pp. 8–9.

[c] Elisabeth Mann Borgese and Norton Ginsburg, eds., *Ocean Yearbook 3,* Chicago: University of Chicago Press, 1982, pp. 565–568.

[d] Data for Brunei is from Central Intelligence Agency: *National Basic Intelligence Factbook,* Washington, D.C.: Central Intelligence Agency, January, 1977.

[e] V. K. Ranganathan, Citibank, Hong Kong.

[f] Data for South Vietnam only.

[g] Michael MccGwire and Wilma Broeren, *Politics of the Sea: Components of National Interest Information Package,* Halifax, Nova Scotia: Centre for Foreign Policy Studies Department of Political Science, Dalhousie University, Table 4A (mimeo). Data reported are for recoverable reserves. Figures for other entities are either nil or not available.

[h] *Lloyd's Register of Shipping; Statistical Tables 1982,* London: Lloyd's Register of Shipping, 1980, pp. 4–5.

[i] *Statistical Yearbook for Asia and the Pacific,* Bangkok: ESCAP, 1974.

[j] Data for Singapore include transshipments.

	Controls			
	Jurisdictional Claims and Dates			
Contiguous Zone[q,r]		*Continental Shelf[o,r]*		*Extended Jurisdiction[s] (to 200 nmi)*
Width (nmi)	*Date*	*Dimensions*	*Date*	
6 nmi exclusive 6 nmi "outerbelt"	1964		30 Jun 54	82[p]
12	Apr 77	Natural prolongation	9 Apr 77	9 Apr 77
		To where depth admits of exploitation	17 Feb 69	Mar 80
12	1 Dec 78	Natural prolongation	27 Sep 69	Jan 78[t]
			28 Jun 66	Apr 80
		To where depth admits of exploitation	20 Mar 68	11 Jun 68
			May 73	May 80
12	12 May 77	Natural prolongation		12 May 77[u]

[k] *Lloyd's*, pp. 6–8.

[l] *Jane's Fighting Ships 1982–1983*, New York: Jane's Publishing Co. Ltd. 1982. See Table 7.4 for more detailed accounting of naval strengths.

[m] *Lloyd's*, pp. 11–13.

[n] Numbers of military aircraft used in this calculation are from *Pacific Defense Reporter 1983*, Victoria, Australia: Annual Reference Division, 1983.

[o] L. M. Alexander, "Indices of National Interest in the Oceans," *Ocean Development and International Law*, Vol. 1, 1973, pp. 21–49.

[p] The policy of the United Kingdom applied to the protected Sultanate of Brunei until 1984; Brunei declared a 12-mile territorial sea and a 200-nmi EEZ in 1982.

[q] Waters within the straight baselines joining appropriate points of outermost islands of the archipelago are considered to be territorial waters.

[r] C. M. Siddayao, "Southeast Asia's Offshore Petroleum Resources and the Law of the Sea," *Southeast Asian Affairs*, Singapore: Institute of Southeast Asian Studies, 1977, pp. 73–88.

[s] J. R. V. Prescott, *Maritime Jurisdiction in Southeast Asia: A Commentary and Map*, Honolulu: East-West Environment and Policy Institute, Research Report No. 2, 1981, p. 6.

[t] N. Chanda, "All at Sea Over the Deeper Issue," *Far Eastern Economic Review*, 3 February 1978, p. 23.

[u] R. Yao, "Gun Law of the Sea," *Far Eastern Economic Review*, 17 June 1977, p. 25.

Table 2.2   Major National Marine Interests in Southeast Asia

Country (prominent maritime feature)	Marine Interests
Australia (island)	Defense against a possible invasion from the north; favorable resolution of boundaries with Indonesia; development of hydrocarbon and fisheries potential there; unhindered passage through the region.
Brunei (zone-locked)	Obtaining the maximum EEZ and continental shelf areas; development of any hydrocarbon resources there.
Burma (historic bay and island-fringed coast)	Acceptance of Gulf of Martaban and Mergui archipelago baselines by neighbors and by maritime powers, and resolution of related continental shelf disputes with Thailand and India; development of fisheries and hydrocarbon potential on the shelf.
China	Coastal surveillance and defense against the Soviet Union; defense of continental shelf claims in the Gulf of Tonkin and of the Paracel and Spratly islands vis-à-vis Vietnam; defense of South China Sea when it serves a larger political purpose; development of hydrocarbon resources on the shelf.
China (Taiwan Island)	Coastal defense against a possible mainland blockade and against mainland or Vietnamese attacks on Spratly forces; recognition of the EEZ claim and resolution of boundary disputes with the Philippines and Japan; development of hydrocarbon resources in the Taiwan Strait (and north of Taiwan); unhindered commercial transit and fisheries access in the region.
Indonesia (archipelago)	Defense of oil fields in Natuna area and limited transit of aid to subversive movements; maintenance of the archipelagic claim with neighbors and maritime powers; resolution of outstanding boundary disputes with Vietnam, Australia, Malaysia, and the Philippines; development of any hydrocarbon and fishery resources; evolution of acceptable regime for the Malacca Straits.
Japan (maritime power)	Unimpeded transit of oil and goods; access to tuna and shrimp resources, and to hydrocarbons.

Kampuchea (shelf-locked)	No major marine interests; resolution of continental shelf boundary disputes with Thailand and Vietnam; development of any hydrocarbon resources.
Laos (land-locked)	Access through Thailand, Cambodia, and/or Vietnam; access to port facilities and fisheries resources.
Malaysia (peninsular; zone-separated)	Coastal defense against a Vietnamese invasion; unrestricted access to and communication through Indonesian archipelagic waters between peninsular Malaysia and Sarawak and Sabah; agreement with maritime powers, Indonesia and Singapore, on an acceptable regime for the Malacca Straits; maintenance of its continental shelf and island claims vis-à-vis Brunei, China, Vietnam, and the Philippines; development of hydrocarbon and fisheries resources.
Philippines (archipelago; treaty waters claim)	Defense of the archipelagic claim; acceptance of the treaty waters as a territorial sea claim; resolution or muting of jurisdictional disputes with Malaysia, China (including Taiwan), Vietnam, and Indonesia, particularly those on the "Dangerous Ground"; development of hydrocarbon resources; acceptable sealane sites and regimes.
Singapore (zone-locked)	Unrestricted transport of goods and oil in and through the region; access to fisheries resources in Malaysian and Indonesian waters.
Thailand (shelf-locked in South China Sea)	Coastal defense against Vietnam; resolution of continental shelf boundary disputes with Kampuchea and Vietnam; access to fisheries resources within and outside the region; development of hydrocarbon resources.
United States (maritime power)	Unimpeded transit of commercial and military vessels and of oil to Japan; access to port facilities; surveillance of Soviet surface vessels and submarines; direct access to hydrocarbon resources.
USSR (maritime power)	Unimpeded transit of commercial and military vessels; access to port facilities; surveillance of United States surface vessels and submarines.
Vietnam	General defense against China and other hostile neighbors and maritime powers; defense of claims in the Gulf of Tonkin and the Spratlys; resolution of the continental shelf boundary dispute with Indonesia; development of hydrocarbon resources in the Gulf of Tonkin and the Mekong Delta–Natuna area.

nei, and Thailand, are geographically disadvantaged both in area gained and loss of possible "common-heritage" resources in the South China Sea that they might have shared.

All of the political entities except the Chinese province of Taiwan, Indonesia, and the Philippines have marine access only on semi-enclosed seas. Hong Kong, Vietnam, Kampuchea, Singapore, and Brunei only have access to the South China Sea, so their vessels moving to and from their ports from outside the region must pass through one or more strategic straits. The juridical regime for these straits and archipelagic waters has important implications for marine access.

Dependence

Some nations are dependent on the sea for conceptual unity, physical communication between water-separated components, as a buffer zone between unfriendly neighbors, maintenance of cultural traditions, resources to further rural development, subsistence for coastal people, recreation and tourism, and waste disposal. These are not readily quantifiable, but often they are significant factors in national marine interests.

GNP per capita and population growth rates give a rough indication of a state's potential demand for marine resources and services. With the exception of Singapore and the British colonies, the South China Sea states are in a "developing" status, although Malaysia, Macao, and the Chinese province of Taiwan appear to be the most advanced in terms of GNP per capita. Nevertheless, the recent global recession has restricted the rate of economic growth in the region in general, while population growth rates continue to comprise one-third or more of total GNP per capita growth rates. Brunei, Hong Kong, and Singapore already depend heavily on the sea for their fortunate economic status. Thus all the entities of the South China Sea region have a national interest in developing marine resources and related activities, if only to satisfy the increasing expectations of their burgeoning populations.

For example, if income should rise by about 10 percent throughout the region, the demand for the services of the ocean would rise by about the same amount. A 10-percent growth rate would mean that the economies would double in seven years and quadruple in fourteen. The impact on the sea and its resources could be staggering. The cost of land-based activities has been rising relative to sea-based activities for many years, and these relative costs will continue to shift in the same direction, perhaps ultimately making more and more substitution necessary between land-intensive and sea-intensive technologies. Dependence on the sea in a strict sense can be indicated by such measures as the share of national income and employment derived from the maritime sector, the per capita consumption of seafood, and the volume of seaborne trade. Low incomes and medium-to-high marine accessibility historically have fostered usage of the sea, particularly as a food resource, by these littoral countries.

The value of the fish catch averages about 3 percent of these nations' GNPs, whereas in most economically developed states of the world the value of the fish catch constitutes less than 1 percent of the GNP. Thailand, Malaysia, the Philippines,

Maintenance of the archipelagic concept and its attendant regime is at the core of Indonesian national marine interests. A 12-nmi territorial sea and a 200-nmi EEZ measured from the archipelagic baselines accompany the archipelagic claim. Almost all Indonesian marine policies, and some others outside the marine sphere, are directly or indirectly based on the archipelagic concept and are part of a strategy designed to gain its recognition. The concept is embodied in the phrase used to connote the archipelagic concept or principle, *Wawasan Nusantara*, which implies that "the seas and the straits must be utilized to bridge the physical separations between the islands, regions and manifold ethnic groups."[10]

Aside from forging a sense of national unity, the concept is of prime security concern to Indonesia. Full control over these waters inhibits external material support to the numerous separatist movements in the archipelago and facilitates interception of violators of regulations in the various jurisdictional regimes. As an indication of this concern, Indonesia's territorial waters constitute a formal "security zone," which means that advance notice and permission are required for foreign military vessels to enter these waters.[11]

The archipelagic concept may also underlie Indonesia's strong territorial waters claim in the Strait of Malacca, since this strait can be seen as providing a route into the archipelagic waters. According to Article 53 of the CLS, Indonesia must designate and obtain approval for sea-lanes through the archipelago. Japanese tankers larger than 220,000 deadweight tons (DWT) (those that when fully loaded fail to achieve the minimum required underkeel clearance of 3.5 meters [m] in the Strait of Malacca) may use the Lombok–Makassar route instead. Indonesia might wish to tap this "floating oil pipeline" to enhance development projects and thus promote political integration of rural and border areas.

As detailed in Chapter 3, Indonesia has already negotiated and established agreed boundaries on the continental shelf with most of its neighbors. Apparently it has taken the view that it is more important to divide the area and resources than to maintain an inflexible position that would prevent resource development. There are still several important continental shelf boundaries to be negotiated, however, including those with Vietnam, Malaysia, and Australia; each area in question has hydrocarbon potential.

Within its archipelagic waters and territorial seas, Indonesia wishes to reserve all fisheries resources for itself for food, foreign exchange, and as a base for rural development. Exceptions are being made for traditional fishing in archipelagic waters. A major concern may be management of the exploitation of transnational tuna stocks that migrate through Philippine, Indonesian, and Australian waters into the Pacific and of other fish stocks shared with India, Malaysia, Australia, and the Philippines.

Kampuchea

Next to Laos, Kampuchea's marine activity has been the lowest in the region. It has the lowest total sea trade, the lowest tonnage of merchant marine vessels both in toto and relative to GNP, no tankers, the third smallest naval fleet, and the smallest number of air force units (thus limiting its surveillance capabilities). Although

Kampuchea has in the past been highly dependent on fish as a contributor to GNP, most of its fisheries production is from fresh water. Kampuchea has ratified all four 1958 Geneva conventions and has participated in many multilateral marine treaties, possibly following the lead of the United States, its close supporter at the time of ratification.[12] In declaring its EEZ, Kampuchea established "liaison zones," which apparently are designated sea routes. Kampuchea also has a security zone approximately 35-nmi wide.[13]

Kampuchea, already one of the poorest countries in the world, has experienced the region's lowest (actually negative) GNP per capita growth rate. Prior to the end of the Indochina war there was exploration for hydrocarbons in the northern area claimed by both Thailand and Kampuchea,[14] and there is hydrocarbon potential in the area of overlap between Kampuchea and Vietnam.[15] Kampuchea may wish to settle these boundaries in order to speed up development of its marine resources there.

Laos

Landlocked Laos wants guaranteed access to the sea as well as compensatory access to the marine resources of neighboring countries. Laos has sought transit rights through Kampuchea to Kampong Som Port, which may now be possible, given the compatible views of their governments. However, given the greater abundance of fisheries resources in the South China Sea, Laos may seek transit and living resource access through its close ally, Vietnam. Indeed, the Soviet Union is constructing an all-weather road to link Laos to the sea at Danang.[16] Until this road is completed or arrangements are made with Kampuchea, Laos must depend on Thailand for access. Thailand has used transit rights as a political-economic weapon to influence Laotian internal politics and to control incursions along their long common border.[17] An agreement on transit rights concluded on 1 June 1978 is quite favorable for Laos, but Thailand has continued to insist on reciprocal transit rights in the event it wishes to trade with China and Vietnam through Laos.

Malaysia

As a water-separated state, Malaysia has a national security interest in unrestricted access and communication between peninsular Malaysia and Sarawak and Sabah. Commercial and naval communication is particularly important since both Sarawak and Sabah have demonstrated secessionist tendencies in the past.[18] Hydrocarbon exploitation is ongoing off both Sabah and Sarawak, and these states are rich in other natural resources such as timber, coal, and copper. Moreover, one of the largest Malaysian development projects — an LNG plant and aluminum smelter— is located at Bintulu, Sarawak.

A recently negotiated Indonesian–Malaysian treaty guarantees unrestricted communication between peninsular and east Malaysia.[19] Malaysia has accepted the Indonesian archipelagic concept with the provision that the legitimate and existing rights of states adversely affected would be protected by international law. Such rights include traditional fishing. However, Indonesia is already establishing a naval base on Natuna Island,[20] and the long-term stability of this agreement may have to be considered in the light of Sukarno's *konfrontasi* (confrontation) with Malaysia and Indonesia's past expansion in Irian Jaya and Timor.[21] Malaysia also eventually may be concerned about passage from Sarawak to Sabah through Brunei's waters when Brunei extends its jurisdiction.

Security and sovereignty considerations have been strong factors in Malaysia's strict enforcement of its territorial waters claim regarding use of its "front yard," the Strait of Malacca. Environmental protection in the strait, formerly a minor issue, has also become of prime importance to Malaysia. Malaysia has negotiated a separate package agreement on the use of the strait with the United States, the Soviet Union, and other concerned coastal and maritime powers. The package agreement underscores the right of Malaysia to establish maritime safety and traffic arrangements in the strait.[22] For example, there is a provision in Malaysia's Environmental Quality Act of 1974 requiring the party causing oil pollution to bear the cost of removing it. Further, the act enables enforcing officials to detain any ship involved in a spill or discharge and, with court permission, to sell it if the owner is unable to pay the fines and costs.[23]

In order to provide a bigger piece of the "economic pie" to *bumiputras* (indigenous peoples) without direct transfer of Chinese citizen holdings, the pie must expand rapidly. Malaysia is thus anxious to proceed with oil and gas development on the continental shelf and to settle shelf and EEZ boundaries and island claims with Vietnam, Brunei, and the Philippines on the Sunda Shelf, and with Indonesia and the Philippines in the Celebes Sea. China's claims in the South China Sea may include prospective hydrocarbon areas off Sarawak and possibly the producing Tembungo field 120 km (75 mi) off Sabah.[24] As explained in Chapter 6, Malaysia has negotiated a memorandum of understanding with Thailand for joint management of continental shelf resources in a small sliver of disputed offshore territory extending eastward onto the Sunda Shelf.

Malaysian fisheries policy is directed to alleviating poverty and unemployment among fishermen, particularly *bumiputras*. Presently, little Malaysian fishing extends beyond 30 nmi from shore. Resources are overexploited within the nearshore zone, resulting in violent competition between indigenous Chinese trawlermen and Malay traditional fishermen.[25] Malaysian fishermen could be tempted to fish in Indonesian or Thai waters if the nearshore resource proves insufficient to support increased fishing capacity. Malaysia thus could become concerned with management of shared stocks on the Sunda Shelf and in competition with Burma, Indonesia, and Thailand over fisheries resources to the west toward India and to the north of Langkawi.

The Philippines

The archipelagic Philippines has the highest population growth rate in the region, the second longest coastline, and the region's highest proportion of employment in the fisheries sector.

The Philippines' principal marine interests appear to be international acceptance of its archipelagic claim, its treaty waters, and their accompanying regimes of
internal and territorial waters.[26] Philippine archipelagic interests are similar to
those of Indonesia: maintaining conceptual national unity, preventing maritime
power conflicts in its vicinity, maintaining sovereignty over resources, and maintaining coastal defense and security, especially with respect to the transit of supplies to Communist and Muslim secessionist movements. In 1982, when Philippine
Air Force planes struck a Japanese tanker 9 mi off Mindanao carrying petrochemicals from Libya, the explanation for the attack was that the tanker was thought to
be carrying weapons for the secessionists.[27]

The Philippines has a national security interest as well as an economic interest in
finding and developing hydrocarbons within its claimed jurisdictional areas. Imports of Middle East crude oil absorb much of its available foreign exchange. The
Islamic Conference has encouraged some Middle East countries to use their exports as a weapon to constrain the Philippine government's options in dealing with
the Muslim secessionist movement in the south.[28]

One particular area of hydrocarbon interest, the "Dangerous Ground," including Reed Bank, is also claimed in part or in whole by China, the Chinese province of
Taiwan, Vietnam, and Malaysia. China, Vietnam, and the Philippines have agreed
to settle the dispute by peaceful means.[29]

Areas claimed by the Philippines and the Chinese province of Taiwan in the
Bashi Channel; by the Philippines, Malaysia, and Indonesia in the Celebes Sea; and
by the Philippines and Indonesia near Miangas Island are good tuna fishing
grounds. The presence of this valuable resource may exacerbate disputes among
these states. In the south, Philippine purse seiners are luring tuna with *payaw*
(floating platforms anchored to the bottom) to save fuel. Indonesian fishermen are
operating in the southern Celebes Sea, and there is Philippine concern that they
may migrate northward and come into conflict with Philippine fishermen.

Potential pollution from tankers rerouted from the Strait of Malacca through
the Lombok–Makassar straits and the Sulu or Celebes seas is a concern, as is the
passage of surface and subsurface vessels of great powers.[30] According to the CLS,
the Philippines must designate sea-lanes. The Philippines has voiced strong objections to the provision in the CLS that the Intergovernmental Maritime Organization must approve its sea-lane designations. The Philippines also has objected to
the "right of archipelagic sea-lanes passage," corresponding to transit passage, preferring instead a regime of innocent passage.[31]

Singapore

Singapore has the smallest area in the region and the second smallest population
but the second highest GNP per capita. Singapore is at a geographic disadvantage,
having the shortest coastline, being shelf-locked and having the least potential offshore area accruing from a 200-nmi EEZ. The small area of the island of Singapore
imposes a forced intimacy of its people with the sea.

Singapore already has the second largest volume of sea trade and of petroleum sea trade, overall and relative to GNP, because it serves as a trade, transshipment, and refining center for the southern South China Sea region and beyond. Singapore also has the region's largest tanker fleet and merchant marine tonnage relative to GNP, even when flag-of-convenience vessels are excluded. Because of the small offshore area it obtains under a 200-nmi regime (100 nmi^2 at maximum), Singapore will have the least logistical problem in enforcing its regulations in the zone despite its extremely small navy.

Singapore's fisheries contribute the smallest portion of GNP in the region, and it has the lowest ratio of personnel employed in fisheries to total labor force, not counting Laos. Although Singapore has a high rate of fish consumption and is a distant-water fishing nation, its projected total demand for fisheries products is the region's lowest due to its small population. Also, Singapore is distinguished by having relatively few marine scientists and engaging in little national marine research.

Singapore intends to enhance its status as the maritime center of the Association of Southeast Asian Nations (ASEAN) and the region, serving as an entrepôt for the Europe–Southeast Asian trade and as a center for warehousing and for servicing marine exploitation operations. Its principal marine interest, and indeed the basis for its economy, is unrestricted transport of goods and oil in the region. Singapore also is interested in compensating for its geographic disadvantages by pressing for unhindered marine transit for its trading partners, for unencumbered air transit over territorial seas surrounding Singapore, and even for "regionalization" of fisheries. Singapore would like to gain access to any declared fisheries surplus in its neighbors' EEZs since there are insufficient fish for its fleet in the small area within its jurisdiction.

Thailand

Thailand has shown a strong interest in marine research, especially fisheries research. It has more research vessels and spends more for this purpose than any other of the region's political entities. Thailand maintains a large distant-water fishing fleet, and it is developing gas deposits discovered in its shelf-locked gulf waters. Thailand has ratified all four 1958 Geneva conventions but has participated in only two other multilateral marine treaties.[32] Thailand is zone-locked in the Gulf of Thailand and in the Andaman Sea and thus has interests in the marine transportation regimes promulgated by its neighbors. Communist and Muslim irredentist movements in the southern Isthmus of Kra far from the power base in Bangkok make the south a potential trouble spot. Thailand has a prime security interest in maintaining unrestricted naval and commercial transit between the east and west coasts of the mountainous Isthmus of Kra through Malaysian, Singaporean, and Indonesian territorial waters in the Strait of Malacca. Further, Thailand attaches great importance to the 1954 Manila Pact,[33] which pledges U.S. support to Thailand in the event of external aggression. Implementation of this agreement may require maximum mobility for U.S. military assistance through archipelagic waters and the Strait of Malacca. Thailand may also be concerned with coastal defense and with the possible shipment of material to insurgent groups. Control of smugglers, pirates, and illegal domestic fishing are also important. Thailand imports 90 percent of its oil from Singapore in small coastal tankers an average of twenty years old. Thus, enforcement of special or even international environmental standards on shipping in Singaporean and Malaysian coastal waters could affect Thailand's oil supply routes.

Thai boats fish throughout the South China Sea. Access and joint ventures have been sought with countries outside the region, including Oman, Bangladesh, and India,[34] and informal arrangements have been sought and made with Vietnam and Kampuchea. It appears that Thailand is seeking access to fisheries in many places by any legal means. Thailand's arguments for access depend on relations within ASEAN and the ideal of technical cooperation between developing countries (TCDC), as well as historic fishing rights, preferential regional treatment, and its alleged geographic disadvantage.

Borders in the eastern Gulf of Thailand remain a problem for Thailand, especially because of the potential for hydrocarbon resources there. The major jurisdictional disputes between Thailand and Kampuchea and Vietnam will probably continue until the Indochinese situation has settled somewhat and contacts with the new Kampuchean regime can be established. As long as these areas remain in contention, however, potential offshore hydrocarbons in Thailand's claimed portion will go undiscovered and unexploited (see Chapter 5).

Vietnam

Vietnam was the second of the region's entities to claim a 200-nmi EEZ. With the largest naval fleet and the second largest air force in the region, it should have little trouble patrolling its offshore claim, including its security zone. Vietnam is developing its fisheries capability with ADB assistance and may phase out Thai fishing in its EEZ. The proportion of the labor force employed in fisheries is the second largest among the region's nations.

Because of hostilities with China, Vietnam's prime marine interest is probably defense of its Gulf of Tonkin coast and of claimed and occupied islands in the South China Sea.[35] In addition to its claims in the Spratly Islands, Vietnam has unsettled continental shelf disputes with Indonesia north of the Natuna Islands, with Thailand in the eastern Gulf of Thailand, and with China in the Gulf of Tonkin. Vietnam is interested in rapid development of offshore hydrocarbons to support its industrial development and energy independence. However, as long as hostilities continue, marine boundary disputes will remain unresolved and development of hydrocarbon potential in these disputed areas will be retarded.

With pressure from the north and west, Vietnam should be eager to avoid aggravating its new immediate marine neighbors to the south and east — Malaysia, Indonesia, and the Philippines. However, if Chinese pressure subsides or ASEAN continues to pursue an anti-Vietnamese united front, Vietnam may be less interested in accommodating the interests of ASEAN countries.

SOUTHEAST ASIA MARINE INTERESTS
OF OUTSIDE NATIONS

Australia

Australia's long common marine border with Indonesia and its proximity to Southeast Asia motivate its general interest in the stability and economic development of the region. Indeed, Australia is a member of an agreement (ANZUK) including Malaysia, Singapore, New Zealand, and the United Kingdom that provides for military assistance in the event of external aggression. The Royal Australian Air Force maintains a base at Butterworth in Malaysia. (The United Kingdom maintains contingents in Brunei, Singapore, and Hong Kong.[36]) Australia is concerned with the adequacy of its northern coastal defense system. Unexpected arrivals of Vietnamese refugee boats on Australian territory and Australia's apparent difficulty in curbing drug smuggling and illegal fishing in this area have apparently rekindled fears of an Asian invasion from the north.

Mutually satisfactory settlement with Indonesia of as yet undetermined boundary portions off northwest Australia, south of Christmas Island, and south of Timor would be of importance to Australia. As indicated in Chapter 6, the latter boundary is particularly important because there is good hydrocarbon potential there.

Unrestricted commercial transport in the Southeast Asian region is a principal marine interest for Australia because iron ore mined in the state of Western Australia is shipped to Japan through the archipelagos and the South China Sea. When Australia begins to export uranium ore, the transport issue will become even more important. Also, any further restrictions on transport in the Strait of Malacca or in the South China Sea or any marine conflict within the region could deflect tanker traffic to Australian waters. Australia is affected by fisheries policies and activities in Southeast Asia because some of the tuna stocks that migrate into Australian waters spawn and grow in Indonesian and Philippine waters.

China

China's huge population and area set it apart from other South China Sea coastal nations in terms of measures such as projected total demand for fish and numbers of naval personnel and marine scientists. When these parameters are compared with its GNP or total population, however, it becomes apparent that China has a relatively low preoccupation with the sea, perhaps due in part to its low ratio of coastline to land area and its focus on development of terrestrial agricultural and mineral resources. Of the countries bordering the South China Sea region, China has the lowest per capita consumption of fish (but the highest catch), the lowest total petroleum sea trade, the lowest sea trade and petroleum sea trade relative to GNP, the second lowest merchant marine tonnage relative to GNP, and the smallest number of naval personnel and ocean scientists per capita. China is unquestionably the dominant power in the South China Sea region, with the largest number of air force units and the second largest naval fleet.

Only about half of China's coast fronts the South China Sea. With the abandonment of its policy of self-reliance and isolationism and its continued efforts to transform from an agricultural to an industrial economic base, however, China is expanding its activities in hydrocarbons, transport, naval maneuvers, and fisheries in the South China Sea.[37] There is considerable hydrocarbon potential on the Mainland Shelf,[38] and offshore hydrocarbon exploration by Western companies west and southwest of the island of Hainan has been successful. As its foreign shipping, seaborne commerce, and naval mission expand, China is becoming more interested in safeguarding passage in the South China Sea.

China's prime marine interest at present probably is security. The missions of the Chinese navy are coastal defense, primarily against attack by the Soviet navy, "liberation" of Taiwan, perhaps through a blockade, and the "recovery" of the Spratly and other islands.[39] Future missions may include strategic deterrence by means of ballistic missile submarines and the establishment of a naval presence in foreign waters. Such a projection of naval power implies a necessity for passage of warships through waters claimed by other countries. This would be contrary to traditional Third World efforts to restrict passage of warships through their waters — efforts China has supported in the past. China does not yet have an oceangoing navy, and thus at present it supports restricted passage because of its interest in limiting the usefulness of its enemies' navies.[40]

China faces a dilemma in enforcing its island and attendant marine claims in the South China Sea. While China is engaged in hostilities with Vietnam and has already occupied the Paracels by force, similar hostile moves against Vietnamese claims and troops in the Spratlys could be construed as acts against the other claimants as well. China is already nearly encircled by the Soviet Union and its allies, and provocation of other Southeast Asian nations would not be in China's interest. China has not specified its claims in the central and northern South China Sea. Their vagueness may be used as leverage to coerce the other claimants into complying with China's anti-Soviet and other policies.[41]

China (Taiwan)

The Chinese province of Taiwan borders the South China Sea along its western and southwestern coasts. Its export-oriented economy is highly dependent on the sea for trade. Taiwan also obtains the largest catch among the distant-water fishing countries in the region. The continuing hostility with mainland China accounts for Taiwan having the highest proportion of naval personnel to population in the region. Insular Taiwan is isolated politically and faces a rapidly increasing population in what is already the world's second-most densely populated political entity.[42]

With normalization of U.S.–China relations and the resulting abrogation of the U.S.–Taiwan mutual defense treaty, Taiwan is in an unstable political situation. Its main marine interest is coastal defense against a possible Chinese blockade and against possible attacks against its forces on claimed islands in the South China Sea.

Taiwan has declared an EEZ and as a result has conflicting claims with the Philippines in the Bashi Channel, with Japan to the northeast, and possibly with China in the Taiwan Strait.[43] Its claims and occupation of islands in the Spratlys area and the resulting disputes with Vietnam and the Philippines are additional problems. Settlement of such claims and boundaries may be difficult due to a lack of political recognition by other countries. Lack of recognition eventually may affect both transit passage of its flag vessels through the Indonesian archipelago and also its access to any fisheries surplus in its neighbors' EEZs.

Hong Kong

Hong Kong is highly dependent on the sea for trade and is a distant-water fishing nation in the South China Sea.[44] Hong Kong's principal marine interests are thus transport and access to fisheries in the EEZs of other nations. Specifically, access to China's EEZ fish "surplus" may be sought on the basis that Hong Kong is disadvantaged by being shelf-locked, i.e., until reversion to China in 1997.

Japan

Japan's prime concerns in the South China Sea are unimpeded transit of potentially polluting cargoes (such as oil, LNG, commercial toxic chemicals, nuclear spent fuel, and uranium ore) as well as normal commercial goods; access to tuna, shrimp, and mackerel fisheries; and access to hydrocarbons.

Japan relies on transport through and from the Southeast Asian region for more than 70 percent of its oil. It is or will soon begin receiving LNG from Bintulu, Arun, Badak, and Brunei.[45] Spent nuclear fuel apparently is shipped through the South China Sea and the Strait of Malacca for reprocessing in Europe. These waste shipments are likely to increase in volume and frequency until Japan either reprocesses its own spent fuel or ships it elsewhere.[46]

Japan's perspective on transportation issues has been primarily economic but is now of necessity becoming political. Japan considers that extensive rerouting will adversely affect its economy and possibly its energy policy. These effects could be passed on to the Southeast Asian nations as higher prices for Japanese exports. Japan has a national security interest in maintaining its raw material supplies from Southeast Asia and its markets there for its manufactured commodities. The Strait of Malacca will remain important, but Japan will probably diversify its routes and develop floating oil storage areas, transshipment points, and refineries along these routes.

In the face of the new restrictions on access for its fishing vessels, Japan has been successful in establishing numerous fisheries joint ventures in Southeast Asia for private Japanese fishing companies, especially in Indonesia and the Philippines. But few Japanese long-distance fishing boats are being built, and Japanese labor and fuel costs are rising. Japanese companies may increasingly purchase fish directly from local fisheries in Southeast Asia, thus using cheaper capital and labor and less fuel to fulfill its fish requirements.

Japan is permitting its national oil company to enter into joint ventures to explore and exploit hydrocarbons directly in Southeast Asia;[47] thus it has an indirect interest in the resolution of boundary disputes in the region such as those offshore China and Burma.

The Soviet Union

The Soviet Union has strong interests in unimpeded transit of both commercial and military traffic through and within the South China Sea. The Soviet Union has direct military interests in Southeast Asia, having signed a mutual defense pact with Vietnam. The Soviet Union is using Cam Ranh Bay as a naval base,[48] and it deployed warships in the Gulf of Tonkin and in the South China Sea during the 1979 Vietnam–China hostilities. The Soviet's Far East fleet of 750 vessels uses the South China Sea for transit from the Sea of Japan to the northwest Indian Ocean and the Persian Gulf. Also, the South Seas Soviet fishing fleet regularly unloads its catch at Jurong in Singapore for processing by the USSR–Singapore joint-venture scheme and for maintenance. The Soviet merchant marine has been undercutting shipping conference rates for the region and is seeking to build refueling bases there. The dispute between Vietnam and China over the Spratlys is of considerable interest to the Soviet Union, because the controller of those islands could control major sea-lanes of communication in the South China Sea. The Soviet Union supports the Vietnamese claim.

The United States

The United States has direct military interests in Southeast Asia. It maintains troops and strategically important naval and air force bases and stations in the Philippines, and the United States fleets use Hong Kong and Singapore for logistical support. The United States has a mutual defense treaty and a bilateral mutual assistance agreement with the Philippines and Thailand, the 1954 Manila Pact.

Unimpeded transit is a prime military interest of the United States for several reasons. The United States is without a naval base on the Southeast Asian mainland and now relies more heavily on mobility as a deterrent in honoring its treaty commitments and for showing the flag in the region. During hostilities, the United States would have to convoy seaborne oil headed both for Japan and the United States from the Middle East. The South China Sea is also one of four alternative routes for the movement of oil from the Middle East to the United States. The South China Sea is used as one supply route to Diego Garcia in the Indian Ocean, a base of increasing importance to the United States in support of its Middle East interests.

The terms and conditions of commercial and military transit in disputed areas like the Spratlys, the Gulf of Tonkin, and near Natuna will be determined by the eventual owners, which the United States would prefer to be any nation other than Vietnam. Freedom of navigation is an important long-range consideration in the strong involvement of U.S.-based multinational corporations in exploitation of natural resources from Southeast Asia, including offshore oil and gas.

The nuclear submarine is a vital component of the U.S. nuclear strike triad capability. In order to attack or defend against a nuclear submarine, its location must be known. If innocent passage regimes were strictly applied, submarines would have to surface during their passage through territorial and archipelagic waters other than archipelagic sea-lanes or straits used for international navigation. Since the strategic value of a submarine lies in its stealth, there is little likelihood of the United States (or the Soviet Union) abiding by such a regime. Permanent and accurate submarine detection systems require a land base. Thus, territory-bordering straits can be of strategic value.

Because of the strategic importance of submerged launch ballistic missile (SLBM) submarines in the Soviet–U.S. arms race, control of the deep waters with seabed detection and attack devices could become the crucial factor in a great power conflict. Strategic placement of such devices requires unimpeded access for oceanographic research.

COOPERATION AMONG NATIONS: STATUS AND PROGNOSIS

Article 123 of the CLS provides that states bordering enclosed or semi-enclosed seas should cooperate with each other in the exercise of their rights and duties, and that to this end they shall endeavor directly or through an appropriate regional organization: (1) to coordinate the management, conservation, and exploration of the living resources of the sea; (2) to coordinate the implementation of their rights and duties with respect to the preservation of the marine environment; (3) to coordinate their scientific research policies and undertake, where appropriate, joint programs of scientific research in the area; and (4) to invite, as appropriate, other interested states or international organizations to cooperate with them in promoting these provisions.

There have been some indigenous subregional efforts regarding marine matters in ASEAN; however, these efforts are incipient at best. Permanent ASEAN committees of marine importance include Fisheries (as a part of food production and supply), Meteorology (as part of air traffic service), Science and Technology, and Shipping. The Federation of ASEAN Shippers' Council sponsored the formation of a Federation of ASEAN Shipowners' Association, presumably to present a united bargaining position vis-à-vis the European-dominated Far Eastern Freight Conference, which controls trade and sets rates for transport of goods between Europe and Asia. There also is a 1975 ASEAN Agreement for the Facilitation of Search for Ships in Distress and Rescue of Survivors of Ship Accidents in which the contracting parties undertake to provide assistance to ships in distress in their territories and neighboring seas.

The ASEAN Committee on Science and Technology (COST) Subcommittee on Marine Sciences has discussed the possibility of a cooperative approach to extraregional access for marine scientific research and has approached the European Economic Community (EEC) and the United States for assistance in funding cooperative marine scientific research. COST also spawned an informal committee on pollution and an ASEAN Subregional Environment Programme. As part of this program, member nations have discussed a coordinated approach to marine environmental protection with the Regional Seas Programme of the United Nations Environment Programme (UNEP). The Regional Seas Programme has as its goal to produce a Mediterranean-type protocol for the "ASEAN Seas" and to upgrade awareness and capabilities for its implementation.[49] The ASEAN Committee on Petroleum (ASCOPE) also has within its terms of reference the development of subregional contingency plans for oil spills. ASCOPE has been discussing standardization of environmental and safety regulations concerning offshore oil exploration. The Strait of Malacca Safe Navigation Scheme between Malaysia, Singapore, and Indonesia (well-described elsewhere[50]), and the concomitant US$1.3 million revolving fund established by Japanese shipping interests and these nations to cover costs of cleaning up and preventing oil spills from tankers are the most concrete indigenous examples of marine regionalization to date.

Finally, there is some evidence of growing military cooperation among ASEAN members, although only on a bilateral basis for the present. Indonesia has conducted joint air, naval, and army maneuvers with Malaysia, and the two countries have cooperated in patrolling their common South China Sea border areas for Vietnamese refugees. Indonesia has conducted joint naval surveillance in the Celebes Sea with the Philippines. Moreover, Thailand and Malaysia have signed the first bilateral defense pact in Southeast Asia since the end of the Indochina war, and in addition to the 1954 Manila pact, Thailand and the Philippines have agreed to cooperate on security matters.

The development of a consolidated, Vietnamese-dominated, Soviet-influenced Indochina is deeply troubling to ASEAN governments, as it may confirm their nightmares of two groups of ideological and political adversaries embarked on an economic and military race for regional supremacy. Such common fears eventually may stimulate ASEAN military cooperation, possibly including cooperation among national naval and coastal patrol forces.[51]

There are also several marine-relevant international organizations operating in the region, such as the Indo-Pacific Fisheries Commission, the South China Sea Fisheries Development and Co-ordinating Programme, the Southeast Asia Fisheries Development Centre, the International Center for Living Aquatic Resources Management, The Committee for Co-ordination of Joint Prospecting for Mineral Resources in Asian Offshore Areas, and the Working Group for the Western Pacific of the Intergovernmental Oceanographic Commission.[52] These organizations are not indigenously derived or majority funded and include among their membership both extra-ASEAN and South China states. Nevertheless, these organizations may serve as models, platforms, or stimuli for indigenously initiated marine regional arrangements.

Several specialized United Nations agencies whose terms of reference include marine problems also have offices in the region, such as the UNESCO Regional Office for Science and Technology for Southeast Asia in Jakarta, the United Nations Environment Programme Regional Office in Bangkok, and divisions of the

Economic and Social Commission for Asia and the Pacific, concerned with transportation and natural resources. The many U.N.-sponsored or supported national projects and bilateral assistance programs in the marine sphere also have helped to stimulate and support national marine awareness in the region.

When the mosaic of national jurisdictional regimes is superimposed on transnational resources and activities, there is an evident need for increased bilateral and multilateral consultation and policy coordination. However, Southeast Asian states are only now beginning to examine their national marine interests. At this juncture, commonalities among national interests are neglected and differences tend to be emphasized. There is perhaps, at base, a lack of shared understanding by policymakers of transnational marine environment and resource interdependencies; of the consequences of diverse national marine policies regarding resource exploitation and environmental management; and of other nations' socioeconomic and political goals that may affect the environment and resources in national marine jurisdictional zones. Further, the form, substance, effectiveness, and net benefit of national management designs will both influence and be influenced by the interests, activities, and policies of the maritime powers and nations with adjacent jurisdictional zones.

For most transnational marine issues in Southeast Asian seas, bilateral cooperation will be the rule for some time. A carefully constructed web of similar bilateral agreements eventually may form the basis for multilateral negotiations and adjustments toward common policies. Nevertheless, in the final analysis, necessity will be the mother of cooperation.

CHAPTER 3

MARITIME JURISDICTIONAL ISSUES

J. R. V. Prescott

INTRODUCTION

Even though the Convention on the Law of the Sea (CLS) has not been ratified by all countries, it seems certain that most will reserve the right to claim the maritime areas that are designated in it. If states are sufficiently remote from overseas neighbors, they may claim five maritime zones: internal waters, territorial seas, a contiguous zone, an exclusive economic zone (EEZ), and a continental shelf. Archipelagic states also may claim archipelagic waters. The zones have been listed in the order in which a mariner sailing directly away from the coast generally would cross their outer boundaries. Internal waters lie landward of the baselines that have been proclaimed by the governments. The next three zones are all measured seaward from the baselines. Territorial seas may be up to 12 nautical miles (nmi) wide, and the contiguous zone may then extend for an additional 12 nmi. The EEZ occupies the area between the outer edge of the territorial sea and a line 200 nmi seaward of the baseline. Some countries such as Australia have claimed a fishing zone, rather than an EEZ. It is expected that such fishing zones will be replaced by EEZs with the adoption of the CLS.

Claims to the legal continental shelf vary with the morphology and structure of the geophysical continental margin; the outer limit of any country's claim must be determined in accordance with a set of complex rules, which apply only to continental margins that are wider than 200 nmi. These rules permit any country with such a margin to use either of two formulae, both of which are subject to absolute limits. With the first formula, a country may define its boundary by connecting points where the thickness of sedimentary rocks is at least 1 percent of the shortest distance to the foot of the continental slope. The second formula entitles a state to define its boundary by points not more than 60 nmi from the foot of the slope. For the first formula to provide access to larger claims than the second formula, it would be necessary for a drilling program to record layers of sedimentary rocks more than 1,216 meters (m) thick at distances greater than 60 nmi from the foot of the slope.

Regardless of which formula is used, the boundary must not be located either more than 350 nmi from the baseline used for fixing the territorial seas or more than 100 nmi seaward of the 2,500-m isobath. In the region under consideration, only Australia possesses margins wider than 200 nmi. Off its northwest coast fringing the Indian Ocean, Australia would gain the widest shelf by following a formula defining its boundary by points not more than 60 nmi from the foot of the slope and the distance limit of 350 nmi from its baseline.

The rights of states to exercise authority vary depending on the zone. A state's rights in its internal waters are indistinguishable from its rights on land. However, according to Article 8 of the CLS, if the baselines enclose waters previously considered to be high seas or territorial waters, then other states have the right of innocent passage.[1] Innocent passage means continuous and expeditious navigation through the territorial sea in a manner that does not prejudice the peace, good order, and security of the coastal state. The right of innocent passage is the only restriction on the authority of the coastal state in its territorial waters. Where straits used for international navigation fall entirely within the territorial waters of adjoining states, as do the Strait of Malacca and Singapore Strait, foreign vessels and airplanes enjoy the rights of transit passage. In practical seafaring terms, such passage is indistinguishable from innocent passage except for submarines, which may travel submerged. The contiguous zone is a buffer zone that enables a coastal state to enforce its customs, fiscal, immigration, and sanitary laws or regulations.

In the EEZ, states have complete authority over the economic use of resources in the waters and on or under the seabed. Thus, for example, no foreigners may fish or prospect for minerals without the agreement of the claimant state. Vessels may navigate through the EEZ and airplanes may fly over it, however, subject only to normal safety requirements. Where states claim continental shelves wider than 200 nmi, their rights apply only to the seabed; foreigners may fish in the waters above the shelf, sail and conduct research in the waters, and fly aircraft over them. Where states claim archipelagic waters, foreign vessels and aircraft have the right of archipelagic sealanes passage through them along sea- and air-lanes designated by the archipelagic state and approved by the Intergovernmental Maritime Organization.

Southeast Asian states border semi-enclosed seas, share a serrated continental coast, and include island chains, part of which lie close offshore and near one another and are connected by continuous continental margins. This geographic arrangement necessitates the delineation of many international maritime boundaries.

This chapter on the international maritime boundaries of Southeast Asia has three parts: (1) claims, agreed boundaries, and the general factors that complicate settlement; (2) unresolved boundary areas, specific boundaries remaining to be drawn, their complexity, and degree of urgency; and (3) responses and details of unresolved boundary situations.

THE SITUATION

The jurisdictional issues that arise in Southeast Asia are not based on claims to exceptional types of jurisdiction; instead they are founded on disagreements about the areas within which conventional claims to jurisdiction will operate. As indicated in Table 2.1, only three countries have claimed the entire suite of maritime zones consisting of territorial waters, a contiguous zone, a continental shelf and an EEZ; they are Burma, Kampuchea (Cambodia), and Vietnam. The claims were made in April 1977, January 1978, and May 1977 respectively; in each case the countries have claimed territorial seas measuring 12 nmi, contiguous zones of the same width, and EEZs of 200 nmi. While Burma and Vietnam have cast their claims to the continental shelf in terms identical to those in the CLS, Kampuchea has referred only to the natural prolongation of its territory; it does not specify a distance of 200 nmi where the shelf was narrower than this distance. In 1972, however, the government of Kampuchea (then still called Cambodia), specified the outer limits of its continental shelf claim. It is not known whether the present government of the country still regards the 1972 claims as being in force.[2]

Australia, Brunei, China (Taiwan), Indonesia, Malaysia, the Philippines, and Thailand each have claimed three of the four possible zones; none claims a contiguous zone. All of the countries claim an EEZ 200 nmi wide, with the exception of Australia, which claims only a fishing zone of that width. The claims were made by the Philippines in June 1978, China (Taiwan) in September 1979, Australia in November 1979, Indonesia in March 1980, Malaysia in April 1980, Thailand in May 1980, and Brunei in 1982.[3]

Only slight differences exist in continental shelf claims. Australia, Malaysia, China (Taiwan), and Thailand are parties to the 1958 Convention on the Continental Shelf. China (Taiwan) made two reservations when it adhered to the Convention. First, it insisted that the shelf boundaries between adjacent and opposite countries are to be determined in accordance with the principle of the natural prolongation of their land territories. Second, the Chinese province of Taiwan noted that exposed rocks and islets shall not be taken into account in determining its continental shelf. Indonesia and the Philippines claim the continental shelf in terms that could be adjusted easily to fit the definition in the 1982 Convention. In 1954, the United Kingdom claimed a continental shelf for Brunei out to the 200-m isobath.[4]

Malaysia and Thailand, however, have unilaterally claimed areas of the seabed. In May 1973 Thailand claimed seabed areas underlying the western part of the Gulf of Thailand. This claim likely was in response to those made to parts of the gulf's seabed by South Vietnam in June 1971 and by Kampuchea in July 1972. Malaysia's unilateral claim to the continental shelves off the east coast of peninsular Malaysia, Sarawak, and Sabah was published in 1979.[5]

Brunei, China (Taiwan), Indonesia, Malaysia, and Thailand claim territorial waters 12 nmi wide, while Australia claims only 3 nmi. The Philippines defines its territorial waters as those between the archipelagic baselines and the limits set in treaties between the United States and Spain in 1898 and 1900 and between the United States and Britain in 1930. Mainland China also claims three maritime zones. The Chinese fishing zone, however, is only 12 nmi wide and coincides with its territorial waters. Singapore claims only territorial waters 3 nmi wide although it announced in 1980 that it planned to declare a 12-nmi territorial sea and an EEZ.[6]

Baseline designations have created controversy in several locations. The segment of the Philippines' archipelagic baseline closing the Moro Gulf is 136 nmi long, 11 nmi longer than the 125-nmi maximum specified in the CLS. It could be adjusted easily to adhere to the maximum. The Burmese baseline closing the Gulf of Martaban is 222-nmi long, much longer than the 24-nmi maximum for bays specified in the Convention. Also, sections of the Burmese baseline system along the Tenasserim Coast are justified only by reason of the geographical conditions along the coast and for safeguarding vital economic interests. They are controversial because they depart appreciably from the general direction of the coast, and some of the islands used as turning points are not in the vicinity of the coast. Thai baselines in the eastern and extreme southwestern Gulf of Thailand are controversial for the same reasons.

In some areas, baselines have not been declared and must be inferred from territorial sea claims; such inferences, while hypothetical, produce some controversial baselines. Because of the two changes of government in Kampuchea and the important role Vietnam is currently playing in the country, it is not clear whether the baseline proclaimed for Kampuchea in 1969 is still in effect. This baseline extended along the coast of Kampuchea and surrounded Dao Phu Quoc, an island occupied by Vietnam then, as now. In 1969, Kampuchea claimed Dao Phu Quoc, but there were unconfirmed reports that Kampuchea abandoned this claim during talks with Vietnam from 4 to 18 May 1976. If those reports are accurate, then the 1969 baseline will need to be modified to exclude Dao Phu Quoc, which was not included in a list of Kampuchean islands published by that country in May 1977. The sections of the baseline that pass through the islands named Kusrovie and Prins would be hard to justify in terms of the CLS because the baseline departs considerably from the general direction of the coast and the islands are not near the coast.

Malaysia has never promulgated straight baselines, but baseline positions can be inferred by taking the straight line segments of the outer edge of Malaysia's territorial waters shown on its map of continental shelf boundaries of Malaysia and drawing parallel lines 12 nmi closer to the coast.[7] Some sections of those inferred baselines cannot be justified according to existing or proposed rules for drawing straight baselines. In the Strait of Malacca, the baseline links the remote islands of Perak and Jarak and results in claims to territorial waters that in one place are 59 nmi from the nearest fragment of Malaysian territory. The baseline along Sarawak's coast links headlands, but only the short segment linking Tanjung Sipang and Tanjung Po, near Kuching, seems justified, since these headlands enclose a legal bay. The baseline along the coast of Sabah links the islands of Keraman, Labuan, and Mangalum; it is then extended west of Keraman toward Brunei and east of Mangalum to the treaty limits of the Philippines. These extensions do not terminate on land; they are located in the sea, and the effect of the eastward extension is that Malaysia claims territorial waters 57 nmi wide when measured from Malaysian territory. The baseline of southern Sabah in the Celebes Sea linking Malaysian territory on Pulau Sebatik with Pulau Sipadan and Pulau Ligitan deviates appre-

Table 3.1   Agreed Maritime Boundaries in Southeast Asia

Country	Boundaries	Signature	Ratification
Indonesia–Malaysia	Continental shelf	27 Oct 1969	7 Nov 1969[a]
Indonesia–Malaysia	Territorial sea	17 Mar 1970	10 Mar 1971[b]
Australia–Indonesia	Continental shelf	18 Apr 1971	8 Nov 1973[c]
Indonesia–Thailand	Continental shelf	17 Dec 1971	16 Jul 1973[d]
Indonesia–Malaysia–Thailand	Continental shelf	21 Dec 1971	16 Jul 1973[d]
Australia–Indonesia	Continental shelf	9 Oct 1972	8 Nov 1973[c]
Australia–Indonesia	Continental shelf	26 Jan 1973	8 Nov 1973[c]
Indonesia–Singapore	Territorial sea	25 May 1973	3 Dec 1973[e] (Indonesia) 29 Aug 1974 (Singapore)
India–Indonesia	Continental shelf	8 Aug 1974	17 Dec 1974[f]
Indonesia–Thailand	Continental shelf	11 Dec 1975	18 Feb 1978[g]
India–Indonesia	Continental shelf	14 Jan 1977	15 Aug 1977[g]
India–Thailand	Continental shelf	22 Jun 1978	15 Dec 1978[g]
India–Indonesia–Thailand	Continental shelf	22 Jun 1978	2 Mar 1979[g]
Australia–Papua New Guinea	Continental shelf Territorial sea Fishing zone	18 Dec 1978	—[h]
Malaysia–Thailand	Joint zone	21 Feb 1979	—[i]
Australia–Indonesia	Fishing zone	29 Oct 1981	—[i]
Kampuchea–Vietnam	Joint zone	7 July 1982	?[j]

Sources:
[a] The Geographer, "Continental Shelf Boundary: Indonesia–Malaysia," *Limits in The Seas (LITS),* No. 1, Washington, D.C., 1970.
[b] The Geographer, "Territorial Sea Boundary: Indonesia–Malaysia," *LITS,* No. 50, Washington, D.C., 1973.
[c] The Geographer, "Territorial Sea and Continental Shelf Boundaries: Australia and Papua New Guinea–Indonesia," *LITS,* No. 87, Washington, D.C., 1979.
[d] The Geographer, "Maritime Boundaries: Indonesia–Malaysia–Thailand," *LITS,* No. 81, Washington, D.C., 1978.
[e] The Geographer, "Territorial Sea Boundary: Indonesia–Singapore," *LITS,* No. 60, Washington, D.C., 1974.
[f] The Geographer, "Continental Shelf Boundary: India–Indonesia," *LITS,* No. 62, Washington, D.C., 1975.
[g] The Geographer, "Continental Shelf Boundaries: India–Indonesia–Thailand," *LITS,* No. 93, Washington, D.C., 1981.
[h] P. J. Boyce and M. W. D. White, eds. *The Torres Strait Treaty,* Canberra: Australian National University Press, 1981, pp. 143–168.
[i] Published versions of these two agreements are not available.
[j] The Geographer, "Straight Baselines: Vietnam," *LITS,* No. 99, Washington, D.C., 1983.
Notes: — designates treaty not yet ratified. ? designates date unknown.

ciably from the general direction of the coast and does not connect islands fringing the coast or enclose a deeply indented coast. The base points nominated for the north coast of Sabah all lie on islands east of Mangalum Island; they do not justify the territorial waters claimed on Malaysian charts.

Seventeen international agreements, listed in Table 3.1, currently define twenty-six boundaries that separate national claims.[8] There is a striking concentration of such boundaries in the southern part of the region. Only four of the boundary segments lie in the seas located north and east of the Singapore Strait; two of them separate Indonesian waters around the Natuna Islands and off northwest Kalimantan from peninsular Malaysia waters to the west and Sarawak waters to the east, a third concerns Malaysia and Thailand in the Gulf of Thailand, and a fourth is between Kampuchea and Vietnam around Dao Phu Quoc. The other twenty-two segments are located in the Andaman Sea, the Malacca and Singapore straits, and the waters south of Indonesia and Papua New Guinea.

Eleven of the seventeen agreements deal with lines separating continental shelf claims; two settle territorial sea limits, and one divides fishing zones. One of the remainder, involving Australia and Papua New Guinea, deals with territorial seas, fishing zones, and continental shelves; two others are concerned with the jurisdictional division of an agreed joint zone defined by Malaysia and Thailand and by Kampuchea and Vietnam. It is evident that Indonesia has played a major role in promoting international agreement, being involved in thirteen of the seventeen agreements; in contrast, Brunei, Burma, China, the Chinese province of Taiwan, and the Philippines have not entered into any international maritime boundary agreements. Of the seventeen agreements, thirteen are known to be ratified; the status of the agreement covering the joint Kampuchea–Vietnam offshore area is unknown. Only the very complicated Australia–Papua New Guinea treaty, the recent Australia–Indonesia fishing zone agreement and the joint zone of Malaysia and Thailand are known to await ratification. It is understood, however, that even in these cases the countries concerned are observing the terms of the agreements.

Apparently at least two historical boundaries have been accepted as international limits by the states concerned. During the colonial period, three boundaries, all for Malaysia, were drawn in offshore areas. On 2 January 1930 Britain and the United States agreed on a division of islands in the Sulu Sea, and instead of naming each island they simply defined a line separating them. That segment has been incorporated in the treaty limits claimed by the Philippines and in the limits of Malaysia's continental shelf. Indeed, that segment of the line is shown on the map by the symbol representing an international boundary. Therefore, it seems that Malaysia and the Philippines intend to retain the 1930 Anglo–American line as their common maritime boundary separating territorial waters and the continental shelf in the Sulu Sea. In September 1958 Britain proclaimed continental shelf boundaries separating the offshore margins that attached to Brunei and the adjoining British territories. The Malaysian map mentioned previously shows these lines as international boundaries even though the limit between Brunei and Sarawak is drawn to give more area to Brunei. It therefore seems possible that Malaysia is prepared to accept the unilateral British boundaries as lines defining Brunei's offshore zones. Brunei's attitude is not known. The third boundary of the colonial period also was drawn by Britain to separate its colonies of Malaya and Singapore. This was not strictly a unilateral boundary because there was agreement between representatives of the British monarch and the sultan of Johore. Negotiations are proceeding to define this 1928 boundary more closely to satisfy the needs of modern, independent states.

The seventeen agreements span thirteen years from the Indonesia–Malaysia seabed agreement of 27 October 1969 to the Kampuchea–Vietnam joint zone agreement of 7 July 1982, but it is evident that in recent years the rate at which concluding agreements occur has declined. Table 3.1 shows that since 1978 there have been only three agreements, two producing joint zones and the other an interim fishing line. It is reasonable to conclude that the easy boundaries have been drawn, although some complicated issues, such as those involving Australia and Papua New Guinea, also have been resolved. Agreements on many segments were less complex because there was little at stake, as in the case of the deep seabed between India's Nicobar Island and Indonesia's Sumatera Island and between Indian and Thai possessions; because little was known about the area; because of relatively simple coastal configurations and the absence of conflicting claims to islands; or because one of the parties eventually took a self-denying attitude as Indonesia did in negotiations over the seabed with Malaysia in 1969 and with Australia in 1972, and in negotiations over territorial waters with Singapore in 1973. The agreement between Australia and Papua New Guinea resulted mainly from major Australian concessions over the ownership of three islands and large areas of seabed. In the remaining cases where boundaries are necessary there are various complications.

THE ISSUES

Unresolved Boundary Areas

General areas where boundaries need to be drawn include the following (see Figure 3.1):

• Malaysia–Thailand — a quasi-triangular-shaped area in the southwestern Gulf of Thailand resulting from disagreement over the effect to be given to Thai islands in drawing an equidistant line, although the two countries signed a memorandum of understanding on 21 February 1979 recognizing the overlapping claims and agreeing to establish a joint authority for the exploitation of seabed resources in the disputed area.

• Indonesia–Vietnam — a large trapezoid-shaped area north of the Natuna Islands where Vietnam claims natural prolongation of its land territory to a depression just north of the Natuna Islands, and Indonesia claims the equidistant line between Indonesia's archipelagic baseline and Vietnamese territory.

• Malaysia–the Philippines — a triangular-shaped area off northeast Sabah in the Celebes Sea where Malaysia's continental shelf claim from a controversial baseline extends beyond lines of equidistance using various islands. There also are two

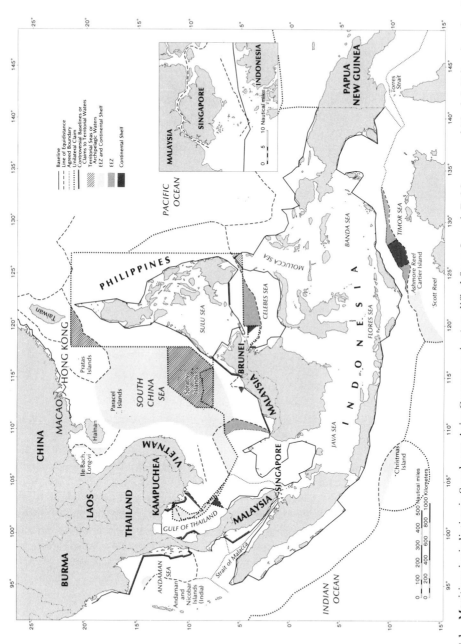

Figure 3.1 Maritime jurisdiction in Southeast Asia: Controversies (modified from Joseph R. Morgan and Mark J. Valencia, eds., *Atlas for Marine Policy in Southeast Asian Seas*, Berkeley: University of California Press, 1983, p. 43).

small slivers of area here disputed by Malaysia and Indonesia because Malaysia's unilateral claim does not give effect to the Indonesian islands of Batuan Unarang and Pulau Maratua.

• Indonesia–Malaysia—a contorted triangular-shaped area extending northeast from the Sarawak–Kalimantan land boundary where the agreed continental shelf boundary is not coincident with an equidistant line.

• Brunei–Malaysia—a triangular-shaped area where the United Kingdom, on Brunei's behalf, claimed more shelf area than it was entitled to by an equidistant line.

• Indonesia–Australia—a rectangular-shaped area south of East Timor where Indonesia claims the equidistant line and Australia claims a direct line joining existing agreed boundary segments.

• Burma–India—a small semicircular-shaped area produced by Burma's controversial baseline across the Gulf of Martaban.

• Thailand–Kampuchea–Vietnam—a large part of the eastern Gulf of Thailand resulting from disagreement on ownership of islands and the effect to be given to various islands in drawing equidistant lines, and on the azimuth of projections of land boundaries into the sea.

• Malaysia–Vietnam–the Philippines–China—most of the central and northern South China Sea is claimed by China on historical grounds; all claim ownership of some of the Spratly Islands on various grounds.

• Vietnam–China—an hourglass-shaped area resulting from Vietnam's claim that the boundary should be an 1887 Sino–French treaty line intended to allocate ownership of islands, and China's apparent claim of the equidistant line as the boundary.

• China (Taiwan)–the Philippines—a large triangular-shaped area in the Bashi Channel resulting from Taiwan's declaration of an EEZ following the equidistant line and the Philippines' adherence to the treaty limits as territorial waters.

• Indonesia–the Philippines—a small triangular-shaped area south of Mindanao where Philippine treaty (territorial) waters extend beyond an equidistant line between Philippine and Indonesian archipelagic baselines.

• Indonesia–Australia—a large area to the west of the Timor "gap" where Indonesia and Australia disagree as to the effect to be given to the Australian Scott Reef and Ashmore, Cartier, and Browse islands.

• Indonesia–Australia—a large semicircular-shaped area between Christmas Island and Java where Indonesia argues that the island does not generate a right to a continental shelf because it is far closer (within 200 nmi) to Indonesia than Australia.

• Malaysia–Singapore–Indonesia—a small belt of disputed area generated by conflicting claims by Malaysia and Singapore to Horsburgh Light or, more accurately, to the feature on which it stands; the result could affect Singapore's boundary with Indonesia.

Specific Boundaries Requiring
International Agreement

States are not required to draw any maritime boundaries, but eventually most find it convenient to do so. If the maritime claims of states are known, and a reliable

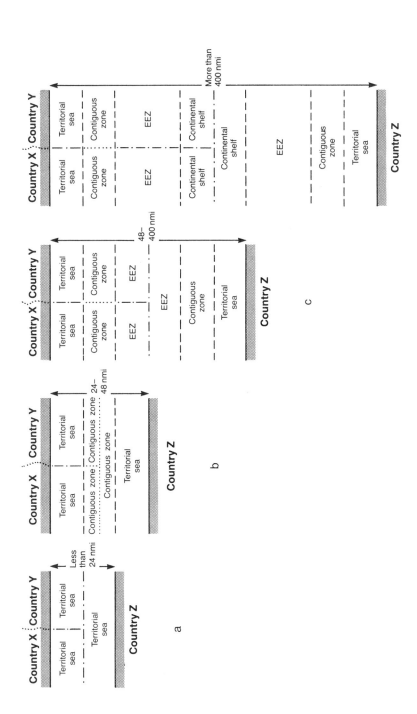

Figure 3.2 Potential maritime boundaries with different distances between opposite shores.

large-scale chart of their coasts is available, it is possible to identify the specific maritime boundaries that each state might wish to draw with its neighbors.

Figure 3.2 shows how the distance between opposite shores influences the range of international boundaries to be constructed. In Figure 3.2a, the opposite shores are less than 24 nmi apart, and because each country presumably claims territorial seas 12 nmi wide, territorial sea boundaries would have to be drawn between each pair of countries. In Figure 3.2b, where the width is between 24 nmi and 48 nmi, the adjacent states would need to draw segments separating their territorial seas and contiguous zones, whereas the opposite states would only need to draw boundaries separating their contiguous zones. Thus, adjacent states would usually have to draw more kinds of boundaries than opposite states.

In the four diagrams the distance between the shores is uniform. However, if two opposite states had coasts set at an acute angle to each other so that the distance between them varied from, say, 22 nmi to 410 nmi, it would be necessary for the states to agree on territorial sea boundaries where the shores were closest and continental shelf boundaries where they were farthest apart. Because the contiguous zone and the EEZ overlap, normally occupying the band of water 12 nmi seaward of the outer edge of the territorial waters, wherever a line separates contiguous zones that line will also separate EEZs.

In establishing specific but hypothetical boundaries, some assumptions must be made. First, it is assumed that there is no dispute over ownership of territory — mainland coast, island, or rock. Second, it is assumed that baselines generally follow the shoreline. Third, since it is impossible to guess where an equitable boundary might be located, the boundaries that have been drawn and measured are all lines of equidistance. Fourth, it is assumed here that the continental margin is continuous between any two states and thus has no physical division.

Table 3.2 identifies the potential boundaries and provides estimates of boundary segment lengths. The list is limited to those cases in which there is no doubt about the ownership of territory. No attempt has been made to include EEZ boundaries between states that have already agreed on an equidistant continental shelf boundary through waters less than 400 nmi wide. It is assumed, here, that if any EEZ boundary is drawn, it would occupy the same equidistant position. Where continental shelf boundaries have been drawn in other than an equidistant position, however, the length of an equidistant boundary separating EEZs has been calculated. Table 3.2 confirms that boundary designation in waters of Southeast Asia has concentrated on the continental shelf. Much remains to be done in designating territorial waters and EEZs, or fishing zones in the case of countries such as Australia.

In settling any maritime boundary issue, states face the basic problem that there are no precise rules governing the way in which negotiations should be conducted and the principles on which the final decision should be based. The CLS treats negotiations about territorial seas and other zones separately. Article 15, which deals with the delimitation of territorial seas between adjacent or opposite states, reproduces the exact sense, and almost the exact wording, of Article 12 of the *Convention on the Territorial Sea and the Contiguous Zone*[9] produced by the 1958 United Nations Conference on the Law of the Sea. In the absence of agreement, neither

Table 3.2   Boundaries Requiring International Agreement[a]

Boundary Segment	*Approximate Segment Length Based on Equidistance (nmi)*
Burma–India	
Territorial sea	14
Contiguous zone	29
Exclusive economic zone–continental shelf[b]	604
Burma–Thailand	
Territorial sea	70
Contiguous zone (Burma)–exclusive economic zone (Thailand)[c]	12
Exclusive economic zone–continental shelf	119
Malaysia–Thailand	
In Strait of Malacca, territorial sea	68
In Gulf of Thailand, territorial sea	12
In Gulf of Thailand, exclusive economic zone–continental shelf	98
Malaysia–Singapore	
In Johore Strait, territorial sea	49
Indonesia–Singapore	
Territorial sea[d]	6
Kampuchea–Thailand	14
Territorial sea	14
Contiguous zone (Kampuchea)/exclusive economic zone (Thailand)[e]	28
Exclusive economic zone–continental shelf	208
Kampuchea–Vietnam	
Territorial sea	55
Contiguous zone	12
Exclusive economic zone–continental shelf	124
Thailand–Vietnam	
Exclusive economic zone–continental shelf	115
Indonesia–Philippines	
Exclusive economic zone–continental shelf	605
Malaysia–Vietnam	
Exclusive economic zone–continental shelf	147
Indonesia–Vietnam	
Exclusive economic zone–continental shelf	230[f]
China–Vietnam	
Territorial shelf	18
Contiguous zone (Vietnam)–exclusive Economic zone (China)[g]	39
Exclusive economic zone–continental shelf	384
China–Taiwan	
Around Quemoy, territorial sea	?
Exclusive economic zone–continental shelf	1,457

Table 3.2   Boundaries Requiring International Agreement (Continued)

Boundary Segment	Approximate Segment Length Based on Equidistance (nmi)
Philippines–Taiwan	
Exclusive economic zone–continental shelf	526
Malaysia–Philippines	
In South China Sea, territorial sea[h]	61
In Celebes Sea, exclusive economic zone–continental shelf	84
Indonesia–Malaysia	
In South China Sea, territorial sea	12
In South China Sea, exclusive economic zone[i]	202
In Celebes Sea, territorial sea	18
In Celebes Sea, exclusive economic zone–continental shelf	118
Australia–Indonesia	
North of Christmas Island, exclusive economic zone[j]	420
South of Timor, continental shelf	136 (Australian view)
South of Timor, continental shelf	267 (Indonesian view)
West of Ashmore Reef, continental shelf	280

Note: While the boundary segment lengths measured here are recorded to the nearest nautical mile, countries may use larger, more accurate charts than were available for this exercise and thus may establish more precise measures. Also, they may by mutual agreement disregard certain small islands or rocks, and they may decide to simplify the alignment of some boundaries to make administration easier. For these reasons the measurements recorded here should be regarded as approximate. They do, however, show the order of boundary segment lengths that states might wish to construct.

[a] This list includes all equidistant boundary segments where there is no dispute over the ownership of islands; there may be disputes over whether full claims may be made from islands.

[b] Unless it is specified otherwise, it is assumed that a single boundary will separate the exclusive economic zone (EEZ) and continental shelf claims. The term EEZ includes fishing zones claimed by some countries such as Australia.

[c] Because Burma, Kampuchea, and Vietnam claim contiguous zones, there will be areas where their contiguous zones are bordered by the EEZ of neighbors.

[d] The agreed line must be extended 5 nmi west and 1 nmi east to join with the Malaysian tri-junction.

[e] See note c.

[f] This distance would be 284 nmi if Indonesia recognized Vietnam's sovereignty over the Spratly Islands.

[g] See note c.

[h] This represents an extension west of the terminus of the 1930 Anglo–American Agreement, which appears to have been recognized by both successor countries.

[i] A continental shelf boundary has already been agreed upon.

[j] The continental margin is not continuous between Christmas Island and Java.

state is entitled to extend its claim beyond the median (equidistant) line, except where historic title or other special circumstances require this provision to be varied. Since there is no definition of how historic title is established or which special circumstances would be properly invoked under this article, there is no restriction on any country to oppose the use of the equidistant line to settle the issue.

The CLS does not stipulate how boundaries separating contiguous zones should be drawn. According to the CLS, international boundaries separating economic zones and continental shelves will be based on international law, as referred to in Article 38 of the Statute of the International Court of Justice, in order to achieve an equitable (fair) solution. Article 38 enjoins the court to reach decisions by applying international conventions expressly recognized by the contesting states, international custom, the general principles of law recognized by civilized nations, judicial decisions, and the teachings of the most highly qualified publicists.[10] There appears to be nothing in this prescription to prevent any state raising any arguments to support its case in favor of a particular boundary alignment. It is this lack of restriction on the scope of argument that accounts for the wide range of circumstances that might create complications that could hinder the settlement of maritime boundary issues.

Difficult Circumstances

The circumstances that might complicate boundary negotiations can be grouped into three categories — political, geographic, and economic. International boundary determinations likely to be affected by such difficult circumstances are summarized in Table 3.3.

In deciding whether particular circumstances existed, the following ad hoc rules were applied. There was no attempt to guess how present relations between Vietnam and the countries of ASEAN might change from their present conditions in 1983. Reference to the nature of the seabed was included only in respect of gradient. It is possible that the structure or geology of some seabed zones might complicate the negotiation of seabed boundaries by encouraging states to claim across the line of equidistance on the basis of natural prolongation, as Vietnam has done. The circumstance of questionable baselines was included whenever a state had claimed or appeared to claim baselines that contravene either the spirit or letter of the CLS, if adherence to those baselines would deflect equidistant boundaries in favor of the state that drew the baselines. The complicating circumstance of distracting domestic problems was recorded only for Kampuchea in its boundaries with Thailand. It is possible that other countries could develop severe internal problems that would make it inconvenient to negotiate maritime boundaries with neighbors.

There are no immutable forces guaranteeing that if a particular circumstance exists, then difficulties are sure to attend boundary negotiations. The critical circumstance will always be the relations between governments and their attitudes toward the issue. If relations are cordial and governments are determined to reach a fair solution, then the chances are excellent that such a result will be achieved no

Table 3.3 Boundaries Requiring International Agreement Classified by Complexity

Complexity	Countries	Boundaries Requiring International Agreement				Difficult Circumstances — Political						Difficult Circumstances — Geographical				Difficult Circumstances — Economic	
		Territorial Sea	Contiguous Zone	Exclusive Economic Zone	Continental Shelf	Poor Relations	Conflicting Claims to Territory	Domestic Problems	Questionable Baselines	Historical Attitudes	Continuation of Previous Boundary	Nature of Islands or Rocks	Location of Islands	Geographical Disadvantage	Nature of the Seabed	Disparity in Wealth	High or Unknown Economic Potential
Very complicated	China–Malaysia–Philippines–Taiwan–Vietnam in the Spratly Islands	•	•	•	•	•	•			•		•	•		•		•
	China–Taiwan	•	•	•	•	•	•						•		•		•
Complicated	Burma–India	•	•	•	•										•		
	Kampuchea–Thailand	•	•	•	•			•	•			•	•				•
	Kampuchea–Vietnam			•	•				•				•				•
	Indonesia–Vietnam	•		•	•				?				•				•
	China–Vietnam	•	•	•	•	•				•							
	Indonesia–Malaysia	•		•					•		•						
	Malaysia–Philippines, in Celebes Sea			•	•				•	•							
	Indonesia–Malaysia, in Celebes Sea	•		•	•				•			•	•				
	Australia–Indonesia, south of Timor			•	•						•				•	•	•
	Australia–Indonesia, west of Ashmore Reef			•	•							•	•		•	•	
	Singapore–Malaysia and Indonesia near Horsburgh Light	?					•										

	1	2	3	4	5	6	7	8	9
Burma–India	•	•							
Burma–Thailand	•	•	•						
Malaysia–Thailand, in Strait of Malacca	•							•	
Malaysia–Thailand, in Gulf of Thailand	•		•	•				•	
Malaysia–Singapore, in Johore Strait	•								
Indonesia–Singapore	•								
Kampuchea–Vietnam	•	•				•			
Thailand–Vietnam			•	•				•	
Malaysia–Philippines, in South China Sea	•								
Philippines–Taiwan			•	•		•			
Indonesia–Philippines (Miangas)	•	•	•	•		•			
Indonesia–Philippines (Celebes Sea)			•			•	•		
Australia–Indonesia, north of Christmas Island			•			•			
Malaysia–Vietnam			•	•		•			
Malaysia–Brunei	•	•	•				•		

matter what other circumstances exist. Ancel's dictum on land boundaries holds
true for maritime limits also:

> Il n'y a pas de problèmes de frontières. Il n'est que des problèmes de Nations.[11] [There are
> no boundary problems; there are only problems of nations.]

If good relations are likely to promote a fair and prompt solution, the converse
must also be true. If relations between governments are poor and clouded with
distrust or hostility, it would be a simple matter to raise difficulties in negotiations
over maritime boundary issues. The lack of formal relations between countries or
poor relations may even prevent the start of negotiations. For example, presently it
is unthinkable that China would consent to discuss its maritime boundaries with
Taiwan, and it is unlikely that in the near future China and Vietnam will be able to
reconcile their different interpretations of where maritime boundaries should lie
in the Gulf of Tonkin.

The next most important political circumstance concerns conflicting claims to
territory from which maritime claims may be made. In the South China Sea the
plethora of claims by China, the Chinese province of Taiwan, Malaysia, the Philippines, and Vietnam to the Spratly Islands makes it unlikely that maritime boundaries in this area will soon be settled.

There will be occasions when a government is preoccupied with domestic problems and feels unable to conduct negotiations about maritime limits; this has probably been the situation in Kampuchea. It is also possible that neighbors will be
unwilling to enter into negotiations with unstable governments that seem likely to
be replaced soon, for such a change may require a fresh start to negotiations.

Baselines that seem unreasonable to others may be used by some countries as the
basis of claims to a particular boundary; this could be a source of difficulty. Burma,
Thailand, Kampuchea, Vietnam, and apparently Malaysia have drawn baselines at
variance with existing and proposed rules. If these countries insisted that these
baselines be taken into account in drawing maritime boundaries, affected countries would be entitled to feel aggrieved.

Negotiations can be complicated if one of the parties has a set historical view
limiting its scope for compromise. In Southeast Asia both China and Vietnam have
insisted repeatedly that all of the Nansha or Spratly Islands and associated submerged banks have belonged to each exclusively from time immemorial. This will
make it difficult for any countries to negotiate with either of these two countries or
with each other over maritime limits there. The Philippines' reliance on the historic virtue of the treaty limits set down in the 1898 American–Spanish peace
agreement as limits of their territorial waters could similarly create difficulties in
negotiations with Indonesia, China (Taiwan), and any states with successful claims
to some of the Spratly Islands.

Another major difficult political circumstance may arise when boundary negotiations are incomplete and have to be resumed at a time when national views have
changed. It is best for two states to draw all the necessary maritime boundaries at
the same time, if that is possible. There are several factors supporting this view.

First, at the time of agreement, teams of experts will have been assembled, mastered the technical facts, and often agreed on a common body of knowledge. If new teams have to be reformed some years later, much work may have to be done again. Second, the chief negotiators will have established a working relationship that might well generate a certain momentum to make it easier to overcome problems. At such times it is sensible to make as much progress toward a complete solution as possible. Third, if a total package of boundaries is considered, more scope is provided for trading mutual advantages in different areas than would exist if only a single type of boundary or a boundary in only one area were being considered. Finally, the fact that the countries have decided to engage in bilateral negotiations means that their relations must be reasonably cordial. Changes in governments, the international climate, or domestic circumstances might cause a worsening of relations and reduce the prospect of bilateral negotiations.

In many cases countries have agreed on seabed boundaries without any reference to boundaries separating EEZs. If a seabed boundary is drawn first and does not occupy an equidistant location, there is a possibility that the country that obtained the smaller area of seabed may insist that it obtain an equal share of waters when the EEZ boundary is settled. That has happened in the case of Australia and Indonesia. The seabed boundaries of 1971 and 1972 gave a larger share of the intervening seabed to Australia. Indonesia subsequently argued that the overlying waters should be divided equally, and the interim agreement reached in October 1981 delivers to Indonesian fisheries jurisdiction some waters above the Australian seabed. A similar situation may arise in the waters east of the Natuna Islands. In 1969 Indonesia and Malaysia agreed on a seabed boundary north of Tanjong Datu in Kalimantan that deviates from an equidistant position in Malaysia's favor. It is quite possible that Indonesia will require any boundary between EEZs to follow the equidistant course, which would give Indonesia control of some waters above Malaysia's seabed.

From a consideration of geographical circumstances it is evident that the presence of islands is a common cause of difficulties in negotiating maritime boundaries. Article 121 of the CLS stipulates that an island is a naturally formed area of land surrounded by water and is above water at high tide, and that such features may be used to claim all maritime zones. The definition of an island follows the language of the 1958 *Convention on the Territorial Sea and the Contiguous Zone*. The last part of Article 121 provides that rocks that cannot sustain human habitation or economic life of their own shall have no EEZ or continental shelf. There is no provision enabling rocks to be distinguished with confidence from islands. There are two distinct problems associated with islands: it is difficult to determine the nature of islands, and it is difficult to assess the location and stability of islands.

In determining the nature of rocks and islands, it is difficult to decide when an undoubted rock might be considered to have an economic life of its own. For example, would the collection of bird or turtle eggs from the rock by traditional fishermen satisfy this condition? Is human habitation sustained if a lighthouse is built and occupied on the rock? Can the economic life of a rock be distinguished from the economic life of the reef on which it stands, and which might be exposed at low tide? In the Spratly Islands there are many reefs surmounted only by rocks; Royal Charlotte Reef at 6°56′N and 113°36′E and Swallow Reef, which is 27 nmi to the north-northeast are two such reefs, and both are claimed by Malaysia.

Then there is the problem of ephemeral islands. Cays, sometimes called keys, are low islands built of sand and coral rubble constructed by wave action on reefs that are awash.[12] Sometimes these features are stabilized by vegetation, including palm trees; sometimes the formation of beach rock following the precipitation of calcium carbonate in the zone of repeated wetting and drying will offer greater resistance to erosion than unconsolidated material. But cays can be destroyed by exceptional waves in severe storms, and it must be asked whether a country's claim to maritime zones from a cay disappears if the cay is washed away. There is also the problem associated with claiming new islands as they are formed. China's claims to submerged banks in the South China Sea may be partly designed to claim any new islands that might form on them.[13]

For some countries the inconvenient location of islands controlled by others may be the most serious adverse circumstance in the settlement of maritime boundaries. Because islands act as national outposts from which maritime claims can be made, their fortunate location close to the shores of another country can augment the claim of the state that owns the island and confine the claim of the opposite or adjacent state. This circumstance was the crux of the difficulty in the Torres Strait, where Australian islands lay within a few hundred meters of the coast of Papua; because of the pattern of colonial claims in 1879 no islands in the Torres Strait were attached to Papua. In Southeast Asia, Kampuchea is disadvantaged because Thai and Vietnamese islands are located near Kampuchean territory, while Australian outposts, such as Ashmore and Cartier islands and Scott Reef, give that country an advantage in claiming an equidistant boundary with Indonesia.

If a foreign-controlled island is small and close to another country's coast, the maritime zones claimed from it could form an enclave within the zones claimed from the mainland. If the present pattern of ownership in the Spratly Islands were confirmed, there would be enclaves of waters belonging to one state surrounded by waters claimed by another. Enclaves would also exist if maritime boundaries were drawn around Quemoy or Hong Kong. Enclaves have generally been avoided by countries negotiating maritime boundaries. They create a potential for friction because citizens of the state that owns the enclave clearly have the right to travel to it through waters controlled by another country. The volume and regularity of traffic to the enclave and its inherent legality creates opportunities for poachers, smugglers, and spies and creates difficulties for the authorities supervising the waters surrounding the enclave. Enclaves on land often pose administrative, political, and strategic problems for the countries involved; there seems to be no reason why maritime enclaves should be less troublesome to the states concerned. However, the unratified agreement between Australia and Papua New Guinea in the Torres Strait has left seven Australian cays, with their surrounding belt of territorial seas 3 nmi wide, surrounded by waters and seabed included in Papua New Guinea's shelf and fishing claims.

The CLS employs a narrow definition of states with special geographical characteristics; such states are deemed to be those whose geographical situation makes them dependent on the exploitation of living resources in the EEZs of neighbors and states that can claim no EEZ. In fact, there are several countries whose claims are severely restricted because of the coastal configuration and the nearness of neighbors. Singapore provides a classical example of a zone-locked state, and Kampuchea and Brunei also are restricted. The presence of Thai and Vietnamese islands restricts Kampuchea's claim from a comparatively short coast. Brunei's disadvantage stems from its very short coast, much of which lies in Brunei Bay, and Malaysia's claim to features off that coast. States that regard themselves as geographically disadvantaged in a broader sense than that used by the CLS might seek redress from neighbors when maritime boundaries are negotiated.

It is not possible to predict the success of such efforts, because many complex factors will be involved. For example, a claimant state will have a better chance of success if the state being asked for concessions attaches a great importance to good relations with the state making the claim. This was one of the strongest factors favoring Papua New Guinea in its negotiations with Australia over the Torres Strait. If a claimant state is able to offer some concessions in trade, or military bases, it might have a better chance of securing larger areas of the sea and seabed. Although force has not yet been used for gaining desired maritime boundaries, it is possible that some disadvantaged country might exert military pressure against a weaker neighbor more fortunate in terms of maritime claims.

A further geographical circumstance that might complicate the settlement of boundary issues concerns seabeds shared by adjacent or opposite states. This is important for the countries of Southeast Asia that have not yet agreed on seabed boundaries because the region shares a single, continuous continental margin. It can be claimed entirely from Australia in the south to China in the north, and from the Andaman Islands in the west to the Philippines in the east.[14] This potential difficulty arises because the CLS is a legal abstraction that does not reflect the real complexity and variety of the world's continental margins.

There are three features that might be examined to determine the direction and extent of the natural prolongation of a state's territory. First, the gradients of the seabed could be considered. For example, Indonesia might claim beyond the line of equidistance in the direction of the Spratly Islands because the seabed slopes in that direction. The Philippines also might use the fact that the margin slopes from its western islands toward the Spratly Islands when justifying claims to Kalayaan.

Second, the structure of the seabed could be examined to discover whether it was formed or deformed by the same forces that molded the coastal regions. Or a minimum continental crustal thickness and density could be the criterion for the seaward limit of natural prolongation. Finally, the geology of the coast and seabed could be compared to reveal whether there are continuities among the rocks of both areas.

Perhaps a case based on gradient, structure, and geology would be stronger than one based on gradient only. In Southeast Asia the sharpest debate over the natural prolongation of territory has been that between Australia and Indonesia over the relevance of the Timor Trough. Australia has argued that this trough, close to the

Indonesian coast, divided the margins that each country could claim. Indonesia asserted that the trough was merely an incidental depression in a continuous margin linking Australia and Timor and that therefore a proper division would lie along a median line. The disagreement could be conclusively settled only by establishing whether the trough marked the northern edge of the Australian plate, or whether Timor itself was the leading edge of the northward drifting plate.

Economic circumstances also might make negotiations about maritime limits difficult. If there is a marked disparity between the resources and wealth of two states seeking to divide waters and seabed they both can claim, the poorer state is likely to argue that an equitable decision would give it the larger share of the area. This argument was used effectively by Papua New Guinea when it sought a larger share of the marine resources of the Torres Strait than lines of equidistance would have provided. It is possible that Singapore, in any negotiations with Malaysia or Indonesia, would draw attention to its restricted resource base and its high population density. Elsewhere in Southeast Asia, major discrepancies in wealth are found only between Australia and Indonesia, and reference to such matters may have helped to persuade the Australian authorities to make major concessions when the provisional enforcement and surveillance fisheries line was drawn in January 1982.

The economic potential of the area might prove to be a critical factor in negotiating maritime boundaries if it is known to be high or if it is unknown. The scramble for the Spratly Islands by China (Taiwan), Malaysia, Vietnam, and the Philippines is partly related to the hope of those countries that the Spratly area will yield commercial hydrocarbon deposits and rich harvests of living marine resources. Other areas of unresolved boundaries involving hydrocarbon potential include the eastern and southwestern Gulf of Thailand, the Natuna area, the Gulf of Tonkin, and the Arafura Sea.

In the 1880s Britain and Germany engaged in a long debate over the ownership of a comparatively small area on the West African coast, on what is now the border between Nigeria and Cameroon. Neither side would give way because the disputed territory "might prove to be an Eldorado or a worthless swamp."[15] That is likely to be the attitude of states seeking control of the seabed under the Gulf of Thailand and north of Brunei.

Complexity

The suggested classification of potential maritime boundaries by degree of complexity (Table 3.3), is not so rigorous that if another scholar applied it he or she would be certain to obtain the same result. The variety of circumstances that might complicate the negotiation of boundaries is divided in the table into categories of very complicated, complicated, and uncomplicated boundary segments. The chief reasons various boundary segments were placed in the first two categories were poor relations and disputes over the ownership of islands. Another important reason was the location of islands belonging to one country in a position to severely curtail the area a neighbor can claim. For example, relations that are sometimes less than cordial and rival territory claims underlie the problems of drawing maritime boundaries in the vicinity of the Spratly Islands. Also, most of the countries involved have no successful experience in negotiating maritime limits with a neighbor. China's negotiations over fishing zones with an eager Japan and Malaysia's agreements with Indonesia do not indicate the difficulties these two countries will face in reaching accommodations with Vietnam and the Philippines. It must be stressed that particular segments could easily be transferred from one category to another by unexpected developments. For example, a sharp deterioration in relations between Malaysia and Singapore could make the drawing of a boundary through Johore Strait a difficult matter, while an Australian decision to settle its seabed boundary with Indonesia on the same terms as the provisional fisheries line would quickly transfer that boundary segment to the uncomplicated class.

The thirteen very complicated and complicated potential maritime boundaries are scattered throughout the region, occurring in the South China Sea, the Gulf of Thailand, the Singapore Strait, the Celebes Sea, the Andaman Sea, and the Timor Sea. The largest concentration of potentially difficult issues, however, is in the South China Sea and its adjoining waters. Only the agreed Indonesian–Malaysian seabed boundaries of 1969 penetrate this area. Although joint zones have been established between Malaysia and Thailand and between Kampuchea and Vietnam, these are admissions that it was impossible to reach agreement on a single line. It has also been suggested that Malaysia and Brunei, and Malaysia and the Philippines, might adopt the lines drawn during the colonial period, but a recent inquiry to the authorities in Brunei elicited the response that Brunei had not concluded any agreements with Malaysia.[16]

Urgency

In mid-1983 there was no evidence that any of the countries concerned regarded any of the potential maritime disputes as a matter of acute urgency. When states regard boundary questions on land or water as vital, there is generally no difficulty in obtaining background information from embassies and information offices, but there is a marked lack of availability of such information concerning offshore boundaries in Southeast Asia. This does not mean that discussions are not being held. Indeed, it is known that Indonesia is negotiating with Australia and Vietnam. It means that the issues are not urgent, and that for the various parties it is not critical whether the boundaries are negotiated this year or in the future. It is also possible that some countries would prefer not to negotiate so that recent claims to islands in the Spratly group can mature and be dignified by age.

It is possible to guess about situations that would encourage states to treat the settlement of boundary issues as a matter of urgency. First, when there is the risk of conflict between navies defending fishermen or oil drillers, or armies defending claimed islands close to each other, states may consider boundary negotiations as one way to reduce tension. Second, states that have limited terrestrial resources and spend large sums on the import of petroleum or natural gas and can claim only small areas of undisputed seabed might attach great importance to securing maritime boundaries that would permit the search for offshore fields to proceed rapidly. As indicated in Chapter 5 on hydrocarbons, given the reluctance of drilling companies to commit their expensive rigs in disputed waters, settled boundaries are often necessary. For example, for Kampuchea, there is only a comparatively small area close to the coast where drilling could be conducted with confidence that neither Vietnam nor Thailand would object. And unless Singapore can make good its claim to Horsburgh Light as an island, its prospects of finding offshore deposits are very limited.

Two countries may seek rapid agreement on offshore boundaries to prevent a third party from raising a claim in the intervening seas or to bolster their claims to islands in the South China Sea. It is not inconceivable that two of the claimants to the Spratly Islands might reach an agreement in the hope of preempting existing claims by other parties. Also, it would be a reasonable policy for Malaysia to offer an independent Brunei a generous settlement in the offshore area in return for Brunei's recognition that Malaysia owns Louisa and Royal Charlotte reefs. Alternatively, the Philippines might consider trying to persuade Malaysia to draw a common boundary near the latitude of Amboyna Cay that would buttress Malaysia's claim to areas to the south and the Philippines' claim to northern parts.

Finally, a state might decide that it is important to settle maritime boundaries quickly while it holds an ascendent position. It is logical for Vietnam to negotiate its common boundary with Kampuchea while Vietnam holds such an important position in that country. There is always the risk that a subsequent Kampuchean government in different circumstances might repudiate the treaty on the grounds that it was signed under duress, but that could be viewed as a risk worth taking.

Thus, there are many segments of potential maritime boundaries still to be negotiated in Southeast Asia. These segments differ from each other in degree of complexity, and some, especially those in the South China Sea, are likely to be difficult to negotiate. At present there is no obvious sense of urgency on the part of any states to reach boundary agreements. Changes in the nature of relations between states, domestic economic and political developments, and the discovery of offshore petroleum or gas fields are all factors capable of changing the level of difficulty of any negotiations, and all could affect the views of the states about the urgency of settling boundary issues.

POSSIBLE RESPONSES TO THE NEED
TO SETTLE UNRESOLVED BOUNDARIES

Table 3.4 shows some possible state responses and the types of boundaries that might be generated; where possible, examples from the region of each type have been provided.

There are two responses that any state can make. The first is to take no action in maritime boundaries; this would involve refusing to publish any claims and declining to take part in any negotiations proposed by a neighboring country. Although they have published their claims, Burma and Vietnam do not appear to have been anxious to conclude maritime boundary agreements with neighbors.

Table 3.4 Difficult Circumstances in Boundary Negotiations: Possible State Responses and Types of Boundaries, with Examples

Types of Boundaries	Responses			
	No Action	Unilateral Claim	Bilateral Talks	Refer to Arbitration
Single multipurpose line		Philippines (Kalayaan)	Indonesia–Malaysia (in the Malacca Straits)	?
Multiple lines		China (Paracels) Kampuchea (Gulf of Thailand)	Australia–Papua New Guinea (Torres Strait)	
Joint zones			Malaysia–Thailand (Gulf of Thailand)	?

The second action is to make a unilateral claim and defend it. The prime example in Southeast Asia is China's military enforcement of its claims to the Paracel Islands and the surrounding waters. Many countries, such as Kampuchea, Malaysia, and the Philippines, have made unilateral claims, but there is little evidence that they have been able to compel respect for those claims to islands, waters, or seabed.

A decision to take no action would not result in the formation of maritime boundaries. Unilateral action could produce two boundary types. Unilateral action could be designed to construct a single multipurpose boundary to separate the fisheries and seabed zones of the claimant state from those of neighboring countries. The claim to the area known as Kalayaan by the Philippines in June 1978 is in this category.[17] The decree claims the islands, waters, seabed, subsoil, continental margin, and air space in 70,150 square nautical miles (nmi^2) of the South China Sea. It is more usual for countries to claim lines that delineate separate maritime zones. Most commonly in Southeast Asia such unilateral claims deal with the seabed, and such claims form the multiple lines. Unilateral action cannot generate a joint zone.

Other active responses require agreement between at least two states. First, neighbors can engage in bilateral talks to produce a common maritime boundary. This is the course by which all maritime agreements have been reached in Southeast Asia. Such negotiations can last for varying periods. The early Australian–Indonesian agreements were concluded quite quickly, whereas the negotiations between Australia and Papua New Guinea lasted for about six years. Before bilateral negotiations begin, government agencies generally collect detailed information, which is then used to justify a particular approach to negotiations. That approach usually centers on support for an equidistant or median boundary, an equitable boundary, or a line that is part equidistant (or median) and part equitable. As in most bilateral negotiations, governments will delineate their minimum acceptable positions and then seek a compromise between those limits. Increasingly, the negotiations are conducted between groups of officers expert in surveying, hydrography, geology, or the economics of fishing, and only when they have reached agreement according to their instructions do the senior government representatives begin talks to produce the final document.

Such bilateral negotiations may create a joint zone as well as single multipurpose boundaries and multiple boundaries. The 1978 treaty between Australia and Papua New Guinea produced boundaries separating territorial waters, fishing zones, and the seabeds, and it also delimited a joint protected zone. This protected zone, the Malaysian–Thai seabed zone, and the Kampuchean–Vietnamese "historical" zone are the only joint zones in Southeast Asia at present.

The establishment of a joint zone may be used to resolve difficult and inconclusive bilateral negotiations. Another solution is to argue the matter before the International Court of Justice or some tribunal of arbiters provided that each side agrees in advance that it will accept the outcome. While a joint zone means that the two states are unable to produce a compromise on a single line, it also means that both sides recognize that the other party's arguments have some force. Thus, the joint zone created by Malaysia and Thailand results from the fact that there is a basic disagreement on how much effect should be given to the Thai island called Ko Losin, which stands only 1.5 m (5 ft) above high tide, 39 nmi off the Thai coast. It is possible that Thailand felt unable to make concessions to Malaysia over the use of Ko Losin as a base point because the island could also be a base point in drawing maritime boundaries with Vietnam.

Arbitration has not been used to determine boundaries in Southeast Asian waters. It was employed by Kampuchea and Thailand over a land boundary, however, when the Temple Case was heard by the International Court of Justice.[18] To resort to arbitration, both parties must be certain that the avenues available through bilateral negotiations have been exhausted and be confident that the tribunal, court, or assessor appointed to deliver a judgment can be trusted to deliver an impartial decision. Or arbitration may simply be considered cheaper and more expedient than other avenues. Part of Australia's determination to reach agreement with Papua New Guinea, which involved making major concessions, is attributed to Australia's desire to avoid being brought before the International Court of Justice, which some officials thought might propose even larger concessions. An examination of arbitral decisions dealing with land boundaries leads to the conclusion that arbiters generally are aware of the politics of the situation and devise proposals that steer an intermediate course between the extreme demands of each contestant. Globally, arbitrations on maritime boundaries have suggested multiple limits and a joint zone and could suggest a single multipurpose boundary. There has been no evidence that any of the countries in the region wish at this stage to take any maritime boundary issue to a third party or to anything like the ASEAN dispute settlement mechanism.

Very Complicated Boundaries

Most of the very complicated and complicated boundary issues in Southeast Asia have been surveyed in detail in an earlier study.[19] The very complicated and complicated boundaries are usually the EEZ and continental shelf segments. The territorial sea and contiguous zone segments are predominantly uncomplicated, but where convenient, all the boundary elements for each situation are described together below.

Unfortunately, boundary disputes are rarely settled by careful academic arguments on facts of geography, history, or law. When solutions are obtained they are generally the result of the governments' determination, strength of will, readiness to act, and the political compromises they are willing to undertake.

Because the Spratly Islands occupy a central position in the South China Sea and are the subject of claims by China, the Chinese province of Taiwan, Malaysia, the Philippines, and Vietnam, progress on bilateral boundaries has proved impossible. China, Taiwan, and Vietnam claim all the islands and associated features in the Spratly group, although none of these countries has ever listed them or provided detailed maps showing the outer boundaries of the claim. These three claims are of long standing, according to the various countries, and China and Vietnam have presented documents to the United Nations in support of their claims.[20] The Philippines has claimed some of the Spratly Islands only since about 1968, when its forces occupied Kota, Pagasa, and Parola. The claim was given a degree of exactness when in 1978 Kalayaan was proclaimed. The boundaries of this zone exclude Spratly Island in the west and all reefs and associated features south of Amboyna Cay. If this area is linked to the archipelagic baseline system or if the Philippines claims for other reasons that the boundaries of Kalayaan may be used as baselines, the Philippines may claim an EEZ and continental shelf far to the west and south of the islands. Malaysia also made a claim to some of the southern features in 1979 by the publication of a map showing its continental shelf claim. Curiously, this Malaysian map shows territorial seas claims only from Amboyna Cay and Swallow Reef, although the latter is reported to be capped only by rocks at high tide, and fails to show territorial seas about Commodore and Mariveles reefs, both of which are reported to be capped with cays.[21]

If the ownership of all or part of the Spratly group were to be decided on current occupation and activity, then the Philippines would be a successful claimant. If the decision were based instead on historical arguments, then China and Vietnam would be the contenders. If geographical factors were considered to be decisive, then Malaysia and Vietnam would probably believe they had strong cases.

The solution of the Spratly Islands issue must await agreement by the majority of the concerned states. A majority is needed because it seems likely that if China, the Philippines, and Vietnam could come to some agreement then Malaysia and Taiwan would not be allowed to frustrate it. However, a simple majority is not enough; China certainly, and probably Vietnam, must be involved in the settlement, because their navies are strong enough to make any agreement excluding those countries difficult to enforce. There is no indication of possible agreement by the concerned states on the question of island ownership. A calculation of whether or not one country could impose a military solution in the region would have to be made by a military strategist. China appears to be the only country that could consider this option, but such action might well draw in the Soviet Union on the side of Vietnam.

If the islands are eventually apportioned to various countries, it will still be difficult to determine how maritime boundaries should be drawn among the multitude of islands, reefs, and low-tide elevations. Indeed, it is possible that at least some of the countries would consider the formation of joint zones. (Detail on joint zones is provided in Chapter 5.)

In the other very complicated boundary issue, between China and the Chinese province of Taiwan, there is no likelihood that China will agree to discuss maritime issues with Taiwan at present.

Complicated Boundaries

The boundary issue between Burma and India has two main elements. It should not be difficult for the countries to agree eventually on lines separating their territorial seas and contiguous zones through the Coco Channel. But the extension of these lines eastward into the Andaman Sea encounters twin difficulties. First, there is the question for India of whether it will accept the Burmese baseline, which closes the Gulf of Martaban as the line from which legitimate Burmese claims will be measured. The recognition of the straight baseline by India would mean abandoning its claim to 595 nmi^2 of the seabed and overlying waters. Second, there is the question for Burma of whether it would accept India's Narcondam Island as a base point in generating common boundaries. In 1967 Burma claimed the island, but the claim was rejected by India, and as recently as early 1981 the Indian navy repelled Burmese craft from the territorial waters around the island.[22] India has the stronger case in this issue, but the resolution of the matter does not seem to be a prime concern for either administration; both control large undisputed areas where offshore hydrocarbon exploration can proceed.

It is probable that any solution of the boundary issue between Kampuchea and Thailand will have to wait until Kampuchea's domestic problems have been settled and good relations have been restored between the two countries. When that time comes there will still be difficulties to overcome. Between June 1971 and May 1973, South Vietnam, Kampuchea (then Cambodia), and Thailand made unilateral claims to overlapping portions of the seabed in the Gulf of Thailand. The area of each overlap was: Kampuchea–South Vietnam, 14,580 nmi^2; Kampuchea–Thailand, 5,798 nmi^2; Thailand–South Vietnam, 233 nmi^2; and Kampuchea–Thailand–South Vietnam, 3,610 nmi^2; for a total of 24,221 nmi^2. In making these unilateral claims, each state chose an interpretation of lines of equidistance that gave the maximum area of the seabed to the claimant. Some small islands were ignored and others were given special effect in establishing lines of equidistance. Thailand appears to have drawn its boundary as a line of equidistance between the Thai mainland and large islands such as Kao Rong that are close to the Kampuchean and Vietnamese coast. Such a procedure involves discounting the Thai islands of Ko Kra and Ko Losin, the Kampuchean islands Kao Wai, and the Vietnamese islands Hon Panjang. Because the islands of the other two countries are farther from their coasts than the Thai islands are from the Thai coast, this discounting shifts the boundary eastward in Thailand's favor. Between 7°30′N and 9°30′N, the boundaries proclaimed for Kampuchea and South Vietnam ignored the Thai islands Ko Losin and Ko Kra, and this moved the boundaries westward to Thailand's disadvantage. There is even a small overlap with the Malaysian continental shelf claim in the southwestern gulf.

However, even these interpretations are inconsistent. For example, the Thai boundary proceeding southwestward from the Thai–Kampuchea land boundary terminus bears no relation to the line of equidistance and appears to be reproducing the azimuth of the final segment of the land boundary. The northern limit of the claim made on behalf of Kampuchea intersected the Thai island of Ko Kut. This island was retroceded to Thailand by France in the boundary treaty of 23 March 1907. The western terminus of this northern segment is situated midway between the Thai baseline and the Ilot Kusrovie; such an interpretation ignores not only Ko Kut but also the entire Thai coast in the northeast Gulf of Thailand.

While it is doubtful that Kampuchea is entitled to the straight baselines it claims, it is entitled to use the offshore islands as base points. When good relations are restored, Thailand and Kampuchea will have to agree on what effect should be given to each of their offshore islands. Because the area has petroleum potential, both sides will seek to secure the largest possible area.

Any Kampuchean administration probably would urge the point that Kampuchea is a poor country, with an unfavorable location from which to make maritime claims, and that therefore an equitable, rather than an equidistant, boundary should be drawn. While this argument might carry some weight with the Thai authorities in discussions over the seabed boundary, it is likely that for security reasons the Thais will insist on an equidistant boundary separating the territorial seas. This means that Thailand may refuse to recognize the straight baselines, which were drawn by an earlier Kampuchean government and do not appear to have been rescinded. The Thai objection to the baselines would presumably rest on the argument that the islands do not fringe the coast, that the waters east of the baseline are not linked closely enough to the land, and that the baseline departs appreciably from the general direction of the coast. In January 1978 Thailand and Vietnam agreed to settle their rival claims on the basis of equitable principles, but as yet there has been no progress in settling the dispute.

There was a serious territorial dispute between Kampuchea and Vietnam over Dao Phu Quoc and some other smaller islands farther from the coast. The dispute originated in a French declaration of 1939 that allocated islands to the French colonies of Cochin China and Indochina, which became Kampuchea and Vietnam, respectively. The allocation was made by a straight line, drawn at a defined azimuth to the coast, which passed through Dao Phu Quoc. That island was specifically allocated to Indochina, but it was noted that the boundary was established only for administrative purposes, not to resolve questions of sovereignty. Subsequently, Kampuchea claimed Dao Phu Quoc and even showed baselines drawn around it. On 7 July 1982 Kampuchea and Vietnam agreed to proclaim a joint area of historical waters, which they have placed under the regime of internal waters.[23] This area measures about 4,000 nmi². Its roughly quadrilateral shape is bounded by the terminus of the land boundary between the two countries; the islands of Tho Chu and Poulo Wai; and a point on the Kampuchean coast near Veal Renh. The two countries will select a boundary to separate their areas of historical waters in due course. The same solution of creating a joint zone while negotiations continue has been adopted on both sides of the Gulf of Thailand.

Negotiations have been proceeding for some time between Indonesia and Vietnam to divide an area of overlapping claims north of the Natuna Islands. The area measures 11,270 nmi² and is bounded by a unilateral claim made by South Vietnam on 6 June 1971 that the Vietnamese government has apparently maintained, a median line between Indonesian archipelagic baselines, and Vietnamese baselines. Measurements on charts make it appear that the Vietnamese claim totally discounts Indonesia's Natuna Islands; the Vietnamese line appears to be roughly equidistant between the Vietnamese coast and the coast of Indonesia's Kalimantan. The Vietnamese case seems weak, and it is a measure of Indonesia's reasonableness in the question of maritime matters that it is prepared to discuss it. One report suggests that the area of dispute has been narrowed to 1,000 nmi² and that Indonesia is satisfied that it has secured the gas and oil reserves discovered in the region under Indonesian contracts.[24] Unconfirmed reports suggest that the disputed area will be divided into a western Indonesian section and an eastern Vietnamese part, rather than into north and south segments for Vietnam and Indonesia, respectively. There seems to be an excellent chance that this dispute will be resolved despite differences that might exist between the two countries over the Kampuchean situation.

If they wished, it would be possible for China and Vietnam to decide their common boundary through the Gulf of Tonkin without any reference to disputed islands in the Spratly group. The dispute arises because of Vietnam's questionable position that the Sino–French Treaty of 1887 created a maritime boundary in the gulf. This treaty allocated islands east and west of a specified meridian to China and Vietnam, respectively. That was a fairly common technique among colonial powers at the time. Britain used it to claim islands in the Torres Strait in 1879; Spain and the United States drew straight lines instead of naming all the islands in the Philippines Archipelago; and as late as 1969 Australia used this simple method to lay claim to all of the islands and reefs in the Coral Sea.

It seems rather implausible for Vietnam to suggest that the meridian 108°3'30"E of Greenwich marks the maritime boundary between China and Vietnam in the Gulf of Tonkin. The treaty does not specify any southern terminus for the meridian, which means that China would be entitled to argue that its southern terminus is located where the meridian cuts the Vietnamese coast, or the outer edge of its territorial waters, just south of Hue! So long as Vietnam insists on maintaining this claim there is little chance of a settlement in the Gulf of Tonkin, even if relations between the two countries improve.

As for the boundary between Indonesia and Malaysia north of Tanjong Datu, it might be considered necessary to separate territorial seas and EEZs there. There will be two difficulties. First, Malaysia appears to have drawn its territorial seas from baselines that have never been proclaimed. The inferred Malaysian baselines are shown in Figures 3.3 and 3.4. East of Tanjong Datu the inferred Malaysian baseline proceeds directly to Tanjong Sipang. There is no obvious justification for this line; the coast is not deeply indented nor is it fringed with islands. Reliance on that baseline would distort in Malaysia's favor a line of equidistance separating territorial seas or EEZs. There are unconfirmed reports that Indonesia has indicated to Malaysia that it cannot rely on unproclaimed baselines; they must either be proclaimed or abandoned. The second difficulty arises because the EEZ is claimed on a different basis from the seabed, and Indonesia may press for an economic zone boundary that occupies an equidistant position. If those efforts were successful, Indonesia would acquire economic rights in waters overlying the seabed that was delivered to Malaysia by the 1969 agreement. Indonesia and Malaysia have enjoyed good relations in recent years, and if they continue to do so they should be able to solve this problem.

The potentially complicated issues involving Malaysia with Indonesia and the Philippines in the Celebes Sea can be considered together. They arise because Malaysia has claimed territorial seas and a section of the continental shelf which intrudes across the line of equidistance with its two neighbors. Figure 3.5 shows the

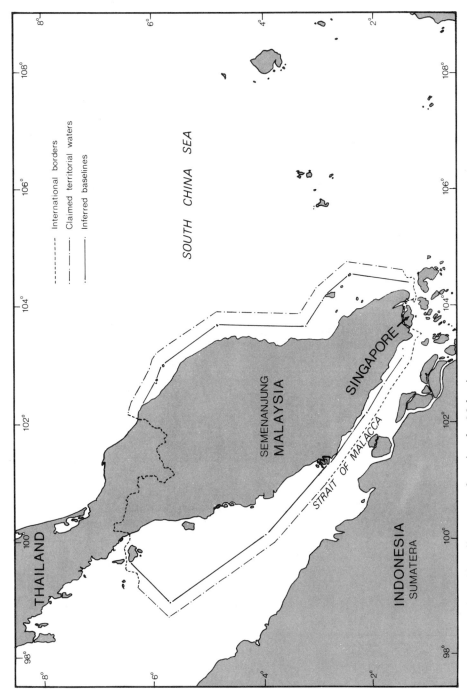

Figure 3.3   Inferred baselines around peninsular Malaysia.

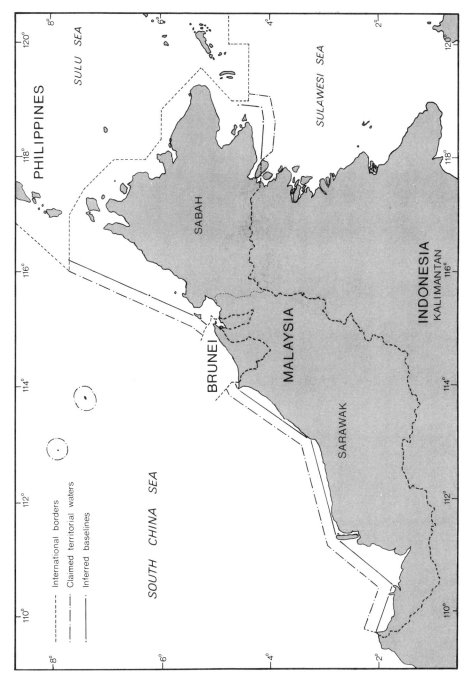

Figure 3.4 Inferred baselines around Sabah and Sarawak.

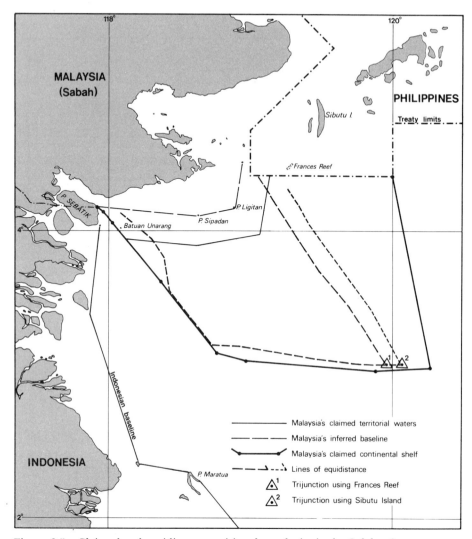

Figure 3.5   Claimed and equidistant maritime boundaries in the Celebes Sea.

Malaysian claims and the line of equidistance. Looking at the boundary between
Indonesia and Malaysia first, it appears that Malaysia has unilaterally drawn the
common territorial sea boundary as a line that bisects the angle formed by Indonesia's archipelagic baseline and Malaysia's inferred baseline. Such a line ignores Batuan Unarang, a rock from which Indonesia is entitled to claim territorial seas.
This feature is the southern outer danger for the entrance to the waters north of
Sebatik Island. It appears that the inferred baseline, which links Malaysian territory on Sebatik Island with Pulau Sipadan, does not connect islands fringing the
coast nor does it enclose a deeply indented coast, and it deviates appreciably from
the general direction of the coast. There is a length of the boundary claimed by

Malaysia that closely follows an equidistant course, but it eventually extends too far to the southeast and therefore discounts the importance of Pulau Maratua as a base point. This feature forms part of Indonesia's archipelagic baseline.

The basis for the Malaysian claim to the continental shelf in the direction of the Philippines is unknown. The area Malaysia appears to have claimed beyond the line of equidistance is 2,420 nmi^2 assuming that Frances Reef, which is part of the Philippine archipelagic baseline system, may be used to calculate the line of equidistance. If Malaysia successfully resisted the use of this low-tide elevation, then a line of equidistance using the southern tip of Sibutu Island as a point of reference would slightly reduce the area of potential dispute.

Because the seabed in this region of the Celebes Sea descends steeply to depths in excess of 2,000 fathoms, competition for this zone of continental shelf might not be very intense. However, if Malaysia's seabed claim is an indication of the EEZ it might eventually claim, there could be disagreements over the control of the waters above the deep seafloor of the Celebes Sea.

The boundary problem on the continental shelf between Australia and Indonesia south of Timor arises because of Indonesia's recent acquisition of Timor. While Timor was still a Portuguese colony, Australia and Indonesia negotiated seabed lines east and west of any potential Portuguese claim. Those lines were not equidistant boundaries because Australia was able to persuade Indonesia that it was making a sufficient concession by agreeing to move the claimed boundary from the axis of the Timor Trough to the continental slope that marks the trough's southern border. The Indonesian authorities subsequently decided that they were too generous in accepting the lines in 1971 and 1972 and, accordingly, the gap south of Timor must be filled by a boundary following an equidistant course. It is generally believed that there are at least two promising basins in the disputed area that might contain oil or natural gas. There are no reports that either side has shown any willingness to compromise over this zone.

West of Ashmore Reef it will be necessary to extend the seabed boundary westward toward the Indian Ocean. While both sides agree that an equidistant line should be drawn, there is no agreement on which Australian base points should be used. Australia wants a line of equidistance related to all Australian offshore islands, including Ashmore Reef, Browse Island, and Scott Reef. Indonesia wants those islands to be discounted and the base points located on or close to the Australian mainland. In Figure 3.6 lines of equidistance have been constructed to show the Australian and Indonesian views. The base points used in constructing the Indonesian line of equidistance are the Lacapede Islands, Cape Veleque, the Champagny Islands, the Maret Islands, and West Holothuria Reef. Although it is not known if those are the base points on which the Indonesian case rests, that line represents the sense of the Indonesian claim. The area between the two lines and the 200-nmi limit drawn from Indonesia and Scott Reef and Rowley Shoals is 52,120 nmi^2.

There is no indication of how that zone will be divided, but Australia and Indonesia agreed on 29 October 1981 to a provisional fisheries surveillance and enforcement line through this region and the area south of Timor. South of Timor the line is

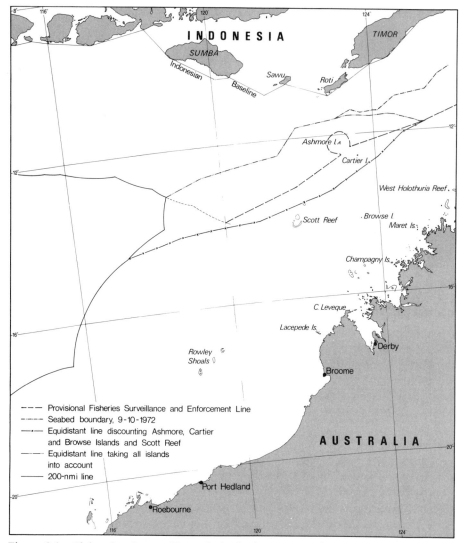

Figure 3.6   Claimed and agreed boundaries in the western Timor Sea.

close to an equidistant position; west of Ashmore Reef the line lies much closer to the
Indonesian proposal than to the Australian claim. Even if it is assumed that in the
west Indonesia's claim is limited by the 200-nmi line (shown as a solid line in Figure
3.6), it is still clear that Indonesia has received the largest part of the disputed area.
While the agreement of 1981 stipulates that this line is drawn without prejudice to
the final line, it is difficult for countries to regain waters they have willingly placed
under the administration of another country. It would be surprising if that interim
boundary does not fossilize in that location. Fishing zones and continental shelves
are claimed on different bases, and thus it is open to Australia to argue for a conti-

nental shelf boundary north of the provisional fisheries line. Indeed, it is possible that the fisheries concession was given in the hope or promise of a concession by Indonesia on the shelf issue. The four maritime boundary issues involving these countries might be treated as a package.[25] The announcement of only a provisional fisheries line still leaves this opportunity open for both parties.

The maritime boundary that Malaysia and Singapore are in the process of drawing through Johore Strait should not pose any difficulties for either country. In the Strait of Malacca there is a gap of 17 nmi between the two Malaysia–Indonesia agreements on territorial waters. These two countries and Singapore will have to agree on boundary segments linking the two existing sections and extending the line through Singapore Strait. In doing this, the issue of Horsburgh Light could become complicated for Singapore and Malaysia. The lighthouse is located on Pedra Branca, a feature that rises about 8 m (24 ft) above water and marks the southern edge of the Middle Channel, the passage generally used by vessels passing through Singapore Strait. The northern edge of the channel is marked by Remunia Shoals. There are two questions to be decided about Horsburgh Light. First, does it belong to Malaysia or Singapore? It is claimed by both and it is apparently used as one of the termini of the inferred baselines used by Malaysia. Singapore claims that the navigation aids on Pedra Branca have been administered from Singapore since the beginning of the first half of the nineteenth century. This ought to be a matter easily settled by reference to historic documents in archives in London, Singapore, and Kuala Lumpur and to contracts for repair work that must have been carried out on the light from time to time.

The second question is important only if the light is confirmed as belonging to Singapore. In that case it will be necessary to decide whether the feature on which the light stands is an island or rocks that have no economic life of their own. If the Horsburgh Light is proclaimed as standing on an island belonging to Singapore, that country can make a claim to a lens-shaped area of sea and seabed measuring 240 nmi². That is not a large area, but to a zone-locked country such as Singapore it is potentially valuable.

This lens-shaped area lies mainly on the Malaysian side of the 1979 seabed boundary drawn by Indonesia and Malaysia. Point 11 of that agreement is located 6.5 nmi northeast of Horsburgh Light, which was apparently ignored in selecting that point.[26] Point 11, which is reproduced as Point 32 in Malaysia's unilateral claim to the seabed, is 11 nmi from the nearest Indonesian territory and 12.5 nmi from the nearest Malaysian territory. While this dispute is between Malaysia and Singapore, its development will be watched with keen interest by Indonesia. Indonesia might prefer to avoid negotiating a new boundary with Singapore.

Uncomplicated Boundaries

Burma and India defined their territorial waters, contiguous zones, EEZs, and continental shelves in 1977 and 1976, respectively. The claims were made in almost identical language. The boundary separating their EEZs and continental shelves east of meridian 90°E remains to be defined. It will also be necessary to draw boundaries separating territorial waters and contiguous zones near the Coco Channel. Between 90°E and the Coco Channel there do not seem to be any difficulties in fixing maritime limits. East of the Coco Channel, however, in the northern part of the Andaman Sea, there are three circumstances that will complicate the construction of common maritime limits. First, the Burmese claim is measured from an exceptional baseline that closes the Gulf of Martaban. Second, India's claim may be measured from a small, isolated, uninhabited volcanic island called Narcondam. Third, an Indian claim from Narcondam will extend onto the continental shelf of the Irrawaddy Delta. The combined effect of the unusual Gulf of Martaban and Tenasserim Coast baseline segments is to deflect the line of equidistance with India southwestward, transferring 1,375 nmi^2 to the Burmese side of the line. It is the closing line across the Gulf of Martaban that causes most of the deflection.

Narcondam Island is a craterless, extinct volcano with an area of 7 square kilometers (km^2). It stands 710 m above sea level and is bounded by wave-cut cliffs 100 m high. According to the Indian census of 1961, the island is not inhabited. The CLS permits India to claim the entire suite of maritime zones from Narcondam Island. In view of the major effect the island has in determining the line of equidistance between India and Burmese territory, it would be possible for Burma to argue that the effect of the island should be discounted and equitable principles should be used in fixing the common boundary.

If the line of equidistance is related to the Burmese baseline, then the area enclosed is 580 nmi^2; if the median line is drawn between Narcondam Island and the Burmese coast, then an additional 595 nmi^2 fall on the Indian side. The CLS allows countries to claim the continental shelf throughout the natural prolongation of their land territory to the outer edge of the continental margin or to 200 nmi where the margin does not extend to that distance. Although the term "natural prolongation" is imprecise, there can be little question that the areas totaling 1,175 nmi^2 referred to earlier form part of the continental margin that extends seaward from the Irrawaddy Delta. Unfortunately for any case that Burma might seek to establish, the edge of the margin south of the Irrawaddy Delta is broken at one point by a submarine ridge connecting it with Narcondam Island. If India agreed to forego its claim to the segment of the continental margin south of the Irrawaddy Delta by discounting the effect of Narcondam Island, it would still be possible for India to request an equidistant line separating the EEZs of the two countries.

Indonesia owns Miangas Island, through a decision of the Permanent Court of Arbitration in The Hague. However, Miangas, formerly called Palmas Island, lies within the treaty limits of the Philippines as described in the Treaty of Paris between Spain and the United States on 10 December 1898. This treaty encompassed all the islands transferred from Spain to the United States. Indonesia and the Philippines proclaimed archipelagic baselines around their islands in 1957 and 1961, respectively. Indonesia's declaration regarding its baseline system fixed Miangas Island as Point 56; it is the most northerly point of the baseline segments that enclose the Molucca Sea. Waters within the Philippines' proclamation of its archipelagic baselines and the treaty limits were considered territorial waters of the Philippines. Thus an ocean area of about 4,300 nmi^2 in the southeast corner of the treaty limits is claimed by Indonesia as internal and territorial waters and by the Philippines as territorial waters.

If Philippine treaty limits prevail, Indonesia's claims in the region could be restricted to territorial waters around Miangas Island, forming an enclave within the territorial waters of the Philippines. If the Indonesian baseline system is paramount, it will be necessary to draw a maritime boundary somewhere between Miangas and Mindanao islands. If Indonesia only advances a claim to territorial waters, however, the boundary could be fixed by lines parallel to and 12 nmi distant from the Indonesian baseline. The Indonesian government, however, wishes to claim other zones beyond the territorial waters, and it will be necessary to consider whether the common boundary should be based on the principle of equidistance or on the principle of equity. An equidistant line related to the baselines would be a smooth, uncomplicated boundary that would give Indonesia rights over 6,200 nmi^2 of ocean and seabed within the treaty limits of the Philippines. An equidistant line related to the coasts of both countries would be less regular and would reduce slightly the area that would fall to Indonesia.

An EEZ boundary between Indonesia and the Philippines remains to be determined in the Celebes Sea. The Philippines might use its treaty limits in the sea as a basis for further claims, which are certain to be disputed by Indonesia. A large portion of the northern Celebes Sea would then be territorial waters, a status unlikely to be accepted by maritime powers. The Philippine baseline that closes Moro Gulf is 11 nmi longer than the maximum 125 nmi in the CLS. If the Philippines uses this archipelagic baseline to claim a 200-nmi EEZ or an equidistant line, Indonesia may object.

On achieving complete independence on 1 January 1984, Brunei was entitled to claim a full suite of maritime zones and to negotiate maritime boundaries with its neighbors. The only existing maritime boundaries were established by two British Orders in Council in 1958 proclaiming continental shelf boundaries between Brunei and the neighboring Malaysian territories. Where these boundaries traversed territorial waters, they also formed the boundary between the adjacent territorial seas of the three territories: Sarawak, Brunei, and North Borneo (now Sabah). The eastern and western boundary lines terminate at the 100-fathom isobath, close to the 200-m depth nominated by the 1958 Geneva Convention on the Continental Shelf as part of the definition of its outer limit.

The western limit of Brunei's seabed begins at the land boundary between Brunei and Malaysia and initially follows a line of equidistance. However, at the 10-fathom isobath, the boundary diverges from the equidistant line, giving Brunei about 300 nmi^2 of seabed it would not possess if the equidistant line were continued. The line passes between two wellheads only 0.75 nmi apart; it is possible that the desire to apportion one wellhead to each entity was decisive in defining this boundary.

The outer limits of Brunei's zones must be fixed. Amboyna Cay and Mariveles Reef are recognized as islands and the full range of maritime zones can be drawn around them. Swallow Reef, Royal Charlotte Reef, and Louisa Reef are rocks and should only be able to possess territorial seas and contiguous zones. If it is agreed by the country or countries that own Louisa, Royal Charlotte, and Swallow reefs that such features are rocks, the line of equidistance between Brunei's baseline and Mariveles Reef would apply. However, if the country or countries owning Louisa, Royal Charlotte, and Swallow reefs successfully insist that they are islands rather than rocks, or that even though they are only rocks Brunei may not claim beyond the median line between its baseline and these features, the triangular area would be truncated due to Louisa Reef.

Another complicating factor in establishing Brunei's maritime zones is the baseline from which the claims should be measured. Ampa Light is located on an off-shore feature, Ampa Patches, a shoal of sand and coral. If Brunei's baseline could be drawn to include Ampa Patches it is possible to construct other lines of equidistance. There are two possibilities, depending on agreement by the negotiating nations, on whether or not Swallow, Royal Charlotte, and Louisa reefs are rocks or islands. If they are held to be islands, or if the nation with which Brunei negotiates insists that Brunei may not claim across the median line between Brunei and these rocks, the area that Brunei can claim is severely reduced.

The northern boundary of the Philippines-claimed territorial waters is unclear. The 1898 treaty reads in part, "A line running from west to east along or near the 20th parallel of north latitude and through the middle of the navigable channel of Bashi from the 118th to the 127th degree meridian of longitude east of Greenwich. . . ." The middle of the Bashi Channel is at 21°30′N latitude, not 20°N as stated in the text of the treaty. Official maps of the Philippines show the northern limit as a straight line through Bashi Channel between meridians 118°E and 127°E in the vicinity of parallel 21°30′N. Thus, the government of the Philippines has chosen the most favorable interpretation of the northern boundary of its territorial waters. If it is decided the line was straight but the specification of 20°N an error, it will be necessary for the Philippine authorities to prove that satisfactorily. It would be plausible for China (Taiwan) to argue that it was the reference to Bashi Channel that was wrong, although it is not seriously suggested that Taiwan might thereby lay claim to the Philippine Islands lying north of parallel 20°N. It is possible the Philippines could argue that even though the line shown on charts cannot be reconciled with the treaty's description, it has been claimed without objection from other states for a sufficiently long time to become established in international law.

With respect to the seabed boundary between Chrismas Island and Java, Australia would be prepared to agree to a line that followed the insular margin; however, Indonesia has questioned whether the island generates any rights to continental shelf resources. Apparently this view is advanced because Christmas Island lies within 200 nmi of Indonesia and is comparatively remote from Australia.

CONCLUSIONS

Most maritime jurisdictional issues in Southeast Asia arise because conventional claims taken to their legal limits would overlap. Most of the boundaries that have been drawn occur in the southern part of the region, where there is only one dispute over ownership of territory, between Malaysia and Singapore. Other factors that have promoted settlements in the south are the simple structure of the seabed, except between Australia and Indonesia, and the stimulus provided by Indonesia's determination to reach boundary agreements, even when this involved making some concessions. The concern of countries in the region with offshore mineral and hydrocarbon exploration is revealed by the high proportion of seabed boundaries among agreements reached.

The construction of any of the potential international maritime boundaries identified may be difficult or simple according to the combination of political, geographic, and economic circumstances that apply. The most critical circumstances appear to be the nature of political relations between the states concerned, the presence of offshore islands, and disputes over their ownership.

An attempt was made to classify the various boundaries requiring international agreement according to the degree of difficulty that appears to attend their solution; the three categories identified were very complicated, complicated, and uncomplicated. This is not a rigid classification. Changed circumstances, especially changes in state relations, might transfer boundary segments from one category to another.

Only two types of responses of states to boundary issues have been used so far in Southeast Asia. States have made and defended unilateral claims, and they have engaged in bilateral negotiations. The result of most bilateral negotiations has been to produce multiple boundaries, that is, several lines each of which separate only one type of jurisdiction, such as the seabed or territorial waters. Joint zones have been used three times; by Malaysia and Thailand, by Kampuchea and Vietnam, and by Australia and Papua New Guinea.

States may seek to modify perceived adverse effects of fixed maritime boundaries by reaching understandings about the operation of rules. For example, in 1974 the Australian and Indonesian governments produced a memorandum of understanding regarding the operation of Indonesian traditional fishermen in areas of the Australian fishing zone and seabed. By this memorandum those Indonesian fishermen who had traditionally taken fish and sedentary organisms from the Australian waters and seabed by methods in use for decades were permitted to continue this activity in specified areas. Malaysia and Indonesia have reached agreement about Malaysia's transit rights through, and fishing rights in, the archipelagic waters surrounding Indonesia's Natuna Islands, which lie opposite of a direct course from the Malay Peninsula to Sarawak. The techniques of constructing joint zones and providing supplementary agreements to modify the operation of rules in national areas may be used to help solve some of the potentially difficult problems that exist in the northern part of the region.

PART II.
OCEAN USE SECTORS

CHAPTER 4

FISHERIES

Elizabeth D. Samson

Fisheries issues are rooted in people — their history, customs, traditions, habits, aspirations, and emotions. In Southeast Asia at least five million people are directly dependent on fishing for their livelihood, and at least twenty-five million people are affected by decisions regarding the fishing industry in the region. The fishermen in Southeast Asia produce about 17 percent of the world's fishery catch. The region's marine catch is about 11 percent of total world catch and is taken from a resource composed of some 2,500 species of fish and a large number of invertebrate species.

Few countries in Southeast Asia have established firm and clear policies with regard to their marine interests, and in fisheries, certainly none has. The Convention on the Law of the Sea (CLS) has stimulated much discussion and planning in this direction, but policies are still being formulated. National marine interests and specific indicators of those interests were reviewed in Chapter 2. Within that setting, this chapter examines the interests and activities of Southeast Asian countries in fisheries. Issues that might arise out of national positions are then considered. Finally, the chapter presents some options that the nations might consider in responding to the issues.

SOUTHEAST ASIAN NATIONAL INTERESTS IN FISHERIES

A nation's involvement in fisheries can be examined by considering its geographic features, its resources and resource use patterns, its dependence on fisheries, its development thrusts, and its ability to enforce its marine interests. Tables 4.1 through 4.4 summarize this information about the nations of Southeast Asia, plus China, the Chinese province of Taiwan, and Hong Kong, in a form designed to facilitate comparative analysis. Figures 4.1, 4.2, and 4.3 show the geographical distribution of production for demersal (bottom) species, coastal pelagic (midwater) species, and oceanic species. Figure 4.4 shows shared and migratory stocks.

101

Table 4.1   State of Marine Resources Presently Fished

Country	Internal Waters	Bay of Bengal	Andaman Sea	Strait of Malacca	Gulf of Tonkin
Brunei					
Burma		Underex-ploited	Underex-ploited		
China					
China (Taiwan)					Pelagics under-exploited
Hong Kong					Pelagics under-exploited
Indonesia	Coasts of Java Sea, Bali Strait overexploited; offshore under-exploited			Over-exploited	
Kampuchea					
Laos	(LANDLOCKED)				
Malaysia		Over-exploited		Over-exploited	
Philippines	Demersals, large pelagics depleted; small pelagics underexploited in some areas				
Singapore				Over-exploited	
Thailand			Mackerels over-exploited	Demersals over-exploited	
Vietnam					Pelagics under-exploited; demersals under-exploited in deep waters

South China Sea	Gulf of Thailand	East China Sea	Others (e.g., Pacific Ocean; Indian Ocean)
Underexploited			
Overexploited			
Demersals overexploited; pelagics underexploited		Pelagics under-exploited	
Demersals overexploited; pelagics underexploited		Pelagics under-exploited	
			Offshore underexploited
	Overexploited		
Offshore fishing may be expanded off Sarawak; coastal and offshore fishing may be intensified off Sabah			
Potential for exploitation offshore			Potential for exploitation
Offshore demersal fishing may be expanded			
	Overexploited		
Demersals and pelagics underexploited			

Table 4.2   Dependence on Fisheries

Country	Total Marine and Inland Fisheries Production (MT)	Annual per Capita Consumption (kg/capita)	Animal Protein from Fish (%)	GNP from Fisheries (%)
Brunei	2,800	38	—	.75
Burma	585,100	16.8 (1979)	substantial	n.a.
China	4,200,000	4.3 (estuarine)	low	0.7
China (Taiwan)[a]	929,176	n.a.	substantial	
Hong Kong	194,560	37	45	<1
Indonesia	1,850,000	12	65	1.8
Kampuchea	20,900	n.a.	n.a.	n.a.
Laos	20,000	—	—	—
Malaysia	736,674	25	65	2–25
Philippines	1,506,024	30–32	62	4.8
Singapore	16,000	30	35	.2
Thailand	1,650,000	15	n.a.	1
Vietnam	1,000,000	15 (1977)	50 (mid-70s)	4.1 (mid-70s)

Country	Percent of Labor Force		Percent of Fishing Units	
	Commercial	Small-scale	Commercial	Small-scale
Brunei	n.a.	n.a.	substantial	n.a.
Burma	nil	substantial	nil	substantial
China	n.a.	n.a.	4	96
China (Taiwan)[a]	—	—	—	—
Hong Kong	n.a.	n.a.	75	25
Indonesia	.5	99.5	.1	99.9
Kampuchea	n.a.	n.a.	n.a.	n.a.
Laos	—	—	—	—
Malaysia	10	90	30	70
Philippines	12	88	.9	99.1
Singapore	n.a.	n.a.	n.a.	n.a.
Thailand	50	50	80	20
Vietnam	—	substantial	—	substantial

Source: Yearbook of Fishery Statistics, 1980, Rome: United Nations, Food and Agriculture Organisation, 1981.
[a]From *Fishery Statistics of Southeast Asia, 1978,* Bangkok: SEAFDEC, Oct. 1980.

Table 4.2 Continued

Production (%)		Labor Force in Fisheries	
Commercial	Small Scale	Number	Percent of Total
substantial	n.a.	nil	.5
2.4 (1977)	97.6 (1977)	350,000	2–3
n.a.	n.a.	860,000 (marine only)	1.4
96	4 (1978)	285,000 (1972) (marine capture only)	n.a.
88	22	36,000	3
5	95	2,200,000	4
n.a.	n.a.	—	—
–	–	–	–
20	80	110,000	2
40	60	450 (1978)	.3
n.a.	n.a.	2,000	.13
90	10	75,000	1.7
—	substantial	355,000 (1973)	n.a.

Predominant Gears in Commercial Fisheries	Trade in Fisheries (Millions of $U.S.)		
	Exports	Imports	Net Exports
Lines	—	—	negative
Trawlers, gillnetters	n.a.	n.a.	n.a.
Trawlers, purse seiners (1978)	n.a.	n.a.	n.a.
Trawlers, liners	670 (1979)	84 (1979)	n.a.
Trawlers	189	355	166 (1981)
Trawlers, liners	22	37	194
n.a.	n.a.	n.a.	n.a.
–	—	—	–
Trawlers, purse seiners	–	–	179
Trawlers, purse seiners, bag nets	128	26.4	101.6
n.a.	—	—	negative
Trawlers, push nets, gillnetters	235	68	167 (1978)
Shrimp trawlers (1973)	13.3	1.3	12 (1973)

Note: Figures for Brunei, Kampuchea, Laos and Vietnam are FAO estimates. Figures are generally for 1980 except where indicated otherwise.

Table 4.3   Development Thrusts in Fisheries

Country	Marine Production	
	Gears/Species	*Fishing Areas*
Brunei	Some development programs	
Burma	Prawn	Development projects
China	n.a.	Resource management
Hong Kong	Trawling; conversion to gears effective outside restricted zones	Potentials of pelagics offshore in north South China Sea
Indonesia	Expand size and range of state fleet; trawlers should phase out; conversion to purse seines, lines	Exploration of offshore, e.g., for purse seining
Kampuchea	Low priority	
Laos	n.a.	n.a.
Malaysia	Vessel/gear design for artisanal fisheries	Exploration of nontraditional waters; resource surveys of EEZ
Philippines	Selective gears will be promoted	Exploration of oceanic waters for tuna fishing
Singapore		
Thailand	Selective gears being tested	Joint ventures/bilateral agreements sought; seeks new areas outside EEZ's particularly for demersals
Vietnam	Trawlers	Shift to offshore

Demersal catches in the region are highest in the eastern Andaman Sea, the Strait of Malacca, off the east coast of peninsular Malaysia, in the Gulf of Thailand, off the Mekong Delta, along the entire Mainland Shelf including the Gulf of Tonkin, and in the Sibuyan and Visayan seas and adjacent waters of the central Philippines (Figure 4.1). Substantial though somewhat smaller catches are made in the eastern Bay of Bengal; around the Anambas and Natuna islands of the Sunda Shelf; around the island of Borneo; around southern Sumatera, Java, and central and southern Sulawesi; in the Arafura Sea off the southern coast of Irian Jaya; and in the Philippine waters around the islands of Mindanao and Palawan.

Coastal pelagic catches, including coastal pelagic fish, squid, cuttlefish, and jellyfish, generally follow the same basic regional distribution pattern as the demersal catches, with the highest catches being obtained from the Strait of Malacca, the Gulf of Thailand, along much of the Mainland Shelf, in the central and southern Philippines, and around eastern Java (Figure 4.2). Smaller though still substantial coastal pelagic catches are made in the eastern Andaman Sea; around northern

Table 4.3 Continued

Inland Culture Production			
Freshwater	Brackishwater	Coastal Mariculture	Utilization and Postharvest
Intensification	—	—	—
—	Development projects	—	Some support infrastructure
Advanced techniques	—	Advanced techniques	Quality improvement; market development
Management, breeding and polyculture	—	—	Attention
	Accelerating	—	Joint ventures with shore facilities encouraged
High priority	—	—	
n.a.	n.a.	n.a.	n.a.
Being promoted		To further develop potentials in cockles	
Incremental production is expected to come from aquaculture sector; target production is more than 100 percent of present product			Improvement of marketing and other postharvest activities and facilities
		Some priority	Processing and transshipment
—		Target is doubling of outputs from this sector	Postdevelopment from external assistance

and southern Sumatera; around western Java, Borneo, Sulawesi, and the Sunda islands; in the waters of the eastern, western, and northern Philippines; along the eastern seaboard of Vietnam; and off the island of Hainan.

Oceanic catches in the region are much smaller than the demersal or coastal pelagic catches (Figure 4.3). The largest catches are made in the Philippines, particularly in the central and southern Philippines where *payaws* are used to attract and concentrate skipjack, yellowfin, and bigeye tunas. Moderate oceanic catches are taken in the Strait of Malacca, in the Gulf of Thailand, in the Indian Ocean west of northern Sumatera, around the island of Java, in the Makassar Strait, and in the Celebes Sea north of Sulawesi. Elsewhere in the region, the oceanic catches are small.[1]

The migration routes of tuna have been charted on the basis of tagging and recapture studies and analysis of catch reports (Figure 4.4). Skipjack, yellowfin, and other tunas swim through the archipelagic and exclusive economic zone (EEZ) waters of Indonesia and the Philippines at various times of the year. Mackerels

Table 4.4   Trends in Production and Fishing Fleet Composition

Country	Marine Areas			
	Demersal	*% of Total*	*Pelagic*	*% of Total*
Brunei	Stagnant	100	Stagnant	—
Burma	Medium but sustained growth rate	73	Medium but sustained growth rate	17
China	Declining	75	Presumed	25
Hong Kong	Declining growth rates; negative in 1979–1980	96	Negative growth rate	4
Indonesia	Lower growth rate	75	Lower growth rate	25
Kampuchea	Sharp decline	52	Sharp decline	48
Malaysia	Lower growth rate 1978–1980; high proportion of trash fish	99	High growth rate; also for cockles	1
Philippines	Minimal growth rate in commercial fishing	76	Minimal growth rate in commercial fishing	24
Singapore	Minimal growth rate; negative in 1979–1980	97	Minimal growth rate; negative in 1979–1980	3
Thailand	Declining	90	Declining	10
Vietnam	n.a.	83	n.a.	17

Notes: Data generally are for last half of the 1970s. "% of Total" refers to 1980 unless indicated. Trends refer to growth rate. Sources indicated in text.

migrate around the Gulf of Thailand and also through the Strait of Malacca to the Andaman Sea, passing through Indonesian, Malaysian, Thai, and Burmese territories. Mackerels are believed to be shared by Malaysia and Indonesia in northeast Borneo and by China and Vietnam in the Gulf of Tonkin; Malaysia and Indonesia share the mackerel and roundscad stock within a wide radius off Natuna Island; Kampuchea, Vietnam, and Thailand share the mackerel, roundscad, and sardine stock in the northeast portion of the Gulf of Thailand; Malaysia, Thailand, and Indonesia share the mackerel, roundscad, and sardine stock in the Strait of Ma-

Table 4.4   Continued

	Inland Waters		
	Freshwater Culture	*Brackishwater Culture*	*Capture*
	Good prospects but qualities nil	Some possibility	—
	Medium growth rate, including inundated fisheries	—	Medium in growth rate
	High growth rate	Medium growth rate	Declining
	High growth rate	High growth rate	
		Sharp decline	
	High growth rate but quantities still minimal	High growth rate but quantities still minimal	n.a.
	Good prospects for further development	Good prospects for further development	
		Declining	
		Medium growth rate	
	n.a.	n.a.	n.a.

lacca; and Thailand and Burma share the mackerel and sardine stock in the Andaman Sea. Various demersal species are shared by Hong Kong and China in the inshore areas of the South China Sea; demersal and pelagic species are shared by Brunei and Malaysia off the coasts of Brunei and Sarawak; pelagic species are shared by Indonesia and Burma around the Nicobar Islands in the Andaman Sea.

Brunei

The Brunei government has appraised the demersal stock outside the 3-nautical-mile (-nmi) territorial zone where some commercial-scale fishing is done and de-

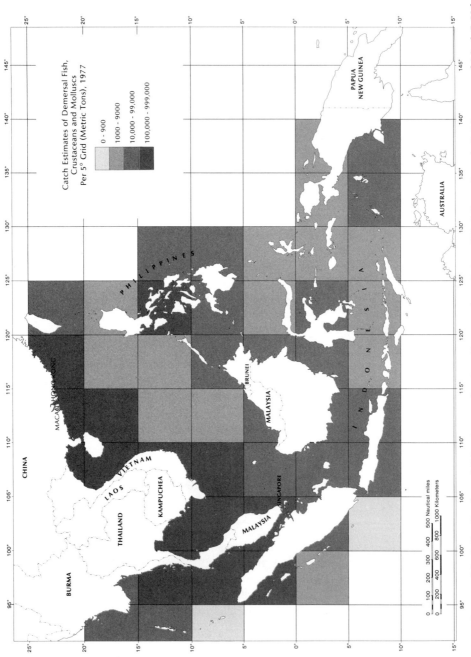

Figure 4.1 Geographical distribution of fisheries production: Demersal catch (modified from Joseph R. Morgan and Mark J. Valencia, eds., *Atlas for Marine Policy in Southeast Asian Seas*, Berkeley: University of California Press, 1983, p. 66).

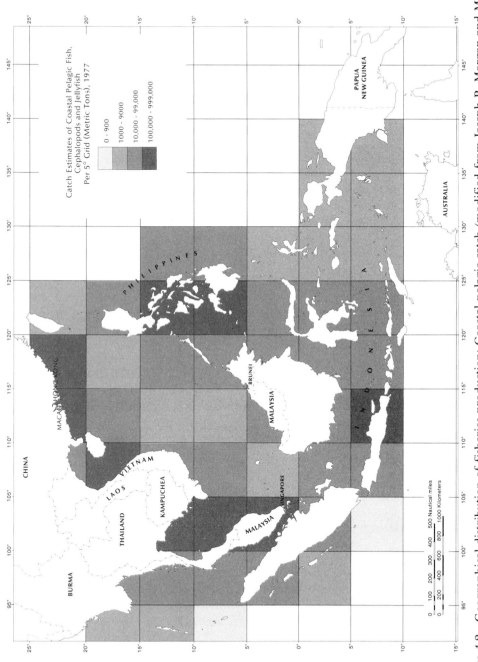

Figure 4.2   Geographical distribution of fisheries production: Coastal pelagic catch (modified from Joseph R. Morgan and Mark J. Valencia, eds., *Atlas for Marine Policy in Southeast Asian Seas*, Berkeley: University of California Press, 1983, p. 67).

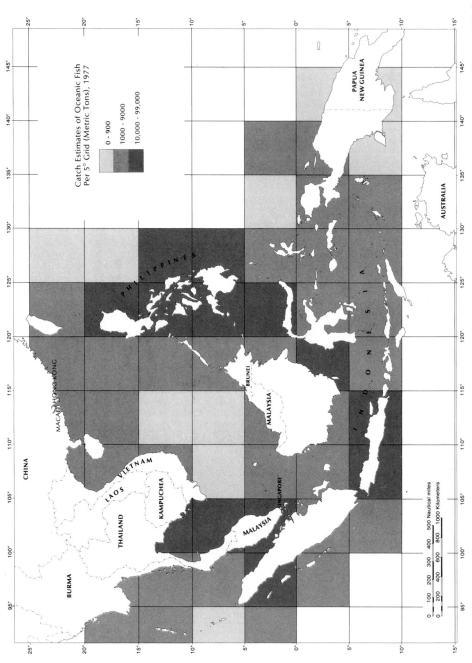

Figure 4.3 Geographical distribution of fisheries production: Oceanic catch (modified from Joseph R. Morgan and Mark J. Valencia, eds., *Atlas for Marine Policy in Southeast Asian Seas*, Berkeley: University of California Press, 1983, p. 68).

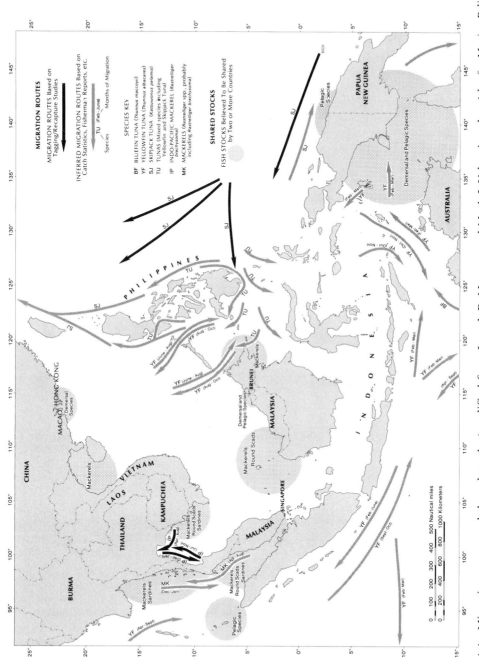

Figure 4.4 Migration routes and shared stocks (modified from Joseph R. Morgan and Mark J. Valencia, eds., *Atlas for Marine Policy in Southeast Asian Seas*, Berkeley: University of California Press, 1983, p. 61).

termined that 76 percent of the continental shelf claimed by Brunei is probably trawlable and 24 percent untrawlable.[2] The United Nations' Food and Agriculture Organisation (FAO) assessment of resources of the Sunda Shelf in 1977 pointed to the possibility of increasing demersal catch from the waters around Brunei by at least three times the peak demersal catch in 1974.[3] These and other indicators suggest that both the demersal and pelagic fisheries of Brunei could be expanded.

Total fish production in 1980 was estimated by the FAO at 2,800 metric tons (MT) (marine catch, 2,700 MT), almost all from capture. In 1979 there were 435 powered vessels.[4] Gillnets and lines were the most common gears, and there were numerous traps and portable fish pots. Portable pots, handlines, and longlines are operated offshore, while bottom set gillnets for Penaeid shrimps are concentrated on the extensive estuarine system in the northeastern part of the nation. It is believed that there are good prospects for the development of freshwater fisheries in Brunei. The northeastern end of the nation is bordered by mangroves that have potential for shrimp culture. The FAO estimated the level of inland fish production of Brunei at a token 83 MT per year up to 1980.[5]

Licensed fishermen numbered only 528 in 1978, accounting for less than 1 percent of the labor force; the effective rate is actually around 0.5 percent because 30 to 40 percent of the fishermen were temporary migrant workers from adjacent states. According to the National Development Plan, the gross national product (GNP) from fisheries was 0.75 percent in 1970. More recent estimates are not available. Of the total fish supply of 5,156 MT in 1977, 48 percent was imported, mostly from Sabah and Sarawak.[6]

The development strategy declared for the 1970s was one of diversification and balanced development, with fisheries mentioned as one of the target recipients of development inputs. Fisheries, however, have a relatively low priority. Expansion of Brunei's fishing industry is subordinate to development of its immensely more valuable petroleum industry. The pollution of marine waters from its offshore oil installations is an issue that Brunei will have to resolve with other countries sharing the same fish stocks as well as with its own small fishing population.

Burma

The potential resources over the continental shelf of Burma that could be harvested on a sustainable annual basis are approximately 780,000 MT demersal and 730,000 MT pelagic. The peak catches are still much below the potential and suggest room for industry expansion.[7]

Total fish production was 585,100 MT (marine catch, 429,000MT) in 1980, increasing at 4 percent per annum for the preceding four years. Some 73 percent of the catch is from marine waters, mostly inshore.[8] Nearly half the marine catch is pelagic fish harvested by artisanal fishermen who typically use stationary lift nets, bagnets, handlines, and other traditional gears. In 1979 there were 30,000 small vessels fishing inshore and 52,000 vessels inland.[9] The state-owned and controlled People's Pearl and Fishery Corporation conducts all offshore operations. In 1976–1977 PPFC accounted for only 2.4 percent of total fish production.[10]

Inland fishery activities are undertaken mainly on floodplains adjacent to three river systems (Irrawaddy-Chindwin, Sittang, and Salween) that are inundated four to five months a year.[11] The FAO placed inland fishery production in 1980 at 155,800 MT, with an apparent annual growth rate of 4 percent from 1977.

Per capita consumption of fish in 1979 was 16.8 kilograms (kg) (37 pounds [lb]), contributing a substantial proportion of animal protein to the diet.[12] In the same year, some 350,000 people (or around 2–3 percent of the labor force) were believed to be involved in fishing activities; 94,000 were in marine fishing, 58,000 in freshwater capture/culture, and some 200,000 were fishing seasonally in the flooded surfaces.

The Five-Year Investment Program for 1977–1982 emphasized marine fishing.[13] Of the total planned investment of US$118 million for the period, 21 percent was intended for marine fishery development in Mergui, 34 percent for marine fishery development in Arakan, 33 percent for marine shrimp fishery development, and only 13 percent was for freshwater ponds. Some of the planned investment probably covered support for infrastructure for marine fishing. (In 1979 there were no fishing ports in the country due to strong river currents and heavy sedimentation, and there are few shore facilities. Two Asian Development Bank (ADB) projects, for which loans totaling US$36 million were incurred, are underway to construct landing sites and install ice plants in major fishing areas. In 1979 US$25 million was invested in freshwater aquaculture and in the collection, processing, and marketing of Macrobrachium prawns.

Illegal fishing by its neighbors is a nagging problem for Burma's navy. Thai trawlers are the main offenders, though the Thais contend that their vessels are only transiting from Bangladesh waters. Burma's existing patrol craft have difficulty monitoring the EEZ, but there are plans to enlarge this capability. The government also has publicly requested citizens and regional organizations to detect illegal fishing vessels.

In summary, Burma's need for fish as food for its impoverished population and employment for its small-scale fishermen, along with indications of its enforcement orientation toward fisheries, suggest a national interest in attaining the benefits offered by its vast marine waters. There are also moves to explore the prospects of aquaculture to reduce dependence on marine waters.

Indonesia

The maximum sustainable yield (MSY) of Indonesia's marine waters has been estimated at 4.7 million MT, of which 2.9 million MT are in archipelagic waters and 1.8 million MT in additional waters gained as a result of the EEZ.[14] The rate of exploitation suggested by its 1981 production is 43.5 percent. This, however, is not quite indicative of the true state of the resource, given the lopsided intensity of fishing in various parts of the archipelago. The nearshore or coastal portions of the Strait of Malacca, the Java Sea, and the Bali Strait are fished by small-scale fishermen to the point of overexploitation. The adverse effects of mechanization on the catch per unit effort (CPUE) are most evident in these bodies of water and to a lesser extent on the nearshore or coastal areas elsewhere in the country. On the other hand, the offshore areas of the EEZ and the eastern part of the archipelago are underutilized.

Demersal fisheries comprise around one-third of the industry. Most demersal fishing is done in coastal waters (10–12 nmi offshore), generally by small-scale fishermen using traditional gears despite the advent of trawling. The inshore waters of the Java Sea and the Strait of Malacca are, however, good trawling grounds, with more than 40 percent of the demersal catch in recent years being hauled in by commercial trawlers. Conflicts between trawling operators and those using traditional gears are frequent. On the Indian Ocean side of Java the main fishing grounds are the areas near Cilacap, particularly for shrimp. In the South China Sea along Sumatera and Kalimantan 25 percent of the demersal catch is landed by trawlers. In 1977 the South China Sea accounted for 18 percent of demersal catch; the Java Sea, 22 percent; the Strait of Malacca, 24 percent; Cilacap on the Indian Ocean, 5 percent; and Irian Jaya, 32 percent. Most of these demersal fishing grounds are trawlable, and shrimp is the most attractive commercial species fished, particularly by trawlers under joint venture arrangements.[15]

The volume of fish production increased from 1.33 million MT in 1974 to 1.84 million MT in 1980, at an average annual growth rate of 6 percent. In 1980 marine catch contributed 1.39 million MT or 75 percent to total production.[16] Motorization of vessels and the successful promotion of more productive gears like purse seines and gillnets spurred the expansion of the marine sector. It grew at an average rate of 6.7 percent from 1974 to 1978 but slowed to 5.8 percent from 1976 to 1980.[17] The decline in growth rate despite an increase in production units substantiates earlier observations of overexploitation in certain areas.

The number of fishing boats dropped between 1974 and 1978 but recovered by 1979; in 1980 there were 271,856 vessels. The recovery is apparently a response to REPELITA III (the development plan for 1979–1983), which targets an increase in production through both modernization of existing fishing units and the augmentation of the fleet. The plan calls for the entry of 1,400 inshore vessels within the five-year period. As of 1980, 17 percent of the marine fleet was motorized, compared with only 5 percent in 1974. There is a notable shift to gillnets, purse seiners, and line gears and a reduction of trawlers.

For inland waters, potentials are placed at 1.4 million MT, assuming certain production inputs.[18] In 1980 inland waters yielded 0.45 million MT or 25 percent of total production.[19] In contrast with the performance of marine fisheries, inland fisheries improved dramatically from a growth rate of only 2 percent in 1974–1978 to 5.6 percent in 1979–1980, evidence of increasing attention to culture activities as an alternative means of livelihood for fishermen operating in highly exploited areas. Data for 1979 and 1980 confirm the government's declared emphasis on freshwater pond culture (11.8 percent growth rate), paddy field culture (21.9 percent growth), and cage culture (51.7 percent growth). These subsectors are still too small in relation to the capture sector to have significant impact on industry production and employment levels. In accordance with the development plans, the area under culture increased from 285,633 ha (705,513 acres) in 1974 to 316,044 ha (780,629 acres) in 1980.[20]

With the development of oil and other major industries in Indonesia, the importance of fishing in the national economy has been reduced. In 1975 fisheries activities accounted for 3.4 percent of GNP. In 1980 this contribution had declined to 1.8 percent.[21] The country has a major dependence on fisheries, however, because fish is a major source of protein for the people and fishing and related activities are a major labor sector. The potential of fish exports as a source of hard currency is also being pursued. Fishing is the main source of livelihood for 2.2 million fishermen and fish farmers, most of whom operate on a small scale and produce some 95 percent of national fish output. Fishermen in the labor force increased from 2.4 percent in 1974 to 4 percent in 1980, indicating that fishing as a means of livelihood is gaining even more importance.

In Indonesia's fish trade, export volume grew 3.7 percent per annum during 1974–1978; the growth rate abruptly rose to 15.3 percent in 1979–1980. In these two periods shrimp was the major export item, with skipjack tuna having increased importance. The export volume of shrimp has been on a general decline, however; and with shrimp being the high-valued species on the export list, this negative growth rate has affected the value of exports, particularly in 1979–1980. Thus, the growth rate in export value was 20 percent during 1974–1978, and −4.4 percent in 1979–1980. Data for 1981, however, show a positive growth rate of 2 percent between 1980 and 1981 export values.[22]

Although important to the incomes of small fishermen (who account for 70 percent of the volume of shrimp exports), the trade in fish products in Indonesia is not a major component of its total trade. Imports have consistently increased since 1974. Import quantities (especially canned fish and fish meal), increased at 40.4 percent per year in 1974–1978 and 27.4 percent in 1979–1980. The value of imports had an annual growth rate of 42 percent in 1974–1979 and jumped to 212 percent in 1979–1980. Price increases for fish meal, among other products, apparently caused this sudden increase.[23] The figures for 1981 show a further rise in import values by 76 percent.[24]

The government hopes to improve its export performance through the development of commercial-scale fishing, particularly in the relatively underexploited eastern parts of the archipelago and the offshore deep-sea areas.[25] The species caught by the commercial vessels are shrimp and skipjack and other tunas that are largely exported.

To obtain the needed capital and technology, commercial fisheries have become open to foreign investors and local private investors who are enticed with investment incentives and favorable legislation and regulations. Foreign equity starts at 80 percent and phases out to 49 percent within ten years. The government augments the activities of joint ventures and domestic enterprises with state-owned fishing ventures. By 1981, twenty-three joint ventures had been established with US$113.5 million in committed investments; sixteen were operational with US$64.5. million worth of capital invested. Twenty-six domestic enterprises had been organized with a planned capital investment of US$76.8 million; eighteen were operational with US$35.2 million actually invested.[26]

Six state enterprises have been established since 1973 to engage in pioneering activities not attracting private investment and to catalyze development in the small-scale fisheries sector. Three of these state firms have been assisted by the ADB, two by the World Bank, and one by Japan's Overseas Economic Cooperation Fund (OECF). Capital resources for those state enterprises total US$58.6 million, of which US$37.4 million was borrowed from the aforementioned sources while US$21.2 million was derived from local loans and government equity.

Over the last decade commercial fisheries earned US$670 million in foreign exchange. In 1981, US$123 million was realized from the exports of these enterprises. More than 95 percent of the export proceeds of private firms has been from shrimp. The state firms, however, concentrate on tuna catching and buying from small fishermen.

Among joint ventures, strict rules are stipulated on fishing areas, gears, and species allowed. In 1976, the entry of new ventures in the shrimp fishery was prohibited. Later, skipjack and other tunas formerly allowed to be fished in internal waters were permitted to be caught by joint ventures only in the EEZ. Commercial fisheries are required to supply the government with resource data, particularly on less exploited and underexploited areas. Investors had been allowed to spend a maximum of six months test fishing and surveying the resource, but this practice has been discontinued because the government decided to shift the responsibility entirely to the state.

While commercial fisheries play a prominent role in expanding exports and have the distinct role of utilizing the newly claimed fishing areas, they are also to be used to uplift the extensive small-scale sector. Large fishing enterprises, particularly those run by government, are expected to provide a ready market for the catch, although this objective has not yet been fulfilled, considering that government purchases of fish in 1981 amounted to only 7,281 MT, less than 1 percent of small-scale production. It is also envisioned that commercial fishing would indirectly benefit small-scale fishermen through demonstration effects and more directly by providing infrastructures to service the larger vessels.

The general thrusts of REPELITA III for fisheries during 1979–1983 are directed at nutritional, socioeconomic, and resource management problems.[27] The plan aims to increase the incomes of fishermen by creating employment opportunities through diversification and development of linkage industries and to improve conservation and management measures for the resource. To correct imbalances in production, consumption, and producers' incomes, diversification to less heavily fished areas is being attempted. There is increased attention on aquaculture, in both brackish water and fresh water, and also in marine waters.

A successful phaseout of trawlers from Java, Bali, and Sumatera to protect the interests of small-scale fishermen and to allow the resource to regenerate would have reduced the supply of shrimp for export. To compensate, the primary tool used was credit provided to trawl operators for the conversion of their gear to purse seiners, gillnets, and selective gear; to small-scale fishermen to increase their shrimp production; and to brackishwater fish farmers to promote shrimp production.

The ADB has provided Indonesia with a technical assistance grant of US$98,000 for fisheries development in Sumatera. The ADB also has provided a loan of US$7.95 million for Irian Jaya fisheries development and a loan of US$13.2 million for Java fisheries development.[28]

Research activities center on resource assessment for marine fisheries and on new and improved techniques for culture. There are many proposals for resource surveys and exploratory fishing for purse seiners in the eastern portions of Indonesia's marine jurisdiction. The postharvest handling of fish in Indonesia is still substandard, although the government has made some headway in providing infrastructure. There are now 24 fishing ports and 140 other landing places. Of the 24 fishing ports, 21 are for coastal fishing, 2 are "interinsular fishing ports," and only 1 is specifically for deep-sea fishing.

The Indonesian government's major plan for fisheries in the EEZ is the development of industrial fisheries, now seen as a major producer for export. Meanwhile, fishing remains largely coastal and small scale. The objectives of increasing fish consumption and improving the incomes of small fishermen can be attained substantially within national waters, at least within the short term.

Kampuchea

Total fisheries production for Kampuchea in 1980 is estimated at 20,900 MT, a sharp decline from the 84,700 MT estimated for 1977.[29] Some 10,800 MT were estimated to have been from the sea; the inland sector was believed to have produced 73,900 MT in 1977 and 10,100 MT in 1980, presumably due to the country's war-torn condition.

Traditionally consumer preference has been for freshwater fish, often live, and distribution to the interior has been a problem due to the absence of preservation and transportation facilities. The fish protein needs of the Kampucheans have been met almost entirely from river and lake resources, centering on the enormous and perennially renewed supply of freshwater fish available in the Tonle Sap (Great Lake).[30]

Currently, all available indicators point to minimal interest in sea fisheries for Kampuchea. If its main economic concern is rehabilitation and attainment of economic stability, it may in time be expected to cooperate with friendly nations that make favorable offers for exploring and developing marine resources under its jurisdiction.

Laos

In landlocked Laos, fish production from inland waters is estimated at 20,000 MT.[31] The country's traditional outlet had been the port of Bangkok, but Laos now has new roads and other infrastructure linking it to Vietnam and its ports. As a geographically disadvantaged state, Laos's marine interest lies in maintaining access to adjacent nations' marine resources.

Malaysia

Estimates of available fisheries resources MSY for peninsular Malaysia are as high as 350,000 MT for the west coast and 215,000 MT for the east coast. Rough assessments for Sabah and Sarawak suggest a potential of more than 500,000 MT consisting of 350,000 MT demersals and 152,000 MT of pelagics.[32] Viewed against actual production reported from Malaysian waters, it appears that industry expansion is feasible.

Expansion should be pursued selectively, however, because studies have advised reducing catches in certain fisheries. For instance, results of trawl surveys conducted by the government found that the optimal yield within the operational range of vessels operating in the west side of peninsular Malaysia (only 110,000 MT) for demersal fish has been reached since 1973. The pelagic resources of the west coast are also heavily exploited. (Undoubtedly a factor accelerating resource depletion in the west coast is the pressure on the stocks by Thai and Indonesian fishermen as well as by Malaysian fishermen; Thailand and Malaysia are engaged principally in trawling.) On the east coast, demersal fisheries can be expanded beyond a 60-m depth. The east coast could also bear additional fishing efforts for pelagics. In Sarawak, there is room for expanding demersal fishing, particularly beyond 30 nmi offshore. In Sabah, the considered judgment is that both the coastal and offshore waters could withstand more intensified fishing.[33] It may be beneficial to shift fishing operations out of the west coast of peninsular Malaysia (Strait of Malacca, Andaman Sea) toward the South China Sea, particularly in areas facing Sabah and Sarawak.

Malaysia's production was estimated by the FAO at 736,000 MT in 1980, having increased at an average growth rate of 6 percent since 1977.[34] More than 99 percent of the catch is from marine waters, including output from coastal mariculture of cockles. Government reports indicate that landings in peninsular Malaysia account for more than 80 percent of the total for the federation, increasing at an annual growth rate of 15 percent in the west coast and 9 percent in the east coast.[35] This high growth rate maybe attributable to landings of fish caught in Indonesian waters. Sabah had a modest increase of 5 percent from 1975 to 1979. Sarawak exhibited a slightly higher growth rate of 7 percent in the quantities landed during the same period. Growth rates in 1978 and 1979 were only 1 percent due to poor landings of all major species except for pelagic fish and cockles.

The rapid increase in the fishery production of peninsular Malaysia is accounted for to a large part by the commercial trawl fishery that goes after high-valued fish species and marine shrimps. Official statistics for 1979 show that almost one-half of the marine catch in the west coast and one-third in the east coast was brought in by trawlers. For both coasts, however, total trawl landings showed a high proportion of trash fish hauled in along with the desired shrimp and other commercial species. During 1975–1979, the shrimp component of trawl landings averaged only 16 percent; commercial fish, 32 percent; and trash fish, 51 percent. The continued increase in trawl landings in peninsular Malaysia, despite evident resource depletion in the west coast since 1973, was boosted by the introduction of trawling on the east coast. Nevertheless, more than two-thirds of the total fleet of the country is still concentrated on the inshore waters of the west coast of peninsular Malaysia.

That trawling accounts for about half the total value of landings suggests the economic reason for the persistent use of this gear, even in the face of the known detrimental effects on the resource: the low returns from trash fish are offset by the high returns from the small proportion of shrimps and marketable finfish caught in trawl nets. This gear is gaining acceptance in Sabah, where 42 percent of the vessels licensed in 1979 were trawlers. In Sarawak, however, the proportion of trawlers was 10 percent, against driftnets or gillnets (62 percent) and bagnets (14 percent).[36]

The other major gear in the large-scale fishery subsector is the purse seine, aimed at the small pelagics. In 1979, purse seines accounted for 20 percent of marine landings in the west coast of peninsular Malaysia and 39 percent in the east coast. In Sarawak (and presumably in Sabah, although no data breakdown is available) purse seines are not as popular as small-scale gears such as driftnets and gillnets. Among the pelagics, the important fisheries are scads, anchovies, and sardines. Production statistics show that tuna has been of relatively minor importance.[37]

In 1980 only 20,000 ha (49,400 acres) (out of a potential 350,000 ha [864,500 acres]) were devoted to aquaculture activities in peninsular Malaysia. Production by culture in peninsular Malaysia in 1980 was 132,000 MT, of which 121,000 MT was from mariculture of cockles. Output from freshwater pond culture was less than 10,000 MT. In Sabah, freshwater aquaculture yielded 5,600 MT.[38]

The value of fisheries to the Malaysian economy lies in fish as a source of protein, foreign exchange, and employment. Per capita consumption is around 25 kg (55 lb), which supplies as much as two-thirds of the animal protein intake for the population. The high dependence on fish as food is explained by its low price relative to other animal sources and its acceptability by all ethnic groups in the country. Malaysia has a negative balance of trade in fisheries in terms of volume but is a net exporter in terms of value (US$170 million) due to the exports of high-value species, particularly shrimps. More than 110,000 persons were engaged in fishing activities in Malaysia in 1979, representing around 2 percent of the labor force. Some 75 percent of the fishermen operate on or from peninsular Malaysia, (two-thirds of whom are on the west coast; one-third in the east), while 15 percent are in Sabah and 10 percent in Sarawak. Aquaculture employs less than 10 percent of the total fisheries labor force. Contribution to the GNP ranged from 2 percent to 2.5 percent in the 1970s.[39]

Artisanal fisheries are the mainstay of the Malaysian fishing industry. Small-scale fishermen constitute around 90 percent of the fishing population and contribute some 80 percent to total fish landings. More than half of the artisanal fishermen have incomes below the poverty level, and some two-thirds of these live on the east coast. Among marine fishermen, the earnings from fishing are depressed by the high trash fish composition of their catches and rising costs, particularly among those operating small trawlers.

The Fourth Malaysian Plan, covering 1981–1985, is now operative. Its main thrust is the eradication of poverty, a carry-over from the third plan, under which the government is said to have been successful in meeting the targets. Fishermen are a major rural-based group that could benefit from government programs for rural improvement. Within this framework, the development thrusts for fisheries are for improving the standards of living of fishermen by increasing their productivity, promoting development in aquaculture, and consolidating investments (through the formation of associations and other fishermen's groupings and using the estate or the plantation-industry approach to large-scale investments in aquaculture), and managing the EEZ.

The alleviation of poverty is emphasized, and the shift to aquaculture is highlighted as promising if the labor force is to remain in fishing. Nonfishing alternatives include settlement in agricultural land schemes and absorption into urban-based industries. In marine fishing, investments are being diverted to the nontraditional waters within the EEZ. These measures are consistent with the companion objective of increasing fish production, given the state of the resource in traditionally fished marine waters.

The ADB has provided Malaysia with two technical assistance grants for fisheries development, one for US$167,000 and another for US$100,000. The ADB also has provided a loan of US$27 million for fisheries development.[40] The United Nations Development Programme (UNDP) has funded two projects for aquaculture development (US$290,000 and US$600,000) and, with the Canadian International Development Agency (CIDA), an integrated fisheries development project. UNDP also is financing acoustical surveys in EEZ waters off peninsular Malaysia, Sabah, and Sarawak to the extent of US$1.15 million.

Marketing reforms will complement the formation of cooperatives, and credit and subsidy programs are intended to enable fishermen to increase their incomes. Marketing infrastructure is fully funded by the federal government. Four fishing port complexes located in rural areas have been completed while four more are being built along the east coast. One of these will service deep-sea vessels; US$45 million has been allocated by the government for fishery infrastructure in the Third Malaysia Plan and a similar sum will likely be extended in the fourth plan. (This amount represents 0.3 percent of the government's development spending for economic activities in the third plan and 1 percent of development spending for agriculture.)

Poaching by Thai, Singaporean, Indonesian, Taiwanese, and other foreign fishermen; the use of illegal gears by foreign and local fishermen; and piracy and smuggling are enforcement problems that have plagued the Malaysian navy, its fisheries, customs officials, and marine police, even prior to the extension of Malaysia's fisheries jurisdictions. The problems are expected to magnify now, following the declaration of an EEZ. The Malaysian enforcement forces have the major responsibility for protecting the peninsula's heavily populated west coast from piracy and smuggling and for maintaining its interests in the Strait of Malacca, an important transit route shared by Singapore and Indonesia. In addition to the need for protecting the coast of peninsular Malaysia, the navy must pass through intervening Indonesian waters to monitor the coastlines of Sabah and Sarawak. The Borneo states are the basis for a large portion of the area claimed by Malaysia under the EEZ and the continental shelf, but the predominant interest in this region is offshore oil installations in the South China Sea. With government plans to expand offshore fishing operations in the east, however, coupled with the long-existing resolve to keep out poachers and to impose gear and net regulations on the local fleet to maintain the productivity of the resource, the enforcement capability of Malaysia's maritime forces will require effective coordination. The immediate objective of Malaysia's extension of jurisdiction relating to fisheries matters was to keep the straying foreign fishermen, largely from neighboring countries, away from already depleted resources. Its concern with tankers in the Strait of Malacca is directly related to the strait as a major fish source for the country and a fishing ground for small-scale fishermen.

Malaysia has been concerned with its disadvantaged situation with respect to Indonesian islands close to Sabah and Sarawak. At the third United Nations Conference on the Law of the Sea (UNCLOS III) Malaysia insisted on maintaining access to certain "traditional" fishing grounds that came within Indonesia's control by archipelagic principle and on maintaining unrestricted passage between its western and eastern regions. Malaysia places great importance on facilitating its access to waters in the South China Sea. Improvement in its marine fisheries can be accomplished primarily in the South China Sea. However, considering the many disputes and other complex problems likely to arise in that area, Malaysia may invest proportionately more effort and resources in the other alternative it has identified — aquaculture.

The Philippines

The Philippines' 22,540-km (13,974-mi) coastline has a productive continental shelf measuring approximately 266,000 km² (77,459 nmi²). This shelf area gives rise to fishing grounds that are within easy reach of both commercial and municipal fishermen. (In the Philippines, "municipal" fisheries are inshore artisanal fisheries in which vessels of 3 GT or smaller are used.) Extensive coastal fishing areas are found off Lamon Bay, Lingayen Gulf, Manila Bay, San Miguel Bay, Visayan Sea, northern and western Palawan, and northeastern and southwestern Mindanao. Various estimates from the South China Sea Programme and FAO place the MSY of Philippine-claimed waters at 1.45– 1.85 million MT.[41] Of the estimated 1.85 million MT maximum potential yield, 1.60 million MT is from internal waters and 0.25 million MT is from waters gained as a result of the Philippines EEZ declaration. Most of the major fishing grounds within the country's internal waters, such as the Visayan Sea, Lingayen Gulf, Manila Bay, and Samar Sea, are overexploited. On the other hand, the offshore waters, such as off the eastern coast of the Philippines and in the South China Sea, are underexploited.

Production from demersal fishing, primarily with trawlers, has declined steadily from 396,000 MT in 1976 to 349,400 MT in 1980.[42] This may be attributed to the depletion of demersal fisheries resources in soft, trawlable areas such as the Visayan Sea, the San Miguel Bay, and Manila Bay. The potential for increased demersal fisheries is projected to come from reef areas and hard, nontrawlable grounds that can be exploited rationally using only passive gears.

It is generally believed that pelagic fisheries in a number of traditional fishing grounds can be further exploited. This is particularly true for small pelagic fisheries whose production of 456,800 MT in 1980 was far below the estimated potential yield of 600,000– 1,000,000 MT. However, some small pelagic stocks, such as the anchovies and chub mackerels in the Visayan Sea, are known to be overexploited.

The most dramatic development in Philippine marine fisheries in recent years has been the development of the tuna fishery. Production of tuna and tuna-like species increased from 138,500 MT in 1976 to 218,000 MT in 1980.

The total production from marine fisheries was 1.14 million MT in 1980. There was a decline in marine production from 1975 to 1976 and only a minimal increase in catch from 1977 to 1980. The performance during this recent period pales in comparison with the 7-percent average annual growth rate from 1971 to 1975. In 1980 the marine catch accounted for 76 percent of the total fish production of 1.7 million MT. Of this, 762,400 MT, or 45 percent of the total, was contributed by the municipal sector. For commercial fisheries, 34 percent of the 488,000 MT production was caught by trawler, 33 percent by purse seine, and 22 percent by bagnet.

The number of commercial fishing boats was 2,571 in 1976, dropped to 2,269 in 1977, and then increased again to 2,993 in 1980. During this period, there was a marked increase in the number of tuna purse seine vessels. The number of municipal fishing craft increased from 258,600 in 1977 to 312,500 in 1979 or by 10 percent per year. Of the total for 1979, 42 percent were motorized and 58 percent nonmotorized. The number of motorized municipal fishing craft is expected to increase over the next ten years in response to the government's Integrated Fisheries Development Plan, which aims to increase production through both the maintenance or replacement of the present *banca* canoe fleet and fleet expansion.

Capture fisheries in inland waters accounted for 17 percent of total production in 1980. In contrast with marine fisheries, inland fisheries exhibited a remarkable increase in growth rate, from 6 percent in 1976–1977 to 36 percent in 1979–1980. Although culture activities accounted for only 8 percent of total production in 1980, as recorded in the official fisheries statistics of the country, the sector's actual contribution is believed to be higher, considering that the data pertain only to milkfish production in brackishwater fish ponds.

Fisheries accounted for 4.8 percent of GNP in 1980, with a production of 1.7 million MT valued at US$1.4 billion. Fish is the main and cheapest source of animal protein. Per capita consumption of fresh fish for 1978–1980 was placed at 30 kg (66 lb) or 62 percent of animal protein intake. Fishing and its ancillary activities also constitute a major source of livelihood, particularly for the rural poor. Fishing was the main source of livelihood for 450,000 members of fishing families in 1978.

Foreign trade in fish grew impressively in the last half of the decade. Between 1977 and 1979, the volume and value of fish exports almost doubled, reaching US$98 million in 1979 while imports remained at around US$25 million. In 1980, exports leaped 40 percent while imports increased 34 percent in volume and value. Tuna has been the major export item. Dried seaweed and shrimp have also been significant export items, but in much smaller quantities and values than tuna. In 1980, 47,300 MT of frozen tuna valued at US$62 million was exported, comprising 62 percent of total volume. Dried seaweed accounted for 21 percent of total volume exported (15,700 MT) and frozen shrimp only 4 percent (2,633 MT). The major import items were fish meal and canned fish, which together accounted for 99 percent of the total volume imported in 1980. The two import items, however, followed contrasting patterns: fish meal imports increased steadily to 24,662 MT in 1980, while canned fish imports dropped to 28,760 MT. This leveling off encouraged by government policy resulted in greater utilization of local canneries.

The government encourages commercial fishing to expand its range of operations to the relatively underfished waters adjoining the eastern and western parts of the country. The species caught by large vessels is primarily skipjack tuna for export. Commercial fishing in recent years has been opened to foreign investors primarily to obtain much needed capital. Foreign participation is mainly in the form of joint ventures in which foreign equity is limited to 30 percent and is renewable annually. Due to this restriction, contractual joint ventures that involve the use of the partner's vessels are preferred. As of 1981 there were five companies involved in joint ventures operating thirty-seven vessels with a total of 10,157 GT. Of these vessels, twenty-two were longliners, fourteen were purse seiners, and one was a refrigerated carrier. All of these operations are geared for tuna. The strategy to lure commercial fisheries to the nontraditional fishing grounds of both territorial waters and EEZ emphasizes local industry buildup rather than foreign participation. Policies and regulations on joint ventures and other forms of foreign participation are relatively stringent.[43]

One major objective of the government in fisheries development is the maintenance of self-sufficiency in fish supply. The underlying reasons for this are the traditional reliance on fish as food and fishing as a rural activity. The government has a declared commitment to the rational exploitation of the country's fishery resources, improved handling and distribution, enhancing the livelihood of rural fishing families, and generating foreign exchange through exports. Production increments during the plan period are expected to come primarily from aquaculture and the exploitation of nontraditional waters. The target growth rate for aquaculture from 1981 to 1985 was placed at 20 percent, leveling off to 8 percent from 1986 to 1990. This will be met by dramatic increases in yields and the promotion of freshwater, cage, and mariculture farming. It is desired that production increases for commercial operations in internal waters be achieved through full utilization of existing fleet capacity instead of increased fishing effort. Fleet expansion will only be encouraged in oceanic waters. Development of the municipal fishing sector will be pursued primarily through area-specific integrated projects and the promotion of alternative sources of income. In line with the thrust, the government has launched the "livelihood movement," referred to as the KKK program, and the Biyayang Dagat Program, both of which are credit-and-technology programs financing projects of artisanal fishermen at concessionary terms.[44]

Because of the reported depletion of resources in internal waters and more recently the reported decline in tuna catch, the government has realized the need for rational fisheries management. The development plan proposes the adoption of a selective licensing scheme for fishing vessels limiting their operations in specific fishing areas. The implementation of limited entry policies will be hindered by opposition from fishermen unused to being regulated and by limited enforcement capability. The proliferation of fisheries joint venture arrangements (many using large numbers of Taiwanese longliners) in recent years is viewed with apprehension in the private sector and the fisheries science community because of the possi-

ble depletion of the country's tuna resources. A moratorium on the further acceptance of applications for joint ventures in tuna is now pending approval.

Credit granted to fisheries increased from US$72 million in 1976 to US$430 million in 1981. About 65 percent was used for the financing of production-oriented
projects, i.e., purchase of fishing equipment and fish pond development. The estimated financial requirement to pursue the integrated fisheries development plan is
US$2.2 billion, of which less than half is expected to be financed by the credit system.
During the latter half of the decade, the government borrowed around US$108 mil-
lion from foreign sources to finance fisheries infrastructure projects such as fishing
port complexes and fish markets. This figure does not include technical assistance
grants and loans to financial institutions for sublending to the fisheries sector. Major
sources of credit are the World Bank, the ADB, and multilateral institutions.[45]

Fisheries research conducted by the government, universities, and international
organizations is focused on aquaculture. Research on marine fisheries is limited in
scope, diverse in nature, and scattered in area of coverage. The government bureau responsible for fisheries research has an average of US$823,000 allocated for
research, or 7 percent of its budget, and only one research vessel, which is more
often than not drydocked. The University of the Philippines augments the research effort in marine fisheries with its average annual budget of US$120,000 and
two research vessels. However, the great bulk of government research funds for
fisheries (US$5.5 million in 1980) was channeled to the Aquaculture Department
of the Southeast Asian Fisheries Development Center (SEAFDEC). Scientists,
planners, banks, and the private sector are getting more vocal about the urgency of
assessing the resource, in view of the reported depletion of marine catch. Resource
assessment activities initiated include improving and expanding the present statistical system, monitoring changes of fish stock abundance, and estimating the potentials of major fishery stocks.

In the Southeast Asian region the Philippines is second or.ly to Indonesia in the
vastness of the marine area and the length of the coastline to be monitored. The
Philippine navy and coast guard enforce fishery laws at sea. Illegal fishing by locals
goes unabated in many areas, while reports of poaching by Taiwanese, Korean, and
other foreign vessels produce a feeling of frustration among policymakers eager to
move to a higher level of fishery management. ·

On 11 June 1978 the Philippines declared a 200-mile EEZ by virtue of Presidential Decree No. 1599. The effect of the EEZ on the fishing industry remains to be
established. Except for tuna, fishing activities are generally confined to archipelagic and territorial waters. This trend in fishing is not expected to change in the
near future because of the limited capability of the existing fleet (which is primarily medium scale) and the high cost of fuel involved in exploring the potentials of
offshore waters. Moreover, fishery scientists believe that the potential yield from
oceanic waters is likely to be much lower than the potential yield of archipelagic
waters because of their great depth and the lack of major upwelling areas.

In the short run, responsibility for the EEZ poses more costs than benefits for
the country. Upgrading of monitoring, control, and surveillance capabilities and
exploratory research on resources would entail massive expenditures. Since local

fishing companies are not financially able to expand, foreign participation with capital and equipment will play a major role in the exploitation of the EEZ. The immediate impediments to expanding the fishing effort farther from shore enhance the attraction of aquaculture activities. There is burgeoning interest in commercial-scale aquaculture for high-value species in brackish, fresh, and salt water.

Singapore

There are no known resource surveys of Singapore's waters, although studies on the Sunda Shelf and Strait of Malacca may provide a general idea of the state of the resource. The FAO studies on the east coast of peninsular Malaysia conclude that demersal fisheries have potential beyond a 60-m depth.[46] The Strait of Malacca is overexploited, and the inability of the resource to sustain further fishing efforts may be surmised from the almost flat production curve in Singapore's fish landings in the past decade, settling at an average of 16,000 MT per year. Slightly less than two-thirds of this amount is caught offshore, one-third inshore, and the small residual (3 percent) is derived from inland waters.[47]

The inshore fleet, using small vessels and traditional gears, has declined through the years, ostensibly due to the limited area available for fishing and the lure of industry-based jobs. There are areas south of Singapore that are designated exclusively for shipping; fishing in these areas is banned. Traditional fishing grounds for small craft have been the Singapore Strait, the former international waters of the Strait of Malacca, and the South China Sea along the Indonesia islands and peninsular Malaysia. The commercial fleet of inboard powered fishing vessels has expanded to a total registered tonnage of more than 7,000 GT, apparently being in a better position to respond to the tremendous market for fish in Singapore, both for local consumption and export. In 1979, licensed fishing vessels numbered 666.[48] There is some potential for intensive cultivation of fish along the coast using cage nets or impounded areas.[49]

Singapore has an unusually high per capita consumption of fish, as much as 40 kg (88 lb) per capita per year. Consumption leveled off to 30 kg (66 lb) in the 1970s, still representing at least one-third of animal protein intake.[50] Considering Singapore's good supply of other animal protein sources, this dependence can be explained only by the population's strong preference for fish.

The difference between production and consumption is supplied by net imports in the range of 40,000–50,000 MT per year, mostly from peninsular Malaysia, Indonesia, and Thailand. Total imports are higher than this figure, however, because 10–40 percent of imports are re-exported.[51] The contribution of local production to GNP is around 0.2 percent, but the total contribution of the fisheries sector is certainly higher. Some 2,100 fishermen licensed in 1979 comprised 0.1 percent of the population and 0.13 percent of the labor force.[52] The ornamental fish industry in Singapore is particularly important.

Commercial fisheries in Singapore include both the offshore fishing fleet and the fish processing sector. The latter consists of freezing and manufacturing specialty products from fish. The manufacture of fish products generally is done by small single proprietorships, with the exception of that undertaken by the large Central Fish Processing Market. The rest of the processing sector is large scale, mostly with foreign participation. Foreign partners supply the raw material to be processed for export. The processing industry is controlled by a few large companies and some smaller ones. Marissco Pte., Ltd., the largest fishery enterprise in Singapore, is a joint venture between a local company, Straits Fisheries, Ltd., and Sovrybflot, the Soviet Ministry of Fisheries, in operation since 1975. The volume of fish handled averages 22,000 MT, three-fourths of which is exported to Japan, Korea, and other buyers. Tri-marine, a company organized in the early 1970s and recently reactivated, has Societa Participazioni Alementari, an Italian agricultural and fishing entity, holding 98 percent of ownership, and the Korean Development Industry holding the rest. Tri-marine imports some 25,000 MT of tuna from Taiwan, Korea, the Philippines, and Indonesia and re-exports more than two-thirds of this in semiprocessed form to the Italian partner, while smaller quantities go to the United States and Japan. Marissco Pte., Ltd., and Tri-marine had planned to expand and diversify to product items that have more value added and to species of higher value, but operations have reportedly slowed down due to competition from processors in producing countries. Among the smaller companies, Montana Frozen Foods started in 1975 as a cold-storage facility and subsequently expanded to importing fish from ASEAN neighbors, Burma and New Zealand, as well as purchasing from the local auction market and processing these for re-export and local sale.

Due to its geographically disadvantaged status in fishing area, Singapore's primary development thrust in fisheries emphasizes its comparative advantage: processing and transshipment. Processing or postharvest activities can be developed due to Singapore's access to manufacturing technology and equipment and the presence of trained or highly educated personnel. To support this thrust, fishing ports and supportive infrastructure are being upgraded to cater to the increasing number of foreign vessels landing in Singapore. There is an aggressive investment incentives program to attract local and foreign investment in offshore fishing, particularly for pelagics, and there are liberal policies for foreign trawlers landing their catch in Singapore.

To meet the objective of import substitution and to attend to the welfare of the small number of people who choose to remain in fishing, Singapore encourages intensive aquaculture, particularly in highly marketable species such as grouper (a species successfully bred in Singapore), marbled goby, snappers, and mussels and other shellfish. Aquarium fish, an item with high export and local demand, is also the object of research and development efforts.

To maintain the continuity of its modest fishing industry, Singapore has argued for the right of geographically disadvantaged states to derive economic benefits from waters claimed by neighboring states, particularly in the context of traditional fishing rights in archipelagic waters. It also has favored a regional zone approach but has expressed its willingness to negotiate bilaterally on conservation and management rules. Singapore's interest in maintaining access to fishing grounds beyond its own area of jurisdiction may be attributed to its desire to reduce its dependence on fish imports, given the high consumer preference for fish among its population.

Thailand

In the Gulf of Thailand (including the zones of Kampuchea and Vietnam) the estimated potential catch of demersal fishery resources is 844,000 MT and of small pelagic fish (*Decapterus* only) is about 100,000 MT. Off the west coast of Thailand, the potential catch for that country has been estimated at approximately 85,000 MT for pelagic fish and around 200,000 MT for demersal fish.[53]

The demersal fishery in the Gulf of Thailand is heavily exploited, particularly in the shallower parts.[54] Though the offshore areas present some possibilities for further fishing, trawling is difficult in the deeper mud zones. Pelagic fisheries on the west side of the gulf are overexploited. Demersal fisheries are some 30 percent overexploited in the Strait of Malacca off the coast of Thailand. In the Andaman Sea to the northeast of Sumatera, the mackerel stock is also overexploited.

The operation area of the Thai fleet is apparent from the state of the resources in waters that surround the country. Around 80 percent of production comes from the gulf and adjacent waters, the rest comes from the Andaman Sea. Thailand is a distant-water fishing state with around one-third of its marine catch taken from other countries' waters. Thai trawlers continue to fish "traditionally" in what are now the EEZs of other countries, notably Vietnam, Kampuchea, and Burma, thereby inciting hostilities directed at Thai fishermen. Overfishing in the Gulf of Thailand is believed to have been evident as far back as the 1960s, a situation that impelled Thailand to explore the waters of Vietnam, Kampuchea, Burma, Bangladesh, India, and Malaysia. This was also the decade when trawl fisheries in Thailand accelerated at a pace that later turned out to be counterproductive.

Thailand's fishery production peaked at 2.2 million MT in 1977 from 1.45 million MT in 1970, or an average growth rate of 7 percent. That is a relatively high rate but one that is quite modest compared with the growth rate in the 1960s of around 50 percent. From 1977 to 1980, production dropped to 1.79 million MT. The marine catch, which accounted for more than 90 percent of production from 1977, fell rapidly. Inland production has increased since then at around 8 percent annually, though incremental and absolute quantities are still insignificant.[55] The drop in marine catch was brought about by declining yields and the high cost of fuel oil that reduced fishing effort. The prediction of the Thai government that it stands to lose 660,000 MT of fish per year due to extensions of jurisdiction is affirmed by the trend. Equally alarming is the declining value of the Thai catch due to the large and increasing proportion of trash fish. Estimates that the share of catch used for human consumption is only about 30 percent suggest that fishing now largely serves as a raw material supplier to the fish meal industry. The predominance of trash fish (and indeed the depletion of the resource) is explained by the fact that trawlers fish for shrimp using small mesh nets that catch juveniles of other species and inhibit the growth of adult fish.[56]

Until the introduction and widespread use of otterboard trawling in the 1960s, the catches were predominantly small pelagics caught inshore by small purse seines and stationary gears. A contraction in total investment in vessels is seen in the number of registered vessels in selected years: 33,600 in 1967, down to 27,500 in 1970, further declining to 26,400 in 1973, and settling at the 26,100 level in 1976 and the latter years of the decade. The motorization program improved the ratio of powered to nonpowered vessels from 56:44 in 1967 to 80:20 in 1976. In 1978, 44 percent of the boats were more than 14 m long. Some 70 percent were trawlers, 21 percent pushnets and gillnets, and 8 percent purse seiners. The fleet started with 201 trawlers in 1961, expanded rapidly to 2,395 in 1965 and 8,114 in 1970, but contracted to 6,041 trawlers by 1978.[57] Overcapitalization has set in. In 1979, some 6,000 vessels failed to sail.[58] Although there are some unverified reports that Thailand's marine catch improved during recent years due to the opening of new fishing grounds, it is unlikely that the situation has been improved significantly, particularly if one considers the costs of the new thrusts. Thailand's distinction in the 1970s of not only being in the top ten fishing nations but also the leader in Southeast Asia (excluding China) in fish production is now precarious. Indonesia's latest production statistics suggest that it has surpassed Thailand's records.

Thailand is putting more resources into aquaculture to fill the gaps in production and employment caused by the decline of its marine fisheries. Counting paddy fields in the central plain in Thailand and coastal plains suitable for culture, some 4.5 million ha of inland waters are available and hardly utilized.[59] Indeed, more than half of freshwater fish production comes from the central region and more than one-third from the northeast, although many lakes, rivers, and estuaries are polluted.

Thailand's per capita consumption of fish was estimated at 20–26 kg (44–57 lb) in the early 1970s and at 19 kg (42 lb) in the mid-1970s. Given declining productivity and the high proportion of trash fish caught, one can extrapolate current per capita consumption to 10–15 kg (22–33 lb) per year, against the target of 20 kg (44 lb). Likewise, the percentage contribution of fisheries to GNP reportedly declined from higher than 3 percent in 1968–1973 to 2.8 percent in 1974–1978.[60] (A review of national accounts figures shows that these rates probably pertain to GDP and that percentage-to-GNP was actually 1.5 percent in 1975 and less than 1 percent in 1979.)

Because Thai fisheries have been mainly commercial scale since 1962, employment in fishing occupations has not been a significant fraction of the total labor force. It has been estimated at 1.7 percent for 1974[61] and has probably also declined or at most remained constant. The fisheries employment figure has been placed at 70,000–75,000 persons.

The contribution of small-scale fishermen to total production has dropped from 20 percent a decade ago to only 10 percent currently. The size of the artisanal fishing sector shrank from 51,000 households in 1967 to 40,200 in 1976. Artisanal fishing is considered unviable due to cost factors and resource depletion. In contrast to marine fishing, aquaculture is primarily small scale.

Only about 10 percent of the quantity of fish produced is exported, but Thailand is a net exporter in terms of value because of the trade in high-value species like shrimp and squid. Export revenues from fishery items rose consistently from US$18.5 million in 1970 to US$235.5 million in 1978.[62] Imports in 1978 were valued at US$67.5 million. Recent reports, however, indicate a reduction in exports due to import cutbacks by Japan and the inability of Thai exports to meet the standards of importing countries such as the United States.

The Thai government recognizes that there is little room for expanding or even maintaining its marine activities unless new approaches are found. For this reason it has actively sought bilateral agreements and joint ventures with other countries, particularly those of ASEAN. Unlike Indonesia and Malaysia, which categorically reject the concept of a regional community for fisheries and opt for two-way governmental consultations leading to agreement, Thailand supports a regional approach that would facilitate access. The growing consciousness of resource management on the part of countries with large jurisdictions makes it doubly difficult for Thailand to "sell" its trawling operations. In Indonesia, for instance, trawling is now virtually banned. The Philippines, to whom Thailand only recently made a joint venture offer, allows foreign participation only for selective gears and discourages trawling even among its own citizens.

Thus, problems arising from the EEZ declarations of other countries are a primary concern, as is management of the waters under Thai jurisdiction. Despite signs of declining productivity in freshwater fisheries, inland fisheries and coastal aquaculture still present real possibilities as gap-filling measures, particularly since they are aimed at the socially and politically important small-scale sector. There are concrete projects aimed at meeting the target of doubling output from this source by 1986. The target for total production is a stabilized 1.8 million during 1982–1986.[63] This means that Thailand will yield its rank as the lead fishing state in the region to Indonesia and the Philippines, both of which have more ambitious targets, at least within the adjustment period of the early 1980s.

In the early and mid-1970s, Thailand's marine research activities focused on assessment of resources and testing of gears to support trawling operations in the Gulf of Thailand and parts of the Andaman Sea adjacent to Thailand. The thrust of marine research currently is the search for new fishing grounds in the jurisdictions of other countries, particularly Burma, Bangladesh, India, Indonesia, Malaysia, and Sri Lanka. Though selective gears are being tested, potential resources of demersal fishes are still the main point of inquiry, suggesting that Thailand must utilize the very large investment, in the form of both capital and technology development, it has thus far sunk into trawling. The potential fishing grounds being considered by Thailand, however, may not be that rewarding given their depths and the fuel costs of fishing there.

The ADB is a major source of funds for development projects with some research components. Another is the World Bank. The thrust of research and investment activities is in culture and not capture. The ADB lent US$14 million for an aquaculture development project in which the fishpond component is joint-financed by the World Bank to the extent of US$2.72 million. There are other programs and loans for aquaculture, including mariculture, and infrastructure financed by the World Bank, the European Economic Community (EEC), and the United States to a small extent.[64] Extension, utilization, training, and selective gear-testing projects are supported by the UNDP and the FAO.

The development of ports and associated facilities is imperative to resolving Thailand's distribution and handling problems. This has been pursued through bilateral and multilateral assistance. The major deep-sea port in Laem Chabang was constructed with the assistance of the Netherlands, at a cost of US$160 million.

Two proposed deep-sea ports in the south, Phuket and Songkhla, have elicited
ADB interest. A naval port in Sattahip will be developed to accommodate and
service deep-sea fishing vessels with a US$150-million loan from the World Bank.
There are thirty-two existing coastal ports that the World Bank has shown interest
in improving.[65]

Thailand's enforcement problem rarely concerns the protection of its EEZ except possibly for security or retaliation. A greater concern is the imposition of disci-
pline on its own fishermen who have been used to fishing in distant waters and now
stray into other backyards, intentionally or unintentionally. To deal with this situation, an interagency body has initiated programs to increase the fishermen's ability
to comply with the rules. It has installed communication and monitoring mechanisms to assist the fishermen in preventing undue incidents related to the closure
of other coastal states' waters to Thai fishing.

Vietnam

Vietnam's 200-mile EEZ and its other marine claims give it access to vast fishing
grounds that are rich in resources and have hardly been tapped. In the early 1970s
it was estimated in an FAO–South China Sea Programme study that the MSY for
demersal species over the northern Sunda Shelf of the South China Sea was
150,000 MT and that over the central Sunda Shelf it was 290,000 MT. These areas
are adjacent to the southern part of Vietnam. The study also identified offshore
trawling grounds within the range of vessels operating out of Ho Chi Minh City
(formerly Saigon) and other southern towns, as well as shrimping grounds along
nearly half of the inshore waters ringing southern Vietnam's coastline, and gillnet-
ting grounds within 100–150 km (62–93 mi) of the entire coastline. A UNDP–FAO
report estimated the MSY of pelagics in the fishing grounds off the southeast coast
of Vietnam (Mekong Delta), east coast (South China Sea) and west coast (Gulf of
Thailand) at 680,000 MT and suggested that Vietnam's own pelagic catch could be
increased to 165,000 MT, or three times the estimated landings at that time.[66] The
area covered by such estimates represents around 55 percent of the fishing area
claimed by united Vietnam.

A later FAO–SCSP workshop on the Sunda Shelf and related areas established a
potential demersal yield of 484,000 MT in approximately the same area covered by
the previous study. It suggested that expectations for additional realizable yields
should be lowered. Due to a lack of data, no conclusions could be ventured for the
pelagic species in the area. An FAO–UNDP purse seine survey done in 1971–1972,
however, identified fishing areas for pelagic species in the waters off the Mekong
Delta and in the Gulf of Thailand.[67] One may interpret from reports for other
countries such as Hong Kong that in the Gulf of Tonkin there are potentials for
increased catches for pelagics, while for demersals it is only the deeper, costlier-to-
fish areas that show promise for additional exploitation.

FAO calculations place Vietnam's total fish production at more than 1 million
MT since 1973, of which 83 percent is believed to be from marine production and

17 percent from inland production.[68] Total fish production of South Vietnam in 1973 was 714,000 MT, growing at the rate of around 10 percent over the preceding ten-year period.[69] In the same year there were more than 92,000 fishing boats, 69 percent of which were motorized. Most of these boats were small and were fishing in coastal waters and along the rivers. There were 20 steel trawlers, all below 300 GT, fishing offshore, particularly for shrimp. A more recent report on united Vietnam states that the number of active fishing vessels has declined due to fuel shortages and the loss of some 5,000 boats by people fleeing the country.[70]

Inland fishery resources of southern Vietnam consist of around 500,000 ha (1,235,000 acres) of mangrove swamps and marshes and about 4,000 km (2,480 mi) of waterways. In 1973 production in South Vietnam from inland waters was 128,000 MT, or 18 percent of total fish output.[71] At that time the government was encouraging aquaculture in both freshwater and brackishwater areas through the distribution of fry and other stocking materials at subsidized prices.

The figures for the early 1970s indicate that per capita annual consumption of fish in South Vietnam was at least 35 kg (77 lbs), but a U.S. government report of January 1977 gave an estimate of only 15 kg (33 lb).[72] It appears that the industry deteriorated during the intervening years. The higher figure, however, is indicative of the traditional dietary practices of the Vietnamese who derive around 50 percent of their animal protein from fish.

The percentage of South Vietnam's GNP attributable to fisheries activities was 4.1 percent in the middle 1970s.[73] The labor force in fisheries at that time was estimated at 5.4 percent. There were 355,000 fishermen in 1973, of which around half were fishing full time.[74] Clearly, artisanal fishing has been the dominant sector of the industry. In the early 1970s the government was promoting cooperatives, with little success. The industrial and corporate fishing sector was then composed of eight entities operating twenty-three offshore trawlers.

Fishery products, particularly shrimp, were a leading export of South Vietnam, accounting for at least 20 percent of foreign exchange earnings in 1973. Export value in 1973 was US$13.3 million, with marked signs then of rapid growth. There is a possibility of expanding exports of frozen shrimp and other items to neighboring trading centers like Hong Kong and Singapore, as well as to Japan and Europe. Vietnam imported canned fish worth US$4.4 million in 1972 and US$1.3 million in 1973.[75] The development plans of South Vietnam in 1973 included the promotion of commercial pelagic purse seining, the shift of demersal fishing to offshore areas, protection of shrimp resources from overexploitation, improved postharvest handling and preservation techniques, the construction of ports and ancillary facilities and even heavier emphasis on aquaculture.[76]

Since the fall of Saigon, Hanoi's reconstruction efforts have reportedly emphasized seabed oil, fisheries, and oceanography. Population pressures and limited alluvial flatlands have made the coastal basins very densely populated and accentuated "the seaward outlook."[77] The new government is reportedly committed to the development of the marine sector and intends to invest more capital in trawler construction to assist in enforcement work.

OUTSIDE STATES' FISHERIES INTERESTS IN THE REGION

Extraregional states that influence the direction of fishery policy and development in the region include the South China Sea states of China, the Chinese province of Taiwan, and Hong Kong, plus Australia, Japan, New Zealand, the United States, the European Community, and the Scandinavian countries.

China

It appears that most of China's important sea resources are heavily exploited. The main demersal species in the East China Sea and the Yellow and Pohai seas are overfished. Most of the species taken from the South China Sea are, likewise, heavily exploited. However, pelagic stocks, particularly mackerel, in the northern fishing areas are believed to be still abundant. The FAO attributes this generally depressed state of China's marine resources to slackened conservation measures during the past decade. In 1979, however, regulations to rejuvenate the resource "were tightened."[78]

In 1978 there were 39,000 motorized fishing boats, mostly small craft. There is also a substantial industrial fishery consisting of 1,600 vessels exceeding 100 gross tons (GT), powered by engines above 200 horsepower. Trawl is the predominant gear, although purse seining with lights has caught on since the mid-1960s. Freshwater fish culture is practiced widely and successfully. Culture accounts for some 70 percent of output from inland waters; the rest of the inland production is by capture in rivers and lakes. Production from the latter source has decreased markedly since the 1960s, apparently due to industrialization and urbanization, as well as overfishing.[79]

China's fishing industry contributes only 0.7 percent to GNP.[80] In 1978 there were some 860,000 fishermen operating in marine waters. Aggregate employment in fisheries was placed at 1.4 percent of labor force and per capita fish consumption is 7.6 kg (17 lb). Comparing population with production (and assuming no fish imports), per capita consumption may now be as low as 4.34 kg (10 lb). China exports 90,000 to 100,000 MT of fresh and frozen fish (mostly carp), largely to Hong Kong and Macao.[81] This quantity is only 2 percent of production, thus, dependence on fisheries is among the lowest in the region.

In 1979 the Chinese government adopted policies aimed at fisheries resource management, active development of marine and freshwater aquaculture, adoption of advanced techniques, strengthened research, quality improvement, and market stimulation. Investments in infrastructure include preservation and processing facilities to improve the reputedly poor quality of China's aquatic products. There are now more than 160 cold storage facilities with a total capacity of 136,000 MT and ice plants with a total capacity of 114,000 MT.[82]

China's marine interest consists of continuing or improving its level of fish production for food and maintaining open sea routes, particularly in the South China Sea. Because of China's reputation in aquaculture technology, there has been a long-prevailing belief that most of its fish supply derived from aquaculture. China does have a long history of successful freshwater fish farming, but its output is not sufficient for the needs of its enormous population. Capture fishing in marine waters is actually the major fishing activity and will likely remain so.

China (Taiwan)

Of the Chinese province of Taiwan's total output of close to 1 million MT (929,176 MT in 1979), at least one-third is caught by deep-sea fishing boats in offshore waters outside its own jurisdiction, another third in inshore areas around 30 nmi from shore, less than 5 percent along the coasts, and the rest by culture activities.[83] The rapid expansion and modernization of the Taiwanese fishing fleet after World War II led to the widening of the scope of fishing operations to various parts of the globe, extending well beyond the Southeast Asian region to the Pacific, Indian, and Atlantic oceans. Many of the fishing grounds covered by Taiwan's past operations now are within the recent declared EEZs of other countries as well as their territorial and archipelagic waters. Its trawling grounds in the South China Sea had been the same ones exploited by mainland China, Hong Kong, Vietnam, Malaysia, and Indonesia.

Although Taiwan is currently known for its successful application of tuna longlining techniques, 30 percent of its large-scale marine fish catch in 1978 was hauled in by otter and pair trawlers of the 300–1,900-GT size. Longlining for tuna and other fishes accounted for 25 percent of 1978 commercial landings. Longline fisheries use smaller boats and fish both inshore and distant waters.

Aquaculture production grew from 114,000 MT in 1974 to 184,000 MT in 1979 and was valued at US$409 million. Taiwan's aquaculture production accounted for 19 percent of total fisheries production. The brackishwater and freshwater areas under culture were 18,665 ha (46,103 acres) in 1978.[84] Tilapia and milkfish are the most important cultured species but obtaining fry is a problem, especially for milkfish; so they have been imported. Due to highly attractive prices offered by Taiwanese aquaculturists, there is a high traffic of fish fry smuggled from countries protecting their aquaculture industries such as the Philippines.

There is no recent estimate of the composition of the Taiwanese fishing fleet. Production figures for 1979 reveal that the deep-sea catch increased by 8.1 percent over that of the previous year, the inshore catch dropped slightly and the coastal catch improved by 2 percent.[85]

Fish is an important part of the Taiwanese diet, but per capita consumption figures are not readily available. The importance of the artisanal sector appears to be relatively low, as suggested by its minimal contribution to fish supply. The major influence of the fishing industry on the economy lies in its being a foreign exchange source; US$670 million was earned from fish exports in 1979. Imports have diminished through the years, remaining at only US$84 million in 1977.[86]

During the postwar era up to 1972, Taiwan already had 2 deep-sea fishing ports equipped with shore facilities and 108 fishing harbors of varied sizes and stage of development. Another deep-sea port was reportedly nearing completion in 1980. Two important and highly prolific fishery research institutes and an institute of oceanography conduct resource surveys and multidisciplinary studies. Their latest preoccupation is searching for new fishing grounds. In 1980 the government announced a new US$220 million program to expand the deep-sea fishing sector through the addition of ten 500-GT purse seiners, fifty trawlers, twenty-five squid vessels, fifteen large tuna longliners, and fifty gillnet boats. A ten-year incentives program was established involving the cooperation of fishing associations with foreign counterparts in joint venture activities. Fish culture and more fishing ports were also among the priorities.[87]

Taiwan's major interest in fisheries is the exploration of new grounds, meaning either finding unclaimed physical areas in which to fish or collaborating with other countries to gain access to fishing grounds now under their jurisdiction.

Hong Kong

The potential yield of demersal species in waters within the fishing range of Hong Kong vessels (the northern shelf of the South China Sea, the Gulf of Tonkin, and the eastern shelf as far south as 13°N), has been estimated at 956,000 MT. The stock of pelagics in the northern shelf has been assessed at 1.1 million MT, with potential yield at 444,000 MT in the northern shelf and in the rest of Hong Kong's fishing area at 209,000 MT. Based on the declines in CPUE of trawlers, it is believed that the demersal fishery in the northern shelf is overfished. On the other hand, offshore pelagics in the three areas are underexploited.[88]

Most of the commercial fleet conducts trawling operations outside Hong Kong's waters, principally on the northern shelf of the South China Sea as well as in the Gulf of Tonkin and the east South China Sea between Taiwan and Hainan islands. In the early 1980s there was some shift of vessels toward the east South China Sea, though the northern shelf remains the major fishing area. Shrimp is the major species fished by some 1,000 vessels that operate inshore at depths of less than 40 m along the coast of China from Hainan to Swatow. In areas deeper than 160 m fishing is limited by mud and corals.[89] However, research vessels have reported possibilities for fishing edible or potentially commercial species in these deep areas. Some Chinese vessels operating in the area land their catches in Hong Kong.

During 1976–1981 total fish production increased by 3 percent per year. The peak of 194,560 MT was reached in 1980. Landings of trawlers averaged a 34.5-percent growth rate from 1974 to 1978 but slowed during the following three years and declined in 1981. Thus, the composite growth rate in 1976–1981 was only 5 percent. Purse seine landings followed a negative trend from 1974; during 1976–1981, the growth rate was −9 percent per year. In 1981 fish production dropped to 182,330 MT.

In 1982 there were 4,756 vessels operating, of which 38 percent were trawlers, 22 percent gill netters, 19 percent liners, 6 percent purse seiners, and 15 percent using miscellaneous gears. Practically all of these vessels were mechanized. Of the commercial-size vessels 1,799 were trawlers, the majority of which were in shrimp operations. The fishing fleet of Hong Kong declined in numbers by an aggregate rate of 13 percent during the decade of the 1970s. (Only those using "miscellaneous" gears increased in number.) The number of trawlers reached a high of 2,174 in 1979 and fell back to its 1970 level by 1982. Over the last half of the 1970s at least two-thirds of the marine catch was brought in by trawlers, and the contribution of purse seiners was down from 8 percent to 4 percent at the end of the decade.[90]

The trends in composition of fish production and of the fishing fleet suggest that the private sector pursued activities resulting in immediately visible returns. The commercial capture sector continues to pursue the high-value species despite the declining state of the resource and the overcrowding in the industry. Recent indications, however, show that the untenability of the situation is starting to affect investments. There has been a significant reduction in investment in new vessels in the 1980s, reportedly due to the increase in oil prices and the need for vessels to go farther offshore to seek better yields.

Production from culture activities is still an insignificant proportion of total fish output. In 1981, only 6,780 MT (or 4 percent of total) was contributed by inland culture and only 990 MT by mariculture. Freshwater aquaculture improved by 6 percent per year during 1976–1981; mariculture, a new but apparently promising activity, had a growth rate of 11 percent.[91]

Per capita consumption of fish in Hong Kong is currently around 37 kg (82 lb),[92] quite high in the region but a substantial drop from the 48-kg (106-lb) level of 1974. Fish supplies 45 percent of the animal protein needs of the city's five million inhabitants. The contribution of fisheries to GNP is less than 1 percent. Employment in the industry has declined by 2–3 percent per year since the 1950s. In 1979, some 36,000 persons were involved in fishing, representing 0.7 percent of population and around 3 percent of the labor force.[93]

The magnitude of trade in fishery products has followed an accelerating upward trend that continued into the early 1980s. By 1981, Hong Kong's external trade in fishery products was valued at US$544 million, of which US$90.4 million represented exports, US$354.8 million imports, and US$98.7 million re-exports. The quantity and value of exports increased despite lower production. The value of imports increased at an annual rate of 7 percent, and authorities expect this trend to continue due to anticipated supply shortfalls in the face of the growing population and their greater incomes plus the increasing limited resources available for exploitation following the ban on trawling in the inshore waters of China and the enforcement of Vietnam's EEZ in the Gulf of Tonkin.[94]

Small-scale fisheries accounted for 20 percent of marine landings and 22 percent of total fish production in 1978. Less than 10 percent of the trawl fisheries are classified as small; artisanal operations dominate the purse seine and culture sectors. Statistics suggest that the small-scale sector generally is declining. Resource depletion in nearshore waters and high fuel costs are the primary constraints. On the other hand, the government expects that the familiar sight of small boats parked along the harbors will remain, if only because of the deteriorating housing situation in Hong Kong. Fishermen live in these boats and this added benefit could be a motivating factor for staying in the industry until it has exhausted its possibilities. Land-based fishery activities such as aquaculture may be an alternative source of employment for some fishermen, but the expansion of aquaculture must compete with more valuable potential uses of land such as housing. The expansion of mariculture to sites identified as biologically appropriate has met opposition among recreational and other interests.[95]

Demersal fisheries, principally trawling, remain the foundation of Hong Kong's fishing industry, despite the problems that have beset this subsector.[96] Development inputs in the form of improved vessels, gears, credit, and training facilities continue to be invested in this type of fishing operation. Conversion to other gears that are effective outside the restricted zones has been attempted on about 100 vessels. A complementary objective is the utilization of trash fish and offals. Intensive fish culture practice to increase yields from the limited area available is also being promoted.

Marine research, which used to emphasize the assessment of demersal stocks, is now investigating the potential for pelagic species, particularly in the offshore grounds of the northern shelf of the South China Sea. Further research is required on the deep-water demersal stocks along the edge of the continental shelf. In freshwater aquaculture, the focus is on water management and techniques for hybrids and polyculture, and in mariculture, the focus is on high-priced species such as grouper.[97]

The industry is adequately serviced by efficient postharvest systems and facilities. Cooperatives are well developed in Hong Kong, and the linkages between fishermens' groups, fish markets, and credit are well established. Wholesale marketing is a function of the government-administered Fish Marketing Organization (FMO). The FMO operates seven wholesale markets for fresh fish, one for cured fish, and a collection service for outlying areas. There are several natural harbors protected by breakwaters.

The high dependence of Hong Kong on fish for consumption and trade impels the government to maintain the present level of production through incentives and direct government inputs. Unfortunately, there is little room for expansion in Hong Kong's limited marine waters for capture fishing and in its scarce land area for culture activities. Hong Kong's maritime interest in fisheries would be one of holding on and improving the state of the resources within its immediate coastal area while seeking opportunities for collaboration with neighboring countries, both in the use of its vessels and in exploring arrangements to maintain a steady supply of fish for domestic consumption and re-export. Due in part to restrictive requirements of most Southeast Asian countries on foreign fishing, Hong Kong businessmen have been offering joint venture arrangements in aquaculture. The capability of the Hong Kong market to absorb high-priced species makes even the capital-intensive joint ventures viable. The 26-percent share of net import of fish supply is expected to increase, making import substitution an even more attractive goal.

Non–South China Sea Nations

The non–South China Sea countries have supplied bilateral credit, technical expertise, research and commercial vessels and gears, postharvest equipment, and markets for the region's fishery exports. Japan's influence has been particularly strong. Second-hand Japanese vessels are the mainstay of the commercial fishing fleet in many countries (notably the Philippines) to the point that the Japanese government has enforced certain restrictions on the export of used tuna fishing vessels. Japan's lending and assistance programs are channeled through its national organizations (such as the OECF) and indirectly through its contributions to the ADB and SEAFDEC. Japan's preference in development assistance has been for infrastructure and equipment-based endeavors. During his state visit to ASEAN countries in January 1981 the Japanese prime minister, through his fisheries minister, renewed his support for ASEAN fisheries development.

Japan's imports of fishery products from the region have induced a large degree of dependence among Southeast countries, which over the years have been charting their activities with an eye on the Japanese market. In 1978 Japan's fishery imports from the region totaled more than US$400 million, almost half of the region's total exports. Some 75 percent was for shrimps, prawns, and lobsters. Indonesia, Thailand, and Hong Kong are particularly dependent on the Japanese market for shrimp. For these three countries the value of their exports to Japan comprise 40 percent to 75 percent of their total fishery exports. During the same year, Japan's fishery exports to the region totaled US$500 million, most of which went to Hong Kong and Singapore.[98]

The United States, in contrast, has been a rather small trading partner for fish products. In 1978 total U.S. imports from Southeast Asian countries amounted to only US$44 million (11 percent of the region's total exports), mostly shrimps and other crustaceans, predominantly from Thailand and Hong Kong. United States exports to the region were only $12 million.[99] The United States' influence on fishery matters in the region has been through the activity of the U.S. Agency for International Development (USAID) and, indirectly, the World Bank.

INTERNATIONAL ORGANIZATIONS' FISHERIES INTERESTS

A few United Nations instrumentalities, two development banks (one based in the region), an association of six Southeast Asian countries, a research and development center with Southeast Asian and non-Southeast Asian membership, and a private corporation with external funding perform advisory, research, and development activities relating to fisheries in the region. Except for the U.N. programs, which have consciously promoted the regional approach with partial success, these organizations have maintained a country focus in their fisheries-related efforts. The activities of these organizations in fisheries so far have tended to revolve around a core group of four countries (Indonesia, the Philippines, Thailand, and Malaysia) with Singapore, Brunei, Hong Kong, and Burma forming the first periphery and the three Indochina states along with China and the Chinese province of Taiwan forming the outer periphery.

Indonesia, the Philippines, Thailand, Malaysia, and Singapore established the ASEAN in 1967 with the avowed objective of cooperating on matters related to economic growth, social progress, cultural development, technical and scientific research, trade, peace, and security. The headquarters and the secretariat are in Jakarta. Fisheries is subsumed in one of nine ministerial committees called COFAF

(Committee on Food, Agriculture and Forestry). Thailand heads the Fisheries Subcommittee. ASEAN's regional projects in fisheries involving third countries (notably Australia, Canada, and groups like the EEC) are capital-based undertakings in infrastructure, transportation, processing, quarantine, quality control, and other postharvest activities. ASEAN has started to address the EEZ questions only recently and then cautiously. In December 1980 when the Fisheries Subsector of the then Working Group on Food, Agriculture, and Forestry was constituted, the agreement reached was threefold: (1) the proclamation of the 200-mile EEZ must be accompanied by a thorough survey of fish potentials to supply more protein to meet domestic and world needs; (2) aquaculture, as a relatively new field, needs to be developed; and (3) postharvest technology must also be developed to make better use of fresh catch.

The Indo-Pacific Fisheries Commission (IPFC), the first regional undertaking of the FAO, came into operation in 1948. The IPFC is concerned with the development and proper utilization of fishery resources, not only for Southeast Asia but for the larger Indo-Pacific region. The IPFC is a purely advisory body, with no powers of regulation. The IPFC has a Standing Committee on Resources and Research Development (SCORRAD).

In May 1980 the IPFC established a new Committee for the Development and Management of Fisheries in the South China Sea (CDMSCS). The committee was created specifically as a response to the new jurisdiction acquired by the littoral states over fisheries in the South China Sea. Its members are Kampuchea, Indonesia, Malaysia, the Philippines, Thailand, United Kingdom (Hong Kong), and Vietnam. The committee was created as a subregional body with the same functions for the South China Sea as IPFC has for the Indo-Pacific area as a whole.

The South China Sea Fisheries Development Programme (SCSP) was established by the IPFC in 1974 to formulate country and regional programs in the region and to assist the countries in the development of the rational use of the international resources of the South China Sea for the maximum benefit of the regional participants. It was based in Manila and funded by UNDP, with auxiliary or specific project support from numerous bilateral and multilateral AID agencies.

The program advised member countries on policies, rules, and regulations regarding maritime jurisdiction. Among its major continuing activities were resource assessment surveys and management studies, including tuna tagging and gear-test fishing projects, aquaculture research and development studies, socioeconomic and technical studies for small-scale fisheries, and statistical improvement programs. In December 1981 the SCSP brought the ASEAN countries together to discuss their respective problems on monitoring, control, and surveillance (MCS) of their EEZs. The five countries agreed to mount a regional training program for policymakers, implementers, and enforcers of the EEZ. The SCSP was formed with the expectation that member countries would ultimately contribute to its maintenance. Aside from the Philippine's hosting the project offices, no such contributions were extended. Funding cutbacks by the UNDP forced the program to phase out in 1983.

The SEAFDEC was established in 1967 as an autonomous regional technical body for the acceleration of fisheries development in Southeast Asia. Japan, Malaysia, the Philippines, Singapore, and Thailand are members. The secretariat and the training department are in Bangkok, the Marine Fisheries Research Department is in Singapore, and the Aquaculture Department is in the Philippines. Japan provides equipment, funding, and scientists. SEAFDEC's training programs are focused on artisanal and inshore fisheries. The Marine Fisheries Research Department has contributed studies on resources and oceanography of the South China Sea. Recently, however, it has emphasized postharvest technology. The Aquaculture Department develops culture techniques for milkfish, shrimp, freshwater species, and seafarming.

The International Center for Living Aquatic Resources Management (ICLARM) started in Hawaii in 1975 as a research corporation and was incorporated in the Philippines in 1977. Initially funded by the Rockefeller Foundation, it has since 1980 attracted substantial USAID support. Small amounts of funding also come from Australia, Germany, the UNDP, and institutions with which ICLARM has had joint projects. Staffed by a small group of scientists and support personnel, one of ICLARM's major programs related to marine resource management is the development of techniques for multispecies stock assessment and an analysis of catch and effort data, so far solely for the demersal fisheries of the Philippines.

Inspired by the success of INFOPESCA in Latin America, the FAO established INFOFISH in 1981 to catalyze and promote the exchange of marketing information and technical advice on postharvest matters and trade in Asia and the Pacific. It has seventeen member countries including Brunei, Hong Kong, Indonesia, Malaysia, the Philippines, Singapore, and Thailand from the Southeast Asian region. Core-funded by a Norwegian trust fund and headquartered in Kuala Lumpur, INFOFISH expects to be self-supporting by charging the subscribing organizations, business entities, and member governments for its services.

The ADB and the World Bank have supplemented the credit systems in the developing countries of the region for the development of fisheries. Member countries in the region include Indonesia, Malaysia, the Philippines, Thailand, Burma, Hong Kong, Singapore, and China. From 1969 to the end of 1978 the ADB had approved US$218.8 million as fisheries loans for Asia and the Pacific; US$153 million of this total went to Southeast Asian countries. The focus of bank lending was for marine fisheries projects with vessel and shore-based facilities components. Substantial aquaculture loans, particularly to the Southeast Asian countries, have been extended for fish ponds, pens, and cages and supporting preharvest and postharvest facilities.[100] In recent years, ADB and World Bank loan packages have incorporated small study components aimed at assessing the state of the resource as a prerequisite to project viability. These studies generally have been confined to the review of secondary data and verification surveys in proposed project sites.

COMMON FISHERIES PROBLEMS

The two archipelagos, Indonesia and the Philippines, have the largest marine areas and water-to-land ratios in the region. These two countries may be expected to maintain their alliance on the archipelagic principle and on the rights of coastal states to determine their surplus at their own pace. At the other extreme are some states that are geographically disadvantaged by being landlocked, shelf-locked, or having gained only a limited incremental marine area under the EEZ regime. These countries are Burma, Kampuchea, China, Laos, Malaysia, Singapore, and Thailand. Island countries with high coastline-to-land ratios share a similarity of interests through their high exposure to sea-related activities, including fishing. In this category are Indonesia, the Philippines, Hong Kong, and Taiwan. Singapore and Brunei are not considered here because their capture fisheries are very small.

The preceding sections of this chapter, together with Tables 4.1 through 4.4, have indicated a variety of similarities in the fisheries interests of Southeast Asian nations. The concern most common to the entire region is the actual or potential depletion of the resource. The depletion of coastal resources and decreasing productivity in centers of fishing populations and the overfished status of the demersal species within respective national jurisdictions, and analogous concerns. It is in the interests of all countries in the region to have an accurate assessment of the stocks and to employ resource management measures, particularly for demersal, inshore, and coastal fisheries, and to explore nontraditional fishing grounds, both for large- and small-scale operations. The shift to pelagic fishing calls for additional resource assessment effort.

The need to protect previous investments in trawlers is strong in the case of Thailand and Hong Kong. For Taiwan, the more evident investment is in longliners. These distant-water fishing countries may be expected to continue reaching out for partnerships and cooperative arrangements within and outside the region and to cooperate in seeking less restrictive conditions for foreign participation.

Shared fishing stocks and areas create a natural commonality of interest while also presenting a potential source of conflict. The South China Sea is shared by all mainland and littoral states in the region except Laos and Burma. Other shared areas include those in the Strait of Malacca by Indonesia, Malaysia, and Singapore; the Andaman Sea by Malaysia, Thailand, and Burma; the Gulf of Thailand by Thailand, Kampuchea, and Vietnam; and the Gulf of Tonkin by Vietnam, and China.

Economic, social, and cultural factors give fish and fishing a dominant place in national development priorities of all countries in the region except Laos and Brunei. The origin and degree of importance of these factors, however, vary from country to country partly with variations in their dependence on fishing, as indicated by per capita consumption, nutritional value, size of the labor force, and magnitude of external trade and foreign exchange contribution.

The problems of the artisanal fisheries sector in these countries are similar but differ in magnitude. Indonesia, the Philippines, Burma, China, and, to a lesser extent, Malaysia have dominant artisanal sectors. In Thailand, the Chinese province of Taiwan, and Hong Kong the larger commercial scale operations are dominant.

The most consistently expressed goal in a region where the high seas have been virtually appropriated is the development of inland, brackish, and marine aquaculture. This commonality of interest presents a ready area of cooperation in technology exchange. Singapore is unique in that it is focusing on land-based commercial and industrial activities. The Chinese province of Taiwan is even more unique in that it seeks to maintain the level of its catching activities while concurrently maintaining its supremacy in aquaculture and trading. Illegal fishing by countries from outside the region is a common complaint, and enforcement against these parties is a shared interest.

JURISDICTIONAL AND RESOURCE ACCESS ISSUES

Disputed Areas (Figure 4.5)

Chapter 3 analyzed the jurisdictional problems in Southeast Asia arising from the extension of maritime jurisdictions. These are reviewed here only for their particular relevance to fisheries.

The center of the Gulf of Tonkin poses an unsettled boundary dispute between China and Vietnam. Vietnam's interest in the area for fishing purposes may be presumed to be more intense than that of China, considering that the gulf is one of Vietnam's principal fishing grounds. Pelagic species abound in the area; demersals can also withstand more exploitation. Given the state of the fishing fleet of Vietnam and the alternatives available to China to increase its fish production, it is unlikely that the fisheries factor will bear heavily on a relativistic evaluation of this issue.

In the heart of the South China Sea Basin lie the Spratly Islands, which have been hotly contested over the latter half of the century by China, the Chinese province of Taiwan, Vietnam, the Philippines, and Malaysia. The pelagic resources in the area are dominated by the mackerel fishery off Palawan. A tuna migration route traverses the Spratlys. A fishery based in the area is unlikely to be economically viable, however, given the depth of the waters and distance of the island group to any major port of the contending parties. For Taiwan, which is the only distant-water fishing entity among the contenders, the demarcation of the boundary lines of the other countries could be important to its tuna longlining operations. On the whole, however, the significance of the Spratly dispute lies more with petroleum and military considerations than with fishing.

The Paracels lie farther north in the South China Sea Basin. They are claimed by China, Vietnam, and the Chinese province of Taiwan. Apart from the possibility that the area might be suitable for deep-water pelagic fishing, no hard evidence exists of its immediate economic importance for fishery purposes.

On the west side of Borneo, north of Tanjung Datu is an area with an unresolved EEZ boundary between Malaysia (Sarawak) and Indonesia. This portion of the Sunda Shelf is an offshore fishing ground for both countries where the pelagics are believed to be underexploited and the demersal species could probably withstand further fishing effort. The area figures importantly in Malaysia's eastward thrust, and to some extent in Indonesia's dispersal of people and fishermen away from the Java Sea and the Strait of Malacca.

Miangas (or Palmas) Island south of Mindanao is owned by Indonesia but lies within the territorial claims of the Philippines according to the Treaty of Paris. The island is very close to a large population center of the Philippines and adjoins small fishing communities of that country. Due to existing military-oriented cooperative

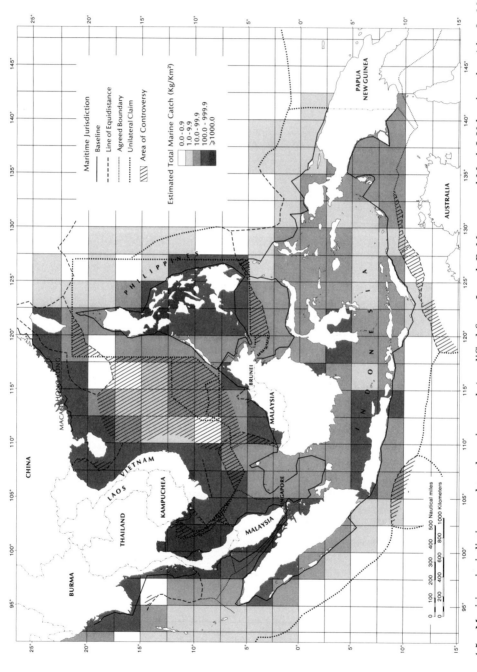

Figure 4.5 Maritime jurisdictions and total marine catch (modified from Joseph R. Morgan and Mark J. Valencia, eds., *Atlas for Marine Policy in Southeast Asian Seas*, Berkeley: University of California Press, 1983, p. 133).

arrangements between the two countries, however, the issue may be expected to be dormant for some time.

Some 24,000 nmi² in the Gulf of Thailand are within overlapping claims of two or three countries circling the gulf, i.e., Kampuchea, Thailand, and Vietnam. Resolution of these overlaps is needed for the division of management responsibilities pertaining to the overfished trawlable species. The quality of management could determine the survival of the trawl-based industries in the contending countries and also affect the economic value of the presumably underexploited pelagic species in the east side of the gulf. Conflicts are common among the numerous fishermen in the three countries. These conflicts are fueled by economic, ideological, and political considerations.

Issues Related to Archipelagic Claims

Two countries in the region have archipelagic status under the new CLS. For the Philippines there is a very complicated issue arising out of its claim to the Kalayaan Islands in the Spratly group that if incorporated into its archipelagic baseline system would result in an incremental water surface of 124,000 nmi².[101] The eastern portion of this incremental area adjoins the rich fishing grounds of Palawan. The latest working maps on the Philippine EEZ incorporate the Kalayaan claim.

The claim of the Philippines to a territorial sea based on the 1898 Treaty of Paris has spawned two other problems — the overlap with Indonesia with respect to Miangas Island and the apportionment of the northern waters along the Bashi Channel between the Philippines and the Chinese province of Taiwan. The difference between using the treaty limits rather than lines of equidistance to delineate the zone of jurisdiction between the Philippines and Taiwan is in the magnitude of 14,400 nmi².[102] This area is more important for fishing purposes to the Chinese province of Taiwan than to the Philippines.

In the case of Indonesia, the relevant provision in the CLS is Article 47, par. 6 to the effect that "if a part of the archipelagic state lies between two parts of an immediately adjacent neighboring State, existing rights and all other legitimate interests which the latter State has traditionally exercised in such waters and all rights stipulated by agreement between those states shall continue and be respected."[103] This provision applies to the rights of fragmented Malaysia in the waters around Indonesia's Natuna Island.

In accordance with Article 51 of the new CLS, which provides for recognition of agreements concerning traditional fishery rights, Indonesia and Malaysia conducted a bilateral agreement that acknowledges Malaysia's traditional fishery rights in specified areas of the Indonesian archipelago and EEZ waters off the northern Anambas Islands.

Issues Related to Disadvantaged Status
and Historical Fishing Rights

The Southeast Asian states adversely affected by the EEZ regime are Laos, Singapore, Thailand, Hong Kong, and the Chinese province of Taiwan. Laos is land-

locked, and Article 69 states that landlocked states shall have the right to participate, on an equitable basis, in the exploitation of an appropriate part of the surplus
of the living resources of the EEZs of coastal states of the region taking into account
the relevant economic and geographical circumstances of all the states concerned.
However, Laos is not particularly keen nor able to bear the costs of developing a
fishing industry under its present economic circumstances. Singapore has shifted
its interests to postharvest activities, including processing, transshipping, and
trading, with apparent success. The three distant-water fishing countries have suffered economic dislocations after being blocked from important fishing grounds
following the EEZ declarations of their neighbors, as well as of countries outside
the region. Article 62 of the CLS enjoins the coastal state to recognize "the need to
minimize economic dislocations in states whose nationals have habitually fished in
the zone or which have made substantial efforts in research and identification of
stocks." A related provision, Article 70 grants coastal states "whose geographical
situation makes them dependent upon the exploitation of the living resources of
the exclusive economic zones of other states . . . for adequate supplies of fish for the
nutritional purposes of their population or parts thereof" the right to share "on an
equitable basis" in the surplus resources of the coastal state. Article 62, which deals
with historical or traditional fishing rights, applies to the distant water fleets of
Thailand, Taiwan, and Hong Kong, as well as to the inshore fishing fleets of the
countries whose boundaries have dense fishing populations, such as Indonesia–
Malaysia, Thailand on the Strait of Malacca, Thailand–Burma on the Andaman
Sea, Thailand–Kampuchea–Vietnam on the Gulf of Thailand, and Brunei–Malaysia in Brunei Bay.[104]

Foreign Fishing

Illegal fishing by foreign vessels from neighboring or distant-water fishing nations
is a common complaint in the region. Due to weak surveillance and enforcement
capabilities, most of the countries whose maritime zones are violated can respond
only with token arrests, diplomatic *notes verbales,* loud denunciations in the press,
and a general feeling of frustration. Host states, however, may tend to exaggerate
in assessing the poaching issue. Violent confrontations involving the Indochinese
states are believed to be motivated more by political differences than by the desire
to enforce fishing boundaries and regulations. The right of passage of distant-
water fishing vessels gives rise to opportunities to fish illegally while in transit.
What can be done to alleviate these problems?

Resource Management Issues

Jurisdiction and control over fisheries resources entail serious management responsibilities. The framework for these responsibilities is defined in the CLS in
Articles 61 and 62:

> The coastal State, taking into account the best scientific evidence available to it, shall
> ensure through proper conservation and management measures that the maintenance of

the living resources in the exclusive economic zone is not endangered by over-exploitation
. . . Such measures shall also be designed to maintain or restore populations of harvested
species at levels which can produce the maximum sustainable yield, as qualified by relevant environmental and economic factors, including the economic needs of coastal fishing communities and the special requirements of developing States, and taking into
account any generally recommended subregional, regional or minimum standards. In
taking such measures the coastal State shall take into consideration the effects on species
associated with or dependent upon harvested species with a view to maintaining or re-
storing populations of such associated or dependent species about levels at which their
reproduction may be seriously threatened.

The coastal State shall promote the objective of optimum utilization of the living resources in the exclusive economic zone. . . .

The CLS also describes the tasks required of the coastal state for attaining the
foregoing objectives such as the determination of allowable catch and of the nation's capacity to harvest the living resources within its zone. The CLS prescribes
the modes and areas of management cooperation among states as follows:

Contribution and exchange of scientific information through competent international
organizations, where appropriate and with the participation by all states concerned, including states whose nationals are allowed to fish in the exclusive economic zone;

Agreement on the measures to conserve and develop "shared stocks" (the same stock or
stocks of associated species occurring within the zones of two or more coastal states
or behind and adjacent to the zones), either directly or through international organizations; and

Cooperation directly or through appropriate international organizations to ensure conservation and optimum utilization of highly migratory species (e.g., tuna, frigate mackerel, etc.).

How and where can such management be implemented?

Conservation vs. Exploitation. Management of fish stocks requires an understanding of the biological and economic forces bearing on the resource. Biological overfishing occurs when the MSY has reached the point where additional fishing effort
brings proportionately less catch. Economic overfishing occurs when additional
investment in the industry results in proportionately lower incremental returns.
Maintaining fishing levels at or below MSY does not guarantee the health of the
resource, however, because changes in the food chain could occur even with fishing
below MSY.

Scientific studies on the state of resources in the waters of the Southeast Asian
region are inadequate for making hard conclusions but sufficient to sound the
danger signals. The increasing proportion of trash fish caught by trawlers in shallower waters, the high percentage of juveniles in net hauls, and the leveling off or
outright decline of catch volumes of some countries are clear signs of biological
overfishing. The demersal and semipelagic species of the west coast of peninsular
Malaysia are already fully exploited, showing a decrease in total landings and an

increase of trash fish as a percentage of total catch. In Indonesia, the Strait of Malacca and the near coastal seas north of Java are probably overexploited.[105] Decreasing yields in the Philippines have been noted in Manila Bay; Pangil Bay; Sorsogon Bay; Pagapas Bay; Tinagong-Dagat, Capiz; San Miguel Bay, Camarines Sur; Bantayan Island, Cebu; Maqueda Bay and Villareal Bay in Samar; a portion of Zamboanga Channel; Lingayen Gulf; San Pedro Bay; Asid Gulf; Polillo Island in Quezon; and Puerto Galera in Oriental Mindoro.

Economic overfishing is evident from overinvestment in and overcapitalization of certain fisheries where profit rates have fallen, boats are idled, unemployment or underemployment occurs, subsidies are sought, and shifts to alternative activities are pursued. Unlike biological waste, economic waste also may be brought about by factors extraneous to the resource, such as the prices of fuel and the cost of investment, the presence or absence of alternative investment opportunities, and, on the demand side, the market prices for the fish produced. The biology and economy of fishing activities are, however, closely interlocked. Government intervention alters the nature and direction of biological and economic waste to the extent that it takes social, cultural, political, and other factors into consideration in promoting or discouraging certain fishing activities. Thus, small-vessel acquisition and motorization programs of many governments have contributed to depletion of coastal resources even as their effect on the beneficiaries' standards of living are in question. The intensive promotion and support of trawling has in some places led ultimately to the collapse of the industry. Biologically sound practices may be economically deficient, but the reverse also may be true. Thus, purse seines are economically efficient but tend to catch juveniles because they use small-mesh nets. More selective gears do not abuse the resource but are costly to operate.

Another aspect of the conservation versus use issue is the choice between present and future benefits.[106] Intensive utilization of the resource has filled pressing and immediate needs of the countries concerned for food, employment, and foreign exchange. To what extent the filling of some of these needs should or could have been deferred or tempered by management restraints in favor of maintaining the continuing productivity of the resource for future generations is debatable; five to ten years of bad fisheries practice is enough to destroy a fishery. Because available information cannot supply the answer with reasonable certainty, governments tend to hedge on limited entry regulations in favor of pleasing the majority. Without these controls, directing fishermen's actions toward alternatives becomes an impossible task. As Christy puts it, "no individual user can afford to restrain his own catch in the interest of future returns . . . because there is no reason to believe that he will be able to capture the benefits if anyone who wants to can enter the fishery."[107]

Shared Stocks. From a multicountry perspective, the question of shared stocks poses some difficulty. No individual country will regulate its own fishermen in the interests of future returns unless it is assured that all other fishermen are regulated.[108] The principle of shared stocks is the core of the biological and economic bases for cooperation among countries in a region. Theoretically, all species of fish could come under the category of shared stocks, whether they are sedentary or mobile, pelagic or demersal, if an EEZ boundary is placed across the stock distribution. Migratory species such as tuna that move across long distances seasonally are most readily recognized as shared stocks, but governments tend to find difficulty in defining their responsibility toward these species precisely because they are not "in place."

Pollution and Ecologically Harmful Practices. The age of environmental consciousness has touched Southeast Asia. Conservation measures in the form of protecting endangered species, controlling the conversion of mangroves to industrial uses, limiting the exploitation of corals, and demarcating marine parks are some of the manifestations of environmental concerns. (These are detailed in Chapter 9.) At this stage, however, socioeconomic priorities and political expediencies still overpower ecological considerations. Thus, pressure remains strong for the conversion of mangrove swamps to fish ponds and for the exploitation of coral reefs for export. These destructive practices as well as sedimentation of estuaries, pollution of coastal areas, and dynamiting and other forms of illegal fishing all affect fish stocks adversely. A major impediment to the successful implementation of ecologically sound programs is their inability to communicate effectively their rationale to fishermen and other resource users. Without this understanding, the long-run goals have little chance to prevail over the socioeconomic imperatives of providing food, employment, and incomes to poverty-ridden fishing communities as well as providing earnings to profit-oriented businessmen.

RESPONSES

Unilateral Policies

Although influenced to some degree by what the rest of the region is doing, the fishery development activities of the Southeast Asian countries are based on unilaterally determined policies. Such policies are official expressions of reactions to industry preferences and to social and political problems; they also relate to broader country priorities. Thus the emphasis on small-scale fisheries development, common in around three-quarters of the region, is dictated by the high and persistent incidence of poverty in those countries and by their predominantly rural population. The countries are reacting in various ways to the problems of extended jurisdiction. The Chinese province of Taiwan and to some extent Hong Kong are intensifying research and exploratory activities for new fishing grounds and for other exploitable species in their own areas of jurisdiction. Thailand and Taiwan are placing even more emphasis on culture activities, and Hong Kong and Taiwan are further enhancing and capitalizing on their capabilities for trade in fishery products.

With extended jurisdictions still new, management responsibilities take a back seat to exploitation opportunities. These in turn are sometimes handled with overflowing confidence and overwhelming nationalistic fervor. Thus, in the Philippines, severely restrictive requirements are imposed on foreign participation in fishing ventures, primarily to protect local industry from undue competition for the resource and secondarily to conserve the resource for future generations of Filipinos. Indonesia's trawling ban around Java and the Philippines' ban on commercial fishing within the inshore waters of Palawan were imposed more for social than for conservation considerations. In both cases, national interests in order of priority shape policy.

Many of the major concerns related to fisheries in the region can in fact be handled by unilateral action, with regional cooperation confined to technology exchange. Small-scale fisheries and aquaculture are at the top of this list. The management aspects of the broader program covering these concerns (i.e., coastal zone management) have regional implications for which the individual countries feel no sense of urgency. Because the sovereignty factor governs their attitude toward their zones, most Southeast Asian states may be expected to continue acting unilaterally on EEZ issues in the short term.

Harmonization

An intermediate step between unilateral and multilateral action is provided by the concept of harmonization defined as "the deliberate alignment of the laws of different nations for the purpose of fulfilling their national interests. Alignment is done by adjusting the laws of two or more nations so that they are similar, complementary, coordinated, or linked in some other way."[109] This approach has a wide range of applications in the region, given the commonalities of fisheries interests. The most common type of harmonization, the pursuit of similarity, is already applied widely although no formal arrangements have been instituted for deliberate harmonization for regional ends. Thus, the extended jurisdiction declarations of most states in the region have common formats; so have the bilateral agreements, investment incentives laws, and certain regulations to control fishing effort. These similarities, however, merely show that through avenues opened to them by regular dialogues, the countries can readily draw from the experiences of others "to simplify their own work and not for any larger purpose.... There may be international benefit, but it may be unintended."[110] ASEAN started to introduce the concept of uniform regulations in 1981 with its common position on fish quarantine. There may be other comparable cases in which nations of the region could benefit from harmonization of laws relating to fisheries. Possibilities include a common treatment of illegal fishing by both intra- and extraregional elements, standardization of laws against pollution of offshore areas and other environmental issues, and establishment of similar mesh size regulations.

The other types of harmonization (i.e., *complementary* legislation and *conditionality* in national law [where the action of one nation is predicated on that of another]) may be best understood as forms or consequences of bilateral agreements and will be discussed in the following section. It is worth noting, however, that a distinct advantage of harmonization is that, once established, its continued operation does not depend on any supranational agency.[111] Thus, international bodies like the South China Sea Programme or ASEAN might facilitate harmonization but fade out as soon as the arrangement is operational.

Bilateral or Multilateral Agreements

Developing countries closely guard and firmly assert their rights to self-determination. While country representatives who attend international conferences are quick to agree on broad principles, the operationalization of these agreements invariably is predicated on individual national interest and beneficial trade-offs. Thus, bilateral agreements are the preferred approach to the issues described in the preceding section as well as to the cooperative solution of common economic problems. Boundary disputes and traditional fishing rights and other resource access issues lend themselves to bilateral and multilateral agreements. So far, however, only a few international agreements on boundaries have been made within the region. The more important jurisdictional disputes, such as those of the Spratlys, the Paracels, the Gulf of Tonkin, and the Gulf of Thailand, remain to be resolved. Agreements with fisheries implications within the region include

- Malaysia and Indonesia on the delimitation of their continental shelves in the Strait of Malacca and the South China Sea (1969);
- Thailand, Indonesia, and Malaysia on the delimitation of their continental shelves in the northern part of the Strait of Malacca (1971); and
- Indonesia, Malaysia, and Singapore to protect the marine environment of the Strait of Malacca and Singapore against oil pollution (1975).

The Indonesia–Philippines agreement on naval liaison enforced since 1963 establishes cooperation on matters of security, smuggling, piracy, illegal entry, and illegal fishing in all areas between the two countries, including the disputed Miangas Island area. The agreement between the Philippines and Indonesia in 1974 to grant "most favored country" treatment to nationals or legal entities of the other country in matters of trade, investment and other economic activities related to fishing "with due regard for their respective bilateral or multilateral commitments" was never operationalized.

Resource access issues have been treated with much caution and hesitation. Legitimate means of access can be made available, and such arrangements are proliferating in the region. Fee fishing has not gained acceptance because the countries so far have not developed licensing procedures, and the inadequacy of resource data poses a serious constraint. Meanwhile, joint ventures, which started with extraregional maritime fishing powers negotiating for access to Southeast Asian countries, are now gaining popularity as countries within the region enter into more fishing partnerships. Indonesia is using equity joint ventures to expand its industrial fisheries. To explore newly gained EEZ areas and to disperse fishing activity from saturated areas, Indonesia entered into an agreement with Japan, renewed in 1979, enabling Japan to fish for tuna by longline in designated areas of its archipelagic waters. The Philippines has restrictive equity provisions so that most joint ventures approved and applied for are contractual, involving the charter of vessels. Such arrangements also have elements of control by the foreign partner and are seen in some quarters as merely an indirect means of gaining access to the resource. Thailand has been negotiating for access to portions of the South China Sea controlled by other countries with little success, although it did negotiate a transit agreement with Burma. Taiwan has several idle tuna longliners, some of which have been offered to Philippine businessmen. Philippine operators have offered purse seine fishing vessels to Indonesia and Malaysia.

Although joint ventures may be the most legitimate and acceptable answer to the problem of access, there are many potential conflict areas associated with it. For example, the displaced fishing vessels are mostly trawlers; the countries to which they are offered are phasing these gears out of the inshore areas for social and resource management reasons. The operation of trawlers in offshore areas, on the other hand, is constrained by the high price of fuel, which accounts for as much as 70 percent of the operating costs of trawling selective gears for demersal species. Purse seiners for the less-exploited pelagic species may be more within the requirements of the host countries involved in joint venture arrangements. Considering that these host countries employ joint ventures to achieve certain economic and resource management goals, however, the ultimate value of these arrangements depends heavily on the enforcement of prescribed policies and regulations. In the face of feeble enforcement abilities and cunning partners from host and cooperating countries, it is doubtful whether the expectations for joint ventures can be fully attained.

From the earlier overview of the many unresolved access and boundary issues it is apparent that the official preference for bilateral agreements has not been translated to formal commitments. Particularly in the case of resource access, it seems that the countries are not ready to commit themselves to pinpointing fishing grounds, gears, and species open to exploitation by their regional neighbors. The provisions of the CLS regarding sharing of surplus and allowing access to disadvantaged states contain numerous qualifications that allow the coastal state to take its time. The inadequacy of resource information is the major rationale offered for the inability of coastal states to operationalize the sharing concept. Another reason for hesitancy could be that in entering into formal agreements there is an implied acceptance of the relevant unilaterally declared rights and demarcation lines. Some countries are not ready to concede these points. The solution, therefore, is to start with exploratory talks that would lead to a phased agreement among governments on the issues. It is time for these dialogues to begin.

Regional Arrangements

Polomka enumerates the limiting factors to regionalism in Southeast Asia, as

- The needs of states to give priority to solving more urgent domestic problems;
- The reluctance to compromise newly gained sovereignty over economic matters;

and Indonesia are net exporters of fish products. Kampuchea, the Philippines, and Vietnam derive the greatest proportion of their GNP from fisheries; Singapore and Brunei are least economically dependent on fisheries. An average of about 3 percent of the labor force in the region is engaged in fisheries; subsistence and part-time fishermen would comprise a significant addition. The Philippines and Vietnam have the greatest proportion of their labor force employed in fisheries; the populace of Brunei and Singapore are considerably less involved in fishing.

Seafood provides a significant portion of animal protein in the diets of Asian people. The annual per capita consumption of fish in the South China Sea region is two to four times the world average of 11 kilograms (kg) (24 pounds).[2] Singapore consumes the most fish per capita per year. The Chinese province of Taiwan, Thailand, Hong Kong, and Singapore engage in distant-water fishing in the South China Sea, as does Japan. Thus the South China Sea countries all need fish as a contribution to the physical sustenance of their populations and also as significant components of their economies.

In Southeast Asia the traditions of the coastal peoples are derived from their interaction with and dependence on the sea and its resources over many generations. These coastal peoples have developed and maintained harvesting and processing techniques and equipment particularly suited to their needs. This cultural dependence on a particular resource or occupation tends to be strongly held and can create a politically volatile situation when traditional coastal people are confronted with the dynamics of modernization. This high economic, nutritional, and cultural dependence on fisheries is expected to continue.

The Philippines, Indonesia, Brunei, Malaysia, and Thailand have offshore hydrocarbon production operations. However, given the generally underdeveloped economic status of the South China Sea nations and their hopes, economic growth plans, and the impatient expectation of their growing populations for an increased standard of living, production alone is not a reliable measure of these nations' dependence on development of potential offshore hydrocarbons to solve their domestic economic and political problems. The current producers, and possibly Vietnam, have the highest offshore potential, and Kampuchea and Thailand have somewhat less potential. Awareness of the importance of these resources has risen dramatically over the past five years, and leasing and exploration has been or is being conducted in the offshore areas of all Southeast Asian countries with potential resources.

Nations dependent on maritime transport are likely to be concerned with maintaining unrestricted passage. The data for Singapore reflect its status as the region's principal entrepôt. Hong Kong is also an important transshipment center, and Indonesia relies heavily on seaborne trade. At the other end of the scale, Kampuchea has little to export and is unable to purchase many imports. Brunei's relatively large GNP, which is comprised almost totally of oil production for export, dwarfs its seaborne trade at a ratio of 0.03×10^{-3}. The rest of the region's littoral nations have remarkably similar proportions of seaborne trade relative to their GNPs (1.6–4.4) though they vary widely in the absolute amounts of goods exchanged.

Thus the South China Sea countries generally rely only moderately on seaborne trade and petroleum compared with the rest of the world. But this low degree of reliance on trade reflects the countries' undeveloped economies rather than a high dependence on sea transport for export of primary agricultural and mineral commodities and importation of manufactured goods and petroleum products. In fact, the entities of Southeast Asia depend on sea transport more than any other region; 75 percent of the population lives on islands, and almost all capital cities are on or have links to the sea. This dependence will increase as development proceeds.

Investment

Investment indicators include money, human capital, and other resources allocated to infrastructure, and activities such as shipping, port construction, naval development, marine scientific research, offshore hydrocarbon and mineral development, fishing, and marine tourism and recreation. Education can raise the level of output in the marine sector. Thus, other forms of investment are marine-oriented education, general marine awareness campaigns, and an awareness of historic interaction with the marine arena.

The relative size of a nation's merchant fleet, particularly its tanker tonnage, indicates the level of national investment and interest in this use of the seas. Singapore's total merchant and tanker tonnages reflect its flag-of-convenience status for tax purposes, but the locally owned component of the merchant fleet is by itself the largest in the region. This again shows Singapore's dependence on unrestricted passage for its economic well-being. The Philippines has the second largest investment in commercial shipping in the region, whereas Kampuchea has the smallest investment relative to its GNP. Brunei relies almost totally on Japanese carriers for its oil exports and other trade. The remaining countries have made a low-to-moderate investment in commercial shipping relative to their GNPs. Marine scientific research expenditure, expertise, and education, as well as marine technology and investment capital, are generally insufficient for the indigenous development of their potential marine resources.

Control

Control may be estimated by the extent of offshore area claimed under each type of jurisdictional zone together with the particular regulations imposed within these zones and a country's ability to enforce these regulations. Control can be a manifestation of accessibility and dependence and is perhaps the best indication of how nations perceive their current and future national marine interests.

The capability of Southeast Asian nations to deter unwanted entry into their claimed marine areas or to patrol them is generally inadequate. Singapore, with its extremely small marine area, is an exception, and Vietnam might also be able to control its marine perimeter and area adequately. As indicated in Chapter 7, the remaining states have thousands of square kilometers of ocean area or hundreds of kilometers of marine perimeter to cover per patrol vessel or aircraft. Of course a vessel or an aircraft equipped with radar would be able to patrol a considerable expanse, and certain areas such as rich fishing grounds would be more likely sites of intrusion than others. However, only a portion of a total marine fleet or aircraft fleet would be suitable or expendable for marine surveillance.

All political entities except Singapore in the core group being discussed here have now claimed a 12-nautical-mile (nmi) territorial sea, a 200-nmi exclusive economic zone (EEZ), and a continental shelf (see Chapter 3). The territorial sea claimed by the Philippines includes nearly 2 million square kilometers (km²) situated between straight baselines drawn about the outermost islands of the archipelago and the boundaries defined by treaties of 1898, 1900, and 1930.

Indonesia, the Philippines, Thailand, and Malaysia have ratified the 1958 Geneva Convention on the Continental Shelf. Singapore has not made such a claim. Only the British colonies of Brunei and Hong Kong, whose international affairs were then handled by the United Kingdom, prerevolutionary Kampuchea (then Cambodia), and Thailand ratified all four 1958 Geneva conventions — High Seas, Territorial Seas and Contiguous Zone, Continental Shelf, and Fishing and Conservation of the Living Resources of the High Seas. Malaysia ratified all but the Convention on Fishing and Conservation of the Living Resources of the High Seas. Indonesia ratified the Convention on the Continental Shelf and the Convention on the High Seas (with a reservation). Except for the Philippines' ratification of the Convention on the Continental Shelf, the remaining countries have not participated in these Conventions.

As for participation in other marine treaties, it is somewhat anomalous that Kampuchea — with its relatively low marine accessibility, dependence, investment, and control — has, along with the Philippines and Vietnam, participated in the largest number of marine treaties. Thailand and Indonesia have ratified the smallest number of marine treaties. The treaty categories having the participation of the most states in the region are fisheries, in particular the Agreement on the Indo-Pacific Fisheries Council, and the safety of life at sea. Treaties concerning technical and legal shipping standards and those concerning pollution have apparently been of low priority for the region's littoral nations.

THE NATIONS OF SOUTHEAST ASIA
AND THEIR MARINE INTERESTS

Brunei

Brunei, until recently a United Kingdom protectorate, has the smallest population and the third smallest area of the region's political entities. However, Brunei enjoys the region's highest GNP per capita, derived almost entirely from offshore hydrocarbon production that is the third largest in the region. Brunei — or more accurately, the United Kingdom acting for Brunei — demonstrated an awareness of the importance of offshore areas for hydrocarbons as early as 1954 by annexing the continental shelf.[3] Brunei, reluctantly on its part, became independent on 1 January 1984 and is now solely responsible for its foreign affairs.[4] Most likely it will negotiate EEZ and continental shelf boundaries with Malaysia and other maritime neighbors. Brunei, with a short coastline, is zone-locked and nearly shelf-locked and has marine access only on the semi-enclosed South China Sea.

Brunei's prime marine interest is to obtain as much offshore area as possible, particularly that with petroleum potential, while avoiding serious disputes that could elicit destabilizing economic and political pressures. Such disputes could arise from disagreements over EEZ and continental shelf boundaries, hydrocarbon deposits divided by boundaries, or transnational oil pollution from offshore drilling. Another interest is in unhampered transport of its oil and liquefied natural gas (LNG) exports to Japan, the United States, Taiwan, South Africa, and elsewhere.

Burma

Burma maintains a strong interest in obtaining recognition of its offshore claims. It has rigidly enforced these claims, by arresting a Singapore-based scientific research vessel intruding in its EEZ, and by arresting several hundred Thai fishing vessels and fishermen over the past decade.[5] Burma's claim to much of the Gulf of Martaban as internal waters closed off by a 222.3-nmi baseline has been challenged by the United States,[6] among others, and Burma's baseline enclosing the Mergui archipelago is not recognized by Thailand. Burma's baselines, continental shelf and EEZ claims also have resulted in disagreements with India and Bangladesh.[7] Burma recently has demonstrated an increased interest in offshore hydrocarbons and fisheries, offering acreage and seismic survey contracts in offshore areas formerly "reserved,"[8] and negotiating an Asian Development Bank (ADB) loan for development of a deep-water fishing fleet. Burma has issued oil exploration leases in an area that lies on India's side of any line of equidistance, even if the Burmese baselines are accepted.[9]

Indonesia

Indonesia has the largest population and the largest land area in the region. It also has the longest coastline and has acquired the largest offshore area in the region under the archipelagic concept and a 200-nmi EEZ. Only a small portion of the Indonesian offshore area, the Natuna "salient," includes waters of the South China Sea. Although Indonesia has the largest number of ports and the second largest naval air force in the region, it has the greatest difficulty patrolling its offshore area simply because of its size.

Indonesia's economy is heavily dependent on hydrocarbon production. Its offshore production is the largest in the region, as is its sea trade in petroleum and its total sea trade. Per capita consumption of fish is the lowest in the region and its absolute and GNP-relative expenditure on marine research has been by far the lowest in the region not counting landlocked Laos. Of the four ocean law conventions adopted at Geneva in 1958, Indonesia has ratified the Conventions on the High Seas and on the Continental Shelf. It unilaterally claimed the archipelagic principle, now legitimated by the new Convention on the Law of the Sea (CLS).

- The sociocultural heterogeneity of the region and the great disparities in level of development, technology and economic social structure; and
- Incompatibility in economic policies, with some favoring "inward looking" industrialization through tariffs while others favor "outward looking" industrialization through foreign investment.[112]

The first two factors inhibit all forms of regional cooperation. The last two factors, however, are major insurmountable obstacles to the establishment of a fully integrated regional fisheries community in this part of the world. Nevertheless, the management and allocation of shared stocks, including highly migratory species, the prevention of pollution and other environmentally harmful practices, and the exchange of scientific information are appropriate objects of more modest programs of regional cooperation.

Although resource studies have been far from exhaustive and catch and effort data are incomplete and often inaccurate, there seem to be sufficient theoretical basis and biological and economic evidence to treat shared stocks as an object of regional cooperation. Regional organizations, bilateral donors, and multilateral organizations outside the region have offered assistance, and in many cases these have been accepted. Lending institutions operating in the region such as ADB, and the World Bank have started to build small resource assessment components into their project loans. In many cases, the findings of these studies have influenced development policies, as in the case of trawl bans and the closure of some areas to certain types of fishing. But while the beginnings of unilaterally imposed, limited-entry management are discernible, cooperative or coordinated management still has to find acceptance; allocation sharing seems a long way off. Political differences among some of the states involved and sheer suspicion of the motives of others impede the long and complicated process of allocating shared stocks. A competent regional organization that has the confidence of the Southeast Asian countries could be the initiating and umbrella organization for subregional agreements toward this end.

The SPSP and other UN–FAO instrumentalities (e.g., UNEP, IPFC, INFOFISH) have played a mobilizing role in resource management in the region. The resource evaluation studies FAO has undertaken on the Sunda Shelf, the Bay of Bengal, and the Philippines have not only made resource information on the region available but have also catalyzed the exchange of information. The tuna tagging project covering the Philippines and Indonesia contributes primary knowledge of the resource from which the entire region benefits. But the Philippines and Indonesia, with their vast marine areas, still have a long way to go in resource assessment. While there may be a general willingness to exchange scientific information, the greater need lies in the establishment of mechanisms to translate this information into management policies. The scientific community in the region, as in other regions, is separate and distinct from the decision-making community. The efforts of scientists to influence the policymakers is only now starting to show results. The lack of an adequate theoretical framework for evaluating the multispecies resources of the region makes it doubly hard to influence government action.

As Marr aptly stated, "along with appropriate theory, we need to develop 'quick and dirty' methods of applying theory for management purposes, methods which do not require the kinds and amounts of data we cannot realistically expect to obtain."[113]

Enforcement problems and the capabilities of the countries of the region are reviewed in Chapter 10. With few exceptions, the capabilities of the navies of Southeast Asian states to enforce the integrity of their extended jurisdictions are inadequate, even with civilian involvement in some countries such as Kampuchea, China, and Vietnam. These limited capabilities are applied to patrolling marine waters and apprehending poachers. To achieve the resource management objective, however, much more surveillance and enforcement is required. Surveillance and enforcement are essential to maintaining resources and a crucial element in regional cooperation. The advent of the EEZ regime has added an entirely new dimension to the functions of the navies. Navies cannot be expected to assume a fisheries orientation immediately nor to place fishery management above their traditional military and peace-keeping duties. In ASEAN particularly, coordination between national navies and fisheries departments is only beginning. This stage must reach some degree of success before the next stage of bilateral or regional cooperation for fishery management purposes can be institutionalized. The inadequacy of the individual countries' enforcement power theoretically may suggest the benefits of concerted action. The fact that the navies' missions are primarily defense and security, however, renders the practical application of this theory rather ambitious. The best that could be hoped for at this stage is pooled efforts for training and exchange of information on techniques, rather than concerted action for enforcement of management measures.

In Southeast Asia, the more operational levels of cooperation in the areas discussed here would probably be on at least two subregional levels, given the differences in political and ideological orientations of the countries in the region and the uneasiness of some countries in dealing with technologically advanced states like the Chinese province of Taiwan. ASEAN is a clear case where cooperation may take a regional approach. Cooperation in fisheries could follow the lead taken at ASEAN's first ministerial meeting on the environment held in May 1981. The five countries adopted the "Manila Declaration on the ASEAN Environment," which calls for an environmental education program and for the enactment and enforcement of environmental protection measures in ASEAN countries. To cover a wider regional scope, ASEAN could elicit the involvement of non-ASEAN nations in the region. An outside agency could make a lasting contribution to resource management in the region through the support of intensive training programs for Southeast Asian scientists who could later be immersed in the intricate tasks of management.

CHAPTER 5

OIL AND GAS POTENTIAL, OVERLAPPING CLAIMS, AND POLITICAL RELATIONS

Mark J. Valencia

STATUS AND TRENDS IN HYDROCARBON EXPLORATION

A decade ago, many policymakers thought of the Southeast Asian region as a collection of small nations surrounding and separated by the South China Sea. Marine geographers and geologists viewed the region as consisting principally of the broad Sunda and Mainland shelves, the deep China Basin, and numerous small marginal sea basins. But with the extension of jurisdiction over resources and economic activities to 200 nautical miles (nmi) or more, the very shape of nations has changed dramatically. Nations find themselves with new, sometimes unfriendly, neighbors in the marine regions with numerous unresolved maritime boundaries.

In many places basins bearing oil and gas extend into areas of overlapping claims. Eventually exploration and drilling will trend farther offshore into deeper and sometimes disputed waters. Chapter 3 described the details of the jurisdictional issues in the region, and this chapter focuses on the petroleum geology of areas of overlapping claims in relation to the specifics of those claims and then analyzes these unresolved boundary situations in the context of international relations.

In 1983 oil prices were down and supplies were in surplus, so exploration and exploration drilling were reduced. Eventually, however, demand will again outstrip supply.[1] When this occurs, the combination of stable political circumstances, good geological potential, a benign climate, and reasonably competitive legislation will produce an upswing in petroleum exploration activity in Southeast Asia. Indeed, in the second quarter of 1982, drilling activity in the Association of Southeast Asian Nations (ASEAN) area hit an all-time high.[2] There continues to be a wide variety of potential discoveries of every size in many geologic settings providing incentives for both large and small companies. In the ASEAN seas, the success ratio drilling was 50 percent in 1982.[3] Exploration costs, while increasing, have not risen as greatly in Southeast Asian seas as in other areas of the world, and the entry expenditures such as bonuses and work obligations are modest relative to the typically large concession areas.

155

Despite diverse exploration activity throughout the region, Brunei, Indonesia, Malaysia, Thailand, and the Philippines are the only countries with established hydrocarbon potential and account for most of the exploratory wells drilled in the region. China's Mainland Shelf, however, is becoming a major focus of activity. There has also been a growing acceptance by several Southeast Asian countries of investment and direct involvement by the national oil companies of Japan, South Korea, and the Chinese province of Taiwan in exploration and development of hydrocarbon resources.

The trend in Southeast Asia is for new exploration contracts to be offered on relatively small blocks that include only part of a basin area. Also, the expanded use of natural gas and its more realistic pricing as a premium fuel are encouraging companies and governments to explore for additional combustible gas reserves.[4] Although Southeast Asia's proved petroleum reserves are small by world standards, the extensive offshore shelf represents a largely unexplored and prospective area for exploration. Developments in remote sensing and positioning technology, geological stratigraphic correlation techniques, deep-water drilling equipment, and pipeline and transmission technology make operations in deep waters increasingly routine, although extremely costly and not without risk. Offshore exploratory drilling capabilities worldwide increased from a water depth of 412 meters (m) in 1973 to about 2,400 m in 1983, although no discovery in waters deeper than about 1,500 m has yet been developed. One of the then world's deepest wells in terms of water depth (Exxon–Discoverer 534, 1,055 m) was drilled in 1976 in the Andaman Sea off Thailand.[5] The absolute amount of deep ocean drilling that has occurred in the region is negligible, however, relative to the prospective acreage involved. Offshore exploration activity in the region will eventually increase and extend farther offshore and into deeper waters.

Regional Petroleum Geology

Figure 5.1 displays the relationship between the distribution of sedimentary basins and oil and gas deposits.[6] The continental shelves of the region are underlain by thick Tertiary sedimentary basins; in places, such sediments also underlie the continental slopes, rises, and the deep ocean floor. The elongate basins underlying the central and northwestern Sunda Shelf are generally parallel to the surrounding land masses in a double festoon draped around the Natuna Arch. The north-south-trending Thai Basin in the Gulf of Thailand and the northwest-southeast-trending Malay Basin off the northeast coast of the Malay Peninsula are separated by the east-west Tenggol Arch from the east-west-trending Penyu and West Natuna basins to the south. The Malay Basin is the thickest, with more than 9 kilometers (km) (5.6 miles [mi]) of sediment. The Malay and West Natuna basins are largely separated from the Sarawak Basin to the east by a ridge of basement rocks, the Natuna Arch. The Sarawak Basin extends to the west and south and to the east into the Brunei–Sabah basins. To the northeast, the Northwest Palawan Basin hugs the coast of Palawan. To the north of the Sarawak Basin, the Saigon Basin is separated from the Mekong Basin by the Con Son Swell, a buried ridge of basement rock. The

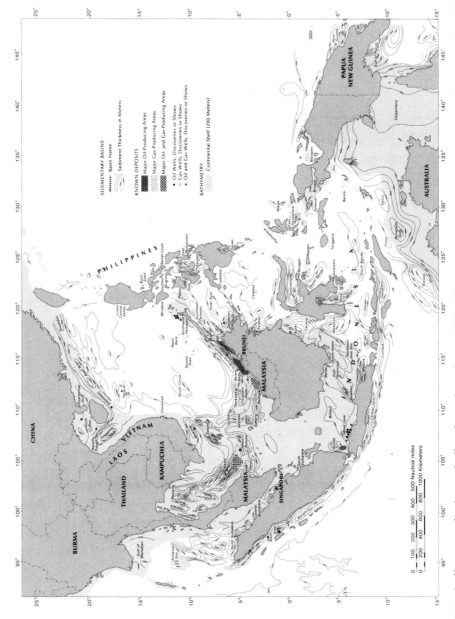

Figure 5.1   Sedimentary basins and oil and gas deposits (modified from Joseph R. Morgan and Mark J. Valencia, eds., *Atlas for Marine Policy in Southeast Asian Seas*, Berkeley: University of California Press, 1983, p. 101).

Mekong Basin is also separated from the Thai Basin to the west by the Korat Swell.

The Mainland Shelf is underlain by some 200,000 square kilometers (km²) (77,220 square miles [mi²]) of fault-controlled Mesozoic–Cenozoic basins. The Gulf of Tonkin contains the seaward extension of the Hanoi Trough, the North Bay Basin, and the elongate Southeast Hainan, Pearl, and Southern basins, all with their long axis parallel to the coast. Sediment thicknesses are 3–4 km (1.9–2.5 mi) except in the more-than-5-km (3.1-mi) and perhaps 10-km (6.2-mi)-thick Yinggehai Basin.

The deep South China Sea proper contains the 2-km (1.24-mi)-thick South China Basin, the shallow Spratly and Reed Bank basins, which rest on a microcontinental block, an unnamed and largely unknown basin parallel to the coast of central Vietnam, several thin subbasins in the Paracels, and an unnamed 2-km (1.24-mi)-thick basin in deep water in the northern part of the South China Basin.

South China Sea basins, which are situated in part or entirely under 200–1,500 m of water, include the outer portions of the Southern, Pearl River and Southeast Hainan basins, the Paracel area, and those on the rim of the Sunda Shelf (the Saigon Basin, the Central Luconia Platform, the Baram Delta, and the Brunei–Sabah, Northwest Palawan and Reed Bank basins). South of Indonesia, portions of the Timor, Sahul, Bonaparte Gulf, and Browse basins are partially or entirely in waters more than 1,500 m deep and thus beyond the economic limits of present exploitation. In the South China Sea such deep basins include the unnamed basin off central Vietnam, the South China Basin, and part of the Brunei-Sabah basins.

Production

Oil production was first established in this region in 1885. Cumulative production to mid-1979, excluding Indonesia, amounted to about 11 billion barrels (bbl). Daily production, excluding Indonesia, is about 2 million bbl of oil and 515 million cubic feet (MCF) of gas (Table 5.1). Even including Indonesia, the region produces only about 3.5 percent of the world's crude oil and 2.5 percent of its natural gas. Asia's first offshore well was drilled on the northwest continental shelf of Borneo in 1957. In 1975, 20 percent of crude oil in the region was produced offshore;[7] in 1980, about 50 percent of crude oil production was from offshore wells.[8]

The predominant offshore discoveries and production have been from basins in the central and southern Sunda Shelf and the Northwest Palawan and North Sumatera basins. The southeastern Malay Basin is oil-prone, whereas the Gulf of Thailand basins to the north and the West Natuna Basin to the south are gas-prone. The Central Luconia Platform is gas-prone and the Baram Delta, Brunei–Sabah, and Northwest Palawan areas are oil-prone. Preliminary indications for the Mainland Shelf are for oil.

For the Sunda Shelf alone, excluding Indonesia, total estimated ultimate recoverable reserves (proved and in some case probable) are 3.8 to 5.3 billion bbl of oil and 56 to 67 trillion cubic feet (TCF) of gas (see Table. 5.1). If the gas is converted to oil-equivalent units, total hydrocarbon reserves are on the order of 13.5–17 billion bbl of oil equivalent. Offshore Indonesia adds some 43.9 billion bbl of ultimate recoverable resources (Table 5.2) with more than 40 percent under water

Table 5.1   Offshore Hydrocarbon Production and Reserves (January 1981)

Country, Basin	Production		Reserves (estimated ultimate recoverable)	
	Oil (thousand bbl/day)	Gas (million ft³/day)	Oil (million bbl)	Gas (trillion ft³)
Brunei				
Baram Delta	262	315	2,000–3,500	7.7–10
Burma	–	–	?	?
Indonesia				
(various basins)	532	–	–ᵃ	–ᵃ
Kampuchea	–	–	?	?
Malaysia				
West: Malay	113.7	–	1,000	6.6–15
East: Sabah	78.3	–	200+	–
Sarawak				
Baram	92.1	–	600	?
Balingian	8	–	Minor	–
C. Luconia	–	–	Minor	15
E. Natuna	–	–	–	?
Philippines				
Palawan	23	–	7–17	–
Reed Bank	–	–	–	Minor
Thailand				
Thai/Malay	–	–	–	19
Vietnam	–	–	?	?

Source: E. P. Du Bois, "Hydrocarbons and the South China Sea," *CCOP Newsletter,* Vol. 8, No. 1, March 1981, Tables 1 and 2.
ᵃSee Table 5.2.
Notes: – = none.   ? = some but amount unknown.

depths greater than 200 m. Offshore southern China adds 10 billion bbl of estimated ultimate recoverable oil reserves to the total.

Potential

Figure 5.2 displays the relationship between undiscovered oil and gas resources (estimated ultimate recoverable), the sedimentary basins of the region, and known deposits.[9] In the South China Sea, high potential for oil is indicated for the Brunei–Sabah basins. High gas potential is indicated for the Central Luconia Platform, the Baram Delta, and the Malay Basin.

Table 5.2   Indonesia's Remaining Ultimate Recoverable Oil and Gas Resources

Basin	Oil and Gas Resources (billion bbl oil equivalent)
North Sumatera Basin	3.5010
Sibolga Basin	1.8250
Central Sumatera Basin	2.7410
Bengkulu Basin	1.3380
South Sumatera Basin	1.4880
Sunda Basin	0.1430
North West Java Basin	1.1260
Billiton Basin	0.1220
South Java Basin	1.0145
North East Java Basin	0.3790
Pati Basin	0.2610
North East Java Sea Basin	0.6880
East Natuna Basin	0.4550
West Natuna Basin	0.1110
Ketungau/Melawi Basin	0.0510
Barito Basin	0.3199
Asam-Asam Basin	3.1450
Kutal Basin	22.9310
Tarakan Basin	2.0650
Sulawesi Basin	0.5500
Makassar Strait Basin	7.1710
Lariang Basin	5.2270
Makassar Basin	12.0640
Gorontalo Basin	3.4850
Banggai Basin	3.0270
Bone Basin	2.4420
Sulawesi Tenggara Basin	4.2440
Flores Basin	0.4470
Bali Basin	0.1230
Sawu Basin	0.3620
Timor Basin	0.7040
Banda Basin	0.5260
Halmahera Basin	0.2900
Walgeo Basin	0.2900
Salawati Basin	0.6550
Bintuni Basin	0.3340
Aru Basin	0.8440
Waropen Basin	1.4550
Akimengah Basin	0.7440
Sahul Basin	0.8950
Total	89.5534

Source: G. A. S. Nayoan, "Offshore Hydrocarbon Potential of Indonesia," in Mark J. Valencia, ed., *The South China Sea: Hydrocarbon Potential and Possibilities of Joint Development,* Oxford: Pergamon Press, 1981, p. 1,238, Figure 12.

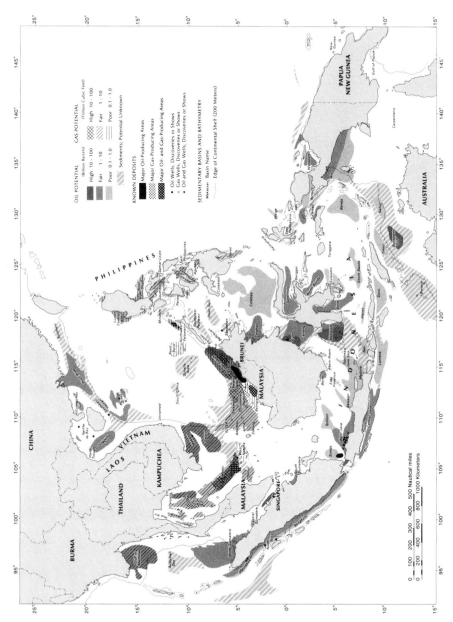

Figure 5.2 Oil and gas potential: Undiscovered resources (modified from Joseph R. Morgan and Mark J. Valencia, eds., *Atlas for Marine Policy in Southeast Asian Seas*, Berkeley: University of California Press, 1983, p. 103).

Poor potential for oil is indicated for the Northwest Palawan Basin, for the central and western Gulf of Thailand basins, and for the northern Andaman Sea. Poor gas potential is indicated for the Northwest Palawan Basin, for the Reed Bank (where only gas potential is indicated), most of the Brunei–Sabah basins and Balingian area, and the West Natuna Basin. Potential for oil only is indicated for the Mainland Shelf. Both oil and gas potential are indicated for the southwestern South China Sea. Large areas of sedimentary deposits greater than 2 km (1.24 mi) thick but with unknown hydrocarbon potential are located mostly in deep water in the northern, northwestern, central, and southwestern South China Sea. Fair gas potential is indicated for the Browse Basin, and high oil potential is indicated for the Bonaparte Gulf Basin. The potential for most of the rest of the southern Indonesian–Australian northwest shelf is unknown.

Exploration Rights

Figure 5.3 shows the relationship between areas under petroleum exploration rights, the sedimentary basins of the region, and known deposits of oil and gas. Such areas are constantly changing in size, shape, and operator; Figure 5.3 gives their distribution at a point when offshore oil exploration activity in the region was at its highest level. The Chinese seismic contract areas have recently been subdivided and awarded to new operators for detailed exploration and eventual drilling. Thus, the areas under petroleum rights can be considered as those of most intense exploration and the most prospective.

Understandably, most of the areas are situated on and around known deposits like the Gulf of Thailand and the southwestern and southeastern Sunda Shelf basins. Others are situated in unproved areas such as the Mainland Shelf, the Gulf of Martaban, and the north and northwest Australian shelves. Areas under petroleum exploration rights appear to be generally limited at present to the continental shelf. Areas under waters deeper than 200 m, with petroleum rights include more than half the seismic exploration rights area on the Mainland Shelf, and also part of the Northwest and Southeast Palawan and Reed Bank basins, the northern Sahul Shelf (particularly in the Browse Basin), and the formerly leased area in the Timor Basin.

HYDROCARBON POTENTIAL AND OVERLAPPING CLAIMS

Figure 5.4 superimposes the jurisdictional claims in the region on hydrocarbon potential. Most countries bordering the South China Sea have laid claim to a continental shelf and all resources thereon and thereunder. Since much of the southwestern and northern South China Sea floor underlies less than 200 m of water, these continental shelf claims overlap in many places. To make matters more complex, all countries bordering the South China Sea except China have also formally and unilaterally claimed exclusive economic zones (EEZs) extending up to 200 nmi from national baselines. Within such zones, nations claim sovereign rights for the

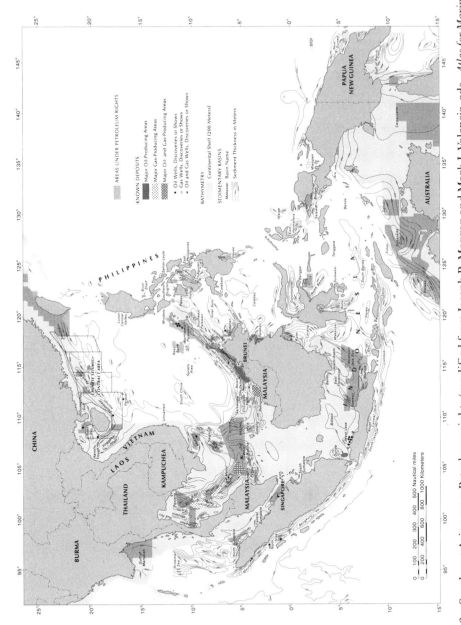

Figure 5.3   Southeast Asian seas: Petroleum rights (modified from Joseph R. Morgan and Mark J. Valencia, eds., *Atlas for Marine Policy in Southeast Asian Seas*, Berkeley: University of California Press, 1983, p. 104).

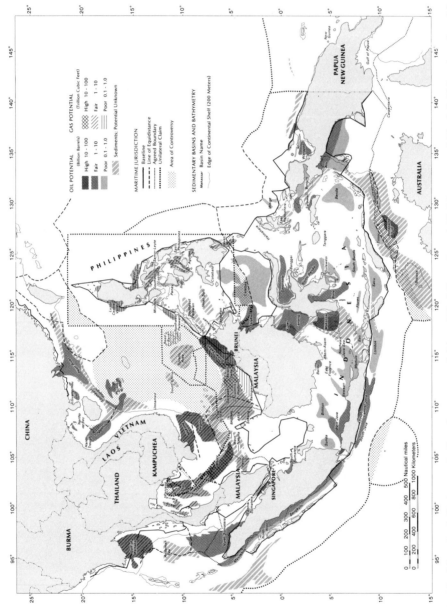

Figure 5.4   Maritime jurisdiction and oil and gas potential (modified from Joseph R. Morgan and Mark J. Valencia, eds., *Atlas for Marine Policy in Southeast Asian Seas*, Berkeley: University of California Press, 1983, p. 132).

purpose of exploring, exploiting, conserving, and managing living or nonliving natural resources; of the seabed and subsoil and the superjacent waters; and jurisdiction for marine scientific research and the preservation of the marine environment. The archipelagic claims of Indonesia and the Philippines, multiple claims to particular oceanic islands as bases for extended jurisdictional claims, and China's possible historical claim to much of the South China Sea all raise additional questions regarding marine boundaries in the region.

Potential hydrocarbon-bearing areas with overlapping claims include the eastern Gulf of Thailand (Thailand, Kampuchea, and Vietnam), the southwestern Gulf of Thailand (Thailand, Malaysia, and Vietnam), the area north, west, and east of Natuna (Vietnam, Indonesia, Malaysia, and China), offshore Brunei (Brunei, Malaysia, China, and Vietnam), the "Dangerous Ground" (Malaysia, Vietnam, the Philippines, and China), the northern Andaman Sea (Burma and India), the Gulf of Tonkin (China and Vietnam), and the Arafura Sea (Indonesia and Australia).

These countries rely on multinational capital, technical expertise, and equipment for offshore hydrocarbon development. While it is not feasible to estimate the precise effects of unresolved offshore boundaries on the progress of hydrocarbon discovery and development in the region, they are an important inhibiting factor. Multinational or extraregional government oil companies are unlikely to invest in hydrocarbon development in disputed areas, particularly if the dispute is potentially serious enough to threaten the security of their investment. Also, the conditions for exploitation and export of any oil found may differ markedly depending on which nation controls the resource. Thus, resolution of boundaries or muting of boundary disputes may be a prerequisite for development of any hydrocarbon resources in such areas, regardless of potential.[10] The following section reviews for each such area the hydrocarbon potential and unresolved boundary situation.

The Eastern Gulf of Thailand:
Thailand, Kampuchea, Vietnam (Figure 5.5)

The Thai Basin occupies the northern part of the Gulf of Thailand and is distinguished from the adjacent Malay Basin to the south by a marked difference in strike of its component element and by a difference in structural character. North-south linear features include, from west to east, the Chumphon Basin, the Samui Shelf, the Western Basin, the Kra Basin, the Ko Kra Ridge, and the thick Pattani Trough. The eastern part of the area is not well known, but named features include the Khmer Shelf, the Khmer Trough, the Central Basin high, and the 3-km (1.9-mi)-thick, north-south trending, pre-Tertiary Panjang Basin. The Pattani Trough contains more than 8,000 m of Tertiary sediments, which thin to a veneer eastward onto the Khmer Shelf and to less than 1,000 m to the west, within the smaller troughs of the western part of the Gulf of Thailand. The Thai Basin is gas-prone. Only the one field in the Thai Basin proper is presently producing, the Erawan structure of block 12.

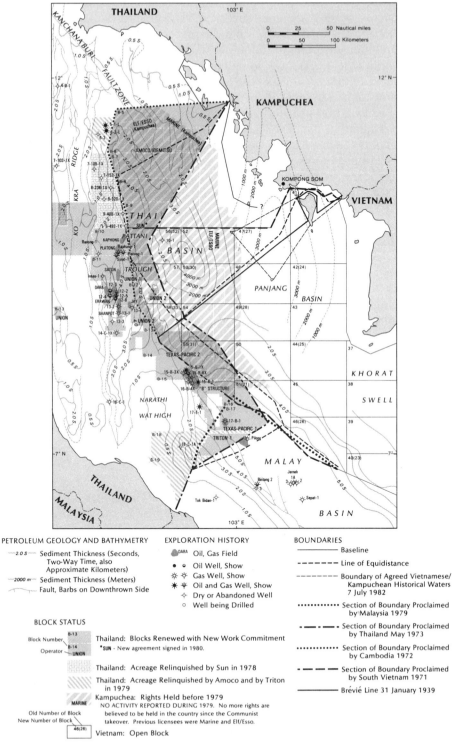

Figure 5.5   The Gulf of Thailand: Maritime claims and petroleum geology (modified from Joseph R. Morgan and Mark J. Valencia, eds., *Atlas for Marine Policy in Southeast Asian Seas*, Berkeley: University of California Press, 1983, p. 108).

Natural gas was first discovered in 1972 by the United States' Union Oil of Thailand, which now has eleven finds of natural gas with commercial potential. The second find was by the United States' Texas Pacific in "structure B" in 1974, increasing reserve estimates to 2.8 TCF. In 1979, Union found the smaller Kraphong and Platong structures, which are located near the route of the gas pipeline constructed between the Erawan field and Bangkok. In November 1980 Union discovered another field, Satun, 8 mi (12.9 km) northeast of the Erawan field. By January 1981 seventy wells had been drilled; natural gas had been encountered in thirty-five, and a small amount of crude, natural gas and condensate in five others. Total discovered reserves are now estimated to be 6.4 TCF.[11]

Kampuchea's only offshore wildcats to date were two holes drilled in 1974 by an Elf–Esso joint venture in which Esso held 35 percent interest. One well was abandoned for nontechnical reasons after a discovery was reportedly made[12] and one was suspended due to the boundary dispute between Kampuchea and Vietnam. In 1972, Elf Du Cambodge (65 percent) and Esso (35 percent) held 39,104 km² (15,099 mi²) in the gulf along the claimed Kampuchean western offshore boundary, thus overlapping with Thai concessions to the United States' Amoco, Sun, and possibly Union. In 1980, Sun and others negotiated a revised contract on their area in the disputed zone.[13] Marine Associates (Hong Kong) Limited acquired petroleum rights to 16,965 km² (6,550 mi²) in mid-1973 and undertook a marine survey in early 1974.[14] Oil exploration came to an abrupt end when Vietnam occupied Kampuchea in 1978.

Including claims of the former regimes, each of the three states has an overlap with each of the others, and each has one area that all three claim.[15] The nearly 6,000-square-nautical-mile (-nmi²) area of overlap between Thailand and Kampuchea includes the entire northern portion of the Pattani Trough and most of its eastern margin. A line of equidistance between Thailand and Kampuchea would give the northern margin of the trough to Thailand and the central-eastern portion to Kampuchea. Most, but not all, of Amoco blocks 5 and 6 would be within Thailand's shelf in an equidistance settlement. In May 1982 Kampuchea protested anew Thailand's granting to Amoco concession areas B-5 and B-6, which lie on Kampuchea's claimed continental shelf, and declared that "any foreign company which searches for oil on the Kampuchean continental shelf without Kampuchea's permission will be responsible for all consequences which may arise from their illegal actions."[16] The greater portions of Sun blocks 7, 8, and 9 would fall to Kampuchea. The Kampuchean boundary claim includes only the easternmost margin of the trough, although it does include gas-bearing Oligocene sediments.

The 14,580-nmi² area claimed by both Kampuchea and Vietnam includes an unnamed, hypothesized basin in the west and part of the pre-Tertiary Panjang Basin in the east. The area to the north that is indisputedly Kampuchean may contain an extension of this unnamed basin. The former or inactive Elf–Esso Kampuchean lease includes the entire unnamed basin, whereas the Marine Associates lease appears to be restricted to the area between the two basins. The Vietnamese lease block system entirely overlaps the Elf–Esso and Marine Associates leases in the area between the Thai claim line and the Brévié line. The Brévié line or an equidistant line slightly to the north appears to cut diagonally across the very core of the Panjang Basin; the equidistant line would give more of the basin, including part of this core, to Vietnam, and it would give the unnamed basin to Kampuchea. In July 1982 Vietnam and Kampuchea agreed on joint historical, internal waters that encompass the core of the Panjang Basin and where hydrocarbons will be developed by "common agreement."[17]

South of the Brévié line is a 233-mi^2 area disputed between Thailand and (South) Vietnam. The Kampuchean leases to Elf– Esso and Marine Associates also included almost all of this area extending considerably to the east, including the most prospective area for Marine Associates. The area is focused on the northern petroliferous, 6-km (3.7-mi)-thick Malay Basin. The Vietnamese claim includes much of the northern part and eastern margin of the Malay Basin, whereas the Thai claim covers the northwestern portion only. In addition to the former or inactive Elf-Esso and Marine Associates leases and the Vietnamese block system in this area, Texas Pacific has leases for Thai blocks 14, 15, and 16. The eastern portions are claimed by Vietnam, whereas the western portions of blocks 15, and 16 adjacent to the Vietnamese claim line are the sites of major gas discoveries, including the B structure. An equidistant line between Thailand and Vietnam would award most of the disputed area and northwestern section of the basin to Thailand.

The (South) Vietnamese claim line and block system also overlaps the western 3,610 nmi^2 of the Thai– Kampuchean disputed area extending to the Brévié line, thus including the eastern third of Union blocks 10 and 13. Union has recently been given the go-ahead by the Thai government to explore in these blocks.

The Southeastern Gulf of Thailand:
Thailand, Malaysia, Vietnam (Figure 5.5)

The area of focus is the extreme northwestern end of the Malay Basin, including an intermediate transition zone between the north-south Thai Basin and the northwest-southeast-oriented Malay Basin. Proven reserves of gas in this part of the basin are 1.3 TCF while proved plus probable reserves are estimated at 5.8 TCF.[18] Ten successful wells have been drilled in structure B located in Thai waters near the northwest extremity of the basin, and Texas Pacific discovered substantial natural gas deposits in its B-13x well in block 15 in 1981.[19] Texas Pacific also had a gas discovery (17-E-1) in block 17 in December 1980.[20] In addition to the Texas Pacific gas discovery, Pilong-1 well is also a major gas discovery; other promising structures are present in the area.

The extreme northwestern end of the Malay Basin is claimed in whole or in part by Thailand, Malaysia, and Vietnam. Although both Malaysia and Thailand agree on their boundaries extending some 50-odd km (31 mi) from land there, their respective boundary claims diverge north and south. The area of overlap is nearly a triangle situated northeast-southwest athwart the northwestern core of the Malay Basin with its apex pointing toward land. The overlap area includes the Texas Pacific gas discovery in 17-E-1. A line of equidistance between Thailand and Malaysia would extend even farther south than the Thai claim and include the gas discovery in Pilong-1. Assuming that the new Vietnamese government has not re-

linquished the 1971 continental shelf claim of South Vietnam, the Vietnamese
claim encompasses the northwestern tip of the area claimed by both Malaysia and
Thailand.

On 21 February 1979, both governments recognized that it was in their best
interests to exploit the resources of the seabed in the area of overlapping claims as
soon as possible and agreed to jointly explore and exploit the nonliving seabed and
subsoil resources in a defined Joint Development Area for fifty years and to share
equally the costs incurred and the benefits derived. During this time the countries
will continue to negotiate the boundary.

Thailand had given concessions in the area of overlap to Texas Pacific and in the
southwestern part to Triton 1. The Texas Pacific concession extends in the northwest into the area claimed by Vietnam. Thailand has extended Triton Oil Company of Thailand's exploration rights in block 18 in the Joint Development Area
for four years, but it has been prevented from undertaking further exploration
due to the boundary question.[21] Texas Pacific won the right to build a liquefaction
plant in anticipation of exports, but the price formula and management control
are in dispute. Petronas also has been granted the right to explore for mineral
resources in the area.[22] In December 1979 Malaysia gazetted maps of its continental shelf claims that, according to an April 1980 Thai *aide memoire* submitted to the
Malaysian Embassy in Bangkok, failed to take into account the Joint Development
Area. Vietnam also raised objections to the map.[23]

The Natuna Sea: Indonesia,
Vietnam, Malaysia, China (Figure 5.6)

The disputed area includes in the west the northeastern West Natuna Basin, in the
north the Khorat Subbasin, in the center the extension of the Natuna Arch, and in
the east much of the "South China Sea Block A, Eastern Part." The central portion
of the disputed area is an extension of most of the Natuna Arch where sediment
thicknesses are about 1 second (two-way reflection time, approximately equivalent
to kilometers of sediment) and thus unprospective. However, thicknesses increase
to 2 seconds across the arch in the northern part of the disputed area, offering
some possibilities.

In 1974, gas was discovered by the Dua well north of the Indonesian claim line.
The AGIP A1-1X gas discovery, approximately 250 km (155 mi) north-northeast
of Natuna Island, near the northern limit of the thick pod of Plio-Pleistocene sediments referred to as the outer basinal area, reported gas-in-place of 130 to 140
TCF, of which 80 percent is said to consist of inert gases, leaving 28 TCF. In late
1981 Conoco and Pertamina announced the discovery of "highly significant" natural gas in its Tembang-1 well in 85 m of water, flowing at 325 million cubic feet per
day (MCFD); the well is located in the disputed area.[24] In April 1982 Sumatera
Gulf Oil reported a significant discovery of high-gravity clean oil in its Anoa-1 well
in block A, flowing at 4,300 bbl of oil per day (BOPD) and 1.7 MCFD of gas.[25] Thus
the disputed area is divided east-west in terms of hydrocarbon potential into two
geologically distinct, unproven, relatively unknown, but prospective basinal ex-

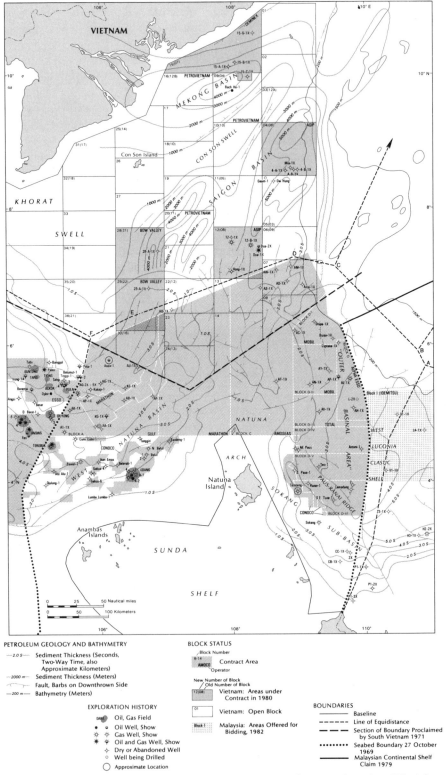

Figure 5.6   The Natuna area: Maritime claims and petroleum geology (modified from Joseph R. Morgan and Mark J. Valencia, eds., *Atlas for Marine Policy in Southeast Asian Seas*, Berkeley: University of California Press, 1983, p. 111).

tensions separated by an unprospective basement high. The eastern area appears gas-prone whereas the west appears oil-prone.

The area originally claimed by both South Vietnam and Indonesia measured 11,170 km² (4,312 mi²) and was bounded on the south by a unilateral continental shelf claim made by South Vietnam on 6 June 1971, and an equidistant line between the Indonesian archipelagic baseline and Vietnam.[26] Malaysia may eventually claim a portion of the South China Sea "Block A Eastern Part."

The South Vietnamese government fell in April 1975, and Indonesia and the new Vietnamese government have met six times. At first the new Vietnamese government adopted the position of the South Vietnamese government. Then it claimed that the deepest points of a trench extending from the northern coast of the Anambas Islands to an area just north of the Natuna Islands formed the effective boundary (the so-called "thalweg" principle), considerably expanding the disputed area. Then Vietnam dropped the thalweg principle[27] only to claim Natuna Islands itself as a response to Indonesia awarding a concession in the area to Marathon Oil Company.

Vietnam divided the disputed area into lease blocks, but the only blocks actually leased that encroached the area were to Canada's Bow Valley (block 29) and to Italy's Agip (block 12) in which the Dua discoveries were made earlier by Shell Oil Company. Indonesia included the area in its production-sharing block system. Holders of Indonesian contracts in the area include Gulf and Marathon (block A), Marathon (block B), and Amoseas (block C). Mobil, Esso, and Total hold D blocks immediately south of the disputed area.

Brunei: Brunei, Malaysia,
China, Vietnam (Figure 5.7)

Beyond the edge of Brunei's continental shelf, sedimentary thickness decreases into the South China Sea; however, there remains sufficient thickness within Brunei's possible offshore area to harbor hydrocarbons. The center of the extension of the Sabah Basin appears to straddle the 200-m isobath offshore Brunei.

Oil was first discovered in the onshore Miri Field in 1910; Seria, discovered in 1929, confirmed the existence of a major hydrocarbon province. Offshore fields include Baram, West Lutong, Baronia, Bakau, Bokor, Betty and Tukau in Sarawak, and Southwest Ampa and Fairley in Brunei.

Ultimate discovered reserves in the Baram Delta part of Sarawak are about 600 million bbl. Remaining reserves in Brunei are variously estimated at 1.3–2.0 billion bbl. Proven gas reserves are in the range of 7.7–10 TCF (1.28 to 1.67 billion bbl oil equivalent). No wells have been drilled near the edge of the shelf in the projected disputed area, although there was a gas and oil show in the Kinarut well in the same basin on the shelf edge in Sabah waters to the northeast.

Brunei became independent on 1 January 1984 and thus is entitled to claim an EEZ. Clearly, the maximum area EFGH in Figure 5.7 would be to Brunei's advantage even though more than half is in waters deeper than 200 m. An offshore area EL2L2H would encompass the thicker part of the Sabah Basin and extend little beyond the 200-m water depth. If Brunei were only able to retain areas CD and EL1L1H, thick sediments in accessible waters would be yielded to its neighbors.

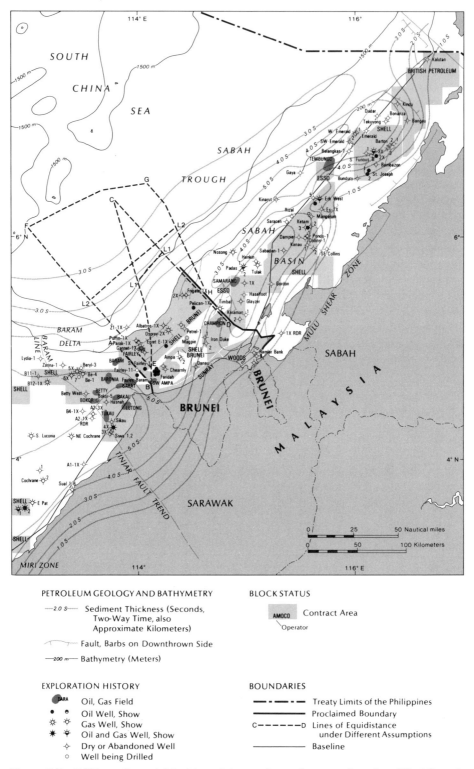

Figure 5.7   Offshore Brunei: Maritime claims and petroleum geology (modified from Joseph R. Morgan and Mark J. Valencia, eds., *Atlas for Marine Policy in Southeast Asian Seas*, Berkeley: University of California Press, 1983, p. 114).

The "Dangerous Ground": Philippines, Malaysia,
Vietnam, China, Brunei (Figure 5.8)

Little is known of the geology of this region. The irregular shoals, submarine plateaus, and small intermediate-depth basins have been interpreted as representing a foundered mass of continental crust. The crust beneath the shoal areas to the northwest of the basin, including Macclesfield Bank and the Paracel Islands, may also be continental. It is hypothesized that the Reed Bank–Calamian microcontinental blocks, possibly extending from the Luconia Shoals in the south to southwest Mindoro in the north, were rifted from the continental margin of China in Middle Eocene time and moved southward. Tertiary thickness of 4 km (2.4 mi) or more are known geophysically and from drilling. The thicknesses of Cretaceous and possibly Jurassic sediments may reach 5–6 km (3.1–3.7 mi) in the southeastern portion of Reed Bank.

In April 1976 a consortium led by the Salen Company of Sweden drilled Sampaguita No. 1 to 4,125 m on the Templer Bank. The well yielded 3.7 MCFD in the interval 3,150 m to 3,160 m from Paleocene sands deposited under deltaic conditions[28] but was plugged and abandoned. However, the well did confirm the existence of good source and reservoir rocks and a thick Tertiary sedimentary section under the Reed Bank.

Midway during the drilling operation the U.S. company Amoco farmed into 38.5 percent of the consortium and became the operator for the subsequent exploration activities of the group using a U.S.-registered drill ship. A geophysical survey revealed several large structures and Amoco drilled two more exploratory wells with the *Glomar Tasman* on the Reed Bank proper, A-1 and B-1. Both wells were subsequently plugged and abandoned as dry holes and Amoco resigned as operator on 15 March 1978. In May, with Salen Exploration Company as operator, a fourth test well, Sampaguita No. 2, was drilled, plugged and abandoned as a dry hole. Salen drilled a fifth well, Kalamansi No. 1, and on the Templer Bank with a carbonate barrier reef as the target. No carbonate buildup was encountered and the well was plugged and abandoned in December 1979. In November 1981 the Philippine government authorized Salen to drill Sampaguita No. 3 in the same area, with unpublicized results.

China, the Chinese province of Taiwan, and Vietnam all claim all the islands on the historical grounds that they have long been part of their territory. Maps published by Malaysia in 1979 showed its continental shelf claim in the southern part of the area enclosing islands and reefs, which they named Amboyna, Terumbu Mantanani, Terumbu Laksamana, Terumbu Layang Layang, Terumbu Semarang, Barat Besar, and Terumbu Perahu. Independent Brunei theoretically could claim an area extending almost to Louisa Reef or even a corridor extending through the Malaysian continental shelf and EEZ. Either claim would be certain to be disputed by Malaysia.[29] On 11 June 1978 President Ferdinand Marcos signed Presidential Decree 1576, which claimed the entire Kalayaan area for the Philippines; the Philippines also specifically claimed Amboyna Island.

In addition to the Reed Bank area, there may be hydrocarbon potential in the southern part of the region. While the Chinese isopachs depicted in Figure 5.8

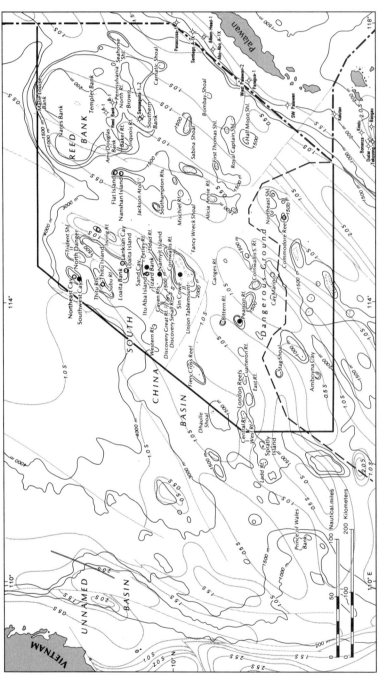

PETROLEUM GEOLOGY AND BATHYMETRY

—2.0 s— Sediment Thickness (Seconds,
Two-Way Time, also
also Approximate Kilometers)

Fault

—200 m— Bathymetry (Meters)

EXPLORATION HISTORY

✧ Gas Show

✧ Dry or Abandoned Well

BOUNDARIES

▪—▪— Treaty Limits of the Philippines

— — — Philippine Presidential Decree 1596; June 1978

—·—·— Malaysian Continental Shelf Claim

———— Chinese Regional Claim

○ Occupied by the Philippines

◇ Occupied by Taiwan

● Occupied by Vietnam

Figure 5.8   The Spratly area: Maritime claims and petroleum geology (modified from Joseph R. Morgan and Mark J. Valencia, eds., *Atlas for Marine Policy in Southeast Asian Seas*, Berkeley: University of California Press, 1983, p. 116).

must be viewed with some skepticism, they do indicate that the area claimed by both Malaysia and the Philippines includes some elongated sediment pods several kilometers thick and reefs such as Amboyna, Barque Canada, Mariveles, and Commodore, which are situated to be used as drilling platforms. There are also some sediment pods under the continental slope in presumed Vietnamese waters to the west of the Malaysian Shelf claim and along the continental margin off Vietnam.

The Gulf of Tonkin:
China, Vietnam (Figure 5.9)

The Red River fracture extends offshore into the Gulf of Tonkin where it finds expression as the northwest-southeast elongated, 60,000-km² (23,166 mi²) Yinggehai Basin in which 8– 10 km (5– 6 mi) of clastic Tertiary sediments may be present. North and northwest of Hainan, 4 km (2.5 mi) or more of sediments are present in scattered pods west of the Luichow Peninsula in the 20,000-km² (7,722 mi²) North Bay Basin.

In the Red River Delta of the Hanoi Trough, fourteen wildcat wells drilled onshore in Vietnam resulted in the discovery of nine favorable structures; rumors of minor production remain unconfirmed. Chinese crews have drilled five wells in the North Bay Basin and have made a total of nine discoveries in eleven wells drilled in the entire gulf. Six of eight wells in the eastern gulf in 1979 had flow rates of 4,400 BOPD of sweet crude. Chinese exploration teams discovered gas, and Total discovered oil in Wushi-16-1-1 about 14.5 km (9 mi) off the southwestern end of the Leizhou Peninsula. In July 1982 Total discovered oil in Weizhou-12-3-1 with tests in the interval 1,410– 1,421 m flowing 850 BOPD of 37° API crude.[30]

In the Yinggehai Basin, oil seeps have been observed at the sea surface for more than a century in more than forty locations over a 10-km² (3.8-mi²) area. A small quantity of oil was previously produced by shallow wells.[31] In September 1981 there was an unconfirmed report that Vietnam, in a joint exploration effort with the Soviet Union, made an offshore discovery west of the disputed sea boundary and Total China's exploration area. That November, China reported that it had found oil south of Hainan Island. In April 1983 Arco completed two wells south of Hainan, Yachen 8-2-1, which was dry, and Yacheng 13-1-1.[32]

In April 1973 Vietnam reportedly reached an agreement with ENI, the Italian state oil company, for exploration in the Gulf of Tonkin. On 18 January 1975 China agreed to hold negotiations with Vietnam at a later date but insisted that a rectangular area in the middle of the gulf, bounded by the 18° and 20° parallels and the 107° and 108° meridians, be kept free from exploration until the two countries could reach agreement on the delimitation of the gulf. Vietnam accepted this proposal for a "neutral" zone and suspended its negotiations or agreements with Japanese, Italian, and French oil companies for exploration of the gulf.

On 15 August 1975 Vietnam asserted that the 1887 Sino– French Convention of the delimitation of the frontier between China and Tonkin (Vietnam) made longitude 108°3′13″E the "sea boundary line" between the two countries in the gulf. In response, China stated that "the sea area here has never been divided, yet you assert that it has. You insist on drawing a dividing line close to our Hainan Island, so as to

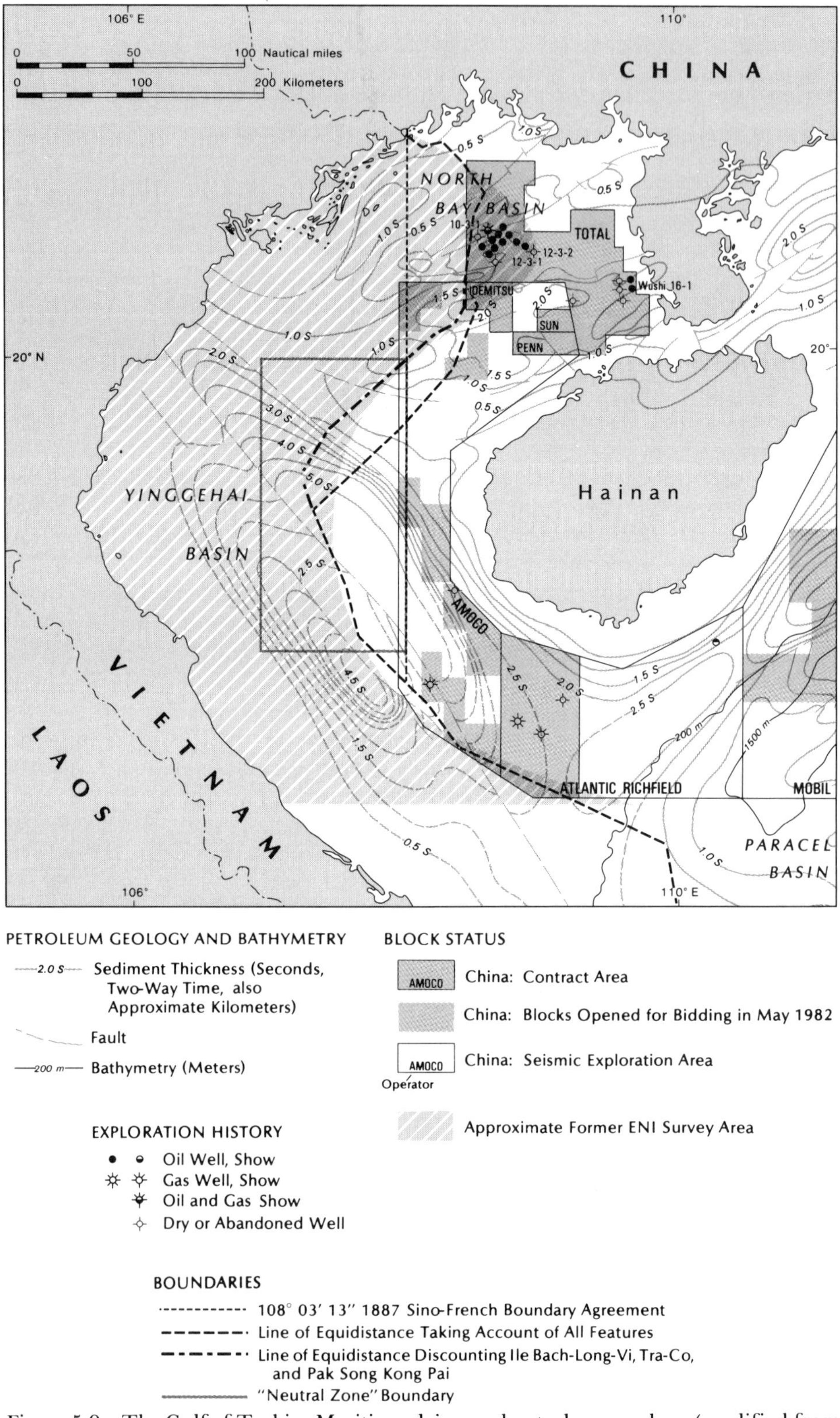
106° E
110°
0
50
100 Nautical miles
0
100
200 Kilometers
CHINA
NORTH
BAY BASIN
TOTAL
10-3-1
12-3-2
12-3-1
Wushi 16-1
IDEMITSU
SUN
PENN
20° N
20°
Hainan
YINGGEHAI
BASIN
VIETNAM
LAOS
AMOCO
ATLANTIC RICHFIELD
MOBIL
PARACEL
BASIN
200 m
1500 m
106°
110° E
PETROLEUM GEOLOGY AND BATHYMETRY
2.0 S
Sediment Thickness (Seconds, Two-Way Time, also Approximate Kilometers)
Fault
200 m
Bathymetry (Meters)
EXPLORATION HISTORY
Oil Well, Show
Gas Well, Show
Oil and Gas Show
Dry or Abandoned Well
BLOCK STATUS
AMOCO
China: Contract Area
China: Blocks Opened for Bidding in May 1982
AMOCO
Operator
China: Seismic Exploration Area
Approximate Former ENI Survey Area
BOUNDARIES
108° 03′ 13″ 1887 Sino-French Boundary Agreement
Line of Equidistance Taking Account of All Features
Line of Equidistance Discounting Ile Bach-Long-Vi, Tra-Co, and Pak Song Kong Pai
"Neutral Zone" Boundary

Figure 5.9 The Gulf of Tonkin: Maritime claims and petroleum geology (modified from Joseph R. Morgan and Mark J. Valencia, eds., *Atlas for Marine Policy in Southeast Asian Seas*, Berkeley: University of California Press, 1983, p. 116).

occupy two-thirds of the Beibu Gulf (Gulf of Tonkin) sea area. Being neither fair, nor reasonable, this is unacceptable to us." Vietnam apparently was using the principal of natural prolongation of the continental margin to claim Vietnamese jurisdiction over the shelf up to China's 12-nmi territorial sea boundary.[33]

The Sino–Vietnamese border war began on 17 February 1979 when Chinese troops crossed into Vietnam along traditional land routes of invasion. In the subsequent Sino–Vietnamese peace talks, China was apparently prepared to share the area "half and half." Vietnam maintained its position that the 1887 Sino–French Convention defined both land and sea boundaries.

China's July agreement with a consortium of Western oil companies (led by Amoco and believed to include Cities Service, Pennzoil, Union Oil, Agip, and British Petroleum as original participants) for seismic survey work off the west coast of Hainan Island was drawn with a western boundary of 108°E so as not to breach the "neutral" zone. It is the nearby 108°3′13″ meridian, however, that Vietnam claims as the "sea boundary line" in the gulf. Indeed, on 10 September 1979 Vietnam accused China of signing contracts with Western companies for offshore "exploration" in what it called "disputed areas" in the Gulf of Tonkin and thus violating the 1979 agreement. On 16 November the U.S. company, Amoco, and its partners began seismic work for China in the Gulf of Tonkin. The work was completed on 18 March 1980. On 19 September 1982 China signed its first drilling contract with an American company, Atlantic Richfield, awarding rights to exploration and production in a 3,500-km² (1,351-mi²) tract south of Hainan Island. Of thirty-five foreign oil exploration companies involved in this round of bidding, twenty were U.S.-based. In November 1982 Vietnam claimed as historic internal waters[34] the waters west of the longitude stipulated in the 1887 Convention.

The intersection of the northeast-southwest diagonal line of equidistance with the 108°3′13″ meridian produces two main disputed areas arranged in the shape of an hourglass: one northwest and another directly west of Hainan. The latter disputed area is expanded if the line of equidistance discounting Ile Bach-long Vi is claimed by China. China has offered areas for bidding that are situated well west of the median line including the Amoco survey area in the south and northwest; one concession even extends 1.9 km (1.1 mi) west of the meridian to the edge of the neutral area.[35] The disputed area in the north encompasses the central portion of the North Bay Basin and parts of three concession areas being offered by China for bidding. Adherence to the meridian as the boundary would transfer much of the prospective basin to Vietnam.

The southern disputed area encompasses part of the central-eastern core of the Yinggehai Basin. The line of equidistance discounting Ile Bach-long Vi expands the portion of the basin that might be claimed by China and perhaps not coincidentally follows closely the margin of the former survey area let to ENI by Vietnam. Chinese concessions opened for bidding stop at the meridian except for one, which extends 1.9 km (1.1 mi) west of it.

The so-called neutral area is mostly unrelated to lines of equidistance or to the shape of disputed areas, being a rectangle that encloses much of the central and northern portion of the Yinggehai Basin and most but not all of the southern disputed area, including the area expanded by considering the line discounting Ile

Bach-long Vi. The southeastern tip of the disputed area in the very center of the basin is not included in the neutral area.

The Northern Andaman Sea:
Burma, India (Figure 5.10)

In 1973 the Burmese government invited foreign oil companies to explore offshore. After spending three years and US$120 million the companies left with neither oil nor gas discovered in the marginal areas they were given to search. In October 1978 the Burmese national oil company, Myanma (MOC), invited bids for exploration licenses offshore in blocks previously reserved for the government. No bids were received, apparently because of a lack of geologic attractiveness, a lack of confidence in the government, and the conditions of the licenses.

Previous drilling offshore Burma included twenty-nine wells, seventeen by foreign companies, and twelve by MOC. The Burmese block system covers the more than 7,000-m-thick Andaman Sea Basin in waters mostly less than 1,500 m. Most of blocks M-11 through M-18, however, are in waters deeper than 1,500 m. Although drilling on the outer Burmese continental shelf has been unsuccessful, 6CC-1 and 3CA-1, 2, 3 on the inner shelf yielded gas discoveries of about 21 MCFD. Also, gas was discovered in the region in AN-1-1 by India off the east coast of South Andaman Island near Port Blair.

Pressed by substantial shortfalls in onshore oil production in 1982, Burma has resumed its offshore exploration for oil and gas in the Gulf of Martaban, this time with the financial and technical assistance of Japanese companies led by the semi-government Japanese National Oil Company. Two test wells were sunk in shallow water off the Irrawaddy Delta in blocks M-2 and M-3 where well 6CC-1 discovered gas. At a later stage, wells may be drilled in blocks M-14 and M-15 off Mergui.[36] The area of overlap is on the southern parts of the Burmese shelf and includes part of Burmese blocks M-8, 9, 11, and 12. The equidistant line ignoring the unusual Burmese baselines would give India parts of blocks M-12, M-9 (formerly of Esso), and M-8, and all of M-11. Block 11 was actually leased to Esso Exploration Company and M-11/A-1 was drilled in an area claimed by India. An equidistant line using the baselines would still give India most of block M-11 and part of blocks M-9 and M-8. All of block M-11 and most of blocks M-8 and M-12 are in waters deeper than 200 m, and half the southern parts are in waters deeper than 1,500 m.

The Arafura Sea:
Indonesia, Australia (Figure 5.11)

In the area between Indonesia and Australia there are four major basins of interest: Browse, Bonaparte Gulf, Timor, and Arafura. Three significant gas discoveries — Petrel 1, Tern 1, and Penguin 1 — were made in the early 1970s in the salt dome province of the Bonaparte Gulf Basin. In the Browse Basin, Scott Reef 1 was drilled in 1971 in the lagoon of Scott Reef atoll on a large anticline. Gas was discovered in Lower to Middle Jurassic and Upper Triassic sandstones and carbonates.[37] Brecknock 1 in 1980 on the Scott Reef trend in 544 m of water confirmed Browse Basin as

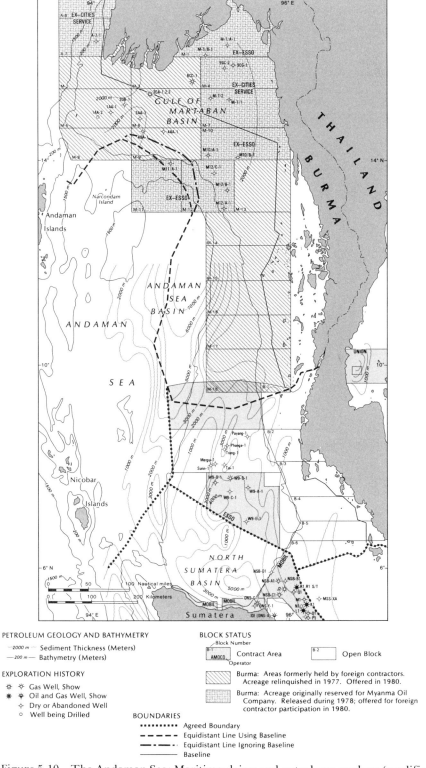

Figure 5.10   The Andaman Sea: Maritime claims and petroleum geology (modified from Joseph R. Morgan and Mark J. Valencia, eds., *Atlas for Marine Policy in Southeast Asian Seas*, Berkeley: University of California Press, 1983, p. 118).

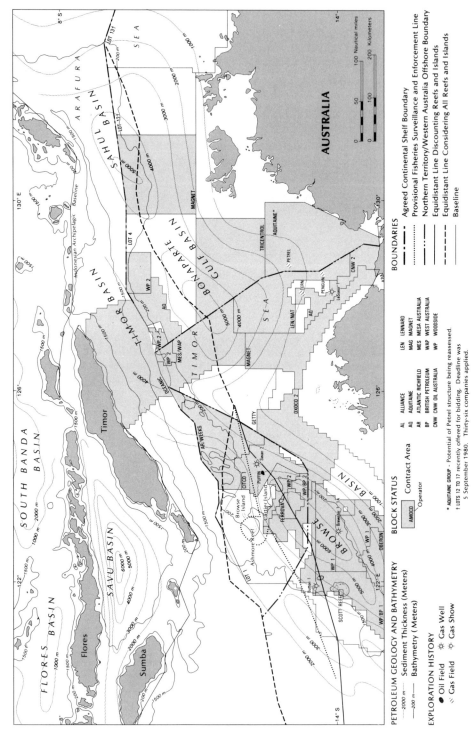

Figure 5.11 The Arafura Sea: Maritime claims and petroleum geology (modified from Joseph R. Morgan and Mark J. Valencia, eds., *Atlas for Marine Policy in Southeast Asian Seas*, Berkeley: University of California Press, 1983, p. 119).

a gas-bearing province. This was the world's deepest-water production test at that time.[38] In 1980 Buffon 1 was drilled in 720 m of water in the northern part of the basin with good gas shows.[39] In June 1982 the Woodside group reported a gas discovery in North Scott Reef 1, with a flow of 26–45 MCFD. Little is known of the petroleum potential of the Timor Basin; it is considered poor, yet the basin is one of the foci of the boundary disputes. The area of dispute is approximately 21,600 nmi^2 out of the 2,000-m isobath.[40]

The closure in the Arafura Basin is divided about one to two in Australia's favor by the agreed continental shelf boundary. An equidistant line would have reversed these proportions. The Magnet Petroleum Company was awarded a contract by Australia in 1979 that extends across an equidistant line to the agreed shelf boundary.

The "Timor gap" presents an interesting problem because it includes two prospective basins, Bonaparte Gulf and Timor. The equidistant line would cut the core of the Bonaparte Gulf Basin's closure in a two to one proportion in favor of Australia. A continuation of the agreed continental shelf boundaries to close the "Timor gap" would place the entire basin in Australian jurisdiction. Several holders of Australian contracts have claims beyond the equidistant line.

The Timor Basin would be completely within the Indonesian "shelf" if the equidistant line were to become the agreed boundary. If the middle of the Australian margin is used as a guide to complete the "gap," a small portion of the core of the Timor Basin would accrue to Australia; Australia has leased some of this portion for exploration. Former Portuguese Timor has leased the area extending to the hypothetical "gap" connection and thus the bulk of the basin to Oceanic Petroleum Company. Almost all of this area is in waters deeper than 200 m, however, and the central half is in waters more than 1,500 m deep.

The Browse Basin situation is also complex. The most important area is that west of the western terminus of the 1972 agreed boundary at point A25 south of Pulau Roti and directly north of Ashmore Island. If the boundary becomes the equidistant line taking all islands into account, Australia gets the entire basin. If the boundary becomes the equidistant line that discounts all the islands, then the northern third of the basin would fall under Indonesian jurisdiction, including the Swan 2 gas discovery and the Puffin oil discovery. If the Provisional Fisheries Surveillance and Enforcement Line becomes the shelf boundary, Australia would get the bulk of the basin including the oil and gas discoveries and Ashmore Island. Much of the extreme western part of the basin is under waters deeper than 200 m. Only Australia has let contracts in the area. The United States' Cities Service company area is the site of the discoveries; it extends beyond both the equidistant line discounting islands and the Fisheries Line. Atlantic Richfield-Weeks holds acreage extending north of the Cities' lease to the agreed shelf boundary.

THE ISSUES AND INTERNATIONAL RELATIONS

Competition between the Soviet Union and the United States for influence in the region, Chinese–Vietnamese tensions, the Kampuchea issue, and the Soviet–U.S.–China triangular relationship affect these disputes. Vietnam is involved in all of the multiple claim areas in the South China Sea. The Soviet Union, an ally of Vietnam, has signed an agreement establishing a joint venture for exploration and exploitation of hydrocarbons from the continental shelf of southern Vietnam. China and the ASEAN countries are seeking total withdrawal of Vietnamese troops from Kampuchea. The Soviet Union's invasion of Afghanistan in December 1979, its military buildup in the Kuriles off Japan, pressures for martial law in Poland, and the downing of a Korean airliner in September 1983 have hardened Western attitudes toward the Soviets and fostered a convergence of interests among the United States, China, and Japan. This has raised concerns in ASEAN capitals about a broadening of the Sino– U.S.– Soviet conflict into the rest of Southeast Asia. The United States is an ally of the Philippines and Thailand and a good friend of the other ASEAN countries, and now China. U.S. oil companies hold concessions in all of the multiple claim areas except the Spratlys, and Amoco in particular is or was involved in exploration in almost all of the multiple claim areas.

The Kampuchea issue is dampening the negotiation process in the eastern Gulf of Thailand, the Natuna area, and the Spratly area. In the eastern Gulf of Thailand it is no accident that drilling activity has followed the constraints of the basin configuration and the edge of the Kampuchean and Vietnamese claim lines. Indeed, the Kaphong structure extends about 5 percent into the Vietnamese and Kampuchean claim area. For that reason, the Petroleum Authority of Thailand planned to ask Union to delay exploitation of natural gas in that structure and to recommend to the industry minister that any gas found there be excluded from international pricing negotiations.[41] The Thai government reportedly applied to the World Bank for a loan to develop the structure itself, but the application was rejected on the grounds that development of hydrocarbons there might lead to international conflict.[42]

In September 1981 Vietnam submitted a proposal through Laos to the United Nations indicating that if ASEAN agreed to deal with Indochina as a bloc, disputes with Malaysia (Amboyna) and Indonesia (Natuna area) over the maritime boundaries could be settled promptly.[43] In the Natuna issue, after five negotiating sessions it was supposedly understood that Indonesia would have jurisdiction over areas contracted to American oil companies since 1970 that are currently exploring or developing known gas reserves (West Natuna Basin). Under this arrangement, Vietnam would have obtained the northeastern portion of the overlap (the South China Sea Block A Eastern Part), which could bolster its claim to the Spratly Islands vis-à-vis that of China and the Philippines. Clearly the two sides were getting closer to a solution and the area in dispute was diminishing, although the northeastern portion remained a problem. Then Indonesia allowed Esso Exploration to take over the Agip concession and guaranteed protection to the company if attacked.[44] Other contract areas in the disputed area were transferred to Marathon and Mobil, also U.S. oil companies.

On 29 November 1981 the Vietnamese Foreign Ministry issued a statement regretting Pertamina's 20 March 1979 invitation for exploration bids in Natuna Blocks A, B, C, and D-1 to D-6 and stated that "foreign companies should pay attention to this matter and should not conduct survey and exploration operations in the disputed area without Vietnam's consent. Any corporation which disregards Vietnam's interests must be held responsible for the consequences arising from its act."[45] As of December 1981 three American oil companies — Amoseas, Gulf, and Marathon — were exploring in the disputed area under production-sharing contracts with Pertamina despite the warning by Vietnam. Thus U.S. companies are exploring on behalf of Indonesia for hydrocarbons in an area claimed in part by Vietnam. Vietnam is being assisted in the offshore exploration of its southern continental shelf by the Soviet Union.

In the Gulf of Tonkin it would appear that China has played the U.S. card in granting contracts to U.S. oil companies for exploration in the areas bordering the disputed claims. U.S. companies are locked out of Vietnam's undisputed claim areas by Washington's trade embargo. The involvement of U.S. firms in and near the Vietnamese claimed areas in the South China Sea effectively merges U.S. and Chinese interests in the event of a flareup of the dispute, and it also preempts Hanoi's hope of wooing U.S. oil companies to aid Vietnam in its offshore oil exploration there. Indeed, Vietnam charged that "by signing such contracts with Western companies China also tries to seek their support for its piratic acts and then to share the profits with them." Vietnam warned that it would resolutely defend its sovereignty over its natural resources and that "Western companies that cooperate with China in the disputed area will share responsibility with China for whatever consequences may ensue."[46]

If large numbers of U.S.-controlled work boats and rigs were operating in the waters around Hainan, some guarantees of security would be necessary — a situation that is an open invitation to the re-entrance of U.S. naval forces into the Gulf of Tonkin.[47] China conducted the seismic surveys on behalf of Amoco in two of four blocks because Amoco and its fellow partners refused to conduct operations in blocks that were likely to be contested by Vietnam. In July 1979 two oil-rig supply vessels were fired upon by a Vietnamese gunboat, and Amoco's surveys west of Hainan were postponed by Beijing.[48] Further trouble followed. These incidents culminated in August 1982 with China rejecting a Vietnamese proposal for a six-week truce along their border, charging deliberate Vietnamese provocations. An Australian newspaper reported that the *Glomar Java Sea* was "blown up" by Vietnam.[49] The Soviet Union, which is now searching for oil on behalf of its ally Vietnam, and the United States, on behalf of its oil companies, could be brought face-to-face in an area disputed by two ancient and bitter enemies.

In the Spratlys, oil is but one factor in the disputes. The Spratlys are considered strategic as bases for sea-lane defense, interdiction, surveillance, and possibly for launching of land attacks. Involved are the security interests of outside powers — Japan, the United States, and the Soviet Union. For China the oil factor is only one element in a more comprehensive Chinese effort to consolidate a position of regional primacy. China, in making far-reaching boundary claims, is not necessarily serving notice that it actually intends to undertake oil development within the entire area claimed but may be motivated by a desire to corner oil development rights as a bargaining weapon in influencing the foreign policy of the other littoral states.

This seemingly innocuous area bears the seeds of open hostilities. The Chinese province of Taiwan, Vietnam, and the Philippines have forces stationed in the area. China has no force stationed in the Spratly Islands nor is it likely to send troops to take control of them unless provoked overtly or a grave situation such as war occurs. However, once it is able to provide fighter cover for operations there, China may seek to dislodge militarily the garrisons maintained by Taiwan, the Philippines, or Vietnam[50] as it did the South Vietnamese in the Paracels in two days in 1974.

Burma has avoided entering joint ventures with foreign companies because of the fear of foreign economic domination. The need for oil has altered this policy; the joint venture between MOC and the Japanese consortium is the first of its kind. The United States, perhaps partially driven by interest in the petroleum resources, has responded to an easing of Burma's rigid neutrality policy with an economic aid program to Burma started in 1980.

India's most recent invitation to prospect for crude oil received a cold response due to the world oil glut, and it is now seeking advice and cooperation from the Soviet Union. India, however, has demonstrated a willingness to cooperate with neighbors in adjacent or overlapping claim areas, an agreement having been signed between the Oil and Natural Gas Commission and Ceylon Petroleum Corporation for a study of prospects in the Palk Strait area. Relations between India and Burma have been cool recently. Prime Minister Gandhi's planned visit to Burma in 1982 was postponed due to protocol snags.[51]

Australian–Indonesian relations have been disturbed by Australia's initial rejection and then grudging acceptance of Indonesia's military annexation of Portuguese Timor and then by Radio Australia's broadcasts in Indonesian to Indonesia of information critical of the Indonesian government and the subsequent outrage and retaliation by Indonesia. Relations will not be improved if new Labor Party Prime Minister Hawke implements two Labor Party resolutions—one calling for suspension of military aid to Indonesia until Jakarta withdraws its troops from East Timor and the other to upgrade bilateral relations and resume economic aid to Vietnam.[52] Many Australians view Indonesia as a restless, volatile, and expansionist neighbor, possibly dangerous to Papua New Guinea, Australia's former colony. The Indonesian government feels Australia is interfering in its domestic affairs.[53]

RESPONSES TO BOUNDARY ISSUES

The following responses have been used singly or in combination by the states involved in these areas of unresolved boundaries. They represent a continuum of low to high degrees of cooperation. A state may

- Occupy the area, either expelling, or defending against, forces of other claimants;
- Unilaterally undertake or license exploration and eventually exploitation in the area;
- Verbally and symbolically maintain the claim while stalling or maneuvering diplomatically for support;
- Refuse to negotiate in conjunction with any of the above;

- Take no action and ignore the actions and verbiage of other claimants;
- Negotiate directly or through intermediaries to resolve the boundary dispute in conjunction with any of the above; or
- Set aside the boundary dispute and agree to jointly explore and exploit any hydrocarbon resources there.

What factors influence the degree of cooperation? The character of the basic relations between the disputants is an important spur or retardant to dispute resolution. Thailand and Malaysia as members of ASEAN found the task of joint development relatively easy because of the ASEAN spirit. Malaysia and the Philippines may find agreement on their overlap in the Spratlys relatively commodious if the Sabah issue does not become linked to it. Similarly, one might expect Kampuchea and Vietnam to reach accommodation in their area of overlap. Burma and India in the northern Andaman Sea and Indonesia and Australia in the Arafura Sea also are likely to resolve their differences. Indonesia and Vietnam in the Natuna Sea and Malaysia, the Philippines, and Vietnam in the Spratly area have tenuous but not openly hostile relations and are at least discussing the problems, although the Kampuchea issue clouds the talk schedule. China largely ignores Malaysian and Philippines claims and actions in the Spratly area in its present interest to cultivate good relations with these countries. However, the general relations between China and Vietnam do not bode well for their disputes in the Gulf of Tonkin, the Paracels, and in the Spratlys. Similarly, although somewhat less tense, Thailand on one side and Vietnam and Kampuchea on the other have difficult relations, with troops facing each other along a common border.

Some states are preoccupied elsewhere either geographically or politically and thus relegate ocean space disputes to secondary importance. For example, Vietnam, Kampuchea, and Thailand do not seem overly concerned with the eastern gulf, and all the claimants in the Spratlys except the Philippines seem preoccupied elsewhere. This may be ominous because the lack of attention could lead to surprises and sudden reactions to actions of other disputants.

The military capability of a disputant may become a factor if tension levels become high. China has in the past chosen and could again choose to exercise its military power to settle disputes with Vietnam, this time in the Gulf of Tonkin and in the Spratlys. Similarly, Indonesia is capable of exercising military might if its relations with Vietnam reach such a point in the Natuna area. And of course it has been demonstrated that Vietnam feels militarily confident to use force in pursuit of its objectives. The remaining Southeast Asian entities are either not capable or do not have the taste for full-scale hostilities without superpower backing, despite belligerent noises from some of them.

The need for oil from the disputed areas, although strong, varies somewhat in degree of urgency among the countries in the region. For Vietnam, the Philippines, and Kampuchea, which have virtually no oil production, the hydrocarbon potential in or near disputed areas is almost the only opportunity that they have to produce indigenous oil. The rest of the countries involved have adequate if not ample potential in clearly undisputed areas.

The degree of knowledge of deposits in disputed areas is also important. If little or nothing is known of hydrocarbon potential, it may be easier to divide a disputed area than if some deposits are already known to exist there. In the latter case each side would be afraid of giving something away. Hydrocarbons are known to exist in the Arafura Sea, the Natuna area, in the Gulf of Tonkin, in the Thai–Malaysian area, and in the Reed Bank portion of the Spratly area. Little or nothing is known of the actual hydrocarbon potential in the southern portion of the Spratly area or in the eastern Gulf of Thailand.

The more these factors reinforce each other in a negative manner, the greater the likelihood of a low-cooperation response such as unilateral action to occupy the disputed area and expel or defend against the forces of other claimants or unilateral licensing or exploration. These low-cooperation responses have been used in the region more frequently than the high-cooperation alternatives.

The Thai–Malaysia Memorandum of Understanding of 21 February 1979 is an example of a high-cooperation alternative, an agreement on the extent of the disputed area, the setting aside of the actual boundary question, and joint exploration and exploitation of hydrocarbons in the area of overlap. It is the first of its kind in the South China Sea, although in February 1983 the charter had still not yet been adopted because some clauses did not have full agreement.[54] There has been some practical difficulty in integrating the different laws of the two countries, particularly on royalties and personal income and corporate taxes. But the differences causing the delay are more fundamental. Both of the prime ministers who supported and signed the Memorandum of Understanding were no longer in office shortly afterward, Kriangsak through resignation due to political opposition and Hussein Onn by resignation due to ill health. In both cases the new prime ministers have significantly different styles and priorities. Kriangsak has been attempting a political comeback and the delay in implementation of the memorandum may be designed to embarrass Kriangsak or at least prevent him from using it as an example of achievements during his tenure.

There have been rumors alleging Thai foot-dragging due to a strong private interest lobby in the Thai government, which holds the view that Thailand should hold out for a larger area or should simply split the area and be done with it. The latter position is based on some evidence that the major discovered gas deposits are on the Thai side of an equidistant line, but Thai experts are not certain that there are no large deposits on the Malaysian side of an equidistant line.

Thailand may also be reluctant to move ahead because of the Vietnamese claim to part of the Joint Development Area and the fear that complications over such boundary claims might be linked to the present border difficulties as well as to boundary disputes in the eastern gulf. But the major factor in the delay is Thai governmental instability and the unwillingness of the politicians to risk their political futures by being involved in a scheme that may fall out of favor with the next change of minister or government. Nevertheless, the shortfall of gas expected to be piped ashore from Erawan and the resultant disruption of development projects may be putting pressure on Thailand to establish its production-sharing formula and to move ahead with joint development.[55]

At the Third United Nations Conference on the Law of the Sea (UNCLOS III), China proposed incorporation of a clause on the continental shelf suggesting joint development as an interim alternative to boundary resolution, and China and Japan reportedly have explored such a scheme for the Senkaku area.[56] There are precedents for such joint development arrangements for the area between Iceland and Jan Mayen,[57] in the Persian Gulf, and on the Japanese–Korean continental shelf.[58] Indeed, relevant provisions of the Convention on the Law of the Sea (CLS) stipulate that pending agreement on the delineation of the continental shelf–exclusive economic zone boundary, "the states concerned, in spirit of understanding and cooperation, shall make every effort to enter into provisional arrangements of a practical nature and, during this transitional period, not to jeopardize or hamper the reaching of the final agreement."

Such arrangements could include joint exploration and development of hydrocarbon deposits in the area of overlapping claims. In the eastern Gulf of Thailand, joint development might be feasible between Vietnam and Kampuchea, but for Thailand and western companies, the Vietnamese occupation of Kampuchea presently precludes such an arrangement. Joint arrangements between Vietnam and Thailand and between Vietnam and Indonesia are possible eventually, but there may be formidable difficulties in finding purchasers of long-term supply contracts. Joint arrangements might indeed be feasible for Burma and India, and for Australia and Indonesia, if complications arising from Australian state versus federal authority can be overcome. The Chinese– Vietnamese dispute in the Gulf of Tonkin seems closer to open conflict than to cooperation. Perhaps one of the best candidates for joint development would be portions of the Spratly area. If Vietnam and the Chinese province of Taiwan could somehow be excluded from the Spratly issue, China, the Philippines, and Malaysia could undertake joint exploration there, perhaps in areas farthest from Vietnamese-claimed islands.

Perhaps the strongest reason for a state's opting for a joint undertaking would be its sense of urgency or obligation to protect its interests in potential oil or gas deposits combined with a desire to maintain good relations with another state with an equally valid claim to the area. Joint development is an idea whose time is coming and that will look increasingly attractive as the need for oil intensifies. Because exploration already is occurring in some areas of overlapping claims, a meeting of countries bordering the South China Sea is urgently needed to discuss possibilities of joint development and other solutions to the problems.

CHAPTER 6

SHIPPING
George Lauriat

Fundamental to the development of the region, shipping is an important feature of life in Southeast Asia. Modern Southeast Asian countries face a number of important decisions concerning shipping policy, some of which are brought about by expanded jurisdictions over marine space legitimized by the Convention on the Law of the Sea (CLS). Designation of archipelagic sea-lanes and control of ship-generated pollution in territorial seas and exclusive economic zones (EEZs) are two issues on which policy decisions must be made. Other problems were with developing nations long before the United Nations Conference on the Law of the Sea (UNCLOS) began deliberations. Examples include cargo reservation rules proposed by the United Nations Conference on Trade and Development (UNCTAD) and development of national shipping conferences.

This chapter provides the historical background for addressing these issues and reviews the current status of shipping in the region and in the world in general. Trade with countries outside Southeast Asia exceeds intraregional commerce, consequently an analysis is presented of the views of important maritime powers on shipping policy issues of interest to Southeast Asian states.

HISTORICAL SHIPPING TRADE

Present shipping patterns throughout Southeast Asia descend directly from ancient intraregional and global trade routes. Traditional sailing craft have long chartered their way through the Indonesian archipelago. Chinese traders in junks followed the monsoonal trading routes of their forebears, and when everything else failed there was always piracy. Trade between the West and China started centuries ago when Western merchants first reached Cattigara in southern China. This set off a wave of travel between the two empires, with China providing silk and Roman envoys providing silver, gold, and trade objects. This was the beginning of the trade and tribute system used by China until the late Ching dynasty in the 1800s. The tribute system

188

was based largely on the pretense that the traders represented nations and hence gave tribute to the empire. In actual fact they were simply trading.[1]

The apex of the tribute system came with the seventh and final voyage of the "five-jeweled eunuch," Cheng Ho, in 1405 when with a fleet of sixty-two ships carrying 37,000 men he sailed through the Strait of Malacca, across the Indian Ocean, and into the Persian Gulf, demanding tribute from more than forty states along the way. With the coming of the Mongols, interest in shipping waned, but the tribute system and the legacy of trade remained. In the 1500s the tide turned, and it was the Western world's turn to dominate sea trade in Asia.

The Portuguese took the initiative, displacing the Moors who previously had monopolized trade between East and West. The Portuguese founded the city of Macau in 1557 and for nearly a century controlled trade among China, Japan, and Europe. The Spanish king, with Papal blessing, declared that Spain was the ruler of the sea, igniting competition among the English, Dutch, and Spanish for control of the world's sea-lanes and thus for control of world trade.[2]

The British set up the East India Trading Company, "Old John," in 1600 and gave the company a monopoly over trade to the Far East. The Dutch followed two years later, forming the Dutch East India Company.[3] Each had fairly standard manning practices, ships, and procedures and thus they were in many ways the forerunners of the modern transnational shipping company.

Both companies faced the problem of trade imbalances. For the Dutch East India Company there was only gold and silver to pay for the goods bought in Canton. The trade was balanced somewhat by opium, but the opium that was shipped from India could only come once a year because of the monsoon. Also, the opium clipper, because of its small size, was suitable for carrying bullion and opium but not general cargo.[4] The opium clippers plying year round put an end to "Old John's" monopoly.

The British empire, forged by unsurpassed sea power, stretched nearly around the world by the end of the Napoleonic wars. Sea power had decided the decisive battles, and sea power guarded the trade routes that brought critical supplies to the island fortress. But the nature of sea power had changed considerably during the three centuries of British ascendancy that started with Sir Francis Drake and reached its climax with Nelson at Trafalgar. Men-of-war were now just that—ships whose sole purpose was war—while merchant ships were becoming more and more specialized. Commerce was now the key consideration, and trade with the Far East was rapidly becoming the key to English commerce. Graceful clippers were built to carry small quantities of tea at high speeds, colliers were built stoutly to move coal, and grain ships were designed specifically to move grain.

This trade specialization called for special shipping institutions to handle its problems. The first to be institutionalized was marine insurance. The concept of insuring a ship against the perils of the sea probably dates back to the Phoenicians, but it took "Pax Britannica" to make insurance international. It started at Edward Lloyd's Coffee House in the 1600s. Knowing that many of his customers were in need of marine insurance, Lloyd began publishing shipping information that would help them in their work. The patrons that went daily to Lloyd's formed a committee and began underwriting marine insurance. An individual member of Lloyd's would underwrite a policy and distribute the risk within a syndicate or group of associates using guidelines that had been agreed on by the committee. By 1871 Lloyd's was formally incorporated by an Act of Parliament and was the dominant organization in the field of marine underwriting. Lloyd's *Register of Shipping* also grew out of the same coffeehouse clientele. In 1760 a group of marine underwriters who were gathering regularly had formed a committee to issue a register giving the details of ships likely to be insured. The first register in 1764 included an assessment of each ship's condition by the vowels A, E, I, O, or U in descending order. Added to this was the letter G, M, or B (good, middling, bad) for the state of the equipment. This register became known as the Green Book and was regarded as confidential.[5] The insurance market branched out further, and associations known as "P and I" (Protection and Indemnity) clubs were formed in Britain from 1855 by shipowners for mutual protection against risks for which they were not covered by ordinary insurance.

The creation of the insurance industry was soon followed by the creation of the Baltic Exchange, where shipowners and buyers and sellers of commodities could meet and set up voyage charters. Thereafter came international conventions, such as The Hague rules that redefined the obligations of shipowners, and countless other small accords that form the basis for modern shipping practices. These rules and procedures were essentially British and Western in concept, because Britain, the world's largest shipbuilder and operator, was the trading center. This Western dominance has persisted. British expeditions charted navigational routes and hazards around the globe and made them available to the merchant fleets of the world. There was no legal or political reason for other maritime nations to follow the lead of the British legislation, but the regulations on seaworthiness, safety, and navigation were eminently practical. The result was that Britain set the standard.

The Victorian age of invention forever altered the face of shipping. Commercial shipping in 1900 was entirely different from that of 1830. The span of one lifetime brought iron and steel, steam and diesels, opened the Suez Canal, introduced the telegraph, and within a few years added the wireless and the Panama Canal. In no place was this change faster than in the Far East.[6] The Europe-to-Asia route was the most demanding on ships and men, and it was extremely important commercially. Any innovations that would cut down the time and losses and increase the profit were of interest to the enterprising shipowners who dominated the route.

Steamers started operating in the Far East in the 1840s, but the tremendous distances and the lack of coaling stations did not allow their general use. Some very fast steamers with small cargo capacities did carry opium and bullion over short routes in the Far East. But it was predominantly the era of clipper ships, especially the tea clippers making their runs through the Moluccas. The major change came with the 1867 opening of the Suez Canal, which drastically reduced transit times.[7] The reduction of the distance and the establishment of coaling stations along the canal made the steamer viable.

Although Western shipping institutions and technology had a profound effect on how trade was conducted, the real power of shipping belonged to a dozen shipowners in Europe (mostly Great Britain) and the Far East. These shipowners controlled the flow of trade from the upper reaches of the Yangtze River, to the Strait of Malacca, through the Suez Canal, to the Isle of Dogs (London). The shipowners on the Far East–Europe trade route quickly adopted the steamship, which was faster, carried more cargo, and could keep a regular schedule.[8]

Yet like the disastrous overordering of tanker tonnage before the 1973 oil crisis, shipowners overordered steamers. The overordering was compounded by a downturn in Far Eastern trade and the development of large iron sailing vessels. These vessels, unlike the tea clippers, could carry as much cargo as the steamers and had smaller operating costs; the wind was free. During the period of depressed rates these sailing ships could afford to wait for cargo, since they were not tied to any fixed schedule.

The situation was exacerbated by the persisting imbalance in East–West trade. Up until 1870 Britain's imports of tea and silk were financed largely by the sale of opium. This meant that there was little outward-bound cargo and heavy return cargo. Tea was seasonal, and for half the year shipowners had to try to fill their ships with whatever cargoes were available in Singapore, Malacca, and to a lesser extent Japan. This situation was not very satisfactory to the merchants who shipped in the region, since there was no stable tariff or regular schedule.

Into this situation of overtonnaging and depressed freight rates stepped John Swire, better known as "the Senior." To Swire and other shipowners the only solution to the problem of overtonnaging and erratic rates was to form some type of liner association. In 1875 the Calcutta Steam Traffic Conference was formed, but without a rebate system it was unable to hold shipper's loyalty and the loyalty of the member shipowners. Within another two years the situation was becoming critical, and a rate war seemed in the offing. Swire cajoled, convinced, and ultimately threatened a majority of the steamship operators into an agreement called "The Agreement for the Working of China and Japan Trade Outwards and Homewards." The seven companies that signed this agreement—the forerunner of today's Far Eastern Freight Conference (FEFC) were P & O; Messageries Maritimes de France; Ocean Steamship; Glen Line; Castle Line; Shire Line; and Gellatly, Hankey and Sewell Company. This collection of one French and six British lines came to dominate international shipping.

The creation of a freight conference, particularly one based on the principle of rebates to shippers to guarantee loyalty, was not received enthusiastically by shippers in the Far East. It was created by Western shipowners for Western shipowners, without concern for the interests of shippers. The conference was tested in court in the Mongul and the Secret Rebate cases. The Mongul case was dismissed by the House of Lords in 1891, thus establishing that a conference was not an illegal monopoly and that the rebate system is a legitimate system for securing shippers' loyalty. It also institutionalized the right of action by the conference against outsiders. Thus it established the ground rules between the conferences and outsiders at an early stage in the life of conferences.

After the Mongul challenge the conference system became stronger and by 1897 included the Straits Outward and Homeward agreements covering the trade among the straits settlements of Singapore, Penang, and Malacca. For most owners this region simply provided the cargoes necessary to fill out a ship. During the 1890s, however, the additional feeder services that connected many small trading stations with the main entrepôt trade at Singapore provided enough cargo to make the straits agreements valuable in their own right.

It was against this background that the most serious complaint against the conference system was launched. The attack on the conference was led by John Anderson, then head of the powerful trading firm of Guthrie and Company. The essence of the dispute revolved around the relationship between the conference and six merchant houses that also acted as freight agents. These firms controlled nearly two-thirds of the export trade from Singapore, and as shipping agents they represented fifteen of the twenty-three conference lines serving the region.

What upset Singapore and Penang merchants was not the standard 10- percent contract rebate that was given to shippers but an alleged rebate of 5 percent on the total freight that was given as a bonus to the six companies: Bousteads, Gilfillan Wood, Behn Meyer, Paterson Simons, Huttenbacks, and Brinkmans; the Borneo Company was added later.[9] The local shipping companies believed that this bonus, or secret rebate, offered an unfair competitive advantage to merchant houses that were already dominating the export trade. A commission set up in Singapore in 1902 found in favor of the shippers, and this led to a Royal Commission of Inquiry in 1909. The conference had argued strongly that the "justification for the rebate was the giving up by these firms of large profits from chartering."[10] This chartering could very well have been in competition with the conference, which made the rebate look more like a bribe than a bonus.

The Royal Commission agreed with the Singapore Commission that there was a problem (although taking a somewhat different view of the source of the problem), and in 1910 the freight agents' rebate was abolished and the freight agents were paid off for whatever losses the ruling might have caused. As a result of the abolition of the secret rebate, freight agents either were brought directly in-house or became third parties between the shippers and the lines. The role of the middlemen was thus defined by the ruling, although the arbitrariness of the original decision to offer the six lines a rebate was lost on succeeding generations.

After the Royal Commission sorted out the secret rebate in 1910, the conference — and the old order—was firmly in place. Although it was always possible for an Indian or Chinese merchant to do well in the trading business, shipping was an entirely different story.[11] Because of the conference, international shipping in the Far East was a members-only club, a situation that was to persist until well after World War II. Asian shipowners were left with the old intraregional trade.

SHIPPING IN SOUTHEAST ASIA: PROBLEMS AND PRACTICES

Four of the five original Association of Southeast Asian Nations (ASEAN) — Indonesia, Malaysia, the Philippines, and Singapore — have gained full independence only within the past four decades.* Initially shipping was of minor importance to these newly emergent nations, because there were other more pressing problems. This situation changed rapidly after the formation of ASEAN in 1967. International shipping had changed a great deal from the end of World War II to the early 1960s. The technology, the trade, and even the style of shipping had undergone an enormous transformation.

The technological changes of the 1960s were nearly as great as those that had occurred in Asia during the 1880s. There were hundreds of tankers from the Arabian Gulf plying the Strait of Malacca destined for a newly rebuilt industrial Japan. It was obvious even to the fishermen in the *kampongs* along the strait that with each passing year the tankers were getting bigger and bigger. Tankers increased in size from a 1960 average of 20,200 deadweight tons (DWT) to a 1973 average of 56,300 DWT. Moreover, very large crude carriers (VLCCs) became a standard class, increasing in number from none in 1965 to 125 eight years later.[12] It was a technological explosion, and the countries bordering the through-routes in the region, particularly the Strait of Malacca, were part of it, willingly or not. The increase in the number of transiting tankers was accompanied by the oil boom in Indonesia and Malaysia and by the growing conflict in Vietnam. Southeast Asia found itself in the midst of a shipping boom over which it had little control.

Even after the founding of ASEAN and the resulting increased regionalism, all of the member states had different maritime priorities. The lack of uniformity in ASEAN's approach to maritime questions was due largely to the varied geographical, historical, and economic nature of the individual states. A review of the shipping developments in the individual ASEAN states during the 1970s will illustrate the point.

Indonesia

Indonesia's maritime development has been heavily influenced by the country's unusual geography. The nation is composed of more than 13,000 islands and has about 650 ports. In order to knit the country together economically, shipping — particularly interisland shipping — is a national necessity. Shortly after independence President Sukarno nationalized what shipping assets the Dutch had left behind; those became the basis for companies such as the national flag carrier, Djakarta Lloyd.

The chief problems have been that the ports and ships serving the interisland trades are inadequate and that the main international ports, Surabaya and Tanjungpriok, are far off the principal steamship routes. Development of ports and the fleet has been slow and difficult. The ocean-going fleet increased from 47 ships totaling 438,930 DWT in 1973 to 1,557 ships totaling 3.26 million DWT (excluding

---

*Brunei became the sixth nation to join ASEAN when it achieved full independence in 1984. Thailand is also a member.

thirty freighters of 86,700 DWT owned by private nonshipping companies). Indonesia has four national flag carriers of which one, PT Jakarta Lloyd, is state-owned. The company operates a fleet of more than 20 vessels totaling 180,360 DWT to Europe, North America, the Far East, and Australia. It dominates the regional and international trade of the country. In 1977 the national fleet share of the Indonesia–Europe traffic was 50 percent; in the Hong Kong–Indonesia service it was 55.3 percent. Although the Indonesian fleet is inadequate for the country's needs, it carries a significant portion of the nation's trade. In 1980 Indonesian flag vessels carried 20 million tons of cargo, of which 16.8 million tons were on domestic routes.[13]

With more than 300 ports in more than 900 occupied islands, control over trade and smuggling has been difficult. That is understandable, since traditional trade routes are much older than and transect the national boundaries, and the attitude in the region has long been that once a ship clears a national port what it does next is its own business. Indonesia has attempted to control this problem by reducing the number of ports open to foreign trade to sixteen and by establishing special ports for loading commodities such as oil and timber. In many respects this move only institutionalized the problem of smuggling. For example, flag vessels in the timber trade from a particular country may have found it more convenient to compensate local officials for the possible awkwardness that the presence of their ships might cause them than to proceed to the official ports. The national cabotage act passed in 1969 backed up this distinction of foreign and local ports by stating that "the right of domestic sailings shall not be given to foreign flags."[14]

Because the Indonesian government has had difficulty controlling trade, its shipping laws are among the most discriminatory in all of Asia. Foreign shipping lines operating in Indonesia must appoint a local shipping company as their agent. For the ten-odd shipping companies operating in Indonesia this means that they have to appoint a local competitor to secure business. In addition, the foreign shipping company is likely to have to back this system up by placing one of its own employees in Jakarta as the owner's representative.[15]

In keeping with the general cabotage policy, the country has a number of cargo reservation schemes. The agreement between Singapore and Indonesia is a 55-percent/45-percent split with the figures reversed on the opposite leg. The Tug and Barge Law, which restricts foreign flag tugs and barges from operating in Indonesian waters, is an extension of the cabotage policies. This legislation was aimed at securing more of the offshore oil support vessel business for Indonesian companies, largely at the expense of Singapore operators. More recently, the Indonesian government has by presidential decree required that all imports and exports under its direct control must go on domestic lines.[16] The impact of the decree on foreign shipping in Indonesia could be enormous, because the government has a hand in a large number of the imports and exports. It is estimated that it will directly affect 40 percent of the imports and 10 percent of the exports. These figures do not include shipments of crude oil and petroleum products, which are largely shipped on foreign flag vessels.

Like the Tug and Barge Law, the decree was not well received by other nations. The United States sent a diplomatic note protesting what it described as blatant flag discrimination. The decree had an almost immediate impact on trade, with two U.S. flag vessels carrying materials supplied or purchased under U.S. aid programs and one Eastern European vessel delayed in unloading as a result. West Germany retaliated by requiring all Indonesian ships loading cargo in West Germany to obtain a permit at each stop. The decree was coupled with a ruling that foreign shipping companies could no longer discharge cargo loaded in Japan, Singapore, or Hong Kong at Tanjungpriok but must take it to Cakung, an inland container base and godown complex (warehouse). Foreign shipping reacted to this ruling by making Pusan or Chi-lung the first port of call, and thus not labeling the voyage as a Singaporean, Japanese or Hong Kong service.[17]

The port system in Indonesia is relatively inefficient, and congestion, damage, and pilferage are common. The major port of Tanjungpriok, located just outside Jakarta, is the most important port in the international and regional trades, handling 50 percent of the country's imports and 10 percent of its exports. In 1971 the port was experiencing pilferage on a massive scale and tremendous congestion of goods quayside. The "Team of Walisongo" was appointed to clear the mess, and by 1974 some degree of order was restored. The team had to remove people who were living in and around the facility.[18] In 1972, the first year of the cleanup, the port cleared 3,872,196 tons of cargo. By 1974, the first year that partial container operations had started, the figure was 5,395,586 tons. Since that time the port has averaged around 5.5 million tons per year.[19] The container terminal, which is composed of two quays with two container gantry cranes, has increased its throughput from 3,920 20-foot equivalent units (teus) in 1974 to approximately 97,000 teus in 1981. The terminal was partly financed by a World Bank loan of US$16.2 million, out of a total amount of around US$80 million. It is estimated that the current capacity for the port is 120,000 teus. It is expected that the port will be handling 18 million tons of cargo by 1990, of which 22 percent will be containerized.[20]

The introduction of containerization to Tanjungpriok has been rife with problems. Initially there was only one access road that was too narrow for two vehicles to pass side by side without a detour into the ditch. People also chose to ignore traffic lights and other safety devices, and foreign shipping companies do not want to use the facilities at Cakung, the inland container station, if they can avoid doing so. Containerization is not always the answer. Many port officials in Asia have expressed anxiety over the reduction in labor that containerization causes. This reduction in labor is particularly difficult to justify to a population that can see no direct benefits from containerization, since the additional goods handled are often luxury consumer goods.

Fleet expansion in Indonesia has taken two courses. One method was the conventional system of subsidies and government incentives, and the other was through the state oil company, Pertamina. Both have experienced the numerous pitfalls that building a fleet can entail.

Pertamina began building up its fleet in the early 1960s when the then director general, Ibnu Sutowo, arranged the purchase of a number of tug and supply vessels and later coastal tankers from a Swiss financier, Bruce Rappaport. Most of these vessels were secured on hire-purchase agreements whereby Pertamina was obligated to pay regular charter fees but at the end of a period of ten to twelve years would own the vessels. In the early 1970s Pertamina, through various agreements, chartered thirty tankers from foreign companies. They were worth a staggering US$3.3 billion, payable over a period of up to twelve years. Pertamina, which had been rolling over short-term debts for a number of years, was in no position to pay the charter fees. The tankers themselves were nearly unemployable. This set off a legal confrontation that stretched around the globe and was not settled until 1977 when it was agreed that Indonesia would pay US$150 million on Rappaport's fourteen vessels (which had claims of US$1.55 billion), with the first US$75 million down and the rest in installments.[21]

The ensuing analysis of Pertamina's plight never really broached the question of just how good or bad the tanker deal would have been if it had gone as planned. The reasoning was that if Pertamina had its own tankers they would generate (or at least save) foreign exchange, create more employment, and allow greater control over the flow of oil. It was hard to argue for the acquisition along purely economic lines because the amount of employment created by the tankers was small, and Indonesian seamen could do better serving on flag-of-convenience ships. Moreover, Indonesia simply did not have either the ports or the shipyards to accommodate large seagoing tankers. A 1974 Pertamina reference book acknowledged that "Not always the economic factor affects the development of the fleet, but the local conditions on which Pertamina is responsible for the stability of supply of fuel oil throughout Indonesia has a vast reaching impact."[22] Unfortunately, economic factors have a great deal to do with the employment of tankers.

The tankers that Pertamina had on charter were generally 20 percent more costly than others on the market. As Rappaport later argued, there was more risk in Indonesia and that meant there had to be more profit. However, assuming that the tanker market had not crashed in 1974, would the additional thirty tankers have been a good deal? Probably not. Thirty tankers were far in excess of the country's needs for oceangoing tonnage. The only port that could handle the tankers was Cilacap, and the only route on which they could have been usefully employed was from the Middle East to Indonesia. As Seth Lipsky wrote:

> It wasn't only the size that bothered them. They were also concerned that the vessels weren't being used to carry Indonesian oil on the high seas. Instead they concluded, Pertamina had made speculative commitments in the hopes of profiting on the spot tanker market. In most cases, particularly with the Rappaport vessels, the Indonesians alleged that the commitments had been made when the market was to its peak and instead of going up, it had gone down — disastrously so. Indeed, when most of the Rappaport vessels were launched and went on hire to Pertamina, they were laid up straight away.[23]

If it were really Pertamina's intention to put its tankers on the spot market, it erred badly, for even in the best of times more fortunes were lost than were ever made on that sort of speculation.[24]

Indonesia has attempted to coordinate the expansion of its fleet through the establishment in 1974 of PT Pengembangan Armada Niaga National (PT PANN).

PT PANN, a state-owned holding, buys vessels from domestic and foreign ship-yards to lease or sell to domestic shipowners. With a US$54 million loan from the World Bank, PT PANN has supplied Indonesia with fifty-four ships totaling 97,893 DWT. Most of Indonesia's purchases come from abroad, because its ship-building and ship repair industry is still in its infancy. The country has seventy shipbuilders, most building ships of less than 200 DWT and none building larger than 5,000 DWT. In addition, the country has a dockyard repair capacity of 137,000 DWT, with fourteen floating docks, twelve graving docks, two side trade docks, and one repair basin. The largest repair dock is PT Dok Dumai, which is owned by Pertamina and is capable of repairing tankers of up to 20,000 DWT.[25]

Malaysia

Malaysia traditionally has been faced with the problem of shipping its agricultural products to a predominantly European market. Yet most of Malaysia's ports were built on shallow, mangrove-lined rivers that were not deep enough to accommo-date ocean-class trading vessels, and the road and railway network was very poor. Thus Malaysia's shipping industry was dominated by its southern neighbor, Singa-pore. It supplies both the feeder ships necessary to collect goods and the major port big enough to ship them. With the split between Malaysia and Singapore in 1965, however, Malaysia was forced to develop its own shipping industry.

Malaysia's reaction was threefold: first, it attempted to build up its own national fleet; second, it built up a port structure that could break the reliance on Singapore as the transshipment center; and third, it supported these moves with laws restrict-ing the use of foreign flag tonnage on Malaysian routes.

The national flag carrier, Malaysian International Shipping Corporation (MISC), was founded in 1968. MISC is 51 percent government owned, with an-other 10 percent held by various government agencies; the remaining 39 percent is privately held.[26] The principal aim of the company was to provide enough tonnage to enable the country to save valuable foreign exchange while providing a service that could show a profit. The ultimate aim of the company and Malaysian shipping in general was to provide enough tonnage to secure 40 percent of its trade, in keep-ing with the 40–40–20 cargo sharing provisions in the UNCTAD Liner Code de-scribed later in this chapter.

The company has been very successful in building up its fleet. After only six years of operation the fleet had fifteen vessels of 420,000 DWT, and by the end of 1982 it had expanded to forty-four vessels of 1.4 million DWT. Under the Fourth Malaysian Plan, the fleet is scheduled to expand to ninety vessels of 2.5 million DWT by 1985.[27] With the launching of the new state shipping company, Perba-danar Nasional Shipping Line (PNSL), this ambitious target might be met.

In order for MISC to secure the liftings in Europe necessary to make the com-pany commercially competitive, it joined the FEFC. This was not a popular deci-sion with Malaysian shippers, since they had hoped the line would run an indepen-dent service. In many respects, MISC has had a difficult time steering a steady course between the expectations of Malaysian shippers, the Malaysian government's own estimation of a national flag carrier's responsibilities, and the rules and regulations of the FEFC.

A collision between the Malaysian shippers and MISC was predictable from the start. MISC's need for the conference liftings in Europe inevitably meant that MISC had to quote FEFC freight rates, follow FEFC policies, and to some degree support the FEFC in its negotiations (now called consultations) with the shippers. It meant sitting across the table from the very shippers whose advice caused the shipping line to be created in the first place. In addition, shippers in Malaysia probably have had the most difficult dealings with the FEFC of any country in the region. A majority of the cargo is bulk, and thus low revenue generating and mostly agricultural, and this presents seasonal and storage problems.[28]

The fights with the FEFC have been severe. MISC's presence in the conference did not automatically entitle the line to all the lifting rights it desired. Lifting rights in the FEFC are decided by the Inter-Group Agreement (IGA). Malaysian shipping policy has always been aimed at securing 40 percent of the trade — which is saying that MISC should be lifting 40 percent of Malaysia's trade rather than the current 24 percent. The battle between the FEFC and MISC came to a head in 1981 when MISC secured the rights to call at ports in South Korea, the Chinese province of Taiwan, and the Philippines, and to load and discharge directly at various Scandinavian ports.[29]

MISC has on occasion had difficulty in fulfilling the government's expectations of its national line. In 1977 MISC ordered five 130,000 cubic meters (m³) liquefied natural gas (LNG) carriers worth US$800 million from three French shipyards. Unfortunately, Petronas, Mitsubishi, and Esso were still arguing over the Bintulu LNG project contract for which the ships were intended. As a result of setbacks at Bintulu, the ships were due to be launched before the project was to start. In the case of less capital-intensive enterprises that might be acceptable, but at a cost of US$120 million each, losing approximately three years out of an expected fifteen-year lifetime for the ships is nearly a disaster. Three of the LNG carriers came out of the shipyards in 1981 and went directly into lay-up in Norway. Never before has a developing state shipping company ordered such expensive tonnage and blundered quite so badly.[30] However, the experience shows the importance of coordination between the various government agencies putting together a project that has a shipping component, especially in dedicated trades such as LNG where there is virtually no hope of alternative employment for the vessels.

Perhaps the most controversial aspect of Malaysian shipping has been the cabotage policy, which allows only Malaysian flag vessels to ship goods from one Malaysian port to another. This ruling was aimed at putting the trade between east and west Malaysia solely in the hands of Malaysian shipping companies. The government encouraged the formation of Malaysian shipping companies by giving twenty-four-year tax holidays and exemption from income tax for trained seamen on international voyages. The system has not worked as planned. In 1980 the cabotage law stated that there were three types of licenses — permanent, provisional, and temporary. Of the 300-odd ships initially registered, 200 were under temporary licenses, mostly owned by Singapore-controlled companies. With the tremendous influx of ships into a route that is worth only 1.3–1.5 million tons of cargo per year, most of the ships found themselves sailing only half full.[31] In 1980 the Domestic Shipping Licensing Board (DSLB) issued 120 licenses for ships carrying dry cargo on the coastal trades. Of the 120 licenses, 95 were issued to Malaysian companies. The government complained that "vested interests in Singapore and to a lesser extent from Hong Kong and Japan were making use of Malaysian shipping companies."[32] Given the historic trading patterns, that is not surprising.

The key to Malaysia's international shipping effort has been the development of the country's ports. All of peninsular Malaysia's major ports — Port Kelang, Penang, Malacca, and Port Dickson — are located on the Strait of Malacca and thus are in competition with Singapore. Also, most of the ports are built on river estuaries. Piles must be driven very deep in order to reach any load-bearing material, and there is the constant problem of silting. The development of Port Kelang, Malaysia's major port, illustrates clearly the impact that the mix of politics, geography, history, and technology has on shipping in Malaysia.

Port Kelang started as a tiny backwater port up the Kalang River. It moved to its present site as a result of the building of the Selangor railway across the Kelang River to the south side. This led to the siting of the port on the river mouth. Port Swettenham, as it was then called, came into operation in 1904 and acted as a secondary port to Singapore.

The decision to turn the port into a major shipping center was taken in 1960 — after independence but before the separation of Singapore — when M\$30,850,000 (US\$13,130,000) was appropriated to build 760 meters (m) of wharves and four transit sheds and to reclaim 10 hectares (ha) of land. The port was officially opened in 1963, and it was thought that it would be adequate until the situation could be reviewed again in 1967. However, the separation of Singapore in 1965 and the almost overnight explosion in container shipping totally altered the situation. It was imperative for Malaysia to build a national port to replace Singapore, and it had to be able to accommodate containers in order to attract the FEFC shipping lines.[33]

The new port was designed to have two 275-m quays serviced by two container gantry cranes. Shortly after construction began, however, the shipping lines released information that the new "third generation" containerships would be 290 m long and draw 31.1 feet (ft) of water. This meant that the terminal stood a good chance of being obsolete even before it was completed.[34]

Although the alterations to the port were relatively simple from an engineering point of view, they required more money. In order for the Malaysian government to justify the loan to cover the unexpected expenditures, it needed some concrete evidence that the port was going to be worth it. The FEFC lines had refused to commit themselves to direct calls to the port — partly out of uncertainty that the facilities would be adequate but more out of the belief that the split between Malaysia and Singapore was not permanent and that Singapore was the best port of call for the Strait of Malacca area.

The Malaysian government decided to tip the scales by declaring that Port Kelang would be the main national container terminal for the Far-East-to-Europe route. This convinced the FEFC operators that the port would become Malaysia's main port of call. The terminal was completed in 1973 and handled 41,887 teus. By 1980 it was handling over 130,000 teus, with that volume expected to rise to 216,000 teus by 1985. Ship calls on the port have risen from eight per month in 1974 to nearly fifty in 1980.[35]

The Philippines

The Philippines has more than 7,000 islands and thus, as in Indonesia, interisland shipping is critical to the economy of the country. Building a fleet and services has been difficult. The Philippines has been more dependent on foreign shipping than any other ASEAN nation except Thailand. The trading pattern of the Philippines is different from that of its ASEAN neighbors in that a majority of its international trade is with the United States rather than with Europe.

In 1974 the Philippine government organized the various maritime bodies into one bureau, the Maritime Industry Authority (MARINA). MARINA's basic job was to design and implement a program that would build up the fleet and port structure so that it would be able to handle a substantial percentage of Philippine trade within the general context of the 40–40–20 UNCTAD Liner Code.

In 1979 the country had 620 vessels of 2,380,420 DWT registered under its flag. The interisland trade has around 242 of these vessels of about 300,000 DWT. It is estimated that more than 54 percent of the interisland fleet is overaged, and that during the current decade 180 vessels will have to be added to the fleet.[36] The Philippine government has attempted to build up the interisland fleet by making vessel acquisition easy. The government policy allows Philippine shipping corporations (defined as companies in which Filipinos hold 60 percent of the issue capital) to charter foreign flag tonnage provided it is managed and operated by Filipinos. The country also has passed legislation exempting the shipping industry from the customary 10-percent *ad valorem* duty and the 7-percent compensating tax on purchases of second-hand vessels. Owners are also compensated for purchases of spare parts and have a tax holiday until 1985.[37]

The government of the Philippines also has tried through legislation to secure a greater cargo share for Philippine flag vessels. Exporters in the Philippines are allowed to deduct from their taxable income the amount of overseas freight expenses and charges in Philippine ports provided the shipments are made on Philippine vessels. The country also has legislation stating that Philippine government cargoes must go on Philippine flag vessels.[38]

Perhaps the most controversial piece of maritime legislation in the country was the recent plan to implement the 40–40–20 UNCTAD Liner Code on the U.S.–Philippine route first and later on other international routes.[39] Under the ruling, Philippine flag vessels would be entitled to 40 percent of the trade, the trading partner 40 percent, and third parties the remaining 20 percent. The proposed plan got a bad reception in the United States and the Organization for Economic Cooperation and Development (OECD), and to a degree at home. The United States warned that it might retaliate with a limitation of sailings and suspension of tariffs for carriage. The OECD also complained that the proposed cargo reservation was discriminatory and pointed out that the order excluded cargoes financed by the Philippine government. The United States wants the legislation deferred until a bilateral agreement can be reached. However, with the United States in the midst of re-examining its own legislation and with Philippine flag carriers lifting less than 20 percent of Philippines' trade, there is a limit to the Philippine willingness to wait for a larger share.

The cross traders, mainly the Japanese, are also perturbed by this unexpected turn of events. In the case of Japan, it is thought that the nondiscriminatory provisions within the Philippine–Japan Treaty of Friendship, Commerce, and Navigation might forestall a head-on clash. The legislation is also under attack at home, since exporters in the Philippines fear that the move will result in increases in freight rates and possible import duties. The Philippine government has countered that it is willing to consider a larger share for U.S. liner operators. A larger share of the 40–40–20 split could be obtained by pooling. A trading partner, entitled to a 40-percent share, could pool its service with a third flag operator (who is entitled to 20 percent) and thus achieve a larger slice of the UNCTAD pie. However, in the case of U.S. lines, this pooling might be in violation of antitrust legislation, putting U.S. operators at a disadvantage.

Despite the Philippines' more than adequate legislation, it has not been successful in operating in the international market. In 1981 the Philippines International Shipping Corporation (PISC), created as a competitor to the FEFC, collapsed. The company was formed in 1978, primarily to compete against conference lines by charging lower rates. The idea received strong backing in the Philippine government, and the company received credits and tax incentives. Nevertheless, the company failed because in the end it could not match the service of foreign operators, even though it could match the price. The failure severely damaged Philippine aspirations in shipping.

PISC was not the only Philippine shipping line that has had problems. National Galleon Shipping, the national flag carrier and often considered the Philippines' most successful operator, was forced to sell a number of its vessels because it had not gained the revenue that it anticipated. This also hurt the Philippines' image, because the government is the major shareholder in the company.[40]

The Philippines has attempted to build up its shipbuilding sector with supportive legislation. The shipyards are exempt from import duties and taxes on equipment imported for use in the shipbuilding and ship repair industry. The government also provides funds at 3 percent per annum for foreign purchases needed by the yards. This legislation was reinforced in 1982 when MARINA issued guidelines stating that "Dry docking and repair of locally owned vessels must be done by shipyards in the country, and the imports of spare parts and machinery must be shipped on Philippine flag vessels." The main shipyard in the Philippines is Philippine Shipyard and Engineering, with a dry-docking capacity of 300,000 DWT. The company is 60 percent owned by the government through the National Investment and Development Corporation, and thus the government is the prime beneficiary of the new guidelines.

Five years ago the Philippine Ports Authority was created to reorganize the country's port structure, beginning with the Port of Manila. It is the main port for both interisland and international trade. It is divided into three sections: South Harbor, International Port, and the North Harbor. South Harbor handles break bulk, International Port handles break bulk and containers, and North Harbor caters to interisland traffic. The port was greatly improved during the late 1970s, with the container facilities handling an impressive 409,000 teus in 1980 compared with 255,000 teus in 1979. International traffic remained relatively steady at 255,000 teus, but there was an unexpected rise in domestic container traffic. Throughput at the North Harbor, where most of the domestic containers are handled, rose from 84,000 teus in 1979 to 154,000 teus in 1980. Aboitiz Shipping, which was in 1978 the only domestic container carrier on the interisland routes, has been joined by four other companies.[41]

Despite these improvements, the port situation is not good. The acquisition of more port equipment is blocked by a lack of funds, and any major increase in the size of the port would mean moving thousands of squatters who live around the port area. "Brownouts" are common, and the loss of electrical power has meant that the international container terminal cannot work to full efficiency. None of these problems is insurmountable, but in the Philippine economic environment it is difficult to see where the money and labor might come from to boost the Port of Manila over these hurdles in the near future.

Singapore

Singapore entered the 1970s with the region's most complete shipping sector. The island state has built up the largest and most modern shipbuilding and ship repair industry, a large, diversified fleet, and the biggest port in the region. It also serves as a base for ancillary businesses such as ship chartering, freight forwarding, crewing, ship chandlering, storage and supply, marine insurance, and banking.

Ever since Singapore's founding, its fleet has been the region's largest. The shipowners fall into three categories: local shipowners serving the regional trades; foreign owners using Singapore as a base for flag-of-convenience operations; and tug and barge operators engaged in the offshore oil industry. With a combination of flag and shipbuilding incentives, Singapore was quick to encourage shipowners to register their ships there. The government offered tax breaks, no specific national crewing requirements, and a line of credit of US$300 million (increased in 1979 to US$600 million) for ship financing.[42] These loans could be worth up to 85 percent of the value of the contract price and were repayable over ten years. The incentives were successful; during the 1970s the registered fleet increased from 153 ships of 550,772 DWT to 11,031 ships of 12,924,332 DWT.[43]

In 1981 Singapore ended its twelve-year-old open registry. Under the new provisions only Singapore citizens, permanent residents, and locally incorporated businesses are allowed to register ships. The move has not affected the more than 1,600 foreign ships already registered in Singapore, but the legislation demands more information on ownership and vessel condition than was previously necessary. However, the essential tax exemption on offshore shipping businesses remains in force. The new legislation has not deterred owners from registering in Singapore. Esso put six vessels of 180,000 DWT under the Singapore flag in 1982 alone.

Most of the local shipping companies are Chinese family businesses that survive on the system of family contacts throughout the region.[44] These lines generally operate older ships on routes linking Indonesia, east and west Malaysia, and Thailand with Singapore. During the 1970s both Malaysia and Indonesia passed legislation that directly affected the Singapore operators by restricting the use of foreign flag vessels in their trade. The Malaysian Parliament approved the Merchant Shipping (Amendment and Extension) Bill in 1976 under which all cargo from one Malaysian port to another must be carried in a Malaysian-registered vessel, and the shipowning company must be at least 50-percent owned by Malaysian citizens. This cabotage law was later reviewed and strengthened to prevent foreign companies from securing the trade.[45]

In an effort to prevent smuggling, the Indonesian government passed another law in 1976 requiring extensive documentation for goods involving high duties. The immediate result was a 50-percent falloff in trade. The Indonesian Shipowners' Association (INSA) and the Singapore Shipowners' Association (SSA) had earlier signed a cargo-sharing agreement whereby 50 percent of the cargo shipped from Singapore was to go on Singapore flag vessels and 45 percent on Indonesian-registered ships, with reverse shares on the other route. When the antismuggling legislation was passed they suffered a 40-percent downturn in trade as a result. Indonesia also passed a Tug and Barge Law, which held that by 1979 tugs or barges would have to either fly the Indonesian flag or be on charter hire to an Indonesian company, and by 1984 all vessels on charter hire would have to be fully Indonesian owned.[46] This sparked a controversy in Singapore because the Tug and Barge Association was not recognized by the Indonesian government, and the tug and barge owners felt let down by their SSA counterparts who were doing the negotiation.

Despite the turmoil, Singapore shipowners have outperformed their ASEAN neighbors. Singapore's national flag carrier, Neptune Orient Line (NOL), started in 1969, has expanded to around twenty-five vessels of 700,00 DWT and is often considered to be one of the developing world's best-run fleets. The company became part of the FEFC and embarked on an ambitious service program that included trans-Pacific routes. Companies such as Strait Steamship and Pacific International Lines (PIL) have managed to do well despite the shipping depression.

Singapore's shipbuilding and ship repair industry is one of the oldest in the Far East. In the early 1960s, however, the island could claim only six small drydocks ranging in size from 4,000 DWT to 40,000 DWT. The industry in 1965 produced only S$40 million (US$18 million) in revenues.[47] The Singapore government was faced with a sizable unemployment problem in the late 1960s. With approximately 9 percent of the work force looking for jobs and with the prospect of the British forces leaving in 1971, Singapore needed to find a labor-intensive industry to put the economy back on its feet. Shipbuilding and ship repair suited the situation. In 1965 the Japanese shipbuilding company, Ishikawajima–Harima Heavy Industries (IHI), entered into a joint venture with the Singapore government at Jurong Shipyard. In 1969 the facilities at the ex-British naval dockyard were incorporated as a private company, adding more shipbuilding facilities to the republic. By 1973 the shipbuilding facilities had been transformed into an international center. The sector continued to build and jumped from a repair capacity of 75,000 DWT in 1973 to 2.1 million DWT by 1977, with five huge drydocks ranging from 150,000 DWT to 400,000 DWT.[48]

What spurred the development of the ship repair industry was Singapore's location. In the 1960s the oil route from the Middle East to Japan became more and more important. A tanker could make a fully laden voyage from the Middle East to Japan, discharge and wash its tanks during the return voyage and be ready for drydocking in Singapore. Singapore's yards were cheaper than Japan's; there was no loss of time because the port was located en route to the Middle East; and because of the massive amount of labor used, the turnaround times were among the fastest in the world. Singapore's shipbuilding and ship repair industry also had the advantage of having the only major facilities in the region. Indonesia, Malaysia, and to a lesser extent the Philippines and Thailand had to use the facilities for annual surveys and other major work.

However, the success of the industry was not without its costs. In the case of IHI, the Jurong Shipyard was convicted six times under the "Factories Act" for being negligent. In 1972 an explosion at the yard killed twenty workers. Two years later the shipyard had another explosion that killed thirteen workers. Then in 1978 a massive explosion aboard the tanker *St. Spyros* killed seventy-six and injured another seventy-six.[49] Partly as a result of these accidents, five contracts reportedly were cancelled when the workers simply refused to work.[50] Despite these problems, the shipbuilding and ship repair industry recorded a revenue of S$1.39 billion, with 52 percent of that total in ship repairs. Although the 1974 shipping slump hurt the Singapore builders, much of the slack was taken up by oil rig building and the demand for smaller vessels. In the 1980s the industry is facing more problems, because other nations in the region are developing their own facilities and the cost of repairing in Singapore is placing it out of the market. In an effort to move up the economic ladder Singapore is emphasizing high technology industries. The resulting increase in wages has caused labor to drift out of the ship repair and shipbuilding sector, a trickle that could become a torrent.

Singapore's position as the major regional port was established because of geography and the clear-cut priority that port development had with the government. Early in the 1960s it was obvious that the liner shipping companies serving the Far East were going to switch to containerization. The impact of this move was hard to estimate at the time because no one was absolutely sure just how much cargo could be containerized and what impact it would have on labor, warehousing, and transport. However, one point was very clear: It was going to be extremely expensive. In 1966 Singapore had been successful in negotiating with the International Bank for Reconstruction and Development (IBRD) of the World Bank to finance the building of conventional piers. With the containerization explosion a revised costing showed that there was an increase of US$2.5 million in the foreign exchange component over the bank loan of US$15 million. In 1967 the project was reappraised by the World Bank and a loan was approved; the work began in 1969. The feeder service berth came on stream in 1970, and the first container terminal was opened in June of 1972.[51]

In that first year, 14,000 teus totaling 185,000 tons were handled. By 1981 this figure had increased to 1 million teus of 13 million tons. It is expected that by 1986, the port will handle 2 million containers of 26 million tons.[52] The port has continued to expand because of the nearly S$100 million (nearly US$50 million) in capital expenditures averaged over the past nine years.[53] Currently, the port has six container wharves and is converting two conventional wharves to handle containers.

Although the container wharves and bulk-handling facilities are the largest of the region, Singapore is still in essence an oil port. In 1973, 53.3 million tons of oil and petroleum products were handled. In the 1960s Singapore refineries were important as swing refineries. They made up the shortfalls that countries' own refineries could not handle. This balance function established the market for Singapore products from India to the United States. Singapore refineries were dependent on Middle East imports, because they were designed for processing heavier crudes, and until the 1980 war between Iran and Iraq, Saudi Arabia accounted for 58 percent of the crude and Iran another 14 percent of oil refined in Singapore. By 1970, with the Indochina war underway, Vietnam had become the main importer of oil from Singapore, absorbing 21 percent of the total exports. Japan was a distant second with 10 percent. However, over the next three years, with the tremendous increases in Japanese consumption and the winding down of the U.S.–Indochina war effort, the roles were reversed, and Japan became the main importer of Singapore products, accounting for 26 percent. This complemented the Japanese shipping movements that were already using the Strait of Malacca.

Thailand

Thailand has the oldest and smallest merchant marine among the ASEAN nations. The fleet, which numbers around 140 vessels of 500,000 DWT, is largely composed of tonnage belonging to state shipping companies. Although the small size of the fleet is a headache for marine officials, Thailand's major shipping problem is the lack of adequate port facilities. The facilities at Bangkok, the country's capital and major port, are inadequate for coping with the heavy concentration of shipping traffic.

Faced with chronic problems that have been strangling the operations of state-run corporations, the Thai government has embarked on a privatisation policy for ten new ports, including Sattahip and Surat Thani. Investment in these facilities will be borne by the government, but the private sector is being invited to manage and operate them on long-term leases. Klong Toey has enough berths to handle ten vessels of 172 m, but a majority of the ships are loaded and discharged in stream by lighters or at private piers. Congestion has always been a problem in Bangkok; the average delays per vessel in 1980 ranged from a June high of thirty-six hours to a May low of fifteen hours. This compared favorably with the previous year's high of a delay of fifty-four hours and six minutes per ship.

The port is located near the mouth of the Chao Phraya River and is at a disadvantage from a lack of water depth and modern harbor facilities. The bar at the entrance to the river has a maximum depth of 8.23 m and the winding nature of the river and frequent obstructions of fish stakes, small fishing vessels, and lighters and riverboats makes the navigation of larger vessels difficult. The maximum size vessel that can enter the port is 172 m. Before 1980, vessels of a larger size could legally enter, providing they were maneuverable, but this permission was suspended after the record during 1972–79 showed that there had been thirty-two groundings and sixteen collisions in the river.[54] Since the port is more than a day's steaming off the main Singapore–Hong Kong–Taiwan shipping route, it has been more often served by feeder services that call at either Singapore or Hong Kong than by direct calls by Europe- or Japan-bound vessels. The port has attempted to pull itself back into the mainstream of Far Eastern shipping by introducing container operations using conventional equipment.

The average monthly throughput of containers rose from 10,012 teus in 1978 to 14,236 teus in 1980. However, the port problems are huge. Most of the containers are packed or unpacked on the dock causing massive congestion in handling operations. The breaking and packing of containers on site also means that the goods are more vulnerable to damage and pilferage. It is estimated that more than 90 percent of the containerized imports are consumed in the metropolitan Bangkok area and that an equally high percentage of the containerized exports originate from there. This fact makes it unrealistic to build another container port any great distance from the city or even to establish a freight container station very far outside the city limits.

Cargo movements to and from Bangkok remained relatively steady throughout the late 1970s. In 1973 the port handled 2,600 ships, and 4,826,821 tons were discharged and 6,826,680 tons loaded. Most of the outbound cargoes consisted of maize, rice, tapioca, and other agricultural products, while the imports were iron and steel, paper, timber, and consumer items.

Thailand has depended largely on foreign shipping lines to move its imports and exports, with a great many of these services being based in Singapore, Hong Kong, and Japan. In 1978, in an effort to reduce the dependence on foreign shipping, the government passed the Merchant Marine Promotion Act. Under the act, the Ministry of Communications was given the authority to direct that imports and exports made on behalf of government departments must move on Thai flag vessels or on vessels chartered by Thai operators. Under the act the government assumes the power to direct, if necessary, all and any Thai-operated vessels and to enter into cargo-sharing agreements with foreign states. The act also offered Thai exporters the right to offset part of their freight bills against their income tax, providing they used Thai vessels.[55]

Vietnam

When hostilities ended in 1975, a unified Vietnam was left with virtually no merchant fleet, since most of the country's ships had either been sunk or used by refugees fleeing the new Communist government. The lack of a fleet had not posed a serious problem during the war against the United States, because a large portion of Vietnam's aid came by rail through Friendship Pass from China. With the Vietnamese invasion of Cambodia and the 1979 Sino–Vietnamese war, however, the overland trade routes were cut and Vietnam became, in effect, an island state.

The Chinese link was important to the Vietnamese as the Hong- Kong-based-but-Chinese-controlled China Merchants Steam Navigation (CMSN) was appointed to act as shipping agent for the Vietnam Foreign Trade and Transportation Corp. (Vietfracht) and the fledgling state shipping company, Vietnam Ocean Shipping Corp. (Vosco).[56] The company acted as the coordinating body for China's considerable offshore fleets registered in Panama and Liberia (and previously in Somalia) and organized the purchasing, chartering, and crewing of vessels for China. The initial advantage of CMSN and its sister companies was that the shipping operations had a relatively low profile—third-country flag and frequently foreign crewing—plus access to international financing. In addition, Hong Kong offered the geographical and political advantages of an open port on China's doorstep. CMSN was attractive for the same reasons to a hard-pressed and nearly nonexistent Vietnamese merchant marine.

The importance of Hong-Kong-based Golden Star Shipping, which acts as shipping agent for Vietnam, is underlined by the tremendous volume of re-exports funneled through Hong Kong to Vietnam. In 1981 re-exports to Vietnam totaled HK$138.35 million (US$17.7 million), but the figure nearly tripled in 1982 as re-exports climbed to HK$349.8 million. This represents just about 23 percent of Vietnam's imports from convertible-currency areas. The main re-export categories were food (HK$83.2 million), machinery (HK$24.9 million), and manufactured goods (HK$170.3 million).

The re-export trade is the result of the political situation, which makes direct trade difficult and in some cases impossible. The United States bans exports to Vietnam while poor relations with China, reflected in the continuing sporadic fighting on the border, make any direct trade an embarrassment. Vietnam also has no relations with either South Korea or the Chinese province of Taiwan though these states along with Japan are the most important sources of Hong Kong re-export cargoes bound for Vietnam.

The Hong Kong connection is particularly important for acquiring such strategic commodities as petroleum and petroleum products, inorganic and organic chemicals, iron and steel, rubber, and industrial machinery. China is the largest source for petroleum and petroleum-related products re-exported through Hong Kong to Vietnam. In 1981 China supplied Vietnam with HK$755,000 worth of petroleum products.[57]

Most of the demand for shipping services is in the bulk sector, and even the main export cargoes, sugar and coal, are bulk items. Vietnam has the potential in the not-too-distant future to become a fairly important purchaser of second-hand tonnage, but for the moment shipping has a relatively low priority since most of the shipping services are directly or indirectly supported by the Soviet Union.

In the Pacific, the Soviet port of Nakhodka is the main base for merchant-shipping operations. The port is also the home of Fesco, the state shipping corporation serving Asia and the Pacific. During the late 1970s the Soviet shipping company came under pressure from Western shipping companies, which accused it of rate-cutting and of building ships simply to support military expansion. This theme was reinforced by shippers' complaints that Soviet carriers were making unscheduled stops in Vietnam, causing delays.

In recent years, Vietnam's dependence of Soviet shipping has shifted to more indirect services. The Soviets' Baltic Shipping Company has weekly services from Europe, and the East German state line also calls weekly from northern Europe. In Asia, Filsov, a Soviet–Philippine service, calls frequently along with Japanese carriers. In addition, the Vietnamese have reportedly been chartering in Eastern-bloc tonnage.

The most active outside company organizing Vietnam shipping services remains Golden Star. The company, acting much like a Vietnamese CMSN, helps coordinate trade, owns vessels registered offshore, sells vessels to the state shipping company, and acts as a chartering and crewing agent for Vietnam.

Golden Star, through a series of secondhand purchases, built up a small fleet of around ten ships. The financing for the ships originally came from (among other sources) Nan Yang Commercial Bank, a Hong-Kong-based, Chinese-controlled bank, and United Overseas Bank of Singapore. Not unexpectedly, some of these early purchases were organized through CMSN's associate companies.

In 1977 Scarbrook was formed and appointed Hong Kong agent for ships going to Vietnam from Hong Kong—an important function in Vietnam's case since the country's shipping laws require an advance notice of one week prior to arrival. Generally, ships going to Haiphong used Golden Star as agent and those going to Ho Chi Minh City used Scarbrook. Neither agent was exclusive, as Eastern Worldwide, Wallems, Hai Thong, and John McRink all have acted for vessels going to and from Vietnam through Hong Kong. From 1978 on, most of the ships purchased were at least partly financed by the Bank of Foreign Trade of Vietnam. Table 6.1 provides further details about Vietnam's fleet.

Vietnam's shipping legislation is in line with that of most centrally planned economies. There are, however, aspects that reflect the high degree of security con-

Table 6.1   Vietnam's Fleet

	No.	DWT	Average Age (years)
Tanker	8	53,324	21
General cargo	37	243,346	20.5
Bulk carrier	2	23,706	9
Ro-ro	2	19,834	14
Tug	2	1,209	39
Coastal	4	11,934	44.5
Research	1	700	38
Dredger	1	4,346	13
Total	57	358,399	–

Source: Far Eastern Economic Review, 17 November 1983.

sciousness with which the Vietnamese view shipping and marine resources. Not only must foreign vessels calling at a Vietnamese port seek permission from the Ministry of Communication and Transport (MOCT) seven days in advance, but they must also notify the ministry twenty-four hours before actually entering Vietnam's territorial waters.

As are many countries, Vietnam is particularly sensitive about foreign ships using a port call as a cover for collecting data on marine resources and geographical features. Consequently, it forbids the use of any electronic measuring devices and also demands that fishing vessels calling must have all their fishing gear stowed before entering Vietnam's maritime zones unless they already have an agreement with the government.[58]

Perhaps the best example of Vietnam's sensitivity is an article in the legislation that states: "While in the internal waters of SRV [Soviet Republic of Vietnam] all foreign ships must seal their communications equipment and liaison apparatus and all their electronic means of observation." This provision is accompanied by another that states ships (even of the same nationality) cannot communicate without going through the port communications authorities.

What makes Vietnam's shipping legislation potentially dangerous is the manner in which it is enforced. Control over shipping is entrusted to the Vietnam People's Navy, the People's Army, People's Police, Vietnamese border guards, and the paramilitary forces. These last are civilians, identified only by a badge, who have the right both to board a vessel and to force it to leave Vietnamese waters.

But since many of the paramilitary vessels, which are predominantly equipped with small arms, look no different from an ordinary fishing vessel it is nearly impossible for a visiting ship to identify them. This makes for a perilous situation, given the conflicting territorial claims surrounding Vietnamese waters and the ever-present menace of pirates roaming the South China Sea.

Other Asian Countries

In Laos, which is landlocked, and Kampuchea, international shipping is nearly nonexistent. Most of the international trade for Laos is funneled through Thailand, and most of the international trade for Kampuchea goes through Vietnam. Burma has a small, active, state-owned line, but expansion is slow and the service is limited to Europe and ports in Southeast Asia.

China, Hong Kong, and the Chinese province of Taiwan all have substantial fleets. It is estimated that the People's Republic of China controls around 50 million DWT of shipping, including China-controlled offshore companies in Hong Kong and Macao flying flags of convenience. Hong Kong controls almost the same tonnage (not counting Chinese shipping but including companies controlled by Hong Kong shipowners in Europe). Taiwan's fleet is around 20 million DWT, although this figure is difficult to determine exactly because of the tonnage that Taiwanese owners control in Southeast Asia. China's fleet has grown enormously in the past decade. It is beginning to be a factor in regional trade, especially with the recent shipping agreement with Malaysia to lift latex that had been previously controlled by the FEFC shipping lines.

For the past thirty years Hong Kong shipowners have been a major factor in regional and international shipping, but China has indicated that it will exert sovereignty over Hong Kong at the expiration of the New Territory lease in 1997. The effect on Hong Kong shipowners is difficult to foresee, but the Chinese province of Taiwan might well benefit from the defection of tonnage from the Colony. Taiwan, for its part, has been building up a more international fleet with the addition of the expanding Evergreen and Yang Ming lines. As in Hong Kong, the future of shipping in the Chinese province of Taiwan depends a great deal on the development of its long-term relations with China.

MAJOR ISSUES

The Model for Shipping Development

What model should be followed in state-shipping development in Southeast Asia? The most natural purpose of a national fleet is to carry international trade, but a fleet also contributes to a nation's economy by contributing to employment, encouraging ancillary industries, and ensuring that shipping services are available to support other industries. In times of war it also can serve to keep the lifelines open. Added to these economic advantages is the intangible benefit of showing the flag, a feeling that seduces young and old nations alike.

Although they are rarely defined, there are five distinctly different approaches to shipping in the world: the Soviet, Chinese, and Eastern bloc centrally planned method; the Japanese quasi-state, controlled approach; noncentrally controlled national fleets; the open registry system; and the traditional maritime powers' private fleet method. In all five methods there is a common underlying objective of carrying as much cargo as is practical, but the means of achieving this end and the secondary objectives vary considerably among systems. These different approaches illustrate how little homogeneity there is in shipping and why there is so little agreement in the international forums.

In the centrally planned model, state-controlled shipping is designed to serve the indigenous industries of the country in much the same fashion as public utility companies. The Soviet merchant marine's principal function is to serve the country's ports, many of which are located in areas where access is limited because of heavy ice. The secondary function of the fleet is to back up the Soviet Union's naval forces; most of the newer vessels have been made to order as naval auxiliaries.

Up until the late 1950s, the merchant fleet was relatively small and ranked low in the list of development priorities. The Soviets' shipping strategy changed considerably in 1971 when under the ninth Five-Year Plan a merchant fleet expansion program included vessels designed specifically for international trade. The Soviet merchant fleet is now divided into a number of smaller fleets based on geographical considerations—e.g., FESCO (Far Eastern Shipping Company of Vladivostok), Baltic Shipping Company—that are answerable to central government. The idea of profit is based on the production levels achieved by the lines. In most cases, a

Soviet shipping company would be expected to remit 6 percent of the gross profit to the state, the gross being previously estimated by the central authorities. Soviet ships, unlike most Western vessels, are depreciated over twenty-six years, and this also reduces the paper cost to a Soviet shipping company. Added to this official production is the relative foreign exchange position of the various lines. A certain amount of foreign exchange is needed for port charges and servicing of vessels, and a Soviet shipping company with a favorable position in respect of foreign exchange can trade this for goods and services inside the Soviet economic hierarchy.[59]

FESCO offered rates 20 percent below conference carriers, but given the service, speed, and problems of the Soviet carriers, 20 percent off was not necessarily a bargain. The centrally controlled fleet could concentrate its assets on one project. For example. FESCO could bid to take Malaysian rubber shipments to Europe, traditionally a cargo handled by FEFC vessels, because if they were successful in their penetration they could increase their ships as necessary from other Soviet carriers. The weakness of the Soviet system is its inherent lack of flexibility in reacting to local shipper problems and the broader political commitments of the merchant fleet, which may be diverted at a moment's notice.

There is diversity among systems of state-controlled shipping. In outward appearances, the Chinese fleet, the China Ocean Shipping Corporation, is a carbon copy of the Soviets'. The Chinese shipping fleet, which expanded so greatly during the 1970s, however, is largely an extension of the traditional system of shipping enterprise in China. The "banner system" employs the use of fleets based at major coastal cities such as Canton, Shanghai, and Fuzhou. The Chinese also have maintained a large flag-of-convenience fleet in Hong Kong, controlled by the China Merchant Steam Navigation Company. It includes companies like Yick Fung, Ocean Tramping, and Nan Fung. Most of the second-hand vessels the Chinese have bought in recent years were funneled through companies for reasons of payment and ease of employment. This offshore fleet has offered China international flexibility that the national flag carrier does not have. It also has proved to be an effective means of chartering vessels needed to adjust to variations in demand, which are considerable because of grain imports.

Japan, whose system of shipping is uniquely a product of the "Inland Sea,"[60] is the most important shipping nation in Asia. Its shipping dominates the traffic through the region's waterways, particularly because of its huge demand for oil. It also dominates the shipyards of the region with its requirements for berthing space. And it dominates the region by the abundance of liner and bulk carriers that move Japanese goods to various countries and carry raw materials back to the factories of the nation. But the system is such that only rarely is the true weight of Japanese shipping enterprise apparent.

Japanese shipping is based on close relationships of Japanese shipbuilders, shipowners, and industry. This vertical integration of industries has been called "Zaibatsu" or, more loosely, Japan Inc. Under this system, the major shipyards and shipping lines are aligned with various trading houses and industrial groups and are ultimately guaranteed by the Japanese government itself. The system was built partly because of historical circumstance and more recently because of economic necessity.[61] Japanese shipyards recovered from World War II much faster than the shipping lines and by 1956 led the world in shipbuilding. The Japanese lines, however, needed to expand and in 1961 were consolidated into six major shipping companies and the "lone wolf," Sanko, which remained outside this merger arrangement. The individual shipping companies had neither the capital nor the access to capital of foreign shipping companies. A system was devised whereby a Japanese shipowner would suggest to a foreign shipowner—often in Hong Kong or Greece—to build a vessel to certain specifications in a particular Japanese yard with which the shipping line was often affiliated and would guarantee a long-term charter to the vessel. The import-export bank would assist with the shipyard credits, and the payment of the charter was guaranteed by a Japanese bank.

This system allowed the foreign shipowner to build an enormous fleet with very little of his own capital involved. Hong Kong's Sir Yue Kong Pao, the world's largest shipowner with 20 million DWT of shipping, built up most of his fleet in this manner. The system also had a built-in "fail-safe" assurance. Since the Japanese government was indirectly involved at each step of the way, the Japanese shipping companies had the shadowy presence of Japan Inc. behind them should anything go wrong. This system hauled Japan Lines, YS Line, and to a lesser degree Sanko, out of severe trouble in the late 1970s. The price that the larger Japanese owners had to pay was to not break ranks. In most international forums, the Japanese acted in unison and voted in a bloc. Rarely did they operate like their corporate competitors in the Western world.[62]

The Western model of shipping has always revolved around the concept of private ownership, no matter how large that private ownership might be, and a minimum of government interference. Traditionally, the attributes of the shipowner have been self-reliance, innovation, and the ability to keep an eye open for finding a new market. He asks and gives no quarter to commercial rivals but is willing to cooperate in what is good for the industry, such as conferences, provided his interests are guaranteed. The relationship between the shipper and the shipowner is based on the shipper's needs. Capital flows to where there is a demand for services and out of those places it is no longer needed. The system is very flexible.

What enables the system to work is the "bankability" of the shipowner. If a shipowner has a well-managed line and a reasonable cash flow situation, he could raise the money necessary for vessel replacement and servicing. If the owner could not raise the necessary capital, then at some stage of the game he would have to cash in his ships.

A real departure from this style came only very recently. Almost simultaneously, traditional Western shipowners began registering their ships in flag-of-convenience countries, and government-controlled state shipping was launched.

The split among owners into two camps has had a major effect on Western shipping. The faction that moved to flags of convenience was generally either the individual entrepreneurial owner attempting to keep his costs down and maximize his flexibility or transnational corporations seeking a tax haven. The result was that the advantages of flag-of-convenience shipping in crewing, taxes, and operations changed the parameters of what was "bankable." A flag-of-convenience-managed

fleet is more bankable because it has lower basic operating costs and less government restriction over its operations. The Western governments' shipping interests
were also split. On the one hand they wanted to protect flag-of-convenience shipping because the beneficial ownership was largely Western and it was a cheaper
method of shipping, but they also wanted to stop the erosion from their own fleets.

Another option in shipping that has found favor in many developing countries is
the establishment of state-controlled national flag carriers, either through outright ownership or controlled indirectly through government organizations. The
prime advantage is that government backing makes the shipping line more "bankable," allowing the company to raise money for ships in the commercial sector.
Since these lines are generally the largest in the country, they often attract top
management talent as well. The chief drawback to the national flag carrier approach is that the companies are frequently not ready, or in some cases able, to
respond to market needs, and at other times they must follow ill-advised government policies that are opposite to the well-being of the company. These companies
are often more acceptable to Western shipping lines than centrally controlled shipping services because there generally exists a willingness to join conferences and
existing shipping structures. Nevertheless these state-controlled carriers have
been attacked as being uncommercial and exercises in national vanity.

As these five systems indicate, there is little uniformity in shipping enterprises. It
is not simply a question of a free enterprise system versus a centrally controlled
system or shipping in developed countries versus that in developing countries, but
what works best given certain geographic, economic, and social conditions. However, shipping touches every part of the body politic. Shipping policies naturally
often are entangled with the larger issues of the day.

The UNCTAD Liner Code

Is the UNCTAD Liner Code good for Southeast Asian countries? The first major
conflict between the traditional maritime powers and developing countries over
international shipping took place at a meeting of UNCTAD in Santiago, Chile, in
1974. The intention of the group of seventy-seven representing the developing
countries was to increase their share of cargo being shipped. The UNCTAD *Code of
Conduct for Line Conferences,* or the 40–40–20 Liner Code as it came to be called,
was approved at the meeting, without support from the West.

The code was to come "into force six months after the date on which not less than
25 percent of the world tonnage . . . have become Contracting Parties to it." It was
hoped that at the UNCTAD V in Manila in April 1979 enough support for the
proposal would have been mustered to ensure that it would be ratified, but by mid-
1982 only fifty-two countries, representing less than 21 percent of the world's tonnage, had ratified the code.[63]

The code's main provision is that the trading partners are each entitled to carry
40 percent of the trade generated and that cross-traders are reserved up to 20
percent. This cargo reservation scheme represented a radical departure from the
historical view that any shipowner has the right to carry as much cargo as he could

contract for in a commercially sound venture. The code was aimed at redistribut-
ing the share of cargoes controlled by the 360-odd liner conferences, estimated to
carry around 25–30 percent of world seaborne commerce. Support for the code
came mainly from the developing nations and the socialist countries, and most of
the opposition came from the traditional maritime powers.

The code leaves many questions open. In liner conferences the intergroup agreements determine the conference shares to be allotted to each carrier. The carriers
are matched against the demands of the ports, demands of the trade, and overall
trading patterns. Most conferences are regional in their approach to route. Even
given some flexibility for pooling under the provisions for third-flag liftings of 20
percent, cargo sharing can be difficult and inefficient. A major question is whether
the implementation of the code actually would help the balance in shipping by
causing liner shipping to move to the registries of developing countries. While it
would be difficult to prevail upon shipowners to move their ships from their home
countries to foreign countries without considerable financial inducements, it is estimated that perhaps 10 million tons of shipping would be transferred from the
developed to the developing countries if 40–40–20 actually were enforced.

Even without ratification the UNCTAD Liner Code has succeeded in giving developing countries the impetus for fleet expansion. In ASEAN it has provided
guidelines for building national fleets. It also has given conferences the incentive
of taking in national flag carriers that probably would have been barred from
membership only two decades ago. Thus, the UNCTAD Liner Code has already
begun to redress the imbalance in shipping services that has existed for centuries.

The developed countries' OECD agreed to the basic principles of the UNCTAD
Liner Code in Manila in 1979, with the reservation that cargo sharing would apply
to the group as a whole and need not apply to trade among themselves. In short, the
OECD established what amounts to a free shipping zone.[64] This principle of applying the code to a group could also apply well to the ASEAN states because of their
geography and cargo mix. It would require a level of unity that has not yet been
achieved in ASEAN, but the trade is in place and the ships would follow the trade.

UNCTAD V and Bulk Cargo

Would application of the UNCTAD 40–40–20 cargo reservation formula to bulk
cargo and the phasing out of flags of convenience be beneficial to the Southeast
Asian countries? At the UNCTAD V meeting in Manila in 1979 the cargo reservation debate was carried two critical steps further. It was proposed that the shipping
of bulk cargoes be treated with the same 40–40–20 cargo reservation formula as
liner shipping. Attached to this cargo reservation scheme was the proposal that
flags of convenience be phased out. During the previous debates on the UNCTAD
Liner Code, some industrialized nations had broken ranks and supported the
adoption of the code, but the bulk cargo scheme and the phasing out of flags of
convenience were so objectionable to Western shipping that the developed nations
closed ranks in opposing the scheme.[65]

The bulk cargo scheme cuts right to the heart of the industrialized world's economic system. Bulk shipments, with the exception of oil, are generally shipped in special bulk carriers on routes that vary widely. Some of these voyages are one-shipment affairs of phosphate, coal, grain, or ore. Other voyages are composed of a series of bulk commodities (often call the neo-bulk trades) such as wastepaper, copra, jute, and cotton. The freight rate on bulk shipping is determined by taking into account all charges such as ports, canals, crewing, and operational expenses. These figures are set against the number of tons to be transported and the route. "There is no necessary relationship between the rate on one route and that on another; the circumstances of every individual voyage and each commodity to be carried will fix the amount of money the shipowner should demand for his vessel if his hire rate is to be compensatory."[66] The profit margin in such shipping is what the competitive conditions permit.

Most vessels operating in the bulk trades are owned either by transnational companies like the oil giants or mineral companies such as Alcoa and U.S. Steel, or by traditional shipowners. The freight rates in oil and other bulk commodities have been extremely volatile and could change overnight with the outbreak of a war, the closing of a canal, or even the rumor of a bad harvest. It has been a high risk business with potentially big profits.

What makes this world of endless risk acceptable is the flag-of-convenience system, the very system that the developing countries are seeking to abolish. The open-registry countries — Liberia, Panama, Honduras, Cyprus, Somalia, Singapore, the Bahamas, and now Vanuatu — allow foreign shipping companies to register their ships, each as a single corporate entity, for a fee that is determined by the size of the ship. The single ship company provides many advantages: it limits the owner's liability in the event of an accident to the ship rather than the fleet; since most flag-of-convenience countries demand only the registration fee, it exempts the shipowner from personal and corporate taxes; and since the crewing requirements do not have a national basis, it allows the employment of cheaper crews. Added to these obvious advantages is the ability to use the vessels to transfer monies and the advantage that the beneficial ownership need not appear on the documentation available to the public.[67] Most ships are registered through lawyers (80 Broad Street, Monrovia, Liberia, is a famous address among shipowners) operating in the flag-of-convenience states. A vessel must pass inspection by an approved surveyor, but this regulation has often been lax on transfers of second-hand vessels.[68]

The development of the flag-of-convenience fleet has had a tremendous impact on the development of shipping in the nations of Southeast Asia. Singapore became a flag-of-convenience state although it is currently phasing out its open registry. China has made use of Hong Kong's access to open registry tonnage to build its fleet and to maintain a large offshore flag-of-convenience fleet. Hong Kong itself has become a major user of open registries and supports 50 million DWT of shipping. The Philippines supplies some 36,000 men to crew open registry vessels, bringing in valuable foreign exchange for the country. Shipowners in all ASEAN nations have taken advantage of flags of convenience to build their fleets.

The ASEAN governments have come out in favor of the resolution passed in Geneva in 1981 to phase out flags of convenience. Although there is undoubtedly some economic advantage in the use of flag-of-convenience vessels, the Third World wants control over its shipping and is willing to wait for the economic advantage. It may be an economic necessity for an individual owner, but for the governments flags of convenience represent just another form of dependence on foreign shipping.

An alternative that has been suggested is an international "super flag" possibly administered by the United Nations.[69] The problems of creating such a flag are enormous. Nothing could be more fitting to the concept of a New International Economic Order, however, than the creation of an international registry that would bring a new and more responsible sense of "freedom" of the seas.

The FEFC

How should the Southeast Asian countries deal with the FEFC? With the boom in the Japanese economy during the 1950s the FEFC blossomed into a huge shipping cartel. There was very little outside tonnage to compete with the FEFC, as Hong Kong, the Chinese province of Taiwan, and the future ASEAN states had yet to build their respective fleets. The FEFC became a classic closed conference. The ASEAN nations agreed that it had become too powerful an economic force in ASEAN affairs. Membership was obtained through selection by existing members. In the United States this system has been declared in violation of antitrust legislation, which requires that a conference must be open to all shipping lines that wish to join.

The full economic impact of the FEFC did not reveal itself until the containerization revolution that began in the 1950s. The advantage of unitized loads was "door-to-door" delivery, a reduction in pilferage, rapid handling, and a reduction in labor. For the European shipowners operating on the Far East and often worldwide routes, containerization became a necessity; if they did not containerize the Far East routes, their U.S. competitors certainly would.

Although containers were perfectly acceptable for the flourishing Japanese trade, they were not suitable for ASEAN ports. ASEAN nations were not much interested in "door-to-door" deliveries, because they did not have the railroads and roads to deliver the containers. Moreover, a reduction of waterfront labor was undesirable in countries with a large cheap labor pool and chronic unemployment. Rapid handling was only a minor concern to countries whose exports were predominantly bulk. Pilferage was a well-entrenched feature of many Asian ports. And containerization would mean rationalization of port calls, which did not suit the ASEAN situation. Ships needed special terminal equipment to unload the 20- or 40-foot containers, and the cost of ships vastly increased.

However, the FEFC was carrying close to 95 percent of the region's trade with Europe, and containerization was necessary if these ports were still to be serviced. Penang, Port Kelang, Singapore, Hong Kong, Kao-hsiung, and Chi-lung all rapidly converted their port facilities to accommodate containers and to avoid being bypassed.[70]

The FEFC set the pace. The governments had to raise the money to convert their ports, railways, and roads to handle containers. The equipment was Western and represented a foreign exchange drain. Although the upgrading of infrastructure was necessary, the element of choice was wrested from the government's hands by the monopolistic nature of the FEFC. The key to the power of the FEFC was the tariff structure of the cartel. As "the Senior" so aptly foresaw, shipper's rebates would ensure shipper's loyalty, providing that the cartel's services were overwhelmingly more comprehensive than those of any rival group.

The main area of disagreement between the conference and the ASEAN shippers in the 1970s was over a series of rate hikes. The development of the third generation of containerships coincided with the closing of the Suez Canal and the tremendous increase in oil prices, especially for bunker fuel, following the 1973–74 oil crisis. From 1971 through 1977, FEFC hikes and surcharges increased the freight rate by 93 percent. The shippers felt that these increases were not all operational and that they were indirectly financing new vessel acquisition programs. During 1974 the ASEAN shippers' councils formed the Federation of ASEAN Shippers' Councils (FASC) to bring some unity into the negotiations between the shippers' councils and the FEFC.

The essence of the dispute was over the method by which freight rate increases were determined.[71] The figures for various cost components were collected from the individual conference members by an independent accounting firm based in London. These figures were then passed on to the shippers' councils in the form of percentage increases. What made the system suspect was that the accounts were unaudited. Although these fundamental disagreements have not been resolved, FASC and its associated shippers' councils in Hong Kong, the Chinese province of Taiwan, Korea, and Japan have at least managed to win a standoff with the FEFC.[72]

Ultimately the power of the FEFC lies in its number of sailings and the shipper's rebate or loyalty clause. The loyalty clause exists in two forms. The conference lines give an immediate 9.5-percent rebate on the gross value of the freight if the shipper will sign an agreement not to ship on a non-FEFC vessel. If the shipper is hesitant about signing such a contract (hence the term contract shipper), he has the alternative of entering into a "gentleman's agreement" whereby he agrees to ship on FEFC vessels and in return is given a 10-percent rebate paid biannually. Should he break his contract by using an independent shipping company, he would either forfeit his shipping rebate for six months or pay a fine equal to two-thirds of the estimated value of revenue lost to the FEFC by the indiscretion.[73] What makes the loyalty clause work is the more than 170 vessels on the Far East route. A shipper with a regular export-oriented business simply cannot afford to take the chance of losing the 9.5-percent rebate, because his competitors will gain the market advantage. The major outstanding issue is that the FEFC has no obligation to any service agreement in the shipper's contract. Therefore, the FEFC has ensured shipper's loyalty with the rebate system but failed to give any assurances that this service obligation will be honored.

The basic reasons for keeping the conference together are to minimize infighting and eliminate rivals. The FEFC has been successful at both. In ASEAN, the FEFC has inducted Neptune Orient Lines (NOL), Malaysian International Shipping Corporation (MISC), United Thai Lines (UNITHAL), and Djakarta Lloyd (an associate member)—the national flag carriers for Singapore, Malaysia, Thailand, and Indonesia. Further, it has added OOCL, part of the C. Y. Tung Group in Hong Kong, Cho Yang, Korean Shipping, and recently Taiwan's powerful Evergreen. This group represents both of the stronger political and economic liner shipping interests in Southeast Asia. The FEFC has fought successfully against smaller independents; both Hong Kong Container Line and the Philippines' International Shipping Corporation have become casualties to the FEFC, and the conference has had a long, protracted struggle with various Soviet carriers and the Trans-Siberian Railway.

Neither the infighting nor the rivals have made any major impact on the conference's strength, however, although the infighting has at times been a threat; Maersk Line left the conference for a year, and MISC fought long and hard to increase its liftings. The main benefit of the tremendous increase in Asian participation in the conference has been a recognition of Southeast Asia as a major economic region. Southeast Asian nations originally wanted to start their own conference through the Federation of ASEAN Shipowner's Associations (FASA), but this suggestion (which was actually put forth by shippers rather than shipowners) has been dropped as impractical. The idea of an ASEAN consortium within the FEFC is still quite possible as NOL, MISC, and UNITHAL have shared services at various times. At least for the moment, the best alternative to the FEFC appears to be a cosmopolitan FEFC in which there is a large ASEAN voice, rather than a competing ASEAN conference that would have to match rates and services with FEFC.[74]

Safety and the Sea

What should be done to improve safety at sea, especially in regard to the new high technology hazards? Any ship that puts to sea is a potential casualty. Ships are lost because of "acts of God," poor charts, substandard maintenance, human error, war, piracy, and in some cases, intent—either the shipowner or crew, or both, deliberately scuttling the vessel. All of these reasons are common to losses in Asia and particularly the South China Sea.

An "act of God" is the marine insurance industry's term for acknowledging that some things that happen at sea are beyond human control. In Asia, God's main act is the tropical storm or cyclone, which can intensify into a typhoon when wind speeds exceed 63 knots. The "typhoon season" is from late April to early October with the prime months being July, August, and September. Most typhoons that affect the South China Sea are formed southeast of the Philippines and frequently pass through that country before moving into the South China Sea. The region usually has about twenty-four major tropical storms per year, but actual typhoons are infrequent—generally less than six per year along the major tracks. However, typhoons do disrupt sailing schedules for the region. The combination of weather flights, satellites, ground radar stations, and direct observation throughout the region usually gives mariners adequate warning time for weather hazards. Endangered ships usually either look for a safe harbor or try to clear the anticipated typhoon path. Hong Kong is reputed to be one of the best safe harbors in the region. The port is well sheltered, and the cargo moorings are fixed firmly to the harbor bottom.

Once a vessel is in trouble in the South China Sea, rescue is difficult. None of the major nations of the South China Sea has a vessel available for deep-sea rescue operations. The last ship to perform such a role was the *HMS Chichester*, which left Hong Kong in 1978. Helicopters and aircraft provide some assistance to vessels in distress, and U.S. naval ships and aircraft are used when available. Salvage vessels are available throughout the region, but they are of only limited value in actual search and rescue operations. Hong Kong is responsible for directing rescue operations in the South China Sea, almost by default. Previously the Royal Navy had been the major force in rescue operations, and thus Hong Kong became the main rescue center. With the withdrawal of British forces, the nature of rescue changed from actual operations to the coordination of rescue by conveniently placed merchant and fishing ships. If a vessel goes down in international waters, any investigation into the loss of the ship must be pursued by the country of registration — often Panama or Liberia. However, with extension of various national jurisdictions over the entire South China Sea, the responsibility for search and rescue falls on the littoral states. It appears that none of these states is at present willing or able to mount any major rescue operation.

A ship's seaworthiness is determined by a system of annual surveys in accordance with the requirements of insurance, international law, its flag, and harbor regulations. When a ship is built it is surveyed by a classification society. The classification society usually represents the country of build — Lloyd's Register (United Kingdom), Det Norske Veritas (Norway), Nippon Kaiji Kyokai (Japan), Bureau Veritas (France) — but the new owner can ask for another society to classify the vessel as well. The system of classification is kept up by annual surveys, and when a ship changes flag the vessel must within a certain period conform to the standards of the new flag. The inspections for this flag are often performed by surveyors in other countries that are recognized by the flag.

It is this system of survey that is the final backstop for preventing vessels from falling below standards and thus becoming dangerous. In the case of flag-of-convenience shipping, however, it is in the interest of the country to encourage registration, the registration fees being a major source of foreign exchange. It is not in the interest of the commercial surveyors, who check these flag-of-convenience vessels, to repeatedly reject ships of an owner. To do so will not encourage the shipowner or the flag-of-convenience country to reappoint the surveyor.

The actual classification societies may have their own aberrations as well. It has often been alleged that Nippon Kaiji Kyokai is much more stringent in its application of standards for Japanese-owned and run vessels than for those of foreign owners. The Japanese officials have maintained that this rumor developed because the guidelines published in English are slightly different in their translation than those in Japanese, but not in their intent. Bureau Veritas, the French classification society, also has among Asian shipowners the reputation of ease of inspection.

The problem is made greatly more complex if states in the region are not overly concerned with safety at sea. For example, the Chinese province of Taiwan has rarely demonstrated any particular concern in the registration of crews and ships. In the early 1970s it was relatively easy to acquire a seamen's ticket or masters' license in Taiwan and to trade this against a license from Panama that could be used to obtain a license in Liberia and in turn could be traded against most nations around the world. Thus a man could receive a valid license without ever working at sea. The problem was attacked and controlled during the late 1970s but still is a factor in shipping in Southeast Asia.

The ultimate arbitrator is the sea, and ships that are lost are more likely to have been less seaworthy than survivors. The flag-of-convenience countries have consistently had a poorer casualty record than the national fleets. In 1968 the flag-of-convenience ships had a casualty rate of 0.80 percent of total gross registered tons while the rest of the world showed a 0.13-percent casualty rate. By 1979 the flag-of-convenience ships were recording a casualty rate of 0.93 percent while the rest of the world had a casualty rate of 0.28 percent.[75]

The high casualty rate is often considered to be simply the results of overage vessels (Panama was the only country allowing the registration of vessels over twenty years) and poor maintenance practices. However, as the UNCTAD Secretariat pointed out:

> It is unreal to talk of "substandard ships" without considering the underlying causes of substandard management and substandard maritime administration; consequently controls by port States will be ineffective unless backed by Flag States which can control owners and managers. In Flag States which have economic links there is no valid reason why maritime administration cannot be improved, given the political will but in States lacking such links substandard administration would appear to be inevitable."[76]

Although Panama and Liberia have tried to improve their safety records, it is extremely difficult to investigate flag-of-convenience casualty and thus determine liability. The nations of the Southeast Asian region have a worse casualty rate than published. Governments have a vested interest in not making things look bad internationally, and unless a vessel actually does sink and unless that vessel has a heavy loss of life or causes a massive pollution problem, it is generally downplayed or forgotten.

It is within the power of the national governments to prevent many shipping disasters and to ensure that vessels trading within their waters are safe. The average age of interisland vessels is eighteen years in the Philippines and more than twenty years in Indonesia. It is sometimes difficult to maintain standards of building and crewing when ships are so important in connecting the nation, but as is so often demonstrated, safety is a necessity. In Asia, casualties have tended to be overaged, relatively small (less than 10,000 DWT) general cargo vessels or bulk carriers registered in either a flag-of-convenience country or in the region itself. This may not be the case in the immediate future. Shipping has grown enormously sophisticated in the past decade and marine casualties likewise have grown increasingly complex. With the CLS reducing the amount of open water in the region, the question of who will ultimately be looking after the safety of these vessels becomes important.

Traditionally the states bordering the South China Sea have shown little concern either for preventing casualties or for pursuing rescue operations after accidents have occurred. The claims and counterclaims to the South China Sea and the almost warlike situation among some of the countries have made unified action impossible. The littoral states have often acted as if a casualty was simply the problem of the vessel and the crew; if they were rescued by nearby vessels that was fortunate, and if they were not it was a risk of the sea that did not affect the country's well-being in any way.

Asia was introduced to high technology marine accidents through grounding of the *Showa Maru* and the resulting pollution in the Strait of Malacca. The specialization of cargoes, the application of space age technology to transport these cargoes, and the often far-reaching impact of these casualties on coastal populations and on the environment set these accidents into a class by themselves.[77] The high technology marine casualty is not as rare as may be assumed. Even after excluding tankers (but including specialized tankships), there were 473 accidents of such vessels reported from 1978 to 1981. Of this total, liquefied propane gas ships accounted for 224 of the accidents, and specialized tankers accounted for 242 accidents. Significantly, internal damage or failures accounted for the highest number of accidents (174), followed by collisions (114).

The real significance of high technology accidents lies in the impact of vessel designs. Ship design is always a compromise between cost, technological considerations, the job to be done, and the physical environment. Traditionally, the principal design concern has been the vicissitudes of the oceans. Beginning with the earliest supertanker, however, a generation of ships was designed more around their economic than their physical environment. In the supertankers, the vessels' size, and thus cargo capacity, increased tremendously, while the actual seaworthiness of the ships remained stagnant or perhaps even decreased. The reasons for this were not readily apparent to naval architects,[78] but it was not sufficient to apply existing shipbuilding practice and operation to these vastly larger vessels. For example, the "M" class supertankers were built originally for Shell Oil and were manned and maintained to the highest standards in the world. Nevertheless, six out of the twenty-one vessels built had major accidents. After extensive investigations by the company, it was thought that the vast size of the tanks allowed the spray from the crude oil washing system to set up an electrical charge similar to a lightning discharge in a thunderstorm.

Ore-Bulk-Oil (OBO) ships are designed to carry either oil, ore, or bulk cargoes such as grain and thus often have triangular trading patterns, carrying oil on one leg, followed by iron on the next, and grains on the third. The *Berg Istra* exploded and went to the bottom of the Mindanao Trench on 18 January 1976. The explosion was so sudden that the only two survivors had been blown off the ship. Her sister ship, the *Berg Vagna*, was last heard of on 29 October 1979 in the South Atlantic. It was suspected that some of the previous cargo of iron ore in the wing tanks had set up an electrical charge that blew the vessels to pieces.

Another aspect of the high technology marine casualty is the helplessness of the crew once things begin to go wrong. In traditional shipping there was always another option — sails could be taken in, spars cut away; furniture burnt; a backup could be used. In high technology shipping, once a fatal sequence begins, the crew can do little to prevent the inevitable, and the ship's fate is literally cast to the winds.

The pressure that high technology shipping places on the crews is often vastly different than that experienced in normal shipping. A hydrofoil, jetfoil, or hovercraft running at speeds of up to 40 knots is a vastly different craft than a normal ship. The vessels fly through the water and a hydrofoil captain's job is more akin to an aircraft pilot's than a ship master's. Unlike an aircraft pilot, however, the hydrofoil master still has the traditional hazards of rocks, debris, and the sea itself.

The risk that high technology shipping presents is related to the cargo or job that the vessel serves and consequently must be weighed against the benefits derived from the service. Because of the cost of the ships and the nature of the cargoes, compensation for an accident is limited. In the cases where the service is of direct benefit to the state, the risk is easy to calculate. The difficulty of assessing the risk is greater when a ship is simply transiting waters controlled by third parties — a situation that will become commonplace with extended jurisdiction.

LNG, liquefied petroleum gas (LPG), nuclear waste, and chemical carriers and product carriers (vessels that carry different grades of petroleum products) all are extremely expensive (LNG carriers cost around US$120 million apiece) and largely built to specific trade. LNG ships are perhaps the most "dedicated," with virtually no spot charter market for the ships — the vessels are built to serve very specific projects. Nuclear waste carriers are similar in their restricted employment prospects. A nuclear fuel carrier is assigned largely to carrying spent nuclear fuel of a reactor in one country to that of another for reprocessing. Chemical carriers and product carriers have more employment options but are still dependent on serving a narrow market that is often connected to specific refineries and discharge ports.

LNG ships designed to carry liquefied gas chilled to 163°C below zero represent potentially the most lethal ships afloat, but after nearly twenty years of service there has been no major casualty, though there have been some very close calls.[79] LPG ships, near cousins to LNG ships, have suffered some terrible casualties. There was an accident in the Philippines in 1973 in which an LPG ship caught fire during discharge after the rupture of a hose, and the fire killed seven people. In an even more gruesome accident, an LPG ship in Japan in 1974 collided with another vessel and exploded, killing thirty people.

In many ways the accidents involving LPG carriers have been useful in designing better ships, but LNG and nuclear waste carriers are still very much unknown quantities. It is uncertain whether an LNG carrier can be vented of its 126,000 m³ of gas in the event of a breach. Most tests have shown that the gas dissipates quickly and does not form a lethal cloud of extremely cold but explosive gas.[80] But the amounts that have been tested are very small. Even less is known about nuclear waste carriers. A fairly typical nuclear waste carrier is the *Pacific Swan,* which was built in 1979 at a cost of US$12 million. The 3,000-DWT vessel was designed to withstand the collision impact of a 24,000-DWT ship moving at 15 knots. The nuclear spent fuel is carried in steel flasks each weighing 45–100 tons and containing around 2 tons of fuel immersed in water. The major hazard that the ships pose is that in the event of a loss of cooling water, the flasks would heat up and inevitably breach the container. If this were to happen in a confined waterway, the ecological results could be catastrophic.[81]

Much the same holds true for chemical carriers and product carriers depending largely on exactly what chemicals or products the vessel is carrying. The Intergovernmental Maritime Organization (IMO) has tried to strengthen regulations concerning chemical shipments, but the littoral state is still largely responsible for what happens within its waterway, if for no other reason than the fact a ship is not responsible for an accident if the navigational aids have not been properly maintained.[82]

There is a price to be paid for safety, but the question is who should bear it. Ultimately the answer must be every maritime nation, but the actual cost of making an international sea-lane safe must inevitably be borne by the user states and the states bordering the waterway. These are the states that derive the greatest benefit from the shipment of hazardous cargoes and endure the greatest risk. International groups like IMO must set the standards for the movement of hazardous goods through these regimes, but enforcement must be in the hands of the littoral states. The dangers are very real in high technology shipping, and the littoral states may not be able to afford the luxury of hindsight.

The Malacca and Singapore Straits

The question of how to control traffic through the Malacca–Singapore straits has been threefold. The initial question was political: Who had jurisdiction over the straits? The second was more of a technological problem: What had to be done to ensure safe navigation in the straits? And the third part of the puzzle was: What would be the economic impact of the changes? The questions hit at the heart of ASEAN unity bringing out the major economic, political, and social differences among the three bordering states — Malaysia, Singapore, and Indonesia.

With both Malaysia and Indonesia claiming 12-nautical-mile (nmi) limits for their territorial seas, for most purposes the straits came under their control. It was suggested briefly and unofficially in Malaysia that the straits should be viewed as the "Suez Canal of Asia,"[83] but this notion was dismissed as it went against the basic principles emerging at UNCLOS III. It was finally acknowledged that the Malacca–Singapore straits were in law as well as in fact a route used for international navigation.

In 1967 the three ASEAN states bordering the straits received their first indication of the potential for catastrophe when the 151,288-DWT *Tokyo Maru* scraped its bottom on Malacca's granite floor. During that fateful year Japan, whose oil lifeline ran through the waterway, proposed that some sort of traffic scheme be adopted for the straits.[84]

The first 200,000-DWT tanker berthed in Singapore in late 1968. It soon became obvious that VLCCs were going to be a fixture in the traffic through the straits and become crucial to the Singaporean economy as well. A preliminary hydrographic survey carried out jointly by Japan, Malaysia, Singapore, and Indonesia in 1969 revealed that five areas of the straits had less than 25 m of water, where a fully loaded VLCC could not transit safely. Thus the survey proved what everybody had suspected for years — that a traffic separation system with specific draft limitations was necessary.[85]

The question of what was necessary was studied over the next three years, and meanwhile the losses mounted. Noël Mostert made the point in his best-seller, *Supership:*

> On one occasion two Japanese VLCCs within the space of one week holed themselves inexplicably on the floor of the Straits, when they supposed they had sufficient water. On 12 March 1973, the 160,000 ton Italian oil-ore ship *Igara* struck an uncharted rock in the South China Sea near Singapore and became, it was later said, the largest single marine insurance loss ever. The ship was a year old and was being navigated, it was said, from charts prepared by surveys which were at least sixty-five years old, made only by lead line, and which didn't indicate the reef on which she foundered.[86]

The point was finally hammered home in 1975 when the 240,000-DWT *Showa Maru*, a Japanese vessel, went aground carrying 224,000 tons of crude from the Persian Gulf for delivery to Japan, spilling thousands of tons of oil into the straits. As a result of a navigational error the vessel, with a draft of 18.3 m (60 ft), grounded in 18.5 m (61 ft) of water on a coral reef 4 nmi from Singapore Harbor. Of its twelve tanks, three center ones and one wing tank were destroyed, and the forepeak was ripped open. The spilled oil moved into the waters of the three littoral countries. And just in case the *Showa Maru* did not make the point abundantly clear, a short time later the 100,000-DWT *Diego Silang* was involved in a collision with two other vessels, resulting in a second baptism of spilled oil.[87]

In considering the design of a traffic separation scheme, a key question was: What draft limitations were really necessary for safety? This question brought into sharp focus the differences among the countries. Recommendations for the minimum underkeel clearance — the distance from the bottom of the channel to the keel of the ship — varied from the Singapore suggestion of 2.5 m (8.2 ft) to the Indonesian and Malaysian recommendations of 4.5 m (14.8 ft). Singapore officials reasoned that, allowing for squat (the tendency of VLCCs to nose down in shallow water), wave action, and a safety margin, 2.5 m would be sufficient. The Malaysians, after considering squat and introducing a "human factor," proposed that 4.5 m was a better margin. Indonesia also supported this figure in the belief that there were bound to be imponderables in the movement of huge VLCCs through restricted waterways.[88]

With their vested interest in the waterway, the Japanese shipowners formed the Strait of Malacca Council in 1968. It was composed of such powerful bodies as the Petroleum Association of Japan, the Shipbuilders' Association of Japan, the Shipowners' Association, the Japanese Maritime Foundation, and the Japanese Hull Insurers' Union. The council's recommendation was for an underkeel clearance of 4 m, although it was proposed that this figure could be "varied" under different conditions of weather, traffic density, or other factors.

Clear self-interest was behind these proposals. Singapore's refining and ship repair industries were built around the VLCC. A change of routes for VLCCs moving between Japan and the Middle East would deal a cruel blow to Singapore's economy since both the shipyards and the refineries had invested in facilities designed to cater to VLCCs.

Malaysia's concerns also were basically economic but focused on fish since a majority of its fish catch was from the straits. Indonesia, unlike Malaysia or Singapore, was not greatly dependent on the straits for any economic reasons. In fact any reasonable diversion of VLCCs on the Middle-East-to-Japan trade route would transit Indonesian waters, passing through either the Sunda or Lombok straits. Thus Indonesia could conceivably derive some economic benefit from this diversion, possibly by establishing ship repair yards and refineries rivaling those of Singapore.

By February 1977 the debate was over and reason prevailed. A compromise underkeel clearance of 3.5 m (11.5 ft) during transit was the agreed figure. On 1 May 1981 the traffic separation scheme went into effect, a victory for regionalism over narrow self-interest. As was observed shortly after the agreement was approved, "the February 24 agreement is a landmark representing one of the first attempts by littoral states on a major waterway to control it—not for the sake of power but for the sake of safety and the ecological well-being of people living and working along it."[89] But traffic density is increasing and further measures will eventually be necessary.

RESPONSES

Regional Approaches

Historically, regionalism often has been an expression of unity against a common foe. In ASEAN shipping the common enemy has been the FEFC and other Western shipping institutions. In many respects, however, the ASEAN nations have been their own worst enemy. The shipping legislation that has been implemented in ASEAN nations, including cargo reservation schemes, cabotage laws, ship licensing policies, and port controls, has largely been aimed at fellow ASEAN nations. It has been easier for the ASEAN countries to tackle the major international political issues of the day generated by events in or initiatives of Vietnam, Kampuchea, the Soviet Union, China, and the United States than to develop a common policy on ships and the sea. There are good practical reasons for this.

Intra-ASEAN trade amounted to 4.9 million metric tons (MT) in 1975, with another 1.5 million MT in transshipment cargoes. This annual total level of 6.4 million MT is expected to remain relatively steady at least up until 1985, with only minor shifts in the composition of specific commodities.[90] A vast majority of this intra-ASEAN trade is composed of what has become known as "neo-bulk"—commodities such as rubber, logs, sawn timber, rice, maize, fertilizer, cement, and oil-bearing seeds that can be shipped as a single homogeneous cargo or as part of a break-bulk shipment. The emphasis on bulk and neo-bulk cargoes has meant that most intra-ASEAN voyages have distinct heavy and light legs, which shipowners have had great difficulty in balancing.

Ship movements are split fairly evenly between liner and tramp services. Singapore and Indonesia have the lion's share of the cargo with 39 percent and 32 percent, respectively, while Thailand is a distant third with 13 percent; the Philippines and Malaysia have less than 10 percent each.[91] Even in the liner services most of the cargo consists of quasi-bulk items like coffee, tea, spices, tobacco, textiles, and rattan. Thus the amount of cargo that could easily be containerized is small.

Many of the routes are impossible to balance. Logs from Sumatera are loaded on barges and towed down the Strait of Malacca to Singapore. The one-way costs are covered, but there is imbalance because there is little that the barges can take to the outback of Sumatera.[92] The one-sidedness of the movements is often reflected in the flag distribution as well; a sample of trading patterns in 1977 revealed that in the 225 full-ship voyages between Thailand and Indonesia (southbound rice was the predominant cargo, balanced only marginally by fertilizer and timber shipments north), 75 voyages were completed by Indonesian flag tonnage, 70 by Singaporean vessels, 23 by Philippine flag ships, 40 by third-flag vessels generally on charter, and only 14 voyages were by Thai vessels, the country that provided a majority of the cargo volume.[93] The only real liner routes that exist totally within ASEAN are Singapore–West Malaysia, Singapore–Indonesia, and peninsular Malaysia–Sumatera. Most of the other routes are extensions of international routes such as Singapore–Bangkok, Singapore–Port Kelang, and Port Kelang–Bangkok. Since the Thai government would prefer for reasons of political and economic security to carry more of its exports in Thai flag vessels, such balancing must be accommodated in any regional arrangement.

The ASEAN nations and Vietnam, Hong Kong, China, and the Chinese province of Taiwan are among the world's leading traders. Under these circumstances regional services are difficult to keep regional. From a shipowner's point of view it makes much better sense to use the triangular shipping route of Hong Kong–Manila–Sandakan–Kota Kinabalu–Hong Kong (which crosses interisland, regional, and extraregional shipping routes) than to undertake a series of two-way voyages with distinctly heavy and light legs. The expansion of national fleets without the rationalization of services among nations would be of little use to ASEAN as a group. Yet the concern of individual ASEAN shipowners engaged in the intra-ASEAN trade is the replacement of existing tonnage. There are around 250 ASEAN flag vessels of around 40,000 DWT operating in the regional trades.[94] An estimated 65 percent of these vessels are less than 2,000 DWT, and nearly all of them are 15–20 years old.[95] It is estimated that Singapore alone has 320 coasting vessels of which 270 regularly ply the intra-ASEAN routes.[96] If the entire fleet were to be replaced the price tag would amount to something like US$400 million, but this figure could be substantially cut by the purchase of second-hand vessels.

For regional or individual fleet expansion, finance is a problem. Traditionally the main sources of ship finance are the shipowner's own funds, national shipping development funds, export credits, commercial lenders, bilateral assistance, and international lending institutions. Financing small shipowners operating on the intra-ASEAN routes is difficult for most commercial lenders for a variety of reasons. Generally the ASEAN shipowners are small, privately owned (frequently family) operations with little collateral other than the ship itself. Often the cash flow situation for such operations is precarious, because the companies are greatly dependent on the success of their particular trade routes. They can be easily disrupted by protective legislation or bad harvests. The actual cost of new small vessels is modest in comparison with the cost of tankers or LNG carriers, but the cost in dollars per deadweight ton is very high, often exceeding US$1,000 for small general cargo vessels. This places an inordinately high risk value on small vessels from the bank's point of view. Also, in the final analysis the commercial lender looks at the exposure to risk of a country and the fiscal responsibility that the country has shown. ASEAN generally has done quite well, but bankers are still cautious about lending to Indonesia and the Philippines, both of which need funds for shipping.

Institutional lenders like the World Bank and the Asian Development Bank (ADB) respond to government programs rather than to individual shipowners. Since this has a tendency to promote "national carriers," these lenders appear to be more interested in nation-building than in region-building. The World Bank in 1974 loaned the Philippine government US$20 million for the development of its interisland fleet and facilities, and Indonesia received a number of loans in the early 1970s designed to build up its interisland fleet.

It is difficult to envision either a rationalization of services or any major changes in the maritime relations of the ASEAN states. Thailand, Indonesia, Malaysia, and the Philippines are all net importers of shipping services, and only Singapore is a net exporter. The majority want the balance redressed. However, should ASEAN nations collectively desire to submerge individual aspirations for the development of a more efficient service for the group as a whole, there are several courses that could be taken.

The conventional procedure is the establishment of bilateral shipping agreements between individual nations. This has already happened with the agreement between Indonesia and Singapore. Such bilateral agreements could contain provisions on commodities, sailings, and flag composition. Knowing approximately what level of trade is to be expected, shipowners could plan their fleets accordingly. These shipowner-shipowner arrangements could be made under the auspices of FASA. However, these bilateral agreements are not likely to be comprehensive enough and often are designed for the preservation of trade rather than its promotion.

Nearly all the interisland shipping companies and intra-ASEAN shipping companies ply routes that take their ships outside their national boundaries. For this reason, the problem of rebuilding an interisland fleet or an inter-ASEAN fleet is one and the same. As the various cabotage laws illustrate, Indonesia, Malaysia, the Philippines, and Thailand are not interested in being dominated by Singaporean shipping services. They do not want either a European monopoly for the international trade or a Singaporean monopoly for the regional services. ASEAN nations are net importers of Singaporean shipping, aggravated by the 1–1.5 million MT of transshipment cargo that passes through the port and by use of Singapore's shipyards. But the problem is to find sufficient items to trade intraregionally.

Malaysia is rebuilding its coastal trading fleet. Indonesia is doing the same for its interisland fleet. Thailand is trying to build a basic international fleet. Singapore shipowners in the intra-ASEAN services have yet to move to replace their vessels. It is likely that an overordering of vessels will result if the individual ASEAN countries pursue an uncoordinated policy of fleet expansion. The region already has had a glimpse of this with the almost overnight saturation of east-to-west Malaysia trade after the introduction of Malaysia's cabotage laws.

The most straightforward means to regionalization would be the formation of an ASEAN shipping line designed to serve the intra-ASEAN routes. The political and economic obstacles to the formation of a regional line are formidable, but it has been done before. The Pacific Forum Line was founded in 1978 by the South Pacific Forum, a regional grouping composed of small Pacific island nations, Australia, and New Zealand. A regional shipping fund was established and the three new Ro-Ro (roll on, roll off) vessels that went into service in 1979 were part of an aid scheme[97] and were registered in Tonga, Samoa, and New Zealand. The company lost US$9 million in its first two years of operation. The problem was severe. The dilemma of trying to serve two masters — profits and politics — is threatening to sink the world's first regional shipping line in a sea of debts.[98]

In the case of ASEAN's trade, the problems would be much the same. The routes are difficult and politics would undoubtedly play a major role, but the problems are not insurmountable. If each ASEAN country registered four vessels of around 6,000–8,000 DWT and placed these vessels into an ASEAN company that operated on a profit-sharing basis, this would provide a solid foundation for building regional shipping and ultimately trade. The advantage that these vessels would have over other lines would be their efficiency based on routes.

Shipping services in a limited regional setting constitute a "commons" of sorts, because all the group shares in the use of the vessels to promote regional trade and development. Conceptually, like a commons, it "should be managed by a corporation in which the owners (states) have a clearly defined share, for instance equity capital."[99] The benefits derived from international shipping, such as improved balance of payments, might be strengthened with improved services at the regional level.

The New Order

Asian shipping has expanded rapidly during the past twenty years. The expansion was partly due to the increase in East–West trade and partly to fulfill the desires of newly independent states to have fleets of their own. The advent of the New International Economic Order (NIEO) philosophy and extended maritime jurisdiction has changed the direction of maritime development in Asia. The emphasis, up until the late 1970s, was largely on building a merchant fleet or training seamen for employment aboard foreign flag vessels. This period is now ending.

The designation of sea-lanes, the use and maintenance of navigational aids, the protection of the marine environment, and the formulation of economic trade policies will all have a bearing on the development of Asian merchant fleets in the immediate future. Asian shipping is now entering a period of qualitative improvement in shipping services. The form that this improvement takes will be based largely on the approaches the governments take toward implementing the accords laid down in the CLS and the attitude of the region toward both regional and international trading agreements.

The future of Asian shipping is inextricably tied to the question of "Who shall inherit the seas?" The CLS, the 40–40–20 UNCTAD Liner Code, and the proposed 40–40–20 bulk-cargo-sharing scheme will forever alter the shipping business. The technology of the sea is changing just as rapidly with the development of LNG carriers, nuclear waste carriers, mammoth drilling rigs, satellite communication and navigation systems, radar, and unmanned engine rooms.

The chief policy decisions that Southeast Asian countries must make regarding shipping concern port development, investment in merchant fleets, membership in shipping conferences, cargo reservation, cabotage laws, flags of convenience, and standards of ship maintenance and crew training. Archipelagic states have some additional decisions to make, brought about by their new status under the CLS, such as the designation of archipelagic sea-lanes. But their principal problem remains that of maintaining and improving sea communications with the far-flung islands of their archipelagos and with the rest of the world.

The written and unwritten rules that have guided shipping enterprises for four centuries are being overturned in less than a generation. The impact of this great "sea change" will affect every aspect of shipping: the ports of call, the ships' flags, size and nationality of crews, where the ships are built, the routes ships will take, and liability in the event of accident. It is the beginning of a new order.

CHAPTER 7

DEFENSE

Joseph R. Morgan
Donald W. Fryer

The use of Southeast Asian seas for national defense is interwoven with the many other uses that nations of the region make of these waters. Although several countries outside Southeast Asia are concerned with the protection of maritime trade that passes through the region, this chapter focuses on Brunei, Burma, Indonesia, Kampuchea, Laos, Malaysia, the Philippines, Singapore, Thailand, and Vietnam. China and the island province of Taiwan are treated here because they have extensive coastlines on the South China Sea and because their interests and responses to maritime defense issues are so directly of interest to nations in the region. The naval forces, bases, and security activities of the United States and the Soviet Union are mentioned only as they relate directly to policy decisions and considerations of the Southeast Asian nations.

The maritime defense interests of Southeast Asian nations are varied, although as developing nations with little money to spare for navies, they have similar problems. Although emphasis here is on the operational characteristics of navies, the role of air power in the region must not be discounted. The relatively compact nature of Southeast Asian waters and the short distances involved make both merchant ships and naval vessels particularly susceptible to attack from land-based aircraft. Notwithstanding air power's undeniable importance, the need to focus on maritime issues, as opposed to general security concerns that might involve land and air forces, precludes detailed discussion of the role or capabilities of Southeast Asian air forces. Air capabilities receive mention here only when particularly applicable to questions of surveillance or the specific question of China's possible attempts to recapture the island province of Taiwan.

Although naval forces may be assigned a variety of missions, there are but three basic functions of navies: defense of the nation against attack, maintenance of citizen and alien order within the nation, and protection of the nation's marine resources.

Sea power serves to keep a nation's sea-lanes open and to deny the use of the oceans to the merchant fleet and navy of an enemy in time of war. Navies can project power from the sea to the land area of an enemy and, in conjunction with air

230

forces, support friendly ground forces in combat. Basic defense occupies navies even in peacetime. Fleets can support a nation's foreign policy objectives by threatening the use of force. The navy can be employed as a deterrent force, and the tactic of showing the flag enhances the deterrence mission. If combat and deterrence capabilities are to be effective, combat readiness must be maintained; hence the principal occupation of navies in peacetime is to train for war.

In nations that have not achieved a high degree of national unity or that have significant dissident groups, the navy may be used in policing roles, supporting the national government against its challengers. Navies may also be involved in antipiracy and antismuggling actions.

Navies, or coast guards in some countries, have always been responsible in some measure for ensuring that the resources in seas under national jurisdiction are not freely available to nationals of other countries. Extension of territorial seas up to 12 nautical miles (nmi) and the establishment of exclusive economic zones (EEZs) that may extend up to 200 nmi from a nation's baselines have made this function both more important and more difficult to carry out. Moreover, the maritime activities that a coastal state can legitimately control now include scientific research, marine pollution, and the exploitation of mineral and biological resources. Surveillance activities and the gathering of intelligence are carried out in support of the mission to protect marine resources and also as part of the defense function. Navies, or coast guards in some countries, also carry out roles only peripherally related to their principal missions. They maintain navigation aids, conduct hydrographic surveys and produce nautical charts, and take a leading role in search and rescue operations.

Distances along typical shipping routes in the Southeast Asian marine region (Figure 7.1 and Table 7.1) suggest both the dimensions of the region and the problems of protecting shipping. Figure 7.1 also shows naval and air bases of both Southeast Asian nations and outside powers.

MARITIME DEFENSE ISSUES IN SOUTHEAST ASIA

In contrast with other uses of the sea in which private individuals and corporations of many kinds participate, maritime defense is exclusively the preserve of the state. Without the physical force to protect its territory from attack and to maintain internal security, the state may not survive as a sovereign entity. In view of Southeast Asia's strong maritime traditions, the limited development of naval defense forces in the respective national military establishments appears somewhat anomalous. The physical shapes of the states of Southeast Asia produce severe administrative problems. Only Singapore and Kampuchea have relatively compact shapes. Others are archipelagic, fractured, or prorupt (with a narrow, elongated land extension, like Thailand or Burma). The disadvantages of a lack of compactness are compounded by the existence in peripheral areas of ethnic or linguistic groups that regard themselves as quite distinct from the dominant national group and from which most of the ruling elite is drawn.

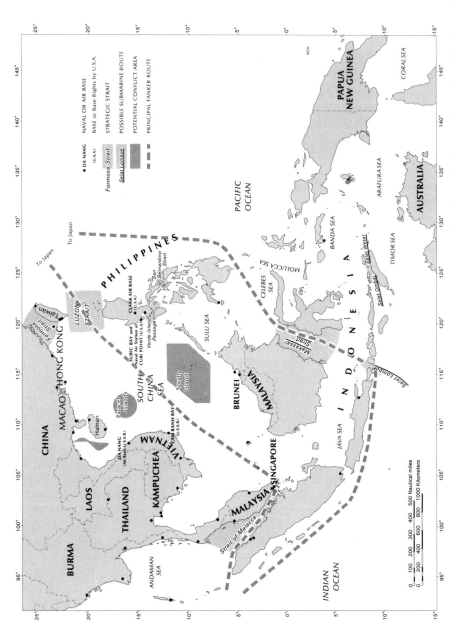

Figure 7.1 Maritime defense (modified from Joseph R. Morgan and Mark J. Valencia, eds., *Atlas for Marine Policy in Southeast Asian Seas*, Berkeley: University of California Press, 1983, p. 54).

Table 7.1   Distances and Travel Times of Selected Southeast Asian Routes

Route	Distance (nmi)	Travel Time (at 15 knots)
Singapore–Manila (via routes N and S of "Dangerous Ground")	1,330	3 days, 17 hours
Singapore–Bangkok	842	2 days, 8 hours
Singapore–Ho Chi Minh City	649	1 day, 19 hours
Singapore–Jakarta	525	1 day, 11 hours
Singapore–Surabaya	763	2 days, 3 hours
Singapore–Torres Strait	2,468	6 days, 21 hours
Singapore–Rangoon	1,109	3 days, 2 hours
Manila–Hong Kong	631	1 day, 18 hours
Manila–Ho Chi Minh City	907	2 days, 13 hours
Manila–Bangkok	1,435	4 days
Manila–Darwin	1,834	5 days, 2 hours
Manila–Selat Sunda	1,578	4 days, 9 hours
Manila–Torres Strait (via Basilan Strait)	2,193	6 days, 2 hours
(via San Bernadino Strait)	2,239	6 days, 5 hours
Manila–Surabaya	1,540	4 days, 7 hours
Manila–Selat Lombok	1,518	4 days, 5 hours
Hong Kong–Ho Chi Minh City	917	2 days, 13 hours
Hong Kong–Jakarta	1,782	4 days, 23 hours
Cam Ranh Bay–Singapore	760	2 days, 3 hours
VLCC Route (Andaman Sea to Luzon Strait)	2,300	6 days, 9 hours
ULCC Route (Andaman Sea to 20°N)	3,300	9 days, 3 hours

Source: Route Chart of Southeast Asia, First edition, Washington, D.C.: Defense Mapping Agency Hydrographic/Topographic Center, 1979.

The primary goal of every Southeast Asian government is to preserve and consolidate the unitary structure of the nation and the integrity of its territory and to develop among its heterogeneous peoples the common sense of nationality that distinguishes the true nation-state. Expressions of regional or sectional interest jeopardize this goal and therefore must be discouraged or suppressed.

The threat of external attack from the sea appears remote. For most Southeast Asian governments the only conceivable source of direct aggression is one of the Communist powers, either in or outside of Southeast Asia itself. But such elements are more feared for their capacity for infiltrating and subverting disaffected ethnic groups. Despite their value in showing the flag, navies are largely useless in combating these activities. Moreover, among the Communist powers only the

USSR possesses the naval resources either to launch or to sustain a serious attack by sea, and these could hardly be committed (either on their own or in conjunction with the naval forces of any "client" state, which in practice means Vietnam) without provoking some reaction and possible intervention by other powers.

Conflict among the Association of Southeast Asian Nations (ASEAN) is a possibility, in view of the conflicting claims to certain South China Sea islands and the numerous overlapping maritime jurisdictions. Hostilities, if they occurred, would almost certainly involve land rather than naval forces. Under these circumstances the relatively low priority given to national navies in total military expenditure appears sensible.

In Southeast Asian waters there are many critical straits that could be defended or interdicted by small, light forces. The number of missile-armed patrol boats recently added to Third World fleets in general has been increasing.[1] These provide great striking power at little cost and are ideally suited to Southeast Asian waters. Under certain circumstances these small but powerful vessels can hold their own against the larger ships of major naval powers. In effect, small, fast ships armed with modern surface-to-surface missiles have become the great equalizers in the relative strengths of naval forces. However, since small naval vessels have limited endurance and sea-keeping qualities, numerous bases well distributed throughout the national territory are desirable.

The navies of Southeast Asia are inadequate even to discharge the traditional duties of suppressing piracy, smuggling, and barter trade. For the archipelagic states at least, it well may be doubted if these activities can ever be eliminated entirely. Many of the navies in Southeast Asia are concerned primarily with defensive patrolling of coastlines and enforcement of regulations in their EEZs. Table 7.2 indicates the scope of the problem.

If governments are to exercise the extended jurisdictional rights conferred by the Convention on the Law of the Sea (CLS), the enormously enhanced surveillance tasks that will fall on some national navies would require a substantial enlargement of naval establishments. Such expansion may not be easy, for the great political strength of the army in most Southeast Asian nations is likely to be exercised to prevent any reduction of its patronage and political influence, and in particular, its share of the defense budget.

The balance between combat-ready and surveillance missions is a function of varying national perceptions on the one hand of the risk of attack and its potential origin and on the other of the present and future exploitation of national resources, including those resources conferred by expanded maritime jurisdictions. Geographic position and archipelagic status might suggest that naval policy in the Philippines and Indonesia should be broadly similar. The reality is very different because of these countries' divergent experiences of decolonization and their differing subsequent relations with the former imperial powers.

Any attack against these archipelagic states must be either seaborne or airborne. For the states of mainland Southeast Asia, on the other hand, any seaborne attack is perceived as likely to be relatively minor support of an overland assault or else designed as a tactical diversion. The status of Malaysia as part of both mainland

Table 7.2   Coastal Lengths, Areas to 200-Nautical-Mile Limits, and Patrol Capabilities for Southeast Asian Navies

Nation	Vessels Available for Patrol Duty (number)	Coastline Length (km)	Hypothetical Area to 200 nmi (km²)	Coastline Length per Ship (km/ship)	Area per Ship (km²/ship)
Brunei	9	161	7,100	17.89	789
Burma	85	3,060	148,600	36.00	1,748
Indonesia	68	54,716	1,577,000	804.65	23,195
Kampuchea	40	443	16,200	11.08	405
Laos	0	0	0	0	0
Malaysia	47	4,675	138,700	99.47	2,951
Philippines	125	22,540	551,400	180.32	4,411
Singapore	20	193	100	9.65	5
Thailand	70	3,219	94,700	45.99	1,353
Vietnam	8	3,444	210,600	40.52	2,478

Sources: J. E. Moore, ed., *Jane's Fighting Ships, 1982–1983,* N.Y.: Jane's Publishing Inc., 1982; Elisabeth Mann Borgese and Norton Ginsburg, eds., *Ocean Yearbook 3,* Chicago: University of Chicago Press, 1983, p. 564.

and archipelagic Southeast Asia affects its defense planning. External attack appears to be more likely to come from the sea than across its land frontiers.

Naval policy is slowly modifying under the aegis of ASEAN, which includes all the states of Southeast Asia except Burma and the Communist Indochinese states. Brunei, now in ASEAN, was given observer status at the ASEAN foreign ministers' meetings in Manila in 1981 and in Singapore in 1982. ASEAN was created to pursue strictly limited objectives of economic and social cooperation. Its members have never considered the organization as a framework for a defense alliance although since 1975 there have been efforts and pressures to turn ASEAN into a military pact. Nevertheless, individual members of ASEAN have cooperated in mounting an impressive array of defense exercises. Indonesia has conducted joint air, naval, and army maneuvers with Malaysia, and the two countries have cooperated in the patrolling of their common South China Sea border areas for Vietnamese refugees. Indonesia also has conducted joint naval surveillance in Celebes border waters with the Philippines. Moreover, Thailand and Malaysia have signed the first bilateral defense pact in Southeast Asia since the end of the Indochina war, and in addition to the 1954 Manila Pact, Thailand and the Philippines have agreed to cooperate on security matters.[2] With the organization's steady growth in stature, as evidenced by the appearance of an ASEAN viewpoint in such bodies as the Economic and Social Commission for Asia and the Pacific (ESCAP) and the United Nations Conference on Trade and Development (UNCTAD), the presumption must be strong that such activities are likely to be an enduring feature. The development of a consolidated Vietnamese-dominated, Soviet-influenced Indochina is deeply troubling to ASEAN capitals, as it may confirm their nightmares of two groupings of ideological and political adversaries embarked on an economic and military race for regional supremacy. Such common fears eventually may stimulate ASEAN military cooperation, including cooperation among national naval and coastal patrol forces.

Of the numerous defense issues in the marine region, eight are predominant and concern the largest number of the region's states. Table 7.3 summarizes these eight important issues and offers a summary assessment of the degree to which they are of concern to the ten Southeast Asian nations.

Fear of Vietnam

Southeast Asian countries fear that Vietnam's occupation of Kampuchea, its domination of Laos, and its attacks across the border between Thailand and Kampuchea presage further attempts by armed forces to expand Vietnamese territory and influence at their expense. The archipelagic nations are less fearful of Vietnam's intentions and capabilities than are the mainland states. The Philippines and Indonesia realize that Vietnam must mount any attack against them from the sea, and they know that the Vietnamese navy is not yet a military force capable of carrying out such a difficult amphibious operation.

Piracy, Smuggling, and Barter Trade

All governments want to suppress piracy and smuggling, but in Burma, Thailand, Indonesia, and the Philippines these activities may also be closely allied with barter trading. These activities can help to finance regional insurgencies or demands for autonomy. Apart from their challenge to national unity, these activities deny foreign exchange to central governments and reduce their capacity to meet obligations to creditors.

Protection of Marine Resources

Disputes over fishing rights either with neighbors or with extraregional parties (Japan, the USSR, or the Republic of Korea) periodically embroil every Southeast Asian nation. Marine resources, however, are not evenly distributed among the nations of the region. Some have long coastlines, sizable EEZs, and valuable mineral and biological resources. Others are short-changed in that they may be landlocked (Laos) or zone-locked (Singapore and Kampuchea). Some can lay claim to offshore oil and gas deposits, others to important fisheries. Some have very small offshore areas they can claim or have not yet been able to develop the marine resources they possess.

Claims to Maritime Jurisdiction

As indicated in Chapter 3, most of the littoral states of the South China Sea make claims to maritime jurisdictions that in some particulars conflict with those of oth-

Table 7.3 Maritime Defense Issues in Southeast Asia

Nations of Southeast Asia	Fear of Vietnam	Piracy, Smuggling, and Barter Trade	Protection of Marine Resources	Claims to Maritime Jurisdiction	Latent Regional Rivalries	China–Vietnam Rivalry	China–ASEAN Rivalry	Freedom of Navigation
Brunei	3	2	2	2	1	3	2	2
Burma	3	1	1	1	2	3	3	2
Indonesia	3	1	1	2	2	3	2	1
Kampuchea	1	3	2	3	2	1	3	2
Laos	1	3	3	3	2	2	3	3
Malaysia	2	2	2	2	1	2	1	1
Philippines	3	1	1	1	1	3	2	1
Singapore	2	2	3	3	2	2	1	1
Thailand	1	1	2	2	1	2	2	2
Vietnam	n.a.	2	1	1	2	1	2	2

Note: 1 = great concern; 2 = moderate concern; 3 = little concern. Assessments are those of the authors of this chapter and do not necessarily represent published or publicly expressed views of the nations.

ers. These conflicts involve claims to territorial waters, to claims of EEZs, or to claims to islands and island groups. Those disputed areas could become the focus of naval activity.

The Spratly and Paracel groups are hotly disputed. The Spratly Islands, claimed partially or entirely by China, the Chinese province of Taiwan, Vietnam, the Philippines, and Malaysia, are important for a number of reasons. The possible presence of valuable oil resources is but one factor in the overlapping claims; the islands are also considered to be strategic locations for controlling the important sea-lanes through the South China Sea. In addition to the claimants, the interests of the United States, the USSR, and Japan are significant. The Soviets, with a base at Cam Ranh Bay in Vietnam, can compete with the United States (with its base at Subic Bay in the Philippines) for control of the vital tanker route that carries more than 90 percent of Japan's crude oil needs.

Control of the Spratly Islands by China might be viewed with concern by the USSR. China vigorously protests Vietnam's claims to the islands, perhaps feeling that Vietnam is actually a puppet of the USSR. The Philippines considers its claim to the islands, which it calls Kalayaan, vital to the defense of the western perimeter of the archipelago, and Manila hopes that its mutual defense pact with the United States will result in American support for its claim to the islands. The Philippines has nearly 1,000 troops stationed on six of the islands and maintains airstrips on two islands. Vietnam also maintains military garrisons, with about 350 troops on five islands, and Hanoi has fortified its main garrison with coastal artillery and antiaircraft guns. The Chinese province of Taiwan occupies the largest island in the Spratly group and maintains a force of 600 troops. China claims the entire Spratly archipelago but occupies none of the islands. Malaysia's claim is based on the fact that its continental shelf extends into the area of the southern Spratlys.[3]

The Paracel Islands are claimed by both China and Vietnam. In 1974 the Chinese defeated Vietnamese forces there and now are effectively in control, enabling China to control access to the Gulf of Tonkin and providing for protection and reconnaissance of China's southern flank. In addition, China wants to keep Vietnam's ally, the USSR, from establishing a stronger military presence in the region. Hostilities in the Paracels have not ceased with Chinese capture of the islands in 1974. There have been skirmishes since, and in 1979 China declared four areas in the vicinity of the Paracels and the island of Hainan to be danger zones and forebade overflights between altitudes of 1,000 meters (m) and 20,000 m.

The conflicting claims of Vietnam and China to an area in the Gulf of Tonkin is the third major region of possible conflict. There are potential oil resources in the gulf, and both countries have been active in exploration activities.

Latent Regional Rivalries

All Southeast Asian nations can find some historical or cultural grounds for claims to the territory of neighbors. Some of these claims arise from the actions of former colonial powers, but others are of longer standing and involve ethnic or linguistic affinities that manifest themselves in a strong sense of identity. The question of ownership of the Malaysian District of Limbang that cuts Brunei in two exemplifies the colonial type. The question of ownership of Sabah between the Philippines and Malaysia involving claims by the Sultan of Jolo illustrates the latter category, although it is compounded by colonial decisions.

In the Sulu Sea area, Philippine, Indonesian, and Malaysian interests and claims converge and conflict in Sabah, the island chains to the northeast, and also in Mindanao, lands that in the nineteenth century together constituted the ill-defined Sultanate of Sulu. Offshore oil and gas production is ongoing here and its potential is great.

China–Vietnam Rivalry

The China–Vietnam dispute also has deep historical roots and was exacerbated by colonial policy. Although the Tonkin boundary and jurisdiction over islands in the South China Sea are also at issue, Vietnam's alliance with the USSR and its aggressive expansion in mainland Southeast Asia, including the potential threat it constitutes to Thailand, are the major causes of Chinese hostility. The USSR is directly involved as a supplier of military and economic aid to Vietnam; the United States could perhaps become involved through similar support to China. Hostilities between China and Vietnam could spill over to other Southeast Asian nations, particularly if the USSR and the United States were to become involved. Geographic location makes this issue of less concern to some nations than to others. In general, nations farthest from the China–Vietnam boundary view the rivalry with less alarm than those, such as Thailand, that have common borders with Indochinese states.

China–ASEAN Rivalries

ASEAN countries have long perceived China as a greater menace than the USSR; China's proximity, the presence in Southeast Asia of large numbers of Chinese of major significance in the region's economic life, and China's historical claim to sovereignty over the entire eastern coasts of the Asian continent all contribute to the Southeast Asian image of the Chinese colossus. The expansion of the Chinese navy would increase Southeast Asian fears of China's ambitions, as would any more forceful demonstrations of China's claim to islands of the South China Sea.

Freedom of Navigation

All countries have some interest in preserving the freedom of navigation in Southeast Asian waters and will carefully watch all attempts at assertion of maritime jurisdictions that constrain this tradition. The issue is of extreme importance to Singapore and of considerable concern to Malaysia and Indonesia, both of which have ports on the Strait of Malacca. Landlocked Laos is less concerned, but it too needs access to the sea, obtained in the past through either Thailand or Vietnam.

NATIONAL CONCERNS, RESOURCES,
AND POSSIBLE RESPONSES TO CONFLICT

National defense concerns in Southeast Asia are influenced by nations' perceptions of current and future threats — both external and internal — and these nations' political and socioeconomic capabilities to develop an appropriate response. However, these perceptions of threat and the role of a navy in meeting it are in turn often influenced by mixtures of ethnicity and history, particularly that involving extraregional powers. National defense concerns, naval resources, and possible responses of the individual Southeast Asian countries are described here. See Table 7.4 for details on compositions and strengths of the region's navies.

Brunei

Brunei's oil wealth, its new deep-water port of Muara, and its runway capable of accommodating the largest aircraft in service, along with its position on the South China Sea, give it great strategic value. Since its beginnings in the early 1930s the petroleum industry has transformed this isolated oddity of the former British Empire set in a forested wilderness into a fragment of the Malay world that, despite its very different physical setting, in many ways recalls the tiny sheikdoms of the Persian Gulf. If Brunei's petroleum output is trifling by Middle East standards, the quality of its crudes and proximity to the markets of Japan and Australia are substantial advantages.

For its neighbor Malaysia, Brunei is a colonial anachronism, a British puppet that refused to join the Federation of Malaysia as its founding in 1963 out of pique. Brunei has since engaged in a propaganda war with Kuala Lumpur, deliberately impeding the closer integration of peninsular Malaysia with Sarawak and Sabah. Sukarno's Indonesia also considered the government of Brunei a problem and supported the 1962 attempt at revolution there. Brunei's ruling house can claim a continuity unmatched by any of the sultanates of peninsular Malaysia, which Brunei regards as an upstart. Moreover, Brunei uses religion in its dispute with Malaysia over Limbang, the territory occupied by Sarawak in 1890 and whose seizure Brunei has never accepted, arguing that under Islamic law property acquired illegally must be returned to its rightful owner. In sum, Brunei claims to be more Malay than Malaysia.[4]

In 1979 Brunei signed an agreement with the United Kingdom in which its status as a British "protected state" was to be replaced by full independence on 1 January 1984. Malaysia was reasonably confident that eventually Brunei would accede to it, thus achieving what Malaysia felt should have been accomplished in 1963. Such an outcome would probably have been accepted by Indonesia. But an independent Brunei again raises the specter of separatism in the Malay world, unless ASEAN, of which Brunei has become a member, successfully manages the problem. The new state will need to show its determination to defend itself and to find acceptable allies.

Table 7.4 Southeast Asian Navies

	Submarines			Destroyers	Frigates	Corvettes	Fast-Attack Craft			Patrol Craft			Amphibious Forces		Mine Sweepers		Personnel
	Missile	Fleet	Patrol				Missile	Gun	Torpedo	Large	Coastal	River	Ships	Boats	Ocean	Coastal	
Brunei							3				3			29			457
Burma					1	4				33	9(2)	41					10,000
China	1	2	102(9)[a]	12(6)	16	3	207(12)	372	255	49(4)	7	110	40	469	23	80	298,000
Taiwan			2	23	10	3	2		9	15	10		28	22		14	11,000
Indonesia			4(2)		10		4(4)		2		8		14	62	4		40,000
Kampuchea											15	25					11,000
Malaysia					2(2)		8	6		22		5				2	6,000
Philippines					7	10	(3)			15	59		31	71			15,000
Singapore							6(3)	6								2	3,000
Thailand					6		6	2		21(4)	27(3)	40	8	41(4)		4	30,000
Vietnam					6	2	8	6	8	6	3	563[b]			1		n.a.

Source: J. E. Moore, ed., *Jane's Fighting Ships, 1982–1983,* N.Y.: Jane's Publishing Inc., 1982.

[a] Numbers in parentheses indicate ships under construction.

[b] Nonoperational. Other nonoperational forces include 181 fast-attack and patrol craft.

Brunei's closer association with Singapore, which could also find itself constrained by Malaysian and Indonesian pressures, is one approach to a solution of
this problem. Singapore's armed forces, which lack suitable facilities within the
island republic, train for jungle warfare in Brunei's Temburong district, and Brunei students, who formerly sought higher education and technical training in Malaysia, now attend institutions in Singapore. Cooperation between Brunei's small
navy and that of Singapore appears likely to increase, and further expansion of
Brunei's naval forces is certain. It is difficult to see how the protected state, which
vigorously proclaims its own brand of Malay identity and nationalism, could do
otherwise; the security of Brunei's present and potential offshore oil industry
alone compels such a development. With full independence Brunei now will begin
enforcing its suite of maritime zones to obtain imputed oil resources of the South
China Sea. Moreover, a Brunei claim to the southern Spratlys would appear just as
valid as the present claim of Malaysia. The tension between Brunei and Malaysia
thus appears likely to be extended to jurisdiction offshore.

The Brunei fleet, although small, should be up to the task of protecting the
offshore oil installations and patrolling claimed maritime zones. There are three
potent missile-equipped, fast-attack craft and three small patrol vessels. The amphibious capacity consists of twenty-nine 60-gross-ton (GT) boats, presumably
used more for logistic purposes than for any potential assault operations.

Burma

Burma has a long and intricate coastline, with numerous indentations and offshore
islands. Such conditions are ideal for smuggling and other illegal maritime activities for which Burma's weak economy generates enormous opportunities. Indeed,
smuggling is essential to the survival of the government for it supplies consumer
goods for the enormous and largely institutionalized black markets necessary to
command the allegiance of the bureaucracy and professional classes. Condemned
in principle, smuggling of rice, livestock, and minerals out of Burma and of consumer goods into Burma is in practice largely condoned. The navy can do little
more than make token attempts at suppression.

Illegal fishing, both in Burmese territorial waters and in areas of extended maritime jurisdiction, by nonnationals (principally Thais) is another major problem for
the naval and ancillary forces. In a singular departure from the policy of national-
izing all economic activity apart from agriculture, Burma has let drilling licenses to
foreign enterprises for oil and gas in the Gulf of Martaban. Thus the protection of
drilling platforms could become an additional responsibility. In view of the nation's
multiplicity of insurgencies, that is a task the navy could not take lightly. Burmese
offshore waters in the Andaman Sea are a rich fishing ground. Burma has made
claims to these waters in a number of controversial ways that appear to violate recognized principles of the CLS.[5]

Despite a long history of conflict with neighbors, Burma's only important
boundary dispute since independence has been with China, and these differences
were largely resolved by agreements made in 1960. The many insurrections that
hinder Burma from achieving a truly national polity and economy concern mainly

the eastern portions of the country, in which naval operations play no part. Burma's position at the northwestern extremity of the Bay of Bengal and east of the Andaman Sea gives it little strategic value except as a back door to China. It is unlikely that this important World War II role will be reenacted in the foreseeable future.

While most of the Burmese fleet is old and probably needs to be replaced the navy does boast a 383-ton Danish-built fishery protection vessel delivered in mid-1980; two more have been ordered.[6] The remainder of the fleet consists of aging coastal and river patrol boats and a number of gunboats. The largest units are a single frigate and four corvettes, all escort-type vessels. The small, modern, fast-attack craft are not present in the Burmese navy, and there is no amphibious or minesweeping capacity. Burma has little need for vessels designed to keep sea-lanes open since the merchant fleet is minuscule.

With a coastline of 3,060 kilometers (km) and 148,600 square kilometers (km²) of EEZ, the fisheries patrol problem is difficult. There are eighty-five ships available, but some (the river patrol and gunboats) can only be used close to shore. As Table 7.2 shows, if the entire fleet were available each ship would have to patrol more than 1,700 km². If half the fleet is operational at any given time, however, each ship must patrol 3,456 km² — an impossible task. Nevertheless, Burmese naval strategy — to concentrate on fisheries protection — is a sound one since there are no other real missions for the navy. There are plans to further increase the size of the fisheries protection fleet so that eventually there will be a total of twelve ships — three coastal patrol vessels, three offshore patrol vessels, and six inshore patrol boats. The most critical fishing areas can probably be protected with a fleet of this size, augmented by other ships in the navy.

China

The official name of the Chinese navy is the People's Liberation Army (PLA) Navy. The name is significant, for the navy literally is a branch of the army, and most naval strategists and high-ranking officers are army trained. The basic naval strategy is largely defensive, with the navy viewed as the seaward arm of the coastal defense forces.[7] In spite of this, the Chinese navy is now the third largest in the world in terms of numbers of naval personnel.[8] The Chinese have long feared invasion of their territory by stronger powers, and times have not completely changed: "Certainly, the Chinese fear the Soviet navy's presence in the Pacific and Indian Oceans and the immense potential for destruction of China's growing maritime concerns that it offers."[9]

Ironically, the Chinese began building their modern defensive fleet with the assistance of the USSR, currently their greatest threat. In the late 1950s the Soviets supplied OSA and Komar patrol boats, Kronstadt antisubmarine escorts, and a large number of Romeo- and Whiskey-class submarines. Between 1960 and 1971 the Chinese began building their own fleet, and more than 800 vessels were completed or commenced during this period. At the same time the argument over the proper role of the navy gained momentum; should the navy be organized for power projection or for defense? The defense argument prevailed because of the growing Soviet threat and the stronger U.S. presence in the Pacific. The inshore-oriented fleet was developed as what might be called the "fortress fleet."[10]

Once the decision was made to build a defensive fleet, an appropriate strategy was outlined. In essence, naval strategy in China is designed to blunt, engulf, and finally to overwhelm an attacking fleet, functions that are assigned to three defensive rings.[11] Tactical command of the navy is in the hands of three separate commands — the North Sea Fleet, the East Sea Fleet, and the South Sea Fleet. For purposes of this volume the principal interest is in the East and South Sea fleets, for the East Sea Fleet defends the coast from the Shanghai area to and including the Taiwan Strait, while the South Sea Fleet guards Guangdong province and the southern flank of the country. The South Sea Fleet has a major interest in Zhanjiang and the Hainan peninsula, which cover the Gulf of Tonkin and the Soviet navy routes to Cam Ranh Bay and the Indian Ocean.[12]

The East Sea Fleet has more than 600 vessels, many of which are patrol boats, but it also includes one submarine squadron. The force is supplemented with air, artillery, and land-based missile support. The strength of the fleet is indicative of the importance attached to the Taiwan Strait region and the possibility of military action against Taiwan. As Lauriat points out,

> The South Sea Fleet is undoubtedly the weakest of the three. The Nationalist control of the Strait of Taiwan prevented any major reinforcements from being transferred, forcing the South Sea Fleet to rely on its own devices. This period was almost immediately followed by the build-up of American naval presence off the coast of Vietnam. Now the fleet possesses around 285 units but, with the current tension, is being reinforced in the Gulf of Tonkin and the South China Sea.[13]

The three defensive rings are deployed as an outer ring of Romeo- and Whiskey-class submarines backed up by bombers and torpedo planes, a middle ring of destroyers and frigates, and an inner ring of fast patrol boats armed with missiles, torpedoes, and guns.

The submarines lack the speed and endurance needed for open-ocean operations but are well suited for controlling the access routes to the South China Sea. They are equipped with six or eight torpedo tubes and have a maximum cruising range of 7,000 nmi or thirty-five to forty-five days at sea. They have a surface speed of 19 knots and can make 15 knots submerged for short periods of time. But they are too noisy and can be detected rather easily by modern antisubmarine ships. Nevertheless, the vessels have sufficient range and numbers to meet an opponent in any of the major straits leading to the Chinese seaboard.[14]

The destroyers and frigates that make up the middle ring have the best seakeeping qualities, and the newer ones have a range of 2,500–4,000 nmi. Equipped with SSN–2 Styx surface-to-surface missiles, they are primarily an antiship force. With virtually no antisubmarine (ASW) or antiair warfare (AAW) capability, they need support from fighters and reconnaissance aircraft.[15]

The inner ring is most impressive. The OSA boats each carry four SSN–2 missiles and have a speed of 36 knots. The patrol boat force is characterized by a great variety of weaponry and great flexibility. Boats can be rapidly moved to a war zone, by rail if necessary. This capability to deploy large numbers of effective craft permits the Chinese to mount a swarm attack that could overwhelm an enemy fleet's electronic countermeasures.[16] However, the small size of the individual units makes this a fair-weather fleet. The patrol boats are inoperable in typhoon and northern monsoon seasons.[17]

Is the defensive strategy sound? Is it likely to be effective? The composite effect of the three rings would enable the PLA navy to launch more than 800 missiles against an invading enemy. But the Chinese fleet generally suffers from a lack of seakeeping ability and is vulnerable to submarines and attacking aircraft. Is it reasonable to assume that China's principal enemy, the Soviets, would launch a naval assault against the Chinese mainland? The Soviet navy has great flexibility and power, and if a naval assault is contemplated it could be launched from beyond the reach of Chinese navy defense forces. Moreover, the USSR could harm China in a number of other ways, one of which would be to interdict Chinese shipping. The large USSR submarine force is clearly capable of this, and the Chinese navy is notably lacking in ASW strength.

China's merchant fleet will soon be the sixth largest in the world,[18] yet there seems to be nothing in the Chinese naval strategy to protect the sea lines of communication and the trade routes. The dramatic increase in Chinese emphasis on maritime trade in the last few years — in 1978 the Chinese merchant fleet ranked fourteenth — is not being supported by a concomitant increase in the types of naval vessels needed to protect seagoing commerce. The naval strategists, largely army officers, seem to have little appreciation for the problem. The nine escorts in the fleet clearly are not enough.

The navy's capabilities can only be evaluated theoretically since the only naval combat by Chinese forces since World War II has been some inconclusive engagements in the Taiwan Strait in 1949, 1954–55, and 1958 and a 1974 assault by China against Republic of Vietnam forces in the Paracel Islands.[19] The Chinese were successful in the Paracels, but against Taiwan they failed. More important, however, is the fact that none of the engagements put the naval fortress strategy to the test.

There is evidence in the navy order of battle that reuniting Taiwan with the mainland, by force if necessary, is an objective to be supported by naval units. The fleet is capable of limited striking operations and has considerable defense capability.[20] The greatest strength of the navy, however, its fast-attack craft, is not available for an invasion of Taiwan, since the patrol craft are not seaworthy enough to operate in the Taiwan Strait. There is need then to rely on the destroyers and frigates, which are showing signs of age.[21]

Amphibious strength and air power are the key elements in an assault on Taiwan. With but 40 landing craft China has limitations. Its 469 landing craft are too small to negotiate the open seas of the Taiwan Strait, and in the past Taiwan has demonstrated clear air supremacy. Consequently, there is a good chance that Taiwan could hold off an attack.[22] Given the balance of military forces, an invasion of Taiwan in the very near future is not likely.

If China chooses another strategy, that of interdicting Taiwan's supply lines, the large navy submarine force could be quite useful. In that case the Chinese submarines would be pitted against the Taiwanese destroyer force. Both forces are getting old, and the outcome might depend more on such things as maintenance and spare parts than on numerical superiority.

If China has ambitions to maintain a sphere of influence over Southeast Asia, its strategic capability is lacking. Neither its navy nor air force are up to the task.[23] It is important to recognize that China claims all the islands in the South China Sea and has used force against Vietnam in the Paracel Islands. There is oil in the South China Sea, and the potential for conflict is clearly present. In Hinton's assessment:

> The potential for conflict is highest in the case of the PRC and Vietnam, because of the extremely strained state of relations between them since 1978. The existence of strained relations between the PRC and Vietnam, and to an even greater degree between the PRC and Hanoi's patron, the Soviet Union, is a major reason why Peking is not likely to seek conflicts with its other neighbors, over oil or anything else.[24]

If China's disputes with Vietnam over maritime claims in the Gulf of Tonkin and the Paracel Islands, or Chinese claims to the Spratly Islands, lead to military action, the navy, with its fortress orientation, may not be up to the task, no matter how large its fleet is in absolute numbers.

Peking maintains a fleet of twenty-three ocean minesweepers, presumably to clear Chinese harbors in the event they are mined by an enemy force. With the great length of China's coast the numbers are not sufficient, but the navy mine force is the largest in the region. The 800 aircraft in the Chinese navy are generally for fleet support and to make up for the deficiency of ASW and AAW capability of Chinese destroyers and frigates. In the past, Taiwan maintained decided air supremacy over China in the Taiwan Strait.

The navy's single nuclear submarine (with one more being built) apparently represents a token attempt to show that China is a world power with a seagoing navy. It is not. With its preponderance of small, light forces that lack endurance, the navy cannot "show the flag" at any great distance in peacetime and consequently cannot contribute much to supporting Chinese foreign policy.

China (Taiwan)

China (Taiwan) has three principal maritime concerns that require naval forces: defense of the island against attack from China, maintenance of sea lines of communication, and enforcement of claims to islands in the South China Sea. The navy of Taiwan is minuscule compared with the fleet of its principal adversary. Nevertheless Taiwan has thus far been capable of maintaining its identity and has successfully withstood forcible association with China. Taiwan, with the deterrent force of the U.S. fleet, has retained control of the Taiwan Strait. As an island polity, Taiwan needs the sea to survive. This need is reflected in ever-increasing shipborne trade and the development of modern ports.

As it regards itself as the legitimate government of China, Taiwan claims all the islands in the South China Sea to which China lays claim.[25] Taiwan actually occupies Tai Ping Dao, a 960-m-by-400-m (.6-mi-by-.25-mi) island in the Spratlys.

An attempt by Peking to capture the island of Taiwan would require amphibious landings by China's forces. These would undoubtedly be supported by land-based naval aircraft. To counter an amphibious attack Taiwan could use the two submarines in its fleet, presumably with a high degree of effectiveness, since, as previously mentioned, the Chinese navy is decidedly deficient in ASW ability. The main strength of the Taiwanese navy lies in its destroyer and frigate forces, which in combination are numerically superior to those of China. But Taiwan's destroyers are more than thirty years old, and it can be assumed that at least some are experiencing engine and hull problems.[26] The ships, all ex-U.S. classes, have been modernized, and some are equipped with guided missiles. Five ex-Sumner-class ships now have Gabriel surface-to-surface missiles, and Sea Chaparral surface-to-air missiles have been added to four ex-Fletcher-class destroyers. The eleven fast-attack craft would provide additional effective firepower. The Chinese navy destroyers are aging also, and four of them are nearly forty years old, having originally served in the Soviet navy. Although much would depend on the state of maintenance and operability of the two fleets, the ability of the Taiwanese to beat off a Chinese amphibious assault seems reasonable.

The twenty-eight landing ships and twenty-two landing craft apparently were added to the Taiwanese fleet when Taiwan had plans to invade the mainland. They would have constituted insufficient resources for the task, and, in any case, the forces available to Taiwan today are clearly inadequate for an invasion against China's much greater personnel and firepower. The amphibious ability might be used to land troops on Taiwanese-claimed islands in the South China Sea, and if coupled with the destroyers, the operation would probably be successful.

The fourteen coastal minesweepers could be used to keep Taiwan's ports open in the event of mining by an enemy, an unlikely possibility, or they could be employed to sweep mines preparatory to an amphibious assault by Taiwanese forces, equally unlikely. Although they appear to be superfluous for their designed purpose at the present time, minesweepers are economical to run and could be used effectively to patrol EEZs where their lack of great firepower makes little difference in enforcing regulations against unauthorized fishing craft.

Indonesia

Indonesia is the world's fifth most populous state and twelfth by size. As the national territory is distributed through more than 13,000 islands strung out over 5,000 km east to west and 2,000 km north to south, on the surface of the globe Indonesia extends over an area equivalent to that of Australia.[27] Through the extended maritime jurisdiction conferred by its archipelagic status under the CLS, all of this area is in practice Indonesian territory. Geographical Indonesia, therefore, is one of the limited group of very large states, a group that includes the superpowers.

Size and an enormous coastline, one of the largest of any state, greatly compound the problems and costs of maritime defense. But of even greater importance in formulating defense policy is Indonesia's location between the Indian and Pacific oceans and its command over their interconnecting epicontinental seas. The great arc of the Indonesian islands outflanks much of the peninsular area of continental Southeast Asia, and the prolongation of the arc westward into the Indian Ocean through the Indian-owned islands of the Nicobar and Andaman groups and eastward into the Pacific through the Philippines virtually completes the envelopment of the Southeast Asian mainland. Does Indonesia envisage itself as becoming the great naval power that its size and location appear to mandate, and does it possess the resources to support such an establishment? The remarkable quickening in Indonesia's rate of economic growth during the 1970s and its greatly increased earnings from the petroleum industry suggest that it could meet the economic costs of such a fleet. This might not be the case, however, if crude oil prices continue to decrease.

As to the question of Indonesia's vision of itself, in the early 1950s a notorious "golden" map in Sukarno's presidential palace in Jakarta showed "Indonesia Raya" as including not only the territory of the former Netherlands Indies, together with West New Guinea (whose status was then in dispute), but also certain islands in the Indian Ocean, the Malay Peninsula (including the southernmost provinces of Thailand), all of Borneo, and the Sulu islands, and Mindanao in the Philippines. In effect it appeared to claim for "Indonesia Raya" the entire Malay-speaking world.[28] Moreover, the president habitually referred to the Indian Ocean as the "Indonesian Ocean." The map had no title and Sukarno denied expansionist intentions. But in the 1960s Indonesia began to acquire the nucleus of a "blue-water" fleet, unique in Southeast Asia, through which the "Indonesian Raya" of President Sukarno's revolutionary fervor might have been achieved. Although the map was soon removed from public view, the uneasiness of Indonesia's neighbors about the country's long-term ambitions has never been entirely allayed.

While accepting the unitary state, many Indonesians, especially on islands other than Java, strongly desire some greater measure of local self-government. In 1957, while Indonesia was in the throes of a serious revolt in Sumatera and Sulawesi, Sukarno laid down the *Wawasan Nusantara* (Archipelagic Principle) discussed in Chapters 2 and 3.

The Indonesian army, which has ruled the country since 1966, traces its prestige and power to its part in the Revolutionary War of 1945–49. Following the Japanese surrender, the army bore the full weight of the struggle against the Dutch and thus regards itself as much the true founder of the republic as the two principal nationalist leaders, Sukarno and Hatta. The suppression of the Communist coup of 1948, the PRRI–Permesta revolts in Central Sumatera and the northern Moluccas in 1957–58, and the *Gestupu* Revolt of 1965, also allegedly Communist inspired, underline the army's claim to be the nation's savior.

The navy, in contrast, was created from assets acquired after the transfer of sovereignty, and its record has been lackluster. The country has encountered difficulties in developing a merchant fleet for both interisland and international trade to replace those services previously performed by foreigners or by Indonesian Chinese. The navy performed reasonably well in supporting the army's invasion of central Sumatera in the revolts of 1957–58. However, in the subsequent confrontation with the Dutch (following the United Nations refusal in 1958 to support Indonesia's claim to West New Guinea), the navy fared badly, for the Dutch easily beat back its half-hearted attempts to invade the island.

For almost a decade thereafter the navy enjoyed a remarkable increase in material and in political influence. Sukarno sought the aid of the USSR, and a great influx of Soviet arms and influence ensued. In building up the navy and the air force, the president found a political counter to the army and rapidly promoted officers sympathetic to his viewpoint. With great rapidity Indonesia acquired what on paper was a formidable combination of air and naval strength, which by 1962 included a renovated 19,000-ton cruiser of the Sverdlovsk class, twenty submarines, several torpedo boats and patrol boats, and a sizable force of long range bombers.[29]

Suddenly transformed from a small patrol force into a service with great offensive potential, the navy promptly launched a large training and expansion program to boost its strength to almost 100,000 troops. But it was never able successfully to maintain its complex new Soviet equipment. Like the air force, it appeared reluctant to engage the British Commonwealth naval forces assisting in the defense of Malaysia following the launching of Sukarno's "confrontation" of 1963. The crushing of the *Gestupu* Revolt of 1965 and the fall of Sukarno ended all prospects of a major role for an aggressive blue-water navy.

The Indonesian "heartland" consists of the two most populous islands, Java and Sumatera. Several other islands have a special significance in national life arising from cultural or historical importance, but strategically all islands outside the heartland are of minor importance, even Kalimantan (Indonesian Borneo) and Sulawesi (Celebes). Their loss through external attack or local uprising would not be critical so long as the government retained firm control of the heartland, which accounts for 80 percent of the country's population and for an even larger proportion of its productive resources.

The deployment of Indonesia's naval resources reflects the basic defense need to protect the core. In the east, the Indonesian government continues to experience sporadic outbreaks of violent resistance from indigenous Papuan people in Irian Jaya striving either for independence or for some link with the relatively new state of Papua New Guinea in the eastern half of the island. In Indonesia's newest territorial acquisition, the ex-Portuguese eastern portion of Timor, guerrillas of *Fretilin* continue their fight against Indonesia's occupation. But none of these regional disturbances presents any difficulties of containment.

Vietnam's political ambitions, its close association with the USSR, and a dispute with Indonesia over demarcation of the continental shelf in the South China Sea identify it as the only potential assailant within the region. Indonesia has already charged Vietnam with providing arms and assistance to *Fretilin* forces in Timur Timor (East Timor), but the evidence is unconvincing. Yet the possible employment of Vietnamese forces in such a role cannot be ruled out. An invasion of this type would necessitate the commitment of large Soviet naval forces and could escalate into a major international conflict. At present it does not appear more than a remote possibility. Because an attack on the Indonesian heartland might be accompanied or preceded by assault on peninsular Malaysia and Singapore, cooperation among the naval forces of Malaysia, Singapore, and Indonesia may be desired, perhaps eventually in a joint command under the aegis of ASEAN. Since they perceive the common danger of a direct attack by Communist powers as extremely remote, however, the three states pursue their own independent interests in the Strait of Malacca and adjacent waters.

Indonesia's defense tasks in the strait are to contain any local aspirations that might risk a repetition of the disturbances of 1957–58 and, closely allied with that end, to pursue yet more vigorously the suppression of piracy, smuggling, and barter trade, which is the bartering in foreign markets of Indonesian products such as rubber or copra for goods that the import policy of the Indonesian government keeps in short supply and highly priced. Or the products may be sold at the world market price, usually far higher than that obtainable in Indonesia, and the proceeds used to purchase desirable consumer goods that are then smuggled back into Indonesia. Barter trade predates the Indonesian Republic, but its growth during the Sukarno regime and the failure to suppress it since reflects, on the one hand, a continued dissatisfaction of the people of outlying areas with their allotted share of the foreign exchange earned by their exports and, on the other hand, the tacit protection often given by local officials who may feel that local resources should contribute more to local development. The elimination of smuggling and barter is a condition of continued support by the international aid consortium, the International Government Group on Indonesia (IGGI).[30]

The failure to eliminate piracy is a standing reproach by Indonesia's neighbors. Piracy has been a hazard to local traders and fishermen ever since independence, but large modern vessels generally have been safe from attack. In 1981, however, raids on some of the largest tankers to use the Malacca–Singapore straits underlined the shortcomings of the Indonesian navy and aroused the ire of the international shipping industry. Most attacks took place where the Strait of Malacca merges with the Singapore Strait just west of Singapore's territorial waters, and there is little doubt that they were launched from Indonesia. The Indonesian navy lacks the fast, modern vessels needed to eradicate these activities.[31]

Malaysia and Singapore, while deploring piracy, have a continued interest in barter and smuggling trade since it supports local industries that generate jobs. For this reason, Singapore for many years ignored all mention of Indonesia in its official trade statistics. In addition to their divergent interests in barter trade, the three countries also have conflicting interests in fishing rights and practices as traditional and essentially conservative methods of fishing are slowly displaced by more capital-intensive and stock-depleting methods such as trawling. This has given rise to occasional outbreaks of violence between traditional and modern groups. Conflicts of this type merge with acts of piracy in which fishers have their catches and equipment stolen.

Another serious problem in the Strait of Malacca is the defense of offshore oil platforms from terrorist attack. Some of Indonesia's most productive offshore oil and gas fields lie off the eastern coasts of northern Sumatera, a part of the country notable for its Islamic extremism and long record of hostility to Jakarta. Acts of violence by Muslim extremists have erupted on both sides of the Strait in recent years, and in 1981 the hijacking of an Indonesian airliner by Muslim extremists ended in a shoot-out in Bangkok.[32] The creation of some specialized force to meet such acts of terrorism may be desired.

A dozen years ago Indonesia had more than 200 ships in its navy, the largest in Southeast Asia except for China. The fleet was largely made up of ex-Soviet ships, 104 of which had been provided by the USSR during the days when Sukarno envisioned that Indonesia would become a true regional sea power. The huge fleet provided by the Soviets has now become largely inoperable, a victim of poor maintenance and lack of spare parts, parts which have been withheld by the USSR as Indonesia turned more to the West.

The new Indonesian navy is a smaller but more realistic armed force. Its largest ships are frigates, four provided by the United States, three built by the Dutch, and three remnants of the old Soviet fleet scheduled for scrapping. The U.S. frigates are ex-Claud Jones-class destroyer escorts, displacing 1,450 tons. Four 9,200-horsepower diesel engines provide a top speed of 22 knots. The frigates are armed with torpedoes and 50-caliber machine guns. Although of distinctly modest capabilities they are nevertheless well suited to patrolling the huge extent of Indonesia's archipelagic waters and EEZ.

The Dutch-built ships are more impressive. They displace 1,500 tons, but more important, they are armed with French Exocet MM-38 surface-to-surface missiles. There are four impressive fast-attack craft, missile-equipped, 40-knot vessels built in the Republic of Korea with four more on order, and a training frigate of Yugoslav construction in the new Indonesian navy. A 1,400-ton submarine constructed in West Germany was delivered in July 1981, and a second was delivered in fall 1981. The old undersea fleet consisting of two Whiskey-class submarines, only marginally operable, were scheduled to be scrapped. The amphibious capability of the fleet has been enhanced by the addition of four Republic of Korean-built landing ship tanks (LSTs). In addition, two more LSTs, capable of handling helicopters, are on order.

The small size of the modern Indonesian navy does not qualify it as a naval power of great consequence, but more important is whether or not the Indonesian fleet is capable of fulfilling its missions. These missions are likely to be

- Patrolling the archipelagic waters and EEZ to prevent illegal fishing and other activities and to protect offshore oil installations;
- Controlling the sea-lanes through Indonesian waters, such as the Sunda and Lombok straits;
- Assisting the small navies of Singapore and Malaysia to control the important Malacca–Singapore straits; and
- Contributing naval forces to an alliance of ASEAN forces in the event of a conflict with Vietnam.

Indonesia has the longest coastline (54,716 km) and the largest area of archipelagic waters and EEZ (1,577,000 km²) of any nation in Southeast Asia. It is not possible to patrol such an area effectively with the available fleet. The patrol function can also be carried out to some extent by aircraft, however. Indonesia has eleven long-range NOMAD patrol planes in its naval forces. Six more NOMADs and three Boeing 737s are on order. Actual enforcement of antifishing regulations requires surface vessels. Even with concentration on the most likely fishing areas the task would be difficult, and if the problems of antipiracy and antismuggling patrols are added, it becomes impossible.

Indonesian naval forces are better suited to operations in the confined waters of the important straits; in conjunction with Malaysia and Singapore it could exercise control over the Malacca–Singapore route. According to one analyst, the Indonesian fast-attack and patrol craft could "seal the Malacca Strait if the Indonesia Government so desires."[33] For a navy such as Indonesia's, however, closing the strait is an easier task than keeping it open against a determined foe. The Lombok and Sunda straits are completely within Indonesian territorial waters, so to keep these important passages open is yet another function of the small Indonesian fleet.

In the event of a conflict with Vietnam it is possible that the ASEAN nations would combine naval forces, and Indonesia's contribution would be welcome. The modern West German-built submarines would prove a useful addition to an anti-Vietnamese navy. They are also earmarked for an important defense role in the Sunda and Lombok straits and other strategic Indonesian waterways.[34]

The modern Indonesian navy appears to be far too small to carry out its missions effectively. The geographic area to be covered is simply too vast. With sprawling archipelagic waters, well-dispersed bases are essential. The Indonesian navy suffers in this respect. The principal naval base is at Surabaya; all ships of the Indonesian fleet are stationed there. There are plans to build a major base at Teluk Ratai, in South Sumatera, and new bases have recently been completed at Tanjung Pinang and on Natuna Island. Ships deploy to other bases for short periods in conjunction with bilateral naval exercises or to operate against illegal foreign fishing and smuggling activities. Belawan, Medan, and Ambon are capable of supporting fleet units, and small ports throughout the Indonesian archipelago can be used for short periods and by small fleet vessels.

The Indonesian government recognizes the deficiencies in its naval power and is taking modest steps to improve capabilities. The maritime patrol mission will be improved with the addition of more NOMAD aircraft to be provided by Australia and ten Wasp helicopters from the Dutch. They will be used for antisubmarine warfare and ship-to-shore movement of marines. The fleet that evolves over the next few years will almost certainly be a modest but realistic one. There will be none of the old delusions of naval grandeur of the 1950s.

Kampuchea

The roughly circular shape of Kampuchea, almost tangential to the Gulf of Thailand, gives the country a restricted coastline that contrasts sharply with the ample endowments of Vietnam and Thailand. The remnant of a state that once extended from the Irrawaddy Delta to the Mekong Delta, Kampuchea has been progressively truncated by the encroachments of its more powerful neighbors. Driven back into the Tonle Sap (Great Lake) Basin, the state has lost almost all of its former extensive access to the sea. Vietnam's occupation of the country thus appears as a further stage in the dissolution of the Kampuchean state, a process that French colonial rule arrested for scarcely more than half a century. But in establishing its colony of Cochin–China, France confirmed and gave legal sanction to what was at the time the relatively recent occupation of the Mekong Delta by the Vietnamese peoples. No Kampuchean government has ever accepted the loss of this territory.[35]

Thus Kampuchea is a country with strong grievances, but it lacks the power to obtain redress and is in danger of becoming a mere puppet. Sporadic armed resistance to Vietnamese overlordship appears likely to continue in the future. Kampuchea may gain some greater freedom to promote its interests through adopting Vietnam's own policy of playing off the two great Communist powers against each other. While China's relations with Kampuchea since 1954 have been generally benign, its ability to provide effective assistance in the struggle against Vietnam has so far proved minimal. A Soviet naval base at Kompong Som would be a sharp rebuff to China while also serving the USSR's immediate strategic interests.

A Soviet presence in Kampuchea would not be new, for the Soviet Union provided substantial aid to the Sihanouk regime, but Moscow's standing was destroyed through its subsequent recognition of the Lon Nol coup. From Kompong Som, which is virtually Kampuchea's only sea port, a Soviet naval force would serve notice to Bangkok that its new *rapprochement* with Peking should not be pressed too far. Even with an absence of the Soviet Union, a greater Communist presence in the Gulf of Thailand appears certain, though the reasons — whether support of Vietnamese, Kampuchean, or joint interests — remain unknown. Thailand's offshore gas development thus appears particularly vulnerable. During the Pol Pot administration of 1975–78, there was a new bellicosity at sea, of which the *Mayaguez* incident was an example. An independent Kampuchea could be equally pugnacious if it desired (as did the Pol Pot regime of 1975–78) to efface the nation's centuries-old image of continuous defeat.

However, the present Kampuchean fleet of fifteen coastal patrol boats and twenty-five river patrol craft is too small to be of any consequence in the defense of the country. Moreover, it is doubtful that many of the boats are now operational.

Malaysia

The Malaysian navy has three coastlines to monitor and defend. The long-standing importance of the Malay Peninsula in commanding the most important route between the Indian Ocean and the South China Sea has increased with the rapid economic growth of Japan and other parts of eastern and southeastern Asia, including both Malaysia and Singapore. With close to 150 transits a day, the Malacca–Singapore straits constitute one of the world's most important sea-land constrictions. Any attempt to close the Strait of Malacca or to interfere with traffic in it would be viewed by Malaysia as serious interference with its sovereignty. On the west coast of the Malay Peninsula are the ports of Pinang, Kelang, and Port Dickson. The latter is an important oil terminal, and unimpeded shipping to it and the other ports must be maintained. The security of the waterway is almost as important to the world as a whole as it is to the bordering states. The Soviet Union has perhaps as much to gain as the non-Communist world in the strait's continued freedom of navigation. In 1972 it joined other powers in repudiating restrictions on traditional rights of passage anywhere, including the Malacca–Singapore straits. Defense of the Malacca–Singapore straits also involves Britain, Australia, and New Zealand through the Five-Nation Pact. The naval forces these countries could contribute in the event of any attack are slender, but such a threat to the waterway appears remote. The defense of the peninsula's heavily populated west coast, together with the quasi-police role of suppressing piracy and smuggling, will continue to be a major task of the Malaysian navy.

The country's eastern wing, almost 965 km (600 mi) distant from the peninsula at its closest point, appears to merit its own fleet. Important oil fields and terminals lie nearly 160 km (100 mi) offshore of both Malaysia's coasts on the South China Sea. The flares in the night sky from the oil platforms helped guide many "boat people" fleeing from Vietnam after Hanoi's conquest of South Vietnam. As a result the impact of the mass emigration was particularly severe on the peninsula's east coast and also on peninsular Thailand and the nearby Indonesian Anamba and Natuna islands.

Whatever its undoubtedly large losses en route, that this cockle-shell fleet could successfully deposit thousands of refugees on the beaches of Malaysia should give the Malaysian defense forces, and those of Thailand and Indonesia, serious pause. Innumerable craft reached shore without the knowledge of the authorities.[36] This suggests that even a hastily mounted seaborne Vietnamese invasion would have stood a substantial chance of success. The last invasion of the peninsula, by Japan in December 1941, was launched from the region of the Mekong Delta and overran the peninsula in a matter of weeks.

Malaysia is the classic example of a state whose territory is fragmented by intervening water. Sarawak and Sabah present Kuala Lumpur with problems of accommodation to local aspirations that resemble those confronting Jakarta in its relations with the provinces. Maintaining communication between the peninsula and Sarawak and Sabah, on the island of Borneo, by sea corridors through Indonesian waters is essential. It was largely to protect Malaysian interests that the CLS specifies that, "If a part of the archipelagic waters of an archipelagic state lies between two parts of an immediately adjacent neighbouring state, existing rights and all other legitimate interests which the latter state has traditionally exercised in such waters and all rights stipulated under agreement between those states shall continue and be respected."[37] Malaysia and Indonesia have recently signed a maritime treaty clarifying Malaysia's rights to transit Indonesian archipelagic waters.

The continued adhesion of the Borneo states to the Federation of Malaysia has become even more important with the evolving law of the sea, for the Borneo states are the basis of Malaysia's claim to a large area of jurisdiction over the southeastern portion of the South China Sea, including part of the Spratly group, where its claims conflict with those of four other countries.[38] Commercial oil and gas production comes from Malaysian and Brunei waters, and the prospects for further strikes in adjacent waters appear very promising. Policing Malaysia's jurisdictional claims in this portion of the South China Sea appears likely to become an increasingly important mission for the Malaysian navy, one that will reflect the tenor of relations between Kuala Lumpur and Manila. While none of these potential conflicts is liable to become the scene of military action, a strong navy will do much to strengthen a Malaysian claim.

Malaysia, like Singapore and Brunei, has a small, efficient navy made even more so by the training afforded by antipiracy and antismuggling operations.[39] The Malaysian fleet would be hard pressed to carry out several of its potential missions at the same time, but for that matter so would the fleets of even much larger navies. With eight missile-equipped, fast-attack craft and six similar boats fitted with guns, the navy seems to be best equipped to control the Strait of Malacca.[40]

Two frigates, the largest ships in the Malaysian navy, can go far from their bases to help defend offshore oil installations and to patrol the extensive area of continental shelf and EEZs that Malaysia claims. Twenty-seven patrol vessels also are available for this mission, and the two coastal minesweepers in the fleet could be used as well.

The naval bases are located at Woodlands (Singapore) on the Johore Strait, Lumut on the Malacca Strait, Kuantan, and Labuan in Brunei Bay. The base at Woodlands (Singapore) is being phased out and a new one is being built in Johore. The bases are thus well positioned to cover the fragmented geography of the nation, but considering the short range of most of the navy units more bases are needed. It is possible, however, that any of the Malaysian ports on the Strait of Malacca could be used to support small naval vessels, and the same is true of Kuching and Kota Kinabalu in East Malaysia.

There are plans for a modest expansion of the Malaysian fleet. Two or three more frigates might be added, as well as four minesweepers, which may be built in Italy. Nine patrol boats will be built at Pinang that, when completed, will augment the present force. There are no plans to build any vessels suitable for amphibious operations. The Malaysian navy currently has little strength in this area, for there is only one small landing craft.

The Philippines

The Philippine Republic is as fragmented as Indonesia but has the advantage of greater compactness. As in Indonesia there is marked regional and linguistic variation, but the Philippines does not have the great religious diversity of its larger neighbor, for more than 80 percent of the population is Roman Catholic. This large Christian majority has a strong sense of national unity, born of a movement for national independence that dates into the nineteenth century. This sense of nationality is much weaker in the Muslim minorities of Mindanao and Sulu, lands never totally subject to Spanish colonial rule and passed under the effective control of the central government in Manila only with the American occupation.

In the 1970s the navy acquired a new role in supporting the operations of the army and of the Philippine Constabulary against the Bangsa Moro army. The Bangsa Moro army is the fighting force of the Moro National Liberation Front (MNLF), in which various Muslim groups from Mindanao and Sulu are represented. This resistance movement is in part financed by profits from smuggling and piracy. As the resistance of various Muslim groups of the south slowly became coordinated in the 1970s, it received support from the Arab world, particularly from Libya, which provided substantial financial and material resources to the Bangsa Moro army. This aid was funneled through the Malaysian state of Sabah, which itself provided assistance, much quite open, to the Moro forces. Kuala Lumpur, though irritated by the unwillingness of President Ferdinand Marcos to abandon unequivocally the Philippine claim to Sabah, had no wish to be involved in a civil war in the Philippines itself. But exigencies of domestic politics at the time deprived the Malaysian central government of effective control over Sabah's Chief Minister Tun Mustapha, whose increasingly personal rule and vigorous policy of Islamization gave rise to deep concern in many Southeast Asian capitals. There was a strong suspicion that Tun Mustapha's ambitions involved the resurrection of the old Sultanate of Sulu in a new independent state that would include all the islands of the Sulu chain and Sabah itself.[41] With Mustapha's ousting in 1975 this danger passed, but the Sabah issue continues to cloud relations between the Philippines and Malaysia.

Direct assistance to the Moro rebels through Sabah has now been halted, but the threat of the Arab oil weapon against the petroleum-deficient Philippines prompted President Marcos to reach accommodation with the Islamic world through the promise of autonomy to the Muslims of the south. The Marcos plan has produced no real amelioration of Muslim grievances, however, and the conflict drags on.

The Moro disturbances are not the only guerrilla war in the Philippines, for in eastern Mindanao and in Samar, as well as in parts of Luzon, the New People's Army (NPA), a Communist-led insurrection, continues to be a challenge to the republic's military forces. There is no evidence that the NPA has received direct aid from any foreign source, but the tremendous quantities of arms left in Vietnam after 1975 by the Americans have helped to equip the NPA just as they have the Moro forces. These arms are smuggled into the south by well-equipped professionals in fast and heavily armed boats. To isolate the rebel groups from their supply sources continues to be a frustrating task for the Philippine navy, ill equipped as it is.

The Philippines has been slower than other states in Southeast Asia in throwing off the pattern of political and economic relations with the former colonial power inherited at independence. The existence of large American defense bases perpetuates the "special relationship" with the United States and discourages the Philippines' own defense; the government is content to leave the principal responsibility for the naval defense of the islands to the United States. The vulnerability of the Philippines to external attack was strikingly demonstrated in 1942 when the large American military and naval presence proved no deterrent. The Japanese invaded from the north and west using Taiwan and the Spratly Islands as launching grounds.

Vietnam could conceivably be a base for future attack on the Philippines. The width of the South China Sea crossing and the difficulties of avoiding detection would make such an invasion hazardous, but the prospects of success could be enhanced by mounting simultaneous strikes at various points in the Philippines from northern, central, and southern Vietnam. Such an enterprise would clearly need to be a large-scale undertaking and is perhaps conceivable only in the context of a major conflict involving theaters other than Southeast Asia as well. As the United States seems prepared to continue to accept major responsibility for meeting such a possible attack, the Philippine government is able to view its own naval role as limited to quasi-police functions. But its archipelagic status implies the acceptance of a greatly enlarged range of responsibilities, far beyond the Philippines' present naval resources to discharge.

The small Philippine navy is largely deployed in the suppression of smuggling and piracy. These activities reach their apogee in Sulu where they have long been part of life. Even interisland commercial freighters operating in Sulu, whose size might appear to keep it from attack, need to be heavily armed. The navy has acquired an additional responsibility to show the flag and to make effective the country's claim to the Spratly group, which Vietnam, China, the Chinese province of Taiwan, and Malaysia also claim.

With a total coastline length of 22,540 km and an area of EEZ totaling 551,400 km²,[42] there is clear need for a sizable, efficient navy. It is not just the size of the Philippine archipelago and its claimed waters that are important. A number of important east-west routes from the Pacific to the South China Sea are under some form of Philippine control. In the Luzon Strait between Taiwan and the Philippine Island of Luzon are the Balintang and Babuyan channels. Farther south are the vital San Bernardino, Surigao, and Mindoro straits. The government of the Philippines considers it important to exercise control over passages into and through its territorial sea. It proposed at the 10th Session of the Third United Nations Conference on The Law of the Sea (UNCLOS III) (on 9 March–24 April 1981) that Article 21 of the draft convention be changed to require prior notification by warships desiring to enter the territorial sea of coastal states.[43]

The United States, with its important naval base at Subic Bay, is also vitally interested in keeping the sea-lanes through the Philippine archipelago open. It is capable of discharging this task, but with all the other missions of the U.S. Seventh Fleet, American naval planners would undoubtedly prefer that the Philippine navy accept the responsibility.

For quite some years the Philippine navy's energies have been spent on coping with religious and political unrest and small-scale piracy.[44] Although the piracy may be small scale to some it is more than the Philippine navy can handle, since "many pirate vessels operating in Philippine waters are faster and better armed than anything the Philippine navy can deploy against them."[45]

The largest ships in the Philippine fleet are seven frigates of World War II vintage; they are being maintained and modernized.[46] The all important patrol function is handled by fifteen large patrol boats and fifty-nine coastal patrol vessels. Nearly eighty additional smaller patrol craft are being built in Manila.[47] The strongest element of the Philippine navy is the amphibious force, with thirty-one landing ships and seventy-one landing craft. It is being maintained and improved with the acquisition and overhaul of a number of ex-U.S. and ex-Japanese LSTs.

The Philippines has the least effective of the ASEAN navies[48] and "piratical activities in the Sulu Sea continue unabated."[49] Vego succinctly summarized Philippine navy capabilities: "This Navy is too small and its ships too lightly armed to present a serious threat to anyone at present, and there is no sign that this situation will change radically in the 1980's."[50]

Singapore

With a strategic location, a bustling port, a growing merchant marine of its own, and little in the way of maritime claims to defend or patrol, the principal mission of the small Singaporean navy is the classical one, to keep the sea-lanes open. With a dozen fast-attack craft, six of them equipped with surface-to-surface missiles, this is a potent force if operations are limited to the nearby straits. The navy also has two coastal minesweepers that would be needed if an enemy chose to mine the Singapore Strait or the harbor complex itself. Three additional missile-equipped, fast-attack craft are being built locally, as are twelve patrol boats for the marine police. The latter have only an inshore capability but could be used to augment the navy. With its concentration on surface-to-surface missile attack craft, the effective strength of the navy is much greater than the size of the fleet or its tonnage might lead one to believe.

Thailand

Thailand's peculiar prorupt shape makes for special difficulties in maritime security. The country's extensive coastline gives it jurisdiction over a large portion of the Gulf of Thailand, but the long peninsula shared with Burma north of latitude 10°N becomes wholly Thai territory south to the Malaysian border and gives the country direct access to the Indian Ocean. The isolated west coast, more than 400 nmi distant from Bangkok at the closest point, is poorly served with communications and, until the proposed improvements for Phuket are completed, lacks a major port.

Thailand's maritime interests in this distant administrative backwater largely concern relations with its traditional enemy, Burma. Beset with a multiplicity of internal problems, Burma is not presently a threat to Thailand, its more populous and affluent eastern neighbor. Thailand's chaotic economy, however, helps to compound the task of both the Thai and Burmese navies on the long west coast. Smuggling of Burmese rice, minerals, and livestock southward and of consumer goods from Thailand northward occurs on a major scale, and Thai rice and tin are smuggled into Malaysia and Singapore. For all of these problems the navy has no effective counter; most of these things also occur in the Gulf of Thailand.

The smoldering issues of the future of the so-called Thai Muslims (Malays) of the south and the depredations of the remnants of the Malaysian Communist Party in the forested border area have done relatively little to upgrade Bangkok's evaluation of the southern peninsula. This attitude and the navy's responsibilities, however, could change radically if the repeatedly deferred proposal for a canal across the isthmus of Kra were ever implemented.

Because it gives access to the nation's heartland — the Bangkok area and the plain of the Menam Chao Phraya — the gulf commands a far higher defense priority than the west coast. With Vietnam's domination of Laos and its invasion and occupation of Kampuchea, Thailand no longer possesses the convenience of a buffer state separating it from the foremost military power in Southeast Asia, one with a long record of territorial expansion. Mui Bai Bung (Ca Mau), the southernmost projection of Vietnam, is scarcely more than 250 nmi from the Thailand–Malaysia border. An assault across that span to seize the southern peninsula could seal off the Gulf of Thailand and deny Thailand seaborne assistance. Support in the field could then reach Thailand only if Burma were prepared to allow transit of its territory. It appears highly unlikely that Burma would be receptive to such a request. Thus, Thailand must maintain a strong naval presence in the gulf to keep its vital supply lines open. Moreover, the gulf is increasingly important as an economic asset. Its natural gas resources could eventually transform the Thai economy, and the gulf still supports a major fishery.

Thailand's physical geography presents naval planners with difficult problems. To the extent that the primary naval mission is patrol of Thai-claimed waters, a "two-ocean navy" is needed with supporting bases in both the Gulf of Thailand and the Andaman Sea. Thailand's limited economic resources and the fact that the Royal Thai Army claims half of the defense budget make such a navy difficult to come by.

A two-ocean patrol could be mounted using present navy resources that include six frigates; six missile-equipped, fast-attack boats; eighty-eight patrol craft of various sizes; and six minesweepers. Even ships of the amphibious squadron such as LSTs could be utilized with some effectiveness, especially in the rough seas encountered in the Andaman Sea during the March to October southwest monsoon.

The Royal Thai Navy's six missile-equipped, fast-attack boats (three have Gabriel missiles and three have Exocet missiles) represent a respectable offensive capability in comparison with other Southeast Asian navies. However, the navy is spread too thin to patrol two areas effectively. With a coastline of 3,219 km and an EEZ of 94,700 km^2, the task would be formidable. Each vessel would have to cover nearly 1,400 km^2, clearly impossible in any realistic assessment of operational readiness and the requirement for in-port time for such things as upkeep and repair, provisioning, and crew rest. The Royal Thai Navy does make occasional forays with task groups of up to ten ships into the Gulf of Thailand for training exercises, but generally patrols remain within 15–20 nmi of the coast.

Naval bases are another problem, considering the limited range of most patrol vessels in the Thai fleet. The majority of the navy's major units are based either at Bangkok or Sattahip. The only other naval base of significance is at Songkhla where a detachment of three patrol craft is maintained on a rotating six-month schedule. There also is a fueling station on an island off the coast of Rayong near the Thai–Kampuchean border. There are plans to build a small naval base capable of refueling and provisioning patrol craft at Ko Samui Island off Nakhon Si Thammarat Province on the east coast about midway between Sattahip and Songkhla.

In the Andaman Sea a naval base at Ban Thap Lamu is partially operational and capable of supporting patrol craft up to frigate size if and when the channel is dredged, for the four months each year of relatively calm seas off the Thai west coast. Since 1977 frigates and patrol craft have sporadically conducted patrols in the Andaman Sea "protecting Thai fishing trawlers and oil exploration operations as well as preventing infiltration from the sea."[51]

Thailand has a naval air wing consisting of nine S2 antisubmarine patrol planes of limited range, four helicopters, and some forty utility aircraft including C-47s of vintage age and six new 0-2s recently obtained from the United States. The principal naval air base is at Utapao, near Sattahip, but a detachment of one or more S2s and C-47s operates from Songkhla in support of the sea patrol effort in the lower Gulf of Thailand. This detachment also conducts infrequent air patrols along the west coast. Consideration has been given to construction of an airfield at Ban Thap Lamu to support naval operations there.

Combating piracy in the Gulf of Thailand is a task the Royal Thai Navy plans to undertake with U.S. assistance in the form of additional 0-2 aircraft and operational funding. For several years pirates in the gulf have preyed heavily on Vietnamese "boat people" and Thai fishermen. Such depredations, which have thus far gone unchecked, indicate the difficulty the Royal Thai Navy faces in controlling even one portion of its large sea area of responsibility.

Little improvement in Thai naval capability is forecast for the immediate future; the only new warships anticipated are two 450-ton gun-equipped patrol craft from the Breda Shipyard in Italy. Three of the six Royal Thai Navy missile-equipped, attack-craft now in the inventory are Breda-built 270 tonners.

Vietnam

The second most populous state in Southeast Asia, after Indonesia, and unquestionably its foremost military power, Vietnam is well placed to dominate both the broad Indochinese peninsula and the South China Sea. Although no formal federation of Indochina under the aegis of Hanoi has been created, Hanoi has clearly made good its long-standing claim to the full inheritance of the former Union of French Indochina.

During the long struggle for a unitary Vietnam, Hanoi had to concede control of the South China Sea to the United States, but with the American withdrawal it quickly began to develop its marine interests. It was also quick to take over those of the former Saigon regime, such as the claim to the Paracel and Spratly island groups, and to resuscitate offshore oil exploration. The sea traditionally has provided the principal means of commercial intercourse between the Mekong and Tonkin deltas, a situation that appears unlikely to change. In theory, the vulnerability of this link to interdiction by potentially hostile powers is a great weakness. But this situation has been transformed by the Soviet naval presence resulting from the granting of base facilities, for the Soviet forces possess the capacity to exploit fully the inherent strategic advantages that arise from Vietnam's commanding position on the South China Sea "lake."

The great bastion of Vietnam divides the South China Sea into a northern basin giving access to the Taiwan Strait and Bashi Channel and a southern basin leading to the Java Sea and Strait of Malacca (Figure 7.1). Where the coast of Vietnam cants southward, from a north-south to a northeast-southwest alignment in the vicinity of Cam Ranh, the width of the "lake" is reduced to scarcely 600 nmi. For most purposes even this distance is effectively reduced to half by the great extent of shoals, reefs, and islands to the west of Sabah and Palawan, the so-called "Dangerous Ground" of which the disputed Spratly Islands form a part. As with the Paracels, the Spratly Islands are too small to permit the construction of genuine bases, and as airstrips they can handle only short-take-off-and-landing (STOL) aircraft.

Vietnam's convex southern coast endows the country with a large area of extended maritime jurisdiction, and this could be further extended were Vietnam to make good its claim to the island groups. These, however, are hotly disputed, and since 1974 when a small garrison of South Vietnamese forces was expelled, the Paracels have been firmly in the grip of China. These islands lie close to the main trade route between the Singapore Strait and the principal ports of eastern Asia. Though small in land area, they could with appropriate equipment constitute a significant mini-base less than 250 nmi east of Da Nang. Their strategic importance to China is thus obvious, for with Hainan Island and Leichou Peninsula, China outflanks the Gulf of Tonkin and northern Annam. If Vietnam appears ideally placed for launching an attack on Japan's petroleum lifeline, China is no less well situated for interdicting Vietnam's supply line from the USSR.

Despite China's aid in Vietnam's war first with France and then with the United States, Vietnam and China have a tradition of hostility going back over many centuries. Although the transition from cooperation to conflict between the two powers in the 1970s involved the irritant of their ill-defined Tonkin boundary inherited from French Indochina and conflict over jurisdiction in the Gulf of Tonkin (*Bac Bo* in Vietnamese), China's post-1975 animosity arose primarily from Hanoi's alliance with the USSR in a "Treaty of Friendship and Cooperation," thus participating in what to Peking was a Soviet grand strategy of the encirclement of China. The granting of bases to the Soviet Pacific fleet appears to China a flagrant act of hostility. So long as Soviet vessels remain at Cam Ranh Bay, no accommodation between the world's second and third Communist powers appears possible. The Spratly group, which Vietnam claims as vigorously as it does the Paracels, has become an eagerly sought prize.[52]

While it is a matter of conjecture whether any of Vietnam's maritime claims will become the reason for military activity, the possibility is certainly there as the 1974 China and Vietnam fight over the Paracel Islands attests. Three entities — Vietnam, the Philippines, and the Chinese province of Taiwan — have established garrisons in the group, and the possibility of an armed skirmish is clearly present.[53]

While enforcement of its claims to maritime regions and islands in the South China Sea and the Gulf of Thailand are its chief naval interests, it is possible that Vietnam, with the assistance of the USSR, wants to become a true regional sea power. The fleet is one of the largest in Southeast Asia, although most of the units are of small size. The largest ships are six frigates, and there are several fast-attack and patrol craft. The Vietnamese navy also has a reasonable amphibious capacity.

There is some doubt about the capability of the Vietnamese fleet. A good portion of the present fleet was captured from the navy of the Republic of Vietnam and may include hundreds of small river patrol craft. These boats were useful when the forces of South Vietnam patrolled the rivers to combat the Viet Cong but are of little value to Vietnam now that the country is reunited. Moore was of the opinion that, "neither navy (Kampuchea's or Vietnam's) has much operational value."[54] It may be assumed, however, that the operational effectiveness will increase rapidly as new Soviet-built vessels are added to the fleet. The Soviets use Cam Ranh Bay and Da Nang as bases, presumably in exchange for assisting Vietnam to build up its navy. According to Sekino and Seno, nineteen ships (frigates, patrol craft, missile boats, and a minesweeper) have been provided to Vietnam by the USSR since 1978, and "the USSR can be expected to continue to rejuvenate the fleet."[55]

It is doubtful that Vietnam has the capability to invade any ASEAN nation except Thailand, which could be attacked from land. The Vietnamese navy is far too small to undertake anything as ambitious as an amphibious assault except perhaps against one of the Paracel or Spratly islands. Moreover, according to Moore, "So far as operational availability is concerned only a very small proportion of this considerable force can be considered fit for sea. Of those that are seaworthy very few can steam any distance due to chronic lack of fuel oil."[56]

CONCLUSIONS

To respond to these issues and concerns, the nations of Southeast Asia must evaluate what they see as the principal threats to their continued survival and welfare and decide what types and sizes of maritime defense forces they require. The decisions will undoubtedly be based on a number of factors: the degree of the military threat, the financial resources available for defense in view of the need for expenditures for other purposes, and the allies they can count on for assistance.

All nations in the region must balance the benefits to be gained from their extended maritime jurisdictions against the cost of enforcing the regulations they impose. An overriding consideration for a number of Southeast Asian nations is the need to maintain naval forces to act as marine police. The extent of the forces required varies from country to country depending on the degree of national unity in the state and the specific character of any incipient insurgencies.

On a regional as opposed to national level the issues are more complex. Organizations with some commonality of interests — ASEAN, for example — need to decide on maritime defense policies and the degree to which they should act in concert against perceived threats. They must also determine what their policies should be concerning the role of outside powers. Should the United States and the Soviet Union be welcomed as allies or shunned as the chief contributors to instability? The Indochinese states comprise another regional organization in Southeast Asia. Unlike ASEAN, Indochina has a recognized "unchallenged leader" in Vietnam, one supported by the Soviet Union. The degree to which Vietnam and the other Indochinese nations choose to remain allies of the USSR is a defense issue that will have implications for the entire region.

There is also the question of the role of China in the security of the region. Both the ASEAN nations and the Indochinese states are wary of Chinese intentions and perceive China as a threat. The Chinese support the Pol Pot–Ieng Sary forces in Kampuchea as opposed to the Vietnam-dominated Heng Samrin regime. Since the ASEAN view is that Vietnamese forces should leave Kampuchea and that free elections should be held, ASEAN and China are, in effect, allies on this issue. In general, however, Chinese military domination of Southeast Asia is feared, and long-standing Chinese claims to ownership of all the islands in the South China Sea give credence to the belief that China is a great threat to Southeast Asian security. Ownership of the islands, no matter how small or otherwise unimportant, would justify Chinese claims to marine resources, including fisheries and offshore oil. If China were to press her claims vigorously, a major maritime defense issue would be brought to the fore.

The Zone of Peace, Freedom, and Neutrality, to which all the ASEAN nations *and* Vietnam subscribe, can be realized only if sufficient military power, including naval force, is maintained to provide for a degree of regional security without excessive help from outside powers. Southeast Asian nations could demonstrate their desire to maintain peace in the region by quantitative and qualitative improvements in their seagoing forces, particularly in view of the increased demands being placed on their navies by extended claims to maritime jurisdiction. A balanced fleet of ships designed to patrol EEZs and engage in naval combat, if necessary, should be the objective. Certainly, no nation in the region needs to become a true sea power with an oceangoing navy capable of projecting great force; yet each requires a navy adequate to its geography. For archipelagic states and those with long coastlines and extensive claims to EEZs, this can be an expensive proposition, and naval requirements must be balanced against other national needs.

PART III.
MANAGEMENT
OF OCEAN SPACE

CHAPTER 8

MARINE POLLUTION: NATIONAL RESPONSES AND TRANSNATIONAL ISSUES

Abu Bakar Jaafar
Mark J. Valencia

Struggling for the past three decades to tackle the urgent issues of economic and social development, the nations of Southeast Asia have only recently become seriously concerned with the degradation of the biological and physical environment. There is increasing realization that development cannot be sustained if the natural environment is irreparably damaged. The emerging environmental concerns in the region have focused on those more immediately visible and terrestrial, with the notable exception of efforts to control oil pollution in marine waters. In terms of scientific understanding and monitoring as well as implementation of controls, pollution in Southeast Asian seas remains a research and policy frontier.[1]

According to the Convention on the Law of the Sea (CLS), pollution of the marine environment means "the introduction by man, directly or indirectly, of substances or energy into the marine environment (including estuaries) which results or is likely to result in such deleterious effects as harm to living resources and marine life, hazards to human health, hindrance to marine activities, including fishing and other legitimate uses of the sea, impairment of quality for use of sea water and reduction of amenities." Further, the convention says that "states shall take, individually or jointly as appropriate, all measures consistent with the Convention that are necessary to prevent, reduce and control pollution of the marine environment from any source, using for this purpose the best practicable means at their disposal and in accordance with their capabilities," and "they shall endeavour to harmonize their policies in this connection." Also, "States shall take all measures necessary to ensure that activities under their jurisdiction or control are so conducted as not to cause damage by pollution to other States and their environment, and that pollution arising from incidents or activities under their jurisdiction or control does not spread beyond the areas where they exercise sovereign rights in accordance with this Convention."[2]

With the extension of jurisdictions, national responsibility for environmental protection extends out to 200 nautical miles (nmi) from shore. Thus the Southeast Asian seas could become a collage of different environmental protection regimes and regulations. The ocean is a continuous, fluid medium, however, and ecosystems, migratory fish, and pollutants do not recognize the new jurisdictional boundaries.

This chapter reviews the status of marine pollution in the region, examines the existing national and transnational responses to it, and formulates transnational issues that arise both from pollution and from the responses to it.

POLLUTANTS, SOURCES, AND DISTRIBUTION

Localized Pollutants[3]

Thermal pollution is not a serious problem in the marine waters of Southeast Asia, although it is of major localized importance where hot waters are discharged directly into rivers from liquefied natural gas (LNG) and power plants. Conventional thermal power plants are scattered throughout the region, with the greatest concentrations in the vicinity of the large cities, particularly Manila, Bangkok, and the Singapore–Johore Baharu area; they are scarce in eastern Indonesia. Several geothermal outfalls are located along the coast in the eastern Philippines.[4]

Organic and biological pollutants include first, human wastes; second, agricultural wastes such as palm oil, rubber, and tapioca processing wastes, animal excrement, and commercial fertilizers; and third, discharges from food and beverage processing and from textile, palm oil, rubber, and paper industries. Figure 8.1 shows the distribution of population concentrations, sewage pollution, and organic pollution in terms of biochemical oxygen demand (BOD). Organic wastes increase biological and chemical oxygen demand and nutrient concentrations and turbidity, possibly leading to structural changes in ecosystems and to increased levels of pathogens.

Almost all large cities of the region are coastal or are on rivers that discharge into the sea. The highest coastal population densities are on the island of Java, the west coast of the island of Taiwan, the Hanoi–Haiphong urbanized region of Vietnam, the southern coast of China (particularly the Hong Kong–Guangzhou region), the metropolitan areas of Manila, Thanh Pho Ho Chi Minh, Bangkok, Singapore, and some additional areas in the Philippines and Indonesia. The most extensive sewage pollution occurs in the Strait of Malacca, near Bangkok and surrounding communities in the upper Gulf of Thailand, in the Hong Kong region, on the north and west coasts of the island of Taiwan, and in the Manila and Jakarta metropolitan areas.

High concentrations of industrial activities are found in the inner Gulf of Thailand, in peninsular Malaysia (particularly along the Strait of Malacca), on Java, and in the Manila Bay area. The west coast of the island of Taiwan also is a notable source of industrial-based pollution. Jakarta and Surabaya are centers of industry, and most industrial plants in these cities lack wastewater treatment facilities. There is little industrial activity in eastern Indonesia. BOD is a primary indicator of the magnitude of organic wastes from land-based sources. Data are available primarily for the five original nations in the Association of Southeast Asian Nations (ASEAN),[5] but extrapolation to other areas in the region with similar population concentrations and industries is justified.

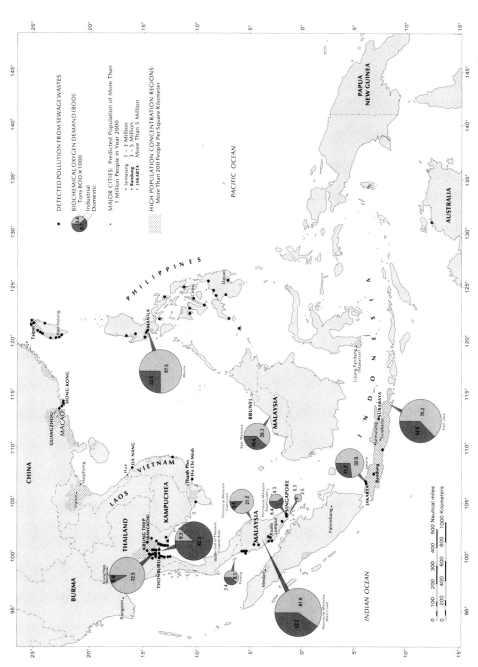

Figure 8.1　Sewage and biochemical oxygen demand (modified from Joseph R. Morgan and Mark J. Valencia, eds., *Atlas for Marine Policy in Southeast Asian Seas*, Berkeley: University of California Press, 1983, p. 126).

Liquid pollutant discharges from Jakarta have been estimated at 43,200 tons BOD per year, while the Indonesian province of East Java including Surabaya has produced 129,700 tons BOD per year.[6] As might be expected in a region so densely populated, the domestic contribution to the overall BOD greatly exceeds that from industrial sources.

In peninsular Malaysia and Sabah and Sarawak, concentrations of BOD from domestic sources are about twice as great as from industrial and agricultural sources such as palm oil and rubber processing mills, pig farming, and food and beverage processing. The greatest BOD load on both an overall and per-coastal-length basis is found on the west coast of peninsular Malaysia. Pinang has the smallest actual BOD tonnage, but with a coastal length of only 80 kilometers (km), the BOD per km of coast is quite high.

Singapore, with a large population in a small area, has impressive controls for domestic and industrial wastes. Consequently, the BOD load is small, only 3,800 tons per year. Eighty percent of the domestic sewage is treated before being discharged into the marine environment. Most of the liquid wastewater is from domestic as opposed to industrial and agricultural sources, which contribute less than 10 percent to the total load.

Metropolitan Manila produces a liquid pollution load of about 130,000 tons BOD annually, most of it from domestic sources. In the Bangkok region the liquid pollutant load is estimated to be about 83,000 tons BOD per year. Water pollution arises primarily from domestic sewage, which is uncontrolled and eventually reaches the marine region. The liquid pollution load from the upper gulf is somewhat larger, 92,600 tons BOD per year, and most of it is from industrial sources, especially on the eastern Thailand gulf coast.

Accelerated sedimentation (silt) from agriculture, logging, terrestrial mining, construction, and offshore mining is the single greatest form of pollution in the coastal waters of Southeast Asia. The increased turbidity reduces light penetration and thus inhibits primary productivity and may cause fish to de-school; siltation changes bottom habitat and smothers corals and shellfish.

Luzon in the Philippines has the most extensive logging-derived sedimentation, but logging has resulted in serious soil erosion also on the south coast of Java, the eastern half of Sumatera, south and east Kalimantan, and on the island of Taiwan. The most extensive regions of agricultural-based sedimentation are the Bight of Bangkok, the west coast of peninsular Malaysia, north Java and Madura, the Philippines, and the waters near Hong Kong. Philippine waters, particularly those off western Luzon, Negros, Cebu, Samar, Balabac, and the Calamian group, receive considerable sediment from terrestrial mining activities. Less extensive patches of polluted waters are located off the coast of Sarawak, north and east of Jakarta, and in Kepulauan Lingga.

To meet the demands of the construction industry during the boom of the late 1950s and early 1960s many rubber plantations in Singapore were converted into sand pits, especially in the eastern part of the island, silting water courses and eventually leading to changes in the coastal marine habitat.

Offshore tin mining and dredging disturbs the bottom sediments, increasing

Table 8.1   Offshore Mining and Mineral Potential in Southeast Asia and China

Country	Active Mining	Potential
China	Sand, iron, nickel, titanium, and other detrital minerals, coral	Gold, diamonds
Indonesia	Tin, titanium, sand, coral, limestone	Tin
Malaysia	Tin (onshore), iron, bauxite, coral	Tin (offshore)
Philippines	Sand, coral sand, coral, limestone	Gold, iron, chromite, silica sand
Singapore	None	Sand
Thailand	Tin	Rock salt, limestone, coal, fluorite
Vietnam	Coal, silica sand, kaolin, limestone, gravel	Coal, iron, titanium

Source: M. J. Cruickshank, "Offshore and Onshore Mining Overview," in M. J. Valencia, ed., *Proceedings of the Workshop on Coastal Area Development and Management in Asia and the Pacific,* Manila, 3–12 December 1979, p. 28.

turbidity and releasing organic material, toxic gases such as hydrogen sulfide, heavy metals, and other persistent pollutants. In Thailand about 70 percent of the tin mined is from coastal waters off the west coast, from Phangna to Phuket. Another extensive area of mining pollution is in the waters surrounding Bangkok and Belitung islands, off southeast Sumatera. In Sabah and the Philippines the mining of living reefs for the construction industry has resulted in noticeable changes in the reef habitat. Dredging for precious corals also occurs in some Southeast Asian waters. Table 8.1 provides an overview of offshore mining and mineral potential in Southeast Asia and China.

Heavy metals such as lead, mercury, cadmium, zinc, and silver are derived from smelting, electronics, plastics, petrochemical and mining industries, domestic wastes, and weathering; lead is derived from antiknock compounds used in automobile engines. Heavy metals may accumulate in fish, shellfish, sea cucumber, and seaweed tissue, rendering them unsafe for human consumption. With the low level of industrialization, heavy metal pollution is not yet recognized as a serious problem in the region, although it is increasing in waters adjacent to urban industrial centers, particularly in sheltered areas. Anomalously high concentrations of cadmium, silver, and mercury were noted in some sediment samples from the inner Gulf of Thailand, but subsequent analysis found all concentrations in seawater, sediment, and organisms used for human consumption within safe limits.[7] Sediment and water from the lower reaches of rivers draining into the gulf, however, revealed high concentrations of mercury, lead, and zinc. In Indonesia heavy metals are a minor localized source of pollution limited to coastal waters off the larger urban centers. In Malaysia the Juru River adjacent to the Perai Industrial Estate revealed dangerously high levels of mercury, cadmium, and copper.[8] In Singapore levels of mercury are high near shipyards and in the Jurong River. In the Philippines heavy metal concentrations in the marine environment are within accepted safe limits except for high mercury concentrations in some sharks.

Transnational Pollutants

Synthetic chemicals such as the insecticide dichloro-diphenyl-trichloro-ethane (DDT) and polychlorinated biphenyl (PCB) in paints, plastics, and paper products are widely used in agriculture, industry, and public health programs in the region but little is known of their distribution and impact. The amount of pesticides and herbicides used has increased in recent decades.[9] In the major rivers of the Philippines monitored for pesticides, 76 percent of the samples contained pesticide concentrations exceeding acceptable standards.[10] The DDT range in the rivers of Thailand is 0.1 to 3.4 parts per billion[11] (ppb) and organochlorines have been found in green mussels and mullets and in sediments collected from the mouths of five major rivers in Thailand.[12] DDT is thought to interfere with reproduction in animals and has been implicated in premature pupping of sea lions in California and, together with PCBs, in reproductive failure in seabirds. There is a higher level of DDT residue in the Gulf of Thailand than in the Andaman Sea due to the larger and more agriculturally developed watersheds draining into the gulf.

Nuclear materials are a potential transnational pollutant. The only functioning nuclear plant in the region is located on the north coast of Taiwan, but there are planned nuclear installations on southern Taiwan, Java, and Manila Bay at Bataan, west of Manila. These plants eventually may create a great environmental problem — how to dispose of nuclear waste. Nuclear spent fuel shipped from Japan to Europe for reprocessing as well as nuclear submarines already pass through the narrow straits of the region.

Petroleum hydrocarbons in the marine environment are derived from discharges from land, the atmosphere, ships, offshore drilling, and natural seeps. Low levels of oil in the oceans can affect biological processes such as reproduction and feeding and can taint edible organisms; higher concentrations can be lethal to animals and plants, from phytoplankton to entire habitats. Aside from the biological effects, oil spills can virtually destroy tourism in coastal areas, and foul boats, nets, and traps.

Hydrocarbon concentrations in Southeast Asian waters range over three orders of magnitude from coastal waters to the open sea, perhaps due in part to the use of different measurement methods. Figure 8.2 shows present patterns of oil pollution in the region. In Indonesian waters, concentrations ranging from 0.3 to 1.1 parts per million (ppm) were found north of Jakarta in the vicinity of the Cinta and Arjuna oil terminals, while in the Riau Archipelago, southwest of Singapore, hydrocarbons ranged from 1 ppm to 11.5 ppm. Other Indonesian locations measured were Pangkalan Susu (0.4–1.2 ppm) and Dumai (1.2–1.5 ppm). The relatively low figures for Dumai may reflect the deballasting facilities available in this location, Indonesia's largest oil port. Concentrations in Manila Bay ranged from 3.6 ppm at Manila's South Harbor to 4.0 ppm at Cavite. In peninsular Malaysia concentrations were 0.1–0.23 ppm for east coast waters and 0.12 ppm at Pinang.

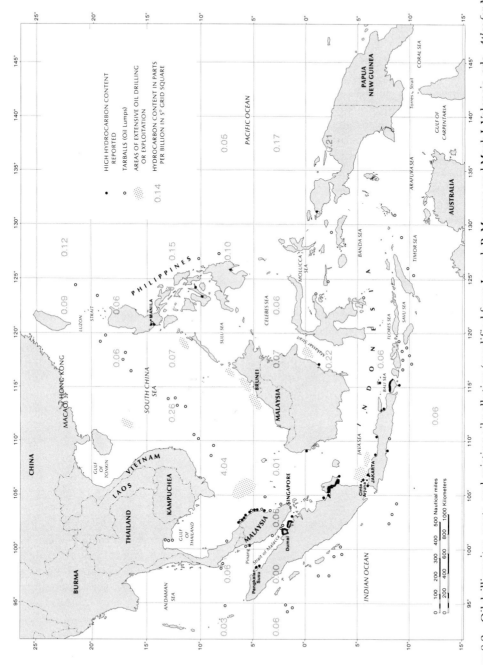

Figure 8.2   Oil drilling sites, ports, and existing oil pollution (modified from Joseph R. Morgan and Mark J. Valencia, eds., *Atlas for Marine Policy in Southeast Asian Seas*, Berkeley: University of California Press, 1983, p. 128).

On a regional basis the highest hydrocarbon concentrations are found in the South China Sea off southern and eastern Vietnam and in the Makassar Strait, and many tarballs are also found in these locales. Tarballs also have been reported beached along both coasts of the Gulf of Thailand, the Thai Andaman Sea coast, both coasts of the Malay Peninsula, and in Pulau Seribu north of Jakarta.

Figure 8.3 shows hypothetical oil spill trajectories for five points of origin in the South China Sea. A spill from the hypothetical point of origin off the coast of Sabah would create an oil slick in Philippine-claimed waters and would cross waters claimed by Brunei. A spill at the hypothetical point of origin east of peninsular Malaysia could result in pollution of Vietnamese and Indonesian archipelagic waters. Oil originating at Bach Ho could penetrate Indonesian and Malaysian waters. A spill originating off the south coast of Hainan Island would cross both the China–Vietnam disputed area and Vietnamese coastal waters before impinging on the coast of Vietnam.

Other more invisible but insidious pollutants such as dioxins may travel across national borders with the surface currents. Chapter 1 illustrates and describes the surface currents of the region (Figure 1.2). Since the current pattern reverses itself twice each year, pollutants could be swept back and forth across jurisdictional boundaries. Moreover, where currents are generally weak such as in the Gulf of Thailand, the eastern South China Sea, the Arafura Sea, and the Coral Sea, presumably so is dispersion and dilution of pollutants.

Airborne pollutants can be carried across national borders by winds and further distributed by surface currents. Table 8.2 indicates the extent to which airborne pollutants are from fuel-burning sources in Southeast Asia. The largest load is contributed by power generation on the west coast of Malaysia followed by internal combustion engines in Jakarta and Manila.

Another means of distribution of pollutants or their effects across national borders is by organisms themselves. Some edible and commercial fish stocks are migratory or shared (Figure 8.4), and their patterns indicate the potential for transnational distribution of accumulated pollutants although no data are available on actual concentrations in the flesh. Mackerel stocks, which move north and south along the western Malaysian, Thai, and Burmese coasts, can be exposed to fishing pressure from all three countries. Yellowfin tuna migrate between northern Australia and southeastern Indonesia. The Philippines shares various tuna stocks with the Chinese province of Taiwan, northern Sabah, Malaysia, and northern Indonesia. Shared demersal stocks of mackerels and other species occur between Thailand and Burma, Thailand and Malaysia, Malaysia and Sumatera (Indonesia), Sarawak (Malaysia) and Kalimantan (Indonesia), Vietnam and China, Hong Kong and China, Sabah (Malaysia) and Kalimantan (Indonesia), and Indonesia, northern Australia, and Papua New Guinea.

PRESENT NATIONAL RESPONSES

The following account of national responses to marine pollution will focus on those nations for which information is available — the five original ASEAN nations of In-

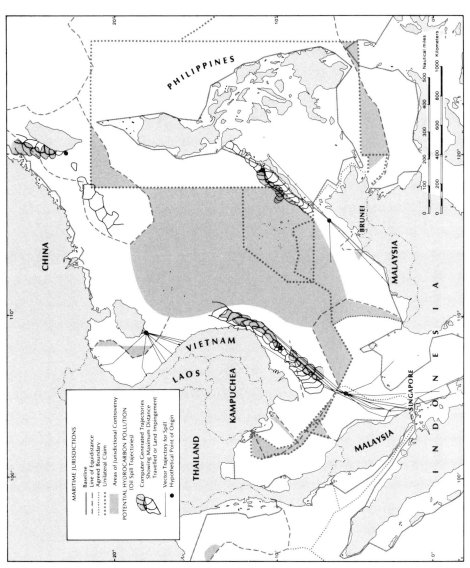

Figure 8.3   Hypothetical oil spill trajectories and jurisdictional boundaries (modified from Joseph R. Morgan and Mark J. Valencia, eds., *Atlas for Marine Policy in Southeast Asian Seas*, Berkeley: University of California Press, 1983, p. 129).

Table 8.2 Airborne Pollutants from Fuel-Burning Sources in Southeast Asia

Location	Total[c] (millions of tons per year)	Share of Total Airborne Pollutants					
		Power Generation (%)	Industrial Share (%)	Domestic Share (%)	Transport Share (%)	Wood-burning Share (%)	Petroleum Refineries Share (%)
Manila	447.0	30.0	8.6	negl	61.4		
Jakarta	545.0	11.7	10.9	6.2	72.2		
East Java	249.0	7.0	24.4	8.9	59.7		
Penang	30.6	–	30.0	0.5	69.5		
Malaysia — W. Coast	876.7	47.4	10.2	negl	24.0	15.8	2.6
Malaysia — S. Coast	76.9	30.6	5.9	negl	51.8	11.6	
Malaysia — E. Coast	65.5	–	35.1	0.5	52.8	11.6	
East Malaysia	65.0	7.0	34.0	0.5	3.2	5.3	
Bangkok[a]	304.0	11.6	31.2	0.4	56.8		
Coastal area around upper Gulf of Thailand[b]	250.0[c]	65.6	14.4	0.1	20.2		

Source: World Health Organization Western Pacific Regional Center for the Promotion of Environmental Planning and Applied Studies (PEPAS), *Preliminary Assessment of Land-Based Sources of Pollution in East Asian Seas, Summary Report,* Malaysia: Universiti Pertanian, Serdang, Selangor, 1981.

[a]The low percentage for industrial water pollution is due to exclusion of industrial discharges upstream of Bangkok.
[b]The high percentage for industrial water pollution is due to the high industrial load from the East Coast.
[c]Based on 300 working days/year for industrial load and 365 days/year for domestic load.

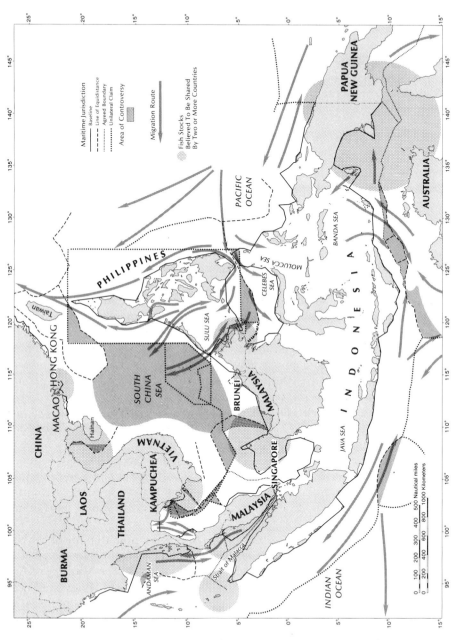

Figure 8.4   Maritime jurisdiction, fish migrations, and shared stocks (modified from Joseph R. Morgan and Mark J. Valencia, eds., *Atlas for Marine Policy in Southeast Asian Seas*, Berkeley: University of California Press, 1983, p. 131).

donesia, Malaysia, the Philippines, Singapore, Thailand, plus China. Existing national regulations and other responses are examined in the following standard order where there is sufficient information:

- Land-based sources — manufacturing, domestic sewage, mining, forestry, and agriculture;
- Offshore exploration and exploitation of minerals and hydrocarbons;
- Vessel sources;
- Radioactive and other hazardous wastes; and
- Overview.

Indonesia

Except where otherwise indicated the information for Indonesia is drawn from T. Karimoeddin, National Report of Indonesia in Dieter Dielenstein, editor, *One World Only: Industrialization and Environment*, Tokyo: Friedrich Ebert Stiflung and Toppan Printing Co., Ltd., 1973.

Land-Based Sources. Indonesia's first step in the control of wastes from land-based sources was taken in 1936 with regulation *Algemeen Waterreglement (Peraturan Perairan Umum, 1936) dat Stble 1936 No. 489 jo. Stble. 1949, No. 98,* concerning the use of water resources, including the disposal of industrial wastes in public streams. Other relevant laws are the Nuisance Ordinance (1926) and its amendment (1940), which regulate disposal of harmful wastes and establish standards for the elimination of harmful wastes from established industries. Safety Law No. 1 of 1970 has provisions on waste disposal and smoke abatement but needs supporting regulations and standards to be effective. Despite this legislation, however, little actual control has been established in the country as a whole.

Jakarta may be an exception. For the capital, a set of regulations, *Peraturan Daerah Khusus Ibu Kota Jakarta No. 12 Tahun 1971, L.D. No. 71 Tahun 1972,* has been introduced to mitigate river and coastal water pollution.

Although the legislative measures have not yet been developed fully, Indonesia has taken action to handle the disposal of human waste. Except for Bandung, Jogjakarta, and Medan, which all have waste treatment plants and sewerage systems for parts of the cities, septic tanks connected to seepage pits are widely used in most urban areas.

In Indonesia, responsibility for the control of marine pollution (or of activities that can pollute coastal waters) is fragmented among several departments at the national level and among various local bodies. For example, the Ministry of Agriculture regulates the import and use of biocides, the Ministry of Mines and Energy controls offshore mining, the Ministry of Health sets water quality standards, and the Municipality of Jakarta regulates sand and coral dredging and the release of industrial effluents.[13] Countermeasures against pollution are coordinated by the Directorate General of Sea Communications, supported by the Department of

Mines, Pertamina Shipping Division, and the Coordinating Body for the Department of Defense (navy and water police), and units of any other agency required under emergency conditions. The Ministry for Research and the Ministry of Justice each has a committee for marine pollution.

A number of study groups have been established in connection with waste problems. The Department of Health Working Group on Environmental Pollution Control was founded in 1971 to study and recommend measures for environmental effects of pollutants in water and in the air. A group composed of the Directorate of Sanitary Engineering of the Department of Public Works and local authorities was formed to study the characteristics of water pollution caused by industrial effluents in Jakarta. There are guidelines used by the Department of Industry in collaboration with the Department of Health in evaluating alternative waste disposal systems for industrial wastes. In 1977 the Ministry of State for Development Supervision and Environment (now Population and Environment) was established to coordinate all work to solve Indonesian environmental problems.

In June 1979 the Directorate for Water Problem Research (Direktorat Penyelidekan Masalah Air) proposed that effluent standards be specified for discharges into four categories of water uses: the drinking water and domestic water supply, fisheries, agriculture and the manufacturing industry, and urban drainage for waste transport.

The use of herbicides to fight weeds in Indonesia is not widespread except for those used in large plantations for killing the grass "alang alang" *(Imperata cylindrica)*. Pesticides are comprehensively regulated in Indonesia by

- Presidential Decree No. 7, 1973, concerning regulation of distribution, storage and use of pesticides *(Peraturan pemerintah No. 7 tahun pengawasan atas peredaran, penyimpanan dan penggunaan pestisida (LN No. 12 tahun 1973);*
- Directive from the Minister of Agriculture No. 201/Kpts/Um/6/1973 concerning application procedure for pesticides registration and use approval *(Keputusan Menteri Pertanian No. 201/Kpts/Um/6/1973 tentang prosedur permohonan pendaftaran and izin pestisida);*
- Directive from the Minister of Agriculture No. 429/Kpts/Um/9/1973 concerning conditions for pesticide packaging and labeling *(Keputusan Menteri Pertanian No. 429/Kpts/Um/9/1973 tentang syarat pembungkusan dan perberian label pestisida);*
- Directive from the Minister of Agriculture No. 437/Kpts/Um/11/1975 concerning registration and approval of pesticide use *(Keputusan Menteri Pertanian No. 437/Kpts/Um/11/1975 tentang pendaftaran dan pemberian izin pestisida);*
- Directive from the Minister of Agriculture No. 125/Kpts/Um/4/1975 concerning registration and approval of pesticide use *(Keputusan Menteri Pertanian No. 125/Kpts/Um/4/1975 tentang pendaftaran dan perberian izin pestisida);* and
- Directive from the Minister of Agriculture No. 201/Kpts/MP/5/1975 concerning directory of offices regulating distribution, storage, and use of pesticides *(Keputusan menteri Pertanian No. 201/Kpts/MP/5/1975 tentang penunjukan*

pejabat yang diberi wewenang mengawasi peredaran, penyimpanan dan penggunaan pestisida).[14]

Offshore Exploration and Exploitation. Indonesia is the major offshore oil producer in the region. Appropriately, Indonesia has the most comprehensive legislation and regulations in Southeast Asia dealing with oil pollution.[15] The earlier legislative measures included The Storage of Oil Ordinance of 1927, The Mine Police Regulations of 1930, and The Basic Mine Law of 1976. Other provisions include

- Presidential Decree No. 17 of 1974 concerning regulation of offshore oil and gas exploration and exploitation (LN No. 20, 1974, TLN No. 3031) *(Peraturan Pemerintah No. 17 tahun 1974 tentang pengawasan, pelaksanaan eksploitasi dan eksplorasi minyak dan gas bumi didaerah lepas pantai (LN No. 20 tahun 1974 TLN No. 3031);* and
- Directive from the Minister of Mines No. 04/P/M/Pertamb/1973 concerning prevention and control of water pollution arising from exploration and/or exploitation of oil and gas activities *(Peraturan Menteri Pertambangan No. 04/P/M/ Pertamb/1973 tentang pencegahan dan penanggulangan pencemaran perairan dalam kegiatan eksplorasi dan atau eksploitasi minyak dan gas bumi).*

The new antipollution supervisory unit within the Oil and Natural Gas Directorate of the Department of Mines and Energy is responsible for establishing environmental policy and regulations and for the enforcement of these provisions. Surveys and research on oil pollution are undertaken by the Center for Technology and Development on Oil and Natural Gas (LEMIGAS), the National Institute of Oceanology, and the State Oil Enterprise, Pertamina. Through its Coordinating Body on Environmental Protection, Pertamina has the operational capacity to clean up oil spills. Pertamina units to combat oil pollution are stationed in the Strait of Malacca, the Java Sea, the Makassar Strait, Irian Jaya, and Cilacap. Pertamina also has a contingency plan to collaborate with similar organizations in Malaysia and Singapore to take countermeasures against oil spills in the hazardous Strait of Malacca.

It is the policy of the Indonesian government that oil pollution originating from offshore operations is of purely national concern and that any problems can be dealt with by the public authorities in charge and the oil companies involved. Legislation stresses repeatedly the obligation of the enterprise to "prevent the occurrence of pollution and to control any that occurs."[16] The operating company is required to have an approved contingency plan and to keep all necessary equipment readily available.[17] The penalty for violations can be as high as one million rupiahs (US$100,000).

Little has been done to develop a system of civil liability for oil pollution damage resulting from offshore exploration activities. As of October 1982 there was no provision for mandatory environmental impact assessment for offshore exploration and exploitation activities.

Vessel Sources. Indonesia participated actively in the International Legal Conference on Marine Pollution Damage in 1969 and in the International Conference on the Establishment of an International Compensation Fund for Oil Pollution in 1971, both held at Brussels.[18] Indonesia, however, still has not ratified the Convention on the Prevention of Pollution of the Sea by Oil of 1954 or its Amendment of 1962.[19] The City of Jakarta introduced a specific regulation, No. Bd. 15/4/36/70 L.D. No. 19, in 1970 prohibiting discharges of oil from tankers into waters around the Thousand Islands group (Gugusan Kepulauan Seribu).[20]

Radioactive Wastes. Indonesia has introduced laws and regulations for controlling the transport and use of radioactive isotopes:

- Law No. 31 of 1964 concerning the basic decision for the development of atomic energy — LN No. 124 of 1964 *(Undang-undang No. 31 tahun 1964 tentang Ketentuan pokok tenaga Atom — LN No. 124 tahun 1964);*
- Presidential Decree No. 33 of 1965 concerning the Atomic Energy Assembly and National Atomic Energy Board — LN No. 88 of 1965 *(Peraturan Pemerintah No. 33 tahun 1965, tentang Dewan Tenaga Atom and Badan Tenaga Atom Nasional — LN No. 88 tahun 1965);*
- Presidential Decree No. 5 of 1969 concerning the use of radioactive isotopes and radiation — LN No. 18 of 1969, TLN No. 2892 *(Peraturan Pemerintah No. 5 tahun 1969 tentang pemakaian Isotop Radioacktip dan Radiasi —LN No. 18 tahun 1969, TLN No. 2892);*
- The Decision of the Director-General of the National Atomic Energy Board — No. 07/DJ/5/11/74 concerning the transportation of radioisotopes *(Keputusan Direktur Jenderal Badan Tenaga Atom Nasional —No. 07/DJ/5/11/74 tentang ketentuan untuk pengangkutan zat-zat radioadktip);* and
- The Decision of the Director-General of the National Atomic Energy Board — No. 14/DJ/16/11/1976 concerning the implementation of Section 2 and regulation 9c of the Presidential Decree No. 12 of 1975 *(Keputusan Direktur Jenderal Badan Atom National —No. 14/DJ/16/11/1976 tentang ketentuan pelaksanaan pasal 2 dan pasal 9c Peraturan Pemerintah nomber 12 tabun 1975).*[21]

Indonesia Overview. Despite a number of laws prohibiting various marine environmental pollutants, Indonesia has not yet developed supporting regulations to make the existing laws effective. The nation has not changed its general view that "the environmental problems of poverty are no less acute and certainly more widespread than the environmental problems caused by affluence." However, since the establishment of the Ministry of State for Development Supervision and Environment in 1977 (now Population and Environment), there has been an effort to integrate the environmental element into the country's socioeconomic development strategy. This ministry's authority is limited to the coordination of environment-related activities and formulation of general environmental policy and guidelines. Regulatory powers remain in the hands of sectoral agencies such as the Department of Industry; the Department of Public Works, Energy, and Electricity; the Department of Agriculture; the Department of Transport; the Department of Mines; and the Department of Public Health.

Malaysia

The Environmental Quality Act of 1974 — Laws of Malaysia (L.M.), Act 127 — authorizes the minister in charge of the environment to regulate releases of wastes from all sources except those of mining, offshore exploration and exploitation, agriculture, logging, and earthworks. The term "waste" in section 2 of the act includes ". . . any matter which is discharged, emitted, or deposited in the environment in such volume, composition or manner as to cause an alteration of the environment."[22]

Land-Based Sources. Under the act, three sets of regulations relating to the disposal of sewage and industrial wastes, palm oil factories, and natural rubber processing factories have been introduced: Environmental Quality (Prescribed Premises) (Crude Palm Oil) Regulations, 1977 — P.U. (A) 342; Environmental Quality (Prescribed Premises) (Raw Natural Rubber) Regulations, 1978 — P.U. (A) 338; and Environmental Quality (Sewage and Industrial Effluents) Regulations, 1979 — P.U. (A) 12.

The maximum oil content in any discharge of treated sewage or effluent from all industries other than those of palm and natural rubber is 10 ppm. The maximum content of heavy metals is specified to be as follows:[23]

Cadmium (as Cd)	0.02 mg/l
Mercury (as Hg)	0.05 mg/l
Chromium (as Cr Hexavalent)	0.05 mg/l
Arsenic (as As)	0.10 mg/l
Lead (as Pb)	0.5 mg/l
Chromium (as Cr trivalent)	1.0 mg/l
Copper (as Cu)	1.0 mg/l
Manganese (as Mn)	1.0 mg/l
Nickel (as Ni)	1.0 mg/l
Tin (as Sn)	1.0 mg/l
Zinc (as Zn)	1.0 mg/l

Where two or more of these metals are present in the effluent, their concentration is not to be greater than 3.0 milligrams per liter (mg/l) in total, or 1.0 mg/l in total for soluble forms.[24]

The allowable BOD[25] and nutrient content for organic wastes discharged into watercourses are shown in Table 8.3.

Under these regulations, pollutants discharged in effluents were to be progressively reduced until by 1981 the BOD content of wastes discharged by palm mills, for example, was to have been reduced to 500 ppm, a 97-percent reduction over the program period. These limits serve only as guidelines, and there are provisions

Table 8.3   Allowable BOD and Nutrient Content for Discharged Organic Wastes

Waste Source	Organic Nitrogen (mg/l)	Ammonical-Nitrogen (mg/l)	Nitrogen (mg/l)	BOD (mg/l)
Palm oil industry	—	200–50	25–10	5,000–500
Rubber industry				
Latex	450–300	—	350–300	450–100
Nonlatex	100–40	—	70–60	300–100
Other industries	—	—	—	50

in the regulations for variance.[26] Even if a variance is permitted by the regulatory agency, an economic disincentive is imposed. The annual effluent-related license fee is computed at the rate of M$10 per metric ton (MT) of BOD and/or M$10 per kilogram (kg) of other pollutants.[27]

The disposal of waste from mining operations is regulated by state authorities but relegated to the Federal Department of Mines in accordance with the Mining Enactment–Federated Malay States (FMS) Cap. 147 (1929) and its counterpart state legislation. As a matter of practice, effluent limits of 800 grains of suspended solid content per imperial gallon (11,320 ppm) or 150 mesh grain size are specified in mining leases issued by state authorities following consultation with the Drainage and Irrigation Department and the Mines Department.[28]

The control of silts and sediments due to soil erosion and runoff is exercised under four separate laws. The Land Conservation Act (No. 3 of 1960) enacted under Article 76(3) of the Federal Constitution has been adopted throughout peninsular Malaysia but seems thus far to have been virtually without effect because it vests broad discretion for state authorities to declare or not to declare that a given tract of land should be cleared or planted with short-term crops.[29] The Local Government Act, 1976 (L.M., Act 171), also has provisions under sections 69 and 70 for the local authorities to prohibit certain discharges within their areas of jurisdiction. In addition, the Street, Drainage and Building Act, 1974, empowers the authorities to issue city bylaws for the control of silt washed away due to improper drainage and improper maintenance of streets.

Proper drainage and frequent maintenance of logging tracks are among the practices required in accordance with various forest enactments enforced by respective state authorities. Also, in accordance with the Waters Enactment, the state authorities can alienate sufficient riparian reserves to prevent inroads of silt into receiving streams and rivers.[30] In fact, the Silt Control Enactment of 1922 for the FMS was the earliest of its kind in the then British Empire, but it has not been followed closely.[31]

The Pesticides Act, 1974 (L.M., Act 156), is administered by the Pesticides Board in the Ministry of Agriculture, with representatives from other ministries, namely, the Ministry of Health and the Ministry of Science, Technology, and Environment. The legislation provides for the regulation of the import, manufacture, sale, and storage of pesticides, but there is no provision for regulating the use of pesticides.[32] In practice, however, the various state authorities can prohibit the use of certain pesticides that directly affect the beneficial uses of any inland waters, any subterranean water resources, and any water in an estuary or sea adjacent to the coast of their respective jurisdictions. This states' provision appears principally as a new section, 7A, of the Waters (Amendment) Enactment, 1970. In one application of the provision, the state of Perak has banned the use of sodium arsenite as a herbicide because its misuse in agriculture and forestry had adversely affected the state's supply of drinking water. This action has been somewhat ineffective, however, because the herbicide is smuggled across the state's border in the southern part of Thailand, and also because of unregulated use in the adjacent states of Kedah, Penang, Pahang, and Selangor, and possibly Kelantan.

Offshore Exploration and Exploitation. The Petroleum Mining Act of 1966, revised 1972 (L.M., Act 95, section 7[5]), empowers the Petroleum Authority (Petronas) to specify in any exploration license that the licensee shall take all steps practicable to prevent the escape of oil or waste from hydrocarbons discovered in the exploration area. The set limit for oil content is 50 ppm, a level considered to be achievable and acceptable in Malaysia.[33]

Vessel Sources. Malaysia has yet to promulgate rules and regulations under the Environmental Quality Act (EQA) for controlling oil or other related wastes. There are deficiencies in the existing act, notably including its liability provisions, which appear to have no application at all to oil spills attributable to collisions and running aground regardless of the cause of the accident.[34] Section 26(1) of the EQA, which specifically prohibits discharges of oil in "any part of the seas outside the territorial waters of Malaysia," is only enforceable for Malaysian-owned vessels and those flying the Malaysian flag.[35] Malaysia has not adopted any of the relevant international conventions such as the 1954 International Convention for the Prevention of Pollution of the Sea by Oil and the 1969 International Convention relating to the Intervention on the High Seas in Cases of Oil Casualties.[36] Further, monitoring of tanker traffic in the Strait of Malacca is not undertaken on a systematic basis.

In the event of an oil spill emergency, Malaysia, under the coordination of the Division of Environment and the operational support of the Marine Department, has a contingency plan involving the ports of Pinang, Kelang, and Johore Bahru with the help of other designated bodies, both private and public, with specific responsibilities.[37] To implement the plan, Malaysia has spent a total of M$23 million in acquiring the necessary capital equipment including booms, skimmers, barges, and fast patrol craft.[38]

Radioactive Wastes. The disposal of radioactive wastes is not totally prohibited. The limits allowable have yet to be specified by the Minister of the Environment.[39] But the Minister of Health has the authority under the Radioactive Substances Act (No. 17 of 1968) to regulate most aspects of the manufacture, storage, sale, and use of radioactive substances and to make rules regarding the safe disposal of radioactive wastes. Such rules have been promulgated and are known as the Radiation Protection Rules, 1974.

Malaysia Overview. Malaysia has quite comprehensive legislative measures to regulate the release of wastes from land-based sources. It has yet to develop a complete set of regulations for controlling oceanic waste sources. Although there is a central pollution control agency at the federal level, the Division of Environment, its jurisdiction is limited to pollution arising from agriculture-based and manufacturing industries, sewage treatment plants, and merchant shipping. Other forms of pollution remain under the general responsibility of the resource development agencies — Petronas for offshore oil and gas and the Department of Mines for other types of mining.

Malaysia has adopted a pragmatic approach to solving environmental problems, an approach that involves the simultaneous application of both long-term planning and rapidly implemented antipollution measures that can be revised with changing circumstances. For controlling water pollution, for example, this dual approach has been implemented by identifying the more important of the nation's forty-nine river basins, based on their beneficial use, and by establishing a sequence of priorities aimed at maintaining water quality. Particular river basins were identified by the Department of Environment as "water pollution prevention areas" in which immediate control was required. In these areas "point" discharge of serious pollutants has been identified and is subject to effluent controls.

Although discharge controls are the main instruments of water pollution control now used in Malaysia, it is recognized that alone they are not enough to cope with the complex and interlocking problems of the nation's freshwater and marine environments. Such controls must be supported by a comprehensive, long-range plan for achieving defined environmental quality objectives. In Malaysia, however, attainment of this goal is made difficult by the sharing of responsibilities between federal and state authorities as well as among several agencies of both federal and state governments.[40]

The Philippines

Except as otherwise indicated, the material in this section is drawn from the Philippine National Environment Protection Council, *Philippine Environment 1978,* Manila, Ministry of Human Settlements, 1979.

In the Philippines, Presidential Pollution Control Decree No. 984 (PD 984) authorizes the National Pollution Control Commission (NPCC) to prevent and control water, air, and land pollution throughout the country. In consonance with the Philippine Environment Code, the NPCC developed various measures specifically for marine pollution control purposes, but the scope of its rule-making authority is uncertain because it is shared with the Philippine Coast Guard. The Bureau of Fisheries and Aquatic Resources is charged with protecting national fishery resources from the effects of pollution resulting from the indiscriminate discharge of hazardous pollutants (PD 704); and PD 856 (1976) authorized by the Department of Health to protect bathing beaches from pollution hazardous to human health. Other aspects of Philippine environmental law, such as those pertaining to watershed protection, for example, also function indirectly to protect the marine environment.

Land-Based Sources. The Philippines has taken an indirect approach to regulating waste disposal. By establishing receiving-water standards under the provisions of section 6 of PD 984, the National Pollution Control Commission is empowered to enforce industrial wastewater treatment requirements so that industrial wastes are reduced to levels that will permit the maintenance of the established ambient quality standards. Less than 21 percent of 724 potential polluting industrial firms have adequate wastewater treatment; 23 percent have inadequate treatment; 10 percent need improvement; 16 percent have treatment facilities under construction; and the remaining 30 percent have no treatment facilities at all. PD 984 also requires environmental impact statements. There are economic incentives that include reimbursement of all duties paid for installed equipment for prevention of water pollution and costs of research studies for pollution control mandated under PD 274. However, the application of these benefits is restricted to industries in metropolitan Manila, particularly those industries within the drainage basin of the Pasig River system. This limitation is expected to be remedied when section 56 of PD 1152 implements the National Environmental Protection Council's (NEPC) guidelines for the grant of tax incentives to individuals or corporations using pollution control facilities.

Large population areas require an extensive network of sewerage systems. At present, only the cities of Manila and Zamboanga have central sewerage collection and disposal systems. The systems provide no treatment for the collected wastewaters, however, and only serve 15–20 percent of the city areas. In other areas residential, commercial, and industrial establishments use septic tanks discharged directly into the street canals and storm drains and ultimately into river systems. The *Metro Manila Sewerage Plan, 1980–2000* does not include treatment mechanisms and would rely upon natural treatment by diffusion and dilution of wastewaters by Manila Bay waters.

Due to the heavy initial capital investment that would be required, and the high volume of wastes generated, no specific measures are designated for the control of mining discharges. Although the Bureau of Mines through PD 463 (1974) has the authority to regulate pollution from mine tailings, most mining wastes are simply disposed of in swamplands and waterways emptying into the ocean. Mining and quarrying are treated as kinds of land use. No local standards exist because the cost of implementation would greatly influence the use of mineral lands.

The only legal measures to prevent siltation are contained in the Revised Forestry Code (PD 705), which authorizes the Bureau of Forest Development to manage, regulate, and monitor shifting cultivation. The Philippine Environment Code instructs the NEPC, established in 1977 by PD 1121, to organize and coordinate an interagency task force to study and evaluate these major problems. The administrative measures taken include determining the extent of erosion in the country, evaluating of major causes of erosion, and mapping the distribution of erosion.

No local standards have been used for pesticides and chemical fertilizers, but there have been current studies to determine the permissible levels of these substances. Currently, the Fertilizer and Pesticide Authority (FPA) adopts the recommended international standards on pesticides by the Food and Agriculture Organisation (FAO) and the World Health Organisation (WHO), as well as the standards set by the Food and Drug Administration of the United States. To prevent pesticides banned by other countries from finding their way into the local market, the Philippines seeks international cooperation in obtaining information on such pesticides. Regulation of local manufacturers, formulators, distributors, and inventors is also the responsibility of the FPA under PD 1144, which protects local users from mislabeling, adulterating, and misrepresenting toxic formulations. The use of DDT is confined to malaria control. The effectiveness of regulations of wastes from land-based sources, including direct river discharges, is very much dependent upon the classification of Philippine rivers as to their "best use." The NPCC has been directed under section 15 of PD 1152 to institute a river classification program in coordination with appropriate government agencies.

Offshore Exploration and Exploitation. Since offshore exploration and exploitation for oil in the Philippines is very recent, there are hardly any regulations for controlling oil spills or wastes from exploration activities.

Vessel Sources. Under PD 602, a National Operation Center for Oil Pollution was created by the Philippine Coast Guard and followed by a National Oil Spill Contingency Plan.[41] The Philippines is one of the few countries in Southeast Asia to have ratified and implemented the 1954 Intergovernmental Maritime Consultative Organization (IMCO) Oil Pollution Convention.[42] PD 600, as amended by PD 979 in May 1977, empowered the Philippine Coast Guard to issue rules and regulations for prevention, containment, abatement, and control of marine pollution. The rules and regulations that were issued required operators of ships of 1,000 tons and above to install antimarine pollution equipment on their vessels not later than 31 December 1978. The rules and regulations also required the installation of oily-water-filtering devices and slop tanks to receive oil residues from the vessels. These measures are currently limited to "territorial waters," "inland navigable waters," and tributaries thereof.[43]

Radioactive Wastes. Republic Act (RA) 5207 bears indirectly on radioactive pollution. This act regulates atomic energy facilities and the release and disposal of radioactive materials into the air and aquatic environment, and it also provides for liability for nuclear damage. The Philippine Atomic Energy Commission has as one of its functions the safeguarding of Philippine waters from pollution by radioactive wastes.[44]

The Philippines Overview. The Philippines has an elaborate set of legal and institutional arrangements and programs regulating wastes that can enter the marine environment. It was the first country in the region to have introduced major pollution control legislation, the Pollution Control Law — RA 3931 — in 1964. However, it has yet to develop environmental regulations for its offshore activities. Its effort to regulate waste disposal by the indirect approach is a monumental task that is considered expensive to implement even in developed countries such as the United States.

Singapore

The material for this section is drawn from the Science Council of Singapore, *Environment Protection in Singapore: A Handbook,* Singapore, 1980.

Land-Based Sources. In 1978, 78 percent of Singapore's two million people were served with sewers. The sewage is treated at the Sewerage Department's treatment works before discharge into the sea. Some of the effluent from the Ulu Pandan Treatment Works is further upgraded by the Jurong Industrial Works to provide a supply of industrial water to certain factories in the Jurong industrial area. The department also encourages siting new factories where public sewers are available to receive industrial trade effluents, because it is less costly to discharge into public sewers than directly into watercourses.

The amount of waste from land-based sources that finally reaches the ocean is regulated by the Director of Water Pollution Control and Drainage of the Sewerage Department, with authorities under the Water Pollution Control and Drainage Act of 1975. A maximum fine of S$5,000 may be imposed for the discharge of a trade effluent that does not meet the minimum standard of quality prescribed by the Trade Effluent Regulations of 1976. Also, under the regulations the discharge of trade effluent must not include pesticides or radioactive materials.

Offshore Exploration and Exploitation. Singapore, with a narrow band of territorial and exclusive economic zone (EEZ) waters, has little prospect of discovering oil or gas offshore. However, it is actively engaged in nearshore excavations and coastal land reclamations. Apparently there are no environment-related regulations governing these activities.

Vessel Sources. Singapore's response to the dangers of ship-generated pollution is perhaps the most comprehensive of all the ASEAN countries. It has ratified and implemented the 1954 Oil Pollution Convention with its Prevention of Pollution of the Sea Act of 1971 and with later amendments put into effect by the 1973 Civil Liability (Oil Pollution) Act and the 1976 Prevention of Pollution of the Sea (Amendment) Act. The 1971 and 1973 acts are enforced by the Port of Singapore Authority (PSA), which coordinates all activities concerning marine pollution in Singapore's coastal waters.

The PSA also provides facilities for the reception, treatment, and disposal of slops, sludges, dirty ballast, and tank washings at the Slop and Sludge Reception and Treatment Centre on Pulau Sebarok. The fees for the deslopping services rendered by the PSA fall into ten categories: collection and disposal per unit volume at anchorage, collection and disposal per unit volume at wharf, dockage per 100 gross register ton (GRT) or per unit time, labor per unit operation, pumping per unit volume, cancellation or amendment or service for each, detention charge per unit time, demurrage per barge or per unit time, sludge disposal and barge freight per unit, and demurrage per unit time.

The reception and treatment facilities at Pulau Sebarok have the following processing capacities:

- Slop/tank cleaning water/dirty ballast, 300,000 cubic meters (m³)/year;
- Contaminated slop, 25,000 m³/year; and
- Sludge, 10,000 m³/year.

Other facilities include two receiving piers with berthing chart datum depths of 10.9 meters (m) and 12.8 m, displacements of 45,800 tons and 23,200 tons, and accommodating ships up to 264 m and 174 m in length; and a sludge pier with a berthing depth of 7.6 m and accommodating ships up to 50 m in length. The slop receiving rate and pressure are 500 m³/hr and 10 kilograms per square centimeter (kg/cm²), respectively. The total receiving tank capacity is 62,000 m³.

Under the Prevention of Pollution of the Sea Act of 1971 the maximum penalty for the discharge of oil or a mixture containing oil is S$500,000 or imprisonment for up to two years or both. Under the Civil Liability (Oil Pollution) Act of 1973, the limit of liability for any damage by oil or its mixture is in accordance with section 295 of the Merchant Shipping Act, which is approximately US$203.70 for each ton of the ship's tonnage. This liability standard is higher than that imposed under the 1969 International Convention of Civil Liability for Oil Damage. This may give rise to difficulties since Singapore is not yet a party to that convention. Should widespread and hazardous oil pollution occur, the PSA would implement the Marine Emergency Action Procedure to mobilize all PSA, Defense Ministry, and Ministry of Environment resources to take countermeasures. In addition, under the provisions of the Prevention of the Pollution of the Sea Act, it will be assisted by oil-based industries, which are obliged to provide antipollution equipment in the event of such an emergency.

Radioactive Wastes.   In addition to prohibiting any discharge of effluent containing radioactive materials under the Trade Effluent Regulations of 1976, Singapore has also imposed restrictions on the marine transportation of radioactive materials under its Radiation Protection Act of 1973. The act provides for the regulation and control of the importation, manufacture, sale, disposal, transport, keeping, and use of radioactive materials and irradiating apparatus. The act is now administered by the Radiation Protection Department of the Ministry of Science and Technology.

Singapore Overview.   Singapore·has the most effective measures in the region to regulate wastes that reach the marine environment. It has maintained high standards in the quality of the environment, and its pollution regulation has been managed effectively despite the difficulty of enforcing pollution controls on international shipping.

Thailand

Environmental protection in Thailand is under the National Conservation of National Environmental Quality Act of 1975. Thailand's effort to control the existing sources of industrial wastes began in 1969 upon the implementation of the Factory Act — Buddhist Era (BE) 2512 and its later amendment, BE 2518 (1975).[45] Order No. 2 of the Ministry of Industry, issued in 1970 under the Factory Act of 1969, reads in part that no wastewater can be let out of the factory unless certain limits are observed.[46] The Industrial Environment Division of the Ministry of Industry is supposed to enforce the regulations.

The penalty for violating section 20 of the Factory Act (which calls for the disposal and destruction of waste or surplus materials containing poisonous elements or flammable materials) is imprisonment for up to one month or a fine of up to 10,000 baht (approximately US$500), or both. The suspected violator has to be served with a prior warning, and any injured party has to institute a tort case to collect compensation for alleged damages.[47] Because of this complicated process, the law has remained ineffective.

For new waste sources the most common measure is the permit system whereby the government agencies concerned are empowered to determine the environmental impact of industries before permits are issued.[48] Section 6 of the amendment empowers the prime minister, on the advice of the Office of the National Environment Board, among others, to prescribe categories and the magnitude of projects or activities of government agencies, state enterprise or private organizations requiring environmental impact studies.[49] With waste treatment systems and subsequent regulations established under the act, the level of discharge reaching the inland waters has been reduced by as much as 65 percent. Two resort areas, Pattaya and Hua Hin, have been considered as sites for ocean outfalls.[50]

Offshore Exploration and Exploitation.   Like the Philippines, Thailand's offshore oil and gas exploration and exploitation activities are quite recent. Although there is no specific legislation covering the control of oil pollution from this source, the statutory basis exists.[51] There has long been offshore tin mining near Phuket. In February 1981 a ministerial resolution was promulgated to stop dredging near Phuket. It appears that this legislation, which delayed new dredging until 1983, was due less to environmental considerations than to the conflict between mining and tourism in the coastal zone.

Vessel Sources. The Act on Navigation in Siamese Waters (No. 12) BE 2522 (1979) applies to marine pollution as a consequence of shipping casualties or accidents in

Siamese navigable waters.[52] The act is administered by the Harbour Department in the Ministry of Communications.[53] A Marine Oil Pollution Control Board was proposed in the Draft Regulations on the Prevention and Abatement of Marine Pollution by Oil.[54]

A cooperative approach has been undertaken by the private sector through the Industry Environmental Safety Group to mitigate oil spills. The group was initiated in 1968 when the refinery and the refineries at Sriracha arrived at an informal mutual aid agreement.[55] The group has developed a contingency plan to respond to major oil spills. The plan includes a set of Emergency Procedure Guidelines and also provides information on properties of crude oils and petroleum products; charts of expanded slick areas due to delay in response time; information on the direction and distance traveled by oil slicks under the influence of current, wind, and tide; and other necessary organizational and technical information.[56] By design, the plan is only to be implemented in response to a spill of crude or petroleum products of more than 1,000 tons.[57]

Thailand Overview. Of the five original ASEAN nations, Thailand has the least legislation governing pollution. Although some laws to control pollution from industrial effluents exist, they are easily circumvented since enforcement is ineffective. Thailand seems to be more concerned with the impact of new development projects or new sources of pollution than with pollution arising from existing sources. It has been very active in developing environmental impact asssessments for new projects.

China

Marine environmental protection in China is governed by Decree No. 9 of the Standing Committee of the 5th National People's Congress, adopted at the 24th Session of the Standing Committee on 23 August 1982, effective 1 March 1983.[58] The provisions discussed in this section are from various parts of the decree. To implement this decree, the State Council subsequently approved the specific marine water quality standards in Tables 8.4 and 8.5.

The law is applicable to the inland and territorial seas of the People's Republic of China (PRC) and all other sea areas under its jurisdiction. The law also applies to the discharge of harmful matter and the dumping of wastes beyond the sea areas under the jurisdiction of the PRC but causing pollution damage to the sea areas under the jurisdiction of the PRC.

The Environmental Protection Department under the State Council is in charge of marine environmental protection in the entire country. Relevant departments under the State Council and people's governments of the coastal provinces, autonomous regions, and municipalities may designate special marine reserves, marine natural reserves, and seashore scenic and tourist areas and take corresponding measures to protect them. The designation of special marine reserves and marine natural reserves must be approved by the State Council.

Table 8.4   Quality Requirements for Sea Water

Type of Pollutants (suspended material)	First-Class Waters (from artificial sources > 10 mg/l)	Second-Class Waters (from artificial sources > 50 mg/l)	Third-Class Waters (from artificial sources > 150 mg/l)
Color, odor, smell	Seawater and sea products with abnormal color, odor, or smell		Seawater with no abnormal color, odor, or smell
Floating material	No surface oil patch, floating froth, and other materials		No clear surface oil patch, floating froth, or other materials
pH	7.5–8.4	7.3–8.8	6.5–9.0
Chemical consumption of oxygen	< 3 mg/l	< 4 mg/l	< 5 mg/l
Dissolved oxygen	< 5 mg/l at any time	< 4 mg/l at any time	< 3 mg/l at any time
Temperature	Not > 4° C above ambient temperature		
Bacterium coliform	Not to exceed 10,000/l (not to exceed 700/l for shellfish culture)		
Disease-producing germs	Industrial liquid wastes containing disease-producing germs must not be discharged through sewage without first being sterilized		
Sediment	Surface siltation cannot hamper the growth of seed plants		
Hazardous material	Must be in compliance with Table 8.5 requirement on maximum concentration		

Source: National Standards of the People's Republic of China: Marine Water Quality Standards, GB 3097-82, 4 June 1982 (in Chinese).

Land-Based Sources. Environmental Protection Departments of the coastal provinces, autonomous regions, and municipalities are responsible for coordinating, overseeing, and checking marine environmental protection in their respective administrative areas and for supervising environmental protection against pollution damage caused by seashore construction projects and by land-based pollutants.

Before working out and submitting their construction plans, units in charge of seashore construction projects must conduct scientific surveys of the marine environment, select suitable sites in the light of natural and social conditions, and submit a report on the possible effects on the environment in accordance with relevant state regulations.

Measures must be taken to protect aquatic resources when building harbors, oil wharves, water conservancy projects, and tidal wave power-generating projects in estuaries. Dams to be built across fish and crab migration routes must be provided with fish ladders. Strict control is to be enforced over land reclamation from the sea, other sea-enclosing projects, and quarrying and sand-collecting work. Damage to seashore shelter belts, scenic forests, scenic rocks, mangrove forests, and coral reefs is forbidden.

Table 8.5 Maximum Allowable Concentration of Hazardous Materials in Sea Water

Pollutant	Maximum Allowable Concentration (mg/l)		
	First-Class Waters	Second-Class Waters	Third-Class Waters
Mercury	0.0005	0.001	0.001
Cadmium	0.005	0.01	0.01
Lead	0.05	0.01	0.1
Chromium	0.1	0.5	0.5
Arsenic	0.05	0.1	0.1
Copper	0.01	0.1	0.1
Zinc	0.1	1.0	1.0
Silica	0.01	0.02	0.03
Oil	0.05	0.1	0.5
Cyanide	0.02	0.1	0.5
Sulfide	calculate as dissolved oxygen		
Volatile phenol	0.005	0.01	0.05
Organic chloride (agricultural chemicals)	0.001	0.02	0.04
Inorganic nitrogen	0.01	0.2	0.3
Inorganic phosphorous	0.015	0.03	0.045

Source: National Standards of the People's Republic of China: Marine Water Quality Standards, GB 3097-82, 4 June 1982 (in Chinese).

Note: The allowable concentrations of inorganic N and P are the limiting value for prevention of "red tide" in warm current bays. Radioactive materials in seawater must not be more than the limit for groundwater defined in GBJ8-74, "The Regulation of Radiation Protection."

The discharge of harmful matter into the sea by coastal units must be conducted in strict accordance with the standards for discharge and relevant regulations promulgated by the state or provincial autonomous regional or municipal people's governments. No new outlet for discharging sewage is allowed within marine natural reserves, aquacultural grounds, and seashore scenic and tourist areas. Outlets set up before the promulgation of the law, if their discharge is not in conformity with state standards, must be rectified within a prescribed time. Medical and industrial sewage containing infectious pathogens can be discharged into the sea only after it is properly treated and strictly sterilized and after such pathogens are exterminated. The discharge of industrial and domestic sewage containing organic and nutrient matter into bays, semi-enclosed seas, and other sea areas with a weak self-purification capacity is to be controlled to prevent eutrophication of the seawater.

When discharging heated wastewater into the sea, measures are to be taken to ensure that the water temperature in the neighboring fishing areas meets the state criteria for water quality to avoid damage to aquatic resources by heat pollution.

The application of chemical pesticides in coastal farm fields must meet state regulations and standards for the safe use of pesticides.

Offshore Exploration and Exploitation. The State Administrative Department of Oceanography is responsible for organizing surveys, for monitoring and surveillance of the marine environment, and for conducting scientific research. It supervises environmental protection against marine pollution damage caused by offshore oil exploration and exploitation and by dumping wastes into the sea.

Before submitting their work plans, offshore oil developers are required to produce reports on the possible effects on the marine environment, including effective measures to protect the marine environment from pollution damage, and submit them to the Environmental Protection Department under the State Council for approval.

Residual oil and waste oil must be recovered and may not be discharged into the sea. Sewage containing oil, oil mixtures, and oil-containing industrial garbage from offshore oil drilling rigs, drilling platforms, and oil extraction platforms cannot be discharged unless after treatment their oil content does not exceed the standards set by the state. When testing oil at sea, oils and oil mixtures must not be discharged into the sea, and the oil and gas is to be thoroughly burned to prevent sea pollution. In exploring and developing offshore oil resources, appropriate antipollution facilities and equipment must be available, and effective technical measures must be taken to prevent blowouts or oil leaks.

Vessel Sources. Harbor superintendents of the PRC are responsible for overseeing, investigating, and dealing with the discharge of wastes by vessels and for maintaining surveillance of the waters of the port areas. The state fishing administration and fishing harbor superintendents are responsible for supervising the discharge of wastes by vessels in the fishing harbors and for maintaining surveillance on the waters of the fishing port areas. Owners of ships from which harmful wastes are dumped may be fined up to US$50,000. The Environmental Protection Department of the armed forces is responsible for supervising the discharge of wastes by naval vessels and keeping watch on the waters of the naval ports.

Harbors and oil wharves must have facilities to receive and treat residual oil, waste oil, sewage that contains oil and other discharges, and to have necessary antipollution facilities and monitoring and alarm devices. All vessels are forbidden to discharge oils, oil mixtures, waste, and other harmful matter into the sea areas under the jurisdiction of China.

Oil tankers larger than 150 gross tons (GT) must have appropriate antipollution equipment and facilities. Oil tankers of less than 150 GT and other vessels less than 400 GT must have special containers for recovering residual and waste oil. Vessels carrying more than 2,000 tons of commodity oil in bulk must have a valid "Certificate of Civil Liability Insurance Against Oil Pollution Damage or Other Financial Guarantees" or a "Credit Certificate of Civil Liability Against Oil Pollution" or hold other financial credit guarantees.

The discharge of oil-containing wastewater by oil tankers of more than 150 GT and other vessels above 400 GT must be conducted in accordance with the state standards and regulations concerning vessel sewage discharge and be accurately recorded in the oil logbook. When accidents to vessels have caused or are likely to cause serious marine environmental pollution damage, the harbor superintendent of the PRC has the right to take mandatory measures to avoid or reduce such pollution damage.

Radioactive Wastes. The discharge of wastewater containing strong radioactive matter into the sea, including that from nuclear powered vessels or vessels carrying radioactive matter, is forbidden. If it is necessary to discharge wastewater containing weak radioactive matter into the sea, it must be carried out in strict accordance with state regulations and standards on radioactive protection.

Dumping. No unit is allowed to dump any kind of waste material into the sea areas under the jurisdiction of China without the permission of the State Administrative Department of Oceanography.

China Overview. The decree is the most recent and comprehensive marine protection law in the region, even addressing pollution in areas beyond China's jurisdiction but likely to affect its waters. As a point of comparison, its concentration limits for heavy metals are ten times as strict as those of Malaysia. In addition to the national marine water quality standards, relevant departments under the State Council and standing committees of the people's congresses and people's governments of the coastal provinces, autonomous regions, and municipalities also may work out concrete measures for the implementation of this law in line with the actual conditions of the specific departments and localities.

The law also provides for penalties and compensation. For violations of this law that have caused or are likely to cause marine environmental pollution damage, the relevant supervising departments may order the violators to remedy the pollution damage within a specific time, pay a pollution discharging fee, pay the cost of eliminating the pollution, or compensate for the loss sustained by the state, or it may give the violators a warning or impose a fine.

Units and individuals who have suffered damage from marine environmental pollution have the right to demand compensation from the parties causing the pollution and damage. Compensation liability may be exempted in any of the following circumstances if pollution damage to the marine environment cannot be avoided despite prompt and appropriate measures: (1) acts of war, (2) irresistible natural calamities, and (3) negligence or other errors in the performance of duties on the part of departments in charge of beacons or other navigation aids. If pollution damage to the marine environment is caused entirely through deliberate acts or errors by a third party, the third party is liable to pay compensation. Where provisions in force concerning marine environmental protection contradict the present law, the present law stands.

Although its marine environment protection measures are the most comprehensive in scope and detail, it remains to be seen whether China will have greater success than other countries of the region in enforcing adherence to them.

Conclusions

Several generalizations can be made about marine pollution in Southeast Asia. First, the countries discussed here share genuine concern about the threat of marine pollution in the region, especially the threat of oil pollution by vessels and offshore drilling installations. Other sources of marine pollution have a lower priority.[59] Second, concern about oil pollution is not matched by appropriate preventive and remedial legislation and enforcement. Third, interest is apparent in various modes of regional cooperation for marine pollution prevention and control — perhaps even in the idea of an appropriate subregional convention[60] — but the diversity of the region limits the feasibility and desirability of bringing the national responses into accord.[61]

The level of concern and the capacity to respond to environmental pollution vary widely from country to country. Although all have some environmental provisions in their earlier laws pertaining to the safety, health, and welfare of the public, their more intense efforts to tackle pollution are recent. Among the ASEAN countries, the Philippines was the first to introduce major pollution control legislation, RA 3931, in 1964. Singapore responded to marine pollution, even earlier than it responded to domestic and industrial pollution, with the passage of its Prevention of Pollution of the Sea Act of 1971. Malaysia enacted its major environmental legislation — the Environmental Quality Act in 1974 — but the act remained ineffective until the three sets of regulations for regulating palm oil wastes, rubber effluent, and sewage and industrial effluents were introduced in 1977, 1978, and 1979, respectively. Malaysia has yet to introduce its marine pollution control regulations under the act.

Thailand and Indonesia have not introduced any new environmental laws but have improvised upon existing laws relating to sectoral matters by introducing subsidiary regulations for pollution control. Thailand issued its Factory Effluent Standards in 1970 under the Factory Act of 1960, but the standards were not observed closely. With the exception of the city of Jakarta's prohibition of oil discharge around the Thousand Islands group, Indonesia has yet to introduce a single regulation specifying rules and standards for waste disposal under any of its existing laws.

The countries have chosen different strategies to combat pollution. The Philippines has opted for a strategy of variable effluent standards. By prescribing what the ambient water quality criteria and standards should be, its regulatory agency theoretically can specify what the discharge or effluent standards need to be for receiving water bodies, the use of which has been predetermined. This strategy is generally recognized to be sensitive to both economic and environmental conditions. However, it demands high administrative skills in the regulatory agency and from the industrial managers. Furthermore, it requires extensive preparation by data gathering, analysis, and interpretation before a single standard for a specific discharge at a selected site can be set. The administrative cost associated with the implementation of this strategy can be prohibitive.

Because of the expected high cost of administering the strategy of effluent variable standards, Singapore and Thailand have adopted the strategy of introducing uniform standards. With its manageable size, Singapore has been able to introduce an additional option in which polluters are encouraged to utilize the state-run wastewater treatment plants. By utilizing these services, polluters do not have to treat their wastewaters fully before submission to these plants; thus, they save some costs.

Malaysia has introduced a mixed strategy: issuing two sets of uniform standards for treated sewage and industrial effluents, and regulating its agriculture-based industries — palm oil and rubber. To regulate these industries, the pollution control agency of Malaysia (the Division of Environment) has the power to exercise many options, such as controlling production or factory operations and specifying the conditions of discharge into watercourses or onto land. Other industries or sources of pollution have to comply with either Standard A or B, depending upon their locations: Standard A is applicable to discharges within drinking water catchments, and Standard B is applicable to those discharges outside such areas.

Indonesia has contemplated adopting a multiple-uniform-standards strategy by issuing four sets of uniform standards for discharges into four types of water bodies designated or used for drinking water and domestic water supplies, fisheries, agriculture and industry, and urban drainage for waste transport.

ACTUAL AND POSSIBLE TRANSNATIONAL RESPONSES AND ISSUES

National responses to the threat of pollution have been described above. The fact that these national responses vary widely in scope and purpose creates transnational issues when a transnational response is required. This section focuses on the major transnational responses and transnational issues related to pollution. Responses and issues are treated together because they are interrelated. Who should respond to *what* and *how* are issues in themselves.

ASEAN and UNEP Programs

The most promising regional pollution control activities now underway in Southeast Asia are those taking place within the ASEAN network. The principal transnational pollutant receiving coordinated regional attention is oil. Two bodies have been established by ASEAN to deal with oil pollution: the ASEAN Council on Petroleum (ASCOPE), which deals mainly with the environmental consequences of the exploration for petroleum and natural gas, and the ASEAN Expert Group on Marine Pollution. ASCOPE has been discussing standardization of environmental and safety regulations for offshore drilling and the local complexities of combating transnational oil spills.

The Expert Group has organized a Contingency Plan for the Control and Mitigation of Marine Pollution that provides for a system for alerting member countries if major oil spills occur within the region. The plan provides for exchange of information on operational capacities to combat pollution within each nation and a program of mutual assistance to cope with oil spills that member countries cannot handle alone. Specific features of the plan include

- Adequate and coordinated contingency planning by the governments concerned;
- Responsibility of the appointed institution to report immediately to the established emergency control centers;
- Availability of sufficient and appropriate recovery and containment equipment, including vessels;
- Availability of adequate slop tanks onshore capable of receiving contained oil spillages; and
- Availability of trained personnel for the cleanup operation.[62]

ASEAN is attempting to develop a regional governmental approach to spill management based on coordinated policies and cooperative programs. The states have also required the national and foreign oil companies to develop their own capabilities to support the governments' policies.

With the assistance of the Intergovernmental Maritime Organization (IMO) and the United Nations Environment Programme (UNEP), Indonesia, Malaysia, and the Philippines developed an action plan for the Celebes Sea that is intended to reflect the underlying philosophy of the ASEAN Contingency Plan.

In June 1979 the First ASEAN Working Group Meeting on Marine Sciences identified marine pollution problem areas requiring strong scientific inputs through regional cooperation.[63] Also, the activities of the Intergovernmental Oceanographic Commission (IOC) of the United Nations Educational, Scientific and Cultural Organization's Working Group for the Western Pacific (WESTPAC) include marine biology and pollution.[64]

In addition to their various national regulations regarding oil pollution described above, Indonesia, Malaysia, and Singapore are signatories to a navigation safety agreement for the straits of Malacca and Singapore. Under this agreement, all tankers and large vessels navigating these straits must carry adequate insurance and compensation coverage. There is also a US$1.3 million revolving fund established by Japanese shipping interests and the straits nations to cover the costs of cleaning up and preventing oil spills from tankers.

The ASEAN Expert Group has developed a proposal for an ASEAN Subregional Environment Program and is coordinating its approach with the Regional Seas Programme of UNEP. The UNEP Action Plan for the Protection and Development of the Marine Environment and Coastal Areas of the East Asian Region was adopted in April 1981.[65] The plan targets the Southeast Asian seas for a Mediterranean-type protocol for the "ASEAN Seas" and for upgrading of awareness and capabilities for its implementation.[66] The plan presently covers only the marine environment of ASEAN nations, but as in the ASEAN organization itself, participation is open to other states in the region.

Some of the marine areas claimed by ASEAN countries are also claimed by other countries not yet party to either the plan or ASEAN — Vietnam and Kampuchea in the eastern Gulf of Thailand, Vietnam in the Natuna area, and Vietnam and China in the "Dangerous Ground." Because pollution does not recognize jurisdictional boundaries, several different issues arise. Should these disputed areas be included in the plan? Should and could the plan and international cooperation in marine environmental protection be expanded to encompass the entire South China Sea and adjacent water bodies? Should extraregional users and polluters such as Japan and the United States participate in the plan or contribute to its implementation? To what degree should the plan be substantively weakened or its priorities changed in order to induce a larger number of countries to participate?

Priorities and Officially Defined Wastes

Scientific experts at an international workshop held in Pinang, Malaysia, in April 1976 identified the major types of wastes in the region. The Scientific Group of Experts also identified the order of priority and the countries or geographic areas having special concern with particular pollutants (Table 8.6). The group expressed no concern with pollutants from Burma, Macao, and Papua New Guinea, or landlocked Laos. The experts also indirectly identified the order of priority of pollutants for different countries. Oil drew the most attention from all fourteen countries or political entities in the region; disposal of radioactive wastes apparently raised little concern in the region.

Table 8.7 summarizes the types of pollutants identified by government-nominated experts at the Baguio meeting in June 1980 and at the Bangkok meeting in December 1980. Under the assessment component of the proposed action plan, there was a reduction in the number of waste categories from the original ten at the Pinang workshop to seven at the Baguio meeting, and finally to five at Bangkok. Pesticides such as DDT—of concern to five countries at Pinang—were dropped from the list. Sedimentation, metals, organics, and nutrients were lumped together and collectively were given a priority equal with oil. A new category — wastes from seabed exploration and exploitation — was added. But seabed, thermal, and atmospheric pollutants were not considered parts of the current action plan. Thus the effective number of pollutant categories in the action plan is now two: oil, and non-oil (metals, organics, nutrients, and sediments).

The Intergovernmental Meeting on the Protection and Development of the Marine Environment and Coastal Areas of the East Asian Region held in Manila on 27–29 April 1981 fully endorsed the Bangkok recommendations.[67] The scope of the plan has thus been drastically reduced from its earlier conception. The persistent and nonbiodegradable wastes (such as pesticides, oil dispersants, organochlorine, vinyl monomers, and radioactive wastes) identified by the scientific workshop

Table 8.6   Pollutant Priorities: Pinang Meeting

Pollutant Grouping	Priority	Country or Area within Region Having Special Concern or Being Affected[a]
Oil	1	*Malacca Strait* (Indonesia, Malaysia, Singapore), South China Sea, Hong Kong, Manila Bay (Philippines)
DDT, pesticides, organochlorines, etc.	1	Philippines, Vietnam, Malaysia, Indonesia, Thailand
Heavy Metals	1	Philippines, Hong Kong, Indonesia, Malaysia
Organic and biological pollutants, fertilizers	1	Singapore, Thailand, Hong Kong, Indonesia, Malaysia, Philippines
Silt	1	*Malacca Strait* (Indonesia, Malaysia, Singapore), *Marinduque* and *Cebu* (Philippines), *Phuket* (Thailand), Hong Kong, Kalimantan and Java (Indonesia), Sarawak and Sabah (Malaysia)
Heat	2	*East Coast of Gulf of Thailand,* Bintulu (Sarawak), Bagac Bay (west coast of Luzon, Philippines), Strait of Johore (Malaysia, Singapore), Hong Kong
Metalloids	2	Indonesia, Malaysia, Philippines
Plastics	3	Hong Kong
Radioactive wastes	3	–
Salt	3	*Hong Kong,* Singapore

Source: Intergovernmental Oceanographic Commission Workshop Report No. 8, Report of the IOC/FAO/(IPFC)/ UNEP International Workshop on Marine Pollution in East Asian Waters, Universiti Sains Malaysia, Pinang. 7–13 April 1976 (Doc. _UNEPIWG).
[a]Areas in italics were specifically identified as high priority areas.

in Pinang received no official attention. The word "research" has crept into the management component of the plan. The exclusion from the plan of the environmental impact assessment along with the development of its methodology and guidelines has effectively reduced the scope of the plan to pollution control aspects only. This narrowing of the pollution control agenda raises several questions. How were the priorities determined, and are there real differences in perception of priorities among the countries? Does each ASEAN country wish to develop its own environmental impact assessment methodology and guidelines to fit its development objectives? How will any such perceptual differences affect the implementation of the action plan? To what degree should politics influence the interpretation of scientific evidence in determining priorities?

There are other concerns as well. The plan includes a subregional effort to combat oil pollution from vessel sources but does not include a similar effort for combating oil pollution from seabed exploration and exploitation. All the ASEAN states except Singapore have offshore oil or gas exploration activities. Singapore, however, has the largest number of tankers either by ownership or by registration.[68] Does the plan impose an inequitable burden on Singapore's merchant shipping industry, and might this perception limit Singapore's participation?

Table 8.7   Waste Priorities: Baguio and Bangkok Meetings

Draft Action Plan Component	Baguio Meeting Priorities			Bangkok Meeting Priorities		
	Pollutant	Priority			Pollutant	Priority
Assessment	Silt and sediment loads	1	Present:		Oil	1
	Organic and nutrient load	2			Nonoil wastes (metals, organics, nutrients, and sediments)	2
	Oil	3				
	Metals and halogenated organics	4	Future:		Seabed exploration and exploitation wastes	1
	Heat-thermal waste	5			Heat-thermal wastes	2
	Seabed exploitation and exploitation wastes	6			Wastes through the atmosphere	3
	Wastes through the atmosphere	7				
Management	Development of principles and guidelines for the disposal of *domestic agricultural, industrial,* and *radioactive wastes*	1		Development of principles and guidelines for the disposal of *wastes*		1
	Identification of the need for, and the *delineation* of, marine sites for ultimate dumping of hazardous wastes	2		Cooperative *research* on the need for ultimate dumping of hazardous wastes		2

Sources: Report of the Meeting of Experts to Review the Draft Action Plan for the East Asian Seas, Baguio, 17–21 June 1980 (Doc. No. UNEP/WG.41/4), UNEP, 1980; and *Report of the Second Meeting of Experts to Review the Draft Action Plan for the East Asian Seas, Bangkok, 8–12 December 1980* (Doc. No. UNEP/WG.52/6), UNEP, 1980.

The Bangkok meeting changed the terms of reference for the management of hazardous waste from identification of dumping sites, as called for by the Baguio meeting, to cooperative research on the need for ultimate dumping of such wastes. Also, the research plan will be confined to hazardous wastes other than radioactive wastes.[69] All the ASEAN states except Singapore, however, have nuclear research capabilities.[70] Eventually they will need to dispose of radioactive wastes from these research facilities, not to mention those from any future nuclear power generation or weapons manufacturers.

The need for disposal sites for hazardous wastes, including low-level radioactive wastes, is still on the public agenda. Marine disposal is the most obvious possible mode of solution in the region, because the small land area and dense population present considerable problems for designating suitable land sites. Suitable marine sites are more likely to be found within the jurisdictions of Indonesia and the Philippines because of their large and deep marine trenches than within those of Malaysia, Thailand, or Singapore. Thus, the feasibility of developing nuclear energy generation in Malaysia, Thailand, and Singapore could eventually depend on acceptance of wastes by Indonesia and the Philippines. Would Indonesia and the Philippines accept the wastes if Malaysia, Thailand, or Singapore were willing to share the electrical power generated?

Standardized Regulations

The CLS provides that states should endeavor to harmonize their policies regarding protection of the marine environment. The countries in the region have similar wastes and a similar level of technology for disposing of the wastes. Theoretically, they might adopt uniform standards. The fact that they do not reflects real differences in national priorities for environmental protection in general and for specific pollutants and pollutant sources in particular. These policy differences are consistent with the CLS since it provides that states "shall use the best practicable means at their disposal and within their capabilities to prevent, reduce and control pollution" (Article 194, par. 2). Yet a mosaic of different pollution regulations could inhibit transnational activities such as the shipping of oil.

Can and should such standards be made uniform or be harmonized among at least the ASEAN countries with large adjacent jurisdictional areas? If so, which standards, where, and at what common base?

Will Differences Be Exploited?

The action plan calls for regional development and application of principles and guidelines for the discharge of wastes into coastal waters. The Philippines has taken the variable discharge standards approach by emphasizing the maintenance of the quality of its waters for various beneficial uses. Standards under the laws of the NPCC could be as lenient as the lowest criteria for water quality, for example, those intended for heavy industrial use. Singapore, Malaysia, Thailand, and apparently Indonesia have taken another approach by specifying uniform discharge standards in their respective pollution control laws and regulations. Normally, a potential investor looks at the various pollution standards set by different countries as part of the economic assessment for project feasibility and siting. From an investment perspective, the Philippines might be projecting a more favorable climate by not explicitly expressing discharge standards in its pollution control laws. By specifying uniform discharge standards in their laws, Singapore, Malaysia, Thailand, and perhaps Indonesia might discourage some polluting industries from investing in these countries. Should countries in the region standardize regulations to avoid offering incentives to polluting industries to locate in a particular country?

Local vs. Extraregional Polluters

There is almost unanimous agreement among the ASEAN states that they should jointly address vessel-source oil pollution but not that they should jointly deal with oil pollution from offshore exploration and exploitation. Offshore exploration and exploitation are less important sources of oil in the marine environment, and they are highly important activities to the countries. Tankers are the major oceanborne source of oil in the marine environment of Southeast Asia. The bulk of the oil carried transits the region from the Middle East to Japan in vessels from outside the region, and international standards do exist. But what of tanker traffic between countries of the region in flag vessels of the region? Should a dual set of standards be developed or applied jointly — one for transiting extraregional flag vessels and one for local traffic and flag vessels?

International Conventions

Many of the international conventions on the prevention and control of marine pollution have yet to be signed, ratified, or acceded to by the original five ASEAN countries (Table 8.8).[71] The only convention relating to marine pollution that has been signed by more than one ASEAN country is the relatively uncontroversial Convention on International Regulations for Preventing Collisions at Sea of 1960 (COLREG 1960). Only six other conventions have been signed; four by the Philippines and two by Indonesia. All are IMO conventions. Thailand and Malaysia have signed none and Singapore only COLREG 1960. Singapore remains committed to maintaining a national registry of shipping, and Malaysia and Thailand simply are not deeply involved in shipping matters, although both are members of IMO.

The countries of Southeast Asia are generally skeptical of international conventions, particularly for the management of ship-generated pollution. Apparently they feel that the costs imposed by implementation and enforcement of the regulations outweigh the benefits to be derived. With increasing economic development and concomitant marine environment damage, however, it may now be asked: Is it time for individual or collective re-examination of the benefits and costs of each of the existing conventions?

Specially Protected Areas

The CLS provides that environmental protection measures taken shall include those necessary to protect and preserve rare or fragile ecosystems as well as the habitat of depleted, threatened, or endangered species (Article 194). The region harbors many such ecosystems and species. Regulations for such areas could exclude, for example, ships carrying potential pollutants. Should proposals for designation of such areas be discussed and approved on a multilateral basis among those countries affected? What criteria should be used, and what should be the balance between protection and use?

Table 8.8 Important Global Treaties Dealing with Marine Pollution

Title and Description	Date of Entry into Force	Dates of Accession (A) or Ratification (R)			
		Indonesia	Malaysia	Philippines	Singapore
Convention on the Law of the Sea, 1982 (CLOS) Stipulates obligation of States to protect and preserve the marine environment. Also, various articles elaborating provisions for global and regional cooperation, technical assistance, monitoring and environmental assessment, international rules, and national legislation to prevent, reduce, and control pollution of the marine environment, enforcement, safeguards, and responsibility and liability.	Not in force				
International Convention for the Prevention of Pollution of the Sea By Oil, 1954, and Amendments of 1962, 1969, and 1971 Provides for prevention of pollution of the sea by oil.	26/7/58 (Convention) 18/5/67 (Amendments) 28/6/67 (Amendments) 20/1/78 (Amendments)			(1963 A) (1965 R) (1971 R, with reservation)	
International Convention for the Prevention of Pollution from Ships, 1973, and Protocol of 1978 Comprehensive attempt to control operational discharge from shipping; establishes operational discharge standards for all substances except radioactive materials and requires certain equipment to	Not in force 2/10/83				

Description	Status	Code
achieve them, e.g., segregated ballast, and record keeping and enforcement.		
International Convention for Intervention, 1969		
The Contracting Parties have agreed to take measures on the High Seas as may be necessary to prevent, mitigate, or eliminate grave danger to their coastline or related interests from pollution or threat of pollution by substances other than oil following upon a maritime casualty or act related to such casualty, which may reasonably be expected to result in major harmful consequences.	6/5/75 Not in force	
International Convention on Civil Liability for Oil Pollution Damage, 1969, and Protocol of 1976		
Provides for liability of a ship owner for all pollution damage caused in the territory or in the territorial waters of another contracting state by oil that has escaped or has been discharged from an owner's ship.	19/6/75 Not in force	(1978A)
Convention on the Establishment of an International Fund for Oil Pollution Damage, 1971, and Protocol of 1976		
Provides for compensation for damages not compensated by Civil Liability Convention.	16/10/78 (Convention) Not in force (Protocol)	(1978A)
Convention on the Prevention of Marine Pollution by Dumping of Waters and Other Matter, 1972, and Amendments on Procedure for the Settlement of Disputes and on the Prevention and Control of Pollution by Incineration of Wastes and Other Matter, 1978	30/8/75 (Convention) Not in force (Amendments) 11/3/79	
International Convention on Civil Liability for Oil Pollution Damage Resulting from the Exploration and Exploitation of Submarine Resources, 1977	Not in force	(1973R)

(continued on the following page)

Table 8.8 Important Global Treaties Dealing with Marine Pollution (Continued)

Title and Description	Date of Entry into Force	Dates of Accession (A) or Ratification (R)			
		Indonesia	Malaysia	Philippines	Singapore
Provides for civil liability for oil pollution damage resulting from the exploration and exploitation of submarine resources.					
Convention on the International Regulations for Preventing Collisions at Sea, 1960	17/6/60	R		A	R
Sets up a system for the establishment of obligatory traffic separation schemes and revises rules for safe navigation practices and navigational signals.					
Convention on the International Regulations for Preventing Collisions at Sea, 1972	20/10/72	Signed			
International Convention on Standards of Training, 1978	7/7/78				
Establishes standards of training.					
Declarations on the Strait of Malacca, 1971	Issued 16/11/71	16/11/71	16/11/71	16/11/71	

- The three governments agreed that the safety of navigation in the straits of Malacca and Singapore is the responsibility of the coastal states concerned.
- The three governments agreed on the need for tripartite cooperation on the safety of navigation in the two straits.
- The three governments agreed that a body for cooperation to coordinate efforts for the safety of navigation in the straits of Malacca and Singapore be estab-

lished as soon as possible and that such body should be composed of only the three coastal states concerned.

• The three governments also agreed that the problem of the safety of navigation and the question of internationalization of the straits are two separate issues.

• The governments of the Republic of Indonesia and Malaysia agreed that the straits of Malacca and Singapore are not international straits, while fully recognizing their use for international shipping in accord with the principle of innocent passage. The government of Singapore takes note of the position of the governments of Indonesia and Malaysia at this point.

• On the basis of this understanding, the three governments approved the continuation of the hydrographic survey.

Sources: Mark J. Valencia, *Shipping, Energy, and Environment: Southeast Asian Perspectives for the 1980s,* Environment and Policy Institute Workshop Report, Honolulu: East-West Center, 1981; Douglas M. Johnston and Norman G. Letalik, "Emerging Legislative Trends in Southeast Asia," in Mark J. Valencia, Edgar Gold, Chia Lin Sien, and Norman G. Letalik, eds., *Shipping, Energy, and Environment: Southeast Asian Perspectives for the Eighties,* Halifax: Dalhousie Ocean Studies Programme, 1982; S. Houston, R. Churchill, M. Nordquist, eds., *New Directions in the Law of the Sea,* Vol. 4, Dobbs Ferry, N.Y.: Oceana Publications Inc., 1975; *IMS Newsletter* (UNESCO), No. 35, 1983, p. 2.

Sea-Lane Siting

Under the CLS, the archipelagic states — Indonesia and the Philippines — must, with the approval of IMO, designate sea-lanes. Should environmental factors be considered in such designations? These designations may influence the routing of some traffic, perhaps preventing fully loaded ULCCs from using the Strait of Malacca. Should designation of such sea-lanes be considered on a multilateral basis among those countries affected?

Hazardous Cargoes

As indicated in Chapter 6 on shipping, there is some doubt that safety technology and regulations have kept pace with technological developments in energy and petrochemicals. Cargoes such as LNG, nuclear spent fuel, and toxic chemicals transit the region, and some even originate in Southeast Asia. Should the nations take some collective action toward regulating the carriage of such substances?

Monitoring, Surveillance, and Control of Pollution

With the extension of jurisdictions, vast oceanic areas have been brought under the authority of individual states. Yet individual national capabilities for monitoring, surveillance, and control in these far-flung areas are inadequate for the task. It has been suggested that a collective effort might be effective and save money and reduce personnel needs. Is such an effort politically, legally, and economically feasible? What are the advantages and disadvantages to each country that might be involved?

A Convention on the Marine Environment

The stated goal of UNEP's action plan is a subregional convention. But within ASEAN there is a general disposition against the notion of a model statute or regulations for environmental purposes, based partially on the diversity among ASEAN nations and the past success of informal coordination of policies. There is a wide range of intermediate steps between no cooperation and a formal convention. One possibility is to establish a series of less comprehensive interlocking agreements within the framework of the action plan. They could be open to nonparties to the plan. Such arrangements could be implemented even while progress is being made toward a convention. Another useful step would be the definitive expansion of the action plan beyond the territorial sea limits of the participating countries to also include their EEZs.

PROBLEMS AND SUGGESTIONS

Scientific knowledge of pollutant types, sources, distribution, and effects is inadequate for remedial action. There remains a need for more baseline studies of the components, processes, and functions of tropical marine ecosystems; for studies of the physical processes that distribute pollutants in coastal waters; and for research on the physical and chemical characteristics of coastal marine environments to better understand the processes by which pollutants are accumulated. There is also an urgent need to standardize the analytical methods used within the region in marine pollution research and monitoring. Such methods must be adapted to the tropical context of Southeast Asia. Among policymakers, there is little awareness of marine pollution and its effects, and there is a need for well-trained and experienced personnel to address pollution policy issues. Preventative and remedial legislation and enforcement of existing legislation are inadequate.

Programs are needed to upgrade awareness and skills of the personnel in the region and to train more people to conduct research, monitoring, and policy formulation to control marine pollution.[72] It would be useful to coordinate regional data exchanges on marine pollution and to gradually increase the number of cooperative research, training, and response programs within the ASEAN network and beyond.

There is interest in multilateral cooperation in the region for marine pollution prevention and control, but more analysis and articulation of the benefits and costs to each country concerned are necessary before cooperative approaches to transnational issues will be fully supported. Although the UNEP Regional Action Plan is a first regional step toward responding to pollution in each country's coastal waters, formidable policy obstacles must be overcome to move toward a truly regional cooperative approach to marine environmental protection in Southeast Asia. The plan has itself created a new set of policy problems, this time intertwined with problems of international relations.

If full protection of the marine environment is desired, countries should first extend their environmental concern and control to their EEZs, including areas claimed by more than one country. Second, the countries should recognize and respond to the transnational nature of some pollutants and their impacts, particularly oil from *all* sources. Third, the region for cooperation should be expanded to include the entire South China Sea, including its transnational oceanographic features and ecosystems. Fourth, the scope of the action plan should be extended to include environmental impact assessment and management of pollutants from seabed exploration and exploitation and atmospheric emissions. And fifth, countries should consider standardizing their approaches to the management of pollution to facilitate the preparation of a regional convention for the protection and managed development of the South China Sea.

CHAPTER 9

CONSERVATION OF THE MARINE ENVIRONMENT

Alan T. White

Human existence depends on a stable and sustainable natural resource base. The marine environment harbors such a resource base. Thus there is value in maintaining the marine environment in a state capable of supporting sustainable use of marine resources. This chapter presents an overview of Southeast Asia's marine environment and of the policy issues and possible responses that arise in its preservation. First, to provide a foundation for this overview, the major marine and coastal ecosystems of the region are examined in their role as environmental habitat for economically important species. Special attention is given to endangered species.

ECOSYSTEMS AND RELATED SPECIES

The Southeast Asian region constitutes a rich biogeographic area in which most higher taxa of shallow-water marine biota reach the peak of their species diversity.[1] This diversity is associated with high primary productivity and high fishery yields. The productivities of some tropical marine ecosystems are given in Table 9.1. Coastal ecosystems and upwelling areas are capable of producing about ten times as much organic matter per square meter per year as offshore waters.

Estuaries

An estuary, a semi-enclosed coastal body of water having a free connection with the open sea, exemplifies the interface between the land and ocean, concentrating a mixture of organisms and nutrients from both environments. Within estuaries, seawater is diluted with fresh water from land runoff. In the tropics, estuaries generally are formed by high rainfall watersheds draining into low coastal floodplains.

Estuaries produce large amounts of organic matter, and associated plant and animal communities are often rich and varied.[2] Many estuaries in the region are

310

Table 9.1   Primary Productivity of Some Major
             Marine Communities

Community Type	Primary Productivity ($g\ carbon/m^2/year$)
Mangroves	430–5,000
Algal, seagrass beds	900–4,650
Coral reefs	1,800–4,200
Estuaries	200–4,000
Upwelling zones	400–3,650
Continental shelf waters	100–600
Open ocean	2–400

Source: A. Soegiarto and N. Polunin, *Marine Ecosystems of Indonesia: A Basis for Conservation,* Bogor: International Union for the Conservation of Nature and Natural Resources (IUCN)/World Wildlife Fund (WWF) Indonesia Program, August 1980 (Draft).

lined with mangrove forests and tend to attract human settlements. Estuaries also serve as nursery grounds for various economic, aesthetic, and ecologically important organisms. The influence of estuaries thus extends beyond the vicinity of river mouths and coastal lagoons into inshore and offshore waters.

Large estuarine systems are found in the deltas of major rivers such as the Mekong, Chao Phraya, Irrawaddy, and Kapuas river systems. Intermediate and small estuaries occur along all the continental and larger island coasts. Only small islands lack estuarine systems completely.[3] Many estuaries are found in the Irrawaddy region of Burma, parts of the eastern Gulf of Thailand, the southern Vietnamese and Chinese coasts, the western Malay Peninsula, the low, northeastern coast of Sumatera, south and eastern Borneo, and scattered areas in Java and Sulawesi. The Philippines and the small islands in the region have few major estuaries.

Increased sedimentation from soil erosion is probably the most important impact of human activities on estuaries in the region. Sedimentation increases the likelihood of floods and shoreline changes, and it affects filter-feeding fishes and other organisms. Estuaries are commonly considered "free" waste disposal sites, so chemical pollution is becoming significant in many estuaries near large cities or industrial sites, such as Manila Bay,[4] the west coast of the Malay Peninsula, the upper Gulf of Thailand near Bangkok, Jakarta, and Hong Kong.

Beaches

Beaches serve as an abrupt transition zone between marine and terrestrial habitats and are a dynamic area of constant fluctuation that requires mobility of organisms. The tidal zones display a marked variety of flora and fauna especially adapted to these environments. A variety of crustaceans, mollusks, and some worms are dependent on a beach habitat, and sea turtles nest exclusively on undisturbed sandy beaches. Numerous beach strand plants both protect the supratidal zone from erosion and provide a habitat for salt-adapted terrestrial organisms.

The beach absorbs wave energy and is constantly changing to best perform this function, thus protecting the shoreline behind, the accompanying flora and fauna, and human settlements.[5] Sheltered beaches may serve as sites for fish fry incubation. Beaches have traditionally provided convenient access to the sea because of the gradual decline to the water and the wave-absorbing morphology. Humans frequent beaches for access to usable marine resources and for recreation.

Indeed, beaches serve a prime function in tourism. The most important coastal tourist sites in the region are associated with white sand beaches and often with coral reefs.[6] Beaches attract tourists because of the aesthetically pleasing natural setting and the opportunities for swimming and surfing. Tourists also are attracted by the possibilities for observing sea turtles, shorebirds, crustaceans, shells, and also the traditional uses of the sea by native peoples.

The primary large sand beaches of the region occur on coasts exposed to wave energy, that is, the south-facing coasts of the Sunda archipelago, the eastern coast of the Malay Peninsula, the gulf of Thailand, exposed coasts on the eastern and western shores of the Philippines, northern Borneo, and the northern New Guinea coast. Smaller beaches are widely distributed throughout the region. These beaches are associated with coral reef formations, small islands, and particular circumstances of coastal geomorphology combined with longshore currents and sediment availability from rivers. Beaches associated with rivers occur throughout the region on one or both sides of river mouths, depending on the coastal currents.

Mangroves

Mangrove forests occur on tidal flats at the mouths of streams and on the shores of sheltered bays or protected seas. Mangrove communities do particularly well on accreting silt-laden shores associated with high rainfall areas. Their distribution is limited to calm and warm areas where the temperature remains above 20 degrees centigrade most of the year. Mangroves represent one of the world's most productive ecosystems in both gross primary productivity and leaf litter production;[7] they may provide more than half of the organic matter available to estuaries. Mangroves also play a role in the pathways of key elements such as nitrogen and sulfur, and they trap inorganic nutrients carried down from watersheds by rivers, converting them into organic compounds that enter mangrove-associated food chains.[8]

Because of the high productivity and the physical structure of mangroves, many coastal land and marine species use mangroves as a source of food and shelter during part or all of their life cycles.[9] Economically valuable organisms of this sort include penaeid prawns, crabs, sergestid shrimps, and various species of fish. Mangroves also are direct sources of firewood and charcoal, some medicinal extracts, roof thatching, minor foods, tannin, and animal feeds. In their natural state, mangroves help stabilize coastal areas by reducing wind damage and wave energy during storms and by checking soil erosion. Mangroves build land through slow, long-term trapping of land-derived sedimentation.

Table 9.2   Mangrove Coverage for Southeast Asia

Country	Area (ha)
Brunei	n.a.
Burma (abundant along Irrawaddy)	517,100
China (small area to 27°N)	67,000
Taiwan	123
India (Andaman and Nicobar islands)	100,000
Indonesia	3,627,000
Malaysia (West)	113,348
(East)	538,959
Philippines	106,133
Singapore	1,800
Thailand	163,349
Vietnam	250,000
Total for the region	5,384,812
Total for world	43,700,000
Regional percent of world	12.3

Sources: S. Snedaker and IUCN, *First Report on the Global Status of Mangrove Ecosystems,* Commission on Ecology, October 1981. For Indonesia, S. Soemodihardjo, "Utilization and Management of Mangrove Resources in Indonesia," in P. Kunstadter and S. Snedaker, *Proceedings of the UNESCO Seminar on Human Uses of the Mangrove Environment and Management Implications,* Dacca, Bangladesh, 4–8 December 1978. For the Philippines, R. Umali, *Coastal Resources Development and Management: Philippine Experience,* Quezon City, Philippines: Natural Resources Management Center, 1980.

Table 9.2 gives estimates of mangrove coverage by country as of 1981. The largest concentration of mangrove forest remaining in Southeast Asia is in Indonesia with an estimated 3.6 million ha (8.9 million acres), three-quarters of which occurs in Irian Jaya and Sumatera (Figure 9.1). Just outside Southeast Asia, another very large concentration is found on the southern coast of Papua New Guinea, one of the least disturbed mangrove areas in the world.[10] Other major mangrove forests are found along the southwest coast of the Malay Peninsula and at various locations along the coast of Borneo.

Mangrove forests often have been viewed as undesirable because of their association with swampy areas and mud flats. As a result the exploitation of mangroves

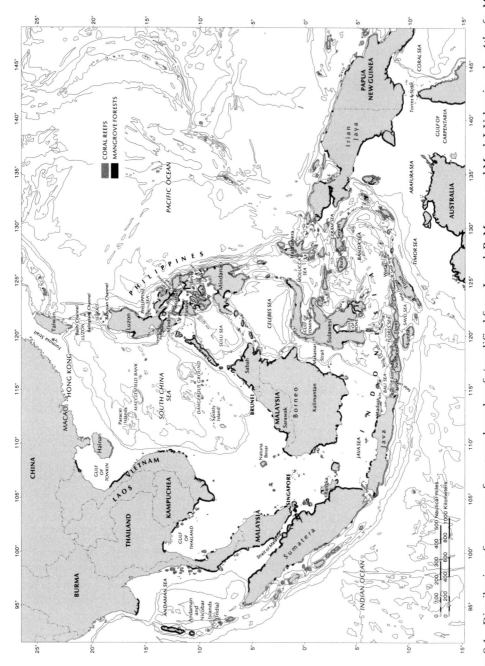

Figure 9.1 Distribution of mangrove forests and coral reefs (modified from Joseph R. Morgan and Mark J. Valencia, eds., *Atlas for Marine Policy in Southeast Asian Seas*, Berkeley: University of California Press, 1983, p. 27).

normally has been uncontrolled. In Southeast Asia these ecosystems are increasingly affected by human activities such as uncontrolled cutting for use as building material, firewood and charcoal; reclamation for agriculture, aquaculture, urban development, dumping sites, or other construction; and waste disposal.[11] The major economic loss caused by mangrove removal probably results from reduction of catch of nearshore fish dependent on mangrove-produced nutrients.

Coral Reefs

The coral reef is a distinctive ecosystem rich in species and highly productive that has as its foundation calcareous rock as a prominent physical structure. The conditions strongly favoring coral reefs are temperatures normally above 20 degrees centigrade, water depths shallower than 50 meters (m), constant salinity greater than 30 parts per thousand (ppt), low sedimentation rates, sufficient circulation of pollution-free water, and pre-existing substrate.

Coral reefs serve humans in many ways: for food production; for coastline protection; as sources on nonfood products such as medicines, sponges, and jewelry items; for aesthetic and related economic benefits; and for scientific and educational use.[12]

As a result of their high productivity and varied physical structures, reefs are inhabited by many organisms of economic value. Coral reef fishes constitute a significant portion of the recorded catch in most Southeast Asian countries. In the Philippines it has been estimated that at least 10 percent of the country's fishery production is reef-associated, and for western Sabah a figure of around 30 percent has been suggested.[13] Thirty-two out of the 132 fish species listed as being of economic importance in Indonesia are associated with reefs.[14] In addition, there are many mollusks, crustaceans, echinoderms, and algae that are of nutritional or other use to humans. Coral reefs supply food for fishes harvested in nonreef areas as well.[15]

Fringing and barrier reefs form wave buffer systems that are generally self-repairing and maintenance free. They have traditionally served as sources for construction materials. A growing number of medicinal products are produced from coral reef organisms. The aesthetic qualities of coral reefs have contributed to the development of tourist industries in areas where reefs are accessible and still pristine. The laboratory qualities of coral reefs make them valuable to educators and scientists for displaying and studying such processes as population dynamics, community interactions, species diversity, and ecosystem stability.

Fringing coral reefs occur throughout Southeast Asia, usually associated with small- to medium-sized coastal islands. Larger island and continental coasts support reefs to a lesser extent due to high sedimentation rates, turbidity, and low salinity associated with river outlets. The Andaman, Nicobar, Mergui, and western Thai coastal islands all support coral reef growth, some in good condition (Figure 9.1). The Gulf of Thailand has limited reef areas. Coastal islands of the Malay Peninsula support coral reefs, but the Peninsular coast generally lacks coral. The most extensive coral reef area for one country occurs in Indonesia, correlating with its very long coastline and many thousands of islands. Coral reefs are well represented in the Mentawai archipelago, along many coasts in the Sunda archipelago, and islands in the Java and Banda seas and north central Indonesia. The Great Barrier Reef and Torres Strait area of Australia offers many high-quality reefs. Southern New Guinea has limited reefs because of terrestrial runoff, but the north coast and islands are fringed with reefs in some areas. The Philippines also has extensive reef growth. The remote, smaller islands support the better quality and the more extensive reefs. The Sulu Archipelago and Sulu Sea islands, Palawan Island, Cuyo islands, some smaller Visayan islands, and some eastern, Pacific-facing coasts support much coral reef area. Most islands in the South China Sea have fringing reefs. The southern Chinese and Vietnamese coasts lack reef growth.

Human impacts on coral reefs may be broadly characterized as physical damage, change in the sediment regime, overexploitation, and chemical pollution (Table 9.3). Irreversible damage to reefs by sediment smothering is the most important threat in Indonesia, Malaysia, the Philippines, and Thailand.

Table 9.3   Human Activities and Their Impacts on Coral Reefs

Activities	*Impacts*
Extraction of coral limestone foundation	Degradation of reef
Extraction of coral sand	Turbidity, water flow dynamics
Explosive fishing techniques	Habitat destruction
Terrestrial sediments from human activity	Turbidity smothering
Physically damaging fishing methods	Habitat destruction
Reef trampling by humans or anchors	Habitat destruction
Overfishing of fish and invertebrates	Changes in ecosystem balance, lowers maximum sustainable yield
Aquarium fish collection	Selectively depletes population
Urban and industrial pollution	Biological degradation
Oil spills	Biological degradation
Oil drilling	Turbidity, habitat destruction
Fish poisoning	Biological degradation
Spearfishing	Selective depopulation of fish
Tourism	Selective depopulation of active coral and invertebrate species
Thermal or salinity changes	Coral polyps and invertebrates

Source: E. Gomez, *Status Report on Research and Degradation Problems of the Coral Reefs of the East Asian Seas,* Manila, Philippines: South China Sea Fisheries Development and Coordinating Programme, May 1980.

Seagrass and Algal Beds

Sea grasses bind shallow sediments and normally grow on sandy substrates, while the larger algae usually develop on, but are not limited to, rocky or rubble substrates. Both flourish only in shallow, well-lighted waters and often constitute a distinct zone on reef flats. Seagrass and algal beds are well represented along Southeast Asian coasts and in particular are associated with protected shorelines inside of coral reefs or in association with mangrove stands.

A large number of species of invertebrates and fishes use seagrass-algal communities at some stage in their life cycles.[16] Both communities commonly fix large amounts of carbon and nitrogen. Organic productivity, exported as leaf litter or finer particulate matter, represents a significant input to neighboring communities and may serve to dampen fluctuations in food availability. Some sea grasses excrete phosphorus, which is then utilized by corals.[17]

Some of the plant biomass is grazed by sea turtles, dugong, or more commonly by smaller herbivores, some of which are valuable in local fisheries. In some areas seagrass beds are important nurseries for penaeid shrimp. Many resident species have food or commercial uses such as locally consumed mollusks, seaweeds, and some plant sources of carrageenans, agars, medicinals, and related organic materials with growing commercial potential. In many cases, seagrass and adjacent habitats are important feeding grounds for wading seabirds.

Seagrass and algal communities are vulnerable to overexploitation of resources, changes in the hydrologic environment, and pollution. Some macroalgae are collected to support industrial demand. Exploitation for food of some invertebrate species is intense, sometimes causing community instability. Dredging and other activities that lead to increasing turbidity and sedimentation can be deleterious to light-dependent algae and sea grasses. Eutrophication caused by sewage or other pollution can dramatically change community composition.[18]

Islands

Islands support ecosystems that are isolated from comparable systems elsewhere. Although more than 90 percent of the land area of Southeast Asia is made up of large island land masses, the many thousands of small islands in the region have significant amounts of coastline. Remote island populations of many marine organisms are genetically distinct even if actual speciation has not yet taken place. Within certain groups of organisms there is also substantial geographical variation in community structure.[19]

The remote islands in the South China Sea and in parts of Indonesia and the Philippines provide habitats devoid of many natural predators including humans. Thus many of these islets are sites of important seabird nesting colonies and provide beaches for substantial nesting populations of sea turtles. Genetic variability maintained by such island ecosystems contributes to the overall marine and terrestrial island species richness of the region. Because of their smallness and ecosystem variability, these islands are useful to science for understanding processes of succession, competition, and evolution and the problems of management. Such environments also are of particular recreational, educational, and tourism value.

Offshore Seas

About half of the offshore seas of the Southeast Asian region lie over continental or archipelagic shelves of less than 200 m depth. The remaining sea area lies over continental slopes and the abyssal plain. Offshore waters are usually highly stratified and vary both horizontally and seasonally. The euphotic layer, in which light is sufficiently intense for significant primary production, usually reaches to less than 50 m, depending on the area.[20] Compared with coastal ecosystems, these deeper waters generally have far more diffuse biological productivity and are of much lower species richness.

Organisms of the offshore seas ultimately depend on phytoplankton production for their food. Productivity is about 2 grams (g) of carbon per square meter (m^2) per day in shallow shelf waters. In offshore waters it is about 0.5 g carbon per m^2 per day. Coastal and upwelling communities are more productive and also are likely to be more efficient at using the available food. Since primary productivity is confined to the surface region, most important fisheries are in shallow water, although pelagic fisheries also are highly significant.

The offshore seas support not only fisheries but also shipping and oil and mineral development, and they also are used for waste disposal. Major damaging human impacts on the offshore seas of the region are pollution and excessive or environmentally degrading exploitation of fish stocks and other ocean resources.

Ecosystem Interactions

Ecosystems, although labeled and studied independently, are in reality interdependent.[21] In the fluid medium connecting marine ecosystems, the organisms, nutrients, and organic matter regularly move through the boundaries. Coral reefs, seagrass beds, and mangroves are all exporters of nutrients and organic matter. Estuaries, with a well-defined flow of water through them, collect and distribute nutrients to surrounding coastal areas. Coral reefs provide conditions favorable for the development of mangroves, stable beach communities, and inshore seagrass and algal beds, and reefs also physically buffer these systems.

Species cross ecosystem boundaries during their life cycles. For example, many prawns, although breeding offshore, are dependent on mangroves for their survival.[22] Many fishes regarded as typical of deep, open waters are associated with coral reefs for feeding or with seagrass beds for nursery grounds. The complexity of the interactions among these species and the diverse and productive inshore ecosystems is far higher than in offshore areas. These ecosystems also interact with offshore waters, and in many ways offshore waters are dependent on inshore productivity. Thus, the potential implications of ecological disruption in the coastal area are greater than in the open sea. In planning for management of marine areas, ecosystems should not be treated on an individual basis. Rather, whole areas comprising interconnected systems should be treated as single, functional units.[23]

ECONOMIC SPECIES AND VULNERABLE MARINE ANIMALS

As discussed in Chapter 4, the Southeast Asian seas support some of the world's most productive marine fisheries. The many economically important marine fish, invertebrates, and seaweeds are dependent on the local and regional ecosystems for habitats and nutrients. The commercially important demersal catches from the region's nearshore, shallow-water, soft-bottom grounds, especially from areas near estuaries or concentrations of mangroves, include shrimps, croakers, snappers, seaperch, catfish, swimming crabs, and blood cockles. The soft-bottom demersal grounds farther offshore, both shallow and deep, provide commercially important catches of sea bream, ponyfish, goatfish, lizardfish, fusiliers, flatfish, conger eels, and slipper lobster.

Some of these are also caught from the many coral reef or seagrass areas and other hard-bottom grounds, both nearshore and offshore, shallow and deep. Others are dependent on reefs for nutrients or as nursery areas.[24] Reef fisheries are often dominated by such commercial species as snappers, groupers, bigeyes, grunts, parrotfish, and spring lobster. Many regional demersal fishing grounds, with varying ecological characteristics, support commercially important specialty fisheries for seaweeds, sea urchins, sea cucumbers, crustaceans, sea turtles, ornamental shells, pearl oysters, and precious corals.

Pelagic fisheries associated with continental shelf areas are primarily those for sardines, anchovies, mackerels, pomfret, squids, cuttlefish, and little tunas. Important pelagic deep-water fisheries beyond the continental shelf are those of tunas, shark, swordfish, and marlin.[25]

The vulnerable marine animals in the region may be divided into two groups according to habitat. Those dependent upon coastal environments, including beaches, estuaries, reef areas, and small islands, are the sea turtles, crocodiles, dugong, seabirds, shorebirds, and selected invertebrates. Those whose habitat is strictly deep water and which migrate within and outside of the region are the whales and dolphins.

Sea Turtles

Sea turtles are the most economically important endangered animals in the region. Sea turtles nest on sandy beaches and breed in protected estuarine or reef waters, with feeding and basking occurring in similar locations, generally over reef flats. The green turtle, *Chelonia mydas*, is the most abundant species and is valued particularly for its meat and eggs. The hawksbill, *Eretmochelys imbricata*, is still abundant in specific areas and is valued mostly for its shell. The leatherback, *Dermochelys coriacea*, although less abundant than the hawksbill, still has important nesting sites on the east coast of peninsular Malaysia. The olive ridley, *Lepidochelys olivacea*, and

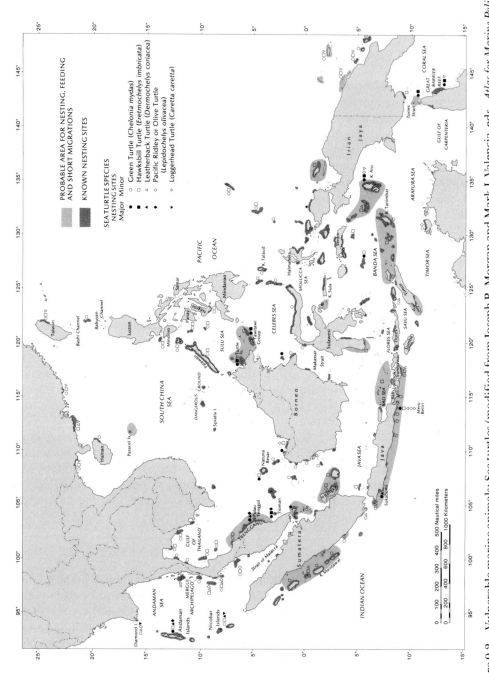

Figure 9.2   Vulnerable marine animals: Sea turtles (modified from Joseph R. Morgan and Mark J. Valencia, eds., *Atlas for Marine Policy in Southeast Asian Seas*, Berkeley: University of California Press, 1983, p. 29).

the loggerhead, *Caretta caretta,* are both uncommon in the region with small, select nesting sites (Figure 9.2).

The single largest concentration of sea turtle nesting in the region occurs along the east coast of Malaysia where more than a million eggs are deposited annually. Other important sites include the Turtle Islands in the Sulu Archipelago and northern Sabah; the beaches and islands off the west coast of Thailand and Burma; the Andaman and Nicobar islands; southern Java, Sumatera, and parts of the Moluccas, Indonesia, northern Irian Jaya; and outside the region, Papua New Guinea. There is evidence that the green turtles of East Kalimantan are part of a larger population shared by Indonesia, Sabah, and the Philippines; that the turtles of northwest Kalimantan are shared with Sarawak; that the leatherbacks of Irian Jaya and possibly the northern Moluccas are part of a population shared with northern Papua New Guinea; and that the leatherbacks of south Sumatera are shared with the Nicobar and Andaman islands.

Extinction or decline of some geographically specific populations of all species of sea turtles is attributed particularly to exploitation for meat, hides, eggs, oil, and other products (including souvenirs), and massive killings of turtles in the trawl nets of fishing fleets.[26] Habitat destruction and disturbances by coastal development and tourism, attraction of hatchlings by inland lights, and other miscellaneous intrusions are important causes of decreased nesting success.

Crocodiles

Crocodiles frequent estuarine, swampy areas near large river mouths and occasionally mangrove areas. They are also infrequently seen in open water over shallow reef flats. The few known breeding sites are located in the Moluccas, the Sunda archipelago and parts of Irian Jaya, in Indonesia, and outside the region, in Papua New Guinea, and northern Australia — away from human population centers (Figure 9.3). Crocodiles are reported to be still abundant in the coastal swamps of southern Papua New Guinea and along the coast and in rivers of Queensland, Australia, where all harvesting is prohibited.

The distribution of remnant populations indicates crocodiles were once common through Southeast Asia. All species in the region have been severely depleted. Declining numbers and distribution have made the crocodile scarce in the few locations where populations still occur, except in Papua New Guinea. This reptile traditionally has been killed when encountered by people primarily because of fear. Now increasing human population has infringed on crocodile habitat, thus decreasing their numbers in recent years. During this century a market has grown for products made with crocodile skin.

Marine Birds

Marine birds include shorebirds, vagrant waders, and oceanic seabirds that frequent and nest on small islands or on shoreline habitat and feed at sea. Colonies of oceanic seabirds are scattered throughout the region, primarily on smaller islands

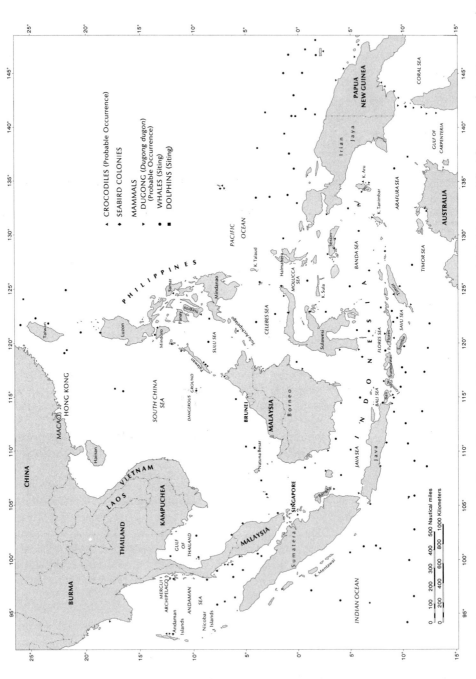

Figure 9.3 Vulnerable marine animals: Crocodiles, seabirds, dugong, whales, and dolphins (modified from Joseph R. Morgan and Mark J. Valencia, eds., *Atlas for Marine Policy in Southeast Asian Seas*, Berkeley: University of California Press, 1983, p. 31).

away from humans (Figure 9.3). These birds are becoming scarce as human populations continue to infringe on their preferred habitats.

Seabirds often have dense breeding concentrations near the shore in undisturbed areas. They are more common near productive waters. Thus important colonies seem to be correlated with established or probable areas of upwelling and associated fisheries. In many areas terns, shearwaters, and boobies are used to locate schools of skipjack tunas and yellowfin tunas. In the central Pacific, 85 percent of tuna schools are associated with birds.[27] In low-nutrient tropical waters, seabird guano locally enhances nitrate and phosphate levels near coral reefs, aiding productivity.[28] Additionally, sooty terns (*Sterna fuscata*) are a source of eggs, and boobies (*Sula* spp.) are a source of meat to subsistence people in the Indo–Pacific.[29] Besides being vulnerable to loss of habitat and subsistence hunting pressure, seabirds are particularly susceptible to oil pollution, and pollutants such as pesticides may accumulate in their food chains.

Dugong

The only inshore mammal occurring in the Southeast Asian region is the dugong (*Dugong dugong*). Dugong inhabit sheltered, shallow tropical and subtropical coastal waters. They feed in intertidal and subtidal areas primarily on sea grasses and some algae. There is little information on their population numbers. The largest protected populations of dugong reside outside the region in Papua New Guinea and northern Australia, and sizable populations survive in eastern Indonesia in the Aru Archipelago (Figure 9.3) where a dugong sanctuary has been proposed. Like turtles, dugong populations are almost certainly shared by Indonesia and Papua New Guinea.

Dugong are exploited for their meat, oil, and teeth.[30] Small fisheries still exist in eastern Indonesia and in parts of Papua New Guinea where the dugong fishery is currently being monitored for formulation of conservation and management guidelines.[31] Overexploitation is the primary cause of population decline. Accidental deaths in nets employed by inshore fishermen and increased pollution, sedimentation, and disturbance of seagrass habitats are having an increasingly negative effect on the dugong as well.

Whales and Dolphins

The diversity of whales and dolphins occurring in the Southeast Asian region is large, including thirty or more species in all; eleven are baleen whales and twenty-four are dolphins and relatives (Figure 9.3). A few species are still abundant, but most are only rarely seen and thought to be remnants of once larger populations or simply outside their normal migratory range. Most sightings are in southern Indonesia and localized near channels between major islands.

The hunting of dolphins traditionally is proscribed in many parts of Indonesia and in some other traditional fisheries.[32] Large, nontraditional offshore fishing operations sometimes inadvertently catch dolphin. A traditional fishery for dolphin and whales still exists in southern Indonesia where up to a hundred whales are taken annually.[33] Modern whaling sanctioned by the International Whaling Commission is done in the northern extremity of the region, but it is not thought to be common. Pirate whaling is rapidly expanding worldwide and may affect the region.[34]

Marine Invertebrates

Hundreds of species of marine invertebrates occurring primarily in the inshore waters of the coastal zone are exploited by humans. Because of the large numbers and wide distribution of these species, most are not endangered. Exceptions include certain precious (black) corals *(Antipathidae)*, giant clams *(Tridacnidae)*, and the coconut crab *(Birgus latro)*.[35]

Black coral is common throughout the region, occurring on the seaward slope of most fringing coral reefs below 10 m. It is collected and sold for jewelry and the curio trade with increasing intensity. Black coral grows very slowly and thus may be easily depleted. The Indo–Pacific giant clams have been overexploited in many localities for their meat and for their shells, a common tourist item. There is widespread commercial exploitation of giant clams in the region by the Taiwanese. With continued collecting pressure, their slow rate of growth and poor juvenile recruitment could result in serious population depletions. The coconut crab, intensively hunted for food, is extinct on a number of islands and survives in a few undisturbed coastal habitats, mostly on small islands.

POLICY ISSUES

The overuse of marine resources has implications for the long-term viability of the resource base. This can create tension between policies for development of ocean resources and resource conservation. Development conservation issues for the Southeast Asian seas include destructive fishing, conservation of endangered marine animals, and habitat destruction.

Conservation and Development

It is assumed here that sustainable utilization of species and ecosystems is desirable. Yet the necessity of ensuring sustainable utilization varies with a society's dependence on the resource in question. For subsistence societies, such as some coastal communities in Southeast Asia, sustainable utilization of most if not all of the living resources is essential. In the sea, humans still have the status of foodgatherers, a form of exploitation that demands the most careful maintenance of the ecological basis of the ecosystems concerned.

Sustainable utilization is also necessary for the rational planning and management of industries using the sea for waste disposal, for mangrove products, and for food. A society that insists that all utilization of living resources be sustainable ensures that it will benefit from those resources virtually indefinitely.[36] With knowledge of marine systems still meager and human impact on them inadequately understood and controlled, the potential for adverse ecological change affecting resources and processes is substantial.[37] Utilization of the sea for food, mineral extraction, waste disposal, and transport will for a long time be dependent on the natural processes of the oceans. Human action at the ecosystem level may have repercussions within and outside of the system that are impossible to quantify. Inadequate planning can lead to conflicts.[38] General conflict categories for resource management include uses of the same resource and short- and long-term interests.[39] Specific instances of use conflicts include those between artisanal and larger-scale fishermen in many coastal areas; those between the exploitation of endangered species for valuable export products, local use, and preservation for genetic reserves and their inherent value; commercial forestry versus fishery uses of mangroves; waste disposal versus fisheries and aquaculture; and mining of reefs and coastal water quality.

Conflicts between short- and long-term interests arise wherever a resource is used faster than natural regeneration provides for recovery. Examples are over-fishing, uncontrolled waste disposal, mangrove cutting, reef blasting or destruction, and other environmental modifications that lower natural production. Rapid development of ocean resources may not deal appropriately with the needs of the majority of the people. To the extent that pollution from shipping, industrial waste disposal, and mechanized destructive fishing methods occurs, it is the large numbers of coastal residents in each of the regional countries who experience the adverse results directly.

Most human-induced environmental changes are, at least initially, the result of actions taken to provide positive benefit to some interested party. It is the goal of marine conservation to balance these positive development benefits with the negative environmental effects and to measure the composite result. Management with this perspective must have reliable information concerning the resources and marine processes affected and the potential development benefits from a proposed environmental change. The concept of "eco-development" — that is, development that is ecologically considerate — takes account of ecological processes, life-support systems, and the potentials for beneficial development within ocean and coastal regions. Eco-development fully acknowledges human dependence on the ocean environment.

Destructive Fishing

Ten years ago the Gulf of Thailand was considered one of the Pacific's richest fishing grounds. The Thai fishing fleet grew to become the seventh largest in the world while competing fishermen increased their profits by using finer and finer mesh nets until even fingerlings were caught. Inshore reef fish were caught with destructive methods, disturbing the habitat. Encroaching pollution has augmented the problem in the northern gulf. Now fishers claim that there are "no more fish" in the gulf and that trawlers travel up to 1,600 kilometers (km) (992 mi) to catch around 350 kilograms (kg) (771.6 lb) of fish in one hour's trawling. The catch in 1981 was down to 70 kg (154 lb) per hour, of which nearly 75 percent was inedible "trash" fish.[40]

Such excessive and wasteful exploitation, coupled with habitat degradation over a period of ten to fifteen years, is proving economically and politically costly to Thailand. Thai fishermen now venture as far as the Arabian Sea coast of Oman and frequently fish in the waters of Vietnam, Kampuchea, Malaysia, and Indonesia where they and their boats are often arrested. Destructive fishing and inadequate enforcement of regulations may be partially blamed for the fishery decline.

Destructive fishing methods do not necessarily imply overfishing but may adversely affect the capacity of the environment to support a full potential fish yield. Destructive fishing methods common in the region include blasting, trawling over reefs, muro-ami fishing, aquarium trade fish collection by using cyanide, use of small mesh nets and traps, and spearfishing.

Although strictly illegal in most countries, blasting is probably the most common destructive fishing technique in the region. Blasting is accomplished by simply dropping one or more charges into the water, moving off to one side with the boat during the blast, and returning to retrieve the fish. The practice is wasteful since fishes of all ages and many invertebrates are killed in far greater number than are harvested. Some fish with sensitive swim bladders may be killed at considerable distance from the site.[41] The most significant impact is to the coral reef, which is shattered for a radial distance of several meters depending on the blast depth and strength. Such areas thereafter support little fish life, are slow to recover (up to thirty years for 50-percent recovery), and encourage infestation by some algae.[42] In Thailand, some 20 percent of the 260,000 m² of reef surrounding Ko Lan Island in the vicinity of Pattaya has been destroyed by blasting.[43]

Since the use of explosives for fishing is illegal throughout the region, a case can be made for strong enforcement of existing laws. Most people agree that it is destructive and wasteful, so it is not a question of education. Sources of explosives should be controlled and there should be active apprehension of those few fishers who use explosives.

Increases in commercial trawling in Southeast Asian waters and declining stocks have led to an increase in the incidence of reef-front trawling.[44] Such trawling for fish has also damaged considerable tracts of coral. Precious coral is also harvested by reef-front bottom trawling or dragging with similar implications. Because of the use of fine-mesh nets, which capture many juvenile forms, this method is a probable cause of the depletion of many fish stocks.[45] Mini-trawlers, purse seiners, and bay netters often ruin nearshore fishery grounds through depletion and habitat disturbance. This cuts off the resource for local fishers and the coastal people who utilize it. Along many coasts in the Philippines, fringing coral reef fish stocks are overexploited and often in a state of productive and physical degradation.[46] Current fears of increased joint ventures with the Chinese province of Taiwan and Japan, whose fishers have been rumored to be guilty of such fishing in the past, is a topic of concern among some communities in the Philippines.

Muro-ami and kayakas fishing techniques, common to the Philippines and reported from Indonesia and Sabah, were inherited from traditional Japanese methods of using swimmers to chase fish into a net.[47] The swimmers bang the bottom substrate to make noise with poles (kayakas) and rocks (muro-ami) to scare fish out and herd them. Although it is an economically efficient means of fish capture, the consequence is a much-disturbed bottom habitat and many broken corals. Most of the fish captured seem to be schooling and shoaling herbivores that could easily be driven in by nondestructive noisemakers.[48]

Bait or aquarium trade fishing often involves the breaking off of colonies of branching and foliose corals and shaking fish out on the boat. Fish toxicants are also used, some of which (such as sodium cyanide) are detrimental to the health of coral and other invertebrates. Also, aquarium trade capture is directed toward certain popular fish such as cleaner wrasses, which serve a particular ecological role in the reef community.[49]

With proper management, the aquarium fish trade could be an acceptable method of utilizing marine resources. Conflicts arise in protected marine areas, however, between this harvest and the maintenance of natural populations of attractive specimens for viewing in their natural state. Many of these fish die in capture and shipping. Since the fish are harvested primarily for export, regulation of the industry on a national basis would help sustain the resource and ensure quality standards for importing countries. Licensing of exporters and designation of collection sites could help.

There has been a drastic decline of shells in Malaysian waters in the past twelve to fifteen years from commercial shell harvesting for food and for collectors. Some species are now rare, and many parts of the Malaysian inshore seabed have become barren, algae-covered rubble as a result of the systematic turning over of bottom material.[50]

Fish traps used judiciously are a legitimate and sound fishing method. At times, however, coral is broken and used for fish trap weights, and abandoned traps are allowed to continue to catch fish until the traps disintegrate. Sometimes large traps are dropped on reef ledges and are retrieved by a line, both of which can smash sizable coral formations. Inshore fishing in reef environments normally is accomplished by numerous small- to medium-sized boats that use anchors designed to hook corals or other substrate. Frequent dropping and removal of such anchors by many boats can have a damaging effect on heavily visited coral areas.

Spearfishing in marine parks and elsewhere has become an issue in some countries of Southeast Asia. Spearfishing may have a marked effect on the species structure and community stability of a reef. Selective overharvesting of larger, more desirable species such as grouper and parrotfish is likely. Fish become exceedingly timid and flee rapidly where spearfishing is practiced. The Philippines has banned scuba spearing from protected marine areas. Traditional spearing normally is not so selective and is done in shallow water. Intensive traditional spearing, however, can also have a marked effect on reef ecological balance.

Endangered Species

The preservation of genetic diversity is both a matter of insurance and investment. Such preservation is necessary to sustain and improve agriculture, forestry, and fisheries production; to keep options open; as a buffer against harmful environmental change; as the raw material for much scientific and industrial innovation; and as a matter of moral principle.[51] Species diversity contributes to the fundamental stability of the natural environment. It cannot be predicted what species may become useful in the future. Indeed, it may be learned that many species that seem dispensable are capable of providing important products such as pharmaceuticals, food, or vital chemical ingredients.

As nations and people in Southeast Asia have come to value the diversity of their marine environment, endangered or threatened species have become the focus of growing concern. The endangered species of the region are few in number and are mostly of large mammalian or reptilian groups that are not of immediate importance to evolutionary genetic flow.[52] Nevertheless, all are of direct usefulness to the coastal peoples of the region, and all are important components of the ecosystem structure and food web; some are of commercial importance as well. The protection of coastal marine habitat is essential to the maintenance of endangered species. As habitat decreases, regeneration of protected species becomes increasingly difficult. Pressure on endangered species comes from diminution of critical habitat where important populations reside and from excessive exploitation.

The exploitation of wildlife and its products is a lucrative commercial enterprise. Individuals and organizations in Southeast Asia supply these commodities for clients, mostly in industrialized countries. Their demand for private and scientific purposes will continue to increase, threatening the survival of those marine species involved in the trade. The Convention on International Trade in Endangered Species of Wild Fauna and Flora (CITES) has formulated excellent regulations governing trade in endangered species.[53] Among the Association of Southeast Asian Nations (ASEAN), Indonesia, Malaysia, and the Philippines have ratified the convention. But conventions and regulations are not enough unless there is political commitment and cooperation among the regional nations. Each nation needs to be an active member of the convention, to enforce internally the agreed restrictions on animal capture, and to inhibit international trade.

The most important aspects of sea turtle conservation concern the migratory routes, breeding, and nesting locations. What occurs at these sites is critical to survival. Normally, the principal parties affecting a site are local residents and fishers who utilize turtle eggs and meat. In traditional contexts such as that in the Turtle Islands of the Sulu Archipelago, island residents only exploit a portion of the eggs and turtles for their use, and the remainder is left for continued reproduction. Sustainable use is an interest of local people.

The national and state governments of Malaysia are actively involved in sea turtle management as a resource for local consumption and as a tourist attraction. Sustainable use and preservation are promoted by regulation of concessions along sea turtle beach habitats to allow both of these activities to occur. This is accomplished by requiring that a percentage of the eggs laid (normally less than 50 percent) be left alone to hatch naturally or to be removed to government-operated sea turtle hatcheries. Poaching is becoming more of a problem because of increased local demand and because some tourists support a market in turtle products for coastal residents to supply.

The problems of maintaining turtle populations in the major nesting or movement areas are similar throughout the region. All of the parties involved — fishers, poachers, coastal residents, exporters, importers, local officials, national government, tourists, and environmentalists — have their own perspectives and interests. The essential element for protection is the maintenance of coastal beach habitat suitable for sea turtles; without this none of the interests can be adequately served.[54] The capacity of local or national governments to protect habitats depends on the promotion of sustainable use in the context of regulation. The concept of multiuse coastal marine reserves could greatly facilitate this end. Rare species need full protection. Coordination with and support of CITES would be important as well to prevent international market forces from outweighing local resource conservation interests.

The various parties affecting the plight of the crocodile are not significantly different from those affecting sea turtles. The main difference is that crocodiles usually have not been considered a significant resource for food. Presently the parties with the largest capacity for further depleting the resource are illegal hunters who supply international trade in skins or skin products of the reptile. Ratification and enforcement of CITES regulations and agreements could facilitate protection for this species. Conservation of dugong populations is also analogous to that of sea turtles. Solutions could include management of harvests at a sustained level through rural extension to fishers and coastal peoples as in Papua New Guinea, protection of critical habitats through marine reserve management programs, and enforcement of CITES regulations on the trade of products derived from dugong.

Seabirds are most susceptible to disturbance at their nesting sites. Small, mostly uninhabited islands — primarily in Indonesia, Malaysia, and in the South China Sea — serve as habitats, as do several coastal wetland reserves in peninsular Malaysia and in Indonesia. Coastal residents and fishers who visit island habitats are the most important groups affecting seabirds. Fishers are a diverse group with varying interests, few of which coincide with the protection of seabirds. Small islands that provide seabird habitat would be good choices for marine reserve sites.

The only documented fishing for whales and dolphin is conducted in southern Indonesia, tolerated by the Indonesian government as a concession to tradition. Incidental kills of dolphins in modern tuna fishing by boats of mostly extraregional origin may become an issue. Indications are that presently there is no commercial whaling in Southeast Asia. Pirate whaling could be a problem where stocks are known to occur as in southern Indonesia.

Possible improvement in the knowledge and protection of these animals could include active regional participation in the International Whaling Commission, better surveillance of population movements and fates of whales and dolphins by coast guard and navy vessels in the region, and regulations for commercial national and foreign fishing boats accidentally capturing or killing dolphins or small whales.

Black corals, giant clams, and coconut crabs officially have status in the International Union for the Conservation of Nature and Natural Resources (IUCN) *Red Data Book* of vulnerable species, although they are not considered endangered. Commercial harvest of giant clams has received little regulatory attention in the region, but in 1981 the IUCN recommended that these animals be added to Appendix II of CITES, which means that trade between member countries would be authorized only with export documentation. Black coral is listed in Appendix II of CITES, so that international trade is supposed to be monitored.

Mangrove Removal

Mangrove forest alteration, harvesting, and alternative uses for mangrove habitat are issues of increasing concern to regional and international policymakers. Mangroves are being rapidly utilized and replaced, with the encouragement of foreign aid and development agencies and local teams responsible for coastal resource management. Recognizing the problem of overfishing of offshore and inshore stocks, these agencies recommend development of fish culture in coastal wetlands to supplement waning fisheries production. They identify coastal wetlands, especially mangroves, as underexploited resources and recommend their conversion to rice fields or brackishwater fish ponds.[55] Indonesia has allowed logging concession leases on 455,000 hectares (ha) (1,123,850 acres) of mangrove forest, or approximately 18 percent of the total estimated mangrove area in the country.[56] In areas of acute population pressure such as Java, mangrove forests have been converted to agricultural fields.[57] Philippine government agriculturalists have asked for scientific evidence showing that mangrove forests are more valuable in their naturally functioning state than well-managed aquaculture projects on the same land.[58]

It has been conservatively estimated that 550,000 tons of fish worth US$194 million caught in Indonesia in 1978 were of species that are directly linked to mangroves and estuaries at some stage of their life cycle.[59] Many of these, especially some shrimp, are species that are already overexploited.[60] Sabah, with 4.77 percent of its land area covered with wetlands, exploits and benefits from a large prawn fishery. There appears to be a direct linear relationship between mangrove area and shrimp production in Indonesia. Thus, every decrease in mangrove area may be matched by at least an equivalent decrease in shrimp production, not to mention reduction in yield of other mangrove-dependent species.[61]

The discrepancy between coastal wetland development and conservation is evident. Depleted fish and shrimp stocks are blamed on overfishing, yet the support systems — mangroves and estuaries — are considered to be underutilized. There is often a direct conflict of interest between the fisheries and forestry departments in Southeast Asian countries over the utilization of specific mangrove swamps. The immediately obtainable forestry and aquaculture value in areas of large forests such as Indonesia must be contrasted with the longer-term food value of the fisheries to local inhabitants, also taking into account the indirect benefits from the ecosystem in relation to species and neighboring ecosystems.

Coral Reef Destruction

More than half the reefs in the Philippines are in advanced states of destruction, with only 25 percent of live coral cover in good condition and only 5 percent in excellent condition.[62] Comparable studies would probably indicate a similar if not worse status for reef quality in Thailand, Malaysia, and Indonesia.

Collecting and exporting of Philippine corals still flourishes today although these activities are illegal by Presidential Decrees 1219 of 1977 and 1698 of 1980, which prohibit the gathering and/or export of stony, precious, and semiprecious corals.[63] Throughout the early 1970s the Philippines was the main world exporter of stony corals. Records of exports (probably conservative) show an increase from 200 tons in 1969 to more than 1,800 tons in 1976, with about 60 percent destined for the United States and the rest going to Japan and Europe.[64] A market survey of the trade showed that the distribution system of corals from source to final customer usually includes a number of local and foreign interests — coral divers, coral traders, manufacturers, wholesale exporters and importers, agents, pet shops, aquaria, retailers, and consumers.[65]

The various middle groups have expanded with the trade. The size and diversity of businesses dependent on the coral trade make it a difficult industry to stop, but the middle points provide opportunities for law enforcement.

The Philippine coral ban was prompted by concern over the condition of many Philippine reefs and by a number of incidents of poaching of precious corals by Taiwanese. Even though official Philippine figures showed a drop in exports after 1977, in 1980 the United States officially imported more than 236 tons of Philippine corals. The coral trade continues, but it is now unmonitored since it is "illegal." Even so, there are indications that Philippine customs agents have been stepping up their vigilance at the major export ports of Manila, Zamboanga, and Cebu. For the ban to be more effective, enforcement would have to be made more comprehensive. Importing countries could contribute to the enforcement by prohibiting imports of Philippine corals.[66]

The Philippines, having ratified CITES, can suggest that corals be added to Appendix III in order to bring trade monitoring and potential international controls. A public awareness campaign to deter people from buying ornamental corals could also have some impact both in the Philippines and in importing countries.[67] Within the Philippines, enforcement could be increased now that there is a legal framework to support it. Education of local people regarding the value of their coral resources is of equal importance. Since a number of people are dependent for at least part of their income on the trade, alternative employment could be considered, such as culture of seaweed, mollusks, or even coral.

The Philippines is the largest precious and common shell and shell product exporter in the world and is a significant contributor to the aquarium fish trade. The rate of extraction is increasing to keep pace with demand from abroad and in local stores.[68]

The total impact of these reef export products on Philippine reefs has not yet been evaluated because it is difficult to separate the effects of such gathering from other disturbing influences. It is likely that as these products become more scarce and prices rise, the industry will not slow considerably because such products will remain inexpensive for foreign customers. Thus, regulation and monitoring of the trade will be necessary.

Interest groups motivated to protect the reefs include scuba divers, snorkelers, swimmers, and reef viewers who visit the actual sites. Some collect specimens or damage coral, but most are concerned with maintaining the resource. The diving tourist industry is taking an active role in coral reef management in the Philippines by financially supporting two marine parks and by voicing strong opinions in public forums in favor of marine conservation. Several small but influential groups have assumed similar roles in Thailand, Malaysia, and Indonesia. Without intact, accessible reef areas, this diving tourist industry would deteriorate.

Traditionally minded fishing communities using ecologically prudent fishing techniques may be willing to share their reef environment with others who want to view and appreciate the reef for its aesthetic value. These two interest groups can be mutually supportive. Unfortunately, most traditional conservation methods have disappeared as the need for fish has increased with population growth. An approach that incorporates some traditional knowledge for management could be extremely helpful in conserving resources.

RESPONSES

International and Regional Responses

As a result of the new Convention on the Law of the Sea (CLS), coastal states are obligated to protect and preserve the marine environment and to cooperate in doing so directly or through international organizations.[69] A Draft Action Plan for the Conservation of Nature in the ASEAN Region has recently been formulated by the IUCN. Priorities set by this plan are (1) establishment of a network of ASEAN reserves, (2) institution of measures to protect endangered species, (3) establishment of mechanisms for information exchange on research and management, and (4) establishment of a regional training program on conservation management.[70] The need to maintain essential ecological processes and life-support systems, to preserve genetic diversity, and to ensure the sustainable utilization of species and ecosystems are emphasized as uniting criteria of potential projects.[71] A network of reserves such as national parks, biosphere reserves, nature reserves, and wildlife sanctuaries is regarded in the plan as one of the most effective ways to conserve ecosystems and their constituent wildlife. Stress is placed on finding common criteria to serve as bases for establishing an adequate reserve system.[72]

Marine Reserves for Protection and Management

The CLS and the IUCN plan reflect two overlapping but distinguishable environmental concerns — conservation of marine species and coastal zone management.[73] A marine reserve, ranging on a spectrum from functional, where resource utilization occurs, to preservational is a cross-cutting response to marine conservation needs. (Pollution control is discussed in Chapter 8.) A marine reserve constitutes a defined space to which some form of management and limited entry is applied. Resources, habitat, ecosystems, species, and the space required for their interactions are common criteria used for selecting boundaries.

In modern times, the first nature reserve on land in the region was set up early in the nineteenth century.[74] From the 1870s onward particular types of fishing were prohibited in some sensitive coastal areas.[75] The first marine reserves were established by national governments some sixty years ago.[76] As the effects of overfishing gradually became obvious during this century, modern, nationally instituted reserves developed. Such reserves have been declared mainly along large continental land masses where abundant terrestrial food supplies coupled with vast seafood resources inhibited recognition of the limitations of marine fisheries resources until only recently.

The effectiveness of reserves is closely tied to the traditional resource use patterns of the people who live within or surrounding a reserve site. Thus ecological knowledge of species is no more important than a complete perspective on humans in their local environment, both in the traditional and modern senses. Reserves do exist in the region, but their effectiveness is in question. Local communities generally do not have jurisdiction over marine areas. And public concern with protection of the marine environment may deteriorate with increased rates of exploitation. For example, in the Philippines the creation of Hundred Islands National Park in 1940 was a first in marine conservation. It has been unsuccessful in preserving marine life. The area was designated with little provision for ecological or sociological field surveys. Hundred Islands has pleasant beaches, but now after years of fishing by destructive methods few living coral reefs remain.

Indonesia's reserves include

- Pulau Seribu (Rambut), an archipelago adjacent to Jakarta with potential areas for a strict reserve, buffer zone, marine park, and recreation sites;
- Bali Barat (P. Manjangan), a coastal, small-island, reef complex in an area of developed international tourism with a potential for a recreation zone, a sanctuary zone, and a buffer zone of traditional but regulated fishing; and
- Komodo National Park, an extensive marine area in a remote terrestrial island reserve with potential for zonation and multiple uses.[77]

Malaysia has four marine reserves, including

- Dungun Beach in Trengganu, which serves as a wildlife sanctuary for nesting sea turtles and as a site for observation of sea turtle nesting;
- Muka Head State Park in Pinang, which serves primarily recreation and tourism needs;
- Bako National Park near Kuching in Sarawak, a terrestrial park bordering the sea with mangrove forest, beaches, and some coral reef and visited by tourists; and .
- Turtle Islands in Sabah, which is a legislated wildlife sanctuary for sea turtle nesting habitat.[78]

The Philippines' marine reserves include

- Malampaya Sound in northern Palawan Island, which is temporarily protected as a fishery reserve for spawning and nursery grounds and in which no commercial fishing is allowed and extensive mangrove forests are protected;
- Sombrero Island in Batangas, which is currently utilized as a snorkeling and scuba diving park; legislation is pending to make it a marine park;
- Sumilon Island near southern Cebu Island, which is a legal fishery reserve and is utilized as a marine park with a strict reserve for scientific research and viewing; it has a buffer zone for regulated traditional fishing; and
- Apo Reef near Mindoro Island for which legislation is pending to make it the largest marine park in the Philippines, with extensive reefs and a potential for a strict zone reserve, recreation areas, and a sizable buffer zone for traditional and sustainable levels of fishing activity.

Thailand's marine reserves include

- Phangna National Park near Phuket Island, formed in 1981, which protects estuarine wetlands, mangrove forests, and shorebird habitat;
- Tarutao Island National Park on the west coast of Thailand with fifty-one hilly islands that protects sea turtle nesting sites, beaches, mangrove forests, coral reef areas, and has potential for tourist visitation; and
- Surin Islands in the Andaman Sea, which are proposed as a marine park with tourism potential and would protect the best coral reefs in Thailand and preserve some sea turtle nesting and mangrove areas.

The various types of reserves represent a spectrum of degrees of control, each type giving particular emphasis to different objectives (Table 9.4).[79] When properly designed and enforced, protected areas constitute a simple, efficient, and logical means of serving various marine conservation needs.[80] The spectrum of possible functions is large, and most are mutually compatible. The maintenance of biotic and genetic diversity through habitat and ecosystem preservation are often cited as prime concerns.[81] Protection of endangered species and subpopulations, management of fisheries, and the maintenance of wild populations important to aquaculture may all be facilitated by reserve management strategies. Restoration of depleted populations can occur and sources of recruitment for depleted areas can be provided. For large, migratory, and other particular species, reserves are difficult to set up, but it is possible.[82] Where specific resources are concerned, the protected area may be subject to multiple use and designation as a "resource reserve" or as a "multiple-use management area." Reserves in most forms serve educational and research functions that are normally not in conflict with strict biotic and genetic protection. Recreation and tourism areas may require separate zoning, but if properly designated and controlled they can be significant assets to protected areas by facilitating education, providing cultural exchange, and generating revenue. Several different types of reserves may be distinguished.

Table 9.4 Priorities Given to the Different Objectives of Marine Observation in Various Types of Protected Areas

Primary Objectives	National Park	Natural Monument	Biological Reserve	Wildlife Refuge	Resource Reserve	Sustained Yield Harvest Zone	Fisheries Management Zone	Water Quality Control Zone	Tourism Management Zone	Cultural Monument	Coastal Zone Management Scheme
Protect ecosystems	1	1	2	1					4	4	4
Protect ecological processes	1	1	3	1					3	2	2
Maintain biotic diversity	1	1	3	1					3	2	2
Conduct education, research, environmental monitoring activities	2	2	1	2	1			1	1	2	4
Safeguard water quality	3	3	3	3				1	4	4	2
Prevent shore erosion and sedimentation	3	3	3	3				4	4	4	2
Produce fish protein	2					4	1	4	4		4
Provide recreation and tourism	2	4		4				1	1	4	4
Sustain yield of particular resource					1	1	4	4			
Protect cultural sites	4	4							4	1	4
Protect aesthetic qualities	1	1	3	3				4	1	4	2
Maintain open resource options					1			2			3
Stimulate rational use and development	3	3	3	3	4	4	4	3	4	3	1

Source: Adapted from IUCN, FAO, 1974 information.

Notes:
  1 = Objective prevails in management of whole zone.
  2 = Objective prevails in management of some parts of the zone.
  3 = Objective is accomplished in parts or all of the zone in relation to other management objectives.
  4 = Objective may or may not have relation to other objectives and resource characteristics of specific area under consideration.

Sectoral Reserves. Sectoral reserves are based on specific uses. Such reserves frequently span natural boundaries of ecosystems, species habitat, or the land-water interface. Coastal zone management areas, tourism management zones, water quality management zones, and fisheries management or sustained yield harvest zones are examples of sectoral reserves (see Table 9.4). In each case, vulnerability to some general threat such as pollution, overfishing, or destructive fishing is the underlying rationale for formation of the reserve.

Ecosystem, Habitat, and Species Reserves. Ecosystem, habitat, and species reserves are established to protect specific vulnerable resources. The motivation for such reserves is the inherent value of the resource. Prime candidates would be the productive ecosystems of the coastal zone such as the coral reef, mangrove, seagrass, estuarine, and upwelling areas. These ecosystems and habitat areas are resources in themselves and provide habitat for commercially important and vulnerable or endangered species. Plans for formation of reserves to provide recruitment for depleted fisheries need to consider factors such as the intervening distance, relative sizes of the protected and fished areas, and the ecology of the species.[83]

Ecosystem, habitat, and species reserves, as contrasted with sectoral reserves, are concerned with the maintenance of specific resources. Such reserves can have stricter control and smaller areas. They may be combined with resource, wildlife, or biological reserves, or with national parks with various zones governing uses within the park.

Regional Biosphere Reserves. Biosphere reserves are designed to protect biotic diversity. Criteria for selecting areas to serve as biosphere reserves would include high species diversity, density and endemism, complexity of ecosystems, outstanding wilderness value, uniqueness in species composition, and the geographical variation of the species richness.[84] Principles of island biogeography could be useful in providing estimates of the isolation of particular communities and the size of area necessary to conserve maximal diversity.[85] Maximum uniqueness and/or diversity should determine geographical location.[86] Regional biosphere reserves could coincide with national reserve sites. They may be compatible with well-maintained habitat, ecosystem, and species reserves or with national marine parks.

Prime candidates for marine biosphere reserves in Southeast Asia include biologically rich areas such as the following (Figure 9.4):

The Aru Archipelago in eastern Indonesia where four species of turtles nest and dugong and crocodile populations survive in an environment of relatively pristine mangrove forests and some coral reefs:

Sites on the northern Great Barrier Reef and islands in the Torres Strait where extensive coral reef areas are intact and are accompanied by sea turtle nesting beaches;

One of several recently formed Indonesian national parks, which include coastal areas with reef and mangrove habitat, some populations of sea turtles, dugong,

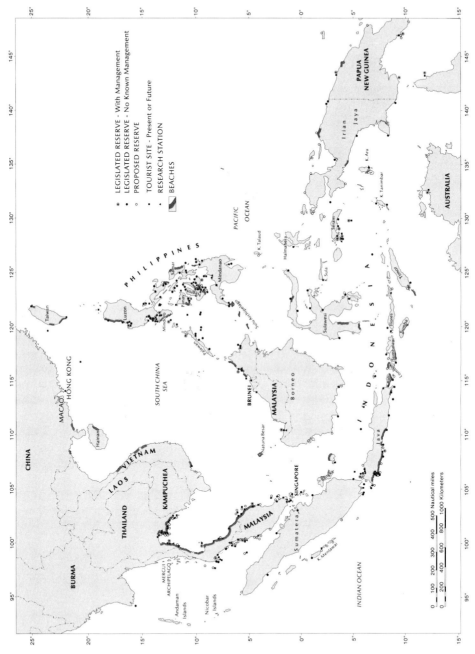

Figure 9.4 Marine reserves, tourist sites, research stations, and beaches (modified from Joseph R. Morgan and Mark J. Valencia, eds., *Atlas for Marine Policy in Southeast Asian Seas*, Berkeley: University of California Press, 1983, p. 35).

few crocodiles, seabirds, and indigenous beach vegetation; these parks are Ujung Kulonn in west Java, Baluran in east Java, Bali Barat in Bali, Komodo in Nusu Tenggara Province, and Manusela in central Seram;

Parts of the east coast of the Malay Peninsula where dense sea turtle nesting occurs;

Apo Reef in the Philippines, an extensive, mostly intact coral reef ecosystem;

Selected smaller islands north of the Papua New Guinea mainland where dugong and sea turtle populations survive supported by seagrass, coral reef, and beach habitat; and

Sites in the Nicobar Islands where four species of sea turtles reside along with some crocodiles, seabirds, and dugong with supporting mangrove, coral reef, and beach habitat.[87]

Marine Parks. National parks, while serving partly as a biosphere reserve, should also be designed for accessibility for people, for recreational value, and for educational value. The various reserve types could all occur within national marine parks. Marine parks should follow international standards set by the IUCN. Variations on the zonation scheme of core and buffer may be appropriate in national marine parks.[88]

Municipal Reserves. This basic reserve system[89] offers simplicity and effectiveness for protection of fish breeding grounds.[90] It fits well with traditional reef tenure and community resource use systems. Most significantly, having been initiated at the municipal level, it generally has the support of and is understood by local residents who facilitate enforcement. Since the concept of community domain over nearby marine areas is well established in many local traditions, the reserve scheme is not alien. Municipal reserves and regulations, like older, local, conservation customs, are devised and enforced by the villagers themselves and thus are tailored to fit specific local environmental and social conditions.[91] Such reserves may serve several ends. They could range from arresting and reversing general degradation of the reef and augmenting fishery yields for local utilization to preservation for scientific research, education, aesthetic values, recreation, and tourism.

Local, National, and Regional Management

As reef degradation has increased, a few communities in the Philippines and elsewhere have recognized the problem and have adopted the reserve concept as a method of conserving local marine resources. This reserve concept is one of strict protection for limited areas of reef, with no removal of organisms allowed within a central core portion. Only ecologically sound fishing methods are allowed in the buffer zone surrounding the central core area. Few of these sites, however, are now being managed in a manner consistent with long-term maintenance of coastal resources. For a long time, residents of Apo, a small island off the southeastern coast of

Negros, had consistently resisted extension efforts of Silliman University to increase awareness of the island-reef ecosystem and its fishery potential. Recently, however, the municipality of Dauin, which includes Apo Island, acknowledged the need for protective measures to prevent further coral destruction and overexploitation of the fishery.[92] The people of Moalboal, on the west coast of Cebu Island, hosted a meeting in May 1980 to formulate plans for protecting the immediate beach-reef area and a small island, Pescador, about 2 km (1.2 mi) offshore. Participants unanimously decided to ban by municipal ordinance the use of fish traps on the reef ledge, since these systematically break corals. Other destructive practices also are to be prohibited, and the entire island of Pescador is to be set aside as a marine park.[93] Even though there has been no official sanction or legislation from the national government, such efforts initiated and managed at the local level may be an effective approach because of the inherent involvement and understanding of those people concerned. Nonformal education can help improve local environmental awareness and communicate reserve management concepts and benefits.[94]

National interests in reserve management are founded in the long-term needs of coastal ecosystem maintenance. Priorities may include the prestige of having pristine coastal areas both for biotic and genetic preservation and for tourism. Purely economic considerations are becoming more important as fishery depletion results from overfishing and destruction of coral reef, mangrove, seagrass, and estuarine habitats. Local cultures may be effected by the dwindling populations of endangered species.

At times, national legislation and management efforts may impede the effectiveness of coastal reserves. If a national reserve is in a relatively remote area, well away from good law enforcement, and if local people do not understand the reasons for such a reserve and tend to be at odds with national government policy, they might plunder the area out of spite. People could rationalize exploitation beyond sustainable limits. Such motivations may underlie management problems in southern Thailand[95] and in parts of the Philippines where national fishery or resource management authorities are looked on with disdain.[96]

In the converse situation, where municipalities take initiative and designate reserved areas for various reasons such as habitat protection and tourism, it may be difficult for such areas to be accepted as valid by the national government. In the extreme, the national government could annul such attempts by forbidding jurisdiction over marine areas, or it could simply refuse to recognize the designation. Or national governments could choose to support municipal efforts logistically and legally after such efforts have proven to be useful. Such attitudes might add to reserve areas while allowing for environmental and cultural needs to be met. In this approach part or all of the burden of selection and management would be assumed by the local community, municipality, or provincial level of government, thus reducing costs to the national government.

Just as community and national levels of reserve management are not mutually exclusive but can complement each other, the interplay of regional and national levels can also be complementary. Most small reserves will fall within national boundaries, but some large threats such as oil spills are most effectively addressed on a regional basis. Moreover, since coastal development in one country may seriously affect another, arrangements are needed for bilateral and regional agree-ments to negotiate the management of broad areas.

On a regional basis, it may be useful to consider establishment of a network of reserves, institution of reserves and legal means to protect endangered species, and establishment of mechanisms for information exchange, research, and manage-ment.[97] Plans could be facilitated by establishing common criteria for selection of a reserve system of regional and national importance and of benefit to the local population, transfrontier cooperation in vulnerable areas, several major marine ecotype reserves in the region to be shared among members, and a regional task force to start pragmatic work on Southeast Asian conservation of marine areas.[98] Emphasis might be placed on workable and functional local reserves as regional plans proceed so that what is practically possible and realistic is kept in sight.

To secure international support for national action in conservation, the nations of Southeast Asia should become parties to the global conservation conventions.[99] The World Heritage Convention affirms the obligation of states to protect unique natural and cultural areas of international significance. The Wetlands Convention concerns the conservation of coastal and other wetlands critical to waterfowl, fish, and species requiring aquatic habitats.[100] The Migratory Species Convention obli-gates parties to protect endangered migratory species and to endeavor to conclude agreements for the conservation of migratory species whose status is "unfavor-able." This convention would be particularly useful for conservation of transfron-tier and specific migratory species in the region. One example is the marine turtle population inhabiting the islands of the Philippines, Malaysia, and Indonesia.

International mechanisms that might be invoked to control trade are CITES and the proposed ASEAN Nature Conservation Convention. Accession to the CITES Conventions is essential for the effective implementation of any regional action to control trade of highly endangered and vulnerable species. It is through such global, regional, national, and local efforts that the vulnerable and valuable genetic resources of Southeast Asia may be protected, conserved, and nurtured for the benefit of present and future generations.

CHAPTER 10

ENFORCEMENT OF MARITIME JURISDICTIONS

Hal F. Olson
Joseph R. Morgan

The Convention on the Law of the Sea (CLS) codifies states' rights concerning resource management under various maritime jurisdictional regimes. The convention provides recognition in international law of the extended jurisdictions that had earlier been declared unilaterally, at least to the extent that those unilateral claims conformed to the specific provisions of the CLS. The major new offshore jurisdictional regime, the exclusive economic zone (EEZ), extends up to 200 nautical miles (nmi) from coastal baselines. According to Article 56 of the convention, in the EEZ the coastal state has

- Sovereign rights for the purpose of exploring and exploiting, conserving, and managing the natural resources, whether living or nonliving, of the waters superjacent to the seabed and of the seabed and its subsoil, and with regard to other activities for the economic exploitation and exploration of the zone, such as the production of energy from the water, currents, and winds.
- Jurisdiction as provided for in the relevant provisions of this convention with regard to the establishment and use of artificial islands, installations, and structures; marine scientific research; and the protection and preservation of the marine environment.

If countries are to make maximum use of the resources of their offshore jurisdictions, they need to establish and enforce management regulations. Enforcement requires an effective series of actions. Surveillance of the area to detect violations must be followed by detailed inspection usually requiring boarding the vessel and examining records, cargo, fish catches, and equipment. If it is determined that the vessel is in fact in violation of the coastal state's regulations, arrest procedures may be initiated, the vessel confiscated, and the crew detained. This must be followed by a trial and the assignment and public announcement of appropriate punishments.

The enforcement of extended maritime jurisdictions presents challenges not normally encountered on land. Surveillance of sea areas to detect the presence of trespassers and to monitor legitimate users of the seas is generally intermittent, except perhaps in some heavily used areas adjacent to ports or developed land areas. Determining placement of enforcement officers on the sea requires far more information than determining placement of their counterparts on land.

Disputes over the location of maritime jurisdiction are not treated in this chapter; only the issues of fishing, shipping, and other activities over which coastal nations have jurisdiction are of concern here. An analysis of selected boundary disputes was provided in Chapter 3.

Much ocean activity, such as shipping or fishing, is mobile. Activities that remain in a fixed geographic position, such as offshore oil and gas exploitation, generally are highly technical in nature. In either case, enforcement action must come primarily from surface vessels, with possible assistance from helicopters. Fixed-wing aircraft can provide surveillance of large areas and can make initial contacts with surface activities but cannot perform actual enforcement actions on the scene.

In Chapter 7 of this volume comparisons are made between the length of nations' coastlines, the areas of their EEZs, and the naval forces available to them for enforcing national jurisdictions. This provides a rough measure of the adequacy of enforcement resources. It should be recognized, however, that economic activity is not uniformly distributed throughout EEZs but is concentrated in specific areas, usually near the shores.

The scope of the enforcement problem in Southeast Asian waters can be gleaned from the enforcement actions of the coastal nations to date. Southeast Asian nations have demonstrated an awareness of the need to regulate certain maritime activities and some willingness and ability to enforce their jurisdictions. Conflicts over fishing thus far have been the most dramatic results of enforcement action and will continue to provide the greatest challenge in the near future. Numerous enforcement actions have resulted in the seizure of fishing vessels, and many of these incidents have been accompanied by gunfire. Most of the details of enforcement activity provided here were gathered from the mass media between 1978 and 1983. It is likely that many more incidents have occurred than have been publicly reported. Data on vessel seizures in Southeast Asia indicate that the Chinese province of Taiwan and Thailand have been the chief offenders and trespassers into EEZs. During the five-year period there were at least 189 Taiwanese fishing boats seized, and there were 114 Thai vessels seized. Neither Taiwan nor Thailand, both distant-water fishing nations, has been able to negotiate satisfactory agreements for access to fish in the waters of its neighbors. The Philippines had three vessels seized, Singapore had three, Hong Kong had one, and Korea had one seized during the period.

Figure 10.1 shows the regions where vessel seizures have taken place. The Tenasserim coast of Burma, the Gulf of Thailand, the Gulf of Tonkin, and the Luzon Strait have been the principal areas, but there have been numerous incidents in Indonesian archipelagic waters as well. The incidents involving gunfire all involved Thai fishing vessels as targets of Vietnamese and Kampuchean patrol boats. In virtually all cases

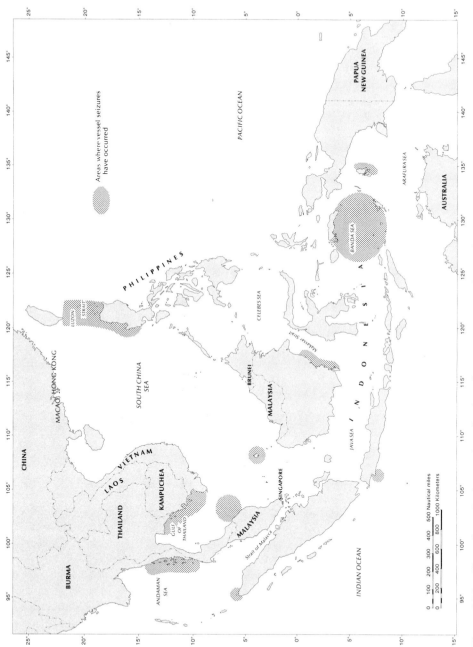

Figure 10.1   Sites of vessel seizures (based primarily on *Foreign Broadcast Information Service* reports).

involving Thai fishing boats there was no reported protest by the government of Thailand, suggesting that the boats were in fact fishing illegally.

ENFORCEMENT ISSUES

Maritime activities subject to regulation by coastal states can be assigned to one or more of the following categories:

- Fishing;
- Energy and mineral resource exploration/exploitation;
- Shipping, including illegal activities such as smuggling, piracy, and espionage;
- Protection of the ocean environment; and
- Marine scientific research.

All of these are receiving some attention by the nations of Southeast Asia, but the emphasis varies from country to country. Indonesia, for example, has a substantial need to carry out surveillance and enforcement in all five categories, while Singapore is most vitally interested in shipping and is little concerned with foreign marine scientific research in its waters.

Each of these activities requires that surveillance and enforcement take place at sea. Some aspects of enforcement can be accomplished in port, however, such as slip inspections to ensure seaworthiness and the prohibition of illegal substances. Such in-port enforcement entails less cost and effort, but it has a rather low degree of effectiveness.

Fishing

Article 62, paragraph 2, of the CLS requires that the coastal state determine its capacity to harvest the living resources of the EEZ. If the coastal state does not have the capacity to harvest the entire allowable catch, it shall, through agreements or other arrangements, give other states access to the surplus of the allowable catch according to provisions of Articles 69 and 70. Articles 69 and 70 discuss the rights of landlocked and geographically disadvantaged states with regard to the resources of the EEZs of coastal states. If the coastal state, after appropriate research, determines that there are no surplus fish stocks, there is no obligation to allow other nations' fishing vessels to be in the EEZ. In such cases, surveillance and enforcement would be simplified. Article 73 of the CLS states:

- The coastal state may, in the exercise of its sovereign rights to explore, exploit, conserve and manage the living resources in the exclusive economic zone, take such measures including boarding, inspection, arrest, and judicial proceedings, as may be necessary to ensure compliance with the laws and regulations adopted by it in conformity with this Convention.

- Arrested vessels and their crews shall be promptly released upon the posting of a reasonable bond or other security.
- Coastal state penalties for violations of fisheries laws and regulations in the exclusive economic zone may not include imprisonment, in the absence of agreements to the contrary by the States concerned, or any other form of corporal punishment.
- In case of arrest or detention of foreign vessels the coastal state shall promptly notify the flag state, through appropriate channels, of the action taken and of any penalties subsequently imposed.

If, on the other hand, the coastal state determines that there are surplus stocks that could be harvested by other nations, appropriate arrangements can be made and agreements drawn up. These agreements might make enforcement more difficult, since they may contain provisions for fishing seasons, size of vessels, size and type of nets, and permissible species and amounts of fish that may be taken, all of which require not only detection of a foreign fishing boat but boarding of the vessel to determine compliance with the myriad regulations. Paragraph 4 of Article 62 of the CLS refers to the requirement for nationals of other states fishing in an EEZ to comply with conservation measures and to keep the coastal state informed as to numbers and sizes of fishing boats, crews, and catches.

The enforcement of fishing laws and regulations requires more effort than any other category of maritime activity. In addition to the large geographic area of concern, surveillance and enforcement in fisheries may include regulating the allowable catch, controlling access to the surplus by other nations, limiting the areas and seasons during which fishing can take place, determining the species that may be taken, establishing the permissible types and amounts of fishing gears, and requiring reports on catch, fishing effort, and position of fishing vessels. These activities serve to protect domestic fishermen from fishing boats and help to conserve important commercial fish species as a renewable resource. In the Philippines, for instance, the illegal catch of tuna by Japanese fishermen in 1977 was estimated as 7,400 metric tons (MT), and catches by Taiwanese and Republic of Korea fishermen in Philippine waters are "presumably comparable if not greater than those of Japan."[1] Japanese fishermen have no fishing agreements with the Philippines, although they have concluded more than 200 agreements with other countries in the Pacific and elsewhere.[2] Even in cases where agreements for access have been negotiated, surveillance and enforcement problems may be severe, since there are frequent instances when catches are not reported. Such has been the case in the Banda Sea agreement between the government of Indonesia and Japanese fishing interests.[3]

To ensure that foreign vessels abide by the established regulations, the presence, specific locations, and activities of those vessels must be known. Surveillance, most efficiently performed by aircraft, must be supplemented by on-the-scene inspection to determine compliance with fisheries regulations. Inspections by personnel from surface vessels is essential to the performance of this task. The mobility of the surveillance and inspection targets can make the task difficult. Located in one position today, fishing vessels may be hundreds of kilometers away by tomorrow. The problem of monitoring large areas can be reduced substantially by concentrating efforts in areas of known fishing activity and by making only occasional patrols into other areas of the EEZ.

Energy and Mineral Resources

Energy resources, now composed of the petroleum and natural gas found in continental shelves beneath the territorial seas and in the EEZs, may later include power generation from ocean thermal energy conversion, wave action, tidal action, or other methods yet to be investigated. Mineral resources may include manganese nodules, tin, metalliferous sulfides, and other ores.

Areas in which exploitation of these resources is actively underway are clearly delineated, and whatever enforcement action is required can be concentrated in those areas. Although drilling platforms can be moved from place to place, those moves require careful preparations and are performed relatively slowly.

The CLS states in Article 60 that the coastal state has the right to establish safety zones up to 500 meters (m) in radius around any installations, a difficult area in which to enforce regulations. Surveillance is needed to detect overpumping, illegal removal of oil, and unsafe industrial practices. Protecting these structures from piracy or terrorist activity also is a difficult task. A small group of well-armed terrorists could assault an offshore platform or rig and hold it and its crew ransom for money or for some political objective. A related security problem is the need for protection from and response to fire or other disasters due to natural or human causes. Rather than post guards on each offshore structure, it may make more sense to have a highly mobile force that can be dispatched quickly to the scene of an incident.

For enforcement action concerning fixed structures, the overall size of a nation's EEZ is not critical; it is the often great distance of the structure from suitable bases that is the important factor. The Pulai and Tapis oil terminals are located in the South China Sea approximately 201 kilometers (km) (125 miles [mi]) east of Kuala Trengganu, the nearest Malaysian port from which a mobile force might be dispatched. Indonesia might have similar problems due to the distance of its Natuna field from suitable ports. Both Burma and Vietnam have offshore exploration sites considerable distances from their coasts.

If the exploitation of mineral resources involves floating equipment, enforcement action may include the boarding of vessels. Much of the offshore tin mining in Thailand, now conducted as only a quasi-legal activity, is a potential target for a strong enforcement effort.[4] In this case, enforcement would be against domestic miners who smuggle much of the tin concentrate to Malaysia or Singapore to avoid government taxes.

The shore-based end of the oil and gas production process poses other problems for enforcement and security personnel. In late 1973 members of the Japanese Red Army hijacked the Laju ferry in Singapore harbor in broad daylight and proceeded to Shell's Pulau Bukom refinery. They carried plastic explosive charges that they attached to several oil storage tanks. Fortunately, the tanks they picked were empty, and authorities captured the terrorists before any damage was done. However, the incident illustrates the type of risk that is present in Southeast Asia, a risk that would become even more serious if major liquefied natural gas (LNG) plants were constructed in the region.

Shipping

Regulations governing shipping can be divided into three groups: those relating to the actions that may be taken from or by vessels in waters over which the coastal state has jurisdiction; those governing the design, construction, staff employment, equipment, and operation of vessels; and those relating to the external measures taken to enhance the safety of navigation or to designate the areas in which vessels may operate.

Navigation is free on the high seas and in the EEZ of coastal states, but within the territorial sea the rights of vessels are limited to those consistent with innocent passage. Exercise of this right of innocent passage requires that vessels make their passage without delay, without the threat or use of force against the coastal state, and without any other action not related to its expeditious transit.[5] Other prohibited activities include practicing or conducting exercises involving the use of weapons; collecting information prejudicial to the security of the coastal state; launching, landing, or taking on board any aircraft or military device; acts of propaganda; and any act against the communications or other facilities of the coastal state. Should a violation be detected, successful enforcement would require means to apprehend the offender and to move the offender to a port or anchorage where a complete investigation and legal action could be initiated. Enforcement of regulations designed to prevent pollution of coastal waters is a function of both the nation whose flag is being flown by a ship (the flag state) and the coastal state.

Normally the flag state of a vessel will take action when violations of staffing, equipment, or operating regulations are detected. Discovery of such violations by the coastal state might occur as a result of inspection or investigation for some other reason, probably in port. Problems arise occasionally with ships flying flags of convenience, since the flag state's regulations concerning crew training, equipment inspection and maintenance, and procedures concerning cleaning of tanks and other activities that might result in polluting discharges are not likely to be stringent. Domestic shipping is subject to internationally recognized standards, and any domestic laws that may be in force.

Article 22 of the CLS says that coastal states may establish sea-lanes and traffic separation schemes in their territorial seas for regulating the passage of ships exercising their rights of innocent passage. In general, the same rights and duties apply to coastal states bordering straits used for international navigation, but in this case there is the further requirement that the coastal states cooperate in formulating proposals to be submitted to the competent international organization (Article 41). In archipelagic waters states may likewise establish and designate sea-lanes and traffic separation schemes (Article 53).

The straits of Malacca and Singapore are among the more congested waterways in the world, and hazards to navigation abound. Traffic separation schemes are in effect, and an underkeel clearance limitation of 3.5 m limits the size of transiting vessels. Aids to navigation have been installed in the straits to assist vessels.

At the close of 1983 neither Indonesia nor the Philippines had yet formally established archipelagic sea-lanes through its waters. The main archipelagic sea-lane in Indonesian waters will probably be the Selat Lombok–Makassar Strait–Celebes Sea route, while the Philippines is likely to establish a route through Surigao Strait and the Sulu Sea as the main east-west lane. Both Indonesia and the Philippines will probably establish other archipelagic sea-lanes as well. Special enforcement action may be required to ensure that traffic separation schemes and sea-lanes are followed by transiting vessels.

Domestic laws of general applicability also are enforceable in the maritime region. These laws cover customs, fiscal, immigration, and sanitation matters, plus those addressing the problems of piracy and, in some places, slavery. Enforcement of these laws at sea poses the additional problem of transportation of enforcement officials to the scene of a suspected violation in a timely manner, perhaps over a great distance.

Enforcement of laws and regulations governing shipping requires surveillance of waters under national jurisdiction that normally are frequented by foreign vessels. Occasional surveillance of infrequently used areas, accomplished concurrently with other enforcement duties, can ensure that changes in traffic patterns or attempts at evasion can be detected. For the most part, surveillance provided by aircraft would suffice to detect the types of violations of greatest importance to the coastal states.

Protection of the Ocean Environment

Part VII of the CLS, entitled "Protection and Preservation of the Marine Environment," provides for enforcement of the applicable provisions. Articles 212–222 are concerned with enforcement of regulations designed to prevent, reduce, and control pollution; Articles 223–233 prescribe various safeguards that must be obeyed in carrying out enforcement procedures.

The problem of enforcement of regulations against pollution of the sea by toxic, noxious, or radioactive materials has two aspects — one concerning pollution from mobile, shipboard sources and the other from fixed sources such as oil wells and coastal sites. The principal source of shipboard pollution is from tankers transiting the region or calling at the oil terminals. Consequently, the main tanker routes through the Malacca–Singapore and Lombok straits are of most concern and would require the highest level of surveillance. The largest oil terminals in Southeast Asia are at Singapore, on both the north and south coast of Java, on the coasts of Sumatera and peninsular Malaysia, on the Strait of Malacca, on the Brunei and Sabah coasts, and on the east coast of Kalimantan. There are other terminals near Manila in the Philippines and on the east shore of the Bight of Bangkok, and at both locations oil pollution is a potential problem. The Tapis and Pulai terminals in the South China Sea are other potential sources of oil pollution that should be kept under some level of surveillance by the government of Malaysia. Where sea-lanes, particularly for large tankers, are close to oil exploitation regions and areas containing valuable and vulnerable marine resources such as coral reefs and threatened animal species, the potential for serious damage to the marine environment is great.

The detection of pollution from shipboard sources requires a patrol effort similar to that for the enforcement of shipping regulations. Coastal pollution sources would be identified by the same patrols that would be enforcing regulations covering energy and mineral resources produced from fixed sources. Deliberate offshore dumping of refuse, dredge spoils, or other materials that may be authorized by permit would have to be monitored during the operation to ensure that regulations are met.

Detection is only the first step in pollution abatement and control; gathering of evidence and apprehension of the violator are also required. Offshore pollution sites and some otherwise inaccessible coastal sites require vessels on the scene to carry out the enforcement duties.

Marine Scientific Research

A real concern to coastal states is scientific research by foreign vessels occurring in their EEZs. Their concern is that information gathered by research vessels may be used to their detriment, or that the research activity may be a subterfuge to mask the acquisition of military or resource information. Hydrographic surveys in some of the important straits might be viewed as an attempt by the research ship to acquire information useful to navies contemplating operation of submarines; the Lombok, Ombai, and Wetar straits are possible foci of such efforts. Scientific research in regions with military potential and that are claimed by more than one nation are particularly suspect. The Spratly Islands are an obvious example.

Whatever the attitude toward the foreign research activity, once it has been sanctioned there will be a continuing need to ensure that provisions are followed. Other vessels, which might be conducting covert investigations without authorization for that purpose, would need to be detected and removed from the area. Authorized research vessels could be located easily, but others would first have to be detected and then examined closely should there be any question about their activities. Both fishing vessels and transit shipping can be bases of such illegal research activities.

RESPONSES

National Priorities and Enforcement Actions

The extent to which each nation in Southeast Asia attempts to enforce its jurisdiction in the maritime region depends upon a number of factors including, but not limited to, the following:

- The need to obtain economic benefits from fisheries, petroleum, and mineral resources of the region;
- The need to demonstrate, for political purposes, that jurisdiction is in fact being exercised over the region; and
- The resources available for the enforcement effort, i.e., ships, aircraft, and personnel.

Even the richest nations are unwilling to provide all the resources necessary for the full enforcement of all laws and regulations in effect in the maritime region. Decisions must be made as to which of them are to be enforced, and how thorough that enforcement effort is to be. Decisions must be made as to where available enforcement resources can be most useful, and what types of enforcement action would provide the greatest results.

Enforcement of maritime jurisdiction may be of concern in relation to fishing, shipping, energy and natural resources, environmental protection, and marine scientific research. Prime fishing areas are found in Philippine, Indonesian, Thai, and Malaysian waters. Smuggling is significant in the Gulf of Thailand, the Andaman Sea, the Natuna area, East Malaysian waters, the Celebes and Sulu seas, western Philippine waters, the Bashi channel, and on the Arafura Sea. The Strait of Malacca has high pollution potential from shipping. Major oil exploration and production areas are found off northwest Palawan, off Sabah, Brunei, and Sarawak, in the Natuna area, off the east coast of the Malay Peninsula, and in the Gulf of Thailand. Refugees fleeing Vietnam are also an enforcement concern. Table 10.1 shows estimates of national priorities for different enforcement activities, based on economic and sociopolitical benefits that are likely to result from enforcement action. The highest priority is given to those enforcement actions that likely would have the greatest immediate impact and could be performed by existing forces. The estimated priorities reflect the concerns of governments demonstrated by their past actions, and those that are expected to arise as a result of their ratification of the CLS.

Figure 10.2 shows the locations of suggested air and surface vessel bases for maritime enforcement, along with the possible areas of coverage. Many of these bases already exist, supporting units of the armed forces. They could be adapted to support vessel and aircraft EEZ enforcement, possibly through separate organizations, if the nations decided to establish such activities.

The following review of maritime law enforcement problems in Southeast Asia indicates areas of major concern to each nation.

Brunei. Having only a small EEZ within which to exercise jurisdiction, Brunei has a small but significant enforcement task. The primary concern of Brunei is protection of the offshore energy sources that provide much of its national income. Surface vessels are adequate for providing quick response to both natural and human-caused emergencies. Aircraft support would further enhance the level and promptness of enforcement action. Even a single patrol boat based at Muara could be effective, and if it were paired with an aircraft it would be very difficult to invade Brunei.

Table 10.1 Inferred Enforcement Priorities in Southeast Asia

Enforcement Activity	Brunei	Burma	Indonesia	Kampuchea	Malaysia	Philippines	Singapore	Thailand	Vietnam
Fishing									
Licensing			1			1			2
Area compliance			1			1			1
Season compliance			1			1			1
Gear compliance			2			2			2
Species compliance			2			2			1
Quantity compliance			1			1			1
Exclusion of foreign fishermen		1		1	1		2	1	1
Protection of domestic fishermen					1			1	
Shipping									
Sea-lanes			1			1			
Traffic separation schemes			3		2		2		
International straits			2		1	2	1		
Surveillance	2			2					1
Energy and mineral resources									
Artificial islands and structures									
License	1	1	1		1	1		1	
License compliance	1	1	1		1	1		1	
Disaster response	1	2	1		1	1		1	
Smuggling of natural resources	1	1	2		2	2		1	
Prevention of unauthorized exploitation or exploitation	1	2	2		2	2		2	
Protection of ocean environment									
Pollution from vessels			1		1	1		1	1

(continued on the following page)

Table 10.1   Inferred Enforcement Priorities in Southeast Asia (Continued)

Enforcement Activity	Brunei	Burma	Indonesia	Kampuchea	Malaysia	Philippines	Singapore	Thailand	Vietnam
Pollution from structures, artificial islands, or seabed installation			1		1	2			1
Dumping			2		2	2			
Land-based runoff or blowoff			3		3	2			
Marine scientific research									
Control of foreign operations			1		2	1		2	2

Notes: 1 = high priority;
2 = medium priority.
3 = low priority.
Blank = no concern.

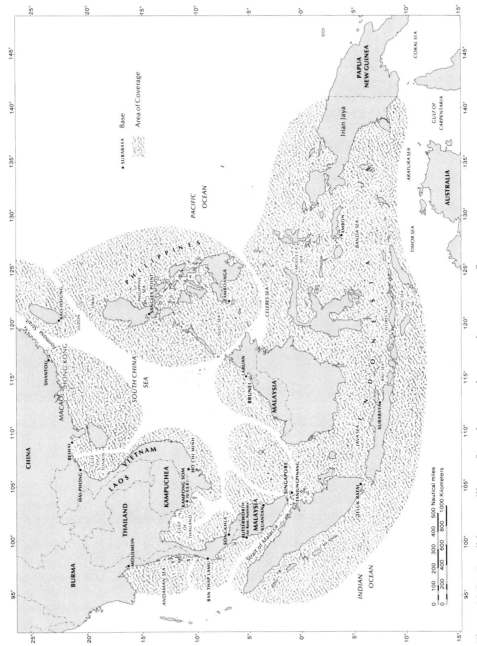

Figure 10.2 Possible surveillance force bases and approximate areas of coverage.

The other areas of enforcement concern are relatively minor compared with off-shore energy production. Any enforcement action necessary in those areas could be accomplished by the same patrol boat and aircraft resources that would be employed in the primary enforcement task. Given its small size, Brunei has no problem of concentrating its forces. Enforcement problems of the type encountered elsewhere in Southeast Asia have not developed but may arise as EEZ claims are more fully defined following achievement of full independence in January 1984.

Burma. The highest enforcement priority for Burma is the exclusion of foreign fishermen from the Burmese EEZ. Burma has been pursuing an active campaign against foreign fishing vessels within its EEZ, including those that may only be in transit to destinations beyond Burmese waters. Thai trawlers have been the principal targets of this enforcement effort, with either encroachment or poaching usually being charged by Burmese authorities.[6] Thailand has claimed that Burma seized more than 120 boats and imprisoned more than 1,100 crew members between 1973 and 1982.[7]

Exercise of jurisdiction over shipping has thus far been limited to surveillance. Such surveillance or related enforcement could be conducted concurrently with the enforcement of fisheries jurisdiction in the EEZ. Burma is apparently concerned with foreign scientific research in its waters; the Burmese detained a Southeast Asian Fisheries Development Center (SEAFDEC) vessel for investigation.

Three 335-ton Osprey-class patrol boats designed and equipped for offshore fishery protection duties were procured during 1980–81.[8] Additional vessels of this type and the use of aircraft for surveillance would permit increased patrol activity resulting in a greater number of illegal fishing boat seizures. They could also be employed against those engaged in the smuggling of natural resources such as tin and market goods. Basing fisheries patrol boats at Mergui and Akyab, and possibly an aircraft at Mergui, appears to be both feasible and potentially effective in providing adequate coverage of the EEZ.

Indonesia. With an EEZ of more than 1.5 million square kilometers (km²), Indonesia has by far the most difficult maritime jurisdiction enforcement problem in Southeast Asia. The many islands of the archipelago are widely scattered, and enforcement efforts must likewise be dispersed. In addition, Indonesia is involved in the full range of maritime activities for which enforcement action might be desirable. Limitations on available enforcement resources require compromises.

That the Indonesians are serious about enforcing their maritime jurisdiction is shown by newspaper and radio broadcast accounts of the seizure of at least seventy-seven foreign fishing vessels between 1974 and 1980. Thirty-one of those seized between 1976 and 1978 were Taiwanese, with two from the Philippines, and one each from Hong Kong and Singapore. Most of these seizures were either for lack of fishing documents or for lack of appropriate security clearances.

Concern by the Indonesians in late 1978 over repeated violations of fishing regulations resulted in a 1980 ban on the entry of foreign fishing vessels into territorial waters and the prohibition of all foreign fishing in the EEZ except by permit.

Three-month, extendable permits granted thereafter required the name, tonnage, crew list, call sign, operational area, and the types and quantities of fish to be caught. Both naval and air force units of the Indonesian armed forces have carried out enforcement actions.[9]

Enforcement activities in fisheries, energy, and natural resources promise the best immediate return on investment in enforcement resources. Enforcement action in these areas can also provide some carry-over into the enforcement of regulations governing shipping, environmental protection, and marine scientific research. A number of strategic straits are under Indonesian control, and surveillance and enforcement of laws prohibiting marine scientific research in such critical ocean areas are important. Scientific research may have both economic and military implications, as mentioned previously.

Concentration of fisheries enforcement activity should be in those areas known to have the greatest number of foreign fishing vessels operating either under permits or as joint ventures. Compliance with area and seasonal limitations can be ascertained by aircraft surveillance, without the need for surface vessel follow-up except for the pursuit and apprehension of *prima facie* violators. Compliance with catch limitations may be ascertained by requiring foreign fishing vessels to call at designated Indonesian ports for inspection prior to departure. In the past, however, Japanese fishing boats have not abided by such agreements.

Enforcement by aircraft patrols and port calls must be supplemented by the presence of surface vessels in the fishing areas if detailed inspection of fishing equipment and records is to be accomplished. The size of mesh and the net materials can be ascertained accurately only by placing enforcement officials on board the fishing vessels. An inspector on board also can determine whether proper records are being maintained, what species of fish are being taken, and if unauthorized species or materials have been retained. With inspections, the costs of enforcement could rise rapidly to a level above which additional boarding operations would not be economically justified.

The geographic expanse of Indonesia makes it impossible to mount an effective patrol effort from one central location. Perhaps four support bases could be considered to provide both broad coverage and concentrated patrols in the most active areas. Bases at Tandjung Pinang, Teluk Ratai, Surabaya, and Ambon would provide the necessary support for surface vessels. Those based at Tandjung Pinang would cover the Malacca and Singapore straits and the South China Sea; those at Teluk Ratai would cover the Sunda Strait and ocean areas south of Sumatera and Java; those at Surabaya would cover the Lombok Strait, the Java, Bali, and Flores seas, and the Makassar Strait; and those based at Ambon would cover the Ceram, Banda, Halmahera, Arafura, and Timor seas and straits in eastern Indonesia. Aircraft based as near to these ports as practicable would facilitate close coordination of patrols.

The protection of artificial islands or offshore oil and gas platforms poses an entirely different challenge, particularly off the northwest coast of Java, the northeast coast of Sumatera, north of Sarawak, and east of Kalimantan. Regulations governing their placement and operation are relatively easy to enforce because of the fixed positions of such installations and the relatively long lead time available for such action. Any military or terrorist attack on such a facility would require an expeditious response. Operational or natural disasters likewise require a prompt response to minimize the loss of life, equipment, or the resource itself.

Indonesia, as an archipelagic state, can be expected to exercise authority over established shipping sea-lanes. Routes between Selat Karimata and Selat Sunda, between Selat Makassar and Selat Sunda or Lombok, and between other straits on the periphery of Indonesian archipelagic waters could be subject to aircraft surveillance. A special problem area is the Natuna salient separating peninsular Malaysia from the Malaysian states of Sarawak and Sabah. An agreement concerning Malaysian shipping rights is in effect for the region. Compliance with pollution control regulations, as well as detection of smuggling, piracy, and prohibited military activities, are of concern to Indonesia in exercising surveillance over its archipelagic sea-lanes. Spot checks would add thoroughness to the effort but would be unlikely to provide any greater benefits except in cases where violations were detected and vessels apprehended. This type of enforcement activity may not be directly productive in the economic sense, but it would clearly establish Indonesian jurisdiction over such sea-lanes.

Patrols of all archipelagic waters merely to locate vessels not conforming to established sea-lanes would not yield adequate benefits to justify the effort, but they could be combined with patrols for other enforcement purposes. Border regions such as the Celebes Sea, the Natuna Islands, Irian Jaya, and the eastern Indonesian Archipelago where Vietnamese refugees might land are areas where surveillance could be concentrated. Protection of the ocean environment from ship-generated pollution could be another benefit obtained from sea-lane patrols, as could the prevention of illegal marine scientific research. Pollution caused by ships is a major concern in the Strait of Malacca and along the Lombok Strait–Bali Sea–Makassar Strait–Celebes Sea route for tankers too large to navigate the Malacca–Singapore straits.

Kampuchea. It appears that recent enforcement actions by Kampuchea are not designed for that country to retain economic benefits from its marine resources.[10] Exclusion of foreign fishing vessels is clearly the policy of Kampuchea, even though repeated approaches have been made by other nations, especially Thailand, to establish a shared fishery. It appears that there has been no attempt by Kampuchea to distinguish between major and minor infringements of its maritime jurisdiction; the only penalty seems to be the seizure and confiscation of vessels and imprisonment of the crews.[11] Numerous incidents have been reported in the press of Kampuchean attacks on foreign vessels, especially Thai fishing trawlers but also including such targets as the United States freighter *Mayaguez.* In these incidents, Kampuchean patrol boats have fired without warning on the foreign vessel with at least one such incident taking place within Thai territorial waters, resulting in the death of eleven Thai fishermen.[12]

Naval units routinely patrol the Kampuchean EEZ, and apparently surveillance duties are also assigned to civilian observers. The threat of the military force, including possible gunfire, has not been especially effective in deterring incursions by Thai fishermen, but it presumably does deter other nations from conducting marine scientific research in those waters. Concern for pollution and offshore energy extraction are not evident except as they relate to activities by Thailand in Kampuchean-claimed areas.

Malaysia. Malaysia shares many Indonesian concerns in establishing effective jurisdiction and enforcement authority in its maritime region. It has a problem unique in the region in that its EEZ is separated into two parts by the intervening Indonesian archipelagic waters and EEZ. Despite the need to combat piracy, smuggling, and guerrilla activities, Malaysia has made little effort thus far to provide enforcement capability in the EEZ off Sabah and Sarawak due to lack of resources and the 965-km (600-mi) separation from peninsular Malaysia.

Protection of the Malaysian fisheries from foreign incursions is of primary concern. The Fisheries Act of 1963, providing for the arrest of persons and the search, seizure, and forfeiture of vessels found to have been engaged in illegal fishing operations,[13] has been enforced often against Thai vessels that have strayed across the maritime boundary line. In a seven-day period in 1979, for example, some forty-seven fishermen were arrested for fisheries violations.[14]

Concern for shipping is concentrated in the international straits of Malacca and Singapore. The possibility of major pollution incidents occurring there has been reduced by the establishment of traffic separation schemes and by the regional (with Indonesia and Singapore) minimum underkeel policy for all ships using the straits.

Enforcement of laws concerning energy and mineral resources is another primary concern.[15] In the past there have been suspicions of overpumping and actual oil theft, but the allegations are unproven. Sites are fixed, and spot checks should be adequate to ensure compliance. Capabilities to respond promptly to problems created by natural disasters or terrorist activity might be strengthened.

Patrol problems for Malaysia are less burdensome than for Indonesia. One of the more serious problems faced by Malaysia, however, is the landing of Vietnamese refugees on the east coast of the peninsula. Patrol routes would roughly parallel the coastline of peninsular Malaysia in the Strait of Malacca and the South China Sea and along the coastline of Sabah and Sarawak. The geography of Malaysia thus suggests a need for four bases from which surface patrol vessels could be operated. Vessels based on each side of the peninsula—at the existing base at Georgetown and at Kota Bharu—would provide surface enforcement capability in the areas of greatest concern. Another base at Labuan could provide coverage of the waters off central Sabah and Sarawak while northeast Sabah could be covered by patrols based at Sandakan.

Malaysia has taken steps to increase the efficiency of its air surveillance. Three Hercules C130H maritime patrol planes equipped with the latest devices for precise navigation, detection, identification, and ship tracking have been acquired. This new air capability will permit closer monitoring of pirate craft, refugee boats, and illegal fishermen.

Protection of the ocean environment, mainly against pollution from shipping in the Malacca and Singapore straits and from offshore oil wells, could be provided by fisheries patrols. These patrols could also make checks on vessels that might be conducting scientific research in Malaysian waters.

   Philippines. The Philippines faces the second greatest challenge in the exercise of maritime jurisdiction in Southeast Asia. Claiming an EEZ of more than 550,000 km^2, it has interests in all five activity categories.

   Fishing poses the most serious enforcement problems. In some areas the task is simply to detect and exclude violators of Philippine waters. Where there are regulations permitting fishing by outsiders, however, enforcing the rules is far more difficult. For example, more than 1,600 boats fish in the Bashi Channel between Luzon and the Chinese province of Taiwan.[16] Enforcement action can be taken against only a few at a time, and it is often difficult to determine whether vessels are within or just outside the Philippine EEZ. The fisheries law enforcement task has become even more difficult with the authorization of joint ventures for tuna fishing in the EEZ beyond a limiting 7-fathom depth.[17] That boundary cannot be determined from from aircraft and may not be located consistently and accurately even by surface patrol vessels.

   Press reports of the seizure by the Philippines of at least 162 foreign fishing vessels between 1972 and 1980 show the government's determination to enforce its jurisdiction in the EEZ. Actions may have been taken in some cases to discourage potential violators, as in the 1980 cases when all ten vessels of a Taiwanese fishing fleet reportedly sank off Batanes "due to big waves" after their crews had been taken onboard Philippine naval vessels.[18]

   Control of shipping in archipelagic sea-lanes that may be established is of secondary importance at the present time. A more serious problem concerns vessels that are entitled to innocent passage through certain Philippine waters. A number of strategic straits in the Philippine Archipelago provide the only reasonably convenient passages from the Pacific Ocean to the South China Sea. For a time, commercial navigation was forbidden in the southern part of the archipelago unless transiting vessels were provided with a naval escort. This resulted from internal problems created by the Moro insurgency. New navigational rules were imposed in March 1981, and the Philippine navy was authorized to prohibit or stop innocent passage and to detain vessels that attempted to evade those restrictions.[19]

   Pollution prevention or abatement efforts could be concentrated in the offshore oil and gas exploration areas and the main shipping lanes through the archipelago. As elsewhere, aircraft patrols can be used to detect pollution initially, with follow-up enforcement action by surface vessels. Land-based sources of marine environment pollution, such as the runoff from copper mine tailings near Marinduque,[20] might also be identified in the course of such aircraft patrols.

   Assigning a high priority to monitoring marine scientific research might be justified in the Philippines on the grounds that such research could be used as a subterfuge for providing supplies to insurgent groups, particularly in the southern provinces. Hydrographic and oceanographic surveys of straits through the Philippines could support unfriendly naval operations and for that reason should be controlled. A combination of air and surface patrols would be needed if detection from the air is to be followed by subsequent interdiction of suspect surface vessels.

A concentration of enforcement vessels in northern Luzon, working from bases at Aparri or San Nicolas, might be warranted in view of the level of foreign fishing activity on the edge of and within the EEZ. Patrol boats at Zamboanga to provide surface coverage in the Celebes and Sulu seas, at Puerto Princesa for parts of the Sulu Sea and the petroleum producing areas in the South China Sea, and at Legaspi for coverage of the Pacific side of the archipelago, could be supported by aircraft at Manila, Zamboanga, and Puerto Princesa for air coverage of these areas.

Singapore. The limited area subject to the maritime jurisdiction of Singapore is an advantage when it comes to enforcement. Gaining much of its livelihood from its position as a shipping center, Singapore would want to protect itself from violations that might result in economic losses. Singapore's concern for avoiding pollution from ship sources is indicated by its participation in the regional agreement prescribing a traffic separation scheme and a minimum acceptable underkeel clearance in the Singapore and Malacca straits. Conceivably, surveillance by land-based radar could be used to determine compliance with the traffic separation scheme in Singapore Strait. Compliance with the underkeel clearance, however, would require a visual check of a vessel's draft or the development of some device to detect a violation and alert authorities.

Singapore has acquired sophisticated early-warning aircraft systems, primarily for military purposes, but such equipment would be useful for detecting violators of Singapore's maritime jurisdiction. Although the area to be covered is small, the port is busy and surveillance is necessary to detect illegal discharges of cargo and wastes and vessels engaged in smuggling and other illegal activities. There have been several instances of pirates boarding vessels in the Singapore Strait, and although the ships were destined for Singapore, the illegal activities took place outside of Singapore's waters. Thus, enforcement and apprehension has been difficult due to jurisdictional problems.

Marine emergency procedures have been developed by Singapore but have yet to be coordinated with neighboring states.[21] Strict domestic laws govern maritime activities and are especially stringent in pollution control.

Thailand. The enforcement problem for Thailand differs from that of other Southeast Asian nations in that it is directed more toward protecting and regulating its own fishing fleet than toward apprehending foreign violators. Because of the depletion of fish stocks in the Gulf of Thailand, and to a lesser extent in the waters of the Andaman Sea off its west coast, Thailand's EEZ holds little attraction for foreign fishing vessels.

The Thai fishing effort has shifted toward more productive distant-water fisheries, a result of the development and construction of a modern trawler fleet. This fleet has been exposed to armed attack and seizure by Kampuchea and Vietnam, and Burma has seized Thai fishing vessels in its EEZ, even when those vessels were reportedly bound for destinations in Bangladesh and beyond. Seizure of Thai trawlers by Burma, Kampuchea, and Vietnam has provided them with modern fishing vessels without the need to spend scarce capital for their purchase.

Thailand has attempted to counter these actions by assigning units of the Royal Thai Navy to protect its fishing vessels from attack and to prevent them from inadvertently straying into foreign waters because of inadequate charts or the lack of navigational skills.[22] It has been necessary also to protect fishermen and Vietnamese refugee "boat people" from piracy and other acts of violence in the Gulf of Thailand.[23]

The widespread practice of smuggling is another problem. Tin concentrates smuggled to Malaysia and Singapore[24] and the illegal exchange of consumer goods for Burmese livestock and minerals make up the bulk of this traffic. Armed patrol vessels are essential to antismuggling operations and could perform those missions from bases at Sattahip, Songkhla, and Ban Thap Lamu near Phuket. Aircraft assistance for surveillance of fishing activity, possible pollution vessel and fixed structure sources, and possible unauthorized marine research could be provided from one base, at either U Tapao or Bangkok's Don Muang airport.

Vietnam. Vietnam claims a military warning zone of 12-nmi wide and pursues a firm policy in dealing with incursions of foreign vessels into its waters, treating them as trespassing violations. Enforcement of this policy, effectively one of straightforward exclusion of foreign vessels, has been performed by naval units, frequently including the use of gunfire. In recent years, numerous foreign vessels, predominantly Thai, have been seized and their crews interned.[25] Surveillance of shipping in general and fishing activity in particular could be performed effectively by aircraft patrols. Interdiction and apprehension, however, would be functions performed either by naval surface vessels or by armed civilian fishing organizations.

There are provisions in Vietnamese policy that would govern foreign fishing activity.[26] Permits would be required, good for one year but renewable for an additional six months. Each fishing vessel would be required to give notice of its intentions one week in advance, stating the place of departure and the direction of travel. A report of position would have to be given daily and again at the end of a voyage. The catching of prohibited species would have to be avoided, and if caught they would be surrendered to a Vietnamese agent. Violators would be subject to warnings, revocation of permits, expulsion of boats and crews, and fines of up to 10,000 tong (payable in the equivalent amount of a foreign currency). The forfeiture of vessels after apprehension can be expected, however, considering previous actions by Vietnam against violations of its EEZ.

Armed "self-defense units" have been established on Vietnamese trawlers, such as those of the Quang Ninh Fishing Enterprise, which act as enforcement units within the EEZ to supplement naval patrols.[27] "All activities concerning geological investigation, research and exploration conducted . . . without the permission of the SRV constitute a gross violation of Vietnam's sovereignty and territorial integrity."[28] Permits for this purpose can be obtained, at least in theory. Particular areas of concern are the Gulf of Tonkin, parts of which are claimed by both Vietnam and China, south of the Mekong Delta, and the Dao Phu Quoc area.

Costs vs. Benefits

Before a coastal state embarks on an enforcement program, consideration should be given to the costs of surveillance and enforcement, and these should be compared with the benefits that such activities would create. Costs can be calculated by referring to the areas to be covered and the forces (both air and surface) needed to provide the desired level of coverage. Planes and patrol boats, personnel, communications, and command and control equipment should be considered. A most important and potentially expensive component of costs is bases for the surface and air surveillance and enforcement units. If the bases already exist for naval, air force, or civilian activities, their upgrading or conversion for use of enforcement craft might be accomplished inexpensively. If no appropriate bases exist, building them can be costly.

Benefits are more difficult to estimate. One economic benefit might be the additional fish that could be caught by local fishermen if foreign fishing activities were forbidden or regulated. Such a calculation requires that fish stocks, sustainable yields, breeding patterns, seasons, and spawning areas, among other factors, be known. The capacity of the coastal nation's fleet to harvest all the stocks, consistent with maintaining the various species at the desired yield, likewise must be determined. There may be other benefits, political or social in nature, such as safety of life and property or environmental protection. However, most states would consider that protecting life and property and protecting the marine environment are activities desirable in their own right, aside from any monetary benefits that might accrue.

Enforcement of regulations designed to improve the safety of navigation, including installation of navigational aids, establishing traffic control lanes and vessel draft or size regulations, monitoring ship movements in crowded ports or approaches, and inspecting vessels to ensure that they meet minimum standards of upkeep and maintenance entail some expense, but the returns from this enforcement effort in terms of reduced insurance premiums for ships might equal the costs. From strictly financial considerations, as well as the general desire for law enforcement, surveillance of offshore oil installations might cost less than the amount of oil that could be stolen if effective enforcement were not carried out.

In the case of archipelagic states, the archipelagic waters may be considered to be so inherently a part of the national territory that enforcement of the various regulations concerning fishing, navigation, and other uses of the waters is considered necessary to maintain national unity and identity. For some nations (Kampuchea and Vietnam, for example) the EEZ also may be worthy of defense and protection to the same degree as the land territory. If the political benefits are considered important enough, no price to be paid in enforcement would be considered prohibitive.

Military Forces or Separate Enforcement Organizations

Most Southeast Asian countries employ military forces in enforcement roles in their EEZs. In the Philippines, however, there is a coast guard with a mission specif-

ically to enforce regulations concerned with the resources of the EEZ and archipelagic waters; the Philippine Coast guard is an integral part of the navy. Vietnam
and Thailand have civilian-staffed patrol vessels to assist naval forces. Malaysia and
Singapore have regularly constituted marine or port police forces. Since existing
naval forces are rarely fully employed in peacetime, their use in enforcement missions would seem to be justified by reason of availability and economy.

But Southeast Asian naval commanders consider that the primary function of a
navy is defense of home territory against attack and to keep sea-lanes open. As discussed in Chapter 7, this function occupies navies in peacetime as well as in war, since
training for war, deterrence, and "showing the flag" are traditional peacetime activities. Protection of maritime resources is a legitimate role for a navy, but it is not the
most important function. Consequently, naval forces generally are not designed for
enforcement roles. There are some exceptions, such as the Burmese navy, which has
offshore fishery protection patrol vessels, but most Southeast Asian naval vessels are
better armed, with higher speed capabilities and less endurance than required for
enforcing EEZ regulations. Thus, the emphasis on the combat mission of navies influences ship design and makes most naval ships needlessly expensive for the enforcement mission. Moreover, they might not be the most suitable for facilitating the
work of boarding parties. Much of what applies to naval surface forces applies to
military aircraft as well. For the most part they are faster, better armed, and more
expensive than the maritime surveillance mission would require.

The temptation to continue using military aircraft and naval vessels because
they are already in existence with crews aboard should be tempered with consideration of the benefits that might accrue from a separate maritime jurisdiction enforcement force. A separate force could serve in a number of other roles, as mentioned previously. Or the maritime enforcement mission might continue to be one
of the navy's missions, but specific ship and aircraft types might be provided. There
are a number of geographic factors that might influence these decisions. For Indonesia and other states with large maritime jurisdictions, swift, heavily armed attack
craft suitable for the control of strategic straits are not well suited to patrolling
archipelagic waters and EEZs. Singapore, however, might profitably continue to
use its small but effective navy to enforce its limited maritime jurisdiction.

There are advantages to establishing separate surveillance and enforcement
units associated with the agency most concerned with the particular activity. Thus,
it seems logical that aircraft, patrol craft, and the entire mechanism of enforcement from apprehension to confiscation of fishing boats, to trial, punishment, and
publicization be more or less under the control of a nation's fishery organization
rather than be separated among a number of governmental units. If the basic mission is to make better use of the fish resources of a state's EEZ, consolidation of all
activities associated with fisheries, including enforcement, makes good sense. Fisheries enforcement officers, familiar with fishing operations, species, and the detailed regulations for management of the fishery region, can serve effectively on
the enforcement vessels and aircraft and do a better job than can naval officers
assigned to the same mission. The same arguments can be made about surveillance
and enforcement of other activities, such as exploitation of offshore oil resources,

tin mining, and regulation of shipping. On the other hand, if the enforcement problem is primarily the control and apprehension of pirates with swift, well-armed vessels, the military capability of naval ships will be more appropriate. Clearly, each country has its own particular circumstances to consider.

Regional Surveillance and Enforcement Agreements

Article 123 of the CLS discusses cooperation of states bordering enclosed or semi-enclosed seas. While not specifically mentioning joint or regional schemes for surveillance and enforcement, it does enjoin states to

- Coordinate the management, conservation, exploration, and exploitation of the living resources of the sea;
- Coordinate the implementation of their rights and duties with respect to the protection and preservation of the marine environment;
- Coordinate their scientific research policies and undertake where appropriate joint programs of scientific research in the area; and
- Invite, as appropriate, other interested states or international organizations to cooperate with them in furtherance of provisions of the article.

Cooperation among countries in Southeast Asia to enforce their rights to the resources of the EEZs is permissible under the CLS. The question is, is it desirable or feasible? Since surveillance and enforcement require ship and aircraft resources and can be expensive, it could be argued that if the necessary resources could be pooled, all nations in the agreement would benefit.

A regional enforcement scheme might be considered in the semi-enclosed South China Sea, although there are several reasons why it might not be feasible. First, nations bordering the sea have very different interests in enforcement; Singapore, with its minuscule EEZ and the Philippines with its very large one clearly do not have the same problems or interests. Second, ASEAN nations do not have the same political ideologies as the Indochinese states of Vietnam and Kampuchea, and the latter have been involved in enforcement activities against Thailand, a member of ASEAN. Third, some of the maritime territorial disputes in the region would make joint enforcement extremely difficult since it would be unclear who was entitled to be in the disputed region and who had sovereignty over the resources. Finally, China probably would be unlikely to participate since the Chinese make general claims to the entire South China Sea.

If cooperative enforcement is not feasible for the South China Sea as a whole, it may be worth exploring for some of the smaller bodies of water in the Southeast Asian region. The Gulf of Tonkin and the Gulf of Thailand do not seem to be real possibilities due to overlapping claims in both of them; Vietnam and China have a serious maritime jurisdictional dispute in the Gulf of Tonkin, and Vietnam, Thailand, and Kampuchea have overlapping claims in the Gulf of Thailand. In the straits of Malacca and Singapore, however, Indonesia, Malaysia, and Singapore already have a cooperative agreement concerning the regulation of navigation. The rules, which are recognized by the Intergovernmental Maritime Organization and the shipping community at large, may need to be enforced. Joint enforcement seems particularly appropriate, since the straits are narrow and easily monitored.

Some of the states in the region have already established cooperative surveillance schemes with their neighbors, and these could provide a framework for additional bilateral and multilateral surveillance and enforcement efforts. Indonesia and Malaysia have cooperated in joint surveillance of their common South China Sea border area for detecting Vietnamese refugees, and the Philippines and Indonesia have a bilateral agreement on joint surveillance in the Celebes Sea. In 1975 the ASEAN states joined in an Agreement for the Facilitation of Search for Ships in Distress and Rescue of Survivors of Ship Accidents.[29] This multilateral pact could become a model for increased cooperative surveillance efforts among the ASEAN countries. Whether the nations will extend their cooperation beyond humanitarian concerns to activities with substantial economic and political connotations remains to be seen.

Regional enforcement might be possible in the Andaman Sea if Burma and Thailand could agree on some formula for allowing Thailand access to the resources of the Burmese EEZ. India might need to be a party to any regional enforcement plan in that area since the Andaman and Nicobar islands are Indian territory. Other possibilities for cooperative enforcement might involve Australia, Indonesia, and Papua New Guinea in the Arafura and Timor seas; Indonesia, Malaysia, and the Philippines in the Celebes Sea; and Malaysia and the Philippines in the Sulu Sea.

Harmonization of Enforcement Policies

Perhaps regional enforcement efforts are too much to expect, considering the differences among the Southeast Asian states. But nations in the region might harmonize their enforcement policies, since harmonization would not imply the sacrifice of any sovereignty over areas in dispute. If some Southeast Asian coastal states were to agree to standard legal and judicial procedures, including levels of permissible punishment in the event of convictions, an important start would be made toward effective management of resources for the benefit of all states in the region. Harmonization efforts could also extend to procedures for detecting and enforcing violations of environmental regulations and to programs for conservation of living and nonliving resources.

As a first step it would be a hopeful sign if all Southeast Asian states implemented the pertinent articles of the CLS, particularly Article 62 concerning access to surplus stocks and Article 73 concerning enforcement procedures and permissible punishments. This might open the way for additional agreements on shared fish stocks, uniform waste disposal rules, and navigation regulations designed to protect the marine environment by reducing the possibility of collisions and groundings. These activities might then be extended to include the establishment of agreed positions regarding other aspects of the CLS and its enforcement.

CHAPTER 11

COOPERATION: OPPORTUNITIES, PROBLEMS, AND PROSPECTS

Mark J. Valencia
George Kent

OPPORTUNITIES

The emphasis in this volume has been on national and transnational marine policy issues created or exacerbated by extended maritime jurisdiction and the Convention on the Law of the Sea (CLS) and the possibilities for international cooperation in their resolution. The major incentives for extended jurisdictions were expectations of enlarged resource bases, and most of the nations of Southeast Asia are now engaged in a conscious effort to identify and pursue their national interests in the ocean arena. For these developing nations, the new resources, activities, and concomitant responsibilities create new challenges and opportunities for national — and perhaps regional — development.

For the Association of Southeast Asian Nations (ASEAN) countries in Southeast Asia, the marine area covered by extended jurisdiction is about 65 percent of their combined land area. For some countries the marine area is greater than the land area. For example, Brunei gains 1.3 times its land area, and the Philippines gains 1.8 times its land area. The direct economic contribution of quantifiable marine uses for ASEAN as a whole is about 8.5 percent of gross national product (GNP), and this will increase with time. Brunei's economy is almost entirely dependent on its petroleum industry, which is increasingly focused offshore. Indonesia, Malaysia, and Thailand also draw significant petroleum from the oceans, and major development projects such as the Eastern Seaboard project of Thailand and the Bintulu regional growth center in Sarawak (Malaysia) are based on offshore natural gas. Singapore's economy is boosted by its port and its shipping and marine services industry. Some offshore marine resources and uses afford opportunities for stimulation of neglected rural areas, as does peninsular Malaysia's oil offshore the east coast, or serve as nodes for population dispersal, as do the rural fishing ports of the Philippines, Indonesia, and Thailand.

Every marine policy issue, even the most problematic, can be an opportunity for gaining new benefits. But the potential value that can come from the extension of maritime jurisdictions — whether from specific actions or from comprehensive programs — should not be overstated. Historically, many countries have hardly used their 3-nautical mile (nmi) or 12-nmi territorial seas. It cannot be expected that they would suddenly find the capacity and will to make full use of new, larger offshore jurisdictions. Some of the fisheries resources that now fall under national jurisdictions had been fully accessible to, but unused by, coastal nations under the regime of the high seas. It has not been so much a matter of legal jurisdiction over resources as it has been questions of capital, entrepreneurship, infrastructure, and access to markets that have impeded the exploitation of ocean resources. Thus, the new jurisdictions may solve some problems, but they will raise others. Policymakers should be wary of overly optimistic suggestions that the new legal control over ocean resources might yield substantial benefits overnight.

The importance of the extension of maritime jurisdictions cannot be assessed simply in terms of the cash value of the resources gained. The major value is the opportunity to reexamine national arrangements for the management of all offshore resources. The extension of jurisdictions creates the occasion for putting the governance of these resources in order, in response to some overriding vision of how and why national resources ought to be used. For example, in some cases it may be wise to reconsider the strong export orientation of fishing industries in relation to widespread chronic undernutrition within a nation. In Malaysia, the Philippines, and Thailand, seafood exports have expanded sharply while at the same time local consumption of this major protein source has declined. It may be useful to broaden the range of functions to which resource management is addressed.

In contrast with land-based resources where they may be deeply vested interests, the recent acquisition of management responsibility over ocean resources provides a virtually unencumbered opportunity for reconsidering the principles under which resources should be managed. Many issues need to be addressed. The courses of action that are finally chosen could be minimal, responding to immediate symptoms — this oil spill, that failed fishery — or they could respond more deeply, addressing the underlying dynamics that cause oil to spill or fisheries to fail, and looking toward the more distant future as well as the immediate present.

National management policies will also both influence and be influenced by maritime powers from outside the region and by nations with adjacent jurisdictional zones. Maritime powers may choose to exploit policy diversities by shifting activities (e.g., shipping of oil, fishing) toward areas of least resistance. Regardless of national agreement with international treaties, legal precedents, and provisions of the CLS, there will remain problems of national and regional implementation of management designs. These and related policy problems will dominate marine affairs in the region during the rest of this century. Thus marine policy in the Southeast Asian seas will be motivated by the exigencies of both national development and international relations. Policies will be largely unilateral, occasionally bilateral where necessitated by the CLS and practicalities, and rarely, multilateral.

PROBLEMS

In the Southeast Asian seas, where all of the coastal nations except China have already extended their maritime jurisdictions, many maritime boundaries have yet to be agreed. The difficulty in resolving these boundaries varies with political, geographic, and economic circumstances, but most important are the nature of political relations between the states concerned and the presence of and disputes over offshore islands. Other factors include domestic problems, questionable baselines, historical attitudes, desire to continue previous boundaries, geographic disadvantage, the nature of the seabed, disparity in wealth, and high or unknown economic potential. States may continue to defend unilateral claims or they may agree on a boundary or multiple boundaries or on joint zones. In particularly difficult areas, they may reach understandings about rules that mitigate the effect of a boundary on a particular activity.

Some maritime areas claimed by more than one country have oil and gas potential. One way to avoid potential disputes in such areas involves agreement on the extent of the controversial area, setting aside the boundary question, and joint jurisdiction, exploration, and development of hydrocarbons in the area of overlap. Factors influencing the choice of this response include the number of claimants and the character of their basic relations, preoccupation elsewhere, military capability and inclination, the need for oil from the area, and the degree of knowledge of deposits in the area. The more these factors reinforce each other negatively, the greater the likelihood of unilateral action, a frequent occurrence in the region. The strongest reason for a nation's opting for a joint undertaking would be its sense of urgency or obligation to protect its interests in potential oil and gas deposits combined with a desire to maintain good relations with another state with an equally valid claim to the area.

The extension of jurisdictions also creates or exacerbates transnational fisheries issues. Multinational fishing in disputed areas may bring conflict with political implications. Nations will have to work out access rights for foreign fishing vessels, especially those from nations that claim adverse geographic characteristics or that now are located within archipelagic waters or exclusive economic zones (EEZs) of other nations. Although joint ventures may seem the most appealing solution to access problems, for nearshore operations inappropriate fishing boats and methods and high fuel costs for offshore operations make this response unlikely. With the enlargement of jurisdictional areas, national responsibilities for management of fisheries resources have also increased and taken on transnational components. Areas important for fisheries development need protection from pollution. Management of shared and migratory stocks, spanning the jurisdictions of several countries, requires transnational cooperation.

The likely initial response to such issues is unilateral action based on industry preferences or on broader country priorities as exemplified by development of small-scale fisheries and trawling bans for social reasons. Harmonization of the laws of two or more nations so that they are similar, complementary, or coordinated is an intermediate response between unilateral approaches and the bi- and multilateral approaches necessary to address the transnational component of fishery issues.

The protection of the marine environment is important for supporting primary uses of the oceans such as fishing, but it should also be seen as being of great value in itself. Major pollutants are oil discharged and spilled from ships and offshore platforms, and silt and human wastes discharged from land. The major resource depletion issues result from destructive fishing, overharvesting, species elimination, mangrove removal, and coral reef destruction. Pollution regulation efforts are a response to the increasingly serious problems in the offshore waters of Southeast Asia. Although national regulations generally are technically sound, their implementation has been disappointing.

With extended jurisdictions, transnational marine pollution and its control have also taken on new emphasis and meaning. A network of reserves in the region could be based on common criteria, transfrontier cooperation in vulnerable areas, and sharing of major marine ecotype reserves, and implemented by a regional task force.

Beyond the separate national problems, there are issues in pollution control of transnational importance. They include standardization of regulations, and the possible foreign exploitation of low standards, dual standards, designation of specially protected areas, pollution control in disputed waters, sea-lane siting, and dealing with hazardous cargoes. A regional convention on the marine environment could unify policies and procedures.

Enforcement of national policies and regulations in the extended jurisdictional zones is the key to national management control of the resources they may contain. Smuggling and piracy remain a virulent activity in the region. Policy issues requiring national decisions include choosing between a separate enforcement organization or assigning the enforcement mission to the coast guard or navy. Regional surveillance and enforcement or harmonization of enforcement policies might be considered.

Marine transport and trade continue to be significant in and through this "mediterranean" between the Indian and Pacific oceans. Policy issues requiring national attention include the model for state-shipping development; implementation (or not) of the various United Nations Conference on Trade and Development (UNCTAD) resolutions relating to the 40–40–20 Liner Code and its application to bulk cargo; the phasing out of flag-of-convenience membership in shipping conferences; and the improvement of safety standards, crew training, and rescue response in light of high-technology accidents. A regional approach could involve an ASEAN shipping line designed to serve the intra-ASEAN routes.

National defense, unilaterally and through various alliances, will continue to be the prime policy concern in Southeast Asian seas. Major decisions are needed on the type and size of navies and their functions. Such decisions in turn depend on conclusions on the degree of threat from whom, the financial resources required versus those available, and the dependability and capability of allies.

Each nation has priorities that will receive immediate national attention; national policies and any attempt at cooperation alike must accommodate these priorities. Brunei, for example, will seek to develop its offshore oil resources and to protect them and related installations from foe and friend alike. Burma, likewise, primarily seeks development of its offshore hydrocarbons. Indonesia must combine defense concerns with offshore oil and gas development in the Natuna area. More general defense concerns for Indonesia include internal security throughout the archipelago and involvement in East–West tensions through its role of maintaining and defending vital sea-lanes.

Kampuchea remains occupied with internal development problems, but keeping its sole port of Kampong Som unencumbered is a persistent national concern. Laos will continue to be concerned with free access to the sea. Malaysia has several defense concerns. It is involved in East-West tensions regarding passage in and security of the Strait of Malacca, and it now also may have to protect its claim in the southern Spratlys, particularly against Vietnam, as well as its offshore oil installations. The concern with unrestricted access between west and east Malaysia has receded for the time being. The Philippines may have to defend its claims in the Spratlys, particularly vis-à-vis Vietnam, and is continuing its desperate offshore search for oil and gas. Singapore is involved in Western security strategies for protecting the Malacca and Singapore straits partly because of its prime economic interest in keeping the straits open.

In addition to a continuing concern with supplies to insurgents, Thailand may have to defend itself at sea against Vietnam; it also must protect and develop its offshore gas resources in the Gulf of Thailand. Vietnam is nearly in a state of war with most of its neighbors, particularly China, and defense against attack, especially in the Gulf of Tonkin, is the prime concern. Development of offshore hydrocarbons is also important to Vietnam.

PROSPECTS FOR COOPERATION

Although national development and unilateral action will remain dominant marine policy themes in the region, cooperation remains a possible policy response for selected issues and countries. Just as the extension of jurisdiction creates an opportunity for the reexamination of all of national ocean management, it also creates an occasion for reexamining a nation's relationships with its neighbors, and an opportunity to move toward a more ideal structure of international relations.

Extended national jurisdiction does not alter the facts that (1) many marine resources are transnational in distribution; (2) the ocean, as a continuous, fluid system, transmits environmental pollutants and impacts; and (3) many maritime activities transcend the new national marine jurisdictional boundaries. There may be insufficient understanding and consideration of the transnational and interdependent character of the ocean environment and the resources and activities that it harbors and supports.

The need is apparent for increased bilateral and multilateral consultations as well as for a new degree of coordination to meet the challenge of changes in marine use patterns and concepts.[1] Indeed, "the extension of national jurisdictions, by a curious dialectical process, increases the need for international cooperation; witness the South China Sea. . . . What had been left unmanaged in the past must now be managed, and purely national management is in many cases frustrated by the overlapping of political and ecological boundaries and by the high costs of exploitative and managerial technologies and infrastructures, which are beyond the means of most small, poor, newly independent countries. These factors should encourage regional cooperation and the development of a new international economic order in the oceans based on that cooperation. . . ."[2]

For any cooperative scheme to enjoy full participation, no participating entity can perceive that it will be more disadvantaged by the application of the scheme than through alternative action or arrangements, including nonparticipation. Categories of benefits (advantages) and costs (disadvantages) are both sociopolitical and economic; time scales are both short and long term. Each entity must decide under what type of arrangement the net benefit would be highest for itself. Some significant categories of political and economic advantages and disadvantages of cooperation in marine issues in Southeast Asian seas are listed in Table 11.1.

Because of the bias for maintaining national control, nations generally shun regional cooperation unless it can be demonstrated that very substantial benefits would likely result from cooperative efforts. For advocates of cooperation, then, one major task is to undertake serious analyses of where cooperation is most likely to be fruitful and to show just how fruitful it is likely to be.[3]

Cooperation can be promoted by showing that the benefits would be substantial and also by showing that the costs and risks of cooperation can be limited. So long as regional cooperation is taken to mean entanglement in some large-scale regional organization, generally of someone else's creation, then nations are likely to assume that regional cooperation is going to be costly and risky. It may be possible, however, to cultivate other means of cooperation that are less onerous.

Several different approaches to regional cooperation can be distinguished: joint activities, regional organizations, treaty arrangements, harmonization of laws and policies, and informal contacts. The most demanding of these approaches is joint activities involving sustained close interaction in specific enterprises or projects such as joint scientific research programs, joint ventures in fisheries, or joint hydrocarbon development.

Participation in regional organizations can range from symbolic to substantial. Where the organization undertakes extensive activities, possibly including management functions, participation can become costly, particularly for developing countries.

Treaties generally are arranged following difficult negotiations relating to specific problems. They result in firm obligations that are not readily adapted to changing circumstances.

Harmonization may be defined as the deliberate alignment of the laws and policies of different nations for the purpose of fulfilling their national interests. In shipping, fishing, and most other sectors, there are likely to be modest adjustments in national laws and policies that would yield significant benefits to all concerned.

Table 11.1 Possible Advantages and Disadvantages of Economic and Political Cooperation in the Marine Arena by Southeast Asian Nations

Advantages	*Disadvantages*
Money saved from economy of scale	Allocation of resources to extranational projects
Contributions of extranational resources	Loss of potential benefit of unilateral approach
Increased amount and efficiency of use of external technical or financial aid	Decreased national share of technical or financial aid
Increased rate of resource development and technology transfer	
Increased efficiency of resource use	Administrative or loss-of-efficiency cost
Better information exchange and better management	Yield of competitive advantage in scientific/technical knowledge
Less strict national enforcement required	Loss of degree of control over decision making
Opportunity for bargaining for national marine interest	
Enhanced power vis-à-vis extraregional interests	Reduction of strong relationships with extraregional nations; possible collective tension with extraregional nations
Enhanced international and regional power and status of leader(s)	Yield of sovereignty to regional group or leader(s)
Strengthening of trends toward regional cooperation in other arenas and the ultimate goal of Zone of Peace, Freedom, and Neutrality	Compromise of other policy or commitments vis-à-vis intra- or extraregional entities

Harmonization is likely to be less demanding than the other more obvious instruments of international cooperation.

Informal contact is the least costly and the least risky method of undertaking regional cooperation, and it does not get the recognition it deserves. With informal communication it may be possible from time to time to find fruitful arenas for cooperation on a modest scale.

For most transnational marine issues in Southeast Asia, informal contacts and bilateral treaty agreements are likely to be the favored approaches to cooperation. A carefully constructed web of similar bilateral agreements could eventually form the basis for multilateral negotiations and adjustments toward common policies on a regional basis. For example, a Southeast Asian nation such as Indonesia, which shares marine borders with several other countries, could take the lead in establishing bilateral agreements on EEZ jurisdictional content as it has done with its neighbors for its continental shelf boundaries. In this way it might eventually lead its neighbors to coordinate the contents of their EEZ regimes. Coordination of policies, jurisdictional content, and enforcement procedures would facilitate formal cooperation. Specific national marine policies could be coordinated to the extent that they would not impinge on national sovereignty.[4]

Two extreme types of circumstances might short-circuit this adaptive process. Marine cooperation could be undertaken on issues that are relatively unimportant and do not impinge on national sovereignty, or at the other extreme, cooperation could be undertaken where there is a clear and urgent need. The first category might include information exchange on fisheries (including biological information and possibly information on various types of cooperative ventures), on hydrocarbons, and on environmental quality and techniques of monitoring, prevention, and control.

Several issues involving political concerns extending beyond the region might create a common sense of urgency sufficient to motivate regional or ASEAN action. For the region's coastal states, the concept of a Zone of Peace, Freedom, and Neutrality (ZOPFAN) might eventually lead to the (perhaps unenforceable) denial of rights of passage of all foreign warships in the South China Sea. Other such issues include common standards for transportation of potential pollutants through the region. There might be dual standards, that is, stricter standards for vessels passing through the region than traffic within the region of coastal state lines. The transfer of marine technology from developed to developing nations might be pursued through the establishment of regional marine scientific and technological research centers of the sort called for in the CLS.

AREAS OF POTENTIAL COOPERATION

Defense

Since maritime defense is a high priority of Southeast Asian nations, this is one possible focus for marine cooperation. Indeed cooperation on general defense matters is ongoing in ASEAN and probably within the Indochina bloc as well. Thailand and Malaysia have signed the first bilateral defense pact in Southeast Asia since the end of the Indochina war, and a recent Thai–Philippine agreement calls for cooperation on security matters, apparently in response to growing Communist-aided insurgencies. Also, Indonesia has conducted joint air, naval, and army maneuvers with Malaysia and joint naval surveillance in border waters with the Philippines. Malaysia, Singapore, Australia, New Zealand, and the United Kingdom have recently concluded naval and amphibious exercises in the Spratly area under the Five Power Defense Pact.

Both the ASEAN nations and the Indochinese states fear Chinese military domination of Southeast Asia, and Chinese long-standing claims to ownership of all of the islands in the South China Sea give credence to the belief that China is a great threat to Southeast Asian security. Ownership of the islands would justify Chinese claims to extensive marine resources, including fisheries and offshore oil. If China were to vigorously press its claims, a major regional maritime defense issue would be brought to the fore.

Nations of the region with considerable commonality of interests need to decide on the degree to which they should act in concert against perceived common threats, as well as their relationship to outside powers. The interest of outside powers in unimpeded transit in general or for specific vessel types in specific waters (such as warships in straits) may unify outside maritime power approaches to the region. Should outside powers—particularly the United States and the Soviet Union—be welcomed as allies or shunned as the chief contributors to instability? The ZOPFAN concept will probably be reevaluated and redefined frequently because the United States and the USSR have security interests in the region and as global powers their presence is perhaps inevitable. However, ZOPFAN may be realized only if sufficient military power, including naval force, is maintained to provide for a degree of regional security without help from outside powers.

Surveillance and Enforcement

Since surveillance and enforcement of marine policies and regulations require extensive ship and aircraft resources and could be costly, pooling resources might be advantageous. Thus, a regional enforcement scheme might be advantageous in the semi-enclosed South China Sea. At the same time, however, there are a number of reasons why it might not be feasible, at least for the entire region. Nations bordering the sea have very different interests in enforcement; for example, Singapore with its minuscule EEZ and the Philippines with its very large one do not have the same problems or incentives. Within ASEAN the surveillance and enforcement activities of Malaysia, Indonesia, and the Philippines are often directed at Thai and Singapore fishing vessels. ASEAN and Vietnam and Kampuchea are at loggerheads, and the latter two have been involved in enforcement activities against Thai fishermen. There are several maritime territorial disputes in the region that would make joint enforcement extremely difficult since it would be unclear who was entitled to be in the disputed region and who had sovereignty over the resources. Finally, China would be unlikely to participate since the Chinese do not recognize others' claims in the South China Sea.

If cooperative enforcement is not presently feasible for the entire South China Sea, it may nevertheless be an idea worth exploring for some of the smaller bodies of water in the Southeast Asian region or along common maritime borders of friendly nations. The Gulf of Tonkin and the Gulf of Thailand do not seem to be real possibilities due to overlapping claims by unfriendly nations in both. In the straits of Malacca and Singapore, however, Indonesia, Malaysia, and Singapore already have a cooperative agreement concerning the regulation of navigation that includes a traffic separation scheme and a minimum underkeel clearance for transiting ships. The rules, which are recognized by the Intergovernmental Maritime Organization (IMO) and the shipping community at large, may need to be enforced and joint enforcement by the coastal states is a possibility.

Joint enforcement might be possible in the Andaman Sea if Burma and Thailand could agree on some formula for allowing Thailand access to the resources of the Burmese EEZ. India might need to be a party to any regional enforcement plan since the Andaman and Nicobar islands are Indian territory. Other possible areas for cooperative enforcement are the Arafura and Timor seas involving Australia, Indonesia, and Papua New Guinea, and the Celebes Sea involving Indonesia, Malaysia, and the Philippines.

If joint enforcement efforts are too much to expect in view of the many important differences among the Southeast Asian states, nations in the region might harmonize their enforcement policies. Harmonization would not imply the sacrifice of any sovereignty over areas in dispute. If some Southeast Asian coastal states were to agree to standard legal and judicial procedures, including levels of permissible punishment in the event of convictions, an important start would have been made toward minimizing conflict. Harmonization efforts could also extend to procedures for detecting and enforcing punishment for violations of environmental regulations and to programs for conservation of living and nonliving resources. If all Southeast Asian states implemented the pertinent articles of the CLS, particularly Article 73 (which concerns enforcement procedures and permissible punishments), this might open the way for additional agreements on other issues such as shared fish stocks, waste disposal rules, and navigation regulations designed to protect the marine environment by reducing the possibility of collisions and groundings.

Hydrocarbons

Since oil and gas discovery and development is a common high priority among the Southeast Asian nations, overlapping claims provide an opportunity for the setting aside of the actual boundary question and provision for joint exploration and exploitation of hydrocarbons in an agreed area of overlap. The Thai–Malaysia joint development agreement is the prime example in Southeast Asia.

In the eastern Gulf of Thailand, joint development might be feasible between Vietnam and Kampuchea. Indeed, the two nations have already established joint historical, internal waters over the Panjang Basin and have agreed to develop natural resources there by "common agreement." Joint arrangements between Vietnam and Thailand and Vietnam and Indonesia might eventually be possible, but there may be formidable difficulties in finding purchasers of long-term supply contracts. Perhaps the best candidate areas for joint development would be portions of the Spratly area or the Indonesian–Australian shelf. If Vietnam and Taiwan were somehow excluded from the Spratly issue, China, the Philippines, and Malaysia could undertake joint exploration there, perhaps in parts farthest from Vietnamese-claimed islands.

Fisheries

The major areas of possible regional cooperation in fisheries are information exchange, research and training, access arrangements, surveillance and enforcement, conservation, production, processing, and marketing.[5] Major advantages and disadvantages of cooperation in these areas are outlined in Table 11.2.

The major appeals of information exchange programs are that they tend to be relatively inexpensive, they do not involve large risks, and they help to build better relationships. Often, however, there is inadequate appreciation of the value of information, so that its producer or supplier is not adequately compensated. Moreover, it can be difficult to create programs that provide information exactly when and where it is needed, and much information is viewed as being proprietary in nature, not to be shared with a potential competitor.

The extension of jurisdictions naturally leads to consideration of licensing or "fee fishing"—access arrangements—since previously accessible waters are no longer open. One form of access arrangements is the single merged zone, with a single license providing equal access to all waters of the region. Alternatively, there could be coordinated licensing arrangements in which fishing vessels could move with relative ease from one nation's jurisdiction to another. Or transiting arrangements could be liberal, with fees and royalties paid to the nation in whose jurisdiction fishing was undertaken. The nations of Southeast Asia have shown little receptivity to simple licensing arrangements, however, or to access by other Southeast Asian nations, preferring to engage in joint venture operations with outside nations. At the same time, nations from outside the region have not shown great interest in obtaining licenses to fish in Southeast Asian waters.

The more ambitious ideas for regional cooperation in fisheries surveillance and enforcement contemplate jointly operated, high-technology schemes such as satellite or high-altitude aircraft systems, possibly together with a joint coast guard.[6,7] More modest proposals suggest the exchange of specific information such as vessel movements or simply information on methods and techniques. In the South Pacific, vessels convicted of poaching in the fishing zone of any member of the Forum Fisheries Agency may be deprived of access to the waters of any other member nation. Members have also agreed to a vessel registration system in which only vessels registered with the Forum Fisheries Agency are allowed to fish for tuna in any member's EEZ.

The major advantage of regional cooperation in fisheries surveillance and enforcement is that it can provide some economies of scale, not only with hardware and other capital costs but also with respect to operations. It can also provide spin-off benefits into other sectors by helping in pollution monitoring, for example, or enhancing regional security. A significant disadvantage of regional cooperation is that nations may not want to depend on one another for any aspect of their security, especially when cooperation might require opening one's own system to observation by outsiders. Southeast Asian nations have substantially different legal systems and political cultures, so cooperation might be quite difficult technically.

Table 11.2   Arenas of Possible Cooperation in Southeast Asian Fisheries

Type of Cooperation	Advantages	Disadvantages
Information exchange, research, and training	Light involvement Inexpensive Virtually risk-free Can minimize wasteful competition Strengthens international relations	Modest benefits Can help competitors
Access arrangements	Yields substantial revenue Helps in stock assessment Can provide technology transfer Can provide political leverage Makes fuller use of resources Relatively light involvement	Can deprive national fishermen May impede national fisheries development Raises security and enforcement problems Risks overfishing No local employment generated
Surveillance and enforcement	Economies of scale Can strengthen regional security Can reduce conflict Can be linked with other monitoring and security operations	May require exposing national security systems Legal systems differ Costly Limited benefits Possibly difficult coordination
Conservation	Fuller use of resources in long term	Little short-term benefit
Production	Increased benefits Risks may be shared	Requires intense involvement Requires substantial capital Possibly high risks
Processing	Substantial benefits Risks may be shared	Possibly high risks Requires substantial capital Requires intense involvement
Marketing	Can yield substantial benefits Limited risks	Can help competitors

Regional cooperation for the conservation of fisheries resources is most plausible for shared and migratory stocks. Article 63 of the CLS deals with stocks that "occur within the exclusive economic zones of two or more coastal States." In such cases the concerned states are called upon to "agree upon the measures necessary to coordinate and ensure the conservation and development of such stocks..." whether directly or through appropriate subregional or regional organizations. Arrangements for fishing these stocks may need to be worked out among the concerned states.

Article 64 of the CLS calls upon those who fish in the region for highly migratory species such as tuna to "cooperate directly or through appropriate international organizations with a view to ensuring conservation and promoting the objective of optimum utilization of such species throughout the region, both within and beyond the exclusive economic zone." Yet fishing efforts off the shores of one nation on the migratory route may damage prospects for fishing by other nations on that route. Some waters of the region are particularly important as spawning grounds for tuna, but because of the migration patterns, a nation protecting such spawning grounds might not benefit from that effort. Another issue is that juvenile tunas are being taken in some areas, either because they migrate out of national waters before they mature or because catching gears are not sufficiently selective.

Joint fisheries production might be considered for shared or migratory stocks. A single corporate structure could manage particular fisheries, with the corporation under the joint control of representatives of several nations, perhaps operating a single regional fleet of fishing vessels.[8] At the first sectoral meeting of the ASEAN–Chamber of Commerce and Industry/Working Group on Forestry and Fisheries (CCI-WGFAF) in 1983 a proposal was made for an ASEAN Fisheries Corporation that would function as a holding company to monitor and manage the investment, manufacturing, and trading activities of five national subsidiaries, one in each member nation.[9] Some fundamental conditions for joint fishing development in the region already exist, including similar development concerns, shared resources and common management responsibilities, distinct fishing skills and experiences that may be exchanged to mutual advantage, developed inshore facilities within easy reach of major shared stocks, and a mass base of low-cost fishing labor in the coastal villages.

Politically, ventures between countries in Southeast Asia could be concrete manifestations of cooperation and unity, particularly in subregional organizations like ASEAN. They could provide cooperating nations with greater leverage for marketing, acquisition of capital, and seeking external development assistance, and they could lead to other forms of cooperation on marine matters such as trade, research, training, and enforcement and surveillance. One major result could be a fuller knowledge of the resource. The direct involvement of citizens, companies, and governments of participating nations in such projects should promote greater compliance with their respective regulations. Compared with the cost of operating distant-water fleets, an indigenous base results in savings in fuel and operating costs. Economies of scale are also achievable in on-board handling and preservation. Joint ventures can eliminate or reduce the motivations for poaching. Funding institutions and regional development and management organizations can more rationally allocate their funds and efforts when assistance is directed at common marine resources since duplication of aid on a per-country basis is avoided.

A major constraint to the creation of joint ventures between nations of Southeast Asia is the common lack of capital and the need for extraregional markets for the products of the venture. But these could be supplied by a third party, at least initially. This party need not be a principal to the venture if compensation could be worked out as a direct business payment or a nonfishery-related trade-off or if the third party were a development institution such as the Asian Development Bank (ADB) or the World Bank. Or, bilateral aid may be sought in the form of credits and grants. Equipment and vessels might be provided by nations that have them in excess as a result of the loss of access to fishing grounds because of the extension of jurisdictions of other nations. Marketing contracts may be explored with nations that would import the product, even if they were not directly involved in its production.

The traditional extraregional partners such as Japan might withhold support or assistance in any or all stages of the venture, however, particularly in marketing and financing of infrastructure. Participation by extraregional nations like Japan might be sought, and its response might be determined by the economics of its new role as well as by the extent to which it was assured of its fish supply.

It also may be possible to undertake cooperative efforts in processing or marketing or some integrated combination of production, processing, and marketing. In Southeast Asia, regional joint ventures in processing might be considered for foreign markets (e.g., tuna canning), for import substitution in regional markets (e.g., to replace canned mackerel presently imported from Japan), or for specialty products for local markets (e.g., fish pastes or snacks). Port infrastructure might be created on a regional basis and accommodate several enterprises of each member nation.

Southeast Asia has already accumulated good experience with one special form of joint venture in its industrial complementation schemes.[10] Comparable arrangements might be considered in fisheries. A major constraint is that most nations inherently resist cooperative commercial ventures, preferring instead to undertake activities fully under national control. Another difficulty is that new commercial ventures might displace operations that previously functioned illegally or informally. Despite the lack of sanctions, those operations may serve national interests.

The nations of Southeast Asia also could work together to increase trade in fishery products among themselves and with nations outside the region. For example, it might be possible to create a regional marketing board that would actively promote legal barter trade, with a central agency to serve as a clearinghouse.[11] The tariff and nontariff barriers to trade in fisheries products among the nations of Southeast Asia might be studied with a view to lowering such barriers, or establishing preference schemes among them. Just as several independent production and processing operations could share a common port area, several independent marketing enterprises could share a common marketplace for wholesaling and retailing, or both.

The major advantage of increasing trade with nations outside the region would be increased foreign exchange earnings. The major advantage of increased in-traregional trade would be promotion of intraregional self-reliance and food secu-rity, thus decreasing dependence on and subordination of local interests to outside forces. Southeast Asian nations' interest in increased intraregional trade or coop-eration in extraregional marketing of exports is likely to be low, however, because their fish exports are similar.

Other Possibilities

Other opportunities for cooperation have been discussed previously in this vol-ume. In marine conservation lie possibilities of joint development of a network of reserves and common criteria for their designation. Transfrontier cooperation could involve shared marine reserves, a regional task force on marine conserva-tion, and possibly harmonization of laws and regulations.

For prevention and management of marine pollution, opportunities for cooper-ation include standardization of regulations, designation of specially protected ar-eas and of sea-lanes and tanker hospitals for potentially polluting vessels, contin-gency arrangements for dealing with emergencies, and formulation of a new, region-specific convention for the protection of the marine environment. In ship-ping, services might be strengthened through bilateral agreements or through the creation of an ASEAN shipping line designed to serve the intra-ASEAN routes.

Dispute management is a marine policy issue in which nations outside the South-east Asian region also have great interest. Mechanisms for dispute avoidance or settlement, so vital for the orderly implementation of the new ocean regime, may be regionalized or subregionalized to conform to regional or local cultural sys-tems. The ASEAN Treaty of Amity and Cooperation in Southeast Asia of 24 Feb-ruary 1976 provides that the contracting parties will be guided by the principle of settlement of differences or disputes by peaceful means and thus may serve as a foundation for settlement of subregional marine disputes.

The Malacca and Singapore Straits

The Malacca and Singapore straits are a microcosm of the coastal activities and conflicts of the region. With the narrowness of the straits and the transnationality of the ecosystems, resources, and activities, effective management strategies de-pend upon the close cooperation of the three littoral nations plus that of extrare-gional users. But these nations have different perspectives, policies, and legal sys-tems. To illustrate the institutional possibilities for cooperation, let us consider a hypothetical regional organization designed to manage activities in the Malacca and Singapore straits. The management system might use existing organizations or establish a new regional organization, perhaps a joint commission or joint au-thority. Each possible system has advantages and disadvantages.[12]

Several existing organizations could be involved in the management of the straits. ASEAN has committees on Trade and Communication (COTAC), Science and Technology (COST), Food, Agriculture, and Forestry (COFAF), and Industry,

Minerals and Energy (COIME). Under COTAC there is the Expert Group on Marine Pollution; under COST there is the Expert Group on the Environment; under COFAF there is the Expert Group on Fisheries; and under COIME there is the ASEAN Council on Petroleum. All of these bodies could include an element of the management of the straits in their deliberations and activities. These committees and groups are already formally established, recognized, and supported politically and financially by the ASEAN member countries. They have an administrative structure, experience, and a system of international communication. Their use for managing the straits could avoid the stress of creating a new organization with its delicate allocation of management responsibility.

These committees and groups are not integrated, however, and they have authority only to recommend action to the national governments. Their terms of reference and members include all of ASEAN, and thus straits matters would have to compete with other regional matters for attention and resources. Further, under the ASEAN style there is no international technical support for these bodies, which are mostly composed of politicians or administrators.

Other relevant existing organizations are the Council on Safety of Navigation and Control of Marine Pollution in the straits of Malacca and Singapore, formed in 1971, and the Tripartite Committee. The Tripartite Committee has been used successfully in the past by the three nations to negotiate with Japan on straits safety and to provide technical support for these negotiations. These organizations have been relatively inactive but could be reactivated. They do exist, and unlike the ASEAN bodies, they focus specifically on the straits and involve only the three littoral countries. They deal only with tanker shipping, however, and were formed initially with a political objective in mind and not specifically to manage the environment of the straits.

A new regional organization could be created to manage all the major activities in and affecting the straits, and it could be structured in a way similar to United Nations (UN) specialized agencies, that is, it could have a governing council of policymakers and a secretariat for technical support. The secretariat might be divided sectorally into shipping (which might include the existing Council and the Tripartite Committee), fisheries, nonliving resources, environment, and security. The organization would centralize policy and provide some stability and predictability to management of use of the straits. It also could have linkages with other international organizations. But its recommendations — UN style — would not be binding on its members, and individual government approval would be necessary for policies affecting them. The issue of allocation of contributions could be difficult to resolve.

Alternatively, a joint commission could be modeled after the regional fisheries councils in the United States. It could be given a legal mandate by the three governments to do research and recommend actions in a way that would make it more independent than most regional organizations. It could have its own arbitration machinery to settle differences, and it could include representatives of the general citizenry and industry as well as government. Technical support could be ad hoc. The individual governments would set the agenda for the body. However, governments might be reluctant to surrender their control over the formulation of policy recommendations affecting their interests.

The most idealistic option for a management body would be a joint authority modeled after the existing Thai–Malaysia Joint Development Authority. It could have a ministerial-rank, intergovernmental, policymaking assembly and an executive branch with separate organs devoted to environment, shipping, fisheries, non-living resources, and security. The decisions or findings of the assembly could be binding upon the member governments.

How would a joint authority work in practice? Development of hydrocarbon resources in the straits could interfere with uses such as fisheries and shipping. Such development eventually may either be constrained by the protests of neighbors or engender use and user conflict, thus reducing the total benefits available to all three states. Under the joint authority, the country with jurisdiction over the hydrocarbon resources would pay the authority to manage the development, thus minimizing conflict. Of course, for this system to work governments would have to yield management control over activities in the straits. Also, the authority, if operating without checks and balances, could become very powerful. Certainly its start-up would take enormous political will and advance subsidies. However, the governments would draw both the short-term and long-term extra revenues and other benefits that would accrue through orderly development and conflict management and would not have the responsibility of direct management. Further, since the authority would combine the political power of three nations, it would be a formidable negotiator with extraregional straits users.

CONSTRAINTS TO COOPERATION

Numerous constraints must be overcome to move toward increased cooperation on marine issues in Southeast Asia.[13] In the wake of the successful Indochinese revolution, the United States, the Soviet Union, and China are vying for areas of influence within the region, thus fostering instability. The political entities surrounding the South China Sea are extremely diverse: the capitalist, Western-oriented ASEAN bloc composing the eastern and southern rim — Indonesia, Malaysia, the Philippines, Singapore, Thailand, and Brunei; the Indochinese states on the northwestern rim — Kampuchea, Laos, and Vietnam — which are under Soviet influence; the politically isolated Chinese province of Taiwan; China, which constitutes the entire northern rim of the sea; the British colony of Hong Kong; and the Portuguese colony of Macao. Burma, outside the South China Sea, is formally neutral.

With the exception of Thailand, all nations in and around the region have achieved independence or have experienced society-transforming movements within the past quarter-century. Many are still struggling with the basic problems of nationhood, thus bringing a nationalistic fervor into regional affairs. Within ASEAN itself, relations are cordial but competitive and perhaps unstable in the long term. The ASEAN nations produce many of the same raw materials, and the resulting direct competition for credit, investment markets, and development assistance may increase with advancing economic development. Southeast Asian nations only now are beginning to perceive clearly their own national marine interests and how these differ from those of neighboring states or outside maritime powers. At this juncture, commonalities are neglected and differences tend to be emphasized. The maintenance of newly acquired national sovereignty over ocean resources and jurisdiction over ocean space has underlying national security connotations, and any proposed coordination or cooperation might be perceived as jeopardizing this basic principle.

With the extension of maritime jurisdiction by the Southeast Asian littoral nations, geography dictates that there will be inequities and imbalances in marine endowments imposed upon an already economically and politically competitive milieu. The marine area and attendant resource base of Singapore, Kampuchea, Laos, and Brunei are negligible compared with the great gains of Indonesia, the Philippines, and Vietnam. Thailand has lost access to important fishery resources. This redistribution of area and potential wealth could endanger ASEAN's progress in cooperation in other arenas. The windfall increases in area and resources for Vietnam and Indonesia open the possibility for competition and conflict between these new marine neighbors. Settlement or the setting aside of jurisdictional boundaries may be a prerequisite for cooperation on other issues.

At present, regional cooperation in marine issues is incipient at best. Perhaps necessity will be the mother of cooperation. It may be premature to hope for extensive cooperation in a region composed of increasingly nationalistic developing states, some ravaged by conflicts instigated and supported by extraregional powers. There are severe political constraints that limit the possibilities for cooperation with regard to marine issues, but political relationships do change over time. The underlying economic potential of the marine resources of the region remain as a more or less constant part of the background, part of the geography of the region. Under changed political conditions an increasing share of this potential might become available to be tapped. Clear analysis of those possibilities may help to motivate and to accelerate the improvement of political relationships throughout the Southeast Asian region.

The CLS calls upon states bordering enclosed or semi-enclosed seas to cooperate with each other in the exercise of their rights and duties. But which specific issues and which aspects of marine policy really can be effectively addressed by a regional approach? Should regional approaches be pursued for such things as management of migratory species, surveillance and enforcement, response to transnational oil spills, dispute settlement, access for scientific research, hazardous waste disposal, environmental regulations for transiting tankers, or regional preserves? What is the appropriate "region" for each of the opportunities for cooperation? What are the various national interests in these opportunities, and what are the likely advantages, disadvantages, and trade-offs for each nation and party involved in or affected by the coordination of particular marine policies? Which recurring issues might require a regional institutional approach? What might be expected of such institutions, and what would they look like? What would they cost, and who would or could pay? What are the possible roles of existing international organizations?[14] These and related questions will be increasingly relevant in national marine policymaking in the region in the years ahead.

NOTES

INTRODUCTION

1. D. W. Fryer, *Emerging Southeast Asia,* second edition (New York: John Wiley and Sons, 1979), 15–16.

2. Scottish Council, *Petroleum Economist* (February 1976):50.

3. *The Economist* (9 July 1983):38.

4. Joseph R. Morgan and Mark J. Valencia, eds., *Atlas for Marine Policy in Southeast Seas* (Berkeley: University of California Press, 1983), 56.

CHAPTER 1 THE MARINE GEOGRAPHY OF SOUTHEAST ASIA

1. Although the equator transects the southern portion of the region, the "thermal" or "climatological" equator lies some distance to the north, in consequence of the large proportion of the Earth's land area that lies within the northern hemisphere.

2. J. O. M. Brock, "Diversity and Unity in Southeast Asia," *Geographical Review* (1944):175–195, is a benchmark study. The theme also appears in the inscription on the Great Seal of the Indonesian Republic, *Bhirreka Tunggal Ika,* usually translated as "Unity in Diversity."

3. Indonesian and Philippine official statistics record nearly 14,000 and more than 7,000 islands, respectively.

4. R. W. Fairbridge, ed., *Encyclopedia of Oceanography* (New York: Reinhold, 1966), 324.

5. Active volcanism at present is confined to archipelagic Southeast Asia.

6. A. C. Hardy, *Seaways and Sea Trade* (London: Routledge, 1927), 41.

7. Except for Greenland. The Antarctic ice sheet also waxed and waned during the Pleistocene, expanding as the sea level fell and retreating as it rose, in phase with the northern ice sheets.

8. J. R. Morgan and M. J. Valencia, eds., *Atlas for Marine Policy in Southeast Asian Seas* (Berkeley: University of California Press, 1983), 6–7.

9. Ibid.

10. K. Wyrtki, *Physical Oceanography of the Southeast Asian Waters,* NAGA Report, vol. 2 (La Jolla: Scripps Institution of Oceanography, 1961), 13–14.

11. Ibid., 17.

12. Wyrtki, op. cit., uses this terminology, which avoids confusion since in Southeast Asia the distribution of land and sea results in wind direction that varies considerably over the region during both monsoons.

13. Wyrtki, op. cit., 17–28; *Defense Mapping Agency Sailing Directions (Planning Guide) for the Indian Ocean* (Washington, D.C.: DMA Hydrographic/Topographic Center, 1978), 152; and Morgan and Valencia, op. cit., 10–11.

14. Wyrtki, op. cit., 17.

15. Wyrtki, op. cit., 24.

16. Morgan and Valencia, op. cit., 14.

17. Wyrtki, op. cit., 139.

18. Wyrtki, op. cit., 143.

19. Morgan and Valencia, op. cit., 8.

20. Wyrtki, op. cit., 48.

21. Ibid., 155–163, contains a good description of tidal types in Southeast Asia. Tidal ranges were obtained from the *Appendix Atlas* to the *Defense Mapping Agency Sailing Directions (Planning Guide) for the Indian Ocean* (Washington, D.C.: DMA Hydrographic/Topographic Center, 1978), 152.

22. Morgan and Valencia, op. cit., 14–16; *Defense Mapping Agency Sailing Directions,* op. cit.

23. Morgan and Valencia, op. cit., 3.

24. Fairbridge, op. cit., 339–342.

25. G. Marten, Y. Matsuda, J. Bardach, S. Comitini, and S. Hardjolukito, *A Strategic Goal Analysis of Options for Tuna Longline Joint Ventures in Southeast Asia: An Indonesia-Japan Case Study,* Environment and Policy Institute Research Report No. 3 (Honolulu: East-West Center, 1981), 8.

CHAPTER 2   NATIONAL MARINE INTERESTS

1. See, for example, L. M. Alexander, "Indices of National Interest in the Oceans," *Ocean Development and International Law* 1 (1973); John King Gamble, Jr., *Global Marine Attributes* (Cambridge: Ballinger Publishing Co., 1974); John King Gamble, Jr., *Marine Policy: A Comparative Approach* (Lexington: Lexington Books, 1977); M. J. Valencia, "Southeast Asia: National Marine Interests and Marine Regionalism," *Ocean Development and International Law,* 5 (1978):421–476; Development Academy of the Philippines, *National Marine Interests: A Comparative Analysis of ASEAN States* (Manila: Exclusive Economic Zone Project, Ministry of Natural Resources, 1981).

2. J. C. Marr, *Fishery and Resource Management in Southeast Asia,* Paper no. 7 (Washington, D.C.: The Program of International Studies in Fishery Arrangements, Resources for the Future, 1976).

3. C. M. Siddayao, *The Offshore Petroleum Resources of Southeast Asia, Potential Conflict Situations and Related Economic Considerations* (Kuala Lumpur: Oxford University Press, 1978), 46.

4. "The First 21 Years Show Some Success," *Far Eastern Economic Review* (1 September 1978):51–52; "Intelligence: Brunei's Bargain Offer," *Far Eastern Economic Review* (11 March 1977):5.

5. Y. L. Lee, *Southeast Asia and the Law of the Sea: Some Preliminary Observations on the Political Geography of Southeast Asian Seas* (Singapore: Singapore University Press, 1978), 10.

6. "Navy Ordered to Contest Sea Claims of Over 12 Miles by Other Nations," *Baltimore Sun* (9 August 1979): 2; "Government Sails Different Courses on Offshore Limits," *Washington Post* (14 August 1979):17.

7. J. R. V. Prescott, *Asia's Maritime Boundary Problems,* Dyason House Papers 2 (March 1976), 1–4.

8. *Energy Asia* 1 (21 December 1979).

9. J. R. V. Prescott, Reader, Department of Geography, University of Melbourne, personal communication, 1982.

10. Y. L. Lee, "Offshore Boundary Disputes in Southeast Asia," *Journal of Southeast Asian Studies* X (1979):178.

11. Lee, loc. cit., note 5; Office of the Geographer, *States with Security Zones* (Washington, D.C.: Department of State of the United States of America, May 1978), Map no. 5037835-78; *States Requiring Prior Notification of Warships Entering Territorial Seas* (May 1978), Map no. 5037845-78.

12. Valencia, loc. cit.

13. R. R. Simmons, *The Pueblo, EC-121 and Mayaguez Incidents: Some Continuities and Changes,* Occasional Paper No. 8 (1978), Contemporary Asian Studies, School of Law, University of Maryland, 41; Office of the Geographer, States with Security Zones.

14. Siddayao, op. cit., 76–81; C. H. Park, "The South China Sea Disputes: Who Owns the Islands and the Natural Resources," *Ocean Development and International Law* 5 (1978):23–60.

15. "Khmers Reject Viet Isle Claims," *Honolulu Advertiser* (21 August 1978):C-1; L. Finely, "The Border Dispute on the Sea," *Southeast Asian Chronicle* (September–October 1978):39–40 plus errata; S. W. Rittenbush, "Marine Resources and the Potential for Conflict in the South China Sea," *The Fletcher Forum* 2 (January 1978):75–84; Prescott, loc. cit.

16. N. Chanda, "Laos Keeps Up a Cold Front," *Far Eastern Economic Review* (15 April 1977):15–18.

17. N. Chanda, "Lao-Thai Gulf is Still Wide," *Far Eastern Economic Review* (25 August 1977):46; Lee, op. cit., note 5, 18; D. A. Andelman, "Indochina is Adjusting to Peace," *New York Times* (19 December 1976):E-4.

18. G. Lauriat, "Costly Alternatives for Asia's Gas," *Far Eastern Economic Review* (1 September 1978):85–89; K. Das, "Reconciliation of Sorts," *Far Eastern Economic Review* (25 November 1977):12–13.

19. Foreign Broadcast Information Service.

20. *Far Eastern Economic Review* (6 April 1979).

21. D. W. Fryer, ed., *Emerging Southeast Asia* (New York: John Wiley and Sons, 1979), 6.

22. Zakaria Yatim, former Solicitor-General, Malaysia, personal communication, 1981.

23. P. Hassan, *Status of Environmental Protection Legislation in the ESCAP Region,* ESCAP/ UNEP Intergovernmental Meeting on Environmental Protection Legislation, 4–8 July 1978, Bangkok, Doc. No. IHT/IMEPL/2, 19 April 1978, 28.

24. P. Fish, "Drawing a Line 50 Years Long," *Far Eastern Economic Review* (9 March 1979):9; Ritterbush, op. cit., 81–82; Ritterbush, *Resources and Changing Perceptions of National Security in the Central and Western Pacific.* Paper prepared for the Conference on Security and Development in the Indo-Pacific Arena, International Security Studies Program, The Fletcher School of Law and Diplomacy, Tufts University, 24–26 April 1978, Map 1, 13.

25. K. Dalton, "Letter from Penang," *Far Eastern Economic Review* (13 May 1977):62.

26. Siddayao, op. cit., 56; A. M. Tolentino, *The Waters Around Us: Why the Archipelagic Doctrine is Vital to the Philippines* (Manila: Bureau of National and Foreign Information, undated), 3–4.

27. *Far Eastern Economic Review* (22 January 1982):8.

28. L. Gonzaga, "A Shot in the Arm for Philippine Oil Search," *Far Eastern Economic Review* (20 August 1976):34–35; S. Ocampo, "Marcos Still Calls the Shots," *Far Eastern Economic Review* (10 August 1979):26–27.

29. "Monthly Political Supplement," *Asia Research Bulletin* 8 (30 April 1978 and 31 March 1979):343, 436.

30. K. Das, "Tankers Face Strict Rules in Straits," *Far Eastern Economic Review* (18 March 1977):82–83; D. P. Finn, Y. Hanayama, M. J. Meimandi-Nejad, T. Pikyakarnchana, and J. N. Reeves, *Oil Pollution from Tankers in the Straits of Malacca: A Policy and Legal Analysis* (Honolulu: Open Grants, East-West Center, 1979), 129–133.

31. Convention on the Law of the Sea (A/CONF. 62/122), 7 October 1982, signed 10 December 1982. Article 53 (Right of Archipelagic Sea Lanes Passage).

32. Valencia, loc. cit.

33. Y. L. Lee, "Malacca Strait, Kra Canal, and International Navigation," *Pacific Viewpoint* 19 (1978):73; "Resurrecting the SEATO Pact," *Honolulu Star-Bulletin* (17 February 1979): A-8; J. McBeth, "Storm Clouds on the Horizon," *Far Eastern Economic Review* (6 July 1979):18.

34. *Asia Research Bulletin* 7 (31 March 1978):430; (30 April 1978):434–435; 8 (31 October 1978):500.

35. Valencia, loc. cit.

36. Associated Press, "British Closing Down Oman Military Base," *The New York Times* (18 February 1977):A-8.

37. S. Uhalley, Jr., "China in the Pacific," *Oceans* (May 1978):33–37.

38. Valencia, loc. cit.; S. Chen, *General Survey of Geologic Structure and Prospects of Oil and Gas on the Continental Shelf on the Northern Part of the South China Sea*. Paper presented at *Offshore China '81*, Guangzhou, 1981; Luo Zhetan, Zhang Ruixiang, and He Liansheng, "Tectonics and Deposits of the Cenozoic Era in the South China Sea," *in* M. J. Valencia, ed., *The South China Sea: Hydrocarbon Potential and Possibilities of Joint Development* (New York: Pergamon Press, 1981), 1,093–1,098.

39. D. G. Muller, Jr., "The Missions of the PRC Navy," *in Proceedings of the United States Naval Institute*, November 1977, 47–52. Indeed, the relinquishment of Vietnamese claims and control in the Spratlys was one of the major items demanded by China in the initial round of China–Vietnam peace negotiations. See "Hsisha and Nansha Islands Belong to China," *Beijing Review* 21 (25 May 1979):23–26.

40. Muller, loc. cit.

41. Park, loc. cit.; M. J. Valencia, "The South China Sea: Prospects for Marine Regionalism," *Marine Policy* (April 1978) 87–104.

42. M. J. Valencia, "South China Sea: Present and Potential Coastal Area Resource Use Conflicts," *Ocean Management* 5 (1979):1–38.

43. D. Ying, "Taiwan Declares 200 nm EEZ," *Asia Wall Street Journal* (8 September 1979):3.

44. Valencia, loc. cit., note 42; J. C. Marr, *Fishery and Resource Management in Southeast Asia*, Paper no. 7 (Washington, D.C.: The Program of International Studies of Fishery Arrangements, Resources for the Future, 1976), 62.

45. Lauriat, loc. cit.

46. M. T. Kavanaugh and S. Shimoyama, "Irradiated Nuclear Fuel Transport from Japan to Europe," *in Proceedings of the First Pacific Basin Conference on Nuclear Power Development and the Fuel Cycle*, Honolulu, 1976, 331–343; B. Hastings, "2-N Waste Ships to Bypass Isles," *Honolulu Advertiser* (25 September 1979):1.

47. J. Lewis, "The Diplomacy of Resources," *Far Eastern Economic Review* (28 September 1979):54–56.

48. D. Bonavia, "China Decides to Sit This One Out," *Far Eastern Economic Review* (25 May 1979):809; N. Chanda, "The Storm That Follows the Calm," *Far Eastern Economic Review* (30 November 1979):15; R. Tasker, "ASEAN Unites in Anger," *Far Eastern Economic Review* (19 January 1979):12–14.

49. United Nations Environment Programme. *Draft Action Plan for the Protection and Development of the Marine Environment and Coastal Areas of the South East Asia Region* (UNEP/EAS. 1) 5 April 1979, 11.

50. Finn, et al., *Oil Pollution from Tankers in the Straits of Malacca: A Policy and Legal Analysis* (Honolulu: Open Grants, East-West Center, 1979), 129–133.

51. M. J. Valencia, "Southeast Asian Seas: National Marine Interests, Transnational Issues and Marine Regionalism" *in* Chia Lin Sien and Colin MacAndrews, eds., *Southeast Asian Seas: Frontiers for Development* (Singapore: McGraw-Hill, 1981), 302–356.

52. Marr, op. cit., 53; International Center for Living Aquatic Resource Management, "Report of the First Meeting of the ICLARM Program Advisory Committee," Manila, March 1977 (ICLARM, July 1977), 18; Louis B. Brow, *Report of the United States Delegation to the First Session of the Working Group for the Western Pacific (WESTPAC) for the Intergovernmental Oceanographic Commission (IOC)*, Tokyo, February 1979.

CHAPTER 3 MARITIME JURISDICTIONAL ISSUES

1. *Convention on the Law of the Sea* (A/CONF. 62/122), 7 October 1982, signed 10 December 1982.

2. J. R. V. Prescott, *Maritime Jurisdiction in Southeast Asia: A Commentary and Map*, Environment and Policy Institute Research Report No. 2 (Honolulu: East-West Center, 1981); J. R. V. Prescott, "Maritime Jurisdictions and Boundaries," *in* Joseph R. Morgan and Mark J. Valencia, eds., *Atlas for Marine Policy in the Southeast Asian Seas* (Berkeley: University of California Press, 1983), 40–52.

3. Ibid.

4. Ibid.

5. Ibid.

6. Ibid.

7. *Map Showing Territorial Waters and Continental Shelf Boundaries of Malaysia* (Malaysia: Director of National Mapping, 1979).

8. The copies of these treaties used to construct Table 3.1 and for the following analysis were provided either by one of the governments concerned or by the Department of Foreign Affairs in Canberra. These copies are preferred to those in collections because they are complete, always accurate, and include any maps that may form part of the agreement. There are three good general sources if official copies are not available. R. Churchill, M. Nordquist, S. H. Lay, and K. R. Simmonds have variously edited a series entitled *New Directions in the Law of the Sea* by Oceania Publications of New York. The first volume was published in 1973. Since 1970 the United Nations has published a part of its *Legislative Series* several volumes entitled *National Legislation and Treaties Relating to the Law of the Sea* (New York). The first volume was published in 1970. Some agreements can also be found in the *Treaty Series* published by the United Nations on a continuing basis, but these volumes include treaties dealing with all subjects, not just treaties dealing with maritime questions.

9. The Society of Comparative Legislation and International Law, *The Law of the Sea* (London: Sijthoff, 1958), 7.

10. S. Rosenne, *The International Court of Justice* (Leyden: Sijthoff, 1957), 538.

11. J. Ancel, *Les Frontières* (Paris: Gallimard, 1938), 196.

12. E. C. F. Bird, *Coasts* (Cambridge, Massachusetts: MIT Press, 1970), 206–207.

13. H. Chiu, "Chinese Attitude Towards Continental Shelf and Its Implication on Delimiting Seabed in Southeast Asia," Occasional Papers/Reprints Series in *Contemporary Asian Studies*, No. 1 (Maryland: University of Maryland, School of Law, 1977), 29.

14. United Nations, *Maps Illustrating Various Formulae for the Definition of the Continental Shelf* (New York: United Nations, 1979); "Face and Floor of the Peaceful Sea" *National Geographic Magazine* (October, 1969): 496–499 (and special map supplement).

15. J. R. V. Prescott, *The Evolution of Nigeria's International and Regional Boundaries: 1861–1971* (Vancouver: Aldine Press, 1971), 14.

16. Letters from the Directors of Information, State Secretariat, Brunei, January 1982.

17. Republic of the Philippines, "Presidential Decree No. 1596 Declaring Certain Areas Part of the Philippines Territory and Providing for Their Government and Administration," *Official Gazette* 75 (February 1979): 1,556–1,557.

18. International Court of Justice, *Receuil des Arrêts, avis Consultatifs et Ordonances,* 2 vols. (The Hague, 1962).

19. Prescott, loc. cit., note 2.

20. Ibid.

21. Hydrographer of the [British] Navy, *China Sea Pilot,* II (British Hydrographic Department, London, 1975), 72, 129.

22. "Burmese Repelled," *Far Eastern Economic Review* (27 March 1981):9.

23. *Petroleum News Southeast Asia (*September 1982).

24. "Sea Dispute Evaporates," *Far Eastern Economic Review* (15 May 1981):9.

25. Prescott, op. cit., note 2, 50.

26. United States Department of State, Geographer, "Continental Shelf Boundary: Indonesia–Malaysia," *Boundary Study* 1 (January 1970), 1 and attached map.

CHAPTER 4 FISHERIES

1. R. Weidenbach, "Fisheries," *in* Joseph R. Morgan and Mark J. Valencia, eds., *Atlas for Marine Policy in Southeast Asian Seas* (Berkeley: University of California Press, 1983), 64.

2. *Regional Seminar on Monitoring, Control and Surveillance of Fisheries in the Exclusive Economic Zones* (Jakarta: Food and Agricultural Organization–United Nations Development Programme–South China Sea Fisheries Coordinating and Development Programme, November 30–December 4, 1981, statement of Brunei delegate).

3. FAO–SCSP, Summary Report of the Workshop on the Demersal Resources of the Sunda Shelf, Penang, Malaysia, 31 October–4 November 1977, 12.

4. Southeast Asian Fisheries Development Center (SEAFDEC), *Fishery Statistical Bulletin for South China Sea Area, 1979,* December 1981, table 6.

5. *Yearbook of Fishery Statistics, Catches and Landings, 1980,* vol. 50 (Rome: FAO, 1981), 50.

6. The Present Status of Demersal Resources and Fisheries Management in Brunei, unpublished paper, 2.

7. A. B. T. Raja, *Current Knowledge of Fisheries Resources in the Shelf Area of the Bay of Bengal,* Bay of Bengal Project, FAO-UN. BOBP/WP/8, Madras, India, September 1980.

8. *Yearbook of Fishery Statistics, Catches and Landings, 1980,* op. cit., 299.

9. *Report of the Burma Inland Fisheries Project Identification Mission* (Burma: FAO, Investment Support Service, Investment Center, 1979), 3.

10. Ibid., 8.

11. Ibid., 2–11.

12. Ibid., 3.

13. Ibid., 7–8, i–iii.

14. The Indonesian Fisheries in Brief, 1981, unpublished paper by Directorate-General of Fisheries, Jakarta, 2.

15. *Country Statement: The Present Status of Demersal Resources and Fisheries Management in*

Indonesia, FAO-DAMODA Seminar on the Management of Tropical Demersal Fisheries, Bangkok, 1979, Appendix I.

16. *Yearbook of Fishery Statistics, Catches and Landings, 1980,* loc. cit.

17. *Fisheries Statistics of Indonesia, 1981* (Jakarta: Directorate-General of Fisheries, 1983), 1.

18. E. D. Samson, *Benchmark Information on the State of Fisheries Development in Selected Asian Countries (As a Follow-up to the World Congress on Agrarian Reform and Rural Development),* Report prepared for the FAO Regional Office for Asia and the Pacific, Bangkok, August 1981, A-4.

19. *Yearbook of Fishery Statistics, Catches and Landings, 1980,* loc. cit.

20. Indonesian Fisheries in Brief, 1981, unpublished paper by Directorate-General of Fisheries, Jakarta, tables 1, 3.

21. Ibid., 1.

22. Ibid., 3.

23. Ibid., tables 11 and 12.

24. Ibid., 3.

25. Adm. A. Rachman, The Development of Industrial Fisheries in Indonesia (Jakarta, unpublished policy statement by director general of fisheries, 1982), 2–3.

26. Ibid.

27. Samson, op. cit., A-1.

28. *Bank Operations in the Fisheries Sector* (Manila: Asian Development Bank, 1979), 51, 52, 54.

29. *Yearbook of Fishery Statistics, Catches and Landings, 1980,* loc. cit.

30. Lim Joo-Jock, *Geo-Strategy and the South China Sea Basin: Regional Balance, Maritime Issues, and Future Patterns* (Singapore: Singapore University Press, 1979), 59–60.

31. *Yearbook of Fishery Statistics, Catches and Landings, 1980,* loc. cit.

32. Samson, op. cit., 3–4.

33. Fisheries Management in Malaysia, FAO-DANIDA Seminar on the Management of Tropical Demersal Fisheries, Bangkok, 1979, 2–4.

34. *Yearbook of Fishery Statistics, Catches and Landings, 1980,* loc. cit.

35. *Annual Fisheries Statistics,* 1979 (Kuala Lumpur: Ministry of Agriculture, Fisheries Division, Malaysia, 1980), xii–xxi.

36. Ibid.

37. Ibid.

38. *Yearbook of Fishery Statistics, Catches and Landings, 1980,* loc. cit.

39. *Annual Fisheries Statistics,* 1979, loc. cit.

40. *Bank Operations in the Fisheries Sector,* loc. cit.

41. FAO–SCSP, loc. cit.

42. Philippines fishery statistical information can be found in Fishery Industry Development Council, *Fishery Industry Brief* (Manila: Ministry of Natural Resources, 1981).

43. Fishery Industry Development Council, *Integrated Fisheries Development Plan for the 1980s* (Manila: Ministry of Natural Resources, 1981).

44. Ibid.

45. Ibid.

46. FAO–SCSP, op. cit., 4.

47. Singapore: Country Statement, Report of the Second ASEAN-COFAF Meeting on Fisheries Resources Management, 21–23 July 1977, Jakarta, table 1.

48. *Annual Report* (Singapore: Ministry of National Development, 1979), 18.

49. A. G. Woodland, et al., *The South China Sea Fisheries: A Proposal for Accelerated Development,* SCS/DEV/73/1 (Rome: FAO, 1974).

50. *Singapore: Country Statement,* loc. cit.

51. J. M. Floyd, *International Fish Trade of Southeast Asian Nations,* Environment and Policy Institute Research Report No. 16 (Honolulu: East-West Center, 1984), 31.

52. *Annual Report,* loc. cit.

53. South China Sea Fisheries Development and Coordinating Programme, *Report of the Workshop on Management of Resources of the Sunda Shelf, Malacca Strait and Related Areas,* Manila, 7–9 December 1977. SCS Gen/78/18 (Manila: 1978), 1–5.

54. Ibid., 2.

55. Samson, loc. cit.

56. T. Sakiyama, Long-Term Trends of Fisheries Development in the South China Sea, unpublished paper, 15.

57. Samson, op. cit., E-7.

58. Sakiyama, op. cit., 4.

59. Samson, op. cit., E-5.

60. *Country Status Report of Fisheries of Thailand.* Paper presented at the 19th session of the Indo-Pacific Fishery Commission in May 1980, IPFL/80/SYMP/CSR/9; and M. J. Valencia, "Southeast Asia: National Marine Interests and Marine Regionalism," *Ocean Development and International Law* 5 (1978):421–476.

61. Valencia, op. cit., table 4-A.

62. Samson, op. cit., E-9.

63. Samson, op. cit., E1-2.

64. *National Marine Interests and the EEZ* (Manila: Ministry of Natural Resources, 1981), III, 5 (Thailand).

65. Ibid.

66. *Country Programme Proposal for UNDP Assistance, 1972–1976* (Saigon: Ministry of National Planning and Development, February 1973).

67. FAO-SCSP, loc. cit.

68. *Yearbook of Fishery Statistics, Catches and Landings, 1980,* op. cit., 300.

69. ADB, Appraisal of the Second Fisheries Development Project in the Republic of Vietnam, unpublished, November 1974.

70. T. A. Clingan, Jr., "Law of the Sea: State Practice in Zones of Special Jurisdiction," *in Proceedings of the Law of the Sea Institute 13th Annual Conference,* co-sponsored by the Center for Economic Development and Social Studies, Mexico City, 15–18 October 1979, 451.

71. ADB, op. cit, 5, 6.

72. Valencia, op. cit., table 4-A.

73. Ibid.

74. ADB, loc. cit.

75. Ibid.

76. Woodland, op. cit., 173.

77. Lim, op. cit., 11.

78. "A Brief Introduction on the Fisheries of China," *Fishing News International* 19 (June 1980):23–24.

79. Ibid.

80. Valencia, loc. cit.

81. "A Brief Introduction on the Fisheries of China," loc. cit.

82. Ibid.

83. *Fishery Statistics of Southeast Asia, 1978* (Bangkok: SEAFDEC, October 1980).

84. Ibid., 132.

85. "Taiwan to Construct 160 New Vessels," *Fishing News International* 19 (June 1980):27.

86. *Fishery Statistics of Southeast Asia, 1978,* op. cit., 7.

87. "Taiwan to Construct 160 New Vessels," loc. cit.

88. Country Status Report on Hong Kong, Indo-Pacific Fisheries Council 19th Session. Symposium on the Development and Management of Small-Scale Fisheries, Kyoto, Japan, 21–30 May 1980, 2–3.

89. Ibid., 2.

90. *Fisheries Profile, Hong Kong,* Agriculture and Fisheries Department, Hong Kong. Prepared for the Second Meeting of the Committee for the Development and Management in the South China Sea, Bali, Indonesia, 8–9 November 1982.

91. Ibid., 1.

92. Ibid., 13.

93. Ibid., 2.

94. Ibid., table 1.

95. Country Status Report on Hong Kong, 6.

96. Hong Kong Annual Department Report (Hong Kong: Director of Agriculture and Fisheries, financial year 1980–1981).

97. Ibid.

98. *Fishery Statistics of Southeast Asia, 1978,* op. cit., 155–161, 179–184.

99. Ibid.

100. *Bank Operations in the Fisheries Sector,* Bank Staff Working Paper (Manila: Asian Development Bank, 1979), 29–30.

101. J. R. V. Prescott, *Maritime Jurisdiction in Southeast Asia: A Commentary and Map,* Environment and Policy Institute Research Report No. 2 (Honolulu: East-West Center, 1981), 20.

102. Ibid., 17.

103. *Convention on the Law of the Sea* (A/CONF. 62/122), 7 October 1982, signed December 10, 1982, 19.

104. Ibid., 25.

105. See T. Sujastani, "The State of Indonesian Marine Fishery Resource Exploitation," *Indonesian Agricultural Research and Development Journal* 3(1).

106. See B. J. McCay, "Development Issues in Fisheries as Agrarian Systems," *in Culture and Agriculture,* vol. II (Champaign-Urbana: University of Illinois, 1981).

107. F. T. Christy, Jr., *Changes in the Law of the Sea and the Effects on Fisheries Management, with Particular Reference to Southeast Asia and the Southwest Pacific* (Manila: International Center for Living Aquatic Resources Management, 1978), 76.

108. Ibid.

109. G. Kent, "Harmonizing Extended Zone Legislation in Southeast Asia," *Ocean Development and International Law* 13 (1983):247–68.

110. Ibid.

111. Ibid.

112. P. Polomka, *ASEAN and the Law of the Sea: A Preliminary Look at the Prospects of Regional Cooperation,* Occasional Paper no. 36 (Singapore: Institute of Southeast Asian Studies, 1975).

113. J. C. Marr, "Southeast Asian Marine Resources and Fisheries," *in* Chia Lin Sien and C. MacAndrews, eds., *Southeast Asian Seas: Frontiers for Development* (Singapore: McGraw-Hill/Institute of Southeast Asian Studies, 1981), 92.

CHAPTER 5 OIL AND GAS

1. F. Fesharaki, *OPEC and the Structural Changes in the Market: The Outlook After the Counter Revolution.* Paper presented at the EAPI/CCOP/ASCOPE/OIC Workshop on Geology and

Hydrocarbon Potential of the South China Sea and Possibilities of Joint Development, Honolulu, August 1983.

2. *Ocean Industry* (November 1982):65.

3. *Business Times* (Kuala Lumpur) (21 January 1983):1.

4. P. D. Gaffney, C. P. Moyes, and J. D. Archer, "Southeast Asia Looks to 1990," and G. L. Fletcher, "Exploration Trends in Southeast Asia: An Overview." Papers presented at *Offshore Southeast Asian 82 Conference,* Singapore, 9–12 February 1982.

5. W. E. Whitney, "Two Years of Drilling in Deepwater," *UNESCAP, CCOP / SOPAC Technical Bulletin* 3 (1980):277–285; "Deepwater Exploration Vital to Future," *Offshore* (5 June 1983):31–38.

6. Sediment thickness contours were compiled from ASEAN Council on Petroleum (ASCOPE), *Tertiary Sedimentary Basins of the Gulf of Thailand and South China Sea; Stratigraphy, Structure and Hydrocarbon Occurrences,* Jakarta, ASCOPE Secretariat (1981); E. P. Du Bois, "Review of Principal Hydrocarbon-Bearing Basins of the South China Sea Area," *in* Mark J. Valencia, ed., *The South China Sea: Hydrocarbon Potential and Possibilities of Joint Development* (New York: Pergamon Press, 1981), 1,113–1,141; W. Hamilton, *Map of Sedimentary Basins of the Indonesian Region,* U.S. Geological Survey, Map I-875-B, 1974; C. L. Mrozowski and D. E. Hayes, "Sediment Isopachs," *in* D. E. Hayes, ed., *A Geophysical Atlas of East and Southeast Asian Seas,* Geological Society of America, Map and Chart Series MC025, 1978; and for offshore China, Luo Zhetan, Zhang Ruixiang, and He Liansheng, "Tectonic and Deposits of the Cenozoic Era in the South China Sea," *in* M. J. Valencia, ed., *The South China Sea: Hydrocarbon Potential and Possibilities of Joint Development* (New York: Pergamon Press, 1981), 1,093–1,098.

Basin names were derived from these sources and G. A. S. Nayoan, "Offshore Hydrocarbon Potential of Indonesia," *in* M. J. Valencia, *The South China Sea:* CCOP/ IOC (1974); *Metallogenesis, Hydrocarbons and Tectonic Patterns in Eastern Asia* (Bangkok: United Nations Development Programme [CCOP]), 158. Areas without contours or basin names lack sediment deposits thicker than 1 km. Where no sediment thickness data were available but basins were known to exist, basin names are indicated. Where contours are incomplete, data are unavailable.

7. D. Jenkins, "Trouble Over Oil and Waters," *Far Eastern Economic Review* (7 August 1981):24–33.

8. *Petroleum News Southeast Asia,* Exploration Annual, 1983. Petroleum News, Hong Kong.

9. Shows of oil and gas in drilled wells were included to display the tendencies of possible deposits. Oil and gas deposits were derived from E. P. Du Bois, op. cit., 1,113–1,114; "Oil and Gas Map," *Petroleum News Southeast Asia* (August 1982); *Petroleum News Exploration Annual,* 1979, 1980, 1981; B. Cooper, ed., *Far East Oil and Energy Survey, 1981* (Geneva–Dublin, Petroleum Economist and Petroconsultants, 1981); ASCOPE Secretariat, Jakarta, 1981.

10. M. J. Valencia, "The South China Sea: Constraints to Marine Regionalism," *The Indonesian Quarterly* 8 (April 1980):16–38.

11. Cooper, op. cit., THA-4, revised downward by new estimate of Erawan's reserves in *Energy Asia* 4 (27 August 1982).

12. *New Straits Times* (27 August 1982):11.

13. G. L. Fletcher, "Far East," *American Association of Petroleum Geologists Bulletin* 65 (1981):2,173.

14. Cooper, op. cit., KAM-1.

15. J. R. V. Prescott, *Maritime Jurisdiction in Southeast Asia: A Commentary and Map,* Environment and Policy Institute Research Report No. 2 (Honolulu: East-West Center, 1981), 5–7.

16. *Energy Asia* 4 (7 May 1982).

17. *Petroleum News Supplement* (September 1982).

18. ASEAN Council on Petroleum (ASCOPE), *Tertiary Sedimentary Basins of the Gulf of Thailand and South China Sea: Stratigraphy, Structure and Hydrocarbon Occurrences,* ASCOPE Secretariat, Jakarta, 1981, 14–15.

19. *Energy Asia* 3 (28 August 1981).

20. *Petroleum Activities in Thailand 1981,* Report no. 7 (Bangkok: Mineral Fuels Division, Department of Mineral Resources, Thailand), 38.

21. *Petroleum News* (January 1983):52.

22. *New Straits Times* (Kuala Lumpur) (24 October 1981):9.

23. "New Map Defines Continental Shelf Limits," *New Sunday Times* (27 January 1980):15.

24. *Energy Asia* 4 (January 1982).

25. *Energy Asia* 4 (16 April 1982); *Energy Asia* 4 (30 April 1982).

26. See Prescott's chapter on maritime jurisdictional issues in this volume.

27. G. Sacerdoti, "Smoothing Troubled Waters," *Far Eastern Economic Review* (12 December 1980):19.

28. Du Bois, loc. cit.

29. Prescott, op. cit., 41–45.

30. *Energy Asia* 4 (30 July 1982).

31. Chen Sengiang, *General Survey of Geological Structure and Prospects of Oil and Gas of the Continental Shelf in the Northern Part of the South China Sea.* Paper presented at *Offshore China '81;* Fan Pow-Foong, "Geology and Bouger Gravity Anomalies of the Gulf of Tonkin and Vicinity," *in* Valencia, op. cit., note 6, 1,099–1,113.

32. *Petroleum News Southeast Asia,* Supplement (May 1983).

33. C. LaGrange, "South China Sea Disputes: China, Vietnam, Taiwan and the Philippines." Environment and Policy Institute Working Paper, East-West Center, May 1980.

34. *Vietnam Courier* 12 (1982):6.

35. K. Woodard and A. Davenport, "The Security Dimension of China's Offshore Oil Development," *Journal of Northeast Asian Studies* 1 (September 1982):3–26.

36. P. Sricharatchanya, "Not Enough Blackgold to Oil Industry's Wheels," *Far Eastern Economic Review* (8 October 1982):76–77.

37. E. F. Durkee, "Petroleum Development in Australia and Oceania in 1973," *American Association of Petroleum Geologists Bulletin* 58 (October 1974):2,179.

38. E. F. Durkee, "Petroleum Development in Australia in 1979," *American Association of Petroleum Geologists Bulletin* 64 (November 1980):1,864–1,865.

39. E. F. Durkee, "Australia," *American Association of Petroleum Geologists Bulletin* 65 (1981):2,241.

40. Prescott, loc. cit.

41. Cooper, op. cit., 67.

42. *Energy Asia* 3 (29 May 1981).

43. Nayan Chanda, "A Surrogate Siren's Song," *Far Eastern Economic Review* (23 October 1981):42–43.

44. Ibid.

45. "S. R. V. Foreign Ministry Statement on Shelf Dispute with Indonesia," *Interasian Affairs* (November 1979), GSO500:41, according to Foreign Broadcast Information Service.

46. G. Lauriat and Melinda Liu, "Pouring Trouble on Oily Waters," *Far Eastern Economic Review* (28 September 1979):20.

47. G. Lauriat, "Another Coming Conflict of Comrades Ahead?", *Far Eastern Economic Review* (5 October 1979):58–59.

48. K. Fountain, "The Development of China's Offshore Oil," *The China Business Review* (January-February 1980):27.

49. *Bulletin Today* (Manila) (1 February 1984):1, 8.

50. S. Harrison, *China Oil and Asia: Conflict Ahead?* (New York: Columbia University Press, 1977), 198.

51. *Far Eastern Economic Review* (29 October 1982):9; *Petroleum News* (January 1983):14.

52. M. Habir, "A Dove Like Hawke," *Far Eastern Economic Review* (16 June 1983):15; M. Richardson, "Man with a Mission." *Far Eastern Economic Review* (14 July 1983):10–11.

53. *Far Eastern Economic Review* (August 1980):30–31.

54. Malaysia–Thailand Joint Development Authority, Petroleum Development Division, Implementation Coordination Unit, Prime Minister's Department, Malaysia–Thailand Joint Authority, mimeograph release, 4 September 1981; *Petroleum News Southeast Asia* Supplement (February 1983).

55. C. Sesthapaisal, "Simmering Union — PTT Dispute Explodes Into the Open," *Petroleum News* (August 1982):12–13.

56. Foreign Broadcast Information Service Worldwide Report, Law of the Sea, no. 124, 21 July 1980 (JPRS F6084), Law of the Sea no. 98, 6 June 1979 (JPRS 073625); "Scrambling for China Oil," *Business Week* (31 May 1982):95.

57. "Report and Recommendations to the Government of Iceland and Norway of the Conciliation Commission on the Continental Shelf Area Between Iceland and Jan Mayen," *International Legal Materials* 20 (July 1981):797–842.

58. Chi Young Pak, "The Continental Shelf Between Korea, Japan and China," *Marine Policy Reports* 4 (Center for the Study of Marine Policy, University of Delaware) (June 1982):4.

CHAPTER 6 SHIPPING

1. D. Howarth, *Sovereign of the Seas – The Story of Seapower* (London: Quarter Books, 1963), 17.

2. K. E. Shaw, and G. G. Thompson, *The Strait of Malacca* (Singapore: University Education Press, 1973), 88–90.

3. C. R. Boxer, *Jan Compagnie in War and Peace* (Hong Kong: Heinemann Educational Books, Asia Ltd., 1979), 9, 11, 28.

4. The opium clippers were generally schooner-rigged and carried double crews and heavy armaments to fight off Chinese "water forces" and pirates.

5. A. E. Branch, *The Elements of Shipping* (London: Champan and Hall, 1975), 80–97.

6. E. Jennings, *Cargoes: Centenary Story of the Far Eastern Freight Conference* (Singapore: Meridian Communications Pte. Ltd., 1980), 19–21.

7. Ibid.

8. Ibid.

9. Ibid.

10. Ibid.

11. Ibid.

12. D. Isaak, "The Future of the Supertanker," *in* M. J. Valencia, E. Gold, N. Letalik, and Chia Lin Sien, eds., *Shipping, Energy and Environment: Southeast Asian Perspectives for the 1980s* (Halifax, Nova Scotia: Dalhousie Ocean Studies Program, 1982), 38–51.

13. *Indonesia Development News* (December 1981):3.

14. Ibid.

15. This system has been heavily criticized by the foreign representatives on the grounds that it created more bureaucracy and yet another opportunity for "pungli" (bribes).

16. S. Awanohara, "No Foreigners, Please," *Far Eastern Economic Review* (28 May 1982):52; S. Awanohara, "Shaping Up to Ship In," *Far Eastern Economic Review* (27 October 1982):74.

17. Awanohara, loc. cit.

18. Pilferage was quite common in Tanjungpriok in the early 1970s. The huge population living on and around the facility made a shambles of any security measures. The lack of uniforms or any organization of dockside labor further aggravated the situation.

19. *Warta Ekonomic Maritime Review* (Jakarta: Maritime Press Foundations, July 1977), 13–66.

20. *Indonesia Development News* (December 1981):3.

21. P. Bowring, "Pertamina—Charter Party Gets Rough," *Far Eastern Economic Review* (11 March 1977):36–44.

22. A. G. Bartlett, R. J. Barton, J. C. Bartlett, G. A. Fowler, Jr., and C. F. Hays, *Pertamina — Indonesian National Oil Company* (Djakarta: Amerasian Ltd., 1972), 107–109.

23. S. Lipsky, ed., *The Billion Dollar Bubble . . . and Other Stories from the Asian Wall Street Journal* (Hong Kong: Dow Jones Pub. Co., 1978), 23–24.

24. Several articles were written on the Pertamina crisis with the first comprehensive roundup being D. Jenkins, G. Lauriat, and P. Bowring, "Tanker Tie Up Spans Four Continents," *Far Eastern Economic Review* (29 January 1977):47–51. An interesting postscript to the Pertamina crisis was the arrest of three vessels in Singapore by Rappaport for nonpayment of charter fees, "A Rap at the Port," *Far Eastern Economic Review* (21 May 1982):78–79.

25. *Indonesia Development News* (December 1981):3.

26. G. Lauriat, "State Shipping — Only Governments Can Finance LNG Costs?", *Far Eastern Economic Review* (2 September 1977):64–66.

27. "MISC Growth Too Slow," *South China Morning Post* (9 July 1982, Business News section):4.

28. The shipment of rubber latex in deep bottom tanks is an example. The conference was unable to supply the vessels necessary to carry the latex.

29. G. Lauriat, "MISC vs. Maersk — First Ever Defection From Far Eastern Freight Conference," *Far Eastern Economic Review* (2 February 1982):51–52.

30. Lauriat, loc. cit., note 26.

31. "Coastal Ships Ply Empty," *South China Morning Post* (31 March 1981, Business News section):3.

32. "Malaysia to Stop Shipping Fronts," *New Straits Times* (November 1981):12.

33. H. Din, "Port Kelang — The First 80 Years," *Seatec III*, 2–6 March 1981 (London: IPC Publ.), 1–13.

34. Ibid.

35. Ibid.

36. "Philippine Ports and Shipping," *Philippine Ship Agents' Association Economic Monitor*, Manila, 1980.

37. Ibid.

38. Ibid.

39. L. Gonzaga, "Manila's Barrier Reef," *Far Eastern Economic Review* (9 July 1982):70.

40. "Two Major Philippine Shipping Companies in Financial Trouble," *Asian Shipping* (March 1981):37–38.

41. Ibid.

42. I. Middleton, *Seatrade's Far East Report 1980* (London: Volker's Publ.), 99–103.

43. Ibid.

44. The interests of the traditional Chinese shipowners are divided along ethnic lines. Some groups deal nearly exclusively with Malaysia and Indonesia while others handle Tai-

wanese trade. Trade to China tends to go through official channels such as Yick Fung, which has an office in Singapore.

45. "Recession, Nationalism Trouble Shipping," *International Herald Tribune* (24 April 1978):12.

46. *Indonesian Shipping Directory, 1976–1977* (Jakarta: Marindo Press, 1977), 18.

47. Lai Park Onn, "Singapore Ship Repair Prospects," *Shipcare Seminar* (2–6 March 1981):3.

48. Ibid.

49. A major government inquiry into the cause of the explosion determined that the ignition was caused by a worker using a torch to loosen some rusted nuts near a vent leading to the bunker tanks. It was also determined that the flash point of the fuel oil in the bunker tanks was extraordinarily low because the ship was siphoning off light crude oil from the cargo tanks. Although there were many other breaches of safety regulations, what caused the heavy loss of life was that there were 167 people working in the engine room at the time of the explosion. As the judge commented in the results of the investigation: "A vessel's engine room is not designed to cater for adequate means of escape for a greater number of persons other than the usual complement of the vessel's engineroom crew. This fact was not recognized by Jurong Shipyard during the repairs of the *Spyros*." *The Explosion and Fire on Board St. Spyros, 12 October 1978 — The Inquiry Report* (31 January 1979):26.

50. Ibid.

51. Loh Heng Kee, "Criteria for Port of Singapore's Containerization Decision," *Port Development for Unit Loads and Containerization — Proceedings of a Seminar in Hong Kong,* September 1976, ESCAP Port Development Series no. 1, 47–54.

52. Chan Bong Soo, "A First Class Port in the Making," *Business Times — Straits Times* (29 April 1978):6.

53. Ibid.

54. Paisal Sricharatchanya, "Passing the Ports," *Far Eastern Economic Review* (3 November 1983):76–78; *Chairman's Report* (Bangkok Shipowners and Agents Association, 1979–1980), 2–14.

55. "Communications Unveils New Shipping Rules," *Bangkok Post* (18 August 1981): Section II, 1.

56. G. Lauriat, "Indochina's Island State," *Far Eastern Economic Review* (17 November 1983):82–83.

57. Ibid.

58. Ibid.

59. G. Lauriat, "Letter from Nakhodka," *Far Eastern Economic Review* (5 August 1977):46.

60. "Inland Sea" is a Japanese expression referring to their own waters.

61. G. Lauriat, "Hongkong's Four Year Gamble," *Far Eastern Economic Review* (24 March 1978):83–87.

62. G. Lauriat, "Support for Japan Line Leaves Lingering Doubt," *Far Eastern Economic Review* (21 April 1978):72–74.

63. *Zosen* (Tokyo: Tokyo News Service, September 1982):12.

64. At the Manila UNCTAD Conference the principal shipping spokesman for the EEC voiced objections to imposing on the whole world the UNCTAD proposals, which were designed only for developing countries.

65. G. Lauriat, "A Refusal to Commit Economic Suicide," *Far Eastern Economic Review* (15 June 1979):44–45.

66. Ibid.

67. The system of using offshore shipping companies to move money from the left hand

to the right is very much an essential purpose of a flag-of-convenience vessel for a transnational company. This was first detailed in two excellent books, *The Energy Cartel* published by the Marine Engineers Beneficial Association in 1975 and Robert Engler's *The Politics of Oil* published by the University of Chicago Press in 1961. Both books were forerunners of Anthony Sampson's famous book, *The Seven Sisters.*

68. It is extremely difficult for shipping researchers to determine the beneficial ownership of a vessel after a series of "sales." Very little documentation is necessary and it is often more difficult to register an automobile than a ship.

69. The idea of a super flag is not a new one. Paul Slater, a shipping banker and strong supporter of flag-of-convenience shipping, recently resuggested it in view of the tremendous opposition to flag-of-convenience shipping among developing nations.

70. Of these six Asian ports, only Hong Kong's Kwai Chung Container Terminal was actually privately financed.

71. G. Lauriat, "Bigger Bill for Asian Shippers," *Far Eastern Economic Review* (6 May 1977):56–57.

72. G. Lauriat, "Getting the Most From Your Shipping Dollar," *Asian Sources* (6 May 1977):180–196.

73. Ibid.

74. G. Lauriat, "Our Cargo, Their Vessels," *Far Eastern Economic Review* (5 June 1981): 48–49.

75. UNCTAD Secretariat, "Action on the Question of Open Registeries," 27 May 1981, Annex.

76. Ibid.

77. G. Lauriat, "Malacca Straits: A Matter of Handling Squat," *Far Eastern Economic Review* (2 September 1977):64–65.

78. There were a great many design problems with the first generation of VLCCs. The vessels often had only a single rudder and propeller which meant that the vessel was effectively disabled if either was damaged. The huge flat bottoms gave rise to the phenomenon of squat while the huge size of tanks created conditions similar to the atmosphere itself.

79. G. Lauriat, "Oceans are More Dangerous Than Ever," *Far Eastern Economic Review* (6 February 1982):57–58.

80. Ibid.

81. The loss of the Soviet containership *Mekanik Tarasov* off Newfoundland on 18 February 1982 upset the Canadians as the ship was supposed to have uranium hexachloride on board, but it was not loaded for technical reasons. The uranium was being sent to the Soviet Union for enrichment.

82. International Legal Conference on Maritime Carriage of Nuclear Substances: Intergovernmental Organization, Maritime Consultative.

83. Shaw and Thompson, op. cit., 75.

84. Ibid.

85. Ibid.

86. N. Mostert, *Supership* (New York: Penguin Books Ltd., 1976), 43.

87. Shaw and Thompson, loc. cit.

88. Lauriat, loc. cit., note 77.

89. Ibid.

90. *Regional Shipping Network*, ESCAP Study 2 (Bangkok, June 1978):119–120.

91. Ibid.

92. Author communication with operators in Singapore in 1980.

93. Ibid.

94. Ibid.

95. Ibid.

96. Y. C. Chang, *Domestic Shipping Tonnage Requirements and Local Shipowners' New Building Program*, 2–6 March 1981, Seatec III (London: IPC Pub. 1), 1–26.

97. G. Lauriat, "Politics on the High Seas," *Far Eastern Economic Review* (6 March 1981):44.

98. Ibid.

99. P. M. Wijkam, *Struggle for the Global Commons* (Boston: Woods Hole Oceanographic Institute, January 1980), 4.

CHAPTER 7 DEFENSE

1. J. E. Moore, ed., *Jane's Fighting Ships, 1978–1979* (New York: Jane's Publishing Co., 1978), 129.

2. M. J. Valencia, "Southeast Asian Seas: National Marine Interests, Transnational Issues and Marine Regionalism," *in* Chia Lin Sien and Colin J. MacAndrews, eds., *Southeast Asian Seas: Frontiers for Development* (Singapore: McGraw Hill, 1981), 302–355.

3. J. R. Morgan and M. J. Valencia, eds., *Atlas for Marine Policy in Southeast Asian Seas* (Berkeley: University of California Press, 1983), 51.

4. D. W. Fryer, *Emerging Southeast Asia* (New York: Halsted Press, 1979), 228–316.

5. J. R. V. Prescott, *Maritime Jurisdiction in Southeast Asia: A Commentary and Map*. Environment and Policy Institute Research Report No. 2 (Honolulu: East-West Center, January 1981); see also Chapter 3 this volume.

6. H. Sekino and S. Seno, "Asian Navies," *United States Naval Institute Proceedings* 107 (1981):58.

7. G. Lauriat, "PLA Navy: Tribute to an Imperial Five-Jewelled Eunuch," *Far Eastern Economic Review* (8 February 1980):45.

8. J. W. Houck, "The Chinese Navy's Prospects for Growth," *United States Naval Institute Proceedings* 107 (1981):69.

9. Ibid., 75.

10. Lauriat, loc. cit.

11. Ibid.

12. Moore, ed., *Jane's Fighting Ships, 1980–1981* (New York: Jane's Publishing Co., 1978).

13. Lauriat, loc. cit.

14. Ibid.

15. Ibid.

16. Ibid.

17. Ibid.

18. C. W. Dragonette, "The Dragon at Sea — China's Maritime Enterprise," *United States Naval Institute Proceedings* 107 (1981):78–93.

19. Houck, loc. cit.

20. Ibid.

21. Sekino and Seno, loc. cit.

22. Ibid.

23. J. Wanandi, "Politico-Security Dimensions of Southeast Asia," *Asian Survey* 17 (1977):771–792.

24. H. C. Hinton, *The China Sea: The American Stake in Its Future* (New York: National Strategy Information Center, 1980), 25.

25. Prescott, op. cit., 36.

26. Sekino and Seno, loc. cit.

27. *Indonesia 1981: An Official Handbook.* Government of Indonesia (1981), 5.

28. Donald W. Fryer and James C. Jackson, *Indonesia* (Boulder: Westview Press, 1979), 241.

29. Ibid., 90–91.

30. Ibid., 156.

31. The Malaysian press has reported that Indonesian naval and customs also engage in "off duty" piracy. See Halim Todd, "Pirates in Uniform," *New Straits Times* (16 August 1983):83.

32. "A profitable rocket," *Far Eastern Economic Review* (3 April 1981):8–10.

33. D. Jenkins, "Indonesia: Launching a New Navy," *Far Eastern Economic Review* (April 1979):23; Prescott, op. cit., 31–33.

34. Jenkins, loc. cit.

35. Fryer, op. cit., 431.

36. "The Exodus and the Agony," *Far Eastern Economic Review* (22 December 1978):8–12.

37. *United Nations Convention on the Law of the Sea,* A/CONF 62/122, 7 October 1982, Article 47–6.

38. Malaysia's claim, first made in 1978, received some teeth when in September 1983 a party of Malaysian naval commandos occupied the atoll of Terembu Layang Layang, some 64 km southeast of the Vietnamese-occupied Amboyna Cay, which Malaysia also claims. Hanoi immediately protested. David Jenkins, "Trouble Over Oil and Waters," *Far Eastern Economic Review* (7 August 1981):24–32; "Perched on a Claim," *Far Eastern Economic Review* (29 September 1983):40–41.

39. Moore, op. cit., 133.

40. Ibid.

41. Fryer, op. cit., 228–229.

42. Prescott, loc. cit.

43. *U.S. Delegation Report,* 10th session, Third United Nations Conference on the Law of the Sea (Washington, D.C.: Department of State, 1981).

44. M. N. Vego, "The Potential Influence of Third World Navies on Ocean Shipping," *United States Naval Institute Proceedings* 107 (5) (1981):111.

45. Hinton, loc. cit.

46. Sekino and Seno, loc. cit.

47. Ibid.

48. Moore, op. cit., Foreword.

49. Ibid.

50. Vego, loc. cit.

51. *Bangkok Post* (27 January 1977):3.

52. Prescott, op. cit., 27.

53. Quoted from *Beijing Review,* no. 21 by Prescott, op. cit., 35.

54. J. E. Moore, ed., *Jane's Fighting Ships, 1979–1980* (New York: Jane's Publishing Co., 1979), 315.

55. Sekino and Seno, op. cit., 59.

56. Moore, loc. cit., note 54.

CHAPTER 8 MARINE POLLUTION

1. K. Ruddle, "Pollution in the Marine Coastal Environment of ASEAN Countries," *in* Chia Lin Sien and Colin MacAndrews, eds., *Southeast Asian Seas: Frontiers for Development* (Singapore: McGraw Hill, 1981), 136–178.

2. *Convention on the Law of the Sea,* A/CONF. 62/122, 7 October 1982.

3. Yoo-Leong Lee and D. Stephen, "Pollution," *in* J. R. Morgan and M. J. Valencia, eds., *Atlas for Marine Policy in Southeast Asia* (Berkeley: University of California Press, 1983), 120.

4. R. M. Umali, *Coastal Resources Development and Management: Philippine Experience* (Quezon City, Philippines: Natural Resources Management Center, 1980).

5. A review of the ability of the tropical environment to assimilate pollutants, the major pollutants, and their impacts appears in Ruddle, op. cit.

6. *WHO Western Pacific Regional Centre for the Promotion of Environmental Planning and Applied Studies (PEPAS): A Full Report on the Preliminary Assessment of Land-Based Sources of Pollution in East Asian Seas.* Universiti Pertanian Campus, Serdang, Selangor, Malaysia, 1981. In collaboration with the UNEP Regional Seas Programme Activity Centre, 56, 58.

7. *Report on the Second Pollution Surveys in the Upper Gulf of Thailand* (Bangkok: National Research Council, 1973); M. Hungspreugs and G. Waltayakorn, *Some Chemical Aspects of Marine Pollution in the Upper Gulf of Thailand* (Bangkok: Department of Marine Science, Chulalongkorn University, 1978).

8. *Pollution: Kuala Juru's Battle for Survival* (Penang: Consumer's Association of Penang, 1976).

9. A. Soegiarto and N. Polunin, *Marine Ecosystems of Indonesia: A Basis for Conservation, Section 1* (Bogor: IUCN/WWF, Indonesia Program, August 1980).

10. A. White, Research Intern, East-West Center, personal communication, 1983.

11. M. Hungspreugs and G. Waltayakorn, "Comparative Studies of DDT Residues in Sea Water, Sediments and in the Gulf of Thailand and the Andaman Sea," in *Proceedings of the Symposium on Marine Pollution Research in Thai Waters, Phuket, March 1977* (Bangkok: National Research Council of Thailand, 1978), 93–100.

12. Ibid.

13. A. Soegiarto, *The Indonesian Marine Environment: Their Problems and Management.* Paper presented to the First ASEAN Expert Meeting on Environment, Jakarta, December 1978, 10.

14. St. Munadjat Danusaputro, *Environmental Legislation and Administration in Indonesia* (Bandung: Alumni Press, 1978).

15. D. M. Johnson, *Environmental Management in the South China Sea: Legal and Institutional Developments,* Environment and Policy Institute Research Report No. 10 (Honolulu: East-West Center, June 1980), 70.

16. Economic and Social Commission for Asia and the Pacific, *Development of Legal Instruments for Protection of the Marine Environment in Southeast Asia, Draft Report* (1980), 29.

17. Mining Regulations (no. 04/P/N/pertamb/1973), S. 11.

18. Danusaputro, loc. cit.

19. Ibid.

20. Ibid.

21. Ibid.

22. Government of Malaysia, Environmental Quality Act of 1974, Section 2.

23. "Environmental Quality Act Malaysia 1974: Environmental Quality (Sewage and Industrial Effluents) Regulations 1979," in *Warta Kerajaan Seri Paduka Baginda* 23:58–76. (His Majesty's Government Gazette, Kuala Lumpur, Malaysia)

24. Ibid.

25. Palm oil and rubber wastes must be incubated at 30 degrees centigrade for three days. For other wastes, the incubation must be at 20 degrees centigrade for five days.

26. Environmental Quality (Prescribed Premises) (Crude Palm Oil) Regulations, 1977.

27. Ibid.

28. Sumun Redzwan, "The Role and Effects of Mineral Resource Exploitation in Development and the Environment in Malaysia," in *Proceedings of the Symposium on the Interdepen-*

dence of Economic Development and Environmental Quality in Southeast Asia: Malaysia as a Case Study (Oxford, Ohio: Institute of Environmental Sciences, 1980), 11.

29. J. N. Shane, *Legal Aspects of Environmental Management in Malaysia* (Bangkok: UN Task Force on Human Environment, 1977), 44.

30. Nik Abdul Rashin, "The Environmental Law in Malaysia: A Survey," in I. Kato, N. Kumamoto, and W. H. Matthews, eds., *Environmental Law and Policy in the Pacific Basin Area* (Tokyo: University of Tokyo Press, 1981), 12–14.

31. C. H. Leigh, "Land Development and Soil Erosion in West Malaysia," *Journal of Developing Areas* 5: 213–217.

32. Shane, loc. cit.

33. J.W.E. Lau, "Oil Pollution Preventions and Controls in Hydrocarbon Exploitation, Offshore Malaysia," in *TENAGA* '80, Kuala Lumpur, 21–23 August 1980 (The Malaysian National Committee of World Energy Conference, 1980).

34. Malaysia Environmental Quality Act.

35. Shane, loc. cit.

36. Johnston, loc. cit.

37. Government of Malaysia, *Straits of Malacca Contingency Plan* (Kuala Lumpur: Division of Environment, 1975).

38. Khalid Ramli, "Safeguards and Contingency Plans of the Government to Combat Oil Pollution in the Sea," in Leong Tak Seng, ed., *Proceedings of the Third Annual Seminar: The Sea Must Live* (Penang: Malaysian Society of Marine Sciences, 1980), 13.

39. Malaysia Environmental Quality Act.

40. Ruddle, op. cit., 168.

41. Johnston, op. cit., 63.

42. Ibid.

43. Ibid.

44. Ruddle, op. cit., 170.

45. Boonyong Lohwongwatana, "The Industrial Pollution Control Program of the Ministry of Industry for the Inner Gulf," in *Proceedings on Protection of the Marine Environment and Related Ecosystems: Thailand National Seminar 26–28 June 1979* (Bangkok: Office of the National Environment Board, 1979), 154; Johnson, op. cit., 82.

46. Twesukdi Piyakarchana, Sunee Mallikarmarl, and Mattaya Jarupan, "Environmental Problems in Thailand: With Special Reference to a Case Study of Lead Poisoning and the Environmental Laws," *in* I. Kato, Nabuo Kumamoto, and W. H. Matthews, eds., *Environmental Law and Policy in the Pacific Basin Area* (Tokyo: University of Tokyo Press, 1981), 55.

47. Ibid.

48. *Legal Aspects for Protection of the Marine Environment and Related Ecosystems* (Thailand: Office of the Juridical Council, 1979), 181.

49. Ibid.

50. H. F. Ludwig and C. Tongkasame, "Environmental Management for the Inner Gulf of Thailand," *in Proceedings International Conference on Water Resources Engineering, 17 January 1978* (Bangkok: Asian Institute of Technology, 1978), 171.

51. Johnston, op. cit., 65.

52. *Legal Aspects for Protection of the Marine Environment and Related Ecosystems* (Thailand: Office of the Juridical Council, 1979).

53. Ibid.

54. Ibid.

55. Suphavit Piamphongsnat, *Thailand Oil Spill Contingency Planning* (Bangkok: Office of the National Environment Board, 1979), 154; Anuchint Supol, "The Industry Environmental Safety Group and the Major Oil Spill Contingency Plan," *in Proceedings: International*

Conference on Water Resources Engineering, 17 January 1978 (Bangkok: Asian Institute of Technology, 1978), 171.

56. Supol, op. cit., 228–247.

57. Ibid.

58. "The Marine Environmental Protection Law of the People's Republic of China," *East Asian Executive Reports,* March 1983, 24–27.

59. Johnston, op. cit., 110 (note 322).

60. Ibid.

61. Ibid., 62.

62. *Proposed ASEAN Sub-Regional Environment Program (ASEP)* (Bangkok: UN Regional Office, 1977), 33.

63. Ibid., 55.

64. Ibid., 56.

65. United Nations Environmental Programme, *Report of the Intergovernmental Meeting on the Protection and Development of the Marine Environment and Coastal Areas of the East Asian Region, Manila, 27–29 April 1981,* Annex V, 25–26 (UNEP/IG. 26/6); UNESCO (1976), *Report of the IOC/FAO/UNEP International Workshop on Marine Pollution in East Asian Waters, Universiti Sains Malaysia, Penang, 7–13 April 1976* IOC Workshop Report no. 8, Paris: UNESCO, 1976; UNEP, *Report of the Meeting of Experts to Review the Draft Action Plan for the East Asian Seas, Baguio, 17–21 June 1980* (UNEP/WG. 41/4, 8 July 1980); and UNEP, *Report of the Second Meeting of Experts to Review the Draft Action Plan for the East Asian Seas, Bangkok, 8–12 December 1980* (UNEP/WG. 52/6, 12 December 1980).

66. United Nations Environment Programme, *Report of the Intergovernmental Meeting on the Protection and Development of the Marine Environmental and Coastal Areas of the East Asian Region, Manila, April 27–29, 1981,* Annex IV-Action Plan, 23, para. 22.2.2.

67. Ibid.

68. See Chapter 2, Table 2.1, and Chapter 7 in this volume.

69. United Nations Environment Programme, loc. cit.

70. ASEAN research reactors and their years of first operation are as follows:

Country	Number	Year
Thailand	1	1962
Philippines	1	1963
Indonesia	2	1964
Malaysia	1	1981

K. R. Smith, "Nuclear Power in the Asia-Pacific Region," in F. Fesharaki et al., *Critical Energy Issues in Asia-Pacific Region: The Next Twenty Years* (Boulder, Colorado: Westview Press, 1982), iv-4.

71. A more comprehensive list of agreements for control of marine pollution may be found in Elisabeth Mann Borgese and Norton Ginsburg, eds., *Ocean Yearbook* I (Chicago: University of Chicago Press, 1978), 692–696.

72. Ruddle, op. cit., 175–176.

CHAPTER 9 CONSERVATION OF THE MARINE ENVIRONMENT

1. A. Soegiarto and N. Polunin, *Marine Ecosystems of Indonesia: A Basis for Conservation* (Bogor: International Union for the Conservation of Nature and Natural Resources [IUCN]/World Wildlife Fund [WWF] Indonesia Program, August 1980 [draft]), section 3.

2. R. H. Whittaker, *Communities and Ecosystems,* second edition (New York: Macmillan Co., 1975).

3. Small islands may have extensive mangrove forest with accompanying lagoon areas, but the freshwater input and retention is normally not sufficient to form an estuary.

4. Environmental reports from the National Environmental Protection Council, Manila, Philippines, show toxic levels of some heavy metals and pesticides for mollusk species from estuarine areas of Manila Bay.

5. B. P. Hayden et al., "Shoreline Erosion in a Reef-Beach System," *Environmental Management* 2 (1978):204–218.

6. *National Plan on Tourism Development: Final Report of the Tourist Organization of Thailand* emphasizes this point. Beaches are particularly important in Thailand and Malaysian coastal tourism.

7. S. C. Snedaker and M. S. Brown, "Primary Productivity of Mangroves," *in* C. C. Black and A. Mitsui, eds., *CRC Handbook of Biosolar Resources, vol. I: Basic Principles* (Boca Raton, Florida: CRC Press, Inc., 1982), 477–485.

8. Ibid.

9. S. C. Snedaker, "Oil Spills in Mangroves." Environment and Policy Institute, East-West Center, unpublished paper 1981, 3.

10. *Proceedings International Workshop on Mangrove and Estuarine Area Development for the Indo-Pacific Region,* Manila, November 14–19, 1977.

11. H. Changsang, "Review of Knowledge on Mangroves in Southeast Asia and the Southwest Pacific, with Emphasis on Management Application," *ICLARM Newsletter* 2 (1979):3–4.

12. E. Gomez, *Status Report on Research and Degradation Problems of the Coral Reefs of the East Asian Seas* (Manila: South China Sea Fisheries Development and Coordinating Programme, May 1980).

13. E. O. Murdy and C. J. Ferraris, Jr., "The Contribution of Coral Reef Fisheries Production," *ICLARM Newsletter* 3 (1980):21–22.

14. Soegiarto and Polunin, loc. cit.

15. R. Grandperrin, "Importance of Reefs to Ocean Production," *South Pacific Commission Fishery Newsletter* 16 (1978):11–13.

16. Soegiarto and Polunin, loc. cit.

17. Ibid.

18. Kaneohe Bay in Hawaii is an example cited by R. E. Johannes, "Pollution and Degradation of Coral Reef Communities," *in* E. J. Ferguson Wood and R. E. Johannes, eds., *Tropical Marine Pollution,* Elsevier Oceanography Series 12 (Amsterdam: Elsevier Scientific Publishing Co., 1975), 21.

19. Soegiarto and Polunin, loc. cit.

20. Ibid.

21. The following discussion is based on that of Soegiarto and Polunin, op. cit., section 4.2.

22. P. Martosubroto and N. Naamin, "Relationship Between Tidal Forests (Mangroves) and Commercial Shrimp Production in Indonesia," *Marine Research in Indonesia* 18 (1977):81–86.

23. Soegiarto and Polunin, loc. cit.

24. R. N. Bray, A. C. Miller, and G. G. Geesey, "The Fish Connection: A Trophic Link Between Planktonic and Rocky Reef Communities?" *Science* 214 (9 October 1981):204–205.

25. R. Weidenbach, "Fisheries," *in* J. P. Morgan and M. J. Valencia, eds., *Atlas for Marine Policy in the Southeast Asian Seas* (Berkeley: University of California Press, 1983), 56–70.

26. International Union for the Conservation of Nature and Natural Resources, *Red Data Book,* 1975.

27. Garth I. Murphy and Isaac I. Ikehara, *A Summary of Sightings of Fish Schools and Bird Flocks and of Trolling in the Central Pacific*, Washington, D.C. Fish and Wildlife Service, United States Department of the Interior (Special Scientific Report: Fisheries No. 154), 1955, 2.

28. G. E. Hutchinson, "The Biogeochemistry of Vertebrate Excretion," *American Museum of Natural History Bulletin*, no. 96 (1950), 373.

29. C. J. Feare, "The Decline of Booby (Sulidae) Populations in the Western Pacific Ocean," *Biological Conservation* 14 (1978):295–305.

30. B. Hudson, *Dugong Conservation Management and Public Education Programme Report 1978–1980, Action Plan 1980–1982* (Papua New Guinea, 1980).

31. Ibid.

32. Soegiarto and Polunin, loc. cit.

33. R. H. Barnes, "Cetaceans and Cetacean Hunting Lamalera, Indonesia," *World Wildlife Fund Project 1428* (England: University of Oxford, 1980).

34. National Wildlife Federation, "Marine Mammals," *Conservation Report* (Washington, D.C., 1979).

35. IUCN, *Invertebrate Red Data Book*, 1981 (draft).

36. *Time Magazine*, 23 February 1981. Cited by *Conservation Indonesia* 5 (December 1981):23.

37. R. M. Umali, *Coastal Resources Development and Management: Philippine Experience* (Quezon City, Philippines: Natural Resources Management Center, 1980).

38. Ibid.

39. Ibid.

40. C. Campbell, "Thai Fishing Trawlers Sail in Narrower Waters," *Business Day* (August 1981):12.

41. Observation of A. White in the Philippines; Gomez, loc. cit.

42. A. C. Alcala and E. D. Gomez, *Recolonization and Growth of Hermatypic Corals in Dynamite-Blasted Coral Reefs in the Central Visayas, Philippines*, Contribution no. 4 (Quezon City, Philippines: Marine Sciences Center, University of the Philippines, 1979).

43. Hunting Technical Services Ltd., *South Thailand Regional Planning Study, Final Report, vol. 2: Physical Planning* (Elstree: Hunting Technical Services Ltd., 1974).

44. E. M. Wood, "Coral Reefs in Sabah: Present Damage and Potential Dangers," *Malayan Nature Journal* 31 (1977):49–57.

45. E. D. Gomez, op. cit., 28; personal communication with P. Castañada, Bureau of Fisheries and Aquatic Resources, Quezon City, Philippines.

46. Gomez, op. cit., 28.

47. K. Ruddle, "Pollution in the Marine Coastal Environment of ASEAN Countries," *in* Chia Lin Sien and Colin MacAndrews, eds., *Southeast Asian Seas: Frontiers for Development* (Singapore: McGraw-Hill, 1981), 139.

48. Ruddle, op. cit., 169.

49. *Bulletin Today*, Manila (27 September 1980).

50. R. B. Lulofs, *Coral Reefs, Marine Parks and Reserves*. Paper presented at a National Seminar on the Protection of the Marine Environment and Related Ecosystems, Kuala Lumpur, 29 June 1979, 3.

51. IUCN, UNEP, WWF, "Preservation of Genetic Diversity," *World Conservation Strategy*, 1980, Article 3.

52. Lack of field observation contributes to the small number of known endangered species and to the bias towards larger size. Some marine invertebrates and fish may be endangered as well.

53. CITES is concerned with the mechanics of trade, such as permits, and with the biological aspects of endangered species. It was concluded at Washington, D.C., on 3 March

1973 and has as a depository the Federal Department for Foreign Affairs of the Swiss Confederation, Bern.

54. J. A. Bullock, "A Blueprint for Conservation in Peninsular Malaysia," *Malayan Nature Journal* 27 (1974):1–16.

55. World Wildlife Fund, *Conservation Indonesia,* 4.

56. P. R. Burbridge and Koesoebiono, *Management of Mangrove Exploitation in Indonesia* (Indonesia: Center for Natural Resource Management and Environmental Studies, Bogor Agriculture University, 1980), 15.

57. Ibid., 19.

58. Arturo Tanco, Minister of Agriculture, Manila, Philippines, personal communications, March 1980.

59. World Wildlife Fund, loc. cit.

60. Ibid.

61. Martosubroto and Naamin, loc. cit.

62. Gomez, op. cit., 9.

63. S. Wells, "Coral Trade in the Philippines," *Traffic Bulletin* (Cambridge, U.K.: WWF Trade Monitoring Unit, 1981).

64. Ibid., 50.

65. J. McManus, "Philippine Coral Exports: The Coral Drain," *ICLARM Newsletter* 3 (1980):18–20.

66. Although the United States has now prohibited import of Philippine corals through an amendment to the Lacey Act, enforcement remains to be implemented. No European countries have yet taken similar steps.

67. Wells, op. cit., 51.

68. Ibid. McManus, loc. cit.

69. D. M. Johnston and N. G. Letalik, *Draft Convention on the Law of the Sea (1980): The Emerging International Obligations for the Preservation of the Marine Environment,* outline for IUCN Commission for Environmental Policy, Law and Administration, 3–8.

70. IUCN, *Draft Action Plan for the Conservation of Nature in the ASEAN Region,* prepared for the Interim Coordinator ASEAN Expert Group on the Environment by IUCN, support from UNEP, first draft February 20, 1981, Gland, Suisse, 2.

71. Ibid.

72. ASEAN, *Report of the ASEAN Workshop on Nature Conservation of the ASEAN Experts on the Environment,* Denpasar, Indonesia, 15–19 September 1980.

73. Johnston and Letalik, op. cit., 10.

74. W. Eshuis, "Protection of Wild Life in the Netherlands Indies," *Bulletin of the Colonial Institute, Amsterdam* 2 (1939), 291–307.

75. *Encyclopaedia van Nederlandsch Indie,* vol. 4 (The Hague, Nijhoff).

76. M. I. Bjorklund, "Achievements in Marine Conservation, International Marine Parks," *Environmental Conservation* 1 (1974):205–223.

77. A. Robinson, N. Polunin, K. Kvalvagnaes, and M. Halim, "Progress in Creating a Marine Reserve System in Indonesia," *Bulletin of Marine Science* 31 (3):774–785.

78. Bullock, loc. cit.

79. N. Polunin, *The Role of Protected Areas in Conserving Marine Genetic Resources.* Paper prepared for the Commission on National Parks and Protected Areas of the IUCN, Gland, Switzerland, September 1981, 12.

80. Ibid., 11.

81. Ibid.

82. G. C. Ray, J. A. Dobbin, and R. V. Salm, "Strategies for Protecting Marine Mammal Habitats," *Oceanus* 21 (1978):55–67.

83. Polunin, op. cit., 13.

84. IUCN, op. cit., 5. See also Polunin, loc. cit.

85. G. B. Goeden, "Biogeographic Theory as a Management Tool," *Environmental Conservation* 6 (1979):27–32.

86. Polunin, op. cit., 13.

87. A. White, "Valuable and Vulnerable Resources," *in* J. Morgan and M. Valencia, eds., *Atlas for Marine Policy in Southeast Asian Seas* (Berkeley: University of California Press, 1983), 26–35.

88. G. C. Ray, "Critical Marine Habitats. A Statement on the Nature of Marine Ecosystems with Criteria and Guidelines for the Description and Management of Marine Parks and Reserves," *IUCN Publication* Series no. 37 (1976):75–90.

89. P. Casteñada, *The Municipal Marine Reef Park: A Community Based Approach on Marine Resources Management.* Preliminary Report for the Bureau of Fisheries and Aquatic Resources (BFAR), Manila, Philippines, 1980.

90. A. C. Alcala, "Fish Yield of Coral Reefs of Sumilon Island, Central Philippines," *National Research Council of the Philippines Research Bulletin* 36 (1981), 1–7.

91. R. E. Johannes, *Implications of Traditional Marine Resource Use for Coastal Fisheries Development in Papua New Guinea, with Emphasis on Manus,* prepared for Conference on Traditional Conservation in Papua New Guinea: Implications for Today (Papua New Guinea: Institute of Applied Social and Economic Research, October 1980), 6.

92. A. Cabanban and A. White, *Marine Conservation Program Using Non-Formal Education at Apo Island, Negros Oriental, Philippines,* presented at the Fourth International Coral Reef Symposium, Manila, Philippines, 18–21 May 1981.

93. A. White, "Management of Philippine Marine Parks," *ICLARM Newsletter* 4 (1981):17–18.

94. Cabanban and White, loc. cit.

95. J. A. Sayer, *A Review of the Nature Conservation Policies and Programmes of the Royal Forestry Department* (Bangkok: UNDP, FAO, July 1981).

96. Personal observation by A. White in the Philippines, 1983.

97. IUCN, *A Strategy for the Conservation of Living Marine Resources and Processes in the Caribbean Region.* Report of the IUCN with support from World Wildlife Federation, September 1979; IUCN, *Draft Action Plan,* 2.

98. ASEAN, loc. cit.

99. IUCN, op. cit., 6

100. Ibid., 7.

CHAPTER 10 ENFORCEMENT OF MARITIME JURISDICTIONS

1. V. L. Aprieto, *Fishery Management and Extended Maritime Jurisdiction: The Philippine Tuna Fishery Situation,* Environment and Policy Institute Research Report No. 4 (Honolulu: East-West Center, 1981), 40.

2. Ibid., 41.

3. See G. Marten et al., *A Strategic Goal Analysis of Options for Tuna Longline Joint Ventures in Southeast Asia: Indonesia-Japan Case Study,* Environment and Policy Institute Research Report No. 3 (Honolulu: East-West Center, 1981) for a description of the Banda Sea agreement and the problems of enforcement.

4. *Mining Annual Review* (London: The Mining Journal, Ltd., 1982).

5. *United Nations Convention on the Law of the Sea*, A/CONF. 62/122, 7 October 1982, Parts II and III.

6. T. Child, "Enforcement of 200-Mile Exclusive Economic Zone Claims Over Living Marine Resources in Southeast Asia," *in* T. A. Clingan, Jr., ed., *Law of the Sea: State Practice in Zones of Special Jurisdiction* (Honolulu: Law of the Sea Institute, 1982), 444.

7. *Dao Siam*, Bangkok (in Thai), February 27, 1981, 3, 10, as reported in *Foreign Broadcast Information Service*.

8. *World Fishing* 29 (February 1980):40–41.

9. Hong Kong AFP broadcast (in English), 1340 GMT, October 15, 1980, as reported in *Foreign Broadcast Information Service*.

10. *Mining Annual Review* (London: The Mining Journal, Ltd., 1982).

11. Child, op. cit., 450.

12. *Bangkok Post* (19 June 1978):1.

13. D. M. Johnston, *Environmental Management in the South China Sea: Legal and Institutional Developments*, Environment and Policy Institute Research Report No. 10 (Honolulu: East-West Center, 1982), 28.

14. Kuala Lumpur Domestic Service broadcast (in English), 1130 GMT, 25 March 1979, as reported in *Foreign Broadcast Information Service*.

15. Johnston, op. cit., 62–63.

16. Taipei CNA broadcast (in English), 0944 GMT, 21 December 1979, as reported in *Foreign Broadcast Information Service*.

17. *Bulletin Today*, Manila (14 May 1981):28.

18. Hong Kong AFP broadcast (in English), 1132 GMT, 6 June 1980, as reported in *Foreign Broadcast Information Service*.

19. *Daily Express*, Manila (11 March 1981):14.

20. *Bulletin Today*, Manila (20 May 1981):22.

21 Johnston, op. cit., 64.

22. Bangkok Domestic Service broadcast (in Thai), 1300 GMT, 16 December 1977, as reported in *Foreign Broadcast Information Service*.

23. *Ban Muang*, Bangkok (in Thai), 30 January 1981, 1, 2, as reported in *Foreign Broadcast Information Service*.

24. *Mining Annual Review*, op. cit., 453.

25. *The Nation Review*, Bangkok (12 September 1981):3.

26. Decision No. 31-CP of the Council of Ministers of 29 January 1980 Regulating the Fishing Activities of Foreign Fishing Boats in the Waters of the Socialist Republic of Vietnam. As published in *Nhan Dan*, Hanoi (in Vietnamese) (26 March 1980):1, 4, and reported in *Foreign Broadcast Information Service*.

27. Nguyen Anh, *Nhan Dan*, (in Vietnamese), 21 February 1978, as reported in *Foreign Broadcast Information Service*.

28. Hanoi Domestic News Service (in Vietnamese), 1100 GMT, 21 July 1980, as reported in *Foreign Broadcast Information Service*.

29. M. J. Valencia, "Southeast Asian Seas: National Marine Interests, Transnational Issues, and Marine Regionalism," *in* Chia Lin Sien and Colin MacAndrews, eds., *Southeast Asian Seas: Frontiers for Development* (Singapore: McGraw-Hill, 1981), 342–343.

CHAPTER 11 COOPERATION: OPPORTUNITIES, PROBLEMS, AND PROSPECTS

1. M. J. Valencia, "Southeast Asia: National Marine Interests and Marine Regionalism," *Ocean Development and International Law* 5 (1978):421–476.

2. E. Borgese and N. Ginsburg, *Ocean Yearbook* 2 (Chicago: University of Chicago Press, 1980), 5.

3. G. Kent, "Harmonizing Extended Zone Legislation in Southeast Asia," *Ocean Development and International Law* 13 (1983):247–268; G. Kent, "Regional Approaches to Meeting National Marine Interests, *Contemporary Southeast Asia* 5 (June 1983):80–94.

4. M. J. Valencia, "Southeast Asian Seas: National Marine Interests, Transnational Issues, and Marine Regionalism," *in* Chia Lin Sien and Colin MacAndrews, eds., *Southeast Asian Seas: Frontiers for Development* (Singapore: McGraw-Hill, 1981), 302–354.

5. *International Cooperation in Fishery Development in Developing Countries,* FAO Fisheries Report No. 201 (Rome: FAO, 1977).

6. *Report of the Regional Seminar on Monitoring, Control and Surveillance of Fisheries in the Exclusive Economic Zones* (Manila: South China Sea Fisheries Development and Coordinating Programme, 1981); Terrin Child, "Enforcement of 200-Mile Exclusive Economic Zone Claims Over Living Marine Resources in Southeast Asia," *in* T. A. Clingan, Jr., ed., *Law of the Sea: State Practice in Zones of Special Jurisdiction* (Honolulu: Law of the Sea Institute, 1982), 438–464.

7. Boeing Commercial Airplane Company, *EEZ Management and Control* (Seattle: Boeing Document B10727, 1982). So far only Indonesia has acquired the aircraft recommended in this study.

8. E. Samson, "Possibilities of Co-operation in Fishing in Southeast Asia" (unpublished manuscript, Environment and Policy Institute, East-West Center, 1983).

9. *Report on the Proceedings,* ASEAN-OCI/WGFAF Fisheries Sectoral Meeting, Kuala Lumpur, 30–31 July 1983.

10. V. T. Paterno, "Southeast Asia Experience in Industrial Joint Ventures," *in* B. Pavlic, R. R. Uranga, B. Cizelj, and M. Svetlicic, eds., *The Challenges of South-South Cooperation* (Boulder, Colorado: Westview Press, 1983), 245–251.

11. A. Goseco, "Barter Need Not be Primitive," *Far Eastern Economic Review* (5 May 1983):146–148.

12. M. J. Valencia and Abu Bakar Jaafar, *Legal and Institutional Issues in the Management of the Malacca Strait,* International Federation of Institutes of Advanced Study, Delft, The Netherlands (forthcoming).

13. M. J. Valencia, "The South China Sea: Constraints to Marine Regionalism," *Indonesian Quarterly* 8 (1980):16–38.

14. M. J. Valencia, *Progress and Plans of the Marine Environment and Policy Program Area,* Environment and Policy Institute Program Report (Honolulu: East-West Center, June 1983).

SELECTED REFERENCES
FOR FURTHER READING

Alexander, Lewis M. *Marine Regionalism in the Southeast Asian Seas Area.* Research Report No. 11. Honolulu: Environment and Policy Institute, East-West Center, 1982.

Aprieto, Virginia L. *Fishery Management and Extended Maritime Jurisdiction: The Philippine Tuna Fishery Situation.* Research Report No. 4. Honolulu: Environment and Policy Institute, East-West Center, 1981.

Chia Lin Sien and C. MacAndrews, eds. *Southeast Asian Seas: Frontiers for Development.* Singapore: McGraw-Hill/Institute of Southeast Asian Studies, 1981.

Child, T. "Enforcement of 200 Mile Exclusive Economic Zone Claims Over Living Marine Resources in Southeast Asia," *in* Thomas A. Clingan, Jr., ed., *Law of the Sea: State Practice in Zones of Special Jurisdiction.* Honolulu: Law of the Sea Institute, 1982.

Christy, F. T., Jr. *Changes in the Law of the Sea and the Effects on Fisheries Management, with Particular Reference to Southeast Asia and the Southwest Pacific.* Manila: International Center for Living Aquatic Resources Management, 1978, p. 76.

Comitini, Salvatore, and Sutanto Hardjolukito. *Indonesian Fisheries Development and Strategy Related to Extended Jurisdiction.* Research Report No. 13. Honolulu: Environment and Policy Institute, East-West Center, 1983.

Finn, D. P., et al. *Oil Pollution From Tankers in the Straits of Malacca: A Policy and Legal Analysis.* Honolulu: Open Grants Office, East-West Center, 1979.

Gilbert, John T. E., ed. *Technical Environmental Guidelines for Offshore Oil and Gas Development.* Tulsa, Oklahoma: PennWell Books, 1983.

Hinton, H. C. *The China Sea: The American Stake in Its Future.* New York: National Strategy Information Center, 1980.

International Union for the Conservation of Nature and Natural Resources. *Draft Action Plan for the Conservation of Nature in the ASEAN Region.* Prepared for the Interim Coordinator ASEAN Export Group on the Environment, first draft. Gland, Suisse, 20 February 1981.

Johnston, Douglas M. *Environmental Management in the South China Sea: Legal and Institutional Developments.* Research Report No. 10. Honolulu: Environment and Policy Institute, East-West Center, 1982.

Lee Yong Leng. *Southeast Asia and the Law of the Sea,* revised edition. Singapore: Singapore University Press, 1980.

Lim Joo-Jock. *Geo-Strategy and the South China Sea Basin: Regional Balance, Maritime Issues, Future Patterns.* Singapore: Singapore University Press, 1979.

Marr, J.C. "Fishery and Resource Management in Southeast Asia," *Resources for the Future.* Paper no. 7. Washington, D.C.: The Program of International Studies of Fishery Arrangements, 1976.

Marten, Gerald, et al. *A Strategic Goal Analysis of Options for Tuna Longline Joint Ventures in Southeast Asia: Indonesia-Japan Case Study.* Research Report No. 3. Honolulu: Environment and Policy Institute, East-West Center, 1981.

Morgan, Joseph R., and Mark J. Valencia, eds. *Atlas for Marine Policy in Southeast Asian Seas.* Berkeley: University of California Press, 1983.

Polomka, P. *Ocean Politics in Southeast Asia.* Singapore: Institute of Southeast Asian Studies, 1978.

Prescott, J.R.V. *Maritime Jurisdiction in Southeast Asia: A Commentary and a Map.* Research Report No. 2. Honolulu: East-West Environment and Policy Institute, 1981.

Siddayao, C.M. *The Offshore Petroleum Resources of Southeast Asia, Potential Conflict Situations and Related Economic Considerations.* Kuala Lumpur: Oxford University Press, 1978.

Soegiarto, Aprilani, and N. Polunin. *Marine Ecosystems of Indonesia: A Basis for Conservation, Section 1.* Bogor: IUCN/WWF, Indonesia Program, August 1980.

Tangsubkul, Phiphat. *ASEAN and the Law of the Sea.* Singapore: Institute for Southeast Asian Studies, 1982.

Tangsubkul, Phiphat. *The Southeast Asian Archipelagic States: Concept, Evolution, and Current Practice.* Research Report No. 15. Honolulu: East-West Environment and Policy Institute, East-West Center, 1983.

Valencia, Mark J., ed. *The South China Sea: Hydrocarbon Potential and Possibilities of Joint Development.* Oxford, New York: Pergamon Press, 1981.

Valencia, Mark J., et al., eds. *Shipping, Energy, and Environment: Southeast Asian Perspectives for the Eighties.* Halifax, Nova Scotia: Dalhousie Ocean Studies Programme, Dalhousie University, 1982.

Wood, E.J.F., and R.E. Johannes, eds. *Tropical Marine Pollution,* Elsevier Oceanography Series 12. Amsterdam: Elsevier Scientific Publishing Company, 1975.

Wyrtki, K. *Physical Oceanography of the Southeast Asian Waters.* NAGA Report, vol. 2. La Jolla: Scripps Institution of Oceanography, 1961.

ABOUT THE AUTHORS

DONALD W. FRYER received his B.S., M.S., and Ph.D. from the London School of Economics. He also holds the M. Comm. degree of the University of Melbourne. He taught at the University of Malaya in Singapore, the Universiti Malaya in Kuala Lumpur, and for ten years at the University of Melbourne. Before joining the University of Hawaii as professor of geography in 1967, he was a senior economic advisor in the Ministry of Overseas Development in London. His interests are in Southeast Asia, resources and development, and geopolitics. He is the author of *World Economic Development* (McGraw-Hill, 1965), *Emerging Southeast Asia* (Philip, 1979), and more than thirty published papers.

ABU BAKAR JAAFAR received his B.E. in mechanical engineering from the University of Newcastle, Australia, his M.E. in environmental science from Miami University, Ohio, and his Ph.D. in marine geography from the University of Hawaii. He is currently the principal assistant director of the Department of Environment in Malaysia. He has represented the government of Malaysia at the Third United Nations Conference on the Law of the Sea (UNCLOS III), the Intergovernmental Council for the International Hydrological Programme of UNESCO, Intergovernmental Meetings to Review the Action Plan for the East Asian Seas of UNEP, the International Conference of IMO on Liability and Compensation for Damage in Connection with the Carriage of Certain Substances by Sea, the Asian-African Legal Consultative Committee (AALCC), the ASEAN Working Group on Marine Sciences, the ASEAN Experts Group on the Environment, and several other international and regional conferences on water and marine resources, pollution control, and general development of international law on the environment. He recently has been elected as the first secretary-general of the Environmental Management and Research Association of Malaysia (ENSEARCH).

GEORGE KENT, professor of political science at the University of Hawaii, served as a research associate at the Environment and Policy Institute of the East-West Center while editing this volume. He received his Ph.D. in communications from the University of Illinois. He specializes in issues of ocean policy and food policy, often combining the two in studies of social aspects of fisheries development. In addition to numerous articles in these areas he has written *The Politics of Pacific Islands Fisheries* (Westview Press, 1984), and *The Political Economy of Hunger* (Praeger, in press).

411

GEORGE LAURIAT, who received his B.A. degree in English from Franklin Pierce College, spent several years as a journalist in Hong Kong specializing in energy and maritime affairs reporting with the *Far Eastern Economic Review.* He also wrote for the *Times of London,* the *International Herald Tribune,* the *Guardian,* the *Financial Times,* and *Seatrade.* Many of his articles broke new ground in the shipping arena, including those on insurance fraud, Vietnam's shipping arrangements, and China's shipping development. He is the author of *China Shipping: The Great Leap Forward* (Lloyd's of London, 1983). He has undertaken various consultancies for the shipping and oil industries and he organized two conferences in China on developments in the South China Sea offshore oil industry. He is now doing private consulting work.

JOSEPH R. MORGAN served for twenty-five years in the U.S. Navy, retiring with the rank of captain. During his military service he spent much time in Southeast Asia. He received his B.A. from the University of Pennsylvania and his M.A. and Ph.D. degrees in geography from the University of Hawaii, where he is currently an associate professor of geography. He also is a research associate in the Environment and Policy Institute of the East-West Center. His research interests are primarily in the field of marine geography, and in addition to teaching courses in this general field he edited, with Mark J. Valenica, the *Atlas for Marine Policy in Southeast Asian Seas* (University of California, 1983). He has also published papers in *Proceedings, U.S. Naval Institute,* the journals *Marine Policy* and *The American Cartographer,* and he wrote *Hawaii: A Geography* (Westview Press, 1983) and made substantial contributions to *The Atlas of Hawaii* (University of Hawaii Press, 1983).

HAL F. OLSON received his B.S. degree in engineering from the U.S. Coast Guard Academy and his M.A. in geography from the University of Hawaii. Retired from the U.S. Coast Guard as a captain, he is currently a member of the faculty at Leeward Community College, Pearl City, Hawaii, and a doctoral candidate in the Department of Geography at the University of Hawaii. He has participated in a study of navigation problems in the Malacca and Singapore straits for the U.S. Agency for International Development, and he holds a U.S. Merchant Marine master's license.

J.R. VICTOR PRESCOTT received his B.S. (honors) degree in geography from the University of Durham. After completing his M.A. degree at the same university, he was appointed to a lectureship at University College, Ibadan, Nigeria, then part of the University of London. During five years in Nigeria, he completed his doctorate at the University of London on the subject of the evolution of Nigeria's boundaries. In 1961 he was appointed to a lectureship at the University of Melbourne, where he presently holds the position of reader. He has written ten books on various aspects of political geography, and since 1975 he has concentrated on questions associated with maritime boundaries. Most recently he was an adviser to the Australian Ministry of Foreign Affairs on maritime boundary questions.

ELIZABETH D. SAMSON received her B.S. degree in business administration from the University of the Philippines and her M.A. degree in economics from the same university. She is currently the executive director of the Fishery Industry Development Council in the Philippines. She is also executive editor of *Fisheries Today,* an international quarterly journal on developments in fisheries in the Philippines and other countries. She has undertaken various assignments for the Food and Agriculture Organisation of the United Nations on Southeast Asian fisheries. Her interests are in research and development in marine fisheries and other marine uses, regional and international maritime issues, aquaculture, agricultural credit and marketing, and rural development.

MARK J. VALENCIA received his B.S. degree in geology from the University of Massachusetts, an M.A. in geology from the University of Texas, a Ph.D. in oceanography from the University of Hawaii, and a Master of Marine Affairs degree from the University of Rhode Island. He was a research associate with the Environment and Policy Institute at the East-West Center while editing this volume. He served as coordinator of the institute's Program on Marine Environment and Policy for five years, and this volume is one product of that program. He is currently an East-West Center research associate in the Resource Systems Institute. His research interests are in ocean management and marine affairs in Southeast Asia. He has served as a lecturer with the Universiti Sains Malaysia in Penang and as a technical expert with the UNDP Regional Project on Offshore Prospecting in Bangkok. He is coeditor with Joseph R. Morgan of the *Atlas for Marine Policy in Southeast Asian Seas* (University of California Press, 1983), and he has written numerous articles and edited other books on the various aspects of marine policy in Southeast Asia.

ALAN WHITE is a doctoral candidate in the Department of Geography at the University of Hawaii and a grantee of the Environment and Policy Institute of the East-West Center. He received his M.A. degree in international management from the School for International Training in Brattleboro, Vermont. He has spent the past four years in the Philippines in research and management of coastal areas. He worked with the Philippines Ministry of Natural Resources helping implement coral reef reserves and parks, and he was a research associate at Silliman University in Dumaguete working on coral reef management problems. His dissertation research took him to the Philippines, Malaysia, and Indonesia, where he studied the effectiveness of marine reserve management. He is the author of the section on "Valuable and Vulnerable Resources" in the *Atlas for Marine Policy in Southeast Asian Seas* (University of California Press, 1983) and other articles on related topics.

INDEX